MANUAL OF MUSEUM EXHIBITIONS

THIRD EDITION

MARIA PIACENTE

A Lord Cultural Resources Book

ROWMAN & LITTLEFIELD
Lanham • Boulder • New York • London

Acquisitions Editor: Charles Harmon
Editorial Assistant: Erinn Slanina
Sales and Marketing Inquiries: textbooks@rowman.com

Credits and acknowledgments for material borrowed from other sources, and reproduced with permission, appear on the appropriate pages within the text.

Published by Rowman & Littlefield
An imprint of The Rowman & Littlefield Publishing Group, Inc.
4501 Forbes Boulevard, Suite 200, Lanham, Maryland 20706
www.rowman.com

86-90 Paul Street, London EC2A 4NE

Copyright © 2022 by The Rowman & Littlefield Publishing Group, Inc.

Cover image courtesy of Smithsonian National Museum of African American History and Culture

All rights reserved. No part of this book may be reproduced in any form or by any electronic or mechanical means, including information storage and retrieval systems, without written permission from the publisher, except by a reviewer who may quote passages in a review.

British Library Cataloguing in Publication Information Available

Library of Congress Cataloging-in-Publication Data

Names: Piacente, Maria, author.
Title: Manual of museum exhibitions / Maria Piacente.
Description: Third edition. | Lanham : Rowman & Littlefield, [2022] | "A Lord cultural resources book." | Includes bibliographical references and index.
Identifiers: LCCN 2021034056 (print) | LCCN 2021034057 (ebook) | ISBN 9781538152805 (cloth) | ISBN 9781538152812 (paperback) | ISBN 9781538152829 (epub)
Subjects: LCSH: Museum exhibits—Handbooks, manuals, etc. | Museum exhibits—Planning—Handbooks, manuals, etc.
Classification: LCC AM151 .M34 2022 (print) | LCC AM151 (ebook) | DDC 069/.5—dc23
LC record available at https://lccn.loc.gov/2021034056
LC ebook record available at https://lccn.loc.gov/2021034057

∞™ The paper used in this publication meets the minimum requirements of American National Standard for Information Sciences—Permanence of Paper for Printed Library Materials, ANSI/NISO Z39.48-1992.

Contents

Foreword ... ix
   Gail Dexter Lord

Preface ... xi
   Maria Piacente

Acknowledgments ... xiii

Chapter 1   **Introduction: The Exhibition Development Process** ... 1
   Maria Piacente

PART I: WHY?

Chapter 2   **Museums and Their Exhibitions** ... 7
   Brad King
- 2.1. The Trust Factor ... 8
- 2.2. Exhibitions as Agents of Transformation ... 8
- 2.3. Museums as Activist Institutions ... 10
- 2.4. Corporate Sponsorship: How Close is Too Close? ... 12
- 2.5. The Way Forward ... 13

Chapter 3   **Where Do Exhibition Ideas Come From?** ... 17
   Barry Lord (updated by Maria Piacente)
- 3.1. Research-Based and Market-Driven Exhibitions ... 18
- 3.2. Planning for Exhibition Research ... 18

PART II: WHERE?

Chapter 4   **Exhibition Facilities**   25
Sean Stanwick and Heather Maximea

     4.1.   A World of Exhibition Spaces   26
     4.2.   Developing Design Criteria for Exhibition Spaces   27
     4.3.   Exhibition Space Characteristics   37
     4.4.   Exhibition Gallery Security   51
     4.5.   Accessibility, Adjacency, and Circulation   55

PART III: WHAT?

Chapter 5   **Permanent Collection Exhibitions**   61
Katherine Molineux

     5.1.   Planning for Permanent Collection Exhibitions   61
     5.2.   Changing Permanent Collection Displays   63
     5.3.   Interpreting Collections   64
     5.4.   Modes of Display   66

Chapter 6   **It's Not Always about Collections**   73
Katherine Molineux

     6.1.   Idea Exhibitions   73
     6.2.   Children's Exhibitions   76
     6.3.   Living History Exhibitions   79
     6.4.   Science Exhibitions   81
     6.5.   Digital Immersive Exhibitions   83

Case Study: Weston Family Innovation Learning Centre, Terms of Engagement at the Ontario Science Centre, by Lesley Lewis and Kevin von Apen   85

Chapter 7   **Virtual Exhibitions**   89
Sarah Hill

     7.1.   What is a Virtual Exhibition?   89
     7.2.   Why Develop a Virtual Exhibition?   90
     7.3.   Thinking About Digital Audiences   95
     7.4.   Virtual Exhibition Considerations   99
     7.5.   Virtual Exhibition Development Process   111
     7.6.   Tips for Smaller Museums that Want to go Digital   112

Case Study: Extending the Life of a Traveling Exhibition, Museum of International Folk Art, Santa Fe, United States   113

Chapter 8	**Temporary Exhibitions** *Maria Piacente and Katherine Molineux*	119
	8.1 Types of Exhibitions in a Temporary Exhibition Program	120
	8.2 Managing a Temporary Exhibition Program	125
	8.3 Making Space for Temporary Exhibitions	127
	8.4 Public and Educational Programming	129
	8.5 Marketing and Public Relations	129
	8.6 Funding and Resourcing a Temporary Exhibition Program	130
	8.7 Generating Revenue	131
Chapter 9	**Traveling Exhibitions** *Maria Piacente*	133
	9.1 Why Create a Traveling Exhibition Program?	134
	9.2 Strategize for Success	135
	9.3 Staff and Professional Resources	137
	9.4 Loan Agreements	138
	9.5 Designing and Preparing an Exhibition for Travel	139
	9.6 Managing the Tour	141
	9.7 Borrowers and Organizers	144
	Case Study: Natural History Museum London's Touring Exhibition Program, An Interview with Jan English, Head of Touring Exhibitions	145
	Interview: Traveling Exhibitions in a Changing World, with Antonio Rodriguez, Chairman of the Board, International Committee for Exhibition Exchange (ICOM, ICEE)	148

PART IV: WHO?

Chapter 10	**Exhibitions and Diversity, Equality, Accessibility, and Inclusion** *Maria Piacente and Karen Carter*	153
	10.1 Implications for Exhibitions	154
	10.2 Reflections: Fulfillment of Our Promise	157
	Case Study: Activating Change: DEAI, Community, and Evaluation, An Interview with Cheryl Blackman, Director of Museums and Heritage Services for the City of Toronto, Canada	160
Chapter 11	**Curiosity and Motivation** *Shiralee Hudson Hill and Barbara Soren*	165
	11.1 Cultivating Curiosity	165
	11.2 Learning and Exhibitions	169
	11.3 Understanding Audience Experiences, Motivations, and Preferences in Exhibitions	171

Chapter 12	**Evaluation**	177
	Gail Lord, Duncan Grewcock, Barbara Soren, and Jackie Armstrong	
	12.1 Measuring Success by Gail Lord	177
	12.2 Before, During, and After: Front-End, Formative, Remedial, and Summative Evaluation by Duncan Grewcock	179
	12.3 Qualitative and Quantitative Audience by Barbara Soren and Jackie Armstrong	187
	Case Study: University of Michigan Museum of Natural History Front-End and Formative Visitor Study Using Multiple Methods by Barbara Soren	201

PART V: HOW?

Chapter 13	**Roles and Responsibilities**	211
	Maria Piacente	
	13.1 Who's Involved in the Exhibition Process?	211
	13.2 Teams and Committees	215
	13.3 Contracting Expertise	217
	13.4 Making Decisions	217
	Case Study: Oakland Museum of California Exhibition Process with Valerie Huaco, Deputy Director and Chief Content Officer	218
	Case Study: Roles and Responsibilities in a Small Museum: The Central Bank Museum of Trinidad and Tobago	221
Chapter 14	**Preparing the Exhibition Brief**	223
	Maria Piacente and John Nicks	
	14.1 Formulating the Exhibition Concept	223
	14.2 Exhibition Brief	226
	Case Study: *Canada Day 1* Traveling Exhibition	231
Chapter 15	**Interpretive Planning**	233
	Maria Piacente	
	15.1 Preplanning, Research, and Visioning	236
	15.2 Interpretive Strategy	237
	15.3 Organizational and Thematic Frameworks	239
	15.4 Organizational and Thematic Frameworks from around the World	241
	15.5 Communication Objectives/Visitor Outcomes	248
	15.6 Interpretive Plan	249
	Case Study: University of Michigan Museum of Natural History, *Exploring Michigan*	250
	Case Study: Capitol Visitor Center Exhibition Hall, Washington, DC: Excerpts from the Interpretive Plan	253

Chapter 16	**Content Development** *Lisa Wright*	257
	16.1 Research Planning	258
	16.2 Collections Research and Selection	260
	16.3 Exhibition Text by Patchen Barss	263
	16.4 Image Research and Procurement	268
	16.5 Hands-On Exhibits, Models, and Dioramas	273
	16.6 Multimedia Exhibits	274
	16.7 Subject Matter Experts	278
	Case Study: Working with Subject Matter Experts: Canadian Museum of Immigration at Pier 21, Halifax, Canada	279
	16.8 Communities and Content	282
	Case Study: Creating with Community *The First Peoples* Exhibition at Bunjilaka Aboriginal Cultural Centre at Melbourne Museum, a Shared Endeavor of Museums Victoria and the Victorian Aboriginal Community	283
	Case Study: Indigenous-Led Design and Content Development: Indigenous Peoples Garden, Assiniboine Park, Winnipeg, Manitoba	287
Chapter 17	**Exhibition Design** *Yvonne Tang and James Bruer*	289
	17.1 The Design Process	290
	17.2 Exhibition Display Cases by Mike Chaplin	301
	17.3 Lighting Design by Kevin Shaw	308
	17.4 Green Design	314
	Case Study: Exhibitions and Museums in India: Challenges and Opportunities by Uttiyo Bhattacharya	317
Chapter 18	**Graphic Design** *Mary Yacob and Jacqueline Tang*	319
	18.1 Semiotics in Design	319
	18.2 Graphic Design Phases	321
	18.3 Graphic Design Elements	323
	18.4 Color	330
	18.5 Imagery	333
	18.6 Design Essentials	333
Chapter 19	**Multimedia** *Cory Timpson*	335
	19.1 Strategic Role	336
	19.2 Types of Multimedia	337
	19.3 Operationalizing Multimedia	351

		Case Study: *Rights of Passage* Exhibition at Canadian Museum for Human Rights	356
		Case Study: *Mandela: Struggle for Freedom* Traveling Exhibition	360
Chapter 20	**Fabrication and Installation** Erich Zuern		363
	20.1	Who Will Produce the Exhibition?	363
	20.2	Design-Bid-Build or Design-Build: What's the Difference?	364
	20.3	Contracting	366
	20.4	The Production Process	368
	20.5	Tracking and Scheduling	375
	20.6	Warranty	376
		Case Study: Creative Contracting by the North Dakota Heritage Center & State Museum by Erich Zuern and Genia Hesser	377
Chapter 21	**Financial Planning** Erich Zuern		379
	21.1	Creating an Exhibition Budget	379
	21.2	Direct Exhibition Costs	384
	21.3	Related Exhibition Costs	386
	21.4	Managing the Budget	387
		Case Study: Budget Stretching with In-Kind Contributions	389
Chapter 22.	**Effective Exhibition Project Management** Robert LaMarre		391
	22.1	The Role of Project Management and Why it is Needed	392
	22.2	A Team Effort	392
	22.3	Applying Project Management Methodology	394
	22.4	Certifications and Continuous Learning	403
	22.5	Completing the Tasks	403
Chapter 23	**Conclusion: The Future of Exhibition-Making** Gail Dexter Lord		405

Glossary	411
Select Bibliography	425
Index	437
About the Editor	457
About the Contributors	459

Foreword

Gail Dexter Lord

The foreword to the third edition of the *Manual of Museum Exhibitions* was written during Lord Cultural Resources' fortieth anniversary. While writing *Planning our Museums,*[1] which turned out to be the first book on museum planning, Barry Lord and I founded Lord Cultural Resources. The premise of that book was simple but new: "Museums are for people." This idea quickly found support around the world because a new generation of museum workers, managers, leaders, and supporters had already decided that museums were for people and wanted to find systematic ways of implementing the idea through planning. And so, the idea grew into a series of museum manuals[2] on planning, management, exhibitions, learning, and strategic planning.

It gives me great pleasure to introduce this third edition of the *Manual of Museum Exhibitions*, which ushers in a new generation of museum leaders through the visionary and capable editorial direction of Maria Piacente, who has directed exhibitions and event projects for more than a quarter century. Maria has realized exhibitions in museums around the world, bringing an exceptional experience to this volume as reflected in the breadth of its contributors, range of topics, and level of practical detail. Above all, Maria brings a respect for cultural diversity, which is essential to the success of the museum exhibition as a communication medium.

Thank you to Maria Piacente and the contributors to this new edition of the *Manual of Museum Exhibitions*, which is destined to be a classic.

NOTES

1. Barry Lord and Gail Dextor Lord, eds. *Planning Our Museums / National Museums of Canada* (Ottawa, Canada: Museums Assistance Programme, National Museums of Canada, 1983).
2. Gail Dextor Lord, *The Manual of Museum Planning* (London: Stationary Office Books, 1999, 1st Edition; 2003, 2nd Edition; 2012; 3rd Edition); Gail Dextor Lord, *The Manual of Museum Management* (London: Stationary Office Books, 1997, 1st Edition, reprinted 1998; 2009, 2nd Edition); Gail Dextor Lord, *Manual of Museum Exhibitions* (Lanham, MD: AltaMira Press, 2001, 1st Edition; 2014, 2nd Edition; 2021 3rd Edition); Gail Dextor Lord, *The Manual of Strategic Planning for Museums* (Lanham, MD: AltaMira Press, 2007); Barry Lord, *The Manual of Museum Learning* (Lanham, MD: AltaMira Press, 2007, 1st Edition; 2015, 2nd Edition); Ali Houssani and Ngaire Blakenberg, *Manual of Digital Museum Planning* (Lanham, MD: Rowman & Littlefield, 2017); Gail Dextor Lord and Kate Market, *The Manual of Strategic Planning for Cultural Organizations* (Lanham, MD: Roman & Littlefield, 2017).

Preface

Maria Piacente

When I began contemplating a third edition to the *Manual of Museum Exhibitions*, I thought my biggest challenge was going to be addressing the mounting complexity and cost of technology and the growing desire for digital and immersive experiences in addition to exploring trends in visitor centered approaches to exhibition development. Then the COVID-19 pandemic struck in early 2020 and the world changed. What did this mean for the role of exhibitions? Would the "blockbuster" as we know it ever make its return, and if so in what form? How would design address the new reality of physical distancing and what would it mean to "interact" in a gallery in the short and long term?

Massive protests also marked societal change as people rightly demanded equality, inclusion, and justice in the antiracism movements that began in the United States and sparked a movement worldwide. In Hong Kong, young leaders protested for democracy and freedom, reminding us of the ongoing changes triggered by the Arab Spring and #MeToo movements.

It's not enough just to present the information—museums are taking a stand—entering the realm of advocacy and reinforcing that "truth" must be sought in facts, science, and public discourse. As museums shine a critical light on their practice and the way in which they engage with diverse communities, how will the relationship between the visitor, the object, and the story change?

Despite these seismic changes and pressures, I still believe that all museum activities, from research and conservation to education and outreach, converge in the very public forum of the exhibition. Since the previous manual was published in 2014, new types of experience-driven venues have surfaced, drawing on the core of what makes museum experiences unique—*authenticity*—while building on the public's desire for storytelling, full-body immersive, and singular cross-disciplinary collaborations.

From the very first version of the publication, visitors have always been at the core of the *Manual of Museum Exhibitions.* What has become clear is that visitor-centricity has become even more prevalent as museums and art galleries are committed to creating exhibitions that appeal to their audiences. Many of the examples and case studies peppered throughout the manual are excellent models of this approach which, considering the growing and justifiable focus on diversity and inclusion, is more important than ever.

Our definition of exhibitions is constantly changing as they can now be virtual; nontraditional migratory and pop-up spaces play host to temporary displays; engaging visits must be story-based, participatory, and experience-driven; social media has shifted authority away from experts to the public; and as time-constrained audiences demand more dynamic, interactive, and mobile applications, museum leadership, managers, staff, and designers are rising to these challenges in innovative ways. This new edition of the *Manual of Museum Exhibitions* aspires to address these cultural and technological changes in the context of professional museum practice.

The third edition of *Manual of Museum Exhibitions,* while addressing new challenges, continues to be, at its heart, a sensible guide to the exhibition development process. New and experienced museum and design professionals will find the technical and detailed methodologies practical and adaptable to any project—big or small, physical, or digital. It will still be your favorite "go-to" guide for *"How do I . . ."* The manual includes more examples of cool exhibitions from around the world that will inspire you.

The manual is organized in five parts:

- Part I: Why? We explore the "why" of museum exhibitions. A new treatise on the purpose of exhibitions provides context, as museums are on the cusp of responding to a changing world and greater community engagement.

- Part II: Where? The physical requirements to mount permanent and temporary exhibitions safely and effectively are described.

- Part III: What? The many different types of exhibitions from science to art to virtual are defined.

- Part IV: Who? This new and expanded section focuses on the importance of understanding visitors, what motivates them, and the evaluation techniques to address their needs. In addition, we explore the impact of Diversity, Equality, Accessibility, and Inclusion (DEAI) on the exhibition development process.

- Part V: How? From concept to opening day, the exhibition development process is analyzed and described in detail. This is the heart of this new edition. New examples and case studies are featured.

Acknowledgments

Firstly, I would like to thank the contributors who have provided all of us with the benefit of their experience and expertise in the field of museum exhibitions. Some are experience experts at Lord Cultural Resources, others are valued collaborators on previous projects, and still others are included simply because I know and admire the work they have done and are doing. Together, their contributions tell as comprehensive a story about this complex subject as we aim to tell in each exhibition.

I would also like to thank the cultural institutions that have allowed us to use photographs, diagrams, tables, documents, or data from their exhibition projects as illustrations or case studies in this manual. These examples demonstrate the exhibition process in action and provide new and experienced professionals with tangible ways of connecting theory and practice to real life solutions.

The *Manual of Museum Exhibitions,* 3rd edition, has benefitted greatly from the professional attention of my editors at Rowman & Littlefield. I know that everyone in the museum profession appreciates their dedication and support of publications in the cultural sector.

Finally, this manual is dedicated to the late Barry Lord, cofounder of Lord Cultural Resources. He was my coeditor for the 2014 version of this book, and his wisdom and guidance continued to inspire me as I prepared this new volume. Barry loved exhibitions, their transformative power, and the way they revealed the world of science, culture, and art in ways like no other medium.

Chapter 1

Introduction

The Exhibition Development Process

Maria Piacente

As opportunities and demand for exhibitions have increased, so too has the need for a broader understanding of where exhibition ideas come from; how they're developed; what the choices are with regard to approach; who makes those choices; what exhibitions cost; how to incorporate complex and expensive new technologies; what impact they will have on museum finances; and what benefits can reasonably be expected from exhibitions in terms of engaging the public and creating new knowledge.

Often, decision makers are aware of neither the high cost of exhibitions nor how these costs can be controlled. Exhibitions may be initiated in the hopes of achieving high attendance levels, yet no market research is conducted. Alternatively, market research and front-end evaluation is conducted, but ignored in the design. Sometimes, the design is completed with minimal involvement of curators and educators, with the result that neither artifacts nor learning objectives fit quite the way they should. With the growing imperative for community consultation and co-curation, exhibition processes need to be further adapted to ensure a responsible and meaningful dialogue that is reflected in the final product.

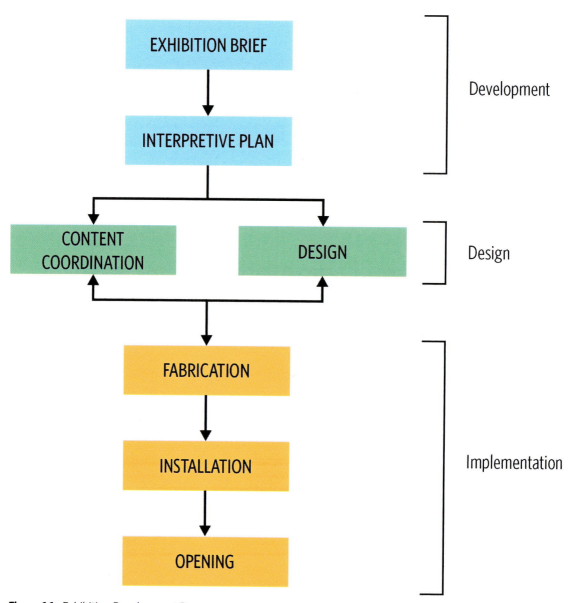

Figure 1.1. Exhibition Development Process. LORD CULTURAL RESOURCES

Figure 1.1 presents a template for the exhibition development process from initial concept to opening day. This flexible and adaptable process holds true for all project types whether a small temporary exhibition on a tight timeframe or a multimillion-dollar renovation of a national museum's permanent collection gallery. If your museum is committed to visitor centricity, the role of **interpretive planning** in your exhibition development process is essential.

As the figure illustrates, the process can be understood in three phases: development, design, and implementation.

1. In the **development phase** the exhibition idea or *concept* is created, tested, and refined. The principal outcome of this phase is a deep institutional understanding of what the exhibition is about and why the museum is doing it at this time, in this way, and at this scale. This understanding is recorded in the exhibition brief. The heart of the development phase is the interpretive plan, which is explored in chapter 15. Many museums fail to develop a robust plan for an exhibition, with potentially disastrous results that are laid at the feet of designers (not enough engagement), or marketing (not enough advertising), or development (not enough money). In fact, the problems are more likely to be rooted in a divided museum staff; lack of clarity of purpose; lack of appropriate funding to match expectations; and insufficient research into the subject, the audience, or both.

2. The **design and content coordination phase** takes place when the interpretive plan and all the research conducted to date is transformed into three-dimensional reality through the creativity and insight of designers working collaboratively with curators, interpretive planners, and evaluators. With the growing use of technology in exhibitions, multimedia specialists should be engaged in the design phase in order to maximize the creative power of digital while keeping an eye on costs. Parallel to the design process is content development and coordination. This is to ensure the content leads design and not vice versa. Object, specimen, and artwork lists are refined, and curatorial research is turned into specific stories, interactive experiences, gallery text, and scripts for multimedia.

3. The **implementation phase** is the production and installation of the exhibition. Project and financial management throughout the development and design phases are crucial to ensure an on-time and on-budget culmination of the exhibition process.

Budget oversight, cost control, and financial evaluation are ongoing throughout the process. As well, curators, designers, and interpretive planners will be quick to point out that their work does not end until opening day or later. Exhibition development is a recurrent and iterative process, adapting and adjusting to exhibitions of varying sizes and budgets, level of complexity, purpose, and the expert teams drawn together to complete them. Ongoing evaluation of exhibitions throughout the planning, design, and installation phase, including a period for adjustments during a "soft opening" is important enough, but a long-range program of evaluating exhibitions over the months or years that they are on view is of even greater value.

The exhibition process and strategies outlined in these pages can be adapted to a project of any type, size, or budget, and can be effectively applied to museums with a staff of five people or five hundred. The key is committing to a process—once agreed upon—and a management approach that will lead you to success.

PART I

WHY?

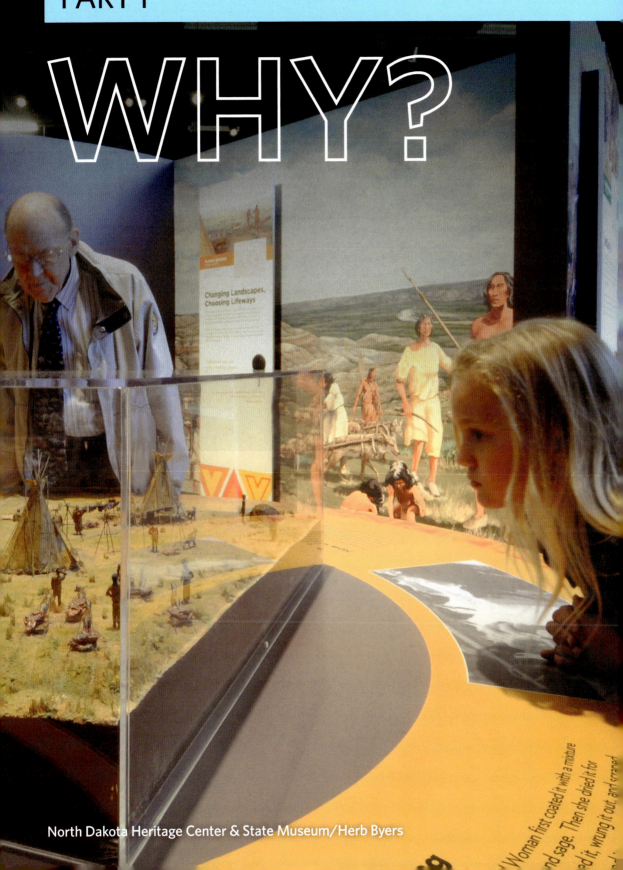

North Dakota Heritage Center & State Museum/Herb Byers

Today, human beings are highly aware of the connectivity among us all. We are acutely informed of how subjects as diverse as our choice and use of energy sources, our tolerance for each other's beliefs and practices, our extreme disparities of income, our understanding of each other's cultures, and many other features of the natural world or what we have fashioned from it are all interrelated. And we question the presuppositions underlying each of these subjects, especially because we can see how one set of assumptions affects all the others.

As trusted sources of information, museums can be of great value as we explore deep, powerful, and sometimes traumatic subjects. The arts evoke the essential meanings of our lives sensually and imaginatively. Understanding human history is necessary for an incisive awareness of the present, and museums of archaeology or historic sites can present and interpret the past more vividly than a textbook or a lecture. Keeping abreast of contemporary science and technology is a bracing challenge that science centers, natural history museums, zoos, botanical gardens, or industrial museums can help us meet. Children's museums and specialized institutions on all subjects can speak to more focused interests. Museums of ideas can directly address such fundamental questions related to human rights, tolerance, and identity.

Exhibitions are the principle means by which museums can be of service to us. They can confirm, question, or shake our beliefs. They may arouse a new interest or deepen our understanding of ourselves or the world we live in. Exhibitions entertain, delight, and amuse us. They transport us to faraway places and tell stories. They have the ability—if done well and responsibly—to present complex and traumatic content and histories from *multiple perspectives* to ensure we are getting the *whole* story. We expect authenticity from exhibitions—original works of art, genuine artifacts, and the most advanced and best informed research on their subjects.

Are exhibitions really necessary? Will they make a difference, and if so to whom? Are they the best way to communicate content? Can we use other types of media to make them more effective? Why are they worth the dedication of the museum's collections, space, time, and money—and most especially—the human resources needed to make them happen?

Chapter 2

Museums and Their Exhibitions

Brad King

Exhibitions are a museum's primary public function. Small wonder: exhibitions, particularly temporary and traveling shows, are often high-profile events involving advertising, media coverage, social media campaigns, and direct marketing. Exhibitions are more prominent than major acquisitions, publications, research, and educational programs and other important but less visible activities. The public knows museums through their exhibitions, which makes them powerful tools of communication. Be they traditional gallery installations or online experiences, exhibitions have a unique power not only to capture the public's imagination, but to transform how people view the world.

In an earlier edition of this book, Barry Lord wrote that "transformation takes place because the visitor is moved by the perceived authenticity of the exhibit to discover meaning in the objects on display . . . the apprehension of that content is itself a transformative experience that the exhibits uniquely make possible."[1] No other public communication medium can accomplish this feat in quite the same way. The long history of museum exhibitions—from the "cabinet of curiosities" in the eighteenth century, to the edification of the working classes in the nineteenth century, to more recent advances in informal learning—have proven the constancy of their transformative power.

This ability to transform is augmented by trust. Public trust in museums is known to be high. This chapter argues that the former is most effective when combined with the latter—that exhibitions' power to capture hearts and minds is directly proportional to the level of trust in which museums are held. Preservation of that trust is one of the keys for maximum effectiveness, but it can never be taken for granted. The goal of this chapter is to provide guidance for exhibition-making during a period of political instability, declining trust, and transformational change in the museum world and in society as a whole.

2.1 THE TRUST FACTOR

Trust is a crucially important factor in society. High-trust societies are more successful economically, more stable politically, and more successful overall.

Overall, trust levels have been declining across Western societies. Tribal media, political parties, race, class, age, geography, and many other forces often divide society and produce declines in trust, whether that be in institutions, individuals, or governments. Unifying, trusted influences are less common, but this is where museums have an advantage: they have unmatched reserves of "trust capital," which puts them in a unique position to create exhibitions that can help heal social and political fractures.

Why is trust so important? Former US secretary of state George Schultz called it "the coin of the realm." Trust, he said, is at the very heart of diplomacy, a necessary precondition to make things happen.[2] Museum leaders who want to "make things happen" need to maintain their trust advantage in their exhibitions.

Studies released over the past twenty years (the most recent cited here is from 2019) document museums' remarkably consistent levels of public trust,[3] even as other public institutions have been diminished. The 2017 National Awareness, Attitudes and Usage Study of Visitor-Serving Organizations highlights how museums are perceived as free from political agendas, which correlates with greater perceived trustworthiness. Data analyst and museum consultant Colleen Dilenschneider calls it museums' "superpower."[4] But this trust cannot be taken for granted. The vast majority of museums are scholarly, fact-based, and scientifically sound. In less polarized times, these virtues made trust something of a given. Today, though, science and scholarship themselves are often under attack. Museums must work to not only maintain trust but to build it.

This is important because, as is widely agreed, museums and their exhibitions can make a positive contribution to society and can be a driving force in solving society's "wicked problems," as coined by designer Jon Kolko. He describes "a social or cultural problem that is difficult or impossible to solve for as many as four reasons: incomplete or contradictory knowledge, the number of people and opinions involved, the large economic burden, and the interconnected nature of these problems with *other* problems."[5] Climate change, social inequality, racial injustice, and a host of other contemporary issues clearly meet these criteria. But preserving their trust capital is vital if museums are to achieve their potential as agents of positive change.

2.2 EXHIBITIONS AS AGENTS OF TRANSFORMATION

The way in which museum exhibitions communicate with the public can benefit society by providing a platform to discuss solutions to wicked problems. As Rebecca Carlsson says in a recent MuseumNext post, museums (via, in large part, their exhibitions) can play a major role in reestablishing common ground and a shared sense of purpose around society's issues.[6] They can be mediators and facilitators, not just between curators and audiences, but also between different audiences themselves. The gallery and its digital extensions serve as connection points, places of discussion and debate. This role reflects recent fundamental changes in exhibition philosophy.

Many authors, including those writing in earlier editions of this manual, suggest *communication* was the primary purpose of exhibitions, in the sense that the effectiveness of an exhibition's ability to communicate is a measure of its ability to transform.[7] In decades past, the nature of communication in exhibitions tended to be one-way: from authoritative museum professionals to the receiving public. This is no longer so. Today, museum exhibitions are more likely to be avenues for two-way or multidirectional communication—from museum professionals and content experts to the museum's audiences, but also from the museum's audiences back to the professionals, and from one visitor to another. Indeed, the very term "visitor" is no longer as accurate as it once was; in many ways, visitors have become participants, actively engaging in the content. That shift puts the building blocks in place to build consensus, or at least meaningful and respectful discussions of opposing viewpoints, making the way in which exhibitions communicate an important building block in problem-solving and social unification.

The origins of this trend stem from a refocus on "visitor centricity," which resulted from a combination of scholarship and a drive for increased relevance. In visitor-centric museums, formal and informal communication between audiences and museum professionals happens all the time—before, during, and after exhibition experiences. Museums stay connected to their audiences and vice versa. Thanks to the work of scholars like John Falk, Lynn Dierking, and others, we now understand far more about how people interact and learn in museums. Didactic, behaviorist approaches where knowledge transmission is authoritative and top-down have been superseded by more participatory approaches. Museums have become places where visitors can "create, share, and connect with one another around content," according to museologist Nina Simon.[8]

This change of emphasis has altered the nature of what people learn in museum exhibitions. A "shared authority" model based on dialogue, participation, and co-curation is a model that moves away from one-way transmittal of facts and conclusions that few visitors absorb and makes it possible to think about learning in a different way. Subject matter content becomes a vehicle for developing soft skills such as critical thinking and active citizenship. Visitors still learn about the subject matter, but they also learn how to critically engage more generally in other aspects of their lives.

Two-way or multidirectional communication also signals the end of single or universal narratives. Exhibitions now need to approach subject matter from multiple perspectives. This means victors no longer write (or interpret history)—at least not in museum exhibitions. Museumgoers have greater power to make their own history, identity, and cultural belonging part of the narrative.

According to the Swedish academic Kersten Smeds,

> Visitors create their own meanings. The museum will become a stage for action, a meeting place, a "switchboard" for information, and a showroom for a pluralistic reality. . . . This mode of organizing exhibitions fits well into the new pedagogy of self-formation . . . thus new narratives of history and social development can be created. . . . The situation has created a "connecting people" kind of experience which opens possibilities to collectively sharing information and resources with others, with people you choose yourself, locally, regionally, nationally, or internationally. In my opinion we

> are witnessing new kinds of collectivism which, in my view, may, in a fascinating way, restore the creativity of memory, the unpredictability of History that was lost at the time of the introduction of national narratives, of the one-way things are.[9]

These principles support the role of museum exhibitions as a unifying force by making room for dissent and debate. They are more democratic than unidirectional communication media. They also benefit museums, making exhibitions welcoming to people with differing mindsets and preferences who would otherwise be alienated by authoritative narratives that dismiss their perspective.

New ideas about exhibition content bolster the multiple-perspective approach. Museums increasingly work to connect content to audience members' lived experiences. Visitor-centered relevance has never been more crucial for museums. Engaging with real-world problems contributes to the idea of the museum as modern-day athenaeums, through which scholars and the public discuss current issues and everyday life. More than ever, museums are civic society institutions supporting both informal learning and also a kind of "school for living" and citizenship. All these trends and techniques make the exhibition's power to transform all the more potent.

2.3 MUSEUMS AS ACTIVIST INSTITUTIONS

As the drive to be more relevant and constructive in society becomes more urgent, some museums have become more strident in how they advocate through their exhibitions. Even pop culture subject matter now explore serious questions about contemporary issues, and increasingly call for real-world action from their audiences. We have seen how the transformative power of exhibitions as communication platforms can inspire such action. The question is how far can they go in this direction before their precious reserves of trust capital—and their overall effectiveness in achieving their goals—begins to diminish. How can museums grapple with divisive current issues without falling into traps of false equivalency (presenting two sides of an issue as if each had an equal claim on the evidence) or the pitfalls of political advocacy? To what extent can museums take a stand on controversial issues? How do museums ensure they heal social divisions rather than exacerbate them? One way to answer these questions is to consider the likely impact of an activist exhibition on trust levels.

There is no doubt that museums exert influence, no matter how much they might try to be neutral. They are, in fact, "soft power" institutions, a concept developed by the scholar Joseph Nye and explored in the museum context by Gail Lord and Ngaire Blankenberg and others.[10] These thought leaders have noted museums' ability to project soft power, a form of diplomacy, in the service of this or that point of view. Museum soft power can be exerted at various levels: at the level of the individual, at the municipal or city level, or even an international level (e.g., the use of museums to advance national pride or status). Persuasion is its stock in trade.

Soft power has a wide spectrum of applications. At one end, it can involve a more-or-less objective presentation of hard facts and their resulting conclusions. As noted, a museum deploying even this mild version of soft power is not neutral. As Marcie M. Muscat says, the museum is "a subtle peddler of influence, promoting an agenda of its own devising" with exhibition narratives "dictated by the objects shown and their means of display, and the prescriptiveness of the story is made less perceptible through careful curation."[11] But the unavoidable fact of curation in and of itself eliminates any possibility of neutrality.

At the other end of the spectrum is more overt activism. Most museums continue to shy away from this "harder" form of soft power, but there are growing pressures for that to change. Some pressures come from within; for museum staff who make morally powerful arguments regarding funding ethics or hiring inequities, a step in the direction of political activism in exhibitions is not a large one. The pressure for change can also extend to museums' relationships with the outside world. External stakeholders can also influence senior administrators and board members toward more activist or even militant directions in exhibition development. For them, morality, ethics, and global existential threats mean unequivocally that if you're not part of the solution, you're part of the problem. This trend has put museum leaders in a very difficult position, since they must now tread carefully between the demands of activist staff, the expectations of their audiences, and their board members and donors, many of whom are wary of wading into politics and other controversial issues.

Some thought leaders believe it is time for museums to become more vocal in their defense of facts and reason and on issues of political and social justice. As Richard Sandell and Robert R. Janes say in the very first lines of their preface to their 2019 book *Museum Activism*, "Only a decade ago, the notion that museums, galleries and heritage organisations might engage in activist practice—marshalling and directing their unique resources with explicit intent to act upon inequalities, injustices, and environmental crises—was met with widespread skepticism and often derision."[12]

This is no longer the case. For Sandell and Janes, museums are a "sleeping giant" and a potentially powerful "force for good."[13] As social and political divides grow broader, as existential planetary crises become deeper, and as society at large and the museums in particular become more diverse, institutions consider the question of activism more and more seriously. In their volume, Sandell and Janes say that museums can communicate an alternative to the corporatist narrative of early twenty-first-century history. For them, activism is a moral duty, necessitated by the failure of political leadership and business elites to confront the emergencies of the times.

Museums are not isolated from the volatility of contemporary society (and never were). But how should they exercise their power in this context? How far can museums go while remaining effective agents of change? Should they "harden" their soft power?

Obviously, some areas are noncontroversial: a museum that did *not* take an unequivocal stand against racism or some other clear-cut moral question would lose all credibility. But for more contentious issues, "hardening" its soft power influence has risks, especially in some societies where basic acts of good citizenship and common decency—such as wearing masks during the COVID-19 pandemic—are politicized. The main **risk** is that activist museums will become "tribal signifiers," especially in low-trust societies, with the practice of museum-going becoming a badge of membership in a specific sociopolitical group. Given the progressive political leanings of most museum staff members, this tribal signifier would likely be characterized as "left wing," "liberal," or "elite" but of course this can vary. The implications must be carefully considered. How will activism affect the value of its well-deserved reserves of trust capital, its ability to build up social trust overall, and, therefore, its ability to effect positive change?

The answer will vary from society to society, but the main point is that museums should consider implications for staff and funding as well as reputation in exhibition planning. There are many instructive examples. One controversy that took place at the Museum of Art and Design at Miami Dade College in Florida in 2020–2021, underscores the potential for damage. The museum had undertaken an exhibition in partnership with a London-based group called Forensic Architecture, which investigates human rights violations. The exhibition, *Forensic Architecture: True to Scale*, was intended to be a vehicle for investigating a nearby detention center for immigrant children funded by the US government through a private operator. This exhibition was seen to have entered the realm of investigative journalism, in essence a three-dimensional version of the press (and it is worth remembering that the press is not nearly as well-trusted as museums, according to the surveys cited above). The exhibition's political overtones likely cost its curator her job while raising alarm among many of the museum's trustees.[14]

Museums must also consider their potential visitors. Some survey results show lower income and younger segments of society much less trusting of institutions and authority.[15] If their goal is inclusivity and effectiveness, museums must understand the psychology of those who are not as open to new experiences, the questioning of formerly accepted narratives, or embracing multiple perspectives. In commenting on the 2020 film *Hillbilly Elegy*, one conservative writer noted how the rural people depicted in the film reject new experiences as a defensive measure against so-called urban elites in order to preserve their established values, and also to avoid the "reverse snobbery" to which they might be subject from their peers.[16] Museums already struggle to attract this demographic; an activist approach is likely to make that struggle all the more difficult, further isolating museums from a large percentage of the population and compromising their ability to maximize unity in the fight against common problems. It is therefore necessary for museums to do the work that will allow them to better understand the questions, concerns, and lived experience of less trusting segments of society in order to properly communicate with them.

Finally, and most importantly, there is the question of how effective activist exhibitions can be at effecting the transformations needed to achieve consensus on wicked problems. If an exhibition reaches only the people who already agree with its position, it is merely preaching to the converted. Can a museum exhibition be a vehicle of inclusivity and reconciliation when a large and influential proportion of the population are neither open nor interested in engaging with it? Is it enough merely to mobilize audiences who are already sympathetic to the cause?

All of this is to say that museums should ponder the likely impact on trust levels—both in maintaining their existing levels of public trust, and in their potential to build it more generally—when considering exhibition projects. It is also important that they try to understand the concerns of a broad swath of the potential audience in order to be most effective in change-making.

2.4 CORPORATE SPONSORSHIP: HOW CLOSE IS TOO CLOSE?

In considering the need to preserve trust capital, the always-present need to generate revenue can also produce problems. With the long-term decline in government subsidies, museums have focused on increased revenues from earned and contributed sources to fill the gap. But there are dangers for museums' credibility as trusted sources of information here as well.

The need to generate increased revenue is real, and while financial pressures long predated the COVID-19 pandemic, that world-historical event was catastrophic for museums' balance sheets. One report stated that the average American museum had lost some US$850,000 in revenue in the first several months of the pandemic, and that many were in danger of permanent closure.[17] As with so many other things, the pandemic accelerated preexisting trends toward innovation in revenue generation, leading museums to think more expansively about increasing nongovernment revenue streams for some time.

The phenomenon of "exhibits for hire" is one manifestation of that thinking. Exhibitions that some have called "sponsored content" skate perilously close to ethical lines, mirroring similar trends in journalism.[18] Just as traditional media, such as newspapers, have tried to reverse losses from declining ad revenue by publishing such content, so too have some museums done the same via exhibitions. And there are other instances of trust-threatening proximity to corporate concerns: for example, the ethical conflicts of for-profit art galleries sponsoring museum exhibitions of artists they represent, since such exposure might increase auction prices or a gallery's future business prospects.[19]

Corporate partnerships have long been a feature of museum business strategies, and these will continue to be important in the future. To maintain appropriate distance, a key issue is curatorial independence where sponsors influence curatorial choices, however questions around credibility thus emerge. The other safeguard is clarity wherein complete transparency around a company's role in exhibit-making is needed. Awareness of these two principles in exhibition development can help museums maintain trust.

2.5 THE WAY FORWARD

This is a time when many formerly unquestioned tenets of museum ethics and operations are being tested. From debates around the use of monies, from collection deaccessioning to questions around ethically correct funding sources, to the proper role of museums in solving our large-scale "wicked problems," what was once taken for granted is now up for revision, and it will be some time before a consensus is reestablished. While this chapter has focused on the latter issue, its topic is of a piece with many contemporary issues in the field. Assessing an exhibition project's impact on trust and effectiveness is one tool to help museums navigate such a fraught landscape.

Due to their prominence, exhibitions are at the center of many of these debates. At their best, they can be effective tools to rally majorities around solutions to serious societal problems. Due to the trust they enjoy, museums can be a force for unification, using the transformative power of exhibitions as a kind of antidote to the division fostered by so many other public platforms. Current trends in exhibitions reinforce this potential, since the "public town hall" nature of many exhibitions fosters debate and discussion, affective learning, and changed perspectives. Multi-perspective exhibitions have all but erased the idea of a universal narrative, which leaves room for competing opinions and, hopefully, some consideration of opposite viewpoints. The ultimate goal is consensus and action.

For this mediation role to work, trust is the single most important factor. We know that museums are trusted, amplifying their ability to influence. George Schultz sums it up:

> Trust is fundamental, reciprocal, and, ideally, pervasive. If it is present, anything is possible. If it is absent, nothing is possible. The best leaders trust their followers with the truth, and you know what happens as a result? Their followers trust them back. With that bond, they can do big, hard things together, changing the world for the better.[20]

Trust is the linchpin: with it, things can happen. Without it, effectiveness is diminished.

It is important to be clear: the need for museums to maintain public trust does not imply they should avoid taking a stand on obvious injustices, nor should they shy away from controversial topics. A major source of museums' trust capital springs from truth-telling: we must go where the facts take us, and not succumb to false equivalency or "alternative facts." Museums actually do have "a duty to be political" as one writer states, not only to help solve existential problems, but also to be on the front lines in the fight against racism, for example, or in the defense of scientific integrity.[21] But they also have a duty to be effective, which means that the preservation of trust capital must be a consideration in exhibition-making.

The process of exhibition development discussed in subsequent chapters of this book lays out all the considerations for creating excellent experiences. This chapter has hopefully provided broad parameters for the approach to those experiences to empower many new exhibitions to generate positive social change in a world that desperately needs it. Museums can provide a venue for discussions that generate the unity to tackle society's wicked problems—even as polarization itself has become a wicked problem. The answers are complex, but a reconceptualization of exhibition development processes is an important component. Staff will likely need to acquire and cultivate new kinds of skills.

Evaluation of exhibition proposals is another angle: Does a proposal preserve and build trust as it tries to advance a social good? Do we truly understand the questions and concerns of the segments of society we are trying to reach, especially those with lower levels of trust? How far can we push boundaries and maintain trust? These types of questions can help build understanding and guide exhibition development, or at the very least help museums approach their exhibitions with their eyes wide open to the potential implications.

To solve our wicked problems, we need to talk to one another. The multidirectional communication in modern-day museum exhibitions can be an effective platform. When founded on public trust, exhibitions have the power to leverage their transformative power as never before by using their trusted status to not only help achieve consensus, but also to build trust in society generally, using this advantage to contribute to a successful, higher-trust society. As the purpose of museum exhibitions continues to evolve, so too must the process of creating them, if we are to fully realize opportunities for positive change.

NOTES

1. Barry Lord, "The Purpose of Museum Exhibitions," in Barry Lord and Maria Piacente, eds., *The Manual of Museum Exhibitions*, second edition (Lanham, MD and Plymouth, UK: Rowman & Littlefield 2014), 12.
2. George P. Schultz, "The ten most important things I've learned about trust over my 100 years, *Washington Post*, December 11, 2020, https://www.washingtonpost.com/opinions/2020/12/11/10-most-important-things-ive-learned-about-trust-over-my-100-years/?arc404=true.
3. There are several such studies. From the United Kingdom, see the Museums Association, "Public perceptions of—and attitudes to—the purpose of museums in society" (2013), https://www.museumsassociation.org/app/uploads/2020/06/03042013-britain-thinks.pdf, a British companion to the oft-cited Lake, Snell, and Perry survey released in 2001 and commissioned by the American Alliance of Museums. For the 2017 study, see Colleen Dilenschneider, "People Trust Museums More than Newspapers. Here's Why That Matters Right Now," April 26, 2017, at https://www.colleendilen.com/2017/04/26/people-trust-museums-more-than-newspapers-here-is-why-that-matters-right-now-data/. A 2019 update appears at https://www.colleendilen.com/2019/03/06/in-museums-we-trust-heres-how-much-data-update/.
4. Dilenschneider, "People Trust Museums More Than Newspapers."
5. Jon Kolko, "Wicked Problems: Problems Worth Solving," March 6, 2012, https://ssir.org/books/excerpts/entry/wicked_problems_problems_worth_solving#:~:text=A%20wicked%20problem%20is%20a,these%20problems%20with%20other%20problems.

6. Rebecca Carlsson, "Why We Need Museums Now More Than Ever," MuseumNext, Oct. 8, 2020, https://www.museumnext.com/article/why-we-need-museums-now-more-than-ever/.
7. Lord, "The Purpose of Museum Exhibitions," 12.
8. Nina Simon, *The Participatory Museum* (Santa Cruz, CA: Museum 2.0, 2010), ii.
9. Kersten Smeds, "On the Meaning of Exhibitions—Exhibition Epistèmes in a Historical Perspective," *Designs for Learning* 5, nos. 1-2 (2012): 69, https://www.researchgate.net/publication/285980155_On_the_Meaning_of_Exhibitions_-_Exhibition_Epistemes_in_a_Historical_Perspective.
10. Gail Lord and Ngaire Blankenberg, eds., *Museums, Cities and Soft Power*. (Washington, DC: The AAM Press, 2015).
11. Marcie M. Muscat, "The Art of Diplomacy: Museums and Soft Power," November 9, 2020, https://www.e-ir.info/2020/11/09/the-art-of-diplomacy-museums-and-soft-power/.
12. Richard Sandell and Robert R. Janes, "Preface" in Richard Sandell and Robert R. Janes, eds., *Museum Activism* (London and New York: Routledge, 2019), xxvii.
13. Richard Sandell and Robert R. Janes, "Introduction" in Richard Sandell and Robert R. Janes, eds., *Museum Activism* (London and New York: Routledge, 2019) 1.
14. See Colin Moynihan, "What did the museum sign up for: exhibition or investigation?", *New York Times*, January 11, 2021, https://www.nytimes.com/2021/01/11/arts/design/forensic-architecture-miami-dade-college.html?action=click&module=Well&pgtype=Homepage&section=Art%20%20Design.
15. While this will vary from country to country, a recent Canadian example can be found at www.cantrustindex.ca.
16. Rod Dreher, "*Hillbilly Elegy*, Class Conflict and Mercy," *The American Conservative*, November 25, 2020, https://www.theamericanconservative.com/dreher/hillbilly-elegy-class-conflict-mercy/.
17. "Museums losing millions, job losses mount as COVID-19 cases surge," American Alliance of Museums, November 17, 2020, https://www.aam-us.org/2020/11/17/museums-losing-millions-job-losses-mount-as-covid-19-cases-surge/.
18. Eileen Kinsella, "'We'd love to work with Netflix again': cash-strapped museums looking for new audiences are increasingly doing exhibits-for-hire," ArtNet, January 4, 2021, https://news.artnet.com/art-world/its-a-deal-is-the-rise-in-museum-sponcon-linked-to-lockdown-1933514.
19. Anny Shaw, "How serious are the dangers of market sponsorship of museum exhibitions?," *The Art Newspaper*, January 27, 2020, https://www.theartnewspaper.com/analysis/public-spaces-private-money.
20. Schultz, "The ten things I learned about trust."
21. Jillian Steinhauer, "Museums have a duty to be political," *The Art Newspaper*, March 20, 2018, https://www.theartnewspaper.com/comment/museums-have-a-duty-to-be-political.

Chapter 3

Where Do Exhibition Ideas Come From?

Barry Lord (updated by Maria Piacente)[1]

If museum exhibitions at their best offer a transformative experience expanding or altering visitors' awareness of, interest in, and valuation of many aspects of themselves and their world, it might be thought that ideas for such exhibitions could originate only with museum professionals who are experts in their respective fields. A few decades ago, this assumption would have been taken for granted, and this chapter would not have been considered necessary in a book on museum exhibitions. Indeed, it is still often true, and the role of the informed connoisseur in sparking museum exhibition ideas remains critical, often crucial, to the genesis of a great exhibition.

Nevertheless, such an approach to the museum exhibition also points to other possibilities. Should the museum exhibition arise from a problem in that discipline's research on the topic? Or should the subject matter respond to public interest, or public demand? What is the role of the community for whom the exhibition is intended, some of whom may not previously have been museum visitors at all? How can they participate in the creation of museum exhibition ideas that are relevant to them? This chapter explores these issues as they affect the planning and development of museum exhibitions and suggests a visitor-centered approach.

3.1 RESEARCH-BASED AND MARKET-DRIVEN EXHIBITIONS

The questions posed above are often presented as an irreconcilable alternative based on the widely held belief that museum exhibitions must either be research-based or market-driven:

1. A **research-based exhibition** program is one that arises from the discipline itself, from an analysis of the museum collection, or from the interests of the museum's curators. It is proposed as worth doing because it will advance our knowledge of the field—our appreciation of the importance of a hitherto undervalued artist, the discovery or interpretation of an archaeological site, or the ecology of an endangered species, for example.

2. By contrast, a **market-driven exhibition** program arises from public interest or demand, as interpreted by the museum. Political events may suggest the need for an exhibition on the culture of a foreign country. The popularity of an artist may prompt a retrospective. Growing concerns with climate might generate a widespread interest in environmental education and climate change. Or health concerns might suggest an exhibition on wellness and mental health.

Although these alternatives have often been presented in professional discussions of the subject as if they were opposed, their opposition is in practice a false dichotomy. This may be expressed in the following statement of principle:

> On the one hand, research, even in the most rarified of disciplines, does not take place in a social vacuum, and on the other hand public interest is always relevant to the direction of socially responsible research. It is precisely the challenge of museum professionals to forge these links. Thus, a successful museum exhibition program should be *both* research-based *and* market-driven. The exhibition policy should articulate this objective in terms relevant to the specific discipline(s) of the museum and should indicate how the museum proposes to be responsive to its community and its audience.

Turner, Whistler, Monet: Impressionist Visions was a major traveling exhibition organized by the Art Gallery of Ontario (Toronto, Canada), the Tate Britain (London, United Kingdom), and the Réunion des Musées Nationaux and Musée d'Orsay (Paris, France). It is a true example of a research-driven exhibition that interprets how each artist changed the course of landscape painting and how a pattern of themes and variations begun by Turner appears to have been developed in the artistic interchange between the younger artists Whistler and Monet.

In extreme contrast, *Game of Thrones: The Touring Exhibition* was created by HBO in partnership with GES Events, featuring actual props and costumes used in the popular series, themed reconstructed immersive environments of the North, Westeros, and Meereen, as well as special effects, interactive multimedia, and of course, the iconic Iron Throne. This market-driven exhibition took advantage of the worldwide appeal of the books and television series. While it can be argued that the *Game of Thrones* exhibition does not have the curatorial and perhaps perceived gravitas of a *Turner, Whistler, Monet* exhibition, both have a place in a museum's responsibility to serve it audiences and meet institutional needs that include the creation of new knowledge, revenue generation, and increased attendance.

3.2 PLANNING FOR EXHIBITION RESEARCH

Desirable as such practices may be, many museum professionals may view the principle of merging research-based with market-driven considerations in an exhibition program as merely a pious wish—a laudable objective, but one that defies achievement in the day-to-day deployment of

Figure 3.1. Banners promoting the *Turner, Whistler, Monet: Impressionist Visions* exhibition, June 12 to September 12, 2004, at the Art Gallery of Ontario, Toronto, Canada. © ART GALLERY OF ONTARIO. A-17661

Figure 3.2. *The Game of Thrones Touring Exhibition* at the Titanic Exhibition Centre in Belfast, Northern Ireland. PA IMAGES/ALAMY STOCK PHOTO

time, money, resources, and personnel to operate a museum exhibition program. Indeed, curators responsible for exhibition programs but also trying to conduct research are often encountered in one or the other of two scenarios, neither of which is desirable:

- Some curators may attempt to oblige the research requirements of a constantly changing exhibition program that is responsive to public interest. In this position they are able to accomplish only a series of brief forays into an unrelated sequence of research topics, developing each subject only as far as the limited time allowed in a demanding schedule. Exhibition catalogs and storylines may get written, and shows are installed on time, but the curator remains a generalist unable to pursue any one topic, while the permanent collection and even new acquisitions may remain indefinitely without the research that is needed in order to realize their full value.

- The other alternative, equally unsatisfactory for both the museum and its staff, is for the curator to withdraw from the exhibition program, delegating their responsibility to an assistant, a designer, or an exhibition officer, freeing the curator to pursue research that may be only tangentially related to the collection, and is often expressed only in the form of scholarly articles in the learned journals of that profession. In this scenario, the curator aspires to become a research professor who does not teach.

Although many museum professionals may not be faced with these dire alternatives, they are likely to recognize them as the opposite poles of a spectrum of options, none of which are entirely satisfactory to the museum or to its staff. The solution is for the museum to develop a research policy, and for the curators, conservators, designers, educators, and exhibition officers to develop research plans:

- A museum's research policy should establish the museum's commitment to research, confirming that time, money, personnel, and facilities will be dedicated to and in keeping with the museum's mission. This may vary from a commitment to keep abreast of the latest developments at a *kunsthalle* exhibiting contemporary art, to a long-term commitment to undertake studies of environmental changes on regional flora or fauna based on the study of specimens at a university's natural history museum. The research policy should articulate the museum's position on supporting grant applications for its staff to pursue research interests, and the museum's approach to intellectual property issues, distinguishing publications or other results of research that are based on work done at the museum from the fruits of research done on the staff members' own time. The policy should describe the range of research to be undertaken at the museum, hopefully including research on the museum's market, its communications, and education programs, as well as curatorial and conservation studies. Above all, the research policy should require all museum personnel who wish to undertake research to prepare an annual personal research plan, which after approval the museum can integrate into a general research plan for the whole institution.

- Each museum staff member who wishes to do research—and this might include docents, volunteers, educators, marketing or development officers, membership clerks, or building managers as well as curators, curatorial assistants, and conservators—should be asked to prepare an annual personal research plan. This plan should set out objectives for that individual's research and relate those objectives to the permanent collection and the museum's public programs, which may include exhibitions, but may also extend to education, market development, or other programs. The research plan should describe the researcher's particular qualifications and propose a methodology that addresses both the academic and practical implications, such as financial or travel needs. The research plan should also project a schedule, over many years, if necessary, for completion of the research. Each annual research plan should be an update of the last, reporting progress or obstacles encountered, and recommending changes if necessary.

Each individual's research plan should be subject to review and approval by the level to which each staff member reports, culminating in a general review and approval by the director, who should undertake integrating all the personal research plans into a general research plan for the entire museum. In this process meetings to discuss each personal research plan may be necessary in order to adjust personal priorities to the mission or corporate plan of the institution, or vice versa.

Many curators and some museum directors are anxious about the introduction of research plans, fearing that they may limit academic freedom of inquiry. With curators especially affected by change on all sides and fighting to retain the role of research within museums, these concerns are understandable. But in fact, research plans as described here can be instrumental in resolving the dilemma implied by the alternative outlined above: of curators being dragged from one exhibition to another versus the equally unsatisfactory option of the curator who withdraws from the exhibition program in order to pursue other research interests. A museum is neither a university nor a research institution, but it can be a vital center of research in all disciplines, both in relation to the permanent collection and in serving the institution's public programs. An annually updated general research plan for the entire museum that is based on the personal research plans of all the interested staff can be a dynamic way of keeping research at the heart of the museum.

For example, the general research plan for a natural history museum might include the ornithology curator's personal research plan to investigate the species relationships within a particular genus of birds based on DNA analysis, song analysis, and field research. The schedule for this work may be projected over several years. The director, advised by the marketing and education departments, may decide that the museum's exhibition program really needs a *Birds in Backyards* exhibition, which will meet a school curriculum need related to climate change and pollution, and will also be fun for family visitors. The decision as to whether to shift the direction of the ornithology curator's research work over the next year in order to plan and develop this exhibition may now be considered in the light of the long-term research plan that has already been integrated into the museum's general research plan. One alternative might be to engage a guest curator for the special exhibition, and to prepare a marketing and retail program that will increase attendance, revenue, private donations, sponsorships, or government grants to justify the additional expense.

An important consideration in resolving this example is that the ornithological species research project should be included in the museum's general research plan only if it is itself related to the museum's public program objectives: a major new display of the permanent collection of birds, together with an associated education program, scheduled to be launched three years from now, for instance. The decision then becomes one of weighing one longer-range museum public programming objective against another, shorter-range one. Whatever decision is made, with the aid of the research plan and a research policy, curatorial research can be integrated with the museum's public programs, the curator is no longer being dragged from one topic to another without regard for continuity or for the museum's long-term needs, and the decision about the exhibition program is now perceived as integrally related to decisions about priorities for the museum's research activity. Museum research can be transformed from its frequent status as a desirable but too often impractical pursuit into the light of museum policy, planning, and prioritizing procedures.

NOTE

1. Maria Piacente has updated the chapter on behalf of Barry Lord, who died March 9, 2017, and who inspired their collaboration on the second edition of this Manual, 2014.

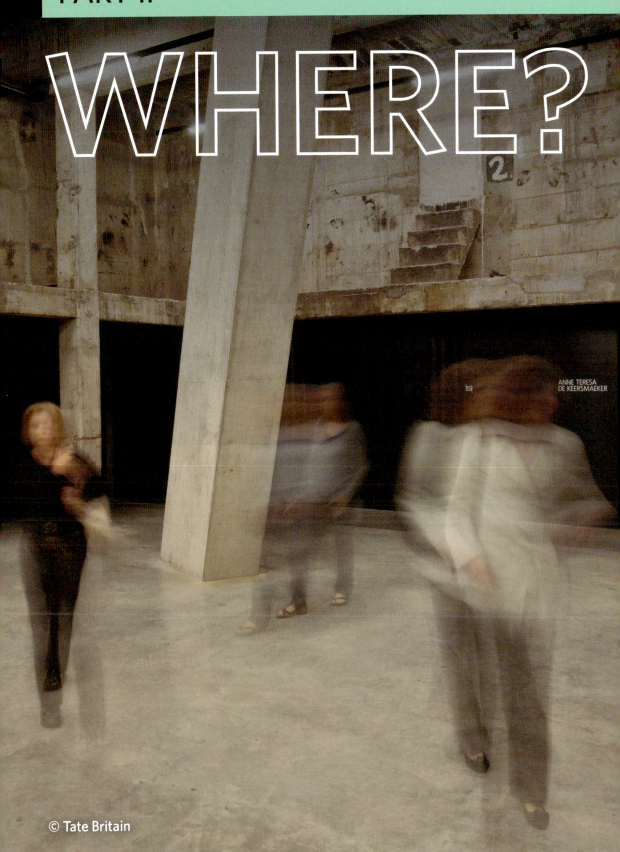

PART II

WHERE?

ANNE TERESA DE KEERSMAEKER

Museum exhibitions are installed in purpose-built galleries, designed to meet the specific needs of the specimens, artifacts, and works of art that will be displayed within them. While exhibitions may be hosted in nonconventional venues and public spaces for pop-up displays as well as contemporary art and multimedia installations, this section focuses on traditional exhibition galleries.

The exhibition gallery provides the space within which objects on display are placed. Yet the gallery itself is conditioned by the museum building as a whole, and that in turn is affected by the building's site. A white cube in a modern building in the heart of the city may be considered appropriate for a contemporary art exhibition or an interactive science center, whereas an exhibition in a historic structure that is itself part of the cultural heritage on display will inform a very different kind of exhibition.

Exhibition galleries used to be predictable boxes, but in recent years their architecture has been far more diverse. Consider the vast swathe of space that accommodates Richard Serra's enormous steel sculpture, which is placed under high ceilings in Frank Gehry's Museo Guggenheim Bilbao, Spain, complete with a mezzanine at one end that allows visitors to appreciate the heft and swoop of the massive sculpture from above. At the other extreme are low-ceilinged spaces of modest size and proportions that provide a comfortable setting for a few visitors at a time to enjoy some rare etchings or drawings at a level of lighting kept deliberately low to reduce the lux-hours of exposure of the precious works on paper.

Understanding the nuts and bolts of what makes galleries work not only ensures that an exhibition will be fully accommodated, but that visitors will enjoy experiencing the gallery space. This section provides an overview of design criteria for exhibition spaces and reviews the vast range of factors that have to be considered when planning to build or renovate a gallery. The differences between permanent collection displays and temporary exhibition galleries are examined, as are the functional requirements for security, environmental control, and set-up or striking of exhibition furnishings.

You might be wondering, "Why do I need to know this? I'm not an architect!" Even though you may not be an architect or facility manager, understanding how exhibition spaces function within the museum building envelope will make you a better exhibition planner.

Chapter 4

Exhibition Facilities

Sean Stanwick and Heather Maximea

A museum's exhibition galleries are its main public areas. They should be splendid spaces that inspire and engage visitors as they move from one experience to another. Planning and designing galleries as part of a museum facility is exhilarating but challenging because it requires planners to envision the completed exhibition product that will someday be housed there, whether it is a long-term permanent collection display or a series of short-term temporary or traveling exhibitions. This visioning must consider the total experience for visitors and the superlative settings for the art, artifacts, specimens, and new media that will be part of the overall story.

The design and layout of the gallery spaces, and the sequence of movement through them, is critical to the experience. Akin to a movie or well-crafted story, the gallery experience should facilitate ease of movement and clarity of wayfinding. Permanent exhibitions must keep the attention of visitors as items are often displayed for long periods of time. Changing galleries, on the other hand, must be flexible enough to accommodate a wide range of works and exhibition styles and sizes.

Unfortunately, many galleries fall short of the ideal. Lack of consideration for exhibit support spaces will have significant downstream effects such as repeated delays in getting exhibitions fully installed in time for openings; insurance claims for damage to art works; and reluctance or refusal of prestigious lenders to become involved in new projects. Why do these problems occur? If staff is asked for a candid analysis, they may well identify inconvenient, inefficient, and poorly planned building services and support areas as well as gallery spaces that do not meet the demands placed on them by the museum's programs.

The ideal time to plan for the best possible facilities to accommodate exhibitions is when new buildings, expansions, or full-scale building renovations are being considered. Every effort made at the early planning stages will reap benefits for years to come in exhibition effectiveness.

4.1 A WORLD OF EXHIBITION SPACES

In many cases, a single art museum will require a range of differently sized permanent collection and temporary exhibition spaces to accommodate its collection and realize its programming needs. Some options may include:

- Exhibition spaces for small- to medium-sized paintings and sculpture, architecture, and design of 1,500–3,000 square feet (150–300sq m) with preferred clear ceiling heights of 15 feet (5.5 m) below all ductwork and light fixtures. These may be interconnecting or stand-alone spaces.

- Small, intimate-scale exhibition spaces for small-scale paintings, sculpture, decorative arts, photography, and works on paper of 1,000–1,500 square feet (100–150 sq m) with minimum clear ceiling heights of 13 feet (4 m) below all ductwork and light fixtures.

- Grand exhibition spaces for contemporary art, installation and performance art, large-scale traditional paintings, textiles, and sculpture of 5,000–8,000 square feet (500–800 sq m) with at least 18–24 feet (6–8 m) ceilings below all ductwork and light fixtures, maximized wall and floor space, and ability to use temporary wall systems to subdivide the space.

- A single special installations hall of 8,000–12,000 square feet (800–1,200 sq m) or more, doubling as a temporary exhibitions hall and capable of accommodating a variety of media. Ceilings would need to be upward of 24 feet (8 m) below all ductwork and light fixtures, with excellent suspension capacity and an opportunity to use temporary wall systems or newly built enclosures to subdivide the space.

- New media exhibition space for art or archives needs to be designed to the specific needs of the media works, in close consultation with curators engaged in acquiring these new types of collections. Requirements may include sound and light locks, multiple projection points, ability to build new enclosures or to change or modify wall and floor coverings, or to incorporate living elements or live performance.

- Thematic or contextual galleries that recreate or evoke the original contexts from which museum objects were taken. A thematic exhibition can vary in format from a walk-through environment to a curated exhibition that may include vitrines, dioramas, or vignettes. The exhibition area may vary widely, from 300–500 square feet (30–50 sq m) in the rooms of a historic house museum to 10,000 square feet (800 sq m) or more of purpose-built museum space. Such spaces are increasingly used for large, immersive projection experiences as a means for creating an environment, requiring adequate power in the ceiling and heights upward of 15 feet (5.5 m).

- "Black box" galleries that feature minimal architectural detailing and exposed structure and services made to disappear by using matte painting and directed lighting. Temporary or movable walls or temporary room structures may be used along with casework, panels, and other exhibition elements to divide the space creatively.

- Children's museums, science museums, and science centers are among the fastest growing museum types around the world and are often oriented toward science and technology, natural or cultural history, ethnology, or art all presented with the intention to foster learning, exploration, and intercreativity. Interactivity in the children's gallery context can be low-tech storytelling or role playing; medium-tech art making; or high-tech multimedia and digital applications. A safe assumption for a single children's discovery exhibition space would be a minimum of 2,000–3,000 square feet (200–300 sq m).

- Study spaces within the exhibition incorporates research and areas for the public for greater access to collections and enhanced learning opportunities. The area required for separate rooms may be as little as 300–500 square feet (30–50 sq m), with ceiling heights not much above 12 feet (4 m).

- An outdoor art display space such as a sculpture terrace, sculpture walk, or sculpture garden that extends the exhibition space providing a different context for selected works.

4.2 DEVELOPING DESIGN CRITERIA FOR EXHIBITION SPACES

For every museum and interpretive program that requires gallery and support facilities, there is a vast range of potential solutions that may be considered, rejected, selected, and modified according to site, building, and budget opportunities and constraints. What are the best solutions for a particular situation? One method is to develop a set of principles, or **design criteria**, that describe, first, the desired result, and second, the means of evaluating success in achieving that result. The subjective and objective design criteria for exhibition space will be instrumental in guiding development of facilities that meet exhibition needs over many years. As figure 4.1

1. VISION: Do the galleries support and enhance the institution's mission and interpretive vision?

2. PLANNING: Are the galleries "right-sized" to meet program requirements, budget realities, and ensure sustainable operations?

3. EXECUTION: Does the implementation reflect an intentional approach that understands the importance of the art environment?

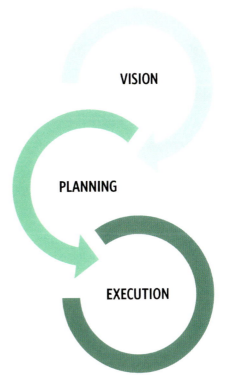

Figure 4.1. Vision-Driven design criteria. LORD CULTURAL RESOURCES

Exhibition Facilities

demonstrates a framework for developing criteria, decisions should ultimately be viewed through three primary lenses: vision, planning, and execution.

1. **Vision**: Do the galleries support and enhance the institution's mission and interpretive vision?
2. **Planning**: Are the galleries "right-sized" to meet program requirements, budget realities, and ensure sustainable operations?
3. **Execution**: Does the implementation reflect an intentional approach that understands the importance of the art environment?

4.2.1 Vision-Driven Design Criteria

Vision-driven design criteria for exhibition galleries center around determining the overall concept for the space based on the vision, mission, and mandate of the museum. A vision or conceptual statement expressing the ethos of exhibition spaces underlies design criteria that suggest their character in conceptual and qualitative terms. The building concept in inspirational terms may be developed by the architect, reflecting a conceptual statement that expresses the institution's vision in more concrete terms applicable to facility planning. This concept can then be applied to the exhibition galleries. Or the design criteria may derive directly from the vision statement itself. Qualitative criteria might include the following:

- **Visionary**: Does it raise aspirations for what the institution can be in the future?
- **Galvanizing**: Does it reflect consensus around shared values?
- **Provoking**: Is it a catalyst for rethinking the institution's larger role?
- **Responsible**: Does it make the best use of capital and infrastructure resources?
- **Flexible**: Can it accommodate present needs and future expansion?
- **Brand building**: Does it express an image reflective of the brand?
- **Integrated**: Is it woven into, and respectful of the local community?
- **Asset building**: Can it be a driver for long-term prosperity?

4.2.2 Planning-Driven Design Criteria

The other essential component of the planning process for new or renovated display spaces is a set of functional or planning design criteria that guide the architects, engineers, building contractors, and exhibition designers working on the project.

One of the most important considerations for planning display facilities is the relative degree of flexibility of use that needs to be designed into the space. Museum exhibition halls may be designed as more or less permanent architectural entities with a strong character of their own; however, a more compelling case for sustainability considers spaces that are easier to transform into new environments as the occasion demands. Museums today are incorporating an array of new types of galleries, specifically designed to meet the needs of particular exhibition types. The new gallery may or may not be subordinate to the exhibitions installed within it; for example, Tate Modern's Tank Galleries carry with them the architectural character of their former use while being redesigned and retrofitted to meet the need for large volumes of space with high technical

Figure 4.2. The Tank Galleries at the Tate Modern, London, Tate Photography. PHOTO © TATE

support for performances, installations, and performance art. Deciding what level of flexibility and technology will be required by a new display is a high-level decision early in the planning process that in itself may require extensive exploration of options and costs, usually benefitting from a dialogue with specialists.

Preliminary objective design criteria begins to emerge in the early stages of planning for a new facility. These may include:

- Meeting national or international museum accreditation standards
- Meeting collection standards for climate control and security
- Planning for operational efficiency and sustainability objectives
- Considering future expansion options or phasing
- Addressing the spatial requirements of both permanent collection display and temporary exhibition programs
- Completing the project on time and on budget
- Meeting the physical needs of distinct audiences, such as children
- Considerations for pandemic planning particularly for queuing and social distancing

Addressing each of these requirements with measurable objectives requires quantification of data on current operations, present and future collections, and close numeric projection of future needs. Comparables or best practice information may be needed to supplement existing data.

Although planning may begin with either a preliminary capital budget or an initial notion of the size and complexity of the exhibition facility, these cannot be taken as given. Various strategies of testing the fit between the desired state-of-the-art display facility and the realities of site, building, capital budget, and future operating budget are imperative to avoid costly design mistakes and cost overruns, and to achieve positive, realistic goals. Testing may include:

- Quantitative and qualitative collections analysis and projection of the "design object"—the largest or most technologically complex and demanding work of art, artifact, specimen, apparatus, graphic, or design component to be likely or most frequently accommodated.
- Quantification of audience and market data and attendance projections for the "design day"—the number of people likely to be in the building and in the exhibition on a busy day.
- Projection of sizes and types of display and support facilities based on the planned exhibition program, considering the workload required to support the given space and activity level.
- Review of the fit between plans for display facilities and overall site and building planning.

To ensure that the galleries fulfill these criteria, an experienced museum planner should work with the museum's staff to prepare a "brief" or "functional program" to guide the architects and designers, and then should work with them to ensure compliance. Most importantly, once developed and agreed by the museum's leadership, the functional requirements or design criteria should be implemented at every stage of gallery design and construction. Changes to the physical space must not be allowed on a whim of the architect, contractor, or museum director, but should be a result of deliberate and balanced reconsideration of all factors by the museum planner and all other members of the planning and design team.

4.2.3 Execution-Driven Design Criteria

At the heart of many museum exhibition projects is the use of collections of art, artifacts, or specimens. These objects are often irreplaceable resources, major assets for their owners, and part of the cultural heritage of mankind. As such, their preservation for posterity is of great importance, and is one of the key mandates of the museum enterprise.

The central decision to be made in setting preventive conservation measures for an exhibition, or for a museum's entire exhibition program, is choosing the **environmental standards** to be maintained. The chosen standards govern the type of building systems installed to serve the galleries, and thus the galleries' capital cost, as well as lifecycle and operating costs. Environmental standards for seven crucial factors affecting museum exhibitions should be considered:

1. Climate control
2. Air movement and outdoor air
3. Air cleanliness
4. Light levels
5. Microclimates
6. Pest management
7. Movement and vibration

4.2.3.1 Climate Control

Best practice for museum and gallery design requires a collection-appropriate climate control system, whether minimal and passive, or a sophisticated active system. The job of the climate control system is to stabilize the interior climate of the building and of each room where collections may be present by regulating swings in **temperature**, **relative humidity (RH)**, and **air movement**, which act on each other to influence the environment of a gallery space.

The risks to collections that unsuitable temperatures and relative humidity levels (particularly fluctuations of those levels) present to museum objects include the development of mold and mildew, chemical deterioration, the detachment of finish layers, and mechanical and structural damage (cracks, breaks, loosened joints) when the object responds to changes in the environment. By providing the optimal environment throughout their collections storage areas, support areas, and galleries, museums can avoid or mitigate these effects both to permanent collections and to museum objects on loan. Therefore, most museums need to think in terms of a stable environment for permanent collections, and in addition, special conditions that may be required for objects on loan. In the exhibition galleries, human comfort is also a factor in determining an acceptable environment.

The professional museum associations of many countries encourage museums to invest in high-quality air-handling equipment and controls as a major criterion of museum accreditation, which in itself provides an assurance to potential donors and lenders that the museum has the facilities to care for the precious objects entrusted to it. Additionally, lending institutions generally require borrowers to fill out a facilities report, which attests to the climate and handling for loans, and lenders may make specific relative humidity, temperature, and lighting requirements.

Determining the requirements for relative humidity and temperature for museums can be a challenge, even for professionally trained staff. The question is often asked whether there is a standard that all museums should meet. The answer to this is that there are indeed standards but that they in turn need to be understood and used with caution; they may provide good protection for *most* objects, but be disastrous for the minority, which tend to be the most fragile. The onus is still on museums to understand their collections and their specialized needs in adapting any standard.

In 1964, R. D. Buck proposed "A Specification for Museum Air-Conditioning" that recommended a general museum humidity level of 55±10 percent relative humidity. During the 1970s, the set point relative humidity recommendation changed to either 50 or 55 percent, and the fluctuation range was reduced to ±5 percent relative humidity as control equipment improved. The standards for museums published in the *1999 ASHRAE Applications Handbook* as a result of this research summarize the maximum fluctuations proposed for collection spaces as five classes of control (AA, A, B, C, and D), and presented the risks and benefits associated with maintaining any particular class of control. The relative humidity set point for all classes of control is 50 percent or the annual average relative humidity in areas like the tropics or cold climate regions where the average annual conditions have been markedly different. The classes relevant to museum exhibitions are AA, A, and B:

- For loan exhibitions, temporary or traveling, the highest standard—AA—will be required by most loan agreements. Class AA requirements should be met by institutions requiring AA standards in their loan agreements or in their own permanent collection display and storage spaces.

Exhibition Facilities

- The difference between AA and A standards for permanent collection display is simply that the lower standard permits two relative humidity fluctuation choices, either with or without seasonal set point adjustments.

- The B standard is relevant primarily to seasonal historic sites in the temperate zone that need to avoid damage to the historic building fabric and may introduce not merely seasonal variations, but also a winter temperature setback aimed at maintaining relative humidity while reducing temperature to a minimum consistent with that relative humidity level.

All three of ASHRAE's (American Society of Heating, Refrigerating, and Air Conditioning Engineers) classes require the same types of equipment to be provided, at similar cost levels. In a building with active control, the equipment would generally consist of air handling units equipped for:

- Heating
- Cooling
- Humidification
- Controlled dehumidification with reheat
- Particulate air filtration
- Gaseous air filtration
- An accurate and stable control system

There is an advantage to acquiring AA-sized equipment—as long as the building is capable of containing an AA environment year-round without deteriorating—since it should be possible to switch the equipment settings between classes at any time. For example, AA may be required for borrowed temporary exhibitions, even though the museum chooses to operate at A or B standards at other times, for reasons of cost and energy savings.

Within the various world climate zones, outdoor temperature and relative humidity may rise and fall rapidly through a daily and seasonal cycle. In some instances, daily cycles may be more significant than seasonal cycles; in all instances, specific regional climatic conditions must be considered. Mechanical engineering consultants can provide extensive analysis of local data and can assist the museum in modeling the best response to hourly, daily, and seasonal climatic variation.

If traveling exhibitions from temperate climates are to be displayed in a tropical region, the temporary exhibition gallery and its support spaces should be capable of maintaining a 50 percent relative humidity set point twenty-four hours per day for the length of time the traveling objects are in the museum. This often means that the suite of rooms used for receiving and displaying traveling exhibitions will require a dedicated HVAC system. At the absolute minimum, air circulation systems should operate twenty-four hours a day to ensure pockets of hot or cold, damp, or dry air do not develop. At those times when local collections are on display, the relative humidity set point would be adjusted to match the level found in the rest of the museum collection spaces.

It should be noted that in 2019 ASHRAE released recommendations suggesting a relaxing of the environmental standards to be attained and maintained within collection spaces with the objective of reducing energy consumption and costs. This research also offered that somewhat broader ranges of temperature and relative humidity fluctuation may be acceptable for most objects. However, the risks involved must be assessed for each class of material, in each climate situation. The differences between tropical, temperate, and arctic climates, and between continental and maritime climates, impact these general recommendations and must be studied in the facilities development stages.

4.2.3.2 Air Movement and Outdoor Air

The quality and quantity of outside air that enters the exhibition space affects visitors and collections alike. Outside air has to be warmed or cooled, with moisture added or removed, for the comfort of visitors and for preservation of the collections. It has to be kept moving in order to promote the right level of exchange and to prevent pockets of stagnant air where mold may grow. At the same time, gusts of air can chill and dry artifacts even when protected by a vitrine—so excessive air pressure and too many air changes per hour should be avoided. Carbon dioxide emitted by visitors can also put additional loads on the climate control systems, as excessive carbon dioxide can be harmful to sensitive works of art. Carbon dioxide sensors should be installed in galleries and collection storage areas to monitor air quality and adjust the amount of outdoor air to be provided by the HVAC system. A museum building and its exhibition spaces should be designed to provide passive protection for the collections so that in case of equipment breakdown or energy outages the museum-quality environmental conditions can be maintained. Thermal gradients should be present in galleries because of stratification—warm air rising and cold air falling—and because of the heat of the lights in the gallery, the thermal influence of visitors, and the presence of any exterior walls, roofs, windows, or skylights. To combat stratification and to provide frequent treatment of the air so that close control is possible, the number of times the volume of air in the space should pass through the air handling unit between six and eight times per hour, compared with the non-museum standard of four to six times per hour. As many as eight to twelve air changes per hour may be required during public hours in popular exhibition galleries.

4.2.3.3 Air Cleanliness

Clean air is essential for a good exhibition environment. There are two main air pollution dangers for collections: particulate pollution, such as the tiny carbon particles that can permanently mark and discolor materials, and gaseous pollution, which can deteriorate fragile materials irreversibly. The museum's air filtration system needs to be designed to combat both types of air pollution. Ideally, the entire museum should be treated so that dirty air does not flow into the galleries from adjacent spaces.

Small, carbon-based particles (less than one micron in diameter) such as diesel soot, which blacken surfaces, require high-efficiency air filters to keep them at bay. Activated carbon filters located in the mixed air stream of the air handling unit should be used, no matter what the exterior gaseous pollutants and their levels are. The use of high voltage electronic (electrostatic) type air filters is to be avoided because of the danger of ozone generation, which can damage collections. The efficiency of filters is measured in either of two ways:

- The North American standard is the efficiency test portion of ASHRAE Standard 52.1-1992: Gravimetric and Dust Spot Procedures for Testing Air Cleaning Devices Used in General Ventilation for Removing Particulate Matter.
- The European equivalent is Eurovent Test 4/5.

Applying these standards, the recommended air filter bank should be composed of:

- A pre-filter that is 30 percent efficient (ASHRAE), class EU 4 (Eurovent)
- A medium filter that is 85 percent efficient (ASHRAE), class EU 7 (Eurovent)
- An activated carbon bed filter providing gaseous pollutant removal
- A final filter that is 95 percent efficient to capture activated carbon dust, class EU 8 (Eurovent)

4.2.3.4 Light Levels

Damage that light can cause to fragile museum objects has long been known to collectors and museum professionals. Increased light on an object will increase surface temperature through infrared heating. This in turn can decrease localized relative humidity and dry out the object. Thus, for both permanent and temporary exhibitions, great care has to be taken not only to control the overall gallery light levels but also to provide appropriate lighting to each object and case.

Figure 4.3 provides light level recommendations that simplify lighting decisions for both temporary exhibitions and permanent collection displays and that also provide safe conditions for most materials.

Class of Objects	Examples	Light Levels	Annual Exposure
Especially Sensitive	Works of art on paper, textiles, feathers, dyed leather, felt pen ink drawings.	50 lux (5 foot-candles)	120,000 lux-hours (11,150 foot-candle hours) per annum.
Sensitive	Oil and varnished tempera paintings; all other organic materials.	200 lux (19 foot-candles)	500,000 lux-hours (46,470 foot-candle-hours) per annum.
Relatively insensitive	Most stone, glass, ceramics, unpainted metal; inorganic materials.	300 lux (28 foot-candles)	NA

Figure 4.3. Recommended light levels for museum exhibitions. LORD CULTURAL RESOURCES

Assuming that the technical standards for lighting can and will be met to preserve the objects on display effectively, there are three systems of artificial lighting within the gallery that need to be considered for different functions:

1. **Exhibition lighting**, intended to highlight individual works, vitrines, or other exhibit components
2. **Ambient light** for safety and comfort of movement of visitors, which may include lighted walkways, ambient room lighting, and emergency lighting

3. **Working lights** that can be turned up and used during exhibition or equipment installation, cleaning, and maintenance

These systems should be part of the lighting plan for a new or renovated gallery space, forming the basic set-up that will be there permanently regardless of future exhibitions. Gallery planning and design should identify the desired degree of flexibility in changing exhibitions, and the demands that this will place on the basic lighting system.

Track lighting is the most frequently encountered system for exhibitions. In an art or archival gallery and most temporary exhibition galleries, it should be possible to light any area of wall or floor surface effectively with an established track lighting system, by moving, adjusting, and refocusing the luminaries. Thus, the track lighting system needs to be designed to provide as complete coverage as possible of the display surfaces. A similar level of overall light coverage using track lighting is a useful basic set-up for thematic and interactive galleries as well, providing the option of focusing a spread of light or a spotlight on a wall, floor, or even a ceiling without having to build this feature into the exhibitry. Having such a basic lighting setup may well help keep costs of special exhibition fabrication down.

Track lighting systems can also accommodate ambient uplighting, working lights, and a drop-down power supply. Control panels for lights in a gallery need to be located near a service entrance, where the person making adjustments can see the entire space. If possible, dimmers and other lighting controls should be accessible to staff, but not to the public. Lamp replacement may be an important consideration in galleries that are high up, requiring a movable sky jack lift or catwalk to access the lights, as in the highest galleries in the Museo Guggenheim Bilbao.

4.2.3.5 Microclimates

Microclimates are special environments found in enclosers such as display cases or dioramas. Microclimates provide protection for certain objects that require different environments from other items in a gallery. For example, the relative humidity set points for many organic objects and for human comfort will not be dry enough for metals that are corroding. Such metal objects can be isolated in sealed vitrines with relative humidity and temperature control to bring moisture levels down to prevent or restrict corrosion.

Microclimates can be useful when a gallery exists within a historic building that cannot provide a good seal against the outdoor environment. Use of microclimates may help to reduce energy costs, depending on the climatic conditions and proposed building systems. Two types of microclimates can be implemented: passive and active.

A **passive microclimate** can be as simple as a framed, matted print with dust-proof backing paper or a more complex system such as an air-tight case with a reconditionable humidity buffer material. Regardless of which method is employed, an important consideration in creating any microclimate is air tightness. Per the 1999 ASHRAE applications handbook, "Most museum cases leak in the range of 10 to 100 air changes per day, but careful design can limit this to 0.1 AC/D." Thus, the better the display case is sealed from outside air, the less need for buffering materials or gallery-wide methods for environmental control.

Figure 4.4. Active climate-controlled cases at the Royal Ontario Museum, Toronto, Canada.
LORD CULTURAL RESOURCES

An **active microclimate** case uses a specially designed and sized air-handling unit that conditions the climate within the display case. In this microclimate, there is less concern about air leakage since the conditioned air is regularly replenished. The air-handling unit may be in a concealed space within or under an individual display case, or in an adjacent room where it may serve one or more cases.

In all microclimate case designs, some means of monitoring the interior climate is recommended, whether it be built-in hygrothermographic equipment, special sensors, or a probe-type wand. In every instance, microclimate case design should be undertaken with professional conservation expertise and extensively tested before being put into operation.

4.2.3.6 Pest Management

Pests range from vermin—mice, rats, and other creatures—to insects, mold, and fungi. Some pests may be endemic to older buildings, others may find their way in with food and supplies, while still more may arrive with new collection items or loans.

The most likely source of an exhibition infestation will be materials brought into the building—food service supplies, office supplies, shop stock, construction materials, new additions to the permanent collection, or objects on loan for traveling exhibitions and their crates. Unpacking of crates in the exhibition galleries is a common practice but is not recommended since infestation of shipments may not be detected until unpacking is underway or even at the point of installation. For this reason, a dedicated crating/uncrating and packing/unpacking area should be designated, and an adjacent isolation room should be dedicated to holding collections for observation prior to being moved into the exhibition spaces. Needless to say, no museum should display an infested artwork or artifact until all signs of active infestation have been eradicated, which may take several weeks.

4.2.3.7 Movement and Vibration

Museum objects and even exhibition components and electronics can suffer harm from careless movement and from sources of vibrations such as uneven and unstable floors, unbalanced or inadequately dampened HVAC equipment, and external vibrations from road, rail, traffic, or construction activities. Equally, security measures inside an exhibition case, such as wax or other stabilizing devices, should also be considered to prevent objects from toppling or "walking" off the edge of a shelf. The case, vitrine, or display platform itself may require an isolating pad to minimize sources of vibration that can loosen case joints, make mounting systems less secure and eventually topple objects.

Smooth floor surfaces are recommended in collection movement and exhibition areas to reduce vibration of carts or dollies. Besides meeting building code requirements for floor loading, the floor structure in exhibition spaces should be constructed of stiff materials that will absorb impact forces without vibrating.

4.3 EXHIBITION SPACE CHARACTERISTICS

This section considers requirements for the exhibition gallery surfaces that bound the spaces within which the exhibition takes place: floors, walls, and ceilings.

4.3.1 The Gallery Shell

The design and construction of the museum building structure provides the container that protects exhibition galleries, support spaces, and their contents from the outdoor environment. The building requires foundations resistant to flooding and earthquakes, along with roof and wall structures and an exterior skin lined with layers of a moisture vapor barrier and insulation that will buffer temperature and relative humidity changes and prevent pests, dust, gaseous pollutants, and the elements from entering. In addition, the building may impact the exhibition gallery through apertures such as exterior doors, windows, and skylights, which could constitute breaches of the security perimeter as well as allowing the outside elements in, or through unnecessary or inappropriate location of building services.

4.3.1.1 A Wall within a Wall

Ideally, collection spaces, including exhibition galleries, should *not* be located on exterior walls. However, in most museum building plans, exterior walls to galleries are inevitable. One way to remedy this is by building a secondary wall inside the exterior shell to frame the gallery and provide additional isolation and buffering. The secondary wall can be extended to a "room within a room" design. The entire internal framing of the gallery—walls, floors, and ceiling—may be used to house and conceal ductwork, wiring, and sprinklers.

4.3.1.2 Exterior Doors

In most cases, for security and environmental stability, exterior doors to a gallery opening directly from the outside world are *not* recommended, particularly public access doors. Even necessary services or fire doors are far better to open from the gallery into an intermediate area such as a vestibule or stairwell, which in its turn may have external access. All exterior doors or other openings should be sealed, weather-stripped, and provided with high-level security alarms and surveillance. The gallery space should be at a slight positive air pressure to adjacent spaces, including the outdoors, so that a pressure barrier is formed protecting the interior environment from contamination.

4.3.1.3 Moisture

Water leakage or flooding is another hazard that can be transferred from the building to the interior gallery spaces. Exhibition spaces should not have water tanks, a water-cooled chiller plant, washrooms, fountains, or pools above or beside them. Exhibition spaces that are below grade should be equipped with moisture sensors monitored by the building management system computer, and exterior basement walls and floors should be treated to prevent water migration. Floor drains should be fitted with backflow preventers, and elevator shaft pits should be provided with a sump pit and pump.

4.3.1.4 Building Systems

Environmental systems and security and life safety systems are usually located and controlled from outside the gallery space. Sprinkler lines, power, and communication connections for video cameras and alarms, and the extensive ductwork needed for air handling not intruding into the gallery. All support systems should be designed and installed in a coordinated manner so as not to take away from usable exhibition space and be as space-efficient and unobtrusive as possible. Design features that should be considered are:

- Design of both structural and mechanical and electrical systems should be coordinated to ensure that services can be tucked up into roof space, run in the troughs between beams, located outside the gallery, or carried in wall spaces.

- Required sizes of openings for supply and return air and electrical and fire panels should be carefully calculated by the mechanical engineers to avoid oversizing. Location and size of these openings should be reviewed and approved by the client to minimize loss of valuable display space.

- Return air should ideally be taken from low level (baseboard) slots within collection spaces with high level supply from the tops of walls or ceiling ducts. This provides the most effective air circulation and reduces harsh air contact with art and artefacts, as well as minimizing the obtrusive appearance of these services.

4.3.2 Load Requirements for Galleries

All gallery structures—walls, floors, and ceilings—must bear the brunt of use and must be designed to support the exhibits, exhibit movement, and visitor traffic. In order to do so, design and construction must take account of the **loading requirements** for museum use of the space. In all cases, the building structure must meet all applicable building codes and should be specified by a qualified architect or structural engineer.

"Loading" refers to the stress placed on a structure by its own weight, gravity, objects placed on it, and/or indirectly by movement and vibration. Loading is measured in three ways:

1. **Line load**: Force or pressure is exerted along a line. The walls themselves and anything attached to them that hangs downward in the same vertical plane, such as paintings, plaques, architectural elements, and screens attached to exhibit walls all exhibit their own structural line load; walls, therefore, must be designed to support or spread line loads.

2. **Point load**: Pressure is placed on a single point or group of points and may be uniform or concentrated:

    - With uniform load, the pressure of the object is spread evenly over its given area. Gallery floors must support the weight of cases or display platforms that may be spread over several square meters or feet. Since it is usually not possible to determine in advance exactly where on the exhibit floor the vitrine may be positioned, it is wise to plan for the entire exhibition floor to be able to support reasonable weights.

    - Sometimes in exhibition areas the weight of objects may not be uniformly distributed across the entire surface, thus concentrated load must often be considered. For concentrated load, the weight of the object is supported on a single point, a small area, and the force exerted on that point multiplies exponentially. In a gallery, this might refer to a tall narrow item positioned on the floor, an aircraft suspended from the ceiling by a single wire, or a painting hung from a single nail.

3. **Drag load**: The extra, but temporary, force exerted by something heavy being dragged across a surface. This refers to moving equipment and objects as well as to the continual passage of visitors' feet across selected areas of the floor. It could cause areas of the floor to become weakened over time or unstable and uneven as a result of timbers moving under pressure. Attention during the design process to expected movement paths from service areas and public access points across and through an exhibition space can allow the structural engineers to strengthen selective floor areas appropriately.

In designing exhibition spaces, architects and engineers need to be aware of established standards and local building codes for occupancy levels (e.g., the number of visitors per square foot or meter of gallery space at peak times) and ensure that this information can be communicated during the building or renovation and refit process. This will help to ensure that no unexpected restrictions on the museum's use of the space will be imposed when it is certified for occupancy. Figure 4.5 provides a rough guide to floor loading standards for different types of exhibition spaces.

Art Galleries	Paintings, prints, small sculpture	5 kN/m^2 - 7.5 kN/m^2
General Museums and Art Museums	Varied art/artifact/specimens and exhibit elements, ranging up to large sizes	7.5 kN/m^2 - 10 kN/m^2
Visible Storage Galleries	Decorative arts, ethnology, archaeology, natural history specimens	8-10 kN/m^2
Specialized Museums	Military, science, technology, transportation artifacts, heavy monumental sculpture and architecture	Over 10 kN/m^2; up to 50 kN/m^2

Figure 4.5. Floor loading standards. LORD CULTURAL RESOURCES

Exhibition Facilities

4.3.3 Gallery Floors

Floor systems for exhibitions spaces can include a wide variety of structures and material types, each with its own characteristics of strength, stiffness, or resilience. Gallery floors may be finished in stone, terrazzo, ceramic tile installed over concrete slab, or the concrete itself may be sealed, colored, and polished—the latter providing the hardest-wearing floor surfaces of all, but also the least resilient. Wood, vinyl tiles or sheets, or carpet installed over wood or composition hardboard subfloors are more resilient and warmer but have shorter life spans. Concrete surfaces must be painted or sealed to prevent dust from rising. A hardening agent should be added to concrete floors, even if carpet or some other finish is to be placed over them.

4.3.4 Gallery Walls: Permanent, Temporary, and Movable

The exhibition space is generally perceived as being enclosed by permanent walls and defined by secondary walls that may be temporary or even movable. Permanent walls may be the exterior walls of the building, and in some contemporary art applications may even be of glass and steel; however, they must still impart security, protection, and support to the exhibition space.

In some cases, such as in heritage structures that cannot sustain proper environmental conditions, or where existing wall systems are relatively inflexible, a "room within a room" design is often implemented. Here, secondary internal walls are constructed separately from the exterior structural wall. The secondary walls have several functions:

- They provide "nailable" walls that can receive repeated installation of security screws or other fastenings in new locations, or patching and reuse of old locations, as exhibitions are changed.
- They can hide sprinkler risers, electrical conduit and communications raceways, electrical panels, electric switches, and dimmers.
- They can form plenums for low level return air ducts.

A repeatedly nailable gallery wall is recommended, constructed of fire-rated gypsum wallboard over fire-retardant treated plywood on studs. A supporting stud wall built to code under this double sheathing is generally strong enough to support the vast majority of art works or other items a museum might want to hang. Extremely heavy items such as stone relief panels would most likely require custom-constructed supports in addition to the wall structure. If the museum's collection warrants it, some or all gallery walls can be upgraded structurally to support heavier items.

The larger the gallery rooms the more likely it will be those individual installations of unusual works, or of changing exhibitions, will require different room configurations. Small galleries may not offer enough open interior space to make it feasible to divide the space with partitions or panels to create more hanging space or to change the feel of an exhibition. Large galleries by their very nature provide the opportunity and the motive to subdivide or reconfigure the space using movable or temporary walls and panels:

- Movable walls that can be rolled away as complete units and used or stored elsewhere.
- Temporary walls, of the same nailable character as permanent walls, which are built in place for the period for which they are needed, then demolished.

The decision whether to use temporary or movable walls is often based on cost, which should be calculated in relation to the exhibition production budget projected over a long period of time. Movable walls involve capital outlay only once, followed by regular patching, repainting, and repair as needed; however, they require a storage bay handy to the exhibition space, which becomes part of the capital cost. Temporary walls allow for unique configurations for each new show but incur repeated costs to exhibition budgets.

4.3.5 Gallery Ceilings

The choice of structure, materials, and finish for the ceilings of museum galleries poses a preliminary question for the architect: Should the ceilings be left open in "warehouse" style, with ducts, sprinkler pipes, and track lighting exposed, or should they be concealed with an enclosed or suspended ceiling? Part of the answer lies with functionality as well as appearance:

- A **suspended ceiling** forms a surface below which the track lights and other service items such as sprinkler heads, supply air duct openings, heat or smoke detectors, and closed-circuit video cameras may be attached or inset. It can be installed at an even height or can follow the lines of the architecture. It can provide an elegant finish to a gallery, absorb sound (given use of high quality materials), and serve as a support for decorative finishes such as plasterwork and acoustic treatments. An existing historic ceiling, which must be retained, can pose problems for the installation of modern lighting and other utilities.

- On the other hand, the honesty of an **exposed ceiling** may be more suitable for contemporary art, thematic displays, and interactive galleries. The open structure offers visual interest, increases clear ceiling height, provides an obvious method of suspension for exhibits, and generally increases flexibility of the exhibition setup. With an open ceiling structure, all service items will be visible but can be painted to match the ceiling surface, thus removing them from the visual consciousness of most visitors. Another advantage of the open or exposed ceiling is the ease and low cost of maintaining these support systems since problems can easily be detected and remedied.

Suspension of objects from a gallery ceiling often poses a concentrated point loading challenge, although sometimes the stress exerted by the weight of an object can be spread over several suspension points to make the load more uniform. An advance assessment of the likely materials that might need to be hung is useful to enable structural engineers to determine likely future suspension loads.

4.3.6 Doorways, Stairs, and Ramps

Since doorways, steps, and ramps are critical to moving people safely, especially in an emergency, they are particularly heavily regulated under most building codes. In many jurisdictions, museums must supply barrier-free access to all exhibition areas for all visitors, with ramps or elevators as required and fire exits meeting code. Doors may have to be provided in larger galleries according to code requirements for the maximum distance for visitors to exit in case of a fire. Only in historic buildings may some of these requirements be relaxed.

Exhibition spaces often require double-leaf doors, rather than single-doors, and should ideally have separate public entry and exit points to prevent bottlenecks. Ideally, a separate service entrance can facilitate movement of exhibits and objects. If possible, service openings for the

Exhibition Facilities

temporary exhibition gallery should be larger to increase flexibility in bringing in occasional oversize items. The height, depth, and width of the design object is a key determinant of necessary door opening sizes.

The consideration for the size and location of doors and exits has become even more important with the rise of COVID-19 and for future pandemic planning. As galleries become required to enact protocols for social distancing, timed entry, and one-way flow, the safe and effective management of large groups of people becomes critical. The location of exits now not only has to meet code-stipulated exit distances but they should also be strategically located to avoid bottlenecks. It is also important to remember that bottlenecks may occur outside the gallery, where people tend to congregate, such as at elevators or washrooms. Also, the consideration for design need not always assume compliance for pandemic line management, but it should be able to accommodate these requirements through simple measures should another pandemic arise.

Door materials may match historic decor or be completely contemporary. Wherever possible, their fire rating should match that of the walls, ceiling, and floors of the gallery, all of which should provide at least a two-hour fire rating. Glazed doors (using shatterproof glass) are often chosen so that users can see others approaching from the opposite side, and to provide light and a more open appearance. Service doors are usually metal hollow-core fire-rated doors, with the gallery side faced with materials similar to the gallery walls. All gallery doors should be fitted with automatic door closers and security hardware.

Providing **vertical circulation** within galleries is always problematic, not least because it eats up a disproportionate amount of potential display space. The structure for stairs and ramps, as for floors, needs to be certified for occupancy levels. Ramp gradients ideally should be no more than 1:30 and preferably 1:50 wherever museum objects are to be moved. Local authorities will be particularly stringent regarding open staircases and ramps between floors, as these openings can conduct fire upward. Passenger elevators built within galleries may be required for handicapped accessibility even when stairs are provided and will likely be required to be fully enclosed rather than open chair lifts.

4.3.7 Natural Light and Fenestration

Natural light adds a special quality of light and color to a room, and architects, artists, and museum professionals are naturally interested to capitalize on this trait where possible. The following guidelines should help:

- Specific classes of objects such as works on paper, in addition to all archival materials, require complete elimination of natural light from the gallery space.

- Objects made of organic materials or combinations of organic and inorganic materials are also vulnerable to natural light and heat build-up, therefore windows, skylights, or clerestories are not recommended for thematic or conceptual galleries.

- Children's museums and science centers featuring nonartifact materials can effectively use natural light, with some means of control such as louvres, shades, or screening to limit glare and allow for different visual effects in the galleries.

- Nonorganic objects (such as stone, glass, ceramics, or metals) can be accommodated in day-lit galleries.

- In all cases, lux (footcandle) and ultraviolet (UV) levels, and heat build-up from light penetrating through glass, must be controlled to meet museum best-practice standards.
- Daylight in study or research areas requires the most stringent controls, and if provided should always be both UV-filtered and diffused.

Considered in terms of their "warmth" and color temperature, there are three kinds of natural light:

1. Sunlight, the "warmest" (most yellow), with the lowest color temperature.
2. Skylight, with medium warmth and medium color temperature.
3. North light, the "coolest," with the highest color temperature.

At the comparatively low light levels encountered in most museums, studies have shown that people prefer warm rather than cool north light (north light is traditionally the favored light for working environments such as artists' studios). On the other hand, direct sunlight is not desirable in galleries due to its high intensity and the potential for local heat build-up. Natural lighting solutions that either mix the lighting sources to provide a medium color temperature and warmth, or which provide indirect light, thus reducing the intensity and heat of sunlight, are preferable.

Natural light can enter a gallery in either of two ways:

1. **Toplighting** strikes vertically, usually from a skylight.
2. **Sidelighting** strikes horizontally, usually from a window or glazed door opening.

Only toplighting is recommended. Sidelighting should be avoided because of the near impossibility of avoiding glare, reflections, and the phototropic effect—the observed phenomenon of the human eye being attracted to the brightest object in the field of view (i.e., a glazed opening). With the eye constantly attracted to a bright window, it is a challenge for the eye to adapt to the relatively low light levels that should be maintained in a gallery. Visitors in such a gallery complain that the space is too dimly lit because their eyes are unable to maintain their low light adaptation.

Where there are windows in an existing building that is being converted to a gallery for art and artifacts, it is usually recommended that these be completely boarded in, or at least blocked with removable panels. The latter approach can be effective in historic structures since it can respect the original architectural detailing.

If fenestration is employed, skylights (roof lights) are preferred. Skylighting and clerestory window systems can be highly effective visually but require some means of light control. Fritting (micro- or semiopaque patterning) is one method that may be used to control light penetration. Many galleries have been designed with both passive and mechanized light control systems. In some instances, these work very well; however, there are too many examples where the design or technology is faulty, and the result is an aesthetic and operating nightmare. At worst, skylighting systems can leak and pour water onto the exhibits below.

Important factors to assess skylight design are:

- Simplicity of design
- Ease of operation and maintenance

Exhibition Facilities

- Effectiveness in reducing light and ultraviolet (UV) levels
- Prevention of heat buildup
- Weather tightness to prevent water and air leakage
- Type of glazing and UV filters
- Choice and location of fluorescent or other electric lights to assist the natural light
- Means of blocking daylight by scrims or baffles when required
- Integration with the track lighting system, which will be used to light items displayed on the walls or the floor
- In cold countries, the need for radiant heating to prevent condensation and build-up of ice and snow on skylights
- Provision of light quality to a desired aesthetic standard

The last criterion is one that requires careful testing by mock-up or prototype. Traditional top-lit galleries illuminate the center of a gallery brightly but leave the walls (where the pictures are hanging) in comparative shade; this can be effective for providing ambient light but requires additional artificial lighting. A close look at the impressionist galleries of the Musée d'Orsay in Paris (renovated in 2011–2012) shows that the skylights are being used only for ambient effect, whereas artificial lights installed along a track at the base of the skylights are actually doing the work of illuminating the pictures on the walls.

Since sunlight varies seasonally and diurnally, all day lighting systems require supplementary electric lighting. Daylight sensors and dimmers may be used to regulate the amount of artificial light needed at any one time. These systems should be prototyped, especially in order to judge the aesthetics of the resultant color rendering and color temperatures under different combinations of natural and artificial light.

The challenge of providing natural light is attractive but complex, and merits close study and attention in the building process.

4.3.8 Power and Communications

The need for exhibition galleries to incorporate new technology has evolved from the provision of artificial light to a multitude of building systems and exhibit components such as audiovisual and multimedia applications, web-based information systems, simulators, and special effects. Each of these is highly demanding of the gallery space in terms of power supply and communications (data networking). This demand points to the need to plan for a "smart gallery" integrating power and data lines into its structure.

With the advent of science centers and commercial exhibition spaces in conference centers and world's fair pavilions over the past half-century, a new type of display space was born. A distinguishing feature of these spaces is flexible use, requiring power and data points dispersed throughout the space, wherever an exhibit needs to be set up. Both vertical and horizontal trunking systems for electrical cables, data cabling, Wi-Fi routing, and fiber optics have become standard for new museum design to meet the technological demands of the coming decades. The special power and data needs of museum spaces to house specific types of new media, as well as new environmental needs such as active microclimates need to be assessed in new project design.

Recessed power and data outlets in gallery walls at baseboard level are often hidden by a kickplate or sections of molding, while three-compartment power and communications trenches cross the floors, generally on a grid of about twelve feet (3.6 m), with access points at the junctures. The power/data grid may be set up to coincide with a column grid or other gallery feature. Outlet points may be concealed by carpet tiles or removable wood sections almost invisible to the eye or may become a design feature with brass or brushed steel fittings to mark the spot. Some form of drop-down power supply from the ceiling is also useful, especially if there is an extremely high roof structure and suspended exhibits.

4.3.9 Acoustics and Sound Control

A gallery's structure, materials, and finishes are the three factors that can be used or misused to control noise levels resulting from visitor load, building mechanicals, and even an in-gallery sound system. In general, noise levels should neither be so low that visitors feel inhibited, nor so high as to be disturbing. **Design Noise Criteria** (NC) ratings should be close to NC 30 in exhibition and research areas, up to NC 35 in related public areas, and as low as NC 25 in auditoria. Noise transmission from the elevators, washrooms, workshops, and mechanical rooms may also require sound attenuation. Acoustic buffering and control materials may be required in some specialized galleries that tend to be noisier, such as orientation or children's galleries, or in-gallery activity areas, to ensure that the sound from them is restricted to these areas. The appropriate **Sound Transmission Class** (STC) number for each space should be determined by the architects and acousticians based on adjacent occupancies.

All spaces within museums should be served by a central **public address (PA) system**, used for both normal and emergency announcements. A PA system should be zoned for selective use, so that announcements can be made within the galleries but not the staff areas, or vice versa, and should override and be separate from the audio systems in public areas.

An audio system, separate from the PA system, is often needed to meet the needs of customized exhibits and programs, with separate distribution to each gallery and to selected public spaces, with centralized equipment storage, set-up, and work area.

4.3.10 Materials and Finishes

Many materials used in construction and finishing have the potential to off-gas chemicals that can cause deterioration to museum objects. Each material has its own aging characteristics; some materials need to be avoided altogether as they will continue to off-gas for years, while others may become relatively stable within shorter periods of time. With green initiatives, materials such as low volatile organic compound (VOC) paints are now available that are safer for humans, the environment, and museum objects. All manufacturers should be asked for specification sheets on their products when these are being considered for gallery use. Conservation institutes such as the Getty Conservation Institute in Los Angeles and the Canadian Conservation Institute in Ottawa, and major museums like the British Museum in London, conduct their own independent tests and can provide detailed advice on materials testing or specific material selection.

The importance of a commissioning period for a new building or a refurbished gallery before the exhibit components and artifacts are moved in, is that it allows not only for a period for systems testing, but also for a "decanting" period in which off-gassing may take place and be monitored. It is especially important that materials used in display cases be tested for off-gassing of harmful chemicals such as formaldehyde and other acidic compounds. Some woods (such as oak) are *not* recommended as display case materials for this reason. If the case construction material proves to be harmful, it may still be used, but only if properly sealed to reduce the emission of harmful vapors.

An area of planning for museum interpretive facilities that always excites a great deal of discussion and debate during the design process is the level of finishes for the new or renovated space, and its cost. Opinions vary widely from "only the best, no matter what it costs" to "we want to be practical—finishes must be able to take a beating!" In considering gallery finishes, many people are likely to think first of appearance—and certainly meeting public expectations of a high quality of finish is one concern.

Both the architect and exhibition designer will be anxious to have control over material selection. Architects may be aware of new materials on the market that may prove an exciting alternative to traditional finishes. However, these professionals need to be guided by what works in the museum setting, and what the desired outcomes are for the use of the space. The criteria for any material used for floors, walls, ceilings, or fittings must include how it will perform within the physical setting of the gallery in terms of:

- Appearance
- Functionality
- Maintenance and replacement

Museum professionals need to be able to specify the performance criteria for materials and finishes so that the architect and designer can come up with the best possible options. Cost correlates with these factors. Establishing a base building allocation helps in planning for the level of finishes that is appropriate.

Keeping up a high standard of neatness and cleanliness day to day is important both for public health and safety, and also to help promote respect for and proper behavior within the exhibition space. Wear and tear from visitors, events, and regular maintenance and housekeeping is inevitable. An unkempt museum gallery is likely to be treated with contempt by the public. Therefore, the museum needs to ask the type of questions every good housekeeper asks when considering the purchase or supply of materials and finishes for the gallery:

- What types of soiling may be expected with this material?
- What is the preferred method of cleaning?
- Will cleaning have an adverse effect: changing the color or finish, or weakening the fabric?
- How long will the material last?
- How long is the same material projected to be available for repair or replacement?
- How long will it take to install?
- Will there be any adverse effects such as fumes during installation?
- Does a specialist have to install this material?
- How much does its cost compared with other options?

In considering gallery finishes, planners and designers should consider sturdy materials and finishes, with a view to prolonging their life expectancy. Quality should not be sacrificed to price if it conveys longevity. All materials have advantages and disadvantages. Figure 4.6 is a summary of common types of materials and finishes found in exhibition spaces today.

Material	Advantages	Disadvantages
Flooring		
Stone, Terrazzo	<ul><li>Elegant, high-quality appearance</li><li>Very hard, long wearing surface</li><li>Easy to clean, dust free</li><li>Generally neutral color value</li><li>Excellent weight bearing</li><li>Excellent fire resistance</li></ul>	<ul><li>High cost</li><li>Hard to walk or stand on</li><li>Cold – hard to heat</li><li>May reflect light</li><li>Reflects and amplifies sound</li><li>Surface may be uneven</li><li>Difficult to attach fixtures and to repair</li><li>Heavy structural load</li></ul>
Concrete Slab (sealed/stained)	<ul><li>Low cost</li><li>Functional, utility appearance</li><li>Very hard, long wearing surface</li><li>Easy to clean, dust free</li><li>Can be color-stained or painted</li><li>Excellent weight bearing</li><li>Excellent fire resistance</li></ul>	<ul><li>Hard to walk or stand on</li><li>Cold – hard to heat</li><li>May reflect light</li><li>Reflects and amplifies sound</li><li>Surface may be uneven</li><li>Difficult to attach fixtures</li><li>Heavy structural load</li></ul>
Ceramic Tile	<ul><li>Moderate cost</li><li>Elegant, high-quality appearance</li><li>Very hard, long wearing surface</li><li>Easy to clean, dust free</li><li>Much lighter to install than stone</li><li>Wide color choice</li><li>Excellent fire resistance</li></ul>	<ul><li>Hard to walk or stand on</li><li>Cold – hard to heat</li><li>May reflect light</li><li>Reflects and amplifies sound</li><li>Surface may be uneven</li><li>Difficult to attach fixtures and to repair</li><li>Less weight bearing – may fracture</li></ul>
Wood, Bamboo	<ul><li>Quality appearance, flexible finish, suitable to many exhibition modes and styles</li><li>Warm, resilient surface</li><li>Relatively quiet surface</li><li>Easy to clean, dust free</li><li>Flexible to install</li><li>Natural colors, or can be painted or stained</li><li>Can be used as a base for vinyl or carpet</li><li>Moderate structural load</li></ul>	<ul><li>Moderate-high cost</li><li>Moderate wearing surface</li><li>Requires consistent labor-intensive upkeep</li><li>Easy to attach fixtures</li><li>Subject to damage from heels, furniture, woodworm, damp rot, etc.</li><li>Moderately easy to repair, but may require replacement</li><li>Only moderate weight bearing</li><li>Flammable</li></ul>

Figure 4.6. Summary of gallery materials and finishes. LORD CULTURAL RESOURCES

Material	Advantages	Disadvantages
Flooring		
Vinyl Sheet (installed over concrete slab or wooden subfloor)	• Low cost • Modern, functional or utility appearance • Durable, moderately long wearing surface • Easy to clean, dust free • Light and flexible to install • Light structural load • Wide color choice • Excellent weight bearing	• Moderate wearing surface, can be gouged or worn off • Not easy to repair, may require replacement, patching • Fire resistance and flame spread may vary
Carpet (carpet intended for commercial installations: low-weave, synthetic blends, stain resistant finish installed over concrete slab or wooden subfloor)	• Low-moderate cost • Excellent short-term solution • Not as durable wearing surface as other options - shorter lifespan • Warm, quiet surface • Light and flexible to install • Light structural load • Wide colour choice	• Range widely in quality appearance, wear and price • Cleaning is labor- and chemical-intensive • Carpet tends to collect dust, mites, pollutants • Not easy to repair, may require replacement, patching • Fire resistance and flame spread may vary
Walls		
Stone	• Elegant, high-quality appearance • Very hard, long wearing surface • Easy to clean, dust free • Generally neutral color value • Excellent fire resistance	• High cost • Cold – hard to heat • May reflect light • Reflects and amplifies sound • Difficult to hang pictures, attach fixtures and repair • Heavy structural load
Concrete	• Low cost • Functional, utility appearance • Very hard, long wearing surface • Easy to clean, dust free if sealed • Can be color-stained or painted • Excellent weight bearing • Excellent fire resistance	• Cold – hard to heat • May reflect light • Reflects and amplifies sound • Surface may be uneven • Difficult to hang pictures, attach fixtures and repair • Heavy structural load

Figure 4.6. *Continued*

Material	Advantages	Disadvantages
Walls		
Plaster (should not be used on uninsulated inner surfaces of exterior wall structure)	• Elegant, high-quality seamless matte appearance • Can be very decorative • Hard, long-wearing surface • Easy to clean • Paintable and moderately nailable • Much lighter to install than stone • Good fire resistance	• High cost • Specialist installation/craftsmanship • Easily damaged by water leaks • Can fracture due to vibration • Reflects and amplifies sound • Must be repaired with care after each use • Can generate some dust • Heavy structural load
Wood or Bamboo Panelling	• Moderate cost • Quality appearance, flexible finish, suitable to many exhibition modes • Relatively quiet surface • Easy to clean, dust free • Easy to attach fixtures – fully nailable • Flexible to install • Natural colors, or can be painted or stained • Can be used as a base for fabric or wallpaper • Moderate structural load	• Moderate wearing surface • Requires consistent, labour-intensive upkeep • Subject to damage from nails, screws, scrapes, woodworm, damp rot, etc. • Moderately easy to repair, but may require replacement • Only moderate weight bearing • Colours cannot be readily changed except by painting • Flammable
Gypsum Board (drywall) (recommended nailable wall of painted 16 mm fire-rated gypsum wallboard over 19 mm of layered plywood on studs, installed so that joints are staggered)	• Moderate cost • Flexible finish, suitable to all exhibit modes as base installation • Relatively quiet surface • Easy to clean, dust-free • Easy to attach fixtures – fully nailable • Flexible to install • Paintable, can be patched and repainted • Can be used as a base for fabric or wallpaper • Moderate structural load	• Moderate wearing surface • Requires patching and repainting for new installations • Fire resistance and flame spread may vary • Only moderate weight bearing

Figure 4.6. *Continued*

Material	Advantages	Disadvantages
Walls		
Fabric-covered panels (installed over studs)	• High-quality appearance, generally most suitable for permanent art gallery installation) • Sound absorptive surface • Relatively easy to attach fixtures – fabric hides nail holes etc. • Low structural load	• Expensive • Flammable; fire resistance and flame spread may vary • Low-moderate wearing surface • Hard to clean, collects dust • Requires specialist installation • Subject to damage from nails, screws, tearing, etc. • Moderate weight bearing • Colors cannot be readily changed
Ceilings		
Exposed structure (concrete, steel)	• Low cost • Functional, utility appearance may match modern, technological or contemporary art exhibition modes • Can increase available ceiling height • Very hard, long wearing surface • Easy to clean, dust free if sealed • Can be color stained or painted • Excellent weight bearing • Excellent fire resistance	• Functional, utility appearance may not be desirable for some galleries • Cold – hard to heat • Reflects and amplifies sound
Plaster (should *not* be used on uninsulated inner surfaces of exterior roof structure)	• Elegant, high-quality seamless matte appearance • Can be highly decorative • Hard, long wearing surface • Moderately easy to clean • Paintable and moderately nailable • Much lighter to install than stone • Good weight-bearing • Good fire resistance	• High cost • Specialist installation and craftsmanship required • Easily damaged by water leaks • Can fracture due to vibration • Reflects and amplifies sound • Must be repaired with care after each use • Can generate some dust • Heavy structural load

Figure 4.6. *Continued*

Material	Advantages	Disadvantages
Ceilings		
Gypsum Board or Drywall (used for suspended ceiling installation below ductwork, sprinkler lines etc., usually as one layer only)	• Moderate cost • Flexible finish, suitable to all exhibit modes as base installation • Relatively quiet surface • Easy to clean, dust free • Easy to attach fixtures • Moderately flexible to install • Paintable, can be patched and repainted • Can be used as a base for fabric or wallpaper • Moderate structural load	• Moderate wearing surface • Requires patching and repainting for new installations • Can be damaged by water leakage and can hide building problems • Decreases clear ceiling height • Only moderate weight bearing • Fire resistance and flame spread may vary
Acoustic panels	• High-quality appearance, generally more suitable for special applications such as auditorium or conference room • Sound absorptive surface • Moderate structural load	• Expensive • Low-moderate wearing surface • Specialist installation • Hard to clean, collect dust • Not easy to attach fixtures • Subject to damage from nails, screws, tearing, etc. • Moderate weight bearing • Colors cannot be readily changed • Fire resistance and flame spread may vary

Figure 4.6. *Continued*

4.4 EXHIBITION GALLERY SECURITY

Works of art and objects continue to be stolen from museums and galleries around the world almost daily, and statistics show that the majority of incidents occur within permanent collection displays and temporary exhibition areas. Of equal concern are the actual and potential instances of fire, flood, building collapse, or acts of terrorism where preservation of life becomes a critical issue. With regard to both security and public safety, museum professionals should strive to ensure that the highest standards of care and protection are maintained in exhibition galleries and support spaces.

When determining security and safety provisions, it should be remembered that acts of theft, willful damage, and arson can emanate from internal as well as external sources. For this reason, access to exhibitions and collections should be controlled and limited to those security personal and exhibition staff with responsibilities for them.

4.4.1 Public Safety

The first consideration in any building or gallery to which members of the public, staff, contractors, and visitors have access is the need to preserve and protect life. People can be at risk from several dangers including fire, smoke, heat, explosion, injury, sickness, and personal attack, and more recently from the spread of infectious diseases such as COVID-19.

Many public safety factors must be kept in mind when designing the layout of exhibitions. The overriding imperatives are preserving life and, in the event of an emergency, evacuating the premises. When designing an exhibition, the following general public safety factors should be considered:

- Does any part of the exhibition structure or the exhibits interfere with visual or physical access to emergency escape routes or doors?
- Does the exhibition contain obstacles (cabling running across floors) obstructing normal safe circulation and exiting?
- Does the layout create bottlenecks or congestion points where people are likely to congregate, both within and outside the gallery that make social distancing problematic and increase the risk to visitors?
- Does the exhibition contain any elements that pose a risk to visitors? Moving parts? Head-high projections? Hazardous materials? Sharp or protruding objects?
- Has the maximum number of visitors allowed in exhibition galleries at any given time been determined according to health and safety regulations (allowing for the space taken up by displayed material)?

The flow of visitors will require careful and constant monitoring of *occupancy levels* to avoid overcrowding, and to ensure ease of evacuation in an emergency. Overcrowding can lead to poor surveillance, unnecessary damage to displays, and in wet weather may have an adverse effect on environmental controls. For popular exhibitions, peak loads must be planned in consultation with security personnel, and timed tickets or similar precautions must be taken to control the number of people circulating in the gallery at any one time. If overcrowding or bottlenecks should occur, security personnel should be trained to handle the situation firmly and courteously.

Although cleaning is an essential part of maintaining an attractive exhibition environment, such operations should not be conducted in the presence of visitors, when wet floors, slippery steps, cleaning materials, and running machines might be dangerous or cause injury. This is a scheduling challenge that should be considered when the public hours of the exhibition are being planned.

Subdued lighting is often desirable or necessary in galleries where sensitive material is being displayed, but there should always be sufficient ambient light to allow visitors and security personnel to see clearly. Insufficient light levels can be dangerous and may cause a feeling of claustrophobia in some people. It may also prevent adequate electronic and human surveillance.

Besides the general safety of the public, the exhibition gallery must also account for fire, terrorism, and medical emergencies. The biggest risk of any confined public event is that of fire. Many museums around the world are also located in areas where they must plan for a terrorist alert or actual incident—and all museums should include such threats in their contingency plans.

Providing first aid or full medical response in case of a visitor injury or illness should be part of exhibition planning; for example, a bench near the gallery exit may be provided in case of light-headedness. A staff member trained in first aid should always be available to respond and should be able to summon emergency crews as required. A first aid room outside the exhibition space but accessible to emergency crews, with a cot and a sink adjacent to a toilet, is invaluable and may be required by code in some jurisdictions. It provides a place to store first aid and emergency equipment needed by first responders, and a base of operations for emergency treatment.

4.4.2 Security Levels

The fundamental objective of security within the exhibition is to wrap the artifact within multiple layers of protection. These objectives can be described as five levels of security:

1. **Level 1: External perimeter**: The outer layer of this protection is the building, constructed to withstand a variety of threats. This perimeter level of protection can be achieved by the installation of metal roller shutters, expanding gates, internal window bars, and bandit-proof laminated glass at openings.

2. **Level 2: Back- and front-of-house separation**: Every museum needs to separate the public front-of-house space from the nonpublic back-of-house space, for security, image, and general operational effectiveness. The exhibition galleries require service access for collections and exhibits from back-of-house, but these service points need to be controlled to forbid public access.

3. **Level 3: Room level–internal gallery perimeter**: Each individual gallery must be provided with secondary perimeter protection so that it can be separately locked off or alarmed. Coverage of the exhibition space and its entrances and exits by CCTV cameras and other gallery-wide surveillance systems reinforces this interior perimeter protection.

4. **Level 4: Case/security hardware**: Each exhibition is individually planned with appropriate physical security structures such as cases, frames, barriers, and hardware affixing art works to walls or artifacts and specimens to secure mounts.

5. **Level 5: Special measures**: Individual objects of value and rarity, or individual cases, can have additional security applied to them in terms of intrusion and approach detection and alarms. These are over and above normal measures that are applied gallery-wide such as normal case hardware.

The nature of the material to be exhibited, which may have monetary value and rarity, or notoriety and subsequent media attention, may dictate particular methods of display and increased levels of protection. Exhibitions involving religious art, ethnographic material, or natural history specimens can arouse hostility in those who associate them with offences against sacred beliefs or animal rights. Contemporary art exhibitions may include controversial material that provokes a violent response. It is important that security personnel are made aware of risks and appropriate response plans are created. In addition, temporary exhibitions that include loan objects may require additional security measures as stipulated by the lending institution.

4.4.3 Electronic Surveillance

Each layer of mechanical defense of external or internal perimeters should ideally be supported by electronic intruder detection, while open display areas should be covered by passive infrared or similar methods of detection. Verified passive infrared motion detectors or digitally analyzed video intrusion detection systems are recommended for gallery spaces. Magnetic switches and glass breakage detectors should be installed on perimeter openings and specific internal doors as appropriate. Specialized electronic detection can be applied to high-risk individual displays, including exhibition cases and restricted zones.

A closed-circuit television surveillance system with color charge coupled device cameras should cover all exits from the galleries and be located facing the exiting person. The cameras should have a low light capability. Cameras should be operative during both open and closed hours and monitored during open hours with all video signals continually recorded.

Security detection and surveillance systems must be supported by an emergency power supply with the capacity to provide twenty-four hour a day monitoring, yet still have power to operate the alarms for five minutes. Electronic systems must be monitored internally or from a central station, with telephone connections to the policing service.

4.4.4 Security Guards

Human surveillance should be used to complement electronic surveillance devices, which are only as good as the people maintaining and monitoring them.

The time of greatest risk to objects and materials on display is during the day due to the presence and activity of large numbers of visitors. Here there is no substitute for the watchful eye of security personnel, who not only invigilate the galleries but also protect visitors in the event of emergencies. Security personnel must be alert and able to respond to any unusual behaviors or diversionary tactics within an exhibition area where an attack or incident might ensue. They must be carefully trained and aware of the legal limits of their powers. Any other duties performed in the galleries by security staff must be secondary (such as counting visitors) to their security responsibilities.

The number of security personnel assigned to each display space must be determined by the exhibition layout and cost factors, keeping in mind expected trouble spots and walking length of each exhibit area. The Smithsonian Institution standard for many years has been one guard per three thousand square feet (300 sq m) of display space. Exhibitions should be laid out so that sightlines across gallery spaces are clear, thereby eliminating blind spots where a criminal could work in seclusion. If clear sightlines cannot be attained, then additional electronic surveillance may be required.

4.4.5 Fire Detection and Suppression

In addition to physical escape plans, the exhibition space must be fitted with local fire alarms (break-glass or pull-station units) plus automatic fire detection and suppression systems designed for the exhibition space and its contents as well as for public safety. When considering the introduction of electronic fire systems, advice should be sought from appropriate professional experts—not just from suppliers. Not only the galleries but the entire museum building should be fully covered by electronic fire detection since a fire in an adjacent space is a clear threat to the exhibitions. The signal from the fire detection system, together with intruder detection alarms, must be relayed to an external monitoring station even if a museum or gallery has twenty-four-hour guarding.

An addressable ionization, photoelectric, or projected beam photoelectric smoke detector system or a Very Early Warning Smoke Detection Apparatus system should be provided. It requires monitoring twenty-four hours per day, 365 days per year, and needs to be connected to an emergency power supply with the capacity to provide monitoring for twenty-four hours and still have power to operate the alarms for five minutes. Heat detectors (addressable) are to be provided only where smoke detectors may be susceptible to false alarms. Addressable pull stations are required. Although sprinklers in galleries remain controversial for some, they are strongly recommended, since a soaked artwork or specimen can be restored, whereas one destroyed by fire is gone forever. However, a strong blast of water from a fire hose can be highly damaging to museum objects. A high pressure pumped mist/fog sprinkler system with stainless steel piping may be considered in appropriate locations. The sprinkler or mist system has the advantage of twenty-four-hour coverage, and of directing and limiting the flow of water specifically to the fire location, and of continual flow until the fire situation is completely contained. In the absence of twenty-four-hour staffing, the sprinkler system chosen for the exhibition areas should meet the same standards as that installed throughout the museum collection areas. It may be necessary for the sprinkler system in a temporary exhibition gallery to be on a separate riser, in order, with a shutoff valve, to enable the museum to meet specific loan conditions.

4.5 ACCESSIBILITY, ADJACENCY, AND CIRCULATION

Accessibility, adjacency, and circulation refer to the efficiency and effectiveness with which museum functions can be carried out within the designated space. Functions relating to museum exhibitions can often be identified from the museum's own policies and procedures, which provide prescriptive guidelines for staff to follow in arranging loans, insurance, travel arrangements, or special events. Studying these processes and describing them as a series of activities or tasks with subtasks can help in understanding what resources of space, equipment, and personnel are needed to carry out the exhibition program.

4.5.1 Controlling Access

Front-of-house space offers the welcoming face of the museum and provides both a buffer and controlled entry for the public to the exhibition spaces. The most convenient arrangement of exhibition space in relation to other public space is to access the galleries directly off the main lobby, but this may not always be possible. Providing fairly direct visitor routes with openings into the galleries allows visitors to navigate the museum easily and to access exhibitions that most interest them. At the Alaska Native Heritage Center in Anchorage, for example, access spines (corridors) curve along each side of the gallery space, allowing random access to any of the displays.

Public entrances to galleries must accommodate the volume of visitors at peak times, the possible need for separate exiting and entry to specific galleries, and the range of choices allowed to each visitor in selecting galleries and movement paths. It is ideal to have separate entry and exit points for each gallery; in large galleries, which may be subdivided for some shows, having two sets of entry and exit doors may be necessary.

Consideration must also be given to appropriate pandemic planning. As noted above, many museums and galleries are implementing reduced gallery occupancy, one-way movement, or timed access, or all the above. To respond, galleries whose point of entry or exit is directly off a large public convening space, such as a lobby, should consider the implications of these measures and the impact they have on queue coordination. In previous years, a long line was considered a negative on visitor experience, whereas today it may be a matter of visitor health and safety. Because of this, it is highly recommended that architects and exhibit designers work together to model and test various socially distanced line scenarios to see the implications of the design. Even small items, such as an ATM or an information pamphlet station can cause congestion if located near an elevator and gallery entry. Again, it is not required that the design accommodate a socially distanced line, but rather the layout should be able to manage a large group safely and effectively should the need arise.

4.5.2 Accessibility

While museums must meet minimum accessibility requirements set forth by their countries' laws, they can make efforts to go beyond the laws to make their exhibition spaces as inclusive as possible. Museum visitors come in all ages and sizes, bringing with them their diverse needs, interests, abilities, and limitations such as:

- Visitors ranging from two to ninety years old
- Visitors with mobility, visual, hearing, or cognitive disabilities

Understanding the needs and wants of visitors is critical for exhibition spaces not only to be attractive and effective for display, but also *accessible*. Incorporating accessible design into exhibition facility planning often benefits not only people with disabilities, but also a large number of other visitors. Incorporating accessible exhibition designs will create an environment of inclusion for the broadest possible audiences, without calling attention to disabilities that some visitors may have.

Ideally, it should be possible to close off individual galleries from public access during installation or deinstallation, during private functions, or in case of an emergency. Having public doors that can be closed off has advantages for climate control as well as after-hours security and crowd control and may be mandatory where a gallery must be maintained at a specific relative humidity and temperature. Glazed doors may be used to retain vistas between the galleries or through a series of galleries. Even when it is desired to have an open free-flow between exhibitions spaces, doors should be provided at the main gallery entrance that can be closed or otherwise secured in case of emergency. Local codes may require fire separations and doors for specific volumes of gallery space, and every gallery will require fire exits, clearly marked, as well as main public entry points.

Service Access

The users of the display space also include building maintenance and housekeeping workers. In addition to regular housekeeping staff, however, the display space must be accessible to the exhibition maintenance, curatorial, and conservation staff who change and adjust lights (sometimes using a cherry picker to get at the higher lamps), clean inside cases, remove and replace objects, and carry out conservation checks. Access from both front-of-house and back-of-house is needed, preferably through a service entrance that is separate from the public entrance.

Service access to the galleries is essential both for bringing in new exhibits and for regular maintenance work. New exhibitions may include large cases, panels, wall-size graphics, and large art works or specimens. Service doors that can accommodate the design object need to be placed inconspicuously but conveniently for access to a major portion of the gallery space. Such doors generally have to be custom-made to a ten to twelve foot (3–4 m) height, but may be designed with additional upper panels to the ceiling to accommodate the occasional extra-tall object.

It is *not* recommended to have the collection elevator opening directly into the gallery space. This is noisy, visually distracting for visitors, and can pose a security problem during loading and unloading. Instead, the freight elevator doors should open into a wide corridor or staging area that in turn fronts directly into the display space. Where the same corridor is used for both public and service circulation, this buffer zone helps to provide some separation between functions.

Staff access to the galleries for installation, cleaning, and maintenance should be restricted to hours and days when the space is closed to the public. Staff presence during public hours should be discreet and carefully controlled to those actually requiring access to do their work, such as docents, gallery assistants, curators, and security guards.

4.5.3 Access to Nonpublic Support Spaces

Nonpublic back-of-house activities related to exhibitions include:

- Organizing, planning, and coordinating the exhibition program
- Receiving and handling loans and traveling exhibitions
- Exhibition design and fabrication
- Preparing, mounting, and installing exhibition material

Users of the back-of-house space include staff, contractors, suppliers, visiting curators, and other scholars, lenders, and their couriers, and that very important "user," the collections and exhibitions themselves. This is nonpublic space, so a security perimeter around it must be imposed to keep the public out. Even among staff, access to the support spaces needs to be closely restricted to those who actually need to be there. The permanent collections storage and curatorial/collections management space does not normally need to be accessed by those building, receiving, or installing exhibition materials, but there does need to be a link to bring works of art, artifacts, or specimens from storage into the space being used for exhibition preparation and ultimately into the galleries. Security personnel need to be able to reach any part of the collections and exhibition space where an alarm may sound or to set up security checkpoints as needed during the receiving and movement of exhibition materials. Support spaces for building maintenance and housekeeping need to be accessible to service entrances to the galleries but are not part of the exhibitions space.

The spaces that directly support the production of exhibitions include:

- The loading dock where loans and traveling exhibitions arrive at the museum
- The packing and unpacking (crating/uncrating) areas
- Transit storage (temporary exhibition storage)
- Crate storage
- Installation storage for lights, scaffolding, ladders, etc.
- The workshops where exhibition materials are produced

Adjacencies to all these spaces are absolutely critical, affecting not only exhibition production and movement of art and artifacts to and from the galleries, but also maintenance of the required environmental conditions for the objects throughout the preparation and installation process.

In addition, support spaces may be needed for activities that are ancillary to exhibitions, such as special retail operations and food services and catering for events. Access, adjacency, and circulation for these amenities must also be considered in the light of their impact on exhibitions. *In general, there should be no access to or movement through the display space for food or waste*, and only limited movement for retail stock and other supplies, preferably during nonpublic hours.

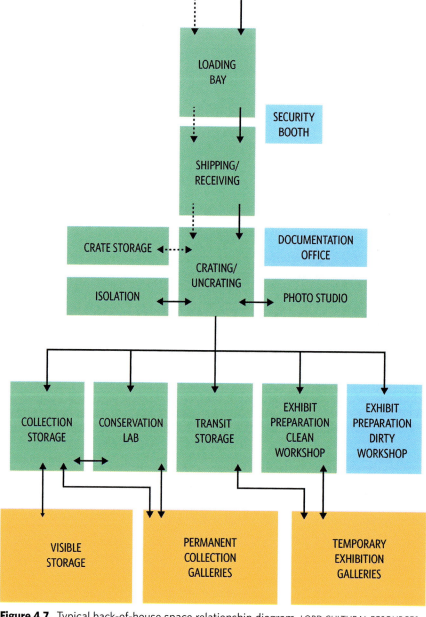

Figure 4.7. Typical back-of-house space relationship diagram. LORD CULTURAL RESOURCES

PART III
WHAT?

Biosphere, Environment Museum, Montreal

The purpose of the exhibition is to facilitate, through interpretation, the transmission of meaning to the visitor. This results in many different types of exhibitions. Some are permanent, some are temporary. Some draw heavily on collections to tell a story, others do not. Some are highly interactive and tactile, while others are more reflective. Some are physical, some are virtual, and some require the input of the public to create them. What all exhibitions have in common, however, is the ability to create powerful, contextual, and meaningful experiences.

Collections-based exhibitions are by far the most common type of exhibition. Works of art are made to communicate meanings, and art museums are increasingly much more willing to help explain those meanings than they used to be. Artifacts communicate meanings only if their context is understood. Specimens may be impressive, or merely curious, but most of us need to read the label to understand what they mean. So, interpretation is needed for most exhibitions based on museum collections to communicate their range of meanings successfully.

Collections are not the only way that museums connect and communicate with the public. Increasingly, visitors are looking to museums as social, interactive, or virtual spaces where one can explore, create, participate, and dialogue around a certain topic, idea, or event. The line between programming and exhibitry continues to blur as exhibitions incorporate live theater, performance, or scientific demonstrations as an integral component of the exhibition experience. As visitors' expectations and demands for museums continue to change and evolve, so too will the form and function of exhibitions.

Part III of the manual examines various types of museum exhibitions, ranging from permanent collection displays through exhibitions without collections to virtual exhibitions. Understanding the type of exhibition you are developing will impact the interpretive techniques employed to meet audience needs; the content needed to be developed; and the materials and technologies required to build them. Temporary exhibition programs are so central to many museums that we have dedicated a chapter to them, and a separate chapter on traveling shows.

Museums are all about meanings, but museums themselves mean many things to many people. This section aims to explore them all.

Chapter 5

Permanent Collection Exhibitions

Katherine Molineux

Collections set museums apart from other cultural, educational, or leisure experiences. While the role, function, and experiences available in and through museums have broadened considerably over time, collections are still central to why visitors go to museums. In an increasingly digital age, the role of the museum in creating opportunities to see "the real thing" cannot be underestimated. Visitors want to have authentic, unique experiences and interactions with objects that they can only get in a museum environment.

5.1 PLANNING FOR PERMANENT COLLECTION EXHIBITIONS

The twenty-first-century museum visitor is a sophisticated, demanding visitor. Some require quiet contemplation of works of art, specimens, or artifacts on their own. For others, simply creating object displays devoid of interpretation or interactive opportunities for engagement and participation will no longer suffice. Both the definitions of and uses for collections have expanded, so that designing a permanent exhibition display may no longer be limited to two- or three-dimensional museum objects. Permanent collection displays today frequently include intangible collections such as oral histories, stories, songs, dances, and presentations of traditional ways of life.

Permanent collection displays can also be an important opportunity to create dialogue among visitors, as well as between visitors and the institution. Thoughtful presentations of the collection can encourage a new or nuanced way of seeing or understanding an object or event. Incorporating layered interpretation of an object, such as multiple perspectives or alternate histories can allow visitors to see an object or event in a new light. As the definition, interpretive methods, and modes of displaying permanent collections expand so do the opportunities to create meaningful visitor experiences.

There can be immense pressure in planning and designing for permanent exhibitions. The time, effort, and funding required to mount a permanent exhibition is extremely resource-intensive, and the stakes can be high. Some art museums rehang their permanent collection galleries of paintings, drawings, prints, and sculpture every year. Other museums with more complex collections remount their permanent collection exhibitions every five, ten, or fifteen years but may have to settle for still longer periods. Some permanent collections with long-term installations of huge dinosaurs or monumental architecture or sculpture may undertake to change their permanent collection display only three or four times in a century. Yet in the digital age in which we live, planning for relevance even six months from now can prove daunting. Given these pressures, which can include meeting the expectations of a diverse range of stakeholders as well as the public, most museums want to open that resource-intensive permanent collection exhibition in a perfect state on "Day 1." There is no room for error.

The implication of opening an expensive permanent collection exhibition that has taken several years to plan, design, and create may be that it is expected to remain relatively static until a new major source of funding is allocated to refresh part or all of the exhibition. All these demands must be balanced with the operational and financial reality of refreshing an exhibition. If it is merely a matter of hanging a different selection of pictures on gallery walls, that is one thing; but if the permanent collection display is of three-dimensional objects in cases or on plinths, some of which are large and heavy, any changes will be challenging. What staff resources are available that allow for rotating collections display, especially if they're necessary because textiles or paper are among the objects on display? Is the budget for audiovisual maintenance and repair adequate? Is it possible to change exhibits within the permanent collection exhibition? And is it advisable? Minor changes in a permanent collection display will seldom result in significant new interest from a public that is familiar with it, but it may refocus outdated interpretation, correct insensitive and incorrect labelling, address the return of long/short term loans, or highlight new research that is object specific.

In order to address these issues, museums must identify from the outset the intended life expectancy of the exhibition or what is meant by "permanent." This helps to set expectations and inform design, content selection, and the degree and scope to which multimedia should be incorporated into the exhibition. Above all, it affects the budget, since life expectancy must make the new permanent collection display cost-effective over the years that it is exhibited. In order to avoid a tired-looking and dated exhibition filled with inaccurate content or dated multimedia, the budget should include an annual allocation for exhibition renewal or rotations. Permanent collection exhibition renewal costs should be allocated as a budget item separate from the maintenance costs for the existing displays to allow for new or refreshed content over the life span of the permanent collection exhibition.

While this renewal budget may help to mitigate the obvious dating of an exhibition, it will not negate the need for a large capital expenditure at the end of the exhibition's lifespan. Often, the "expiration date" of the permanent collection display creates much-needed opportunities for reinterpretation and experimentation. The exhibition planning process allows for opportunities for public consultation and engagement; updates in interpretive planning and display approach based on new theories of pedagogy and museology; and a sense of excitement and renewal to motivate museum staff and stakeholders. Of course, for budget reasons, the expiration date must be postponed, sometimes for years, but eventually it will have this stimulating effect.

5.2 CHANGING PERMANENT COLLECTION DISPLAYS

Most people think that an important purpose for any museum is to display its collection. Yet many visitors' exit surveys attest to the often-well-founded suspicion that this function is not being satisfactorily fulfilled. Indeed, it is often publicly acknowledged by the museum—and even widely publicized as a way of supporting a fundraising campaign—that a relatively small proportion of the permanent collection is on display. Newspaper accounts often cite the low display percentage figures as if they were definitive tests of the institution's merits, deploring the concealment from the public of what may be properly seen as their heritage. While there is a balance to be achieved in displaying a large quantity of collections and creating a rich visitor experience, visitors still expect collections to be seen, not just stored.

5.2.1 Display/Storage Ratios

The degree to which museums are able to display their collections varies by museum type. Art museums often exhibit only 5 percent of the permanent collection. History museums sometimes do better, although their percentage is also likely to be low if they are amassing social history or military artifacts, but they often hover around 15 percent. Natural history museums, especially those associated with universities or research institutions, often have the lowest percentages (as little as 2 percent), since many of their specimens are study collections, and are not intended for display.

Museums are sometimes able to utilize this low display percentage as an impetus for expansion or renewal. In the early 1990s, the Tate Gallery in London let it be known that only 10 percent of its permanent collection was on display before its bifurcation into Tate Britain at its old building at Millbank on the north shore of the Thames, and Tate Modern in the renovated power station at Bankside on the south shore. Having raised the funds to complete Tate Modern, Executive Director Sir Nicholas Serota was able to announce that, henceforth, the public would be able to see 60 percent of Tate Modern's international art collection at Bankside. The phenomenal success of that institution (five million annual visitors instead of the originally projected two million) resulted in another major fundraising effort.

Although increasing the percentage of the collection on display is a standard rationale for an expansion, it is often an elusive target. If a collection consists of 10,000 works of art, of which only 500 (5 percent) are on display in the small existing museum, a 50 percent increase in permanent collection display space will increase the number of works on show to 750. However, if the collection is growing at the rate of 5 percent annually—acquiring 500 objects per year but gradually increasing—and furthermore if the announcement of the expansion project stimulates still more donations of works of art, the increased percentage on display will soon evaporate as the total collection size expands to 15,000 works and more. If it takes three years to raise the funds needed for the expansion and five more years to plan, design, and construct the larger museum, the percentage of works on display will be back to 5 percent—or even drop below that level—within a year or two of opening the larger venue.

5.2.2 Changing or Rotating Exhibitions

A large-scale renovation or expansion as a means of increasing collection display percentages may not always be a feasible option. However, planning for and creating opportunities for changing content within permanent collection displays and creating opportunities for rotating collection displays can be an effective means of:

- Enabling more of the collection to be on display
- Allowing more fragile or light-sensitive pieces to be rotated off display
- Keeping the exhibition fresh and current
- Featuring recent donations/discoveries/acquisitions

For conservation reasons, works on paper, textiles, costumes, and other sensitive materials like ivory should be rotated off display every few months. Planning for rotation, therefore, means that the interpretative plan must find a sequence of objects in the collection that can meaningfully replace each other without disrupting the "storyline" of the exhibition. These items should be identified, and those left in storage at the launch of the exhibition should be earmarked to replace the ones that are on display. The exact length of time on display for such sensitive artifacts needs to be calculated in lux hours of exposure (the number of hours that the lights will be on times the lux level at which they will be exhibited).

If changes are planned for other than conservation rotation purposes, they should be significant enough that they can be expected to attract a return visit by guests who have seen the show in its original edition. Signage and labels need to be planned to accommodate such changes: flexible graphic or multimedia displays that allow for easy updates of labels or interpretive content. In London, Tate Britain pioneered an innovative approach as early as 2000 to changes in permanent collection display of paintings by featuring an annual rehang in its Millbank galleries, which was marketed as an annual temporary exhibition with a highly public opening and reviews. Such an approach is to be preferred to the limited replacement of particular objects that can be one result of an unplanned approach to permanent collection display and is often hardly noticed by the visiting public.

5.3 INTERPRETING COLLECTIONS

While public access to collections is important, it is often the case that the museum can tell its story better with fewer artifacts displayed in more space. This enables sufficient attention to be paid to interpretation and the creation of a memorable visitor experience. In interpreting collections, there is a spectrum of collection-based interpretation that can be employed relative to the character of the collections, as illustrated in figure 5.1. One axis considers the range of interpretive approaches, from didactic to interactive, while the other considers collection types, ranging from intangible to tangible. When planning permanent collection displays, both collection types, as well as the range of interpretation should be considered to ensure a balance in experiences and budget.

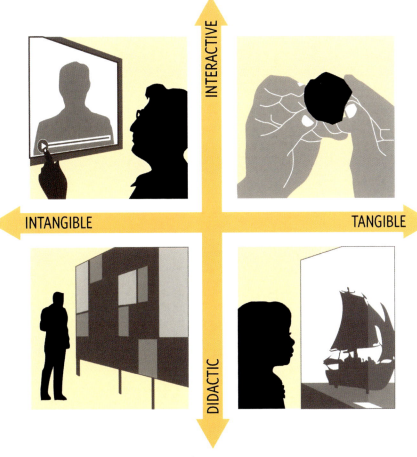

Figure 5.1. Spectrum of collections-based interpretation. LORD CULTURAL RESOURCES

Intangible-interactive interpretive displays present opportunities for:
- Direct visitor engagement
- Visitor-driven learning, exploration, and manipulation
- Meaning-making such as visitor-curated stories
- Highly visual and sensory communication such as an audiovisual display of traditional song and dance

Intangible-didactic interpretive displays present opportunities for:
- Higher degree of museum/curatorial control
- Less resource-intensive exhibits

Tangible-interactive interpretive displays present opportunities for:
- Building layers/depth of interpretation around the collection
- Visitor interest-driven learning and exploration
- Visitor participation

Tangible-didactic interpretive displays present opportunities for:

- Object displays in cases
- Graphic panels
- Budget-responsive design strategies

Before designing for a permanent exhibition display begins, decisions by the planning team should be made as to where on this spectrum their priorities lie. In identifying priorities for display in advance, design and budget allocations can proceed more smoothly.

5.4 MODES OF DISPLAY

In addition to options for interpreting collections as outlined in the foregoing spectrum, there are also several modes by which artifacts can be displayed or drawn upon to communicate to visitors. These modes of display can be characterized as:

- Aesthetic
- Contextual
- Process
- Visible storage

5.4.1 Aesthetic

An aesthetic display is an exhibiting technique whereby works of art (or occasionally outstanding specimens or artifacts) are presented as individual objects to be seen and appreciated in and for

Figure 5.2. Aesthetic display of artifacts from the Asian Collection at the musée du quai Branly-Jacques Chirac, Paris, France, January 2013. © MUSÉE DU QUAI BRANLY-JACQUES CHIRAC, PHOTO BY CYRIL ZANNETTACCI

themselves. There is often relatively little contextual material to interpret the work of art because it has communicative power in itself. The emphasis is placed on the object itself, not on supporting material. Art galleries typically display their collections in an aesthetic mode, but other museums may employ this mode to varying degrees, depending on the character of the collection—if a natural history collection includes magnificent gemstones or large colorful minerals, for instance. Usually, only part of the collection is displayed in this manner, or it is employed when a certain degree of emphasis is to be communicated about the object, such as showcasing a "treasure" in the collection or a featured new acquisition. In Paris, the musée du quai Branly-Jacques Chirac, for example, groups artifacts by geographical region, gorgeously presenting individual objects such as masks or textiles with minimal interpretation and context so that they can be appreciated aesthetically; the interpretation is not far away, but it does not interfere with the aesthetic interaction with the artifacts.

5.4.2 Contextual

In this mode, the priority is on communicating nature, culture, or history achieved through the display of material culture or specimens. Building context around artifacts, specimens, or works of art is the key to achieving greater relevance and telling a bigger story about cultures, people, and natural or cultural history. The technique is often employed in history museums and is part of an overall storytelling or thematic approach to interpretation. A contextual display can help visitors understand an object, including its meaning and importance, in a more clear and evident way. It can reveal stories that would otherwise be "hidden" from the visitor, such as who made it, who used it, why, and when. The emphasis in this mode of display is making connections with the visitor, and building a story around the object, or among several objects.

A contextual display approach is employed throughout much of the permanent exhibition display at the National WWII Museum in New Orleans. Large images, projections, sound, and recreated environments give the objects greater meaning as visitors see how such objects might have been

Figure 5.3. Contextual display at the National WWII Museum, New Orleans, Louisiana.
CAROL BARRINGTON/ALAMY STOCK PHOTO

Permanent Collection Exhibitions

experienced or used in their original settings. Context creates drama for some objects that may seem less than exciting if displayed on their own in a case without much interpretation. Suddenly an event or story comes life, and visitors can see the connections between objects, specimens, and works of art.

5.4.3 Process

Communicating how something works, how it is made, or why something occurs, through the display of a specimen, artifact, or work of art may be called a "process" mode of display. While there may be some story or contextual information supporting this form of display, the emphasis is placed on revealing a sequence of actions or behaviors that lead to a certain outcome. For example, an "exploded" display of an automotive engine might be interpreted in a process mode of display to communicate to visitors how an internal combustion engine works. This approach is often used in science and technology museums but can be employed effectively in a wide range of exhibitions including art and history museums (e.g., how an engraving is made, or how a textile is woven). Archaeology museums often use process displays to show how the artifacts in the exhibition were discovered: the Manuels River Hibernia Integration Centre in Newfoundland, Canada, uses a mixed media display to convey the process and tools employed by a field paleontologist when "digging" for fossils.

Figure 5.4. Process display at a recreated dig of a shale bed at Manuels River Hibernia Interpretation Centre, Conception Bay, Canada. LORD CULTURAL RESOURCES

5.4.4 Visible Storage

The most effective way to increase the percentage of works on display is to introduce visible storage. Individual objects are arranged along shelves, in glazed drawers, or gallery storage walls, identified only by a number code that refers visitors to a catalog book or (more likely) screens on which the visitor can read the museum's entire catalog entry about the objects they have selected because their interest has been drawn to them. Such displays work well for both for casual browsers—who can find out more than they wanted to know about the bright red item that caught their eye—and for serious students who can spend hours or days studying the collections in detail and learning everything that the museum knows about them. Visible storage also facilitates educators' use of the galleries, as students can be assigned to select an object of interest or relevant to a particular subject and to write a report about it, beginning with what they found in the museum's electronic catalog on screens positioned beside the display case. For those parts of the collection that can be meaningfully presented in visible storage, the percentage on display can rise steeply from 15 percent to 85 percent.

In 2021, the Depot Boijmans van Beuningen opened the Boijmans van Beuningen Museum in Rotterdam, Netherlands, with the sole purpose of making the entire collection of more than 150,000 works of art accessible to the public. The Victoria and Albert Museum in London is following close on the heels of the Depot, with its V&A East storage facility expected to open in 2023. The new space will house some 250,000 objects and 1,000 separate archives, which visitors can explore in person during self-guided tours more than sixty to ninety minutes long. As reported in Nina Siegel's article for *The New York Times*, V&A East would be "an endlessly changing cabinet of curiosities" from the collection of furniture, fashion, textiles, and art. Visitors can learn from curators how exhibitions are planned and watch conservators at work.

Granting visitors and researchers a greater degree of access to the collection as well as a "behind the scenes" glimpse into caring for the collection are important trends in planning visible storage displays. Designed to include studio or program spaces, study and research spaces, these areas allow researchers and visitors to interact with collections as well as museum staff. At the Darwin Centre of the Natural History Museum in London visitors are given visual access and even the ability to interact via two-way microphones with scientists or technicians in the Specimen Preparation Area, where visitors can watch the specialists at work as they prepare and conserve specimens.

Creating spaces and programs of this nature reflects a change in attitude about transparency and increased intellectual access to collections—the notion that collections do not belong just to the institution but also to the communities which they serve. For example, the Smithsonian Arctic Studies Center at the Anchorage Museum in Alaska employs visible storage techniques in their exhibition. Part of the experience is encouraging research about Alaska Native culture through an archaeology laboratory and a space where Alaska Native elders, artists, and scholars can study heritage objects up close. While increased access to collections carries some risk, such as balancing collection security with community needs, as well as the time and resource intensiveness of facilitating greater access, it also permits more people to enter the "hidden" world of collections. This creates opportunities to communicate principles of good collections management and the importance of caring for such resources, ideally creating community stakeholders and advocates for the museum in the process.

Macro artifacts, such as automobiles, tanks, or aircraft, can also benefit from a visible storage approach in a large gallery or hangar. Visitors can get up close to these large objects ranged in

Figure 5.5. Macro visible storage at the Canadian War Museum, Ottawa, Canada. LORD CULTURAL RESOURCES

parallel rows to illustrate the changes in style and technology over time. Again, this type of visible storage needs to be supported by visitor access in the same gallery to the museum's complete catalog about these artifacts, usually on monitors nearby. The macro storage display of tanks, aircraft, and vehicles at the Canadian War Museum in Ottawa is an excellent example of dense displays of large artifacts.

With the proliferation of multimedia in exhibitions, there are new opportunities to communicate a depth of information about the objects in a visible storage gallery. Computer terminals, mobile applications, and tablet technologies allow visitors to "select" an object that interests them. They can manipulate the digital image, watch videos that show it in action, or listen to interviews with curators about the object. In short, multimedia has transformed what has traditionally been a rather static or low interpretation display method into one that can accommodate all aspects of aesthetic, context, and process modes of display as well as layers of interpretation. The Teck Suite of Galleries: *Earth's Treasures* at the Royal Ontario Museum in Toronto displays some three thousand geological specimens if not more in an interactive manner that allows visitors to find out more about the objects on display through touchscreen interfaces, but also to pursue their interests by locating similar specimens within the gallery.

Opportunities for interactivity and integrated programming also help to transform visible storage (or other) displays into more engaging and participatory experiences for visitors.

Figure 5.6. Multimedia kiosks provide access to information for all the minerals in the visible storage display. *Earth's Treasures* at the Royal Ontario Museum, Toronto, Canada. LORD CULTURAL RESOURCES

Artist-in-residence programs, artists' demonstrations, curator/community tours, audio tours, scavenger hunts, and more, all serve to engage visitors and to empower them to view the collection through multiple perspectives. In some cases, besides showcasing the viewpoint of the artist or the museum curator, various communities are drawn upon to share their interpretation of the collection. This helps target audiences that might not normally visit the museum and increasingly to address decolonizing strategies now being employed by museums. The Multiversity Gallery visible storage exhibition at the Museum of Anthropology at the University of British Columbia in Canada, which includes important First Nations collections, is used as part of the Native Youth Program. In addition to extensive mentoring and training activities, the program allows students to select various objects in the Multiversity Galleries and develop their own tour based on their research and connection to the objects, often incorporating family histories and information from elders.

In recent years, the effectiveness of visible storage on the visitor experience has come into question. Are visitors getting anything out of the experience? Or are they just taking in the density and diversity? Are displays devoid of interpretation worth it, if a museum can get more of the collection out of storage? The V&A and Boijmans van Beuningen seem to think so. Overall, visible storage displays have plenty to offer visitors. They increase the percentage of the collection on display and appeal to those who enjoy the invitation to discover the collection for themselves. As museums increasingly employ current exhibition design trends to visible storage display, this behind the scenes, free-form exploration has the potential to create new and interesting spaces and visitor experiences.

Chapter 6

It's Not Always about Collections

Katherine Molineux

Although collections are at the heart of many museums, there are entire museums that do not revolve around collections of specimens, works of art, or artifacts at all. Instead, some museums are mission-driven to communicate an idea or ideas. Collections may be present, but they are seen as a means of supporting and communicating those ideas. This diverges from a more traditional approach of shaping a story around a collection.

Other types of exhibitions, such as those developed for science centers, children's museums, and living history sites may be constructed around the notion of communicating a scientific phenomenon, an educational principle, or as a means of creating a historical context for the past. Again, collections may or may not be present, but they support the story rather than the story being based on them.

6.1 IDEA EXHIBITIONS

Idea exhibitions are organized around the exploration of an idea. Unlike many traditional art museums, where the collection is the basis for the development of an exhibition, idea exhibitions are not defined by discipline or constrained by access to museum objects. Instead, they are driven by a topic, concept, or thesis. Exhibitions of this nature tend to:

- Be interdisciplinary and holistic—they can take a 360-degree approach to a topic
- Incorporate multiple interpretations from different perspectives
- Include more oral histories and first-person interpretation devices
- Focus on the visitor experience
- Employ interactive technologies
- Have more opportunities for co-curation with the public
- Provide a forum for social engagement, interaction, and visitor participation

Idea museums are entire institutions dedicated to exploring a particular topic, such as the Museum of Tolerance in Los Angeles or the Canadian Museum for Human Rights in Winnipeg, Canada. Since museums are trusted institutions, idea museums can create an environment where difficult, controversial, or emotional content can be discussed and experienced in a safe, authentic, and moderated manner. These institutions aim to promote dialogue, actively integrating programming, visitor participation, creative activities, and performances into the exhibition experience. In addition to creating dialogue, some institutions emphasize action and advocacy. The International Coalition of Sites of Conscience includes more than two hundred sites globally and advocates conscious action, transforming "places that preserve the past into dynamic spaces that promote civic action on today's struggles for human rights and justice."[1]

While some idea museums are purpose-planned and built, more traditional collection-based museums are also creating exhibitions that are focused on communicating a topic or idea. Taking an "idea exhibition" approach allows these institutions to:

- Engage in popular topics
- Address issues of social justice and identity
- Encourage dialogue with and between visitors
- Stay fresh and current in their appeal
- More easily explore co-created opportunities

Even art museums are exploring other organizational models in addition to chronological, biographical retrospectives, or style-focused displays of their permanent collections. In 2017, the Whitney Museum of American Art in New York City launched a temporary exhibition entitled, *An Incomplete History of Protest*. It explored how artists, past and present, confronted the political and social issues of their day. Whether making art as a form of activism, criticism, instruction, or inspiration, the featured artists saw their work as essential to challenging established thought and creating a more equitable culture.

Collections in idea exhibitions are often utilized in a different manner than traditional exhibitions. Artifacts for display are chosen to illustrate a particular powerful message or story or are significant in a particular way because they are related to an idea or concept in contextual

Figure 6.1. *An Incomplete History of Protest* temporary exhibition at the Whitney Museum of American Art, New York. DIGITAL IMAGE © WHITNEY MUSEUM OF AMERICAN ART/LICENSED BY SCALA/ART RESOURCE, NY

mode exhibitions. Intangible collections such as oral histories and interviews often have a strong representation in idea exhibitions and are powerful tools to communicate a story. In the *Facing Freedom* temporary exhibition at the Chicago History Museum, for example, the content is organized around an idea that postulates that the history of the United States has been shaped by conflicts over what it means to be free. Four themes are explored: Workers' Rights, Armed Conflict, Race & Citizenship, and Public Protest. Artifacts and objects in the exhibition are minimal and targeted, chosen for their power and placed into context. In exploring the topic of slavery, for example, reproduced archival documents and photographs provide context for the iron neck collar on display, and an audio station provides visitors with an opportunity to hear a first-person account of the brutality of wearing the neck collar. Visitors are personally engaged throughout the exhibition by the use of interactives and targeted personal questions such as "What would you do if you lost your freedom?"

As twenty-first-century museumgoers demand an ever more sophisticated and curated thought-provoking and interactive experience, it will be interesting to see how idea exhibitions proliferate and evolve, and the role intangible or digital collections will play in this evolution. Incorporating opportunities for depth of visitor participation and dialogue will also continue to evolve the meaning and relevance of this type of exhibition experience.

It's Not Always about Collections

Figure 6.2. The *Facing Freedom* temporary exhibition is an example of an "idea exhibition," Chicago History Museum. COURTESY OF ADAM JONES, PHD/GLOBAL PHOTO ARCHIVE/FLICKR

6.2 CHILDREN'S EXHIBITIONS

Children's museums and exhibitions have evolved greatly since the Brooklyn Children's Museum opened in 1899. Visitors have become more sophisticated and demanding in their expectations, and these heightened expectations extend to the time spent with family and friends at children's museums.

The Association of Children's Museums refers to children's museums as places "where children learn through play and exploration in environments and experiences designed just for them." This definition can also apply to purpose built spaces or exhibits for children within a broader museum environment. The United States has historically led the way in this development, with major examples in Boston, Philadelphia, Indianapolis, and now almost every large American city. The movement has spread to Europe—with examples like Zoom! in Vienna—and Asia. Two of the world's outstanding children's museums are to be found in Manila and Mexico City.

There is also a strong trend, which began as early as the 1960s, for museums of all types to include a children's discovery room, children's gallery, or children's pathway within their walls. This may be a designated area of a larger gallery, a purpose-built and designed gallery space, or an interpretive pathway through an exhibition not otherwise specifically oriented toward children. Children's exhibits may be focused on science and technology, natural history, environmental sustainability, history, ethnology, or art, and are used to foster learning and exploration.

Children's museums often present exhibits in which children can learn how their bodies function and grow, or how to live safely in a big city. As part of a larger exhibition targeted at the general public, a children's interpretive pathway will take the topics and ideas presented in an exhibition and create exhibits and text specifically targeted at children, thus allowing for an experience that addresses a family's needs. Those pathways are often shown in the galleries at a child's-eye height, running under the adult text that is higher up.

One advantage that specialized children's museums and galleries have over interpretive pathways featuring exhibits for children is that they can target more specific ages and learning stages. Children's museums and galleries are generally aimed at children from preschool age through to about age ten or twelve, often with separate areas designed to serve:

- Infants and toddlers (aged infant to three years)
- Preschoolers and kindergarten-aged children (aged four to six)
- Primary and middle school children (aged six to eight and nine to twelve)

The infant to age three audience is a growing segment in children's museum attendance, with specifically designed infant and toddler rooms to target the particular needs of this age group. For a growing family with children of different ages it is important to have something for everyone to enjoy and learn from in ways that are appropriate to each age group.

Targeting cognitive development stages for different age groups is a key priority in designing for children's exhibitions. Not only should exhibits be interactive, play-based, and multidisciplinary, but they also need to target different developmental skill levels: hand-eye coordination, fine motor skills, and memory development. This consideration of skill and cognitive development underscores the importance of children's museums and exhibits as an integral part of informal learning and as a compliment to formal learning. They help to foster skills and behavior that can prepare children for school and instill a desire for lifelong learning.

Not to be forgotten are all the families and friends (adults and older children) who also attend children's museums and children's exhibitions. Spaces must accommodate the presence and the comfort of accompanying adults. Attendance and participation in a children's gallery are viewed and marketed as a family activity, which parents, grandparents, extended family, and children can enjoy together. Some children's museums, such as the Boston Children's Museum, even offer adults pre- and post–visit resources online not only about practical tips for navigating the museum, but also how to facilitate a successful experience (e.g., advocating the use of repetition in learning, or following your child's lead). A trip to the children's museum is not targeted only at children but is rather a safe and social place where the whole family can spend quality time together.

Caregivers expect that a trip to the museum with children will result in learning, stimulation, and experiences that are responsive to the learning processes of children. These exhibition experiences are expected to enable and include, among others:

- Playful discovery
- Hands-on interactivity
- Creativity through the arts

- Sparking curiosity and discovery through stimulating and engaging experiences
- Exposure to diversity: new ideas, new people, new ways of being
- Learning about community needs and issues and facilitating quality family time

Given the high standard of expectations regarding the outcomes of a children's exhibition experience, it is no surprise that collections are used in a very particular manner. An artifact-heavy children's exhibit lacking in interactivity and hands-on opportunities is destined to fail. Therefore, children's museums or museums with children's displays that *do* have collections are only successful if the exhibits find a way to make their collection engaging. Children's exhibits are often program-based—not collection-based. This means that where collections are employed, they tend to be teaching or study collections that enable children to conduct hands-on discovery or experimentation, as opposed to passive observation. Even traditionally child-unfriendly spaces such as art museums are increasingly recognizing the need to reach and plan for a family audience. For example, the Art Gallery of Ontario opened the Weston Family Learning Centre in Toronto in 2011. This thirty-five thousand square foot (3,252 sq m) space, billed as a "hub for community creativity and learning—a gathering place for hands-on and online exploration of the creative process" includes a hands-on center for young children, a youth center, workshop and studio space, and more. Reaching out to families is central to building community relationships as well as developing a future audience base.

Incorporating community outreach and tapping into and addressing local community needs is an integral part of planning and designing children's exhibits. Communicating values about diversity

Figure 6.3. Play-based exhibits for children at the Zoom! Kindermuseum, Vienna, Austria. COURTESY OF ZOOM KINDERMUSEUM/ALEXANDRA EIZINGER

and tolerance—not just race and ethnicity, but religion, developmental and physical disabilities, or socioeconomic status—are a staple of children's exhibits in the Western world. Not only does such an approach help foster inclusive values and life skills, but it also helps reach a wider and traditionally underserved population. Some institutions are working to dissolve the physical (and social) barriers that face underserved communities by taking the museum to the community by displaying exhibits in a publicly accessible setting such as libraries and community centers, for example.

In an increasingly digitized world, it may seem like site-specific physical exhibits may be of waning popularity and attraction for youth. However, as families and caretakers continue to value educational hands-on, stimulating, and engaging experiences, balancing screen time with physical experiences, children's museums and exhibitions continue to hold an important place in the informal learning milieu.

6.3 LIVING HISTORY EXHIBITIONS

Living history sites are extremely diverse in scope, including forts, historic sites, heritage houses and villages, living historical farms, and battlefields—but they do share a number of commonalities. As Stacy Roth explores in her book, *Past into Present: Effective Techniques for First-Person Historical Interpretation,* living history sites (otherwise known as heritage villages or open-air museums) interpret both tangible and intangible heritage in a setting that replicates parts of a historical environment as a featured exhibit area.[2] Living history sites attempt to bring history to life, to transport visitors across time and place through immersive, sensory experiences. They often employ costumed interpreters who communicate in the first person (in-character interpretation) or in the third person (as docents). These sites are a unique way of communicating lifeways of the past—how a particular culture at a particular time performed their work, formed relationships, thought, acted—in short, lived.

Creating living history exhibitions is extremely resource-intensive. Achieving high standards of authenticity that such an experience demands is difficult, which accounts for the diverse levels of authenticity among living history sites. Interpreters are a vital part of the experience. They make meaning of the historic setting, communicating to visitors what life was like for people of the past through costumes, work, or trades they engaged in and the objects around them.

Collections play an important role in creating this experience, especially since they often include whole buildings as well as their contents. They help to make the past real and create a level of authenticity that an interpreter alone cannot create. Having access to the real thing—whether that be flint for knapping, a quilt, a butter churn, a weapon, or a uniform—is what visitors desire, often asking of any interpreter the question "Is it real?" meaning, "Is this an authentic artifact from the time period that would have been used by people in the past?" The manner in which collections are displayed is integral to creating that immersive, authentic experience for visitors. Unlike museums in which the permanent collection is kept in vitrines, artifacts in living history sites are usually integrated into the building or structure (which is often itself part of the collection) to create a realistic scene in order to communicate themes and messages. For example, in order to communicate to visitors the social norms and expectations of middle-class Victorians, a living room full of artifacts such as chairs, tables, musical instruments, carpets, and paintings will speak to gender roles, design, architecture, leisure, and more. The artifacts are more than props on display—they are critical to the success of creating an authentic experience. The challenge for interpreters is being able to unlock the stories that an object has to tell and communicate that information to visitors in an engaging and, most importantly, *accurate* manner. The challenge for visitors entering living history exhibitions is to be able to observe the environment around them, assess the similarities and differences to their own environment, and engage in discussion with interpreters to learn more about what the objects say about life in the past.

In addition to creating an authentic environment whereby visitors can witness the past, living history sites often have a robust teaching or display collection that allows for an interactive, hands-on approach to learning about history. These collections are often comprised of duplicates or replicas that may be permitted to deteriorate through controlled uses such as interactive exhibitions, hands-on education, and demonstrations. For example, living history sites often display and use artifacts such as spinning wheels, looms, wood-burning stoves, and tools to interpret lifeways of the past. These require skill sets and knowledge not often learned and applied in our urban twenty-first-century lives where most people consume rather than produce goods. Using a teaching collection allows visitors to learn through seeing, listening, and doing, thus creating powerful and memorable experiences.

There are many challenges facing living heritage sites today. In Europe they may recreate prehistoric or protohistoric lifestyles, replicate folk customs in open-air *heimatsmuseums*, or reproduce mining or industrial villages. In North America, the struggle to maintain relevancy and to compete with more entertaining leisure options is a constant challenge. In many cases, these sites were created after World War II in response to a changing (and more visibly diverse) population as a means of preserving the past. What that translates into today are sites that must find ways to connect to their surrounding community, which may in fact bear little resemblance or personal connection to the history that they are portraying. Integrating historically underrepresented or unrepresented groups in the interpretation of these historic sites, such as the role of women, visible minorities, the poor, and Indigenous people is key to telling a more representative story.

Figure 6.4. The Historic Threads website complements and extends the reach of living history experiences such as the weaving demonstration at Colonial Williamsburg in Virginia. THE COLONIAL WILLIAMSBURG FOUNDATION

Figure 6.5. A weaving demonstration at Colonial Williamsburg in Virginia.
THE COLONIAL WILLIAMSBURG FOUNDATION

Perhaps a more fundamental criticism levied at living history sites is whether it is even possible to portray a historical event or a period of time in the seemingly objective manner that such sites purport to portray.[3] Living history sites can be seen as simulacra of the past, but these are, of course, our present-day constructions of that past, fraught with all the pitfalls and nostalgia associated with trying to capture a simplified snapshot in time under an educational mandate. First-person sites have some advantages: at Plymouth Plantation in Massachusetts, visitors can hear the costumed inhabitant of one humble home boasting about the wooden floor she has just had installed, whereas the old man in the next house dismisses them, favoring the hard-packed earthen floor he is accustomed to; thus, we learn that just as today these seventeenth-century settlers had divergent opinions about how to do things. History is not monolithic but abounds in contradictions at any given time.

6.4 SCIENCE EXHIBITIONS

Science centers have their roots in the working technology displays installed in the Deutsches Museum in Munich, Germany, as early as the 1920s, where they inspired an American philanthropist to sponsor similar exhibitions at the Museum of Science and Industry in Chicago. In the 1950s and 1960s, the Evolution at Eindhoven in the Netherlands, the Exploratorium in San Francisco, and the Ontario Science Centre in Toronto were among those setting the pace. Science centers and museums are now presenting interactive exhibits throughout the world, from Paris and London to Singapore and Bangkok. China continues to be a hotbed for science museum development, with some of the most high tech and largest in the world.

Exhibitions featuring scientific discoveries and technological achievements are sponsored by governments and industry anxious to foster scientific and technological learning, and support for high-cost enterprises. As with children's galleries, the range of exhibits in the science gallery can be oriented toward natural history, earth sciences, pure science, or energy and technology. This may include aerospace, underwater exploration, communications and artificial intelligence, or medical and biogenetics applications. The emphasis is on discovery learning with a strong hands-on component. Often, concepts are interpreted through personal connections, such as exhibitions that focus on the body that explain bodily functions to children and other young visitors. The methods of science are often part of the display, either through creating a working lab space within the gallery itself, or by communicating with visitors through changing exhibits and programming what is new and hot in the various fields of science today.

Fostering innovation, creativity, and critical thinking skills through science exhibitions and programming is now seen as just as important as imparting the particular knowledge itself. The *Science Storms* exhibition, opened in 2010 at the Chicago Museum of Science and Industry, explores the basic scientific principles behind seven natural phenomena—lightning, forest fires, tornados, avalanches, tsunamis, sunlight, and atoms in motion—in an awe-inspiring, immersive, and wholly interactive manner. The exhibition includes more than fifty experiments in more than twenty-six thousand square feet (2,415 sq m) and is intended to move visitors from a state of wonder to inquiry, curiosity to observation, an investigation to understanding. Everything about the exhibition is geared toward creating an active experience that invites the visitor to experiment and create.

Taking this emphasis on experimentation and self-discovery to another level is the award-winning Weston Family Innovation Centre at the Ontario Science Centre in Toronto, Canada. A custom-built

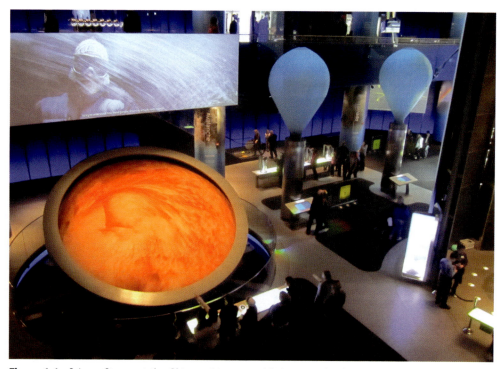

Figure 6.6. *Science Storms* at the Chicago Museum of Science and Industry. LORD CULTURAL RESOURCES

experimentation space, the exhibitions and programs integrate art, design, technology, and science to encourage visitors to be innovative and to think critically to solve challenges. The experimental spirit is infused into the design of the space itself, encouraging the museum team to evolve the space and exhibits based on visitor needs and learning. Efforts to create connections to virtual visitors and online content have also been accounted for through the creation of podcasts, videos, and other pre- and post-visit content.

Besides fostering skills, science museums and exhibitions are also engaged in a battle to create a scientific literate society. This entails, at a basic level, helping to create a generation of people who have a positive view of science and its value in society. Undoubtedly, creating an engaging and empowering science exhibition can go a long way toward encouraging that sense of wonder and curiosity that can lead to greater interest and literacy in science.

6.5 DIGITAL IMMERSIVE EXHIBITIONS

A growing number of exhibitions use a combination of technology, storytelling, and art to create full-body immersive experiences. These installations occur in purpose-built spaces, large warehouses, or outdoor pavilions. Innovations in projection, audio, and gesture-based technologies have made these new types of exhibitions possible. Many of these installations are meant to be experienced for a short period of time like Yayoi Kusama's *Infinity Mirrors* or Random International's *Rain Room*, which has been traveling to museums and art galleries around the world since 2012. *Rain Room* allows visitors to walk through a downpour without getting wet. Motion sensors detect visitors' movements as they navigate through the darkened space, becoming performers in this intersection of art, technology, and nature. These types of installations continue to grow in appeal as museums and art galleries engage with contemporary artists and cutting-edge technology companies to create immersive, experimental, one-of-kind experiences.

At the Wu Kingdom Helv Relics Museum in Wuxi, China, visitors are immersed in a fifteen-minute story about the rise of the Kingdom of Wu during the Spring and Autumn period between

Figure 6.7. Immersive experience at the Wu Kingdom Helv Relics Museum in Wuxi, China.
COURTESY OF TAMSCHICK MEDIA+SPACE GMBH

514–496 BC. The producers created a unique visual style; a mix of cinematic martial arts scenes shot in Shanghai combined with paint-style animations. The linear storytelling is enhanced with interactive elements that reinforce the visitors' feeling of being transported back in time, away to King Helv's coming into power, his fight for hegemony, the victory at the battle of Boju, and other great events of that period.

In addition to museums, private companies are recognizing the power of immersive exhibitions and becoming direct competitors to museums. By January 2021, three companies had created large, immersive Van Gogh experiences. Visitors immerse themselves in lush environments created through high-resolution projections of Van Gogh's masterpieces. Visitors walk through large open spaces, as the images on the walls and floors change. During the COVID-19 pandemic, a Toronto venue was transformed into a drive-through experience so that visitors could still attend during the lockdown. Not a single piece of original art was part of the show, which is housed in a large warehouse space that is not conditioned to showcase rare works of art. The success of this type of show has launched similar experiences with other artists including Marc Chagal, Gustav Klimt, and Claude Monet. With *Immersive Van Gogh* attracting some two million visitors in one year, there is little doubt that museums will need to take stock of this trend and why it appeals to visitors.

Figure 6.8. Visitors are digitally surrounded by the works of Vincent Van Gogh. CBW/ALAMY STOCK PHOTO

Case Study

WESTON FAMILY INNOVATION LEARNING CENTRE, TERMS OF ENGAGEMENT AT THE ONTARIO SCIENCE CENTRE

Lesley Lewis and Kevin von Appen

Figure 6.9. Hands-on experimentation at the Weston Family Innovation Centre, Ontario Science Centre, Toronto, Canada. COURTESY OF THE ONTARIO SCIENCE CENTRE

In 1999—at the turn of a new century and after thirty years as a leader in science engagement—Toronto's Ontario Science Centre saw it was time for a change. Our world had been transformed since our opening in 1969. Our science center brand of interactive engagement had spread to retail stores and restaurants. Science content for the layperson was now widely available in print and on television—or just a click away online. So, we committed to evolving a science center for the twenty-first century by developing new ways to engage our visitors:

- Our focus would continue to be on science and technology, but our approach would foster creativity and innovation across a broad array of disciplines.

- We would move beyond being primarily an attraction-based "place to visit" to building relationships that went beyond the walls of our site or the boundaries of an admission ticket.

We would spark an understanding that science is an essential element of twenty-first-century culture.

- We would strive to make a difference in the life of every young visitor, not just those with high potential who are the focus of specialized programs.
- We would inspire people of all ages to gain confidence through our activities, to become creative problem solvers, and to move from "visitor" to "participant."
- We would cultivate citizens who could imagine and build new solutions to twenty-first-century challenges, who would be curious, confident risk-takers—critical thinkers who would be both creative and science-literate. In sum, we began to think of ourselves as community builders.

Early in the work that would culminate in the opening of the Weston Family Innovation Centre in 2006, it became clear that fundamental to this development was the concept of working *with* our audience, not following typical processes to create exhibits *for* them.

Further, the new experiences needed to be more process-oriented than outcome-driven. Processes can be taken away from a visit as new skills, transferable to real-life situations. The fact that a quickly-rigged contraption to transport water from one point to another might fail is much less important than the innovative thinking, rapid prototyping, and collaboration it takes to try out the idea in the first place—a truth we've since seen confirmed again and again on our gallery floor.

Extensive pilot testing with thousands of participants had a significant influence on understanding the conditions necessary to make our visitors feel comfortable sharing ideas in a problem-solving environment, working with people they may not know.

The result? Fifty-plus experience areas that fostered inspiration and exploration; unexpected connections between art, music, science, fashion and more; observation and analysis; creativity; collaboration; and risk-taking—in short, the skills, attitudes, and behaviors of innovation. These ranged from an art piece transforming a captured image of a visitor's face into a wall-sized pixel-portrait in bubbles to a ground-breaking "makerspace" equipped with tools for constructing a common item like a shoe from unexpected materials such as cardboard or Astroturf.

Acknowledging that physical exhibits rarely lend themselves to the flexibility required to address changing views in science and advances in technology, we created a "Hot Zone" where constantly updated presentations, both digital and "analog" in the form of host-led demos and dialogue keep visitors at the forefront of science while engaging them in activities relevant to them as individuals. This can range from breaking news on a tsunami illuminated by screen animations, live links and physical demos of the wave to on-floor experiments in playing rock/paper/scissors sparked by published research and uploaded to the web.

Our development teams continue to take the processes of innovative thinking to heart. Collaborating with visitors at every step, testing concepts, piloting loose frameworks for activity, engaging teachers and researchers, and rapidly expressing ideas in physical form have all become new modes of development—it has been fun, fast, and uncertain.

And not surprisingly, we didn't get everything right on the first try! In fact, we promised ourselves and our Board that we would make mistakes—if there were none, we hadn't pushed the envelope far enough. By 2010, ongoing evaluations had shown that while our free-range, largely instruction-free new space worked with our target audience of youth aged fourteen to twenty-four, the majority of our visitors—families with kids under twelve and adults without children—needed more: more context, more guidance, and more accessible entry points to begin their explorations.

The next step? Call it Innovation Centre 2.0. We extensively revitalized our space in 2012, driven by lessons we learned as we created a new traveling exhibition called *Imaginate* that was designed to extend our offerings to a broader audience. This project was a catalyst for major changes to the entire Innovation Centre.

Innovation Centre 2.0 connects open-ended activities with broad themes exploring pathways to innovation. For example, there's the theme of "Dream Big," which links making and testing a better paper airplane with trying out a pair of wings to compare your flapping abilities with those of birds and with the iterative testing that produced Canada's Avro Arrow fighter jet, along with background on the earliest dreams of aviation. Elsewhere we reworked areas to make them more useable for visiting school groups, and through the theme of "Look to the World" we are communicating that innovation is not simply about technology, by inviting visitors to test out a "hippo roller" plastic drum that's giving people in developing economies a cheap, simple, and effective way to transport water. (It's also fun to roll.)

In one special case, that engagement has linked our past with our new present. We responded to a visitor-generated petition on Facebook to bring back our beloved "Coffee" voice synthesizer (an exhibit dating back to our opening in 1969 in which a mechanical voice pronounces the word to amusing effect) by renewing the original and placing it in a context of modern voice synthesizer innovations that visitors can try.

Through 2020 and 2021, as the global pandemic closed cultural attractions worldwide, Science Centre teams working from home embarked on our latest cycle of iteration for the Innovation Centre, with refreshed graphics, new artworks, and activity areas and a partner-driven "CoLab" to explore new models in maker-based visitor co-creation.

We can't predict with any certainty where our evolution will take us in the future. But we can close by sharing some lessons our core development team learned that we'll carry forward as we go:

- **Question past practices**: Don't dismiss every skill or process that has led your organization to its present stage, but don't rely on them either.
- **Play**: Laughter is a great indicator of how comfortable people are expressing new ideas. In a playful environment only ideas fail, not people.
- **Change the language**: We purposefully change our language to illustrate that we are working differently. For example, we speak of experiences, not exhibits.
- **Make mistakes**: A fundamental characteristic of innovation is taking **risks**. How can we create environments for participants to be innovative if we don't allow ourselves to make mistakes?
- **Move people around**: Changing processes and practices can be more successful if people are moved out of their traditional environments into new locations.

- **Document**: How can you repeat success if the process isn't documented? Oral traditions are valuable, but they are not transferable. Spread the wealth of knowledge by capturing it in the moment.

- **Read**: There is a wealth of information available on innovation. This has helped us to change processes, sometimes simply by providing a new word or phrase to describe what we're hoping to achieve.

- **Celebrate**: This can be forgotten in the rush toward deadlines and frustrating budget-crunching meetings. This is new work people are putting their heart and soul into trying out uncertain and untested ideas. Celebrate their creativity!

NOTES

1. Please see: sitesofconscience.org.
2. Stacy Roth, *Past into Present: Effective Techniques for First-Person Historical Interpretation* (Chapel Hill: University of North Carolina Press, 1998).
3. Scott Magelssen, *Living History Museums: Undoing History through Performance* (Lanham, MD: Scarecrow Press, 2007).

Chapter 7

Virtual Exhibitions

Sarah Hill

7.1 WHAT IS A VIRTUAL EXHIBITION?

Virtual exhibitions come in a variety of formats and are known by many names (online exhibition, virtual tour, web gallery, etc.) but simply stated, a virtual exhibition is any exhibition whose venue for presentation exists virtually in cyberspace rather than physically within the walls of a museum, gallery, heritage site, or visitor center.

Like any physical exhibition, a virtual exhibition blends a variety of artifacts, specimens, works of art, ideas, multimedia, interactives, models, replicas, or graphics to tell a story and create an enjoyable learning experience for the public. It just so happens that virtual exhibitions convey this story exclusively through a grouping of digital media (images, video, animations, text, graphics, games, etc.) that can only be accessed or experienced online or a via a digital interface.

By using an entirely digital format and existing purely in the virtual realm (typically connected via the internet), virtual exhibitions can be a far more flexible option to physical exhibitions as they are not bound by several key constraints:

- Geography: Usually hosted online, virtual exhibitions are accessible from almost any location you can think of, at any time, on a range of different devices by anyone who has access to a computer or mobile device, and an internet connection. Audiences no longer need to be physically present or travel long distances to attend an exhibition at a museum.

- Space: The extent of content featured, and the number of exhibitions delivered annually is often restricted by the amount of available gallery space. More technical aspects of these spaces such as security and environmental controls can also be limiting. For some heritage sites, there may not even be a defined space in which to host an exhibition. With virtual exhibitions there are no walls, ceilings, or floors to hold you back.

- Time: Available 24/7, virtual exhibitions need never close for the evening or to make way for a new incoming exhibition. They can be offered to the public for as long as desired—or at least for as long as the content produced remains factually correct and relevant. This means audiences can repeatedly engage with a virtual exhibition when they want to, for as long as the want to, and can consume content at their own pace.

Great! So, virtual exhibitions are just like regular exhibitions but online, and with less constraints to deal with. No need to change our approach to planning and devote a whole chapter to the subject, right? Well, not exactly.

The virtual environment is a much different place to the physical environment, with its own limitations, regulations, and architecture. Despite the many advantages of a virtual exhibition, there are also costs and limits to what can feasibly be achieved when communicating entirely virtually through digital media. The pace of change in the virtual realm is also much faster and harder to keep up with, as new devices, platforms, programs, and features are launched at an unprecedented rate. When internet-enabled, the virtual environment is vast and connects the museum to an incredibly large, diverse, and global audience. The technology that people use in their everyday lives significantly shapes their expectations of what a virtual experience should be, and people behave much differently online than they do in person; searching for information differently, consuming content differently, and communicating differently with each other. For museums, galleries, and heritage sites that are thinking about engaging with audiences on this unfamiliar virtual frontier, this creates a new set of considerations and the need to adopt a slightly different approach to planning for virtual exhibitions.

7.2 WHY DEVELOP A VIRTUAL EXHIBITION?

There are countless reasons why a museum might decide to develop a virtual exhibition, ranging from a simple desire to experiment with a new platform, to more strategic decisions aimed at broadening audiences or increasing relevance. It could even be to satisfy a more serious need to quickly capture significant but fleeting stories or preserve artifacts at risk. Below are a few reasons why museums might consider developing a virtual exhibition.

7.2.1 Extend the Life of a Physical Exhibition

Extending the life of a physical exhibition is the most common motivation for creating a virtual exhibition. Producing a physical exhibition, whether permanent or temporary, is resource intensive. It takes expertise, time, and funds to plan, research, fabricate, market, and manage an exhibition. Whether it runs for two months or for two years, the cost of development—planning, design, and implementation—remains pretty much the same. However, the longer the exhibition content is publicly available, the more opportunity there is for people to engage with and learn from it, and for a museum to generate a greater impact and greater return on its investment.

By translating content from a past exhibition into a digital format for presentation in the virtual environment, museums and galleries can create a long-term archive, document the exhibition for posterity, and stretch the resource outlay made to extend its life long after the physical exhibition has closed.

7.2.2 Expand the Experience of a Physical Exhibition

Often, the research and development process generates more information and content than can feasibly be incorporated into a physical exhibition—either due to a lack of space, cost constraints, or the general rules of best practice for creating an engaging experience. Similarly, many visitors are not able to take in all that an exhibition has to offer during their visit; to read every panel, look at every photograph, watch every video, or interact with every kiosk.

Virtual exhibitions provide another outlet through which to continue telling the story and maximize research and content development efforts. This expands the visitor's experience of the physical exhibition, enriching it with additional layers of information that can be accessed by audiences in their own time, from the comfort of their own home, either before, during, or after a visit to the physical exhibition.

Virtual exhibitions are also a great vehicle for promoting your museum and enticing new people to visit. By showing the public what an in-person trip to the exhibition entails, you give them a taste of what the experience will be like, set expectations, and create excitement. In the end, it can be a great motivator for buying a ticket, purchasing a membership, or making a donation. In support of their 2009 Tim Burton retrospective, the Museum of Modern Art in New York City,

Figure 7.1. Screen capture from the virtual experience of the Tim Burton exhibition created by the Museum of Modern Art/Big Spaceship, New York. COURTESY OF BIG SPACESHIP

launched an exhibition website[1] simultaneously with the opening of their physical exhibition (press preview access was granted a few days prior). Taking inspiration from the artist himself, an external web development team hired by the museum created a virtual environment with the same look and feel as one of Burton's movie sets. Virtual visitors could explore a timeline of his career, view art by medium, or watch exclusive interviews. Users were also encouraged to buy exhibition tickets online or the associated publication from the Design Store website; they could review the exhibition checklist to see what works of art would be on display and download a family activity guide.

7.2.3 Present Distant, Iconic, and Sensitive Collections and Sites

Museums and gallery collections contain an array of rare and wonderful objects and specimens, all with their own unique stories that deserve to be told. Some of these collection items are more sensitive and fragile than others and for conservation reasons, are less likely to ever be put on public display. The same is also true for certain heritage sites, which might include precarious features, landscapes, or structures that would be put at risk if too many people were to visit (think of the prehistoric cave paintings in Lascaux, France). Some sites and features may be located at great heights or in remote areas too dangerous to visit. In other cases, certain objects or works of art are so extraordinary that they draw thousands of visitors daily. These collection icons, like the Louvre's *Mona Lisa* by Leonardo Da Vinci, are unlikely to ever be loaned out to another institution regardless of how appealing an exhibition proposal might be.

Using a variety of digital media, virtual exhibitions can help to bring these rare and sensitive objects out of the storeroom for presentation and interpretation, while minimizing any damage that could be caused by overexposure to light, vibrations, air pollutants, or visitor enthusiasm.

Not limited by distance, great heights, or the need to display the actual object itself, virtual exhibitions are a means of creating greater public access to remote areas and "out of reach" features without the associated risks. For example, York Minster Cathedral in the United Kingdom launched the *Stained Glass Navigator*.[2] Standing seventy-seven feet tall (25.5 m) and thirty-two feet wide (10 m), the Great East Window is roughly the size of a tennis court, and to see it up close would require either an extreme telephoto lens or a scaffolding tower. Using photos taken by conservators during the decade-long restoration and repurposing interpretive content from earlier in situ exhibitions, virtual visitors are now free to explore the intricate details of the six-hundred-year-old window online.

Additionally, virtual exhibitions are a fantastic way to bring together iconic or geographically dispersed items in a way that could never be achieved in real life. For example, five international museums, The National Gallery in London, the Van Gogh Museum in Amsterdam, the Philadelphia Museum of Art in Pennsylvania, the Neue Pinakothek in Munich, and the Seiji Togo Memorial Sompo Japan Nipponkoa Museum of Art in Tokyo partnered to virtually unite their five famous "Sunflowers" paintings by Van Gogh in *Sunflowers 360*. For the first time ever, viewers can examine all five paintings "hanging" side by side in a virtually rendered gallery and learn more about the artist and his paintings by watching the special Facebook Live recording from the curators and directors.[3]

Figure 7.2. Screen capture of *Sunflowers Virtual 360 Gallery* at the Van Gogh Museum, Amsterdam.
COURTESY OF VAN GOGH MUSEUM

7.2.4 Be Responsive, Tell More Stories, Stay Relevant

With a small market, limited resources, and minimal exhibition space (perhaps even none at all), some museums cannot feasibly put on more than one or two exhibitions per year. Depending on the format chosen and the amount of preexisting digitized content available, stand-alone virtual exhibitions can be a cost-effective way for cultural institutions to establish or broaden an exhibition program to tell more stories and engage more people.

Planning and building physical exhibitions takes time, often years in advance of opening, but the world moves and changes at a much faster pace. What is a relevant and interesting theme today, might not be as exciting in two years. Similarly, with round the clock news cycles and media coverage, museums may wish to immediately address pressing current issues or help contextualize widespread events. Virtual exhibitions can usually be turned around more quickly than a physical exhibition. This provides museums, galleries, and heritage sites with an opportunity to be more agile and responsive to the topics that are relevant to today's audiences, facilitating dialogue and driving the conversation.

7.2.5 Maintain Audiences During Prolonged Closure Periods

At some point an institution may be closed for a prolonged period. This may be during a time of renewal to accommodate expansion or upgrades, to facilitate a move to a new home, or to enable the rehanging of a gallery or refresh of permanent exhibition. A closure may be the result of political or civil upheaval such as a mandated government shutdown, strike action, or public protest. In the most severe cases, this could be during a period of crisis caused by fire, natural disaster, armed conflict, or even a global pandemic.

Figure 7.3. Ayala Museum home page, Manila, Philippines. COURTESY OF AYALA MUSEUM

Whatever the reason for closure, it is essential that a museum continue to reach and engage people so that when it finally reopens, members and loyal audiences are ready and waiting to visit and provide support. Virtual exhibitions allow museums to continue to deliver great content, stay top of mind, and maintain relationships with members and audiences while closed. In 2019, the Ayala Museum[4] in Manila, Philippines, was planning to make major changes to their fifteen-year-old facility that would require them to close their doors for two years. Not wanting to deny their visitors their "dose of joy and wonder," the museum relaunched its website to bring virtual exhibitions, workshops, lectures, and concerts to the public while the museum was being renovated.

Virtual exhibitions (and other online content) can be an important tool for new museums and galleries that have not been realized yet and are still in the planning and development phase. Before construction has even started, virtual exhibitions that deliver on the stated mission can help a future museum build its audience. Using virtual exhibitions to establish an online presence helps to show people what a museum is all about, attract funders and donors, and generate a following of potential visitors before the doors have even opened. For example, Hong Kong's M+ Museum was under construction in the city's new West Kowloon cultural district with an opening date of late 2021. However, it engaged audiences with a range of virtual exhibitions and digital content since 2012. Rather than making their online presence an afterthought or waiting until the museum finally opened to the public, the M+ Museum embraced virtual exhibitions as a critical aspect of the institution building process from the outset. Its interactive *Neon Signs*[5] virtual exhibition was successful at encouraging locals to engage with the museum. More than four thousand photos of the city's iconic neon signage along with personal stories were received, helping to create a lasting record of a quickly disappearing aspect of the city.

7.2.6 Meet Demand, Satisfy Expectations, and Attract New Audiences

Museumgoers today have become quite tech savvy and expect some element of digital interaction as part of their cultural experiences—both in person and online. With the global pandemic of 2020, demand for virtual content has only increased and looks set to stay. Virtual exhibitions are a great way to give audiences what they want—the ability to revisit the physical exhibition experience later, the chance to gain a deeper understanding of content, and the opportunity to share things online with their various social networks.[6]

Many museums worry that providing virtual content (particularly virtual exhibitions that are available simultaneously with the on-site experience) will create a substitute for a physical visit to a museum and negatively impact attendance and admissions revenue. In fact, research suggests the opposite. High-propensity museum visitors (those most likely to visit a museum or gallery) are motivated to visit based on the museum's reputation and are "superconnected" on the internet. Online, this includes social media engagement, but also the content offered on the website and mobile web, such as virtual exhibitions. Museums generate online visitor satisfaction and excitement when they connect with them with great content and virtual experiences. Excitement about a museum fuels its reputation, and as a result, increases people's motivation to make a visit.[7]

Because virtual exhibitions are accessible from anywhere, a museum can also expand the reach of its exhibition beyond only those people who are able to visit in person. Content can be accessed by more people across the globe and more interest can be generated. During the pandemic of 2020, when people could not leave their homes due to lockdown measures, museums and galleries saw a drastic increase in the number of people engaging with online cultural offerings to entertain themselves, educate their kids, and maintain a sense of hope. Research suggests that many of these people had not physically visited the same kinds of cultural organizations in the past year, thus representing potential new audiences engaging with institutions, collections, and stories.[8]

Whatever its purpose, it is important to pinpoint the motivation for developing a virtual exhibition at the outset of planning. This ensures the articulation of goals for the project and are likely to influence the approach taken to develop and deliver a virtual exhibition.

7.3 THINKING ABOUT DIGITAL AUDIENCES

It is widely agreed that advancement in digital technology is the single greatest disruptor of the twenty-first century. The impact that digital technologies have made and continue to make on our daily lives is profound; think about how much time you spend looking at your smartphone, the increasing number of internet-enabled devices we use, and how more and more personal interactions and business transactions have moved online.

As we begin to adopt new digital "things" into our lives, we too as people begin to adapt and adjust. These digital "things" and experiences change how we gather information, how we communicate with one another, how we see and portray ourselves online, and how we behave. Museum audiences have also changed. They have developed new expectations of what can be accomplished with digital technologies, what they can access and experience online, and what museums can and should do for them.

These new digitally-enhanced expectations require a rethinking of what a museum experience is—no longer merely physical, it is now simultaneously physical, digital, and virtually connected. It also requires a shift to a visitor-first mindset—putting the needs, interests, and expectations of audiences before that of the institution.

Before planning a virtual exhibition consider the following:

- What themes and subjects will audiences be interested in?
- Which ones might work well for a virtual presentation?
- What are the audiences' digital behaviors and expectations of virtual exhibitions?
- How can the virtual experience be inclusive and accessible for everyone?

7.3.1 Behaviors and Expectations

Leading practice for the development of any physical exhibition experience includes identification of core audiences, learning styles, and behaviors in order to attract visitors to the museum and ensure an engaging and enjoyable experience. The same applies for virtual exhibition planning, although considerations for the virtual realm will be slightly different.

Customer perceptions of value and satisfaction are based on how well their needs and expectations are met. Satisfied virtual visitors are more likely to make an in-person visit, support the museum through donations or membership, return to the museum's website to engage with more content, and amplify the museum's message by sharing content with their personal networks.[9] Key elements to keep in mind about digital audiences when planning for virtual exhibitions include:

- **What device are they using?** Smartphone, tablet, or laptop? Android or iOS? Devices come in all shapes and sizes, and various devices display virtual content in different ways. Today's internet users prefer to access online content via their mobile phones rather than from their laptops/computers (50 percent mobile phones, 47 percent laptops and desktops, 3 percent tablet).[10] Knowing what devices audiences are using to access virtual exhibition content helps a museum ensure that virtual exhibition content looks good and displays properly regardless of screen size or operating system.
- **Where are they? (Location)** Audiences can access the internet from just about anywhere—approximately 46 percent of Canadians admit to using their mobile phone while in the bathroom.[11] Considering where audiences might be when accessing a virtual exhibition is important because it has a direct impact on the type of virtual exhibition content they will consume, their attention spans, and how much they will consume. Waiting for the bus, a virtual visitor might spare a few minutes to browse some publicly appropriate, easy to consume content to pass the time. At home people have more time and privacy, so are likely to delve more deeply and consume harder hitting subjects. Location also has an impact on the file

size of content. At home, audiences will use their own Wi-Fi network, whereas waiting for the bus may require a public Wi-Fi network or their own wireless communication provider. Public networks may be free to use but limit the amount of data consumed per user. Personal data plans can vary widely and can be expensive if incurring overages for download.

- **What platforms do they use and have access to?** The virtual realm is vast and expansive. While the majority of virtual exhibitions are typically made available via a museum's website or a standalone microsite, there are instances where museums have been experimenting with publishing virtual exhibition content on social media platforms, using custom apps/interfaces, or providing content to external service providers. Knowing which platforms virtual audiences are familiar with, use regularly, and have access to is important when developing virtual exhibitions to ensure content can easily be found (called discoverability). Web-enabled virtual exhibitions and those available on mainstream social media platforms will attract more virtual visitors and achieve higher rates of engagement. Those that require the download of a custom app, a user to register for an account, or are only accessible by paid subscription may be less likely to attract visitors.

- **What type of content interests them the most?** The interests and preferences of contemporary virtual audiences requires constant monitoring. Currently, virtual museum audience research is scarce but sources like the American Alliance of Museums' *Annual Survey of Museum-Goers*[12] sheds some light on these preferences. Typically, virtual museum audiences are interested in quality virtual content (especially if paying for it) and in bite-sized, easy to consume chunks to help fight digital fatigue caused by excessive screen time and content overload. Virtual audiences consume video content the most, and are looking for content that surprises and delights, that shares hope and beauty, that is entertaining and/or educational (including puzzles and games, fun facts, behind-the-scenes tidbits), and that helps to foster social connections with others at a distance. Giving virtual audiences what they want—in the format that they want it—helps to increase reach and overall engagement.

- **What kind of interaction or user experience do they expect?** Nothing is more frustrating for in-person museum visitors than digital exhibits that are ugly, do not work, and/or are difficult to use. The same is true for virtual exhibitions. Virtual exhibition planners should not underestimate the importance of a good **user interface** (visual design, colors, graphics, layouts, typography, etc.) and a good **user experience** (information architecture, interaction design, etc.). Virtual exhibitions should be easy, seamless, and fast. This means making sure that a virtual exhibition is easy to find, intuitive and simple to navigate, fun and beautifully designed, and in good working order (i.e., functional with no broken links or unavailable content). This also means ensuring an omni-channel experience; the virtual exhibition should be presented in a way that echoes the quality of content, design, and experience that visitors have come to expect from a museum's physical exhibitions.

7.3.2 The Digital Divide

Digital technology is often seen as the great leveler, increasing access to information, and creating greater opportunities for people to express, create, and prosper. At the museum, it is credited with providing greater access to museum collections and content, as well as democratizing knowledge. However, it is not a sweeping solution for improved access.

Museums must remember that not everyone has an equal chance to benefit from the advances of the digital age. Referred to as the "digital divide," this concept recognizes that not everyone has the means to access the internet nor the confidence and capabilities to do so. Those who do not have the means to access the internet include financially challenged audiences who cannot afford to buy a computer or smartphone, or who cannot afford the service fees to access Wi-Fi or mobile networks. It also includes those audiences that live in rural or remote areas where internet networks cannot deliver the necessary bandwidth to stream or download rich digital content. In some cases, internet service might simply not exist at all. Those who do not have the capability of accessing and engaging with virtual exhibition content are typically older audiences who might not be comfortable using digital technology. However, there are others who might not have the ability or the know-how to independently connect to and effectively navigate the virtual realm.

Successful virtual exhibition planners will always keep the digital divide in mind and consider creative hacks to ensure the widest possible access for its audiences. One such idea could include working with local public libraries to develop links to the museum's virtual exhibition direct from the library's website or to host the content directly on their digital terminals. For example, the San Jose Public Library[13] in California provides virtual visitors with an assembly of various links to virtual tours for art museums, history museums, children's museums, and local museums, as well as book suggestions from the library's collection for further reading. Others, like the Toronto Public Library in Canada encourage borrowing and circulation of Wi-Fi hotspots to its more economically-deprived patrons.

7.3.3 Inclusive and Accessible Virtual Exhibitions

With around 15 percent of the global population living with some form of disability and many who have a reading age of around nine years old, a significant number of people experience barriers in their everyday lives that prevent them from accessing both physical and digital experiences. The Interaction Design Foundation,[14] identifies several accessibility concerns that can impact the experience a virtual exhibition visitor may have when using web pages and other digital tools, including:

- Visual (e.g., color blindness)
- Motor/mobility (e.g., wheelchair-user concerns)
- Auditory (e.g., hearing difficulties)
- Seizures (especially photosensitive epilepsy)
- Learning/cognitive (e.g., dyslexia)

Poorly designed virtual exhibitions that adopt a one-size-fits-all approach can create and perpetuate these barriers. Designing a virtual exhibition with consideration for accessibility from the outset results in a more inclusionary and a rich experience for everyone. There is more discourse in creating accessible virtual exhibitions than this chapter can hope to cover, but here are a few items to consider:

- Headings and titles: Use headings and different font styles to create levels of information.
- Typeface and fonts: Stick to simple font styles with clean lines and limit the number of typefaces used so that text is legible.
- Color and contrast: Ensure colors for text and backgrounds are legible and contrast to make things easier to read.

- Image descriptions: Ensure all images, graphics, and diagrams have alternative text so that screen readers can recognize and describe visual media accurately and with detail to those with visual impairments.
- Diverse representation: Feature people of different abilities, ages, and ethnicities in content to be more inclusive.
- Provide context: Add a bit of explanation for animated GIFs and memes as not everyone will understand jokes or culturally and regionally specific references.
- Captions: Use closed captions or subtitles for video presentations so that people with auditory impairments can follow along. It also helps when watching a muted video in a public setting.
- Links (hyperlinks): Create a descriptive title for the link rather than saying "click here" so that it is more obvious where to click.
- Prototype: Test virtual exhibition content with a variety of audiences.

Further resources on web design accessibility and what to consider can be found at:

- Interactive Design Foundation: https://www.interaction-design.org/literature/topics/accessibility
- Digital Museums Canada Accessibility Values and Standards: https://www.digitalmuseums.ca/help-and-resources/toolbox/accessibility/
- World Wide Web Consortium (W3C) Accessibility Guidelines: https://www.w3.org/standards/webdesign/accessibility.html

7.4 VIRTUAL EXHIBITION CONSIDERATIONS

The variety of virtual exhibitions and digital content available demonstrates the creativity and ingenuity of exhibition planners, user experience designers, and web developers. With new devices, platforms, and programs adopted almost daily, new opportunities for virtual exhibitions also arise, reshaping and redefining what a virtual exhibition can be and should look like. Despite this seemingly constant evolution, there are a few key items to take into consideration when producing virtual exhibitions:

- What themes and subjects might work well for a virtual presentation?
- What digital media content does the museum already have?
- What platform(s) will the virtual exhibition use?
- What format will the virtual exhibition adopt?
- When and how will the virtual exhibition be delivered?

7.4.1 Content

A virtual exhibition is made up purely of digital media. While this does include text and sound, virtual exhibitions are more about visuals, movement, and creating moments of interactivity. As such, when developing a virtual exhibition concept, it is important to choose a topic that can be communicated easily and set learning objectives that can be achieved effectively through images, videos, animations, games, and interactive media.

Determine whether the topic and related content is appropriate for the virtual realm. Online, a museum has much less control over who can access and engage with content. There may be topics not suitable for younger audiences without parental supervision, or there may be objects sacred to Indigenous groups that should never be put on display. Other topics might just be too controversial.

In preparing content for a virtual exhibition, museums must consider the online behaviors of potential audiences, and what sort of experiences and content will interest them (namely bite-sized videos). On average, audiences spend seven hours per day surfing the web, so digital attention spans are fleeting, and screen fatigue sets in quickly. This means virtual exhibition experiences will be much shorter than a physical exhibition, requiring less content—although less content does not necessarily mean less effort.

Finally, museums should try to use and reuse digital content that is already available with the requisite permission to publish online. Content production activities like digitizing collections, editing images, and producing videos, all take more time and effort, as does chasing down rights and permissions to feature copyrighted materials. For most museums, virtual exhibition content is often repurposed from an existing (or concurrent) physical exhibition and translated to the virtual environment. This maximizes content production efforts. However, more and more museums are creating **digital first** or **born-digital** virtual exhibitions, meaning exhibition content is developed and customized for exclusive virtual delivery.

7.4.2 Platforms

Choosing a platform to host a virtual exhibition requires careful reflection. Each platform comes with its own specific audiences and publishing features, as well as technical limitations and costs regarding how much content it can feasibly host; the size of the files it can accommodate; the format in which content can be displayed; and the overall user experience that can be provided. Much of this has to do with whether these sites and applications can be held on the museum's existing server or hosting service (see the section on hosting below).

While typically held on a museum's website or on a microsite, many museum professionals with a flair for digital communications are creativity adapting virtual exhibition content to fit a range of platform alternatives. Options to consider include:

- **Museum's website**: The role of the museum website has changed in the past decade. No longer just an information source providing opening hours and admission prices, a museum's website has been transformed into a dynamic content hub—an extension of the museum experience in the virtual realm. As the heart of the museum's online presence and an existing platform, the website is a natural place to feature and host virtual exhibitions. Reasons a museum might not use its website for virtual exhibitions could include an outdated platform that does not have the capabilities needed to do so, not wanting to slow down the functionality of the site or overwhelm it (and the visitor) with too much content, or a limited amount of server/file/cloud space to host additional web pages. In the case of government sponsored institutions, museums only occupy single informational web pages and communication policies may not allow them to do anything else. Smaller museums looking to develop their own website may consider the many cloud-based development platforms like Wix. These services will host the website on their server and allow customers many contemporary designed templates to create a website for a monthly subscription fee.

- **Microsites**: Some museums choose to create microsites or "mini websites." Microsites and websites are similar; they are both the same on a functional level and each one needs a unique domain name (URL) to find it. The key difference is that a museum's website usually contains all the information about the organization and its products and services, whereas a microsite has a special and specific purpose. Because microsites are smaller (fewer web pages), have highly focused segments of content organized around a consistent theme, and are project specific, they are a perfect tool for virtual exhibitions and temporarily housing digital content without bogging down the main website. The disadvantage of microsites lies in the creation of too many web addresses that may confuse audiences and draw attention away from the main website. A good rule of thumb is to link microsites to and from the museum's main web page. There may be additional costs to developing and hosting a microsite for a virtual exhibition, so consider the many free, easy-to-use microsite building tools that are available. In response to the 2020 pandemic lockdown measures and the growing demand for easily accessible and relevant educational content, the San Diego History Center[15] in California quickly built a microsite for its "learn at home" resources. Using the free tools on Google Sites, the center created a special portal for parents and teachers with lesson plans, activity sheets, virtual exhibitions, and recordings all in one place.

Figure 7.4. Microsite for digital resources created by the San Diego History Center.
SAN DIEGO HISTORY CENTER

- **Apps (applications)**: When mobile technology and smartphones exploded in popularity, so too did the mobile app. An app is essentially computer software that allows a user to run a unique, mobile-friendly program from their smartphone or tablet. As many museums adapt to the online environment, apps are a potential solution for creating friendly experiences and interfaces for mobile users. Museums may commission the development of a custom app to run their virtual exhibition, or they might use a company's out-of-the-box app program to

Virtual Exhibitions 101

create and host digital content. These solutions are often expensive to develop and maintain in the long run. More importantly, the popularity of apps has generally begun to wane. Audiences simply do not want the hassle of downloading an app, to have it take up valuable memory space, and to create clutter on their home screen. Instead of an app, museums should consider providing virtual exhibitions as mobile-optimized web content, either from the museum's website or on a special microsite. This will ensure that visitors can access virtual exhibitions through their web browser of choice (no downloads necessary) and that content is formatted for mobile viewing.

- **Content aggregators**: In the digital world there exists many different communities of interest connected by a range of virtual platforms and channels that deliver exhibition-like content similar to museums. Engaging with a content aggregator is a way for museums to address this competition and keep their content top of mind for online users. Third party platforms such as Google Arts and Culture or Artsy.net, as well as other targeted initiatives, act as content hubs, grouping special interest content, like virtual exhibitions, together in one place. Visitors can easily browse a catalog of virtual exhibitions produced by a variety of different museums all at once and without having to navigate between different websites. By participating and uploading virtual exhibitions to these platforms, museums, galleries, and heritage sites can leverage built-in dashboards and development tools to create professional-looking virtual exhibitions and gain an additional platform on which to host their content (sometimes free of charge).

- **Social media**: Social media is not just a resource for broadcasting information and marketing upcoming exhibitions. More museums are using social media to engage online audiences with their content and in a wider conversation. With huge audiences and built-in content features and tools, social media managers and educators are developing nontraditional virtual exhibitions for social media platforms. On Twitter, this might take the form of an extended tweet, which provides interpretive text, images, and/or videos in a single thread like that from the Toronto Dreams Project.[16]

Figure 7.5. Twitter images of the Toronto Dreams Project by Adam Bunch.
ADAM BUNCH/@TODREAMSPROJECT

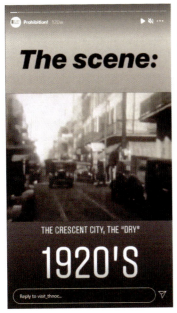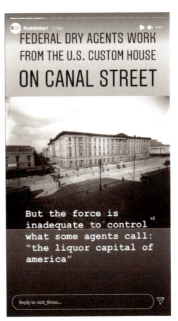

Figure 7.6. Instagram images of *Prohibition*, the mini virtual exhibition created by The Historic New Orleans Collection. COURTESY OF THE HISTORIC NEW ORLEANS COLLECTION, ORIGINAL PHOTO AND VIDEO FROM THE CHARLES L. FRANCK STUDIO COLLECTION

On Instagram, the stories function and the multi-image posting capabilities allows museums to create slide shows of images, video, and text. The Historic New Orleans Collection used these functions to create a mini virtual exhibition called *Prohibition*.[17]

While there are many advantages to using social media platforms and content aggregators to host virtual exhibitions, these sites offer moderate content delivery functionality. These sites also have their own terms and conditions for use that govern the type of content that can be posted ensuring that it is appropriate for public consumption (nudity is frowned upon, even if it is considered art), and they often claim the right to reuse content for their purposes without permission.

7.4.3 Hosting

Hosting is the act of storing and maintaining a virtual exhibition on a web server in order to make it available to the public via the internet. The type of platform a museum chooses to hold a virtual exhibition will often influence, and subsequently be influenced by, the hosting capabilities of the museum's existing server or external hosting service.

In most cases, a virtual exhibition can easily be hosted and managed on a museum's existing website and server. However, there are instances where the museum may need to consider employing an external web hosting service. This may be the result of outdated technology, a server nearing storage capacity, lack of in-house technical expertise to administer it, or when a proposed virtual exhibition format and user experience is too sophisticated for the existing server. For example, virtual exhibitions that expect heavy traffic, that are reliant on several different multimedia files, or that feature larger immersive components will require a higher level of server performance and computing power—processing, memory, storage, and/or bandwidth—to deliver.

There are a few different options with various cost and performance implications when a museum considers using an external company for managing and hosting services.[18] Shared hosting will be the most cost effective, but as many websites share the same machine to run them all at the same time, the virtual exhibition may be lower performing. A private hosting service is probably the most cost efficient and can meet a broad spectrum of needs with customized configuration. Dedicated servers are the most expensive, as they require greater technical expertise and administration, and are necessary for more sophisticated virtual exhibitions. Cloud servers are similar to other services described with the benefit of storing and running everything from the cloud instead of from a physical server and can expand and contract as more or less processing, memory, storage, and/or bandwidth are required. Each option provides a varying degree of technical service and web administration. Costs range anywhere from a few dollars to hundreds of dollars per month, but a target of US$30–$60 per month is the average. It is important for museums to be cognizant of data sovereignty and where hosting services are located; domestic hosting may be required if the museum is collecting personal information from users.

For those virtual exhibitions that use third party platforms such as social media, content aggregators, or conference expos, content is typically hosted on their websites and servers. Because of this, the amount of content and file sizes might be limited, or subscription charges may be applied.

7.4.4 Formats

Virtual exhibitions come in all shapes and sizes and, with the constant pace of change in the digital realm, the format of these digital media presentations continue to advance and evolve along with it. There are a few formats that museums, galleries, and heritage sites typically use and should be familiar with if planning a virtual exhibition.

- **Didactic**: The most simple and traditional of all formats, the didactic virtual exhibition presents information using mainly static text under key headings, with a few illustrative images of relevant objects or works of art. Incorporated throughout, the images help to break up the text field, create visual interest, and reinforce core messaging. Content might be presented on one web page that the user manually scrolls down or can be broken up over a series of themed, hyperlinked web pages to make it easier for the virtual visitor to read and digest. As with physical exhibitions, it is important to limit the amount of text to avoid boring the visitor. Using slightly more advanced features like an image slide deck or parallax scrolling (where the background image is moved at a different speed than the foreground content when scrolling) can help elevate the didactic virtual experience from flat and text heavy to something a bit more stimulating.
- **Carousel or slideshow**: This format adds a layer of vitality to the virtual exhibition by presenting content as a carousel or scrolling slideshow. Depending on how the navigation of the virtual exhibition is designed, the movement back and forth (or up and down) between slides can be initiated by the virtual visitor with the click of a mouse or swipe of a finger. It can also be automated or animated. While reliant on text and images as a means of communication, the carousel/slideshow format is different from the didactic format because it changes the emphasis of communication. High quality, full bleed images or images with macro details become the main vehicle for the story. More advanced virtual exhibitions of this type might include other interactive features on each slide such as an image zoom function or a collapsible accordion menu to provide additional details about an object, artist, or event. The

Figure 7.7. Virtual exhibition of *Women in Service: The War Art of Molly Lamb Bobak* by the Canadian War Museum, Ottawa, Canada. COURTESY OF THE CANADIAN WAR MUSEUM

Canadian War Museum's virtual exhibition, *Women in Service: The War Art of Molly Lamb Bobak*, uses this format with advanced features.[19]

- **Dynamic**: A dynamic virtual exhibition has a highly interactive user interface and experience. For example, the Smithsonian National Museum of the American Indian's virtual exhibition, *Americans*,[20] combines moving content with a variety of attention-grabbing navigation options and control elements. This results in an enlivened virtual experience that encourages visitors to explore, activate, and consume content. Dynamic virtual exhibitions use rich content like looped moving images, video, animations, and interactive maps and games. They may also provide additional features to save content to a personal account, options to buy tickets to the physical exhibition, access to learning resources or activity downloads, and links to the gift shop. Navigation through these additional layers of content may be created with image click-throughs, pop-ups, animations, drag and drops, or graphics that appear when a cursor hovers above them. Given the sophisticated programming and complexity of content needed to produce this type of virtual exhibition, it can be one of the more expensive options and will require a skilled digital content producer and web designer.

- **3D virtual walkthrough**: This type of virtual exhibition format seeks to replicate the physical exhibition experience by recreating the real-life gallery as a 3D virtual walkthrough (also called a virtual tour). Immersed in a complete scene, the visitor navigates through the space to explore the works of art, exhibits, and panels of the exhibition just as they might have done in person. The level of interactivity and quality of imagery for a virtual tour varies widely. Basic walkthroughs provide the virtual visitor with the opportunity to pan around the gallery, merely giving them a sense of what it looks like. More sophisticated walkthroughs, like those provided by the European Museum of Modern Art,[21] offer high resolution zoom functions to get up close with objects, as well as interactive information points on screen that provide interpretive text and links to additional images and video. Walkthroughs are produced using virtual reality photography or 3D scanning to capture the actual physical exhibition in situ and typically deliver it as a wide-angled, panoramic photograph in a full circle to give the visitor a 360-degree perspective. This can be done using specialized omnidirectional cameras or a less expensive technique that digitally "stitches" many photographs of the space together. Resourceful museums are known to have employed the same technology that many real estate agents use for home showings to easily generate virtual tours in a cost-effective way.

- **Virtual reality (VR) and immersive renderings**: Where the walkthrough uses photography to virtually recreate the actual physical exhibition, a VR virtual exhibition creates something entirely new in a computer-generated environment. Using graphics, images, and animations, programmers create the illusion of a museum experience with a limitless series of rooms, filled with any object or work of art imaginable. This format works very well for those situations where no real-life exhibition currently exists or when it might be impossible to borrow certain objects or display them side by side. These experiences typically require the use of a VR headset. However, it is technically possible to develop a VR experience without the need for an additional viewing device. Application programming interfaces like WebXR allow web browsers to present VR content either on a computer or mobile screen, making them more accessible for everyone. The Brooklyn Museum's virtual exhibition *The Queen and The Crown*[22] showcases the spectacular costumes from the two popular Netflix series alongside relevant objects from the museum's collection. The objects are rendered within an immersive virtual model of the museum's soaring Beaux-Arts Court and accompanied by a soundtrack of gallery noises, show clips, sketches, fabric swatches, and interviews with the costume designers.

Figure 7.8. Immersive virtual exploration of *The Queen and The Crown: A Virtual Exhibition of Costumes* from the award winning titles *The Queen's Gambit* and *The Crown*, October 3, 2020, through December 13, 2020. CREATED BY NETFLIX IN COLLABORATION WITH THE BROOKLYN MUSEUM, AND CURATED BY MATTHEW YOKOBOSKY, SENIOR CURATOR, FASHION AND MATERIAL CULTURE, BROOKLYN MUSEUM, NEW YORK.

- **Augmented reality (AR)**: An AR exhibition is where the real world and the virtual world meet. AR exhibitions enhance a visitor's experience of the specific place they are standing in by adding layers of new or missing information using computer generated images, graphics, text, and sounds. For example, "then and now" AR exhibitions layer an archival image over the same present-day scene to illustrate what has changed, or those heritage sites that create a digital skin to reanimate features lost hundreds of years ago. When considering an AR exhibition, look for themes and stories that have a direct relationship with an existing real-life environment or in situ objects. Also, given their strong connection to place (and landscapes), AR exhibitions work best on mobile devices so the program can access the device's camera to capture "reality" in real-time on the screen.

- **Expo booth**: An emerging virtual exhibition format, the expo booth, has gained traction as more and more conferences and events move into the virtual realm. The purpose of these virtual exhibitions is different from the other formats previously discussed in that they are more for promotional purposes than for storytelling and visitor engagement. Despite this, their importance should not be overlooked. Depending on the conference or event organizer, exhibitors are offered a basic design template for a virtual expo booth that usually includes space for a dedicated company profile, logo, and contact details, along with some placeholders to insert content like text and images. Depending on the package chosen, virtual exhibitors can take advantage of other add-ons such as additional images, graphics, and video hosting, as well as chat functionality or one-on-one appointments. This type of virtual exhibition format is important to understand should a museum be a regular part of the conference circuit (perhaps to promote touring exhibitions) or if a museum is considering moving its own annual symposium to a digital format.

7.4.5 Opening/Timing

Another key consideration in the production of virtual exhibitions is timing of the launch. Various options exist and will likely depend on the rationale and goals for developing a virtual exhibition in the first place.

- After the physical exhibition closes: Content developed for the physical exhibition is reused and remixed for the virtual environment, often with the intention of extending the life of the material when the original in-person exhibition is over. This could happen immediately after the exhibition closes or much later as a way to create an online archive and provide content in perpetuity.

- Before the physical exhibition opens: Content for the virtual exhibition is planned and produced in tandem with the physical exhibition and access is granted before the physical exhibition opens. This approach is typically used to leverage the virtual exhibition as a marketing tool to encourage in-person visits to the physical exhibition.

- Simultaneous with physical exhibition: Like the previous example, content for the virtual exhibition is planned and produced alongside the physical exhibition but this time public access is granted at the same time as the physical exhibition. Museums and galleries often use this approach to provide an expanded and digitally enhanced experience to compliment an in-person visit. Once the physical exhibition is over, the virtual exhibition may also close. However, since the virtual exhibition is not beholden to space or time, it can continue to be made available so long as the museum has the hosting capabilities to do so.

- As a standalone virtual exhibition: Content is designed to be presented as a virtual exhibition only, without a physical counterpart. As such, the launch may be associated with a special event, anniversary, or marketing campaign as opposed to a connection with any physical exhibition.

7.4.6 Access and Admissions

Exhibition production costs are recouped by admissions, memberships, surcharged ticketing, associated retail, and sponsorship. Similarly, options for monetization can be applied to virtual exhibitions. Historically, museums have not charged for virtual content. How much people are willing to pay for virtual exhibitions is still yet to be understood.

However, museums, galleries, and heritage sites should begin exploring opportunities for revenue generation. According to research conducted in 2020 by Canada's Business for the Arts,[23] 14 percent of culture-goers would be willing to pay half of the in-person ticket price to experience the same thing digitally, where 41 percent were unsure. Experiment and prototype with various payment options, which might include the following:

- Free: There is no charge to access virtual exhibition content.

- Free with registration: Free access to virtual exhibition content is granted to users who complete a registration process in which they agree to provide you with contact details or sign up for your newsletter.

- Sponsored: Access to the virtual exhibition is free for users. The cost of developing and hosting the exhibition is covered by the virtual exhibition sponsor, so no charge is necessary. The sponsor is recognized in the virtual exhibition, typically on the title page and/or in the web page footers.

- Suggested donation/pay what you can: Virtual visitors are granted free access to the virtual exhibition but are asked to make an online contribution to the museum before doing so. Museums may suggest how much this donation should be or leave it up to the individual. At present, anecdotal evidence from peers imply that the "pay what you can" approach has yielded a greater contribution per visitor than the "suggested donation" model.

- Paid admission: Visitors must pay a set fee through an online transaction portal before access to the virtual exhibition is granted. This could be via an automated redirection or in some cases a password or individualized code. Careful consideration should be given to single price or multiple price point structure. The latter offers virtual visitors greater flexibility and helps the museum to avoid leaving money on the table.

- Benefit of membership/subscription: In order to enhance the value of a membership, some museums and galleries are creating exclusive member-only virtual exhibitions and or digital subscription options. These are often hosted on microsites where existing museum members or subscribers can log in with their membership numbers and a personalized password to access unique content.

In order to optimize access and admission, museums may stagger the release of virtual exhibitions to grant access to different audiences at various times. Much like with first-look previews and members' only events, museums and galleries might choose to limit access during the launch of the virtual exhibition to give members and donors, VIPs, or the press a sense of exclusivity. However, virtual exhibitions do not really have an expiration date. After a certain period of time, access barriers and pay barriers can easily be removed and the virtual exhibition or parts of it can be released to the wider public.

7.4.7 Costs and Budgets

As this chapter has demonstrated, the opportunities for delivering creative and engaging virtual experiences are plentiful, but this also makes it difficult to provide specific guidance on how much developing a virtual exhibition is likely to cost.

By repackaging existing content, using a simple didactic approach, and populating a predesigned website template, some museums can easily turn out a great virtual exhibition in a week and for under US$1,500. Other museums might spend between US$150,000 to $250,000 on cutting edge virtual exhibition projects that create new digital media content from scratch, incorporate more unique interactive digital elements, and seek to provide a truly bespoke immersive experience. The cost of these projects is higher because of their overall ambition and technical sophistication, requiring greater time and investment for research, production, and the specialist technical skills needed to develop those web-enabled 3D virtual reality environments. On average though, a museum should be able to create a good, dynamic-format virtual exhibition with rich content, a decent level of interactivity, and maybe one or two advanced features in the range of US$50,000 to $60,000.

The best way to determine the likely cost for proposed virtual exhibitions is to sketch out a list of all the tasks needed to complete the project and then build a budget around those activities. Digital Museums Canada, the largest funding program in Canada dedicated to online projects produced by the Canadian museum and heritage community, provides some guidance on planning for virtual exhibitions and what cost categories and line items to think about when building project budgets.[24] Each project will have unique requirements but are likely to include, but not limited to, those shown in figure 7.9.

Most museum professionals already have a good idea of how much time is needed for interpretive planning, research, and content coordination. However, the amount of time and effort it takes to produce digital content is often underestimated. Remember, the smartphone most people carry around is a powerful tool; many beautiful photos and videos have been captured and even produced using a smartphone, as well as the array of apps now available. Museums, galleries, and heritage sites should also not forget that the content and digital media created for these virtual exhibitions can be repurposed and repackaged elsewhere—social media posts, promotional videos, in-gallery displays, and more. This helps to maximize use of the content produced and increase return on investment.

Museums should seek out experienced web designers and back-end developers and get competitive quotes for their services. Online research about potential web hosting services will result in an array of cost options. Partnerships are always a valuable way to experiment with digital technology, create new networks, and learn from others. Smaller technology start-ups with an entrepreneurial flare as well colleges or universities with digital media programs may be a source for young talent, low-cost educational initiatives, and competitive pricing.

Category	Potential Costs
Coordination	- Project management - Equipment and software e.g. smartphones, cameras, scanners, livestreaming equipment, video editing software, etc. - Training or skills development - Audience research
Interpretive and Content Planning	- Establishing an interpretive plan - Writing/research - Consultation or specialist expertise - Content sourcing and production planning - Rights and permissions for images, video, performers, etc.
Content/Digital Media Production	- Digitization of objects, artifacts, and documents - Photography and 360-degree imaging - Graphics, design, and illustrations - Audio, voiceovers, and music - Video recording, drone footage, and editing - Educational resources and other downloads - Animations and specialist digital media - Writing text, editing, translation - Transcripts, closed captioning, and alternative text
Website/Platform and Technical Development	- Domain name registration (ongoing cost) - Platform subscriptions or web hosting services (ongoing cost) - Technical audit, upgrades, and integration with existing systems - Populating dashboard or templates - Website design, information architecture and wire-framing - Back-end development (coders) - Website/platform maintenance (ongoing cost)
Evaluation	- Content review - Meeting accessibility standards - Beta testing the prototype - User analytics and audience feedback (ongoing)
Marketing	- Promotional content/materials - Press viewing, VIP/member launch - Paid and unpaid social media promotion
Contingency	- About 15%

Figure 7.9. Sample budget guidelines. LORD CULTURAL RESOURCES

7.5 VIRTUAL EXHIBITION DEVELOPMENT PROCESS

Whether being developed in conjunction with a physical exhibition or as a standalone project, planning for a virtual exhibition follows a similar process to that of developing a physical exhibition. Ideally, planning for virtual exhibitions should receive the same care and attention as any physical exhibition, and consideration for why and how a museum will deliver a virtual exhibition should be incorporated into the annual exhibition program planning cycle.

As discussed throughout this book, the exhibition development process can be understood in three phases: development, design, and implementation. However, as a purely virtual experience with a greater focus on digital media, computer programming, and interactive interfaces, there will be a few key differences that you might encounter.

7.5.1 Development

- **Exhibition brief**: A museum's motivation for developing a virtual exhibition is different from that of developing a physical exhibition; often it is developed in support of a physical experience.
- **Team**: Anyone is capable of developing a great virtual exhibition. At the museum, the core exhibition planning team will still be essential. However, new expertise will be required to help with digital media and more technical aspects. Depending on the approach taken, new team skills might include content production (e.g., filming, image and video editing, graphic design, etc.); on-screen presentation and narration (e.g., lead tours, voiceovers, etc.); website designers, back-end developers (coders), digital specialists (interactives, games, 3D environments, 360-degree photography, animators, etc.); and social media coordination. Virtual exhibition development may require commissioning outside assistance.
- **Interpretive plan**: When developing the interpretive plan, it is important to remember that not all themes and topics translate well into digital media or are appropriate for the virtual realm and certain platforms. A virtual exhibition is also likely to be a much shorter experience with fewer digital exhibits than a physical exhibition would have. The attention span of online audiences is limited, and screen fatigue drastically reduces the amount of time people are willing to spend engaging with content. Remember, digital audiences tend to be younger, and have advanced expectations for what a good virtual experience should be. Best practice and comparable research are a good way to start.

7.5.2 Design

- **Content coordination**: More time will likely be spent sourcing images, audio and video clips, or producing new content from scratch such as filming and editing videos, creating animations, and programing digital interactives and games. Because virtual exhibition audiences are global, there could be additional implications for rights and permissions—both domestic and international laws may apply. Coordination with the registrar or collections manager is essential before uploading any content to the internet. Development of text should follow the good practice of interpretive writing.
- **Design**: Onscreen graphics should be designed to be consistent with the museum's brand and formats used in physical exhibitions, as well as address accessibility. Instead of a 3D designer, a web designer is engaged to assist with information architecture, interfaces, and coding, and a digital media designer will create interactive elements. Throughout design,

the interpretive framework continues to be an important structure for the development of headings and text. It will also act as the wireframe or template on which to build the virtual experience and its navigation.

7.5.3 Implementation

- **Production and prototyping**: During this stage, web designers will create a new website (or web page), establish a new domain name (URL), and build and test an offline prototype of the virtual exhibition. They will also be making sure that servers and chosen platforms are capable of hosting the virtual exhibition content, delivering interactives without issue, and interfacing with other computer systems like the digital asset management system, ticketing point of sale, and membership registration. Digital media/interactive designers will be programming animations or creating games. Much of the coding and uploading of content to the website (or another platform) will happen simultaneously in the prototyping phase, making for a more agile development process.

- **Opening**: Coordinating the launch of the virtual exhibition (as described above) may be different depending on its purpose and relationship to any physical exhibition. Remember, virtual exhibitions are not beholden to time and space, and can be made available for much longer than a traditional physical exhibition.

- **Monitoring and evaluation**: Like any physical exhibition, it is important to set clear performance metrics and benchmarks at the outset to monitor and evaluate the success of a virtual exhibition. A key difference will be the type of metrics used and the focus. Most museum professionals understand exhibition attendance; for virtual exhibitions this is akin to web traffic, especially impressions (total number of unique page views). But the real advantage for virtual exhibitions is the ability to track content-related metrics such as bounce rate (when someone visits the website, does nothing and leaves), dwell time (how long people spend on the website in a session), engagement (any form of interaction taken by a social media user on a page such as video views, likes, comments, shares, etc.), and conversions (did viewing virtual exhibition content lead to ticket sales, membership, or donation?).

7.6 TIPS FOR SMALLER MUSEUMS THAT WANT TO GO VIRTUAL

1. Start small, use what you have: Get your feet wet by revisiting some existing exhibition content you already have and thinking about how you might transform it into a virtual exhibition. Lots of text and images? You could easily put together a didactic or a carousel/slideshow virtual exhibition.

2. Ask your audiences what they want: With so many digital opportunities out there it can sometimes be hard to know where to start. Why not survey your visitors and members to find out what kind of virtual exhibitions they might like to see from you, how they would like to access your content, and if they would be willing to pay a small fee?

3. Put that smartphone to good use: No need for a fancy production studio, these pocket-sized supercomputers are your new best friend. They can capture amazing moments around your museum in fairly high-quality image and video format and can easily upload them to your social media page. Just remember to get the "okay" to post images of copyrighted works, sensitive artifacts, and visitors (particularly children) who appear in them.

4. Experiment with social media: Many social media platforms provide interesting features that can help you tell your story in an alternative and more dynamic way and help you reach out to your online followers.

5. Use "out of the box" templates: There are many online platforms and museum content aggregators that already provide user-friendly tools and preconfigured templates that can be used by those with minimal technology skills to create a professional looking website, microsite, or virtual exhibition quickly and easily. Some are free and others provide design templates and hosting services for a reasonable monthly fee.

6. Do some research: Digital transformation of our museums and increasing virtual content have become big priorities for funders. There may be a grant program out there that will help fund your project idea. Expand your search beyond museum programs to media and innovation funds too.

7. Seek out potential partners: Collaboration is key to making digital work. Technology start-ups and digital media programs at your local college or university are great places to find budding new digital talent and potential partners that can help you produce your virtual exhibitions and level up your own digital skills at the same time. Don't forget your other museum peers and partners. They may have similar ambitions that will allow you to pool resources and learn together.

8. Look inside your organization for tech talent: Canvas your existing museum staff to see if anyone has these skills. You might be surprised to find a budding filmmaker, web designer, or social media influencer already on your team. Don't be shy asking other museums for help too. They may have some great lessons to pass on or a colleague that could mentor you.

Case Study

EXTENDING THE LIFE OF A TRAVELING EXHIBITION, MUSEUM OF INTERNATIONAL FOLK ART, SANTA FE, NEW MEXICO

Founded in 1953, the Museum of International Folk Art (MOIFA) in Santa Fe, New Mexico, is dedicated to advancing our understanding of folk-art traditions and to encouraging dialogue about cultural identity, community, and aesthetics. With more than 130,000 objects from more than one hundred countries on six continents, the museum's holdings represent a diverse range of cultures and constitute the largest collection of international folk art in the world. An integral part of this is the Girard Collection, a vast assemblage of more than a hundred thousand folk art pieces donated by renowned American architect and designer Alexander Girard and his wife Susan in 1978.

Best known for his work with fabric giant Herman Miller Inc., Alexander Girard was one of the most influential interior and textile designers of the twentieth century. He also had an insatiable appetite for collecting and the visual language of folk art. Girard broke the rules, fusing sleek mid-century modernism with vernacular folk-art traditions of the past. His playful designs attest to a passion for colors and ornamentation and were inspired by a lifetime of travel and a love of objects.

Fast forward to the twenty-first century, where MOIFA continues to celebrate the visual beauty and power of folk art and has established an ambitious vision for the future, one that strives to use folk art to change lives and to shape a more humane world by connecting people through creative expression and artistic traditions. To achieve this vision, the museum set out on an extensive strategic planning process and soon recognized a need to increase its online presence and expand its use of current and emerging digital technologies as a way to enhance the visitor experience and create improved local and global access to its exhibitions, collections, and interactive programs.

In 2019, MOIFA found the perfect chance to develop its first virtual exhibition, *Alexander Girard: A Designer's Universe*.[25] A traveling exhibition produced by Germany's Vitra Design Museum, this was the first major retrospective of the designer's work. With more than four hundred objects—textiles, drawings, furniture, graphics, film, and folk art (many from MOIFA's own collection)—the exhibition touches on Girard's early beginnings in architecture, the bright and bold textiles he is known to have produced for Herman Miller Inc., as well as the amazing folk art collection he drew inspiration from.

"A Designer's Universe was the ideal candidate for our first virtual exhibition," said Laura Addison, MOIFA's curator of North American Collections. "Because Girard's textile designs are colorful and graphically bold, it is a show that makes for a great fly-through experience online."[1]

Forgoing a more traditional (and sometimes flat) didactic virtual exhibition format, the museum instead chose to make use of 360-degree camera technology and software that allows visitors to navigate the gallery and interact with content online. After obtaining permission from the

Figure 7.10. Visitors enter the virtual exhibition, *Alexander Girard: A Designer's Universe,* using online navigation tools. VIRTUAL EXHIBITION BY FIVE D MEDIA/LISA HINSON, © VITRA DESIGN MUSEUM/MUSEUM OF INTERNATIONAL FOLK ART

Vitra, MOIFA created a virtual exhibition in the form of an interactive 3D walkthrough tour. The intent being to create a lasting visual archive of this groundbreaking exhibition and providing those who could not visit in person with a chance to engage with Girard's work and legacy even after the exhibition closed and moved on to the next location.

"The digital life of exhibitions used to be secondary to the development of the in-person museum visit experience," said Addison. "The intention has always been there to have exhibitions live on in other ways once a show is over, and to reach an audience that is unable to visit the show in person, but it wasn't always the priority.

"Now the virtual experience is foremost on museum professionals' minds. These can't replace the experience of seeing artworks in person—the scale, the skilled hand of the artist, the materiality. But museums are now adapting to this new reality with creativity and resourcefulness, by sharing ideas and tapping into technical know-how of staff or in the community."[2]

With minimal in-house digital skills, MOIFA needed to seek outside expertise to help produce the virtual exhibition. Experimental in nature, budgets were also limited and necessitated a more creative and resourceful approach. At first glance, Five D Media, experts in producing quick capture virtual home tours for real estate clients, may have been an unusual partner to choose, but quickly became the right partner for MOIFA.

Over the course of a few days at the museum, Five D Media used their Matterport Pro2 3D camera to photograph the temporary exhibition installed in the gallery. Later, they used the images captured to render a 3D "dollhouse" floor plan and recreate the galleries as a 360-degree virtual walkthrough. Collaborating with the museum's curatorial team for content development, Five D Media and MOIFA were able to identify and program key points of interest (or "tour stops") within the virtual exhibition to provide online visitors with an additional layer of on-screen interactivity and information. Navigating at their leisure, virtual visitors can review interpretive text panels and engage with enhanced content such as a time-lapse video of the installation, articles, and links to other information about Girard and his legacy. It even includes a link to the exhibition catalogue for purchase in the Museums of New Mexico Foundation's online gift shop.

Hosted on Five D Media's web platform and embedded in the MOIFA website, visitors can easily explore the virtual exhibition at their own pace from a computer or mobile screen or in VR with the assistance of a headset.

Overall, the creation of this 3D virtual walkthrough exhibition was realized for under US$500 and utilized about a week's worth of staff time to direct the photography technicians, identify tour stops, recast existing interpretive content, and customize it to fit the digital format.

Since its launch, the virtual exhibition has been popular with more than 3,600 visits (for embedded Matterport models like MOIFA's, a visit is counted after a user clicks the play button) and is a fantastic opportunity to relive the in-person experience.

The virtual exhibition also proved to be a critical resource for MOIFA during the COVID-19 pandemic. Like many of the world's museums it was forced to close to in-person visitors for many months in 2020. The Girard virtual exhibition provided a lifeline to MOIFA visitors and the New Mexico community with continued digital access to the museum's exhibitions and collections.

Most importantly, the development of its first virtual exhibition has been an important achievement for the Museum of International Folk Art as it looks to build its in-house digital capabilities

Figure 7.11. Virtual bird's-eye view of the *Alexander Girard: A Designer's Universe* exhibition facilitates visitor choice and navigation. VIRTUAL EXHIBITION BY FIVE D MEDIA/LISA HINSON, © VITRA DESIGN MUSEUM/MUSEUM OF INTERNATIONAL FOLK ART

and advance its vision and strategic objectives for improving statewide impact and expanding its global presence. Already the museum is putting the lessons learned and its experience with 360-degree image capture technology to good use.

"The virtual Girard exhibition has proved a fruitful pathway towards increasing our reach, and we have already created similar virtual tours for the exhibitions currently on view, including Yokai: Ghosts and Demons of Japan; Música Buena: Hispano Folk Music of New Mexico; and Community Through Making: From Peru to New Mexico, the last on view in the museum's Mark Naylor and Dale Gunn Gallery of Conscience," said museum Executive Director Khristaan D. Villela.

NOTES

1. "MOIFA Presents 'Alexander Girard: A Designer's Universe,' a Virtual Exhibition," New Mexico Department of Cultural Affairs, June 10, 2020, https://media.newmexicoculture.org/release/1163/moifa-presents-alexa.
2. "MOIFA Presents 'Alexander Girard.'"

NOTES

1. "MoMa: Stepping into Tim Burton's World," Behance, accessed November 2020, https://www.behance.net/gallery/4351051/MoMa-Tim-Burtons-World.
2. "The York Minster Stained Glass Navigator," The York Glazier Trust, accessed November 2020, https://stainedglass-navigator.yorkglazierstrust.org/.
3. "Sunflowers Virtual 360 Gallery, Facebook, accessed November 2020, www.facebook.com/VanGoghMuseum/videos/10159187334010597.
4. "Virtual Exhibitions," Ayala Museum, accessed November 2020, https://www.ayalamuseum.org/exhibitions/.
5. "NEONSIGNS.HK," NEONSIGNS, accessed November 2020, https://www.neonsigns.hk/?lang=en.
6. "Reports," Culture Track, accessed November 2020, culturetrack.com/research/reports/.
7. "The Visitor Engagement Cycle for Cultural Organizations," colleen dilenschneider, February 1, 2017, www.colleendilen.com/2017/02/01/the-visitor-engagement-cycle-for-cultural-organizations/.
8. "Culture and Community in a Time of Crisis," Culture Track, June 7, 2020, https://s28475.pcdn.co/wp-content/uploads/2020/09/CCTC-Key-Findings-from-Wave-1_9.29.pdf.
9. "The Three Most Important Reasons to Prioritize Visitor Satisfaction (DATA)," Colleen Dilenschneider, April 25, 2018, https://www.colleendilen.com/2018/04/25/three-important-reasons-prioritize-visitor-satisfaction-data/.
10. "The Global State of Digital 2020, Hootsuite, accessed November 2020, https://www.hootsuite.com/pages/digital-2020#c-214756.
11. "2019 Canada's Internet Facebook," accessed November 2020, https://www.cira.ca/resources/corporate/factbook/canadas-internet-factbook-2019.
12. "Data Stories: infographics that tell a story," Wilkening Consulting, accessed November 2020, http://www.wilkeningconsulting.com/data-stories.html.
13. "Exploring Museums, Digitally!" San José Public Library, March 27, 2020, https://www.sjpl.org/blog/exploring-museums-digitally.
14. "Accessibility," Interaction Design Foundation, accessed November 2020, https://www.interaction-design.org/literature/topics/accessibility.
15. "Learn at Home," San Diego History Center, accessed November 2020, https://sites.google.com/view/sdhc-learn-at-home/home.
16. Twitter, accessed November 2020, https://twitter.com/TODreamsProject/status/1345943526924824580.
17. Instagram, accessed November 2020, https://www.instagram.com/stories/highlights/17979680011079117/.
18. "Where should you host?" Digital Museums Canada, accessed November 2020, https://www.digitalmuseums.ca/help-and-resources/toolbox/resources/how-to-choose-web-hosting-services/.
19. "Women in service—The War Art of Molly Lamb Bobak, Canadian War Museum, accessed November 2020, https://www.warmuseum.ca/mollylambbobak/.
20. "Americans," National Museum of the American Indian, accessed November 2020, https://americanindian.si.edu/americans/#.
21. "European Museum of Modern Art," Matterport, accessed November 2020, https://matterport.com/industries/gallery/european-museum-modern-art.
22. "The Queen and the Crown," Brooklyn Museum, accessed November 2020, https://www.thequeenandthecrown.com/.
23. "Arts Response Tracking Study," National Arts Centre, accessed November 2020, http://www.businessandarts.org/wp-content/uploads/2020/06/2020-1642-Business-for-the-Arts-Populated-Report-Culture-Goers-English.pdf.
24. Digital Museum Canada, accessed November 2020, https://www.digitalmuseums.ca/funding/large-investment/?tab=schedule-budget.
25. "Alexander Girard: A Designer's Universe," Museum of Internation Folk Art, accessed November 2020, https://fivedmedia.com/3d-model/alexander-girard-a-designers-universe/skinned/.

Chapter 8

Temporary Exhibitions

Maria Piacente and Katherine Molineux

Temporary exhibitions are an indispensable tool for the museum to attract repeat visitors and engage in new discourse. A strong temporary exhibitions program includes exhibitions loaned from other institutions as well as new experiences generated from the research of the museum's curators. For some museums, where there is no permanent collection on which to base an exhibition, or it is not in the institution's interest or mandate to do so, temporary exhibitions may provide the entire display program. Le Laboratoire in central Paris, for example, is a place where artists and scientists experiment at the frontiers of both disciplines; it does not have a permanent collection but prepares constantly changing exhibitions of experiments-in-progress accompanied by a powerful schedule of public programs. Another example is the Frist Art Museum in Nashville, Tennessee. The museum presents and originates high-quality exhibitions with related programs and community outreach activities. It does not have a collection and as such, its many temporary exhibition galleries showcase a diversity of art and culture.

In addition to encouraging repeat visitation, temporary exhibitions can:

- Offer a "window on the world" to the community that the museum serves by hosting cultural experiences and works art from all over the planet.
- Build membership and loyalty. An exciting temporary exhibition program gives the museum more opportunities to provide their members with special privileges, thereby encouraging new members and maintaining the loyalty of current ones. The subjects of specific

exhibitions may attract the interest of formerly underrepresented groups who can be encouraged to become members if the museum has a membership program.

- Generate additional revenue through special admissions charges, themed programming, food services, and retail.
- Increase access to collections that would otherwise remain buried in storage rooms.
- Allow permanent collections to be remounted or reinterpreted in a new light, according to a theme, topic, or idea, thereby reducing the need to bring in costly rented exhibitions.
- Encourage public participation through exhibitions designed to directly incorporate visitors in the co-creation of the exhibition. In this way, museum's change their relationships with their audience and find new ways to be relevant in the communities they serve.
- Facilitate experimentation with new forms of exhibitions, interpretive techniques, and technologies.
- Develop new partnerships with other museums and public and private organizations to create exhibitions and share research and new ideas.

In practice, every museum operates a mix of temporary shows: small and large, rented or not. Some shows will be on exhibit for three months while others will remain open for a year depending on each organization's priorities for revenue, resource allocation, and audience attraction. In order to manage such a mix and budget accordingly, a museum's temporary exhibition program is usually (ideally) developed three to five years in advance, taking into consideration time allocations for installation, demounting, packing, and shipping. However, even the most well-planned schedule needs to be flexible to make room for a great exhibition that comes along or to respond to a timely news item that requires a response to public interest.

8.1 TYPES OF EXHIBITIONS IN A TEMPORARY EXHIBITION PROGRAM

A carefully formulated **temporary exhibition policy** or **strategy** is essential to managing a temporary exhibition program. This policy controls the number of exhibitions executed or borrowed in a given year, provides criteria and processes for assessing proposed exhibitions, and maintains the integrity of the museum's mission and mandate. The exhibition policy should state the purpose of the temporary exhibition program relevant to the museum's mission and strategic plan, reference research plans or institutional initiatives related to content strategies (e.g., focus on climate change or long-term initiative focused on fashion and textiles), and include a realistic projection of the annual percentage of shows to be drawn from international, national, local, or internal sources so as not to stray too far from a museum's mandate, which may be to focus primarily on regional or community history.

The exhibition policy may address the intended mix of six possible levels of a museum's involvement in the origination or management of temporary exhibitions:

1. A temporary exhibition may consist of a new presentation of the museum's permanent collection, the recognition of a new and impressive donation, or other new acquisitions. The 2010 exhibition *Picasso* in the Metropolitan Museum of Art in New York focused on

Figure 8.1. The twenty-five-meter blue whale skeleton was impressively displayed at the Royal Ontario Museum, Toronto, Canada. WITH PERMISSION OF THE ROYAL ONTARIO MUSEUM © ROM

showcasing the complete holdings of the works by Pablo Picasso in the Met's collection, attracting more than seven hundred thousand visitors in a four-month period. In 2017, the Royal Ontario Museum (ROM) in Toronto launched *Out of the Depths: The Blue Whale Story*, the highly successful exhibition that told the story of nine blue whales that died tragically in the Gulf of St. Lawrence in 2014, and the unprecedented opportunity for research and conservation that it presented. ROM scientists traveled to Newfoundland and Labrador where they collected two complete blue whale specimens that had been towed to shore. The success of this exhibition in delighting ROM's audiences led to the 2021 launch of *Great Whales: Up Close and Personal*, an exhibition that included two additional specimens—the critically endangered North Atlantic right whale and the sperm whale—along with new research and interpretation about whales. Ultimately, a museum's potential for such a program depends on the range and depth of its permanent collection, but it provides an opportunity to create an event and a sense of immediacy that aids in garnering the public's attention.

2. The museum may borrow works related to objects in its collections and present them together as a thematically related show. The result enriches the museum's understanding of its own collection as well as attracting renewed public interest in specific works of art. The 2013 Tate exhibition, *Lowry and the Painting of Modern Life*, was a retrospective and reinterpretation of the artist's work; although Tate has a reasonable representation of Lowry's paintings, the exhibition's curators needed to borrow works from other museums and private collections to assemble the show.

Figure 8.2. The exhibition *Lowry and the Painting of Modern Life* at Tate Britain, London, 2013. © ESTATE OF LAWRENCE STEPHEN LOWRY/SOCAN (2021)/PHOTO © TATE

3. The museum may choose a subject or theme and borrow objects from many sources, possibly including only a few items from its own collections. Exhibitions that document an artist's entire oeuvre, a whole civilization, or all aspects of a species are among the many examples of this type of exhibition. Science centers may rely less on borrowing and more on fabrication of new exhibit apparatus to explore such subjects as chemistry, physics, or astronomy. *The Warrior Emperor and China's Terracotta Army* shown at the Royal Ontario Museum in Toronto in 2011 depended on loans of several of the famous life-sized terracotta figures from the Shaanxi Provincial Cultural Relics Bureau in order to present the exhibition to a Canadian audience.

4. Although the preceding three levels of engagement are applicable to shows originated by the exhibiting institution, museums can also participate in exhibitions initiated by others. Participation may be limited to paying a rental fee or may involve collaboration in research, preparation of catalogs, negotiation of loans, or other services. *Dragons, Unicorns, and Mermaids: Mythic Creatures*, an American Museum of Natural History (AMNH) exhibition from New York City, reveals the relationship between science and legend, tracing the origins of mythic creatures and their enduring hold on the imagination. The exhibition was organized by the AMNH in collaboration with the Field Museum in Chicago, the Canadian Museum of Nature in Gatineau, the Australian National Maritime Museum in Sydney, and the Fernbank Museum of Natural History in Atlanta. AMNH led the process and will manage the exhibition tour for a fee after each of the collaborators has hosted the show. Collaborations such as these share in the cost of developing the exhibition, research, and collection support.

Figure 8.3. *The Warrior Emperor and China's Terracotta Army* temporary exhibition at the Royal Ontario Museum, Toronto, Canada. LORD CULTURAL RESOURCES

Figure 8.4. A seventeen-foot dragon guards the entrance to the temporary exhibition *Dragons, Unicorns, and Mermaids: Mythic Creatures,* created by the American Museum of Natural History in New York. COURTESY OF ROBB MCCORMICK PHOTOGRAPHY

5. A growing level of temporary exhibition engagement in the museum sector is the collaboration between museums and living artists and multimedia firms to develop unique experiences. The artist or media specialist may work with the museum's staff to create a unique installation that takes over an entire gallery or series of galleries and public spaces. Some examples include Olafur Eliasson's *The Weather Project* at the Tate Modern in 2003 or Chila Burman's stunning light installation for Tate Britain in 2020. Alternatively, an artist may develop a series of works that are solely for the benefit of display at that museum. The museum may choose to acquire those objects, or the artist may choose to sell or maintain ownership of the works after the exhibition closes.

6. Finally, museums may simply receive and display packaged shows, exhibitions circulated by museums, or specialized agencies such as the American Federation of Arts or the Smithsonian Institution's Temporary Exhibition Service. For such exhibitions, the receiving institution usually pays a fee and receives a completely prepared, full-scale exhibition, including a fixed number of catalogs, publicity photographs, and the text for a news release. The Canadian Museum for Human Rights traveled a fully packaged exhibition, *Mandela: The Struggle for Freedom* throughout Canada and the United States from 2018 to 2021. The show comes complete with objects, graphics, cases, constructed scenery (including a jail cell), and all the hardware to present the audiovisual materials.

Figure 8.5. The Canadian Museum for Human Rights (Winnipeg, Canada) traveled a packaged show complete with multimedia interactives, reconstructed environments, and graphics across Canada and the United States from 2018 to 2021. COURTESY OF AARON COHEN/CANADIAN MUSEUM FOR HUMAN RIGHTS

8.2 MANAGING A TEMPORARY EXHIBITION PROGRAM

Temporary exhibitions are a demanding activity, sometimes requiring the attention of the museum's entire staff. Balancing their appeal with other museum functions is a major challenge for exhibition planners. Hosting and originating temporary exhibitions involve personnel and contributions from all departments. Ranging from curators who research and develop topics to public programers who create specialized events around particular themes to the marketing team that gets the word out about the show. The operation of a temporary exhibition program revolves around the following core personnel:

- **The curator** researches and develops topics that are reviewed by the museum's exhibition selection committee.
- An **exhibition director/manager** operates the program and selection process that includes organizing original exhibitions and sourcing suitable shows from other institutions. Some larger museums have established entire departments to schedule and manage their temporary exhibition program.
- A **registrar or collections manager** tracks and documents both incoming and outgoing loans as well as temporary displays from collections storage.
- Skilled installation teams of **preparators** or **art handlers** are necessary for any museum with a strong temporary exhibition program. These people are trained to pack, unpack, and install objects and works of art. In addition, a skilled installation team can meet the often demanding schedules required to mount and dismount exhibitions borrowed from other institutions.
- The **conservator** oversees care of any collections that accompany a traveling exhibition and may be required to prepare a condition report to record the conservation status of the works of art or artifacts upon arrival at or before departure from the borrowing museum. If the temporary exhibition consists of collections from the museum's storerooms, the conservator will oversee their preparation which may include conservation and/or the creation of special mounts.
- A **design** and **interpretive planning** team will be engaged to either develop the exhibition envisioned in-house by the museum or enact any changes and additions to the temporary gallery space for rented shows that will make the content more relevant to their audiences. The later may include some gallery adjustments (i.e., temporary walls, lighting), new labels, or additional materials for supporting content from the museum's own collection. The interpretive planner may also lead consultation and evaluation strategies.
- A **project manager** who will oversee the budget, schedule, and procurement requirements of both rented and museum-led original exhibitions.

Managing a temporary exhibition program includes particular tasks related to the logistics of shows that are rented as opposed to those generated in-house. These include loan agreements, insurance, shipping, crating and storage, security, and expenses related to couriers and installation teams that travel with the exhibition.

When temporary exhibitions or collections are rented or "loaned" from other organizations, the museum must adhere to a specific set of conditions outlined in a contract known as the

loan agreement. This is a legal agreement between a lender/organizer and a borrower/exhibiting venue. Such agreements identify the responsibilities of both parties, and specifically focus on the financial, environmental, and legal responsibilities of the borrower in order to ensure the safety and preservation of the objects or works of art.

Insuring the objects borrowed for temporary exhibitions can be costly in the operation of a temporary exhibition program for small- and medium-sized institutions. Many lenders prefer to insure objects themselves and bill the borrowing institution, while in other instances the borrower may be expected to provide what is often called "nail to nail" insurance, which means coverage from the time a painting is taken off the wall of the lending institution until it returns to that "nail." In either case, the insurance cost is proportionate to the monetary value of the objects borrowed.

An alternative developed by many countries that are actively involved in the international circulation of works of art for temporary exhibitions is a government indemnity program, according to which the national government of the borrowing institution agrees to cover the cost of any loss or damage, making insurance unnecessary. One difficulty encountered with such programs can be a divergence between the amount of indemnity required by a lender and the amount that the government may be willing to indemnify; where these differ, the borrowing museum may have to arrange for supplementary insurance coverage. In 2015, one of the few existing original versions of the Magna Carta traveled to Canada for an exclusive exhibition event. The value of the document (US$27,554,275) made it impossible for the participating institutions to insure the document. As such, the Government of Canada stepped in to secure the insurance and indemnify the museums, allowing Canadians a once in lifetime opportunity to view an object of rare historical value.

Figure 8.6. The Magna Carta was valued at $27,554,275, requiring the Government of Canada to insure the document on behalf of the Canadian museums participating in the tour. LORD CULTURAL RESOURCES

Shipping, crating, and storage costs are significant budgetary items, especially if the exhibition is on a global tour that will incur additional customs-related fees. In most cases, the lender will organize the shipping and prorate (or "share") the costs among all participating venues. Knowing where the exhibition is going early in the process enables organizers to plan for shipping expenses. When borrowing works of art or packaged shows from an organization directly, the museum will be responsible to cover round-trip shipping. As such, the farther the works have to travel, the more expensive the exhibition will be. Shipping costs may also be influenced by particular conditions identified in the loan agreement: for example, some lenders will insist that all objects must travel by air rather than truck or sea. Specialized art handlers, air-ride trucks with air-conditioning to protect the goods being transported, and security escorts from the lending institution known as couriers may be required to accompany the shipment and oversee the unpacking and installation of the works on loan. Finally, if the museum does not have adequate temporary crate storage, off-site locations will need to be rented for store crates until the show is ready to be packed and shipped to its next location.

Museums hosting blockbusters sometimes find that visitor demand exceeds the normal operating capacity of the gallery and/or museum. For example, school groups requesting tours of a special exhibition may temporarily eclipse visits to the permanent collection, creating a programming bottleneck. Such shows may require short-term operational adjustments such as timed ticketing, extended hours, supplementary security measures and crowd control techniques to deal with the anticipated level of visitation. Some lenders may also require that museums provide in-person, constant security in the galleries where high value objects are to be displayed. Human security may need to be supplemented by additional CCTV cameras, cased alarm systems, and more.

8.3 MAKING SPACE FOR TEMPORARY EXHIBITIONS

Most "packaged shows" are relatively small, since they are designed for circulation to a relatively large number of possible venues. The opposite extreme is the blockbuster, usually a relatively large exhibition for which there is known to be broad public interest, and for which there is a limited distribution. These exhibitions respond to public demand and are key to increasing or maintaining attendance figures as well as generating revenue. Major art "Masters" exhibitions of the French impressionists, Van Gogh, or other "big name" artists are almost always blockbusters, especially when they travel far from the original lending institution. Ancient Egypt, dinosaurs, and shows that feature precious "treasures" from famous collections also continue to perform well. In recent years, pop-culture, photography, and contemporary art exhibitions have succeeded in drawing large crowds of visitors. For example, *Alexander McQueen: Savage Beauty* organized by The Costume Institute, celebrating the late Alexander McQueen's contributions to fashion, at the Metropolitan Museum of Art in New York drew more than eight thousand visitors a day over a three-month period. In 2019, Ai Weiwei's exhibition—his first ever showing in South America—was the highest-ranking show by a single artist according to *The Art Newspaper*, drawing more than 1.1 million visitors as the exhibition traveled around Brazil.[1]

To accommodate very large exhibitions museums require 10,000–20,000 square feet (up to 2000 sq m) of dedicated exhibition space. At the other extreme, as little as 1,500 square feet (140 sq m) may suffice to mount solo exhibitions of individual artists in smaller institutions. Most packaged shows are designed to fit into 3,000–5,000 square feet (280–465 sq m), although most look best at the higher end of that range. In order to operate a dynamic program capable of initiating creative exhibitions in collaboration with other museums, at least 5,000–8,000 square

Figure 8.7. *Alexander McQueen: Savage Beauty,* The Costume Institute at the Metropolitan Museum of Art, New York. IMAGE COPYRIGHT © THE METROPOLITAN MUSEUM OF ART. IMAGE SOURCE: ART RESOURCE, NY

feet (465–750 sq m) is recommended, while 10,000 to 20,000 square feet (1,000–2,000 sq m) is requisite for larger institutions.

While larger temporary exhibition spaces create greater opportunities for programming, it also means that the museum must commit to keeping those spaces programmed. This can be expensive and time-consuming. Although exhibitions originated by a museum or in partnership with one or two other museums are usually shown for longer periods at each venue, packaged shows and many other borrowed exhibitions are often available for only three to six months. This means that at least two or three packaged shows rented from other organizations would be required in a given year to keep a gallery or series of galleries fully programmed. As such, in addition to projecting the types of exhibitions to be shown, the exhibition policy must also ensure that the museum provides only the temporary exhibition gallery capacity that can reasonably be programmed, considering space and facility limitations, budget, staff, and time available.

Space for displaying temporary exhibitions is not the only requirement for mounting a temporary exhibition. In the public zones, additional spaces are needed to support audio-visual programs, audio tour equipment, and specialty shops with product dedicated to the subject matter of the changing exhibition. Retail is particularly significant as it has become a chief source of revenue generation associated with major shows. There is also the need for an entire suite of nonpublic support spaces—from the loading bay through shipping/receiving to a crating/uncrating area to a temporary exhibition storage area, not forgetting the associated isolation room (in case of infested crates), crate storage, packing supplies storage, a documentation office, workshops for framing and mount-making, and an exhibition staging area where works of art, artifacts, or specimens can be installed in cases or on plinths to test case layouts before they go into the galleries.

Many museums find it necessary to meet the highest standards of functionality, environmental controls, and security in these nonpublic temporary exhibition support spaces in order to guarantee their ability to borrow important exhibitions from major museums. Even if they do not come in person, directors, curators, conservators, or registrars considering a loan request routinely issue a form that requires the borrowing institution to describe these facilities in detail. Most collection policies require that loans can be approved only to institutions that at least match the facilities and conditions of the lending museum or in some cases even exceed the conditions found within the loaned work's home museum.

8.4 PUBLIC AND EDUCATIONAL PROGRAMMING

Planning and delivering education programs and special events related to temporary exhibitions has become an important part of their presentation. In addition to regularly scheduled events, the museum's public programming department may choose to create a series of specially designed programs such as tours, lecture series, after-hours events, and more. A new website, social media activations, and mobile application may be developed in conjunction with the exhibition. The *David Bowie Is* exhibition, mounted by the Victoria and Albert Museum in 2013, was the first international retrospective of David Bowie's career and featured more than three hundred objects. The experience included a celebrity-studded opening event, interviews and content by pop star colleagues, opportunities to win free trips to see the exhibition, lectures and workshops, the creation of an exclusive product line to sell in the shop, and concluded with a nationwide cinema event, live screening from the exhibition to more than two hundred theaters across the United Kingdom.

Programs such as these require additional funding and staff and should be part of the budget (or accounted for in some fashion if absorbed by another department) when the project is first conceived for the museum. Depending on the size and significance of the exhibition, press events, opening night celebrations, and member's only previews should be planned.

8.5 MARKETING AND PUBLIC RELATIONS

Marketing campaigns ensure that potential visitors know about the upcoming temporary exhibition. These campaigns include announcements on the museum's website and social media platforms, television and radio ads, physical posters and banners, press events, contests, promotions, and more. The Victoria and Albert Museum conducted an innovative advertising campaign to attract visitors to the *David Bowie Is* exhibition. According to an article published by *Encore Media Partners* in May 2014, their mixed media strategy included the following:[2]

1. It connected with top social media influencers in addition to traditional press to get the word out about the exhibition.

2. It used both printed banners and digital monitors around the city and in London's underground to advertise the exhibition.

3. It leveraged an experiential distribution campaign to drive audience interaction and social sharing with "instagrammable" moments.

4. It collaborated with private enterprises including the department store, Selfridges in London to launch a concept shop and David Bowie widow display, and Benugo coffee shops featuring branded hot drink cup sleeves.

5. It spent large amounts of money on newspaper, radio, TV, and digital adds to promote the exhibition and related special events.

8.6 FUNDING AND RESOURCING A TEMPORARY EXHIBITION PROGRAM

A dedicated budget for planning, creating, renting, and operating a temporary exhibition program should be included as a line item in the museum's annual operating budget. These budgets are often enhanced by sponsorship and fundraising activities, but no museum can mount a regular schedule of temporary exhibitions without a consistent and committed allocation in its annual operating budget. Here is a checklist of items that may need to be itemized in a budget:

- Rental/participation fees
- Gallery renovations and enhancements (walls, lighting, finishes, media equipment, caseworks, graphics, etc.)
- Exhibition planning, design, and fabrication
- Consultation, evaluation, and topic testing
- Insurance
- Crating and shipping
- Legal fees
- Installation and deinstallation support
- Additional staff such as security, volunteers, ticket takers, or guest curators
- Courier expenses for borrowed works of art
- Translation costs (if the exhibition needs to be bi- or multilingual)
- Marketing and promotion
- Special events, public programming
- Maintenance and operation contingencies
- Conservation

Given the constantly rising costs and the growing popularity of temporary exhibitions, it is not surprising that sponsorship of temporary exhibitions by corporations or individuals has become a substantial factor in their planning and execution, often affecting the decision whether to proceed with a show or not. A **sponsorship policy** or series of guidelines may be important to address potential donor strategies related to exhibitions. A museum's credibility depends on the public's appraisal of its objectivity, and this may be forfeited if the museum allows the sponsor to influence the content of the exhibition. A science center presenting an exhibition about food groups, for example, may be tempted to avoid displays that cast doubt on the food value of a corporate sponsor's products unless it has a clear policy that isolates exhibition content from sponsors' interests. Still other questions are raised when the sponsor is also a collector who stands to benefit from the prestige conferred by the institution that displays their collection. Most sponsors, individual or corporate, understand the need for a policy that preserves the museum's integrity, and are willing to work within its terms as long as it is presented in a positive context.

Nevertheless, the importance of securing sponsors and the increasing tendency of corporations to consider sponsorship as a function of their public relations or marketing budgets and "ownership" of certain topics or ideas, means that museums in their sponsorship proposals for exhibitions must increasingly address such marketing issues as reach, demographic impact, impression, and exposure.

8.7 GENERATING REVENUE

Revenue for a temporary exhibition may be derived from admissions and sales. Whether or not to charge special admission for a temporary exhibition is often a crucial decision. In some situations, it may actually be better for the museum not to charge an additional fee, but simply to benefit from the increased general admission receipts and added value for members. On the other hand, if admission is normally free to the permanent collection, a special admission charge may be necessary to recover at least part of the expense of creating or hosting a temporary exhibition.

Another important consideration is whether to offer a discount—or merely prior access to tickets—to the museum's members or friends. Some museums use high profile temporary exhibitions to build membership, making it advantageous for resident visitors to purchase a membership and get a free or discounted ticket to the special show. The institution's challenge after the exhibition closes is then to retain those new members, who may have been attracted only by the temporary exhibition. This is a particularly interesting challenge if the exhibition has featured the culture or heritage of a local ethno-cultural group that may have become interested in the museum only because of a particular show. Can the museum retain their interest with an ongoing series of programs relevant to them, or is it possible to broaden their interests to respond to other museum programs on offer?

Shops with stock specific to temporary exhibitions have become common at or near the exits from the galleries in which shows are presented. Larger museums now routinely locate temporary shops with exhibition-related merchandise within their galleries in addition to a boutique that may be located elsewhere in the museum.

We also can't forget about the revenue generated from food services. An influx of visitors to the museum as a result of a temporary exhibition will likely result in increased sales at the café and restaurant. Determining the impact of increased food and beverage sales should be credited to the temporary exhibition program. This is part of understanding the complete value that a temporary exhibition program adds to the museum's bottom line.

Another, although more rare option for some museums to generate revenue from temporary exhibitions is making collections accessible through the establishment of **museum branches** where rotating exhibitions drawn from the headquarters are regularly shown thereby turning the liability of collection storage costs into a public asset. New York's Guggenheim Museum has done this most spectacularly through the establishment of branches around the world, including its celebrated museum at Bilbao, its smaller venues in Berlin and Venice, and its Lower Manhattan gallery in Soho. This enterprising policy transforms the Guggenheim's extensive collections from a massive resource requiring expensive storage (and thus a liability in economic terms) into an asset that can be seen by many more visitors elsewhere. Another gain is the capacity to plan facilities in each center to accommodate large individual works of art such as the forty-foot (13 m) tall heavy steel sculpture by Richard Serra that is more or less permanently installed in Bilbao.

In England, London's Tate Gallery established branches at Liverpool and St Ives, and in May 2000 opened Tate Modern at Bankside on the south shore of the Thames, in addition to Tate Britain at its Millbank site in the north. Le Musée du Louvre in Paris has developed a similar model of offering its collections to branch operations, including *Louvre Lens*, which opened in 2013 in northern France. The industrial city of Lens will play host to a number of short- and long-term exhibitions thereby beginning a trend of creating access to great works of art outside of Paris. Even before Lens opened, Le Centre Pompidou had established its branch in eastern France at Metz.

Louvre Abu Dhabi, owned and operated by the UAE, opened in 2017. It showcases loaned works of art from the Louvre in Paris. This arrangement between France and Abu Dhabi has proved to be an opportunity for the Louvre to generate significant revenue for conservation in a consortium of nine French museums as well as to allow residents and tourists in the United Arab Emirates access to one of the greatest art history collections in the world. In general, such arrangements may affect the pattern of traveling exhibitions in the future, with long-term loans and rotating distribution of permanent collections possibly becoming more common, thereby realizing the inherent value in collections that would otherwise remain in storage for long periods.

Pop-up exhibitions are a form of temporary exhibition that last only a few days or a couple of weeks. Some museums have begun harnessing this trend to create exciting, alternative, and fun exhibitions in nontraditional venues such as shopping malls, bus stations, outdoor kiosks, and more. While not a traditional temporary exhibition that will generate a direct fee, pop-ups are a great form of marketing that can drive audiences to the main institution.

NOTES

1. "Art's Most Popular: Here are 2019's Most Visited Shows and Museums," *The Art Newspaper*, December 17, 2020
2. Show Marketing Insights published by Encore Media Partners, May 2014, http://encoremediapartners.com/encore_insights0514_davidbowieis.pdf.

Chapter 9

Traveling Exhibitions

Maria Piacente

Museums create and share exhibitions for various reasons, including to generate revenue, provide greater access to collections and new research, and defray the costs of temporary exhibition programs. While some museums develop traveling—or touring—exhibitions intermittently and opportunistically, others have dedicated traveling exhibition departments and resources.

National museums such as the Smithsonian Institution through its SITES program are mandated to create and circulate exhibitions at little to no cost. These programs allow smaller museums with limited budgets to host good-quality temporary exhibitions for their resident audiences. These exhibitions are offered to museums as complete ready-to-install "packages" and are usually not conceived as profit-making ventures.

Alternatively, institutions like the American Museum of Natural History in New York and the Victoria and Albert Museum in London have dedicated staff resources whose sole purpose is to fund, originate, and operate a traveling exhibition program to generate revenue. Their catalogues of exhibitions tend to include a variety of offerings with rental fees ranging from US$100,000 to $1,000,000 per show.

Private for-profit organizations are another source of "packaged" exhibitions. These companies fund and produce their own exhibitions or manage the tours of exhibitions on behalf of museums for a fixed fee or share in the revenue generated by rentals and ticket sales. This is because many institutions simply do not have the resources to address the enormous requirements of managing the logistics of a traveling exhibition.

This chapter explores some of the fundamental requirements for managing a traveling exhibition program. *On the Road Again: Development and Managing Traveling Exhibitions*, by Rebecca Buck and Jean Allman Gilmore,[1] is a comprehensive publication, complete with sample agreements and forms, checklists, and case studies.

9.1 WHY CREATE A TRAVELING EXHIBITION PROGRAM?

Not all museums have a traveling exhibition business model or wherewithal like the Victoria and Albert Museum or the American Museum of Natural History. So, institutions should carefully consider the reasons for and the impact of developing a touring exhibition program: it's expensive and time consuming.

So why do it?

- **Audience development**: As the museum's content travels around the world, more diverse audiences are exposed to the institution's brand, collections, and research. This will drive audiences to the museum's digital resources and encourage tourist visits to the physical museum.
- **Direct revenue**: Many museum leaders and boards believe that touring exhibitions will generate revenue for the institution. Unless large rental fees can be charged or they can attract sponsorship, it is more likely that, at a minimum, museums may recoup their development costs and capital expenditures.
- **Reputation/branding**: A touring exhibition program may be created to develop and enhance a museum's reputation as a world-class research institution; as a leader in audience engagement and creativity; as an expression of its outreach mandate; or as an industry thought leader in museum best practice. Building the museum's reputation can result in other significant benefits such as the cultivation of donors; access to public funding to support museum functions such as a collection's digitization program associated with a temporary exhibition; greater public awareness; the creation of strategic museum partnerships for future collaborations; and collateral products such as publications, catalogs, and boutique products for sale. These by-products can have more significant impact on the institution than fees collected from the rent.
- **Access to collections**: Museums that have large archival and 3D collections languishing safely in storage will develop a traveling exhibition program to showcase its holdings and make its collections as accessible as possible.
- **Anniversaries/special events**: A traveling exhibition is a great opportunity to celebrate a museum's anniversary and special events; a recent acquisition; a donor-funded prospect; or regional and national milestones. These are more opportunistic activities that, while not a regular occurrence, need to be planned out in advance to ensure that funds and resources are strategically addressed and made available at the right time.

9.2 STRATEGIZE FOR SUCCESS

If your organization has decided to get into the traveling exhibition business, develop a strategy and plan for execution that is articulated in museum policy. That strategy should answer the following questions:

What is the Purpose?

Establish a clear purpose for your program that may be one or a combination of the reasons identified in above. The statement of purpose ensures clear communication with your board, stakeholders, and audience. These values will help you develop the rest of your strategy. For example, if your purpose is about reputation rather than revenue, then rental fees will be lower to ensure that more museums can take your show rather than the few who can afford it.

What is your target market?

A good strategy includes an assessment of your potential museum market and the competition you may face. Will you travel your exhibitions nationally, internationally, or both? What types of museums and sizes of temporary galleries will you target? Will you only travel your exhibitions to museums that have the most stringent environmental controls? Will you travel exhibitions to non-museum venues such as libraries and cultural centers? Consider the following when addressing the potential market for host institutions:

- **Affordability**: Price is a big factor in whether museums, especially small and medium sized institutions, can take a show. Remember that host institutions are not just responsible for the rental fee. Insurance, shipping, marketing, program development, design, and other costs may be a factor in whether your target museums can take a show.

- **Size**: Will your program target museums with small, medium, or large temporary gallery sizes? A majority of museums in Canada, the United States, and Europe have small temporary exhibition spaces ranging from 1,500 square feet to 5,000 square feet (150 sq m to 500 sq m). In China, the museum boom has resulted in very large museums with large temporary exhibition spaces. In the Global South only national level museums have temporary exhibition galleries in excess of 10,000 square feet (1,000 sq m) let alone galleries with stringent environment controls. Many of the top exhibition providers create exhibitions for spaces 8,000 square feet to 20,000 square feet (800 sq m to 2,000 sq m) because those institutions can often afford higher fees and associated costs.

- **Competition**: The traveling exhibition market is quite competitive especially for museums with large exhibition spaces and operating budgets that can afford them. Success can be achieved through careful consideration of the market. Find out which museums are being underserved and create product they can afford. For the more competitive segments—great content, superb design, and partnerships—will make a difference.

How will the program be funded and organized?

Establish early in your strategy the means to fund the design and development costs for exhibitions. A successful program will require a combination of funding sources including a dedicated operational budget, rental revenue, and fundraising. Your funding model must address how your institution defines feasibility. Do touring exhibitions have to be 100 percent funded by the revenue they bring in or will the museum absorb some or all those costs? There are different business and organizational models museums might explore.

From a funding perspective:

1. Sole production: when the museum takes full responsibility for production, cost, and tour.
2. Co-produced: a formal arrangement between two or more museums to share costs, product, and tour logistics. This model often results in a closed tour in which only the participating museums will host the exhibition at their venue.
3. Co-organized: a collaboration between two or more museums, but one organization is the technical producer. This museum takes on a majority of the financial and logistical burden but has the right to the generated revenues once the exhibition tours beyond the original partners. This includes exclusive rights to publications, retail product, and licensing.
4. Export/sale of product: A portion of the exhibition including images, text, video, and media (anything that is not an artifact, specimen, or work of art) is sold or licensed to other museums.

From an organizational perspective:

1. **Embedded operation**: Existing staff within the museum's organization are additionally tasked to create and operate traveling exhibitions in addition to their regular exhibition development tasks. In such cases, it is not always easy to assess the cost and resource requirement of a particular traveling exhibition (except for defined capital expenditures) as those duties are intertwined with the day-to-day, unless outsourced to consultants.
2. **Commercially driven separate division**: Staff and resources are independent from other exhibition, marketing, and programming departments. The traveling exhibition department is distinct and often commercially motivated. It creates its own product (some of the exhibitions might not ever go on display at the museum but are produced for travel only) with the sole purpose of generating revenue and covering all its own costs including staff salaries, outsourced resources, and expenses. These models often include other revenue generating activities including consulting services, product sales, etc.
3. **Hybrid model**: A combination of 1 and 2, which allows for more flexibility and sharing of resources and expertise within the museum. Generating revenue is still a priority but not always. Staff report up to the same supervisor to ensure integration, but some staff salaries may be covered directly by traveling exhibition revenues, while others are embedded as part of the overall operation.

What partnerships, if any, are needed?

Your strategy should include criteria for partnership development. While partners may not be required for every exhibition created, it may be ideal to cultivate sector relationships for several reasons:

- To share the cost of development especially for large blockbuster type shows.
- Access rare collections and research. All partners provide collections and absorb the costs of conservation and preparation.

- Share knowledge and expertise. For example, a show may require disparate requirements for art, science, and archaeology for which each partner has expertise. One partner may have touring management experience and staff to handle logistics. Another may have expertise in multimedia development while the other has a strong design department. Each partner will bring those curatorial and operational resources to best serve the project.
- Built-in access to venues and network. All partners will take the show in their turn and as it generates buzz and success may generate interest from potential venues or with other museums that each partner has relationships with.
- Create new relationships with institutions that may lead to other types of collaborations.

9.3 STAFF AND PROFESSIONAL RESOURCES

Managing one touring exhibition, let alone a program of several that travel, is time-sensitive and specialized work. For museums that irregularly travel one or two shows, the task of touring the exhibition may fall to a registrar, exhibition manager/officer, or a subcontractor. However, museums with a robust traveling/touring exhibition program may have dedicated teams of professionals to market, develop, and manage them.

Here are the core roles whether in-house or outsourced:

- A **tour manager** is a dedicated staff or outsourced position ultimately responsible for the successful tour of an exhibition. This individual manages the schedule, loan agreements, shipping and logistics, and overall coordination with host venues and suppliers. The tour manager creates the business case for each exhibition tour, coordinates its feasibility, and manages any partnerships and supplier relationships.
- The tour manager may be supported by a dedicated **project manager** for robust traveling exhibition programs as logistics management of multiple shows on the road at any given time can be complex.
- **Registrars** document and track all incoming and outgoing loans of collections. Many collections management software packages incorporate features to track objects on tour. However, if this software is unavailable a simple database or excel document should be developed to track objects, condition reports, valuations, insurance requirements, borrower information, shipping information, crate lists, etc.
- The **sales and marketing** team sells the exhibitions to other institutions. These teams prepare printed and online materials, attend conferences, and make direct sales appeals to target institutions in desirable markets. The key sales tool is the **offer package** or **prospectus**, which describes all the salient aspects of the exhibition: show synopsis, size, price, lists of objects, and associated collateral such as educational programs, retail products, and catalogs. Another key tool is a **contact relationship management** system, or CRM. A database of contacts organized by market, museums type, and other relevant data ensures that the sales representative/tour manager is able to maintain a strong relationship with their "customer."
- **Conservators** prepare collections for travel and display. This may include specialized mounts that travel with the specimens and artifacts (although museum preparators may also be responsible for creating mounts). Conservators also repair any damage to collections.

- **Couriers** are registrars, curators, or conservators who accompany the exhibition in transit to ensure the safety of collections. Couriers supervise the packing and unpacking of collections for condition reporting and may also mount some of the more valuable objects.

- Museum **technicians** with expertise in exhibition and multimedia installation may travel with the show as a team or as an individual to oversee a host venue's installation crew.

- Museum **preparators/object handlers** with experience in packing and shipping individual loans or whole exhibitions can be invaluable to the maintenance of a museum's traveling exhibition program. Museums with aggressive traveling exhibition programs will have larger groups of preparators/technicians on staff or a series of dedicated contract specialists whom they can engage in a more cost effective, project by project manner. Several books by the distinguished Canadian conservator Nathan Stolow on this subject (one of which is cited in the bibliography) are useful guides to the safe packing of works of art and artifacts for travel.

Other professionals involved in traveling exhibitions are the expert art shipping companies that can handle all aspects of crating and shipping as well as customs clearance if contracted to do so.

9.4 LOAN AGREEMENTS

The loan agreement is a contract between the borrower and the organizer, stipulating the responsibilities of both parties. Often the loan agreement is the second step in the contractual relationship, the first being a letter of intent or a letter of agreement in which a potential host for the exhibition indicates that it is entering into negotiations for the show in good faith. Such a letter might trigger a deposit, a partial nonrefundable payment of the rental fee. This is because the tour manager will hold a spot in the tour schedule while negotiations are taking place, preventing another museum from taking that time period on the itinerary.

Managing and negotiating the loan agreement is one of the chief tasks of the "tour manager" or registrar as conditions set out in the agreement need to be enforced while the exhibition is on loan. If an exhibition includes works of art and artifacts borrowed from a number of institutions, there may be several loan agreements, each with their own particular requirements and conditions. This may require the organizer to pass on to the participating borrowers the conditions and liabilities that the organizer agreed to in loan agreements. Sometimes the borrower may have to sign separate loan agreements with each of the museums lending objects for the exhibition.

The organizing museum should create a standard contract, reviewed by a lawyer, that will form the basis of negotiation with an intended borrower. All loan agreements have the following categories:

- Agreement to borrow
- Description of the exhibition and its contents
- Participation fees, related costs, and payment schedule (includes provision for insurance and shipping costs that may be prorated across all participants or charged per event)
- Clearly stipulated exclusions so that potential hosts know exactly what is included and what is not

- Security requirements and other special conditions
- Facility conditions required (i.e., environment controls, lighting, disaster plan, provision of facility report, etc.)
- Insurance policy or indemnity, immunity from seizure if applicable
- Crating and shipping arrangements
- Customs and clearance obligations
- Exhibition display restrictions which may include the approval of any design and interpretative additions/adjustments by the lender
- Installation/deinstallation and handling
- Condition reports and damage reporting
- Couriers (requirements, fees, expenses, timing)
- Publicity/marketing (conditions for marketing and promotion with the provision of approved photography, titling, and crediting the lender); the lender may provide additional marketing support under a separate agreement and for an additional fee
- Retail and licensing (catalog, product line, profit share, restrictions); this may be provisioned under a separate agreement
- Copyright and permissions
- Sponsorship and funding (restrictions, requirements)
- Acknowledgments
- Breach of contract/termination provisions
- Notices
- Governing law

Other clauses and appendices may be added, and some requirements will change depending on jurisdiction and the type of traveling exhibition. Appendices to the loan agreement usually include all checklists such as crates, objects and their values, environmental guidelines, custom clearances (if required), and packing and installation instructions.

9.5 DESIGNING AND PREPARING AN EXHIBITION FOR TRAVEL

Although the exhibition will follow the same process for development (planning, design, and implementation as described in this manual), traveling exhibitions have some particular requirements and needs that are different from a permanent exhibition. Budgets need to consider the additional costs of building crates, initial packing, conservation, registration, marketing, and travel expenses. Along with expenses related to the design and development of the exhibition, expenses will continue to be incurred by the staff managing the tour. Some costs like those related to conservators who must travel with the exhibition (couriers) will be offset by participation fees, shared costs, or direct expense reimbursement. If you are planning to be in the traveling exhibition business, then part of your planning process has to be about thinking ahead and anticipating every possible situation that might arise.

While some traveling exhibitions may include only artifacts on loan, which then require the borrower to design and build each showing of the exhibition around them, some traveling shows include some or all the exhibitry as well. Keep the following in mind:

- Make it modular and simple: Types of furniture, equipment, and graphics should be repeatable. This makes them easy to build and replace if parts are broken. The components need to be simple. Complex designs that might make sense in a permanent collection gallery are difficult to take apart and travel over several years. In fact, plan your traveling exhibition to make use of the host institutions furniture, temporary walls, and technology. Not only does this reduce your upfront development costs, but it also reduces the size of the exhibition for shipping, and ultimately the amount of materials that will need to be disposed of at the end of the tour—try and keep waste to a minimum.

- Make it easy to put together, take apart, and pack: The exhibition has to be designed as a kit of parts. Each exhibit cannot have its own crate, as this would make it expensive to move and ship. *Designing an exhibition that is expected to travel is completely different from designing an exhibition that will not.*

- Make it durable: Materials and finishes will take a beating on the road. Often designers will balk at the aesthetics of these materials, but they are not the ones who will constantly have to pay for repairs as a result of wear and tear.

- Make it compact and easier to ship: Furniture or components of the exhibition need to be efficiently packed in order to make the shipping of the exhibition feasible. If this is not done efficiently, a bulky exhibition that is more expensive to ship will be undesirable to other museums. Design items to fit compactly in crates and remember to size the crates to the different types of trucks. The more trucks needed the more expensive it is to ship. Museums may choose not to rent a show that has a reasonable fee because of shipping costs or because the crates won't fit in their freight elevators and will cost a fortune to store off-site.

- Consider collections: The more valuable and fragile collections, the more care required in building adequate mounts and crates. Collections will affect shipping and insurance costs as well as the ability for some venues to adequately display. Consider replicas where appropriate.

- Adapt power: if lighting and media components are traveling with the exhibition, it should include adapters for international destinations with different voltages.

- Prepare for gaps in the tour schedule: If a host institution drops out or a museum cannot be found to fill one of the spots on the tour schedule, adequate storage will be required especially if there are sensitive artifacts traveling with the show. Also, storage may be required for museums who have a stable of traveling exhibitions. These shows will need to be temporarily stored at any given time.

- Plan for disposal and dispersal: Decide whether the exhibition will go into long-term storage or if all non-collection components will be destroyed or recycled. In addition, objects that have been borrowed from other museums to create the tour will need to be returned if they do not belong to the lender. These costs need to be built into the fee, shared costs, or expenses the lender chooses to absorb.

Building quality crates that will protect the museum's objects in transit is paramount to mitigating risk. The first step is to determine which objects need crates and the best ways to pack them. For example, several paintings can be packed in the same crate, but a particularly fragile piece

Figure 9.1. Preparators open a traveling artifact case at the Royal Ontario Museum, Toronto, Canada.
WITH PERMISSION OF THE ROYAL ONTARIO MUSEUM © ROM

of sculpture may require its own crate. Crates need to be sturdy, waterproof, and built for travel. The packing of works of art, artifacts, and specimens for shipment is a specialized trade in itself. Paintings, for instance, may be shipped upright in padded slots, or laid flat in large "cradles" custom-built for them. Crate interiors must be padded and lined, and all packing materials must be tested for low acid content.

Art handlers and companies specializing in crate construction should be hired to do this work as these firms are usually aware of current standards and materials. Objects traveling short distances may be soft packed, but museum quality crates are highly recommended. The expenditure is worth it in the long run. All crates should be numbered, labeled, and measured. Packing instructions with illustrations and photographs should be included in the overall **installation manual** but should also be inserted inside the crate to ensure that preparators pack the crate in the exact same way, using the same materials that came with the crate. A master checklist of the crates, which will be used by shippers and registrars, should include crate numbers, measurements, and contents.

9.6 MANAGING THE TOUR

Tour managers must diligently manage all the logistics associated with scheduling, transporting, and mounting traveling exhibitions that may be on three-month, six-month, or nine-month rotations. A tour schedule may be complicated by long distances between venues; a break in the schedule that requires temporary storage in a suitable and climate-conditioned space; and complex requirements that result from the transport of particularly valuable and fragile works of art. These later conditions may include restrictions on air-conditioned truck transport, or the splitting up of a large collection into two or three shipments to avoid the entire collection being lost in case of a disaster. Some venues may be obliged to drop out late in the preparation for the tour, which may require unforeseen expenditures related to storage or a quick sales job to find a last-minute replacement for that slot in the schedule. Damage to crates, collections, or exhibition components may require changes to the tour to address repairs and conservation. The tour manager has to keep all this straight!

Shipping is a logistical process that concerns both the organizer and the borrower. While the organizer manages the shipping process to ensure on-time and safe delivery of the exhibition, the borrower is concerned with the cost. Most exhibitions will travel by truck and should be contracted to a fine arts company experienced in moving works of art. These companies use air ride trucks that are climate controlled and alarmed. Every truck carries two drivers. Sometimes trucks will be escorted by the police or military if the organizer requires additional security. This is especially required in countries where theft and vandalism are a likely threat. International shipping will include air travel, which is more expensive than trucking but unavoidable when exhibitions need to cross oceans or long distances. Shipping by sea is not recommended for artifacts and works of art, as climate-controlled environments cannot be guaranteed and shipping times between venues can double. However, if the exhibition does not include collections, sea travel may be worth considering as it is considerably cheaper than air travel.

Shipping is organized by the tour manager who works with a trusted series of art handlers, shippers, and customs agents. Once the tour schedule is known the tour manager will prorate the exhibition costs among all the participating venues. As such, costs may not be known at the time the loan agreement is being negotiated, although an experienced tour manager will be able to make estimates to help potential borrowers make the decision to rent the show. For exhibitions that are not a part of a tour or are shipped to venues on an ad hoc basis, borrowers need to cover the costs of round-trip shipping or be responsible for the cost of shipping from the last venue to their loading dock.

International shipping will require the services of a **customs broker** because cultural objects or specimens are carefully regulated to ensure there are no contraventions of international acts related to stolen cultural property and endangered species of flora and fauna. Such individuals understand the necessary clearances, have the security credentials to supervise unloading at the airport, and know the right foreign contacts to complete transactions. Customs documents are complex, legal, and opaque. The right agent will help the organizer, or the borrower, prepare the right documentation to keep exhibitions from being unduly held up in customs warehouses. Serious conservation problems as well as delays in the schedule can occur in customs warehouses.

Condition reports are prepared by preparators, conservators, or registrars, usually as soon as a crate is opened or about to be packed. Condition reporting occurs at the beginning and end of each show in order to track any damage or change in condition. Reporters must pay attention to detail, with any observed variation in condition accurately recorded such as "slight discoloration 7.54 mm from the top of the canvas, 3.5 mm from the left edge," for example. Photographs should accompany condition reports, certainly in case of any perceived variation in condition. For exhibitions showing works with higher insurance values, photographs may be required of every work in the exhibition after each unpacking, and before each onward shipment. These reports are cumulative documents, tracing the history of an artifact's condition during the life of a show.

Careful condition reporting ensures that the organizer knows exactly where and when damage occurred either at the venue or during transit. Since insurance requirements are "nail to nail," there is always a borrower and their insurance policy that will take responsibility and cover repairs and losses. If crates are opened and damage is observed, it is imperative for the reporter to immediately notify both the organizer and the insurer of the loan. If insects or other pests are seen, the crate and its contents must be moved to an isolation chamber which, ideally, is adjacent to the crating/uncrating area.

Simple or low value exhibitions often travel without staff personnel from the lending museum. In such cases, the borrower is responsible for reporting damage and preparing the condition reports. However, exhibitions with large numbers of objects, many of which are precious and valuable—or even one outstanding work of art—require a staff member from the lending institution known as a **courier** to travel with them. Some objects are so valuable that they must never be left unattended—on the road, on the tarmac, or on the loading dock. The courier will be primarily responsible for preparing the condition report and will supervise all handling of the object at the borrowing institution until it is safely installed. A courier may be a conservator, registrar, or preparator.

The courier's travel costs, expenses, and time are almost always paid by the borrower. The tour manager will work with the borrower to schedule the courier's time and agree on class of travel, per diem rates, and quality of accommodation.

Every traveling exhibition must be accompanied by an **installation manual** that describes everything a borrower needs to know about mounting, demounting, and maintaining the exhibition. It will include:

- Name and contact of the tour manager
- Packing instructions: illustrations and photographs
- Installation and deinstallation instructions written and photographed (preferably in the order that they should be installed, including any special equipment that might be needed such as rigging or lifts)
- Crate list (numbered): measurements and contents
- Object list: measurements, photographs, values
- Exhibit list: measurements, photographs, values (of mounts, furniture, cases, or panels)
- Materials and finishes list (to assist with minor repairs such as paint chips)
- Condition reports
- Maintenance guidelines: general cleaning requirements, troubleshooting, and what to do in the case of damage

The manual may include sample design or exhibition layouts envisioned by the designer or from the first venue—often the organizer's own temporary exhibition gallery.

The last task for the tour manager is to arrange to bring the exhibition home and return the objects and works of art to storage, permanent collection display, or other participating museums if loaned objects were used (**final dispersal**). Return transit is usually organized as part of the overall shipping arrangements for the tour and incorporated in the prorated costs paid by the borrowers. In some cases, the museum will need to pay for the final trip home; budgets planned for the exhibition at the very beginning of the process should have accounted for this scenario. At the very least a contingency fund may cover an unscheduled return as a result of some event that requires the cancellation of the tour, such as civil unrest or sudden change in the lending institution's leadership.

If an exhibition includes loan objects from other museums, the organizer may choose to bring all objects home and then disperse or return the objects from the last venue. The latter solution can save time and money but does require the expertise and cooperation of the last venue's staff to assist in the operation. Couriers may again be required to travel with all objects as they return to their home institutions.

Exhibitions with furniture, mounts, panels, multimedia, and cases may be stored in off-site storage for future use in other exhibitions, or if the exhibition was not object-heavy, may be refurbished and sent on the road again. In other cases, the organizer may choose to dispose, recycle, or sell components of the exhibition.

9.7 BORROWERS AND ORGANIZERS

Figure 9.2 provides a brief summary of the responsibilities of organizers and borrowers. While there are exceptions to every rule, this provides a sound understanding of what is expected on both sides.

Organizer	Borrower
• Exhibition packaged and crated • Tour management • Installation manual • Couriers and technicians • Marketing materials • Retail Products and licenses • Loan agreement • Logistics • Customs • Initial condition reports • Check lists (signed by both parties) • Manage incidents • Administer repairs and exhibition upkeep • Final disposal	• Participating fees • Insurance costs • Shipping costs • Courier costs • Security (additional if required) • Installation and de-installation (experienced and qualified team) • Gallery modifications and design • Translations (if required) • Condition reporting • Check lists (signed by both parties) • Repair and conservation costs (as authorized) • Marketing and advertising • Associated programming

Figure 9.2. Summary of responsibilities for borrowers and organizers. LORD CULTURAL RESOURCES

Case Study

NATURAL HISTORY MUSEUM LONDON'S TOURING EXHIBITION PROGRAM, AN INTERVIEW WITH JAN ENGLISH, HEAD OF TOURING EXHIBITIONS

The Natural History Museum (NHM) is a world-class visitor attraction and leading science research centre. The NHM uses its unique collections and expertise to tackle the biggest challenges facing the world today. The museum envisions a future where both people and the planet thrive, and its mission is to create advocates for the planet. One of the longest standing touring programs, NHM has been touring exhibitions globally for more than thirty years. Outside of London, the museum's exhibitions are seen on average by two million people in fifteen countries on four continents with more than forty presentations each year.

Why does the NHM tour exhibitions?

Touring exhibitions at the NHM is an important part of the museum's strategy to expand its global brand and reach the widest possible audience. Touring exhibitions expose international audiences to the museum's collections and scientific research. In addition, touring exhibitions

Figure 9.3. *Treasures of Life* touring exhibition, Natural History Museum, London. NATURAL HISTORY MUSEUM, LONDON/THE YOMIURI SHIMBUN

Traveling Exhibitions

contribute to the museum's soft power, demonstrating the value the NHM brings to the United Kingdom and how it promotes the country's scientific and cultural contributions to the world. Touring exhibitions also generates vital revenue to support the museum's work.

How are touring exhibitions organized at the NHM?

Currently, touring exhibitions are part of NHM's public programs department within the museum's engagement group. The touring exhibition team is a discrete unit that operates somewhat independently and is comprised of ten full-time members and a number of exhibition technicians with expertise in the following areas:

- Sales and marketing
- Project management
- Financial and business management
- Operations and logistics
- Engineering
- Carpentry
- Audiovisual
- Object handling (e.g., conditioning reporting, packing)
- Content development

However, the team is also supported by its colleagues in scientific research, conservation, registration, interpretation, and communications. This ensures an integrated approach to the development of exhibition ideas, access to research and collections, and communication within the engagement group at NHM. Greater cooperation between commercial and noncommercial divisions can help identify topics that appeal more strongly in different markets, to learn from each other, and share relevant best practices in the profession.

Touring exhibitions operates on a three-year planning horizon. This allows enough time to plan and develop new exhibitions while managing the tours of existing products as they travel around the world.

What is NHM's business model?

Touring exhibitions at NHM is regarded as a "commercial endeavor" and self-sustaining unit. All salaries, administrative costs, expenses, and capital expenditures related to the creation of exhibitions must be recouped by the program—from rental fees, publishing, and retail.

Exhibitions for travel are created in two ways:

1. The touring exhibition team plans, designs, and builds exhibitions expressly for the purpose of traveling nationally and internationally. Topics are selected for international and market appeal. Prior to creation, each exhibition is assessed for financial feasibility. An example of this type of exhibition is, *Treasures of the Natural World*.

2. The touring exhibition team also inherits exhibitions, such as *Fantastic Beasts*, created and funded by others in the museum for presentation first in London before launching on global tour. In these cases, the touring team creates a financial plan for its eventual tour, prepares it for travel, and collaborates with interpretive and design colleagues to make any required adjustments to address international markets. *Fantastic Beasts* opened in London in December 2020 and the tour will start in summer 2022.

NHM is flexible in its financial modeling for traveling exhibitions to allow the museum to ensure an exhibition is meeting the strategic goal for brand expansion; to account for potential grants in the cost recovery process; cost sharing with prospective partners; and at times waiving contributions to the museum's bottom line to make exhibitions more accessible in emerging markets.

Who are the museum's partners in touring exhibitions?

NHM primarily focuses on creating exhibitions with its own collections and research as opposed to a participation model that might include partnerships with other select museums. Exhibitions are NHM's product and are driven by the museum's strategy and vision. However, recently the NHM has been exploring non-peer institution or alternative industry partnerships like Warner Brothers for the *Fantastic Beasts* exhibition. Its more about unique selling propositions, market appeal, and alternative funding strategies.

Thoughts on a competitive marketplace for touring exhibitions.

It is super competitive, especially for natural history museums more so than others like art galleries with rare and unique collections, for example a dinosaur verses a Picasso show. Natural history museums have similar collections and research, so being competitive requires constant review of what makes your product unique, how you can adapt to a changing market, and how your product addresses the museum's vision.

What do you think the impact of COVID-19 will have on the business of touring exhibitions?

Museums will need to get people back in the door and exhibitions are critical to driving attendance. COVID-19 will have an impact on touring exhibitions, but mostly by accelerating what was already starting to happen, such as:

- Making exhibitions more relevant to local audiences.
- Flexible and adaptable business models to adapt to changing situations in the market and that are not all commercially dependent.
- Extended runs (at least in the short term) for exhibitions at the same price.
- New and cheaper exhibition products that can change format and size easily, reproduced locally, and rely less heavily on objects.
- More environmentally sustainable (rely on venues to install exhibits, unpack objects, and condition reporting).
- Growing digital offers that can be offered separately or compliment a physical experience and exploring how to make digital exhibitions commercially viable. While they may be cheap to "license out," they can be very expensive to create so funding models need to be studied.

Big blockbusters or shows that have large price tags or complex revenue/ticketing strategies will certainly continue to be attractive in the future as museums look to recover from the pandemic and encourage visitors to return. This being said, we will see changes in the way that exhibitions are toured in terms of new pricing strategies, what travels, how it travels, basically what is core to a successful experience.

Note: Jan English is currently the Collections and Public Engagement Director, American Museum & Gardens, Toulouse.

INTERVIEW: TRAVELING EXHIBITIONS IN A CHANGING WORLD, WITH ANTONIO RODRIGUEZ, CHAIRMAN OF THE BOARD, INTERNATIONAL COMMITTEE FOR EXHIBITION EXCHANGE (ICOM, ICEE)

THE ROLE OF TRAVELING EXHIBITIONS

Traveling or touring exhibitions allow museums to engage audiences with their vision and content beyond their physical walls. Besides revenue generation and reputation, it is an opportunity for museums to understand *all* their potential audiences and not just the ones they interact with daily. Visitors from diverse backgrounds in different parts of the world are immersed in their content.

Traveling exhibitions are of tremendous strategic value to museums.

- They initiate a variety of partnerships with all levels of government, other museums, and the private sector.
- They are a form of cultural diplomacy. Exhibitions travel between countries that are sometimes politically and ideological opposed, creating political, cultural, and social bridges.
- They create educational and learning opportunities for audiences to access new ideas, and for museum professionals to learn from each other.
- They expose museums to new donors and levels of support within their own countries and those of host institutions.

GAPS AND INEQUALITIES IN THE GLOBAL MARKET

The market has been shaped by those museums who can afford to participate in the creation and exchange of touring exhibitions. There is a level of exclusivity in museum-to-museum collaborations that limits participation in some major shows or forms of exchange. Nonprofit organizations like the Smithsonian's SITES program are important equalizers, but there are not enough of them to level the playing field.

Museums in North America (United States and Canada), Western Europe, and some parts of China dominate and skew the marketplace, charging large fees to generate revenue as they seek to place their shows in desirable markets. This has resulted in geographic inequality, especially in parts of the world like South America, Africa, and Southeast Asia where opportunities to access and exchange exhibitions are rare due to lack of funding, inadequate facilities, and few resources to coordinate complex logistics associated with loans.

The private sector has tried to help those institutions frozen out of the current market, but this leads to another problem—the saturation of certain topics. For example, the sheer number of dinosaur shows is staggering. This type of saturation hurts creativity and creates a *market-driven* imbalance in exhibition content.

TRAVELING EXHIBITIONS IN A POST-PANDEMIC WORLD

Traveling exhibitions will be transformed in the post-pandemic world. While the future is unpredictable, here are some anticipated outcomes:

1. Exhibitions will incorporate stronger community voices and more co-curated content. This was already starting prepandemic, but lockdowns and social movements like Black Lives Matter have crystallized the need for multidisciplinary and multiperspective exhibitions.

2. The physical and digital experience of touring exhibitions can no longer be considered separately. The pandemic has demonstrated the important role of technology as lockdowns forced many museums to begin growing their digital content and strategies. Both the American Alliance of Museums and International Council of Musuems have shared recent findings that institutions expect and need to provide more access to content online and in other digital formats.

3. Audiences will behave differently, and we must begin anticipating what those changes might be for both the physical and digital incarnations of traveling exhibitions. What are we going to do with/learn from the increased level of global virtual participation in culture? Will there be a backlash when the pandemic is over due to fatigue in use of screens? Are hands-on and touch screen interactives a thing of the past? Evaluation and outreach will be needed to understand what audiences will need.

4. Temporary exhibitions will have stronger social justice messages because of the post-pandemic environment. Audiences will be looking for meaning and guidance after such a traumatic experience. What does it all mean and how can trusted institutions like museums help people navigate the future?

5. Economic and financial pressures will be immense. Institutions will have less money and less staff to create and exchange ideas. This means smaller exhibitions and new forms of collaboration to offset these restrictions.

6. New business models will emerge in the long term as museums recognize they can no longer rely on participation models, old generative income strategies, and logistic-heavy or bureaucratic working practices that include expensive couriers and complex installation processes. Business models that rely on ticket sales to recoup/generate revenue by pushing the high cost of blockbuster type exhibitions to the visitor will not be sustainable.

7. New types of partnerships with government and the private sector will emerge. Such partnerships will focus on technology and sustainability to help reduce the carbon footprint of touring exhibitions (such as software companies, think tanks, and universities). More collaborative associations like the National Museums of Scotland will develop to help create touring exhibitions with less money and less staff. In addition, creative partnerships with the private sector will ensure parity and accessibility in smaller and emerging markets. For example, La Caixa, a Spanish bank, partners will museums around Spain, Brazil, and elsewhere to make art accessible.

As a result, traveling exhibitions will become smaller, more affordable, more sustainable, more agile, more digital, and more accessible with host institutions adding more of their own content to the show, and using their local teams to do more of the work guided by virtual training sessions with lending institutions.

Will the blockbuster survive?

Yes, but in a new form. Blockbusters will remain because they have powerful narratives, likely even more connected to audiences, and the social and environmental issues relevant today. They will be smaller, more accessible, involve lower budgets, and require deeper collaborations and alliances. They will need to be more diverse and more inclusive in order to be successful as host museums become more selective about which exhibitions they select to host.

Final thoughts.

Since 2010, museums have always been impacted by external drivers or "forces of change," which include social (immigration, diversity), economic (access to funding), political (changes in leadership), technological (virtual reality, augmented reality, artificial intelligence), environmental (natural disasters), and ethical levels (questionable sponsors). Over the years, certain drivers have taken precedence over others, often first impacting museum operations negatively, while at the same time presenting new opportunities for positive change. During the pandemic and in the short-term post-pandemic world, these drivers have been and will be impacting the museum all at once. Now is the time to take risks with exhibitions and to finds ways to respond quickly to forces of change.

NOTE

1. Rebecca Buck and Jean Allman Gilmore, *On the Road Again: Development and Managing Traveling Exhibitions* (Washington, DC: American Alliance of Museums, 2003).

PART IV
WHO?

National Archaeological Museum Aruba

Who is the exhibition for and whose story are we telling? These fundamental questions are more important than ever as museums engage more responsibly with underserved communities; address storytelling gaps in their collections in an effort to decolonize privileged collecting legacies; and seek to facilitate Indigenous voices in their exhibitions. In addition, understanding museum audiences and communities, who they are, how they learn, and why the public visits or doesn't visit museums, is essential to the exhibition development process and how museums measure success—qualitatively and quantitatively.

The increasing cost of exhibitions for permanent collection displays (related to technology and increasing visitor demands for a high-quality experience) and temporary or traveling exhibitions (due to rising costs of shipping, and lending fees) mean that there is more pressure than ever to achieve high attendance levels. Attendance revenue, shop and food sales, sponsorship, membership, and most foundation and government grants are directly and indirectly related to visitor numbers.

This section of the manual explores the critical importance of connecting with communities, and how exhibitions will address Diversity, Equality, Accessibility, and Inclusion (DEAI), and the decolonization of Western Museums. The way visitors behave and learn in museums is addressed in-depth to ensure more empathetic interpretive plans and designs. And of course, evaluation methods are described with detailed examples and techniques.

The pressure to perform financially *and* connect more positively with the community, means measuring engagement is vital to making the case for museums as sites of lifelong learning for their publics. As such it is no wonder that visitor analysis and evaluation will continue to significantly contribute to the exhibition development process.

Chapter 10

Exhibitions and Diversity, Equality, Accessibility, and Inclusion

Maria Piacente and Karen Carter

Elisa Shoenberger stated, "Many museums have legacies rooted in colonialism; their collections were from wealthy donors who benefited from empires. For example, Sir Hans Sloane, doctor and collector, funded his enormous collection that would be the foundation of the British Museum with earnings from his wife's slave plantations in Jamaica. Moreover, his collection profited from the reach of the British Empire where collectors and travelers all over the world acquired items for him."[1] Indigenous peoples around the world were thought of as "other," unable to care for histories, and relegated to ethnographic interpretations—ultimately dead cultures to be preserved by dominant cultures.

As museums strategize how to address greater diversity, equality, accessibility, and inclusion into every aspect of their organization, the role of the exhibition and how it is created is critical to any future action plan. What better way for institutions to demonstrate an honest assessment of their past, substantive change, and truth-seeking then through the powerful communication device of the exhibition?

10.1 IMPLICATIONS FOR EXHIBITIONS

So, what are the implications for the exhibition process?

1. **Collections**: Museums need to scrutinize the gaps and biases in their collections and collecting practices so that new exhibitions can tell well supported stories. Strategies must include prioritizing new acquisitions as well as recognizing the importance of *intangible collections* in telling a more complete history as opposed to traditional "objects" collected. Museums also need to understand what they already have in their collections and spend time learning how best to display them—or not—in consultation with Black, Indigenous, people of color (BIPOC) communities to recontextualize and reindigenize them. As permanent exhibition collections are reinstalled, long-term plans must address the redistribution of narratives to bring forward diverse voices and perspectives on history, culture, and art. This may require enlisting local, national, and international knowledge keepers from communities to help staff reinterpret the way the collection has been positioned in the past. Don't be afraid to use your collections as a point of entry for increased collaboration across the exhibition planning process. Don't just think about bringing those voices in for programming after the fact.

2. **Co-curation, sharing authority, and redefining the role of the curator**: In order to make space for alternative, conflicting, and diverse voices, museums will need to add mechanisms into their exhibition development processes that allow for the sharing of authority. This includes working with community cultural leaders, scholars, artists, and other types of external collaborators who are not what might be considered "traditional curators." New partnerships embedded into the exhibition process can build trust, result in new and exciting narratives, and new collections. These efforts will have the added benefit of building new scholarship and expertise within BIPOC communities, creating a new generation of diverse museum professionals. This will also help the current museum team to gain professional knowledge and understanding into communities to help them to come to the collaborative process with greater comfort and openness. The fear of doing or saying something wrong can often be a hinderance to bringing community knowledge keepers to the table. Start small if you must but start. You will create a better cultural ecosystem for the constituencies you are serving.

3. **Formal and regular community consultation**: This must be fostered throughout the planning and design process. It allows for necessary interpretive critiques and challenge of institutional perspectives. This can be accomplished through regular consultation with advisory groups drawn from BIPOC communities (duly compensated), and focused front-end and formative evaluation strategies related to specific exhibitions. Maintaining the relationship requires demonstration that the consultative process has impacted the organizations overall operations.

4. **More cross department and multidisciplinary collaborations**: This type of collaboration has been a growing trend for the past ten years. Diversity, equality, accessibility, and inclusion (DEAI) social movements and awareness will only accelerate the need to engage multiple perspectives and divergent views as well as across cultures, geographies, and histories. This will make the process more complex. Breathe and jump in. Those community relations will help you address this in both direct and indirect ways over time. The domino effect will be worth it.

5. **Timely exhibiting of current issues**: Museums will need to explore how their temporary exhibition programs can be nimbler to respond quickly to the social, gender, and sexuality

issues that concern their audiences in the moment. This may include fast-track processes with community advisory groups and local partners; the redefinition of the temporary versus permanent galleries, and new spaces dedicated to social discourse. Responsiveness requires that museums have established and trusting relationships with communities and collaborators. This may also mean we need to become comfortable with things not being perfect. Sometimes if we just admit we are sharing what we know, and leave room for community ideas, and expertise to be added, we may end up with better results. We may find perfection in the imperfect.

6. **Funding for long-term sustainable engagement**: Mechanisms for engaging with BIPOC and minority communities need to be funded at the institutional level as well as properly allocated in exhibition budgets. This may mean less money for construction, but more resources for ensuring diversity of voice. This may also open other funding opportunities in the long run.

7. **Development schedules**: Exhibition schedules will adjust to reflect the time required to do more upfront consultation, research, and front-end evaluation. As well, consensus building work with advisory committees can lengthen the planning and design phases.

8. **New and changing roles and responsibilities**: The roles of interpretive planners and evaluators will become more pronounced, and curators will become facilitators in addition to generators of content and original research. New roles such as community engagement officers and community knowledge keepers will help museums build the local partnerships and relationships.

In considering the implications of DEAI on museum exhibitions for this section of the manual, there are wonderful examples that demonstrate the potential.

The death of Minnesotan George Floyd on May 25, 2020, at the hands of police sparked protests across the United States and the world. In the weeks and months that followed, people discussed and debated hard questions: What is racism? How can we overcome systemic racism? How can we be antiracist? In the Canadian city of London, five young women called on the community to join them in a peaceful protest at the museum against the systemic racism experience by Black people, Indigenous people, and people of color. The Museum London collected signs carried by the protesters as well as stories and material culture to keep the discussions and debates going as part of its commitment to antiracist practice. The exhibition was created with the participation of community consultants Ghaida Hamdun, Olivia Musico, and Kiera Roberts.

The Tropenmuseum in Amsterdam, Netherlands, is a museum of world cultures with a massive ethnographic collection, a legacy of Dutch imperialism and trading heritage. In 2016, the museum opened a new permanent exhibition entitled *Things That Matter*. Objects from the museum's collection were reinterpreted from multiple perspectives and shared stories around ten different themes. Authority is shared with the people in the Netherlands and beyond as the exhibition explores ten fundamental themes of social issues impacting people today including identity, migration, and conflict.

The Abbe Museum in Bar Harbor, Maine, has made decolonizing practices part of its strategic plan and everyday operation. The 2015 temporary exhibition, *Coming Home*, explores how the material culture of the Wabanaki culture has ended up in museums all over the world, making it impossible for local people to see and experience pieces of the culture and history. Wabanaki

Figure 10.1. Display of protest posters at the *Black Lives Matter, London* exhibition, August 13, 2020 to February 28, 2021, at Museum London, Ontario, Canada. MUSEUM LONDON (LONDON, ONTARIO)

Figure 10.2. Decolonizing the interpretation of ethnographic collections at the Tropenmuseum, Amsterdam, Netherlands. COURTESY OF JAN REINIER VAN DER VLIET/COLLECTION NATIONAAL MUSEUM VAN WERELDCULTUREN

community curators worked with Abbe curatorial staff to select and borrow objects from museums in the northeastern United States including the Peabody Essex Museum, the Boston Children's Museum, and the Peabody Museum of Archaeology and Ethnology at Harvard University. Collaboration and shared decision-making allowed for the sharing of perspectives and ideas that broadened understanding and interpretation.

10.2 REFLECTIONS: THE FULFILLMENT OF OUR PROMISE BY KAREN CARTER

The year 2020 was a challenging time for those of us working globally in the museum and cultural sector. No matter where you are as you are reading this, you will surely have heard about the direct and indirect impacts of the COVID-19 pandemic and the revolutionary Black Lives Matter movement. For me, as the pandemic forced my work to slow down, and I was provided with the opportunity to reflect on what is most important, I found myself reminded of why I chose to work this sector. I believe we have a responsibility to educate our communities with the goal of dismantling notions of the "other" and, in so doing, we may then help make the world a better place.

As I begin a new position as the executive director of the MacLaren Art Centre in Barrie, Ontario, just north of Toronto, I am especially aware of the particular challenges of working in a regional art museum serving communities that are not as diverse as the major city to which it sits adjacent.

I am a child of immigration. I came to Canada as a child and was raised in a Toronto suburb. The people and the formal and informal cultural experiences of this, the seventh largest city in North America, has formed me. Over my twenty-plus years career to date in the culture sector, I can point to many experiences that underscore the value of working on programs, projects, exhibits, and other experiences that have shaped my approach to working in, for, and with museums. One such experience came during my time as the founding executive director of Myseum of Toronto was working on a major public exhibition, *Cosmopolis Toronto: The World in One City*. This project was the brainchild of artist and geography educator Colin Boyd-Shafer. He had photographed a person from every country in the world who made Toronto their home. This project was presented as a public pop-up exhibition across the Toronto Public Library system and in panels on the public transit system. It gave life to the idea of Toronto as one of the most diverse cities in the world with the 195 photos.

As I was getting ready to move to Barrie, I found myself reflecting on *Cosmopolis Toronto* and many other exhibitions and collaborations that brought the voices of diverse communities forward. I had many conversations with friends and colleagues about how I would manage the change of operating in a community-centered museum model in a place that is not as diverse as Toronto. I had to consider the impact on these ideas of reflecting DEAI of BIPOC when you do not have the world in your city. What does this mean for people with varying physical disabilities and/or those managing mental health challenges? Would I feel overwhelmed? Would I be up to the challenge?

The more I thought about the many possibilities for how to present exhibitions and engage with communities, I found myself reflecting on the roots of the museum's promise, to bring the cultures of the world to local people. I became aware of how this really is an idea that has not yet truly been fulfilled. The Great Exhibition of the nineteenth century is my reference for this idea of museums being the place where people who were unable to travel to see and experience the cultures, ideas, places, and objects of the world, could experience them in some way by having them brought to the museum. The Great Exhibition took place in Hyde Park, London, from May to October 1851. It was to be the first in a series of "World's Fairs" that became popular in the nineteenth century. One can only imagine the lens through which those nations' innovations would have been presented and perceived.

We know that most museums today still present the world through an imperialist, colonized lens. Even within the context of the many conversations about the **decolonization** of the museum, the challenge to this perspective often manifests itself in the analysis or acknowledgment of the colonial constructs serving more to reinforce while explaining the views and positions of this structure rather than to deconstruct it. So many of our global institutions were formed with Eurocentric and stereotypical representations of the rest of the world and become repositories of the spoils of war and imperial theft.

The more I reflected on this and my new position, the more I saw the regional museums as an opportunity to finally show how museums can find a pathway toward the fulfillment of their promise. There is a great deal of talk about the need to have more representation from BIPOC, across organizations and institutions. There seems to be a greater desire to have DEAI principles become the key drivers through which museum operations, exhibitions, and programming are filtered. At first glance it may seem that these ideas and challenges are all more necessary and possible in diverse large cities where the need for the population to be reflected in the museum is much clearer. However, the challenge is that we know the big cosmopolitan city is also where the ocean liner-like institutions are parked and they are not easy to move, even when they really desire a change in direction. In Canada we are seeing qualified BIPOC executives being passed over for leadership positions at our major cultural institutions all while these same institutions have been talking for years about equity and the desire to reflect the communities they serve. I firmly believe that the larger the institution the more likely it is that the right arm may not know how to direct the left in order effect change swiftly.

I am happy to come to a smaller community where the yachts, sail boats, and dinghy-sized organizations reside. I think we will be able to experiment and give our colleagues in the larger institutions some of the tool kits they will need to help them slowly move toward healthier work environments.

I don't have all the answers yet, but I believe, based on where we are in our sector, the first thing we all need to do is build trust. If the community you are serving trusts you, they will come with you on the journey, through rough or calm waters. If we go out into the communities around us and begin to have one-on-one and small group conversations, we will start to build and rebuild the trust across the various constituencies where we need to do our best collaborative work. This means donors, volunteers at governance and community partnership levels, corporate and political leaders, artists, activists, academics, and curators.

Once you go out, the next challenge is what and who are you bringing them into. If in this moment your organization does not have within its inner sanctum the people who can help build and care for or steward these relationships, you are not going to be able to reflect the community you are charged with serving. If the communities can see themselves in the organization, it will be easier for you to keep the relations you need for your long-term success. Think of all the various skills it takes for a cultural organization to be successful. You need to use this same skills matrix to map the community needs and then you will begin to have a path for what your organization's inner circle should look like.

If you cultivate these relationships in and outside of the immediate circle, it will make it possible to have staff (full time, part time, and contract), board members, volunteers, (supporting operations, serving on committees or on specific projects) and supporters (members and individual donors, public sector funders, corporations, and foundations) who reflect the community.

For me, this means I need to begin with the historic context that frames the place. It is always interesting to see how research into a community's historic demographic can sometimes be the easiest way to find some of the diverse connections we are seeking to help us understand the present. The MacLaren is situated in Barrie. It is the largest art museum serving the city of Barrie, Simcoe County, and beyond. The region has an estimated population of 465,000 people. Barrie is politically and administratively separate from Simcoe County but is geographically and economically part of the county.

As of 2020, Barrie, Ontario, has a population of just under 150,000. Of the population, 87 percent is White Anglo/European; 7.6 percent is racialized; and 5 percent is Indigenous. The city may not have a large Black population today but the history of Black people in the region is significant, as it was a part of the Underground Railroad and one of the final destinations for African American slaves who escaped to gain freedom. Simcoe County was also the location of Oro Townships, a designated Black settlement for escaped slaves and Black veterans of the War of 1812. The Indigenous communities that reside in the region today are the Beausoleil First Nation and the Mnjikaning First Nation, however there is a long history for the Huron-Wandat peoples in the region that too can open up opportunities for how a museum may go about engaging with Indigenous communities across Ontario and Quebec in more significant ways.

Do you know the past and present history of the communities your organization or institution serves? This historical and present-day context can help you find a road map to help you understand where your communities may be going in the future. If you build the trust across all these pillars, and the organization reflects the communities it is mandated to serve, you will be able to tell local, national, and international stories that connect to all our collective humanity. You will be able to explore the world through the communities' eyes and they will trust you to lead them down the walkways and portals to explore past, present, and future lives. You will be able to use the museum's exhibitions and programs to educate and support dialogue about challenging ideas and issues, and you will begin to chart a path toward making the world a better place, one informal educational experience at a time.

The promise of the museum is to be a safe place for people to learn about the world. We live in a time that when the world is so much smaller than the one the people of the nineteenth century could have ever imaged. We live in a time where a video of a horrific murder on a street in a city in America galvanized a global movement because of how technology can connect us and our ideas in seconds. We have the tools, knowledge, and it seems we finally have the willingness to build and rebuild our museums into the global community-centered places they were always supposed to be.

Case Study

ACTIVATING CHANGE: DEAI, COMMUNITY, AND EVALUATION
AN INTERVIEW WITH CHERYL BLACKMAN, DIRECTOR OF MUSEUMS AND HERITAGE SERVICES FOR THE CITY OF TORONTO, CANADA

In this interview, Cheryl Blackman, shares her experiences guiding DEAI efforts and transforming museum practices through evaluation, community engagement, and collaboration.

You are known for your work leading audience evaluation as well as diversity, equity, access, and inclusion initiatives in museums. How are evaluation and DEAI practices related?

From my perspective, the saying *"what gets measured gets done"* could not be truer. Understanding this is critical, both in evaluation and in DEAI work. One of the biggest challenges we face with DEAI work is the lack of publicly accessible, Canadian, cultural sector data.

When I search for data to understand trends and set baselines, I end up scouring American, Australian, and European data sets. As Canadian arts, culture, and heritage professionals, we must conduct our own research in order to understand where we are, but more importantly, where we *aren't*, and where we have to go.

In 2016, while leading negotiations between the ROM, and the Coalition for the Truth about Africa, I saw first-hand the fallout from inclusion not being embedded in the exhibition development process for the *Into the Heart of Africa* exhibition. For more than thirty years, museum and art professionals have discussed this case study as an example of what not to do. However, this cautionary example has not resulted in a deepening of diversity, equity, inclusion, and accessibility for decision makers. With the impacts of COVID-19 in 2020, and the global focus on social justice resulting from the murder of George Floyd, we must accept and acknowledge that the work we are doing is central to dignity and belonging. We must accept that access to culture is a human right and then behave accordingly.

Working within institutions to center community voices remains challenging work today. What role do you think audience evaluation can play in DEAI work?

No two museums, art galleries, or living history spaces will have the same metrics. Museum practitioners cannot determine their key performance indicators based on the operation of other institutions. Each community, and each community engagement effort is unique. Cultural workers must appreciate the importance of understanding how the values of their audiences align to the values of their spaces. Working with communities is not a cookie cutter approach.

I have been asked, "Can you share your checklist for working with diverse communities?" I should be clear, that there is no checklist. If we take a checklist approach, then we miss the point. It is critical that we establish an approach to community engagement that allows us to share a vision with stakeholders, gain feedback, and then evolve the idea from mine to ours.

How we think about success and achievement is also changing. Much of past museum evaluation has been similar to counting widgets, that is, How many visitors came past the turnstile? Attended the program? None of this tells us about the impact of our work. The central question right now is how we grapple with the current definitions of essential service. How can we demonstrate the impact of our work? How can we tell the stories about the lives that have been changed as a result of exposure to arts, culture, and heritage? Real impact is hard to measure and strengthening the ways that we demonstrate results will be even more important in a pandemic challenged world.

Instead of a searching for a checklist, can you describe approaches a museum practitioner can take that lead to more inclusive projects?

A framework for action includes understanding that consultation is required to do work that genuinely serves our communities. We should not attempt to channel the voices of community in our projects if we have not spoken to and involved these communities. The days of museums being the sole authority are behind us. We must have participation from the communities we are meant to serve. Don't be afraid to fall back on the basics. The five w's (who, what, when, where, and why) are still extremely important conversation starters—so ask questions and do a lot of listening.

You are in the midst of directing the transformation of the City of Toronto's history museums; can you tell us more about your vision and your work related to that transformation?

When I joined the City of Toronto in 2018, I recognized the need to reimagine the ways in which Toronto history museums develop, deliver, and evaluate programming. In December 2020, we launched *Awakenings*, a multiyear program that features a virtual series of art projects by Black, Indigenous, and artists of color exploring untold stories, awakening new perspectives, and inviting the public to join the conversation.

One of the first actions in my first one hundred days was to co-create a new vision, a new mission, and develop a new programming narrative. I should be clear that my simple sentence is no reflection of the complexity of the work or the importance of change management. Along the way, we have had our share of challenges because change is not easy, but the gains have far outweighed any bumps in the road. I accepted the role of director because of my commitment to see change in action. Even during the pandemic, we continued to move forward. In April 2020, we launched two committees, an Inclusion, Diversity, Equity and Accessibility (I.D.E.A.) committee and an Indigenous Circle to ensure that visitor voice is a part of our change story.

The way we manage projects and timelines is changing. In project management, folks are talking about "Agile," another iterative approach to delivering a project. They are also using MoSCoW Prioritization (Must have, Should have, Could have, Will not have) to move the work forward. Traditional waterfall approaches to project management are less of a fit when consulting to advance outcomes.

Museum planning may be detailed, but this does not mean we cannot revise it to include community voices. We cannot do this work ourselves, and we need community if we are to embrace the opportunity of diverse content creation and meaningful storytelling with the communities we serve.

I appreciate the design thinking process because it allows us to respectfully gather in a room to ideate and experiment without fear of failure. Design thinking is a great way to iterate approaches and to fail fast. We have to get comfortable with being uncomfortable because there is no innovation without failure.

Why is it important for museum leaders and workers to get comfortable with being uncomfortable?

You will do the most meaningful work in your life when you are uncomfortable. When you are comfortable you accept things as they are; you end up accepting the status quo. If you are completely comfortable in your work, I would hazard a guess that you are not talking with the people who feel a part of your museum or art gallery.

If you are doing inclusive work in museums, there won't be many days that are exactly the same. Nothing should be too static because the world is not static. Being uncomfortable means mixing it up by seeking new voices and new perspectives. Ask difficult questions of yourself and your work. I see museums as a conduit, as a vehicle for community expression. The museum spaces I supervise do not belong to me; they belong to the community.

I entered the museum field in my thirties, and it has been the best experience of my life. I have been able to find parts of myself that I didn't even know I was missing. I want to share the journey of personal connection and discovery with all of the communities we serve. After sixteen years in museums, I know more about myself as a Black woman, and as a human being than I knew coming in. I want everybody to feel the power of their story—to have this gift that only culture can give.

What actions can museum practitioners take to move toward operating under principles of anti-oppression, anticolonialism, and antiracism. What kinds of learning needs to take place?

I am going to put that question on its head and ask, what actions can't we take?

One of the most fundamental pieces of the DEAI journey is to reframe how we position what we can and cannot do. I think the reality is we can do anything we really want to. Then the greater question is, how do we prioritize inclusion? I have seen the most amazing work come out of one-person, two-person, three-person shops. How can a large institution or organization justify not activating inclusive practices? It seems odd to me and I have never been able to accept that.

In the fall of 2020, I instructed a graduate course at the University of Toronto's Museum Studies program on equity, diversity, access, and inclusion in the GLAM Sector (Galleries, Libraries, Archives and Museums). The final assignment for the class was a podcast project called "No More Excuses." I wanted to bring attention to the reasons we cite for not taking action. Are these real reasons or just excuses? What does your community need? Start there.

In what ways are collaborating with communities a key part of creating more equitable cultural institutions?

Collaborating with communities is central to the kind of change museum professionals say they want to do. This kind of collaboration can sometimes mean longer timelines, but not necessarily. We pulled together the *Awakenings* project in six months, during the COVID-19 pandemic, working with multiple community partners. The notion that community work is slow and will reduce the quality of the project is not true. *Awakenings* demonstrates the power of equity work. The work was driven by Black, Indigenous, and people of color creatives working with the team at Toronto History Museums. We built brand new relationships during the pandemic, leveraging the work of Umbereen Inayet (supervisor, special events, City of Toronto) who is an outstanding professional. This project was realized by a small internal team working with a large team of external community partners and together we created this beautiful, beautiful thing.

This collaborative process is now the model for all Toronto History Museum work moving forward. Museums need their communities more than ever. And communities need museums. Communities need spaces to tell their stories and cultural institutions have these assets. Communities fund museums, don't they have the right to benefit from them? Museums must figure out how to do meaningful work with our communities, otherwise we become the artifact.

NOTE

1. Elisa Shoenberger, *What does it mean to decolonize a museum?* MuseumNext. December 11, 2019, https://www.museumnext.com/article/what-does-it-mean-to-decolonize-a-museum/.

Chapter 11

Curiosity and Motivation

Shiralee Hudson Hill and Barbara Soren

Visitor-centered exhibition planning requires practitioners to consider exhibitions as learning spaces and investigate questions such as: How do audiences learn? What motivates visitors? How can I design relevant and responsive experiences for diverse publics? Understanding the importance of learning and meaning-making as well as community and curiosity is a core part of the planning process. This chapter provides an overview of a selection of learning theories, visitor studies, and approaches for engaging audiences with meaningful experiences as it underscores the importance of knowing "who" you serve in order to create more meaningful and engaging exhibitions.

11.1 CULTIVATING CURIOSITY

The Oxford English Dictionary defines curiosity as "a desire to know or learn about something, a feeling of interest that leads to wanting to inquire and find out more." Museum exhibitions can inspire curiosity, not only among individuals, but also communities, nurturing and supporting civic and civil society. But why is it important for museum staff to understand the nature of curiosity? What role does it play in engaging communities, meaningful visitor experiences, and life-long learning?

As Susie Wilkening explores in her publications *Curiosity: A Primer* and *Curiosity, Empathy, and Social Justice*, curiosity benefits both individuals and communities.[1] Curious people show improved outcomes in academic achievement, employment, income, health, social well-being, and civic engagement. They tend to be more compassionate and empathetic. Curiosity fuels a continuous circuit of learning: inquiry leads to knowledge, knowledge activates empathy, empathy inspires new questions, and so the circuit of learning continues.

Curious people are open-minded, and experts theorize that this open mindset may be central to curiosity's relationship with social justice and inclusion. People committed to lifelong learning are open to new points of view; open to questioning their own beliefs; and open to being uncomfortable or uncertain as part of learning. Curious people engage with social issues and shift perspectives when they encounter new information.

However, not everyone has equal access to curiosity and its benefits. Socioeconomic, emotional, and physical supports foster curious minds and encourage curious pursuits. Likewise, systemic racism, poverty, health constraints, and physical insecurity can hinder a curious mind. Recognizing that curiosity plays an important role in engagement, how can museums help create exhibitions that support their communities' curiosities?

Curiosity is iterative and generative. Museums can provide a platform, both internally and externally, that encourage a constant cycle of thinking, questioning, learning, and changing. As sites of curiosity, community, and learning, museums are uniquely positioned as potential change agents in society. By encouraging curiosity in all aspects of their practice, museum workers encourage moving toward a more equitable and inclusive society.

11.1.1 Different Kinds of Curiosity

Not all curiosity is created equally. In her work, Wilkening describes different kinds of curiosity and how they lead to different kinds of learning. Curiosity can be about answering questions that arise. Museums answer questions all the time. Why do bears hibernate? What is the difference between a rock and a mineral? Where did the artist create that sculpture? Cultural institutions tend to attract the already curious and many visitors experience learning as fun. These visitors want to learn something new as learning is a part of their identity. As such, museum practitioners aim to create exhibition experiences that invite curious audiences to acquire new information. But are they also sparking curiosity and critical thinking that encourage new outlooks and ideas?

To cultivate the kind of inquiry that supports the continuous pursuit of new ideas and fresh perspectives, museum workers must go beyond presenting and answering questions. Museums must strive to open up new questions within visitors, communities, and their staff's own practices.

The Cooper-Hewitt Smithsonian Design Museum's 2017 exhibition *Process Lab: Citizen Design* centered on communities and their questions. Entirely visitor-centered and issues-focused, this hands-on interactive installation encouraged visitors to engage in civic dialogue about local issues through a series of questions and choices. Using interactive cards, visitors identified issues that personally mattered and brainstormed potential interventions using design-thinking approaches. The exhibition's website also features "The Citizen Design tool kit." Created for audiences to take *Citizen Design* into their own communities, it includes free PDFs of interactive printed materials to promote dialogue and creative thinking.

Figures 11.1 & 11.2. *Process Lab: Citizen Design* exhibition at the Cooper-Hewitt Smithsonian Design Museum, New York. PHOTOGRAPH BY S. HUDSON HILL

Figure 11.3. *Process Lab: Citizen Design* exhibition at the Cooper-Hewitt Smithsonian Design Museum, New York. PHOTOGRAPH BY S. HUDSON HILL

11.1.2 Fostering Curiosity in Museum Experiences

Audience research and visitor evaluation is essential to the work of a curious museum. Operating responsive and relevant sites of lifelong learning requires awareness of a museum's publics, and research helps practitioners appreciate and respond to the questions circulating among audiences and communities. A curious museum incorporates ongoing assessment into its practices, not only gathering information about visitor attendance and demographics but also gaining insights into the resonance and relevance of its exhibitions and programs and its public and social impact.

When planning museum experiences for visitors, consider how to create a culture of sustained curiosity by asking questions such as:

- What and how are you learning from your audiences? What questions do they enter with? What questions do they leave with?
- How are you promoting greater cultural understanding?
- How are you promoting empathy and compassion?
- How is the content and design of your exhibition or program expanding world views?
- How is your museum pursuing questions without easy answers?
- How is your exhibition presenting multiple voices and perspectives?
- How is your exhibition relevant to people's everyday lives? To society?
- How are you collaborating with your communities to co-create exhibition content?
- How are you prioritizing historically marginalized and oppressed voices in your exhibitions?

To become agents of social change, museum leaders and their teams must create experiences that inspire the kind of inquiry that propels beyond themselves and their own knowledge and cultivates a sustained pursuit of new questions and understandings. Curious museum leaders also encourage regular questioning of their internal practices, inquiring about effectiveness, relevance to communities, inclusiveness, and societal impact. They create environments in which questions and new perspectives are welcome—from both visitors and staff members.

Because of museums' potential power to open up questions and build understanding among disparate groups, cultural scholars link inquiry to social cohesion and the viability of democratic societies. Democracy depends on thoughtful and empathetic citizens, purports cultural scholar David Carr, and "cultural institutions deepen, inform and encourage—even elevate—their users toward reflection."[2] Within museums, he asserts, publics safely seek revelation, encounter insights that expand how they see the past and the future and think themselves anew. By acknowledging and activating their roles as sites of collective debate and discourse, and forums for discovering questions and multiple perspectives rather than extolling expert answers, museums can fulfil their responsibilities as public leaders and employ their influence or "soft power"—to encourage social justice and enhance the quality of life in their communities.

11.2 LEARNING AND EXHIBITIONS

In order to spark curiosity and create exhibitions that engage visitors, it is helpful for museum professionals to understand how visitors learn in museum settings. There are a variety of terms and models to describe the types of learning visitors experience in museums, but for the purpose of this manual we will focus on the following:

- Formal
- Nonformal
- Informal
- Experiential
- Free-choice

Figure 11.4 highlights key characteristics of each type of learning, advantages and disadvantages of each, and implications for using different ways of talking about visitor learning.

Type of Learning/ Characteristics	Characteristics	Implications for Museums
Formal learning; Structured learning delivered in a systematic intentional way	• Learning is extrinsically motivated • Facilitated, planned and guided by an onsite or online instructor • Usually occurs in a face-to-face setting or through an online learning platform	• needs structure, has deadlines, and there is a definitive goal
Non-formal learning; Structured learning situations, which typically take place naturally and spontaneously	• Learning is intrinsically motivated but still facilitated • Takes place outside formal learning environments but within some kind of organizational framework	• most museums' learning programs and events, including outreach and exhibitions, fall into the non-formal learning category, as they have visitor outcomes and more often than not, participants expect to learn something
Informal learning; A casual encounter or experience that happens by chance or voluntarily, resulting from daily life activities related to work, family, or leisure	• Learning is intrinsically motivated and self-directed, unstructured, often unintended • Occurs outside of a conventional learning setting	• self-directed, asynchronous, and has no real objectives, rather it just happens naturally, and in most cases is not intentional
Experiential learning; The process of learning through experience or doing	• A hands-on approach to learning that moves away from a teacher at the front of the room imparting and transferring knowledge to students	• strives to bring a more participatory way of learning including performance and active engagement
Free-choice learning; Learning that tends to be nonlinear, personally motivated, and involves considerable choice on the part of the learner as to when, where, and what to learn	• Learning that most typically occurs while people visit museums or other cultural institutions, watch television, read a newspaper, talk with friends, attend a play, or surf the Internet	• learning experiences where the learner exercises a large degree of choice and control over the what, when, and why of learning

Figure 11.4. Comparing types of learning across museums.

Generally, museum workers plan for formal learning experiences with programs (such as school and studio programs), and develop structured, nonformal learning experiences when they plan exhibitions and public programs. People who visit museums come for informal and experiential learning experiences and choose to visit as a free-choice learning experience.

- Informal experiences in museums tend to be spontaneous whereas planning for nonformal exhibition and program experiences is quite intense, as described by Marcella Wells, Barbara Adams, and Judith Koke in *Interpretive Planning for Museums: Integrating Visitor Perspectives in Decision Making*.[3]

- The power of experiential learning for Eileen Hooper-Greenhill in *Museums and Education: Purpose, Pedagogy, Performance*[4] is that experience in exhibitions can include performance with actors, enactment, participation, active engagement, or involvement with active participants, and results in "real knowing."

- Falk and Dierking in their various studies, note that free-choice learning related to exhibitions tends to be visitor-centered with choices about how to use learning during leisure time. Museum workers in the twenty-first century need to think more about visitor barriers to free choice (such as economic, societal, and cultural barriers) and how to remove those barriers. Societal barriers include systemic oppression and systemic racism, as well as exhibition environments in which some visitors do not feel welcome or safe.

11.3 UNDERSTANDING AUDIENCE EXPERIENCES, MOTIVATIONS, AND PREFERENCES IN EXHIBITIONS

Recognizing behavior, personality types, learning typologies, and more helps the exhibition planning team create responsive and inclusive exhibitions. Ongoing evaluation and visitor studies create audience profiles that provide invaluable understanding of target audiences as well as audience types that are not engaging with content or even coming to your museum.

This chapter summaries a selection of learning theories, outlines application to exhibition planning, and demonstrates how visitor-centered approaches to exhibition development consider audience motivation, learning style, and appeal. Whatever theory or model is chosen, addressing audience motivations, profiles, and needs are central to the interpretive planning process. By articulating the target audience early in the planning process, it is easier to select stories that will resonate with visitors as well as design techniques that meet the different ways visitors will engage with content. Rich and layered experiences create more opportunities to support visitors' personal meaning-making and to generate curiosity.

11.3.1 Howard Gardner's Multiple Intelligences

Howard Gardner first wrote about Multiple Intelligences in his book *Frames of Mind*.[5] He believes that just as we look different from one another and have different kinds of personalities, we also have different kinds of minds. Gardner has identified nine distinct intelligences that all human beings have to some extent: linguistic, logical-mathematical, musical, spatial, bodily-kinaesthetic, interpersonal, intrapersonal, naturalist, and existential. This framework encourages us to think of museum visitors in new ways, value different ways of understanding artworks and objects, and to connect visitors with exhibition content via multiple modalities.

Intelligence	Enjoys	Learns best by	Potential Exhibits
Visual-Spatial	Looking at pictures, watching movies, drawing, designing and creating	Visualizing, dreaming, working with colors and pictures	Mini-theaters presenting life of artist; painted mural of wooded environment
Linguistic-Verbal	Reading, writing and telling stories	Saying, hearing and seeing words	Feedback station to comment on art of a particular artist; text panel describing the climate of a wooded environment
Logical-Mathematical	Experiments, asking questions, exploring patterns and relationships	Classifying, working with abstract patterns, categorizing	Compare and contrast two works of art; identify patterns of bird habitats
Bodily-Kinesthetic	Moving around, touching and talking	Doing, touching and moving, physical activity, making things	Create a work of art using tools or themes of a particular artist. Touch replicas; team up to compare and learn about evolution
Intrapersonal	Working alone, pursuing their own interests	Self-paced instruction and thoughtful processes	Aesthetic display of works of art with vistas and appropriate seating for reflection; Compare and contrast animal skeletons
Interpersonal	Being with friends, talking to people and being part of a group	Sharing, cooperating, interviewing and comparing	Cooperative art making activity; Role playing activities that require group problem-solving
Musical	Singing and humming, listening to music, playing instruments	Rhythm, melody, music	Audio kiosks with musings/reflections of the artist on his or her work, Match animal sounds to various species
Naturalist	Understanding living things and reading nature, recognizing, and categorizing plants, animals, and other objects in nature	Comparing, categorizing, observing, discussing	Labs that discriminate among living things (plants, animals), citizen science; comparative exhibits
Existential	Tackling the questions of why we live and die	Reflecting, discussing deep questions about the meaning of life	Religious, mystical, or metaphysical objects, minds-on exhibits with open-end questions that allow visitors to reflect on their ideas

Figure 11.5. Gardner's MI theory and exhibition planning.

Gardner's work provides opportunities for:

- Multiple entry points to rich exhibition topics
- Powerful or telling analogies and metaphors to help visitors make appropriate connections and associations while not misleading them, and have experiences that are familiar and personally meaningful
- Multiple ways to represent and convey the core ideas of a topic and approach interpretation using a range of strategies to address preferences for learning

Gardner's work holds value in museum practice and exhibition planning practice because museum practitioners can target a variety of modes of communication to target different types of learners. This allows for exhibitions that use a variety of techniques in addition to traditional didactic displays of objects and texts such as interactive media, immersive environments, and hands-on activities.

In 2020, Gardner used a computer analogy to demonstrate the differences between multiple intelligences and learning styles, explains Kendra Cherry in Verywell Mind,[6] an online resource about people and events that have shaped the modern mental health landscape. Gardner's recent conception of multiple intelligences provides a sense of his evolving way of visualizing how the mind possesses a number of "computers" that act mostly independently of one another and contribute to different mental abilities. In contrast, learning styles relate to an individual's personality and learning preferences. This computer analogy may be useful for exhibition planners to consider.

In his book *A Synthesizing Mind: A Memoir from the Creator of Multiple Intelligences Theory*, Gardner reflects on his *own* mind as a "synthesizing mind" with the ability to survey experiences and data across a wide range of disciplines and perspectives, which may also apply to exhibition visitors who frequently visit museums.[7]

11.3.2 Audience Fragmentation and Psychographic Segmentation

Audience fragmentation and segmentation is another way to identify and categorize visitor motivation that is driven by a person's preferences, personality traits, attitudes, lifestyles, and values. These characteristics may or may not be observable, but by recognizing the multiplicity and complexity of visitor profiles, exhibition planners can target a variety of needs. John Falk describes identity-related motivations that are useful for attracting visitors and marketing in *Identity and the Museum Visitor Experience*. Antoinette Duplessis elaborates on identity motivations.[8] Falk's identity motivations help us understand why audiences visit museums and how we can better communicate and design exhibition experiences that engage visitors' different desires and interests. See figure 11.6 for a description of these identity motivations.

Andrew Pekarik developed the theory of experience preference, or the IPOP model, which evolved from structured observations and interviews with visitors to the Smithsonian Museums in Washington, DC, from 1990 to 2014. Pekarik's work (in collaboration with James P. Schrieber) seeks to better understand visitor experience preferences and identifies four key dimensions of experience.

Identity	Motivation
Explorers (having curiosity, interest in discovering)	Explorers are most common and visit a museum because it interests them and appeals to their curiosity. They highly value learning but are not experts. This is the group most likely to be attracted by a new exhibition and the rare items on display.
Facilitators (satisfying needs and desires of someone a visitor cares about, for example a parent or caregiver)	Facilitators visit museums in order to satisfy the needs and desires of someone they care about rather than just themselves. This group is price conscious and aware of time. They may visit with kids or grandkids, perceive that learning is fun, but when pressed can't say what they learned. Or they may have come for a social visit with another adult (spouse, friend, visiting relative). Their visit is more about hanging out with friends and chatting and only occasionally glancing at the exhibits.
Experience Seekers (wanting to "collect" an experience, checking it off a list as a tourist)	Experience seekers want to see the destination, building or what's iconic on display. They are often tourists and could just be looking for fun things to do on the weekend. They are socially motivated and want to have fun with friends or family.
Professional/ Hobbyists (having strong ties to the content of a museum or one part of a museum)	Professionals and hobbyists represent the smallest category of visitors and are very influential. They could be museum professionals, art and antique collectors, teachers, or artists, and are often the most critical visitors. They come with a goal in mind and are on a mission, such as a teacher who is planning a lesson on a particular artist and comes to the gallery for information.
Rechargers (visiting to reflect or rejuvenate)	Rechargers visit in order to reflect, rejuvenate or just enjoy the wonder of a place. Art museums, botanical gardens, aquariums have lots of these visitors. They see museums as places that afford them the opportunity to avoid the noisiness of the outside world, as respite from the world. They are rarely attracted by special exhibits or blockbusters.
Respectful pilgrims (visiting out of a sense of honoring)	Visitors who go to museums out of a sense of duty or obligation to honor the memory of those represented by an institution or memorial.
Affinity seekers (speaking to a visitor's sense of heritage or personhood)	Individuals who are motivated to visit an ethnic-focused museum because an exhibition speaks to the visitor's sense of heritage.

Figure 11.6. Identity motivations.

The IPOP framework maintains that individuals are drawn to each dimension in varying degrees and usually have a dominant preference among the four:

- **Ideas**: An attraction to concepts, abstractions, linear thought, facts, and reason
- **People**: An attraction to emotion, human connection, affective experience, stories, and social interactions
- **Objects**: An attraction to things, aesthetics, craftsmanship, use, ownership, and visual language
- **Physical**: An attraction to somatic (bodily) sensations, including movement, touch, sound, taste, light, and smell

Pekarik's framework and typology of experience helps planners make decisions around what stories to tell in exhibitions, appreciate visitor differences, and respect different visitor preferences for sharing stories in ways that activate learning and engagement. The model reminds planners to create exhibits in equilibrium. "Four example a display about early commercial flight could contain facts and figures about the first airliners (ideas), compelling accounts from the early adopters daring enough to fly (people), a flight attendant's uniform (objects), and a simulation of the propeller noise and vibrations passengers endured (physical)."[9] It takes away from the experience preferences of the exhibition planning team and helps them base decisions more in the diversity of visitor interests. Pekarik also talks about the "flip" experience. For instance, if a visitor is an *ideas* person and has a really great *physical* experience, the person's learning is even more augmented. A flip experience is going beyond a usual comfort zone and having a fabulous experience or break through in another realm.

NOTES

1. Susie Wilkening, "Curiosity: A Primer," American Alliance of Museums, October 12, 2020, https://www.aam-us.org/2020/10/12/curiosity-a-primer/; Wilkening, *Curiosity, Empathy, and Social Justice: A Long-Form Data Study*, Wilkening Consulting, December 4, 2019, http://www.wilkeningconsulting.com/datamuseum/curiosity-empathy-and-social-justice-a-long-form-data-story.
2. David Carr, *Open Conversations: Public Learning in Libraries and Museums*. Santa Barbara, CA: Libraries Unlimited, 2011.
3. Marcella Wells, Barbara Adams, and Judith Koke, *Interpretive Planning for Museums: Integrating Visitor Perspectives in Decision Making* (Oxfordshire, UK: Routledge, 2013).
4. Eileen Hooper-Greenhill, *Museums and Education: Purpose, Pedagogy, Performance* (Oxfordshire, UK: Routledge, 2007).
5. Howard Gardner, *Frames of Mind: The Theory of Multiple Intelligences* (New York: Basic Books, 1983).
6. https://www.verywellmind.com/howard-gardner-biography-2795511. March 27, 2020.
7. Howard Gardner, *A Synthesizing Mind: A Memoir from the Creator of Multiple Intelligences Theory* (Cambridge, MA: MIT Press, 2020).
8. John Falk, *Identity and the Museum Visitor Experience* (Oxfordshire, UK: Routledge, 2009).
9. Pekarik, Andrew J., James B. Schreiber, Nadine Hanemann, Kelly Richmond, and Barbara Mogel. "IPOP: A Theory of Experience Preference," *Curator: The Museum Journal*, vol. 57, no. 1, (January 2014), 5–27.

Chapter 12

Evaluation

Gail Lord, Duncan Grewcock, Barbara Soren, and Jackie Armstrong

12.1 MEASURING SUCCESS BY GAIL LORD

There are many reasons why there is an increasing demand to measure what museums do, such as:

- Public accountability (after all, there are many stakeholders involved)
- Financial responsibility (the cost of exhibitions is high)
- Learning what works and what doesn't (so as to ensure continuing improvement)

Since the first edition of this manual in 2001, there has been a fundamental shift in how museums are evaluated by stakeholders, supporters, and the public. Museums are evaluated not according to their good intentions but by the *impacts* they achieve and whether those impacts are socially and intellectually useful or not.

Thus, museums understand the importance of knowing who visits and why. This includes surveying their visitors regularly to learn who they are and why they attend, as well as which museum offering attracted their visit on that particular day. With this information, museums can better communicate with their current audiences and expand them; learn how to be relevant to their needs and to the needs of the communities in which they live; and determine how better to serve them in the galleries, programs, restaurants, shops, and online. Evaluating, tracking, and surveying their guests also serves to help museum staff discover who is *not* attending

In reality no evaluation will have meaning or credibility unless it is grounded in the goals and objectives set for the exhibition in the first place as well as the mission of the museum. So, it's the job of museum staff and leadership to set those goals and to determine how they will be evaluated in an objective (not self-serving) process that is embedded in the exhibition development and design process. Therein lies the biggest challenge because most often museum staff and designers are not given the mandate nor the time to work out their goals. Frequently, the key players just cannot agree on the goals: research and curatorial departments have their goals, marketing and education have theirs, and sponsorship has still others. The exhibition can become a series of compromises that have been (partially) hidden by design.

Before exploring the well-known stages of evaluation—front-end, formative, remedial, and summative—let's consider whether there are some specific evaluation criteria that could be considered inherent to professional museum practice.

There are five inherent criteria by which museum exhibitions should be evaluated:

1. **Creation of new knowledge**: Museum exhibitions really are too complex and too expensive to be undertaken unless they create new knowledge. Such "new knowledge" can be the result of research in any number of fields (archaeology, art history, history, sociology, physics, biology . . . the list is endless) and in this interdisciplinary age, it is the very combination of research fields that yields new knowledge. New knowledge can be sparked when the museum juxtaposes works of art, artifacts, specimens, or archival materials rarely seen together. New knowledge can come from the visiting public (through participatory experiences or the community it services, for example stories, content, and design generated by the Indigenous community to tell its story). In the case of "permanent" exhibitions, the input of visitors and the continuing input of experts helps to ensure that the exhibition stays alive and fresh over its ten- to fifteen-year life expectancy.

2. **Transformative experiences**: The museum exhibition is not a book on a wall. The museum experience involves reading but is different from reading a book or a blog because it is kinesthetic, occurring in space as well as time. This temporal-spatial quality leads to surprise and discovery of new attitudes, new values, and new ideas. Given the human wish to reinforce old ideas, the unique temporal-spatial experience of an exhibition places preexisting ideas in a new context. The challenge for the interpretive planner and designer is to create an effective "mise-en-scène" for the communication of new knowledge. It's a special challenge that differs fundamentally from theater or movies where the audience is seated for a defined period of time and does not physically move. Barbara Soren explores the meaning and potential outcomes of "transformational experiences" through, for instance, the reframing of oneself in relation to an object, expanding vocabulary to describe a museum experience, and/or leaving with a vivid impression or memory that will last beyond a museum visit.[1]

3. **Self-directed experiences**: Visitors may choose to wander, to use an audio guide, a human guide, or their mobile phone to navigate an exhibition. Alternatively, they may visit online. Museum exhibitions are "free-choice learning environments" as John Falk and Lynn Dierking have so incisively theorized in their work over the years. Museum exhibitions are not like courses of study delivered in classrooms or on video or other media. This is a key

differentiator of the museum exhibition and an important reason why we bother to create these extraordinary spaces that we call galleries. In creating successful exhibitions, we must challenge ourselves to adapt and present content to the many different ways visitors may wish to experience it.

4. **Engagement with the full diversity of visitors**: Museums are institutions for the public benefit and their doors are open (at more or less cost) to everyone. An exhibition needs to be meaningful to scholars, students, collectors, escapists, tourists, first-time visitors, diligent autodidacts, leisure seekers, families, and people of varying cognitive and physical abilities. It needs to be intelligible and enjoyable to people with very different cultural backgrounds or religious beliefs, especially in the many countries where recent immigrants are a significant part of the population. There is a well-worn cliché, "You can't be all things to all people," which is actually *not* true of museums. Museums need to engage with the full diversity of the public; and to their credit museums are frequently using research methodologies to help them do so. Some exhibitions may be more focused on the scholar, others on the first-time visitor, but a successful exhibition should engage the broadest spectrum possible, albeit in different ways and to different degrees.

5. **Transparency as to the sources of the viewpoint of the exhibition**: Museums are spaces of *representation*. This means exhibitions are places in which objects and ideas are presented in a way that is fundamentally different from how they were originally used, or found, or created, for the purpose of expressing ideas about them. The idea could be "look, these are beautiful" or something much more complex such as the origin of the universe. Behind the idea is the viewpoint of an individual curator, a school of thought, a research institute, or the wisdom of the originating community; often these viewpoints may be at odds, particularly but not only in ethnographic exhibitions. As a medium of representation, museum exhibitions are ill-suited to the voice of omniscient authority, which until recently was the dominant museum voice. Exhibitions should reveal the sources of their viewpoint and encourage critical thinking by presenting a multiplicity of voices and perspectives. In this case success is measured against the revelation of the museum's sources, encouraged by critical thinking, and by engaging with communities to represent a multitude of voices and perspectives.

The next section of this chapter explores the specific considerations and tools that museum exhibition-makers in the twenty-first century use to measure the success of their work.

12.2 BEFORE, DURING, AND AFTER: FRONT-END, FORMATIVE, REMEDIAL, AND SUMMATIVE EVALUATION: BY DUNCAN GREWCOCK

The ultimate power of understanding a museum exhibition lies with the visitor. As a consequence of this, exhibitions that have not fully understood and acted upon the fundamental contribution made by the user to the process of communication risk qualitative failure. Much has been written on how visitors learn in museums; evaluation is a process through which *museums* can learn.

A commitment to exhibition evaluation does not represent the surrender or compromise of the professional and intellectual capital held by museums and their staff. Evaluation simply recognizes the museum-audience dynamic and facilitates the successful sharing and communication of knowledge and understanding between visitors and museum. Successful exhibition evaluation thus *increases* the intellectual capital of the museum and improves its ability to achieve institution-wide goals and objectives.

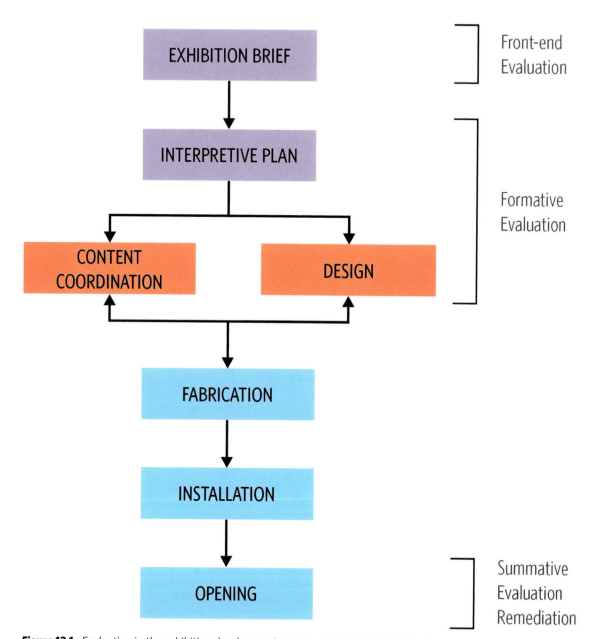

Figure 12.1. Evaluation in the exhibition development process. LORD CULTURAL RESOURCES

At least some members of the exhibition planning team need to have familiarized themselves with the growing body of literature and research on museum exhibitions, evaluation, and theories of learning. This research will often provide the team with important first principles and a conceptual framework within which to conduct the whole program of evaluation. Every stage of the exhibition planning process can be informed by secondary research, and new evaluation should always be informed by a museum's previous evaluation and audience research programs.

Evaluation as generally applied to museum exhibitions is divided into four distinct but interrelated stages. Although terminology may vary, the four most generally accepted stages of exhibition evaluation are front-end, formative, remedial, and summative evaluation. Each stage is defined by its position in the exhibition planning process (figure 12.1), and the specific content and focus of the evaluation. It is useful to begin with a brief definition of each stage before describing their use and value before, during, and after the exhibition development process.

1. **Front-end evaluation**: Arguably the most important stage, front-end evaluation is implemented at the earlier stages of exhibition development, and as such can have a major impact on the concept, content, and direction of the entire exhibition. Front-end evaluation includes the definition of an exhibition's goals and identification of the intended audience. Successful front-end work will provide the next stage of evaluation with a head start in developing a "best-fit" between the exhibition concept and content and will lay the groundwork for successful communication.

2. **Formative evaluation**: After the initial exhibition concept has been agreed—including the goals and interpretive plan—formative evaluation develops the detailed content and tests the proposed methods and modes of communication. Individual exhibition components may be tested at this stage through mock-ups or prototypes to generate specific information of use to designers and to interpretive planners, and text writers for gallery names, labels, and multimedia. An entire installation may be evaluated to determine whether the constituent exhibits interact successfully. Both design and implementation phases of an exhibition are therefore informed by formative evaluation, which may require testing and retesting in order to overcome barriers to the successful communication of the exhibition's content.

3. **Remedial evaluation**: Remedial visitor evaluation is conducted after the installation of an exhibition, when all of the exhibit displays are placed on the exhibition floor. Remedial evaluation can look at, for example, circulation, sight lines that capture attention, and visual competition among objects. As described by Stephen Bitgood, a leading visitor researcher and educational psychologist, remedial evaluation can be used in two ways: to improve the impact of a newly developed exhibition and/or to renovate an exhibition that has been open for some time.[2]

4. **Summative evaluation**: The final stage of evaluation addresses the actual exhibition and actual visitors since it takes place after the exhibition has opened. Many museums decide to conduct summative evaluation during a "soft opening" when the exhibition is complete but not fully open to the public. Invited groups and individuals are invited to test the exhibition when there is still time to make some changes. Summative evaluation measures the success of the earlier stages of evaluation and concludes the evaluation process. Summative evaluations should inform the development phase of forthcoming exhibitions, thus contributing to future front-end studies in an on-going cycle of exhibition evaluation. What worked? What didn't? How can we improve?

12.2.1 Before Exhibition Development: Front-end Evaluation

At the outset of the exhibition development process, there should be a clear statement of why and for whom the exhibition is being planned. Front-end evaluation proceeds to ask: What do the people in the intended audience now understand about the subject or theme of the proposed exhibition? How can their prior knowledge—or their lack of knowledge—be understood and accommodated within the exhibition? Front-end evaluation can also explore what people actually want to see and do in a museum. Are there topics that have particular appeal in the community? If so, what are they and why do intended audiences want to see exhibitions about them?

Clear aims and objectives are crucial for effectively directing the planning process and the later stages of evaluation whereby the exhibition's success can be assessed meaningfully against specific criteria. For example, it is important to determine at the outset whether the exhibition is intended to broaden the museum's audience, or to appeal to specific groups of current visitors. Front-end evaluation should identify the *target audience* for the exhibition. Target audiences should be defined not only with reference to the aims and objectives of the exhibition, but also with regard to the museum's overall role and responsibility within the wider community.

The definition of a target audience for exhibition planning purposes need not be a specific demographic portrait as understood in the world of marketing. However, it is always important to identify at least a notional "visitor" to increase the likelihood of successful communication. Exhibitions are, for the most part, a mass media experience. Therefore, audiences for exhibitions tend to be conceived as a broad and diverse public, from children and families through to specialists and nonspecialists. However, individual exhibitions or their components may be intended for specific groups: a children's gallery or a family learning area, for example. Indeed, it may be more effective to consider both "general audiences" and "specific audiences" for any given exhibition.

Members of the exhibition planning team, "evaluators," assigned to this task need to develop as rich and deep an understanding of target groups as possible within the context of museum visiting and other leisure and learning choices. No one will visit an exhibition unless they can be attracted through the doors of the museum in the first place. This kind of information is not only useful in itself for the museum but can also provide key "requirements" of a visit that the exhibition can satisfy. Key areas to investigate include:

- Visit motivation
- Visitor expectations
- Visitor perceptions
- The physical environment and its use
- Barriers to visiting

The focus of these questions will be dependent on the overall aim of the exhibition and its intended impact, although previous visitor research at the host museum is usually extremely useful. At this stage, an explicit statement of objectives and target audiences will enable later stages in the evaluation process to be directed to relevant areas of enquiry.

Another important criterion to determine at the outset in front-end evaluation is whether or not the exhibition has explicit *objectives for visitor experiences*, and if so, what they are. Like the selection of target audiences, evaluating visitor experiences or engagement is a far broader issue than the exhibition alone, but must be fully analyzed in relation to the institution's mission and mandate. For the purposes of exhibition evaluation, objectives for museum experiencing should not be vague statements of intent. At the same time, it is important to remember that museum experiences are primarily *affective*, not cognitive. A mounting level of research and opinion suggest that the museum exhibition is not particularly effective at communicating complex information or the transfer of knowledge. Rather like television programs (another example of mass media), exhibitions appear to be excellent at generating enthusiasm, challenging long-held opinions, affecting attitudes, arousing interest, raising awareness of specific issues, or generating deep—often long-held—emotional responses. In a paper presented at a seminar entitled "Musing on Learning" at the Australian Museum in Sydney in April 1999,[3] Lynda Kelly summarized research on learning and concluded that museum learning:

- Is the process of applying prior knowledge to new experiences
- Proceeds primarily from prior knowledge and secondarily from newly presented materials
- Is a complex series of interactions and feedback loops
- Involves remembering, and therefore memory
- Is intimately connected to feelings and emotions
- Is long term—a continuous process of reconstructing experience

Therefore, objectives of an exhibition need to accommodate such ideas on what is actually thought to constitute visitor experiencing in museums. These will subsequently be important objectives to evaluate summatively.

In projecting objectives museums often assume a level of knowledge on the part of their audiences. It is not unusual for most museum visitors to have little direct knowledge of specialist disciplines or specific concepts and ideas. An initial assumption on the level of existing knowledge could be wide of the mark, and consequently limit the visitor's appreciation of an exhibition's subject or key message. This is a common problem with history and science exhibitions, where museum curators may assume a more general familiarity with the basic parameters of the subject than is actually to be encountered among the museum's public.

Of course, this can be a problem the other way, resulting in exhibitions that patronize their audiences by "dumbing down" their subjects. Exhibition planners must remember that all visitors bring with them the richness and diversity of their own life experiences and life knowledge and networks of associations and connections with the wider world. Common assumptions or misconceptions about the exhibition's subject matter need also to be considered: the exhibition may confirm, revise, or deny them, but it should not ignore them.

In learning from potential museum visitors, front-end exhibition evaluation should therefore aim to:

- Provide an understanding of visitors' range of knowledge and understanding on a particular subject
- Identify the questions visitors want answered in relation to this subject
- Inform approaches to the "layering" of information for different audiences, inform interpretive techniques through which interpretive planners and designers may tap into visitors' potentially powerful and deep reservoirs of personal and shared experience
- Possibly modify an exhibition's overall objectives on the basis of these findings

Evaluation

Front-end evaluation can also address the exhibition's proposed modes of visitor apprehension or intended presentation styles. At this early stage in the exhibition planning process, it is useful to gauge visitor response to different approaches to display and interpretation, giving designers and interpretive planners a head start when developing components for the next stage of evaluation.

By considering, and possibly reconsidering, exhibition objectives, target audiences, objectives for visitors, and preferred modes of apprehension, front-end evaluation may change the direction of an exhibition, reshape the planners' preconceived aims, and resolve disagreements within the planning team.

12.2.2 During Exhibition Development: Formative Evaluation

The exhibition planning team will now begin to develop a more detailed exhibition or interpretive plan in which the content is worked up and various media for its interpretation and communication are considered and developed. Formative evaluation addresses issues that fall into three broad areas:

1. Content and storytelling
2. Display and interpretative techniques
3. Physical and social environment

Informed by front-end evaluation, in response to feedback from the potential audience and in view of the overall aims and objectives of the exhibition, the planning team is now in a position to develop the detail of the exhibition content. Key decisions concerning the main thematic components of the exhibition may now be made. Formative evaluation of this detailed content is useful for answering such questions as the following:

- How do visitors relate to technical detail and terminology and more complex and subtle concepts?
- Can individual components of the content be understood alone or do they need a more developed context?
- Is the story best told through a linear or modular approach to content organization? Will it be understood better if visitors follow a linear sequence or should they be allowed to choose the sequence of exhibition modules as they prefer?
- Are visitors able to recognize the main messages of the exhibition?

In considering alternative display and interpretative media, formative evaluation proceeds to ask how the content or story may best be communicated within the exhibition setting. A most important issue to resolve within the context of the museum's exhibition policy or strategy is to determine the intended role of the museum's objects—whether these are works of art, artifacts, archival documents, specimens, or apparatus—in communicating the exhibition's content. Exhibition planners are charged with interpreting a subject in ways that make it accessible and engaging without creating an unbridgeable distance between the visitor and the museum objects. Here formative evaluation assists the planner to attain a "best-fit" scenario.

Formative evaluation as it relates to display and interpretative media is very much an iterative process. Exhibition components are developed, evaluated, developed, and then reevaluated. At each step of this process, specific information needs to be generated so that designers can use the findings to greatest effect. Formative evaluation can occur during and after interpretive planning and during the early stages of design to test and retest ideas and techniques.

Since museum exhibitions tell stories through both objects and words, language, whether spoken or written, remains fundamentally important within any exhibition. Yet very often the size and length of graphics, labels, and other exhibition text is written, printed, and displayed without testing. Exhibition text and labeling is one of the more straightforward and inexpensive aspects of an exhibition that can be tested with an audience during formative evaluation. Issues such as readability and legibility can be tested and resolved successfully, affecting every aspect of the exhibition, from the use of terminology through the frequency and placement of graphic panels and labels to the length and type size of their text. Even the mode of address to the visitor can be easily tested: Is a declarative sentence better to express this point or would an evocative question be more effective?

It has long been recognized that the physical and social context of a museum visit also has a tremendous influence on the visitor, both in terms of overall enjoyment and visitors' capacity to learn. Exhibition planners during formative evaluation therefore need to explore specific issues with visitors that can impact the layout of an exhibition and its overall conception. Different visiting groups will require different levels of provision. How these groups interact with each other and the displays will need to be considered in order to avoid design problems and increase the comfort and safety felt by the visitor.

Formative evaluation should be considered as an integral part of the exhibition development process, testing all aspects of the exhibition as they are developed, informing the planners and designers, and often testing the proposed changes in response to its findings. As long as time and budget allow, formative evaluation can continue to improve the end result.

12.2.3 After Installation of an Exhibition: Remedial Evaluation

Remedial evaluation takes place once an exhibition is open to the visiting public. It is helpful in troubleshooting problems and informs museum staff and designers about improvements that can be made to maximize the visitor experience. Remedial evaluation is useful for addressing problems that could not be foreseen during the development of the exhibition, such as lighting, crowd flow, and signage issues. This type of evaluation targets potential problems within and between exhibit displays in order to improve all aspects of an installed exhibition. Physical problems within an exhibition will often become apparent early on. They may be problems of circulation and visitor flow, or heavy use of individual exhibit components such as hands-on experiences, or the more complex audio-visual experiences.

Those exhibition components that break down early are likely to be most heavily used and can provide evaluators with implicit information on visitors' preferences in the exhibition. Through remedial evaluation, developers are able to seek feedback related to how well the exhibition communicates its intended messages. They can produce the best possible exhibition within the limits of what is possible. Evaluation following installation can provide insight into visitor engagement and to what extent the exhibition and interpretive materials communicate effectively.

The primary aims of this type of evaluation include:

- Check that the program "works" in a practical sense
- Determine what maintenance/resources are needed
- Improve the short- or long-term effectiveness of the exhibition for visitors
- Provide some early insights into how visitors use the exhibition

Evaluators can use the following methods/techniques to conduct a remedial evaluation:

- Observations of visitors as they are experiencing the exhibition
- Informal feedback from visitors
- Feedback sheets
- Surveys, exit questionnaires, and interviews
- Comments books
- Staff feedback, especially "front-of-house" and floor staff

Remedial evaluation is defined by multiple dimensions: *when* (after exhibition installation), *how* (a test-modify-retest iterative process), *what* (inter-exhibit factors such as competition for attention among exhibits, movement pathways, as well as effectiveness of communication), and *why* (to improve the overall functioning of the exhibition rather than individual components).

12.2.4 After Exhibition Development: Summative Evaluation

Rigorous front-end, formative, and remedial evaluation enables exhibition planners to feel confident that they have done all they can to make an exhibition a meaningful and enjoyable experience for visitors. Summative evaluation discovers whether they were successful, uncovers mistakes, and recommends improvements both for this exhibition and for others in the future.

Conducted with actual visitors within the context of the finished exhibition, summative evaluation provides the museum with feedback from its audience and can assess overall impact and success. Summative evaluation needs to be conducted in direct relation to the original aims and objectives of the individual exhibition and the museum itself, so that meaningful information may be generated most broadly to answer such impact-oriented questions as, "What difference has the exhibition made to anybody's life?" or to society, and more modestly whether the museum's objectives established by front-end evaluation and/or interpretive planning at the outset have been achieved.

Summative evaluation asks who is visiting the exhibition and how they are using it. Once the exhibition has opened, the museum now has the actual audience to consult. If the museum has conducted previous visitor research or evaluation, it will be useful to structure the collection of information so that it can be compared with previous studies. Much of this information will also be of use to the marketing department. The following represents a baseline of visitor information to be derived from summative evaluation, as it relates directly to a specific exhibition, and as it should be compared with the museum's more general information about its visitors:

- **Demographics**: Age; gender; ethnicity; place of permanent residence; level of educational attainment; occupation/socioeconomic status; special needs (including languages).
- **Visitor motivation and expectations**: Interests in visiting the museum today/purpose of visit; actual and preferred visiting group; length of visit; sources of awareness; frequency of visitation.
- **Physical use of the exhibition/building**: Entrance used; visitor facilities used; take-up of specific interpretative material (audio guides, guided tours, etc.); length of visit.
- **Quality of the exhibition visit**: The most significant indicator of performance and value within the museum, to be evaluated in relation to the exhibition objectives.
- **Achieved objectives**: To determine whether the core message and objectives for exhibition as defined by interpretive planners have been communicated to visitors. Did they get it?

In undertaking summative evaluation of the quality of an exhibition visit, museum professionals need to remember that the exhibition is primarily a venue for affective experiencing. Evaluators need to consider therefore on which criteria an exhibition should be evaluated in order that results have the most meaning and relevance. A test for retention of data or learning may be of little value, whereas a finding that interest in a previously neglected subject has been aroused may be of fundamental significance.

A variety of stakeholders including scholars, private and public funders, government, and sponsors are increasingly interested in more accurately demonstrating and recording the *true* value of museums and the experiences that they offer. However, this requires the development of new and relevant measures of value not wholly reliant on statistics and other classic indicators of performance. As long as the exhibition remains the most visible means by which a museum makes the connection between audiences and content, summative evaluation of finished exhibitions can make an important contribution to this wider debate.

Nor is summative evaluation of one show the end of exhibition evaluation. Like museum visitors, museum staff will continue to learn through applying the knowledge and experience generated through evaluation to the next exhibition. Exhibition evaluation can provide essential information for the management and direction of the whole museum, and as such needs to be considered a necessary part of any new exhibition development, particularly major long-term installations.

Exhibition evaluation does not promise or guarantee a perfect exhibition experience—whatever that may be. Exhibitions are unlikely ever to become a medium that can offer every single visitor what they are looking for, every time. But evaluation of exhibitions does offer the museum a far better chance of successfully delivering a meaningful and enjoyable experience to their audiences.

12.3 QUALITATIVE AND QUANTITATIVE AUDIENCE RESEARCH
BY BARBARA SOREN AND JACKIE ARMSTRONG

How can exhibition planners find out about the visitors who attend an exhibition and the nature of their experiences? Some of the questions that exhibition planners need to ask are identified in figure 12.2.

Audience research related to exhibitions is an umbrella term for visitor studies, evaluation, assessment, and research. Qualitative measures answer some questions about visitor experiences

Motivation	- What are people's motivations for visiting?
- Was the exhibition the main reason for a visit to the museum or cultural heritage organization?
- Where did individuals hear or see the exhibition advertised?
- What was the main influence on their decision to visit?
- If they did see/hear/read about the exhibition, what perceptions and/or expectations did they have about what the experience would be like? (e.g., did the museum clearly communicate about the exhibition, was there a specific aspect of the messaging that caught their attention)?
Demographics	- What groups are visiting (e.g., genders, age categories, members/non-members, race, cultural affiliations, special interest groups, families with children)?
- Whom do they come with (e.g., visitors on their own, couples, friends, extended family, colleagues)?
- Where have they come from (e.g., are they local, national, international)?
- What access needs might visitors have? (e.g., people with low vision or no vision, hearing loss, mobility concerns, sensory processing issues and more)
Visitor experience	- How long do people stay in the exhibition?
- What areas of the exhibition has the greatest 'dwell time' (i.e., where visitors spend extended periods of time)? Which areas do people pass through quickly?
- What do individuals look at and/or read? Do they use audio?
- What do visitors interact with or engage in (e.g. hands-on interactives, taking photographs or selfies, mentioning their visit on social media, audio/video elements)?
- How do visitors move through an exhibition? How does the design of the exhibition affect visitors' movement through the space? How many visitors are using seating, and is more seating needed?
- Are there moments of pause and/or reflection?
- Do they talk with any staff in the exhibition (gallery guides, docents, security officers)?
- Are there any related programs for the exhibition that visitors engage with?
Visitor outcomes	- Is a visitor's experience meaningful? Do visitors connect to aspects of their own lives in the exhibition, and/or of the world around them?
- Are visitors aware of the main ideas conveyed through the exhibition?
- How do individuals feel about the content of the exhibition? What sparks their curiosity?
- What will visitors take away from their experience? What will they tell others about their experience? What will they remember about the exhibition?
- How does the exhibition make visitors feel (their mood, the atmosphere created)?
- Do visitors feel inspired by the exhibition in any way?
Attendance	- How many people have attended over the duration of an exhibition?
- What was the average attendance in the exhibition per day?
- Were there any peak days and/or particularly slow days, and why (e.g., weather, community events, holidays, school holidays, tourist season)?
- How many are first-time visitors vs. return visitors?

Figure 12.2. Asking the right questions (evaluation matrix). LORD CULTURAL RESOURCES

in an exhibition; quantitative measures answer others. A combination of the two approaches, that is a multiple method or mixed methods approach, answers most of the questions:

- **Qualitative** methods are useful for collecting information about behaviors and feelings (observed in real time or through photographs or videos), words (spoken or written), and social media (what can be gleaned from social media through analytics and what is shared in comments). These methods provide depth in that it is possible to study selected issues in detail with a smaller number of people and situations. Qualitative methods also can be helpful for enriching statistical data. It is possible to code and quantify qualitative data, which deepens the impact of findings, understanding and interpreting interactions, and looking at visitor experiences more holistically. Qualitative data adds texture to quantitative methods, bringing narratives and visitor experiences to life in ways that help others better understand them.

- **Quantitative** methods collect numerical data and highlight statistical patterns or trends. These methods provide breadth in that they require the use of a standardized approach and predetermined response categories, measuring the reactions of many individuals to a limited set of questions. Quantitative methods can test hypotheses, make predictions, and look at cause and effect through studying specific variables.

Numbers tend to be straightforward; words provide detail and nuance. Each way of collecting, interpreting, and reporting data has strengths and weaknesses. Together they can create a dynamic picture of visitor experience and findings that are more readily digested.

12.3.1 Qualitative and Quantitative Approaches to Audience Research

Qualitative data offer detailed description, and often take the form of dialogue, conversation, or narratives. Reporting uses details that vividly describe the context of visitors' experiences with direct quotations from observations, interviews, activities, and written questionnaires.

Methods commonly used in qualitative approaches are:

- Firsthand, intensive, long-term participant observation in a setting (i.e., as a participant and/or as an observer in the setting)
- Semi-structured interviews using open-ended questions
- Focused observations in a specific location and for a set time
- Visitor journeys, which combine observation and interviews
- Photographic, audio, or video materials that capture visitor experience
- User testing
- Focus groups
- Community and advocacy dialogues
- Participatory approaches (e.g., card sorts; comment or message boards; a photo booth; voting activities using stickers or dropping a color-coded slip of paper, button, or object into a container; concept or personal meaning maps; reflective journal stems or questions that consist of more than one part, such as "Before this program, I . . . , Now that the program is over, I . . . , Looking ahead, I . . . ;" crowd-sourcing or soliciting contributions from a large group of people or an online community)

These methods are particularly useful for hearing people's stories about their experiences in an exhibition, a shift in perspectives, and new insights. Qualitative approaches to audience research can provide information about:

- What motivates individuals to come to a particular museum and exhibition?
- What interests them or sparks curiosity?
- When people learn something new or unexpected?
- What types of connections do they make or associations do they have?
- How do visitors construct or make meaning?
- What do they find unclear or lacking?
- What they find memorable?

During a study, ongoing analysis of visitor behaviors and comments on-site or online gradually paint a picture of the nature of visitors' experiences. One of the challenges in this type of audience research is finding topics, themes, and patterns in the rich amount of information gathered (e.g., behaviors, attitudes, opinions, values, beliefs, and learning preferences) and deciding how much of individuals' responses to include in reporting to give a sense of visitors' experiences in an exhibition. Another challenge is sharing what the overall response to an exhibition is, and without ignoring individual responses that may fall outside the general feedback. It is important to use balance and open inquiry when looking at data to present the full picture.

Quantitative data facilitate comparisons because all program participants respond to the same questions (or variables) within predetermined categories. Numbers and statistics report quantitative information, most often in tables and charts (e.g., scores, ratings, ranks, or frequencies).

Key factors in quantitative studies are:

- Behaviors that a design team can expect in an exhibition
- Control of variables
- Analysis involving descriptive statistics (e.g., frequency and measures of central tendency, such as mean, mode, median, variability)

The next two sections highlight the uses of more qualitative and more quantitative methods for audience research. Included is the method used, a description of the method, and examples from audience research projects cited in print and online international publications, as well as from professional experiences as researchers and evaluators.

Qualitative Approaches	Quantitative Approaches
• Qualitative data (conversation, narratives) • Naturalistic inquiry methods • Case studies of individuals	• Quantitative data (visitor numbers, statistics) • Experimental designs • Experimental treatment and control groups
• Inductive analysis of visitors	• Deductive hypothesis testing about visitors
• Subjective perspective • Close to the visitor experience or embedded as a participant-observer	• Objective perspective • Aloof from the visitor experience
• Purposeful or random sampling of relevant visitors	• Random sampling of visitors
• Understanding of the overall visitor experience, along with a focus on uniqueness and diversity of experiences	• Standardized, uniform procedures
• Emergent, flexible design of audience research that is responsive to a visitor's experience	• Fixed, controlled design of audience research
• Content analysis related to themes and patterns	• Statistical analysis
• Meaning about audiences extrapolated from evaluation or research	• Generalizations about audiences made from evaluation or research

Figure 12.3. Comparing qualitative and quantitative approaches. LORD CULTURAL RESOURCES

12.3.2 More Qualitative Methods

The following are examples of more qualitative approaches to researching or evaluating visitor experiences in exhibitions.

12.3.2.1 Front-End and Formative Studies

METHOD: PROJECTIVE TECHNIQUES

Description

- Invite individuals to project into ideas the exhibition design team is developing.
- May be participants in a focus group, questionnaire, interview, or survey (i.e., a method of gathering information from a sample of people, traditionally with the intention of generalizing the results to a larger population).

Use for Audience Research

- Exploring people's awareness, knowledge of, and interest in a particular topic using an iterative evaluation process with periods of data collection and analysis, each followed by revisions to interpretation strategies (e.g., develop, test, and refine an innovative program that engages adult visitors in a deeper understanding of how children learn).
- Understanding barriers for visitors and communities who may not typically visit exhibitions in the museum.
- Offering diverse interpretive tools and strategies with awareness of individual preferences for experiencing objects, learning styles, and needs (e.g., didactic materials, text panels, labels, scaffolded experiences progressively providing stronger understanding, catalogs, tactile opportunities, audio/video/photographic elements, interactive media).
- Testing of exhibition titles and marketing images to determine which are most appealing to audiences, and for a sense of messages conveyed.
- Becoming more aware of how visitors want content delivered, whom they want to hear from, and how they might want to participate and/or engage with content.

METHOD: FOCUS GROUPS

Description

- A group representative of target markets and/or stakeholders, led by a facilitator or moderator, focusing on key issues or questions in a structured or open discussion.
- May use prototypes of exhibits and/or objects.
- May be recorded with participant consent.
- May be a catalyst for communication among the observers of the focus group.

Use for Audience Research

- Helping an exhibition design team consider elements they should develop (e.g., for a science fiction (SF) exhibition asking target markets about their SF awareness and preferences, or ideas for the exhibition and complementary programs).
- Exploring perceptions of existing displays and changes for a new exhibition (e.g., orientation, welcoming environment, clear language, layered information, displays relevant to visitors' lives).
- Determining adolescents' self-identified needs and expectations for a visit to an exhibition.
- Using behavioral indicators for family learning to develop exhibit enhancements aimed at achieving family learning goals.
- Receiving feedback from specific audiences such as caregivers, partners, or individuals with Alzheimer's and/or other forms of dementia after participating in an art-making program (e.g., conduct one focus group with caregivers and one with individuals who have Alzheimer's to find out what attracted people to the art-making program, previous experiences, what they enjoyed about the program, how the program affected them, and thoughts on improving the program).

12.3.2.2 Summative Visitor Studies

METHOD: CONTENT ANALYSIS

Description (Analysis of)

- Exhibition planning documents and records of planning meetings to determine goals and objectives.
- Visitor comments and requests for information to examine outcomes for visitors.
- Visitor behaviors in an exhibition using technologies for data visualization (e.g., Tagxedo or Wordle using word clouds, Padlet, or an online post-it board, and Pixton to create comics and storyboards).
- Visitor drawings, photographs, or messages that individuals share with open-ended prompts.
- Staff and exhibition developers' reflective responses before and after a particular exhibition.
- Online surveys using SurveyMonkey, Qualtrics (creates dynamic online surveys), Fluid Surveys (for creating surveys, forms, and questionnaires), iForm Builder (a universal, cloud-based mobile data collection platform), or TrackNTime (tablet software designed for tracking and timing research).
- Social media sites related to an exhibition using metrics (e.g., Google Analytics).
- Participation in programs using Zoom (e.g., professional development for volunteer Gallery Guides and Infoguides).

Use for Audience Research

- At a living history site: Observing staff meetings, volunteer training sessions, Christmas decoration of the heritage house, and several special weekend and evening programs to find out about the history behind objects, ideas selected, and decisions made about how to present objects, intentions for visitor experiencing and learning, and interpretive strategies developed.
- At a science center: Analyzing visitor comment cards to look at visitors' new insights into the nature of science and sociocultural influences on visitor understanding.
- At an art museum: Tracking visitors through an exhibition and seeing which images, phrases, and types of messages appear most frequently in responses to follow-up open-ended interview questions.
- In an online members' survey: Finding out ways in which visitors might "take action" in their community after seeing an exhibition about the power of children.
- On an exhibition's Facebook site: Looking at how many "likes" and "shares" there are; on the exhibition's Twitter site, determining the number of new followers, retweets, and replies; on the exhibition's Pinterest site, counting new followers, repins, and "likes"; on the exhibition's Instagram site, the number of posts, followers, and following.

METHOD: WRITTEN QUESTIONNAIRES, STRUCTURED AND SEMI-STRUCTURED INTERVIEWS, SURVEYS, AND FOCUS GROUPS

Description

- Open-ended questions asked in a systematic way, so it is possible to report on visitors' responses directly.

- May be recorded with participant consent.

- Use objects from the exhibition and/or photographs taken by visitors to discuss responses to an exhibition.

- Conduct exit interviews as visitors leave an exhibition, at a particular location within an exhibition, or after some time has passed since a visit.

Use for Audience Research

- Finding out how, when, and why people visit an exhibition and the effectiveness of information and interpretive materials provided for visitors.

- Exploring how visitors respond to the use of humor in an exhibition (e.g., whether or not visitors find the use of humor to be appropriate in the context of the exhibit, whether or not the humor was understandable to individuals, whether the humor had a perceived positive effect on their visit, and whether the humor changed visitor attitudes about the topic).

METHOD: IN-GALLERY OBSERVATIONS

Description

- Impressions of visitors' experiences in exhibitions, with descriptions recorded by the observer(s).

- Use of a behavioral tracking form or checklist to record movement around an exhibition, reading of interpretive materials, interactions, and length of time at objects and at specific elements in the exhibition.

Use for Audience Research

- Better understanding of the context for an individual's comments during interviews and providing a sense of decisions a range of visitors are making about where to go and what they are interested in seeing in the exhibition.

- Using an observation protocol that includes:
  - Visitor behavior (e.g., initial route decisions, hesitancy; use of a museum map, plan, or guidebook; who is accompanying the visitor if with a group; conversational patterns)
  - Label/captions/wall texts behavior (e.g., reading of wall text and length of time spent reading; number of objects in a gallery compared with number of objects stopped at; length of time reading traditional or tombstone labels, extended labels, and viewing objects; photographing of text with cell phones)

METHOD: IN-GALLERY INTERVIEWS

Description

- Conversational interviews in which an interviewer encourages a visitor to talk freely around key issues or questions.
- May involve an individual or group.
- May be specific to interpretive strategies, art works or objects, and/or programming.

Use for Audience Research

- Finding out about a visitor's conceptions of specific issues.
- Testing the effects of different visitor agendas on visitor learning.

METHOD: SELF-REPORTS, AUDIO/VIDEOTAPES, PARTICIPATORY

Description

- Make recordings of experiences and responses to objects or displays (e.g., in writing, on audiotape or videotape, or on a mobile device).
- Use of reflective journals, personal writing and/or drawing on topics of interest, concept mapping around a given topic or theme, self-tracking or documenting a visit, or photographing areas of interest or confusion.
- Integration of more activity-based forms of data collection into an exhibition.

Use for Audience Research

- Studying the letters and pictures returned after children visited with school groups to compare how children experience an exhibition compared to adults.
- Inviting visitors to take a photo using an instant camera of what most captures their interest in a particular exhibition and using that image as a point of discussion.
- Using "play-testing," in which a selected group of users (random or invited) play unfinished versions or variations of a game to test its "playability," clarity of instructions, design, fulfillment of goals such as looking more closely at works of art, and the fun factor. Usually, those involved in the creation of a game are the first to play-test, and later on in the process outside participants (e.g., museum visitors) might receive invitations to play-test (facilitated or not). "Play-testing" is possible with both analogue and digital games (e.g., a Museum of Modern Art and Institute of Play collaboration on a game called Everyone's a Critic).

12.3.2.3 Longer Term Impact Studies

METHOD: CASE STUDIES

Description

- Focused, intensive inquiry about one or more individuals related to an exhibition, activity, or program experience.

- May be across groups (cross-sectional) or related to one individual over time (longitudinal).
- May be immediately following an experience or after some time has elapsed to determine the longer-term impact of an exhibition experience.

Use for Audience Research

- Probing visitors' memories of their experiences at time intervals after their experience in an exhibition, through telephone interviews.
- Asking about recollections of exhibition experiences (e.g., a field trip from school; visits to a region's outdoor cultural attractions; an online experience browsing an exhibition website or responding to the exhibition's blog, Facebook, Twitter, or Pinterest site).

12.3.3 More Quantitative Methods

The following are examples of more quantitative approaches to researching or evaluating visitor experiences in exhibitions.

12.3.3.1 Front-End Visitor Studies

METHOD: PROJECTIVE TECHNIQUES

Description

- Invite visitors to project into ideas the exhibition design team is developing.
- There are no "correct" answers; frequency of responses is important in analysis.
- They may be part of a focus group, questionnaire, interview, or survey.

Use for Audience Research

- Having focus group(s) with target market individuals or groups react to elements an exhibition design team is considering or elements the team should develop.
- Conducting structured interviews that invite participants to describe an object or exhibit component and predict what would happen as they manipulate objects.

12.3.3.2 Formative Visitor Studies

METHOD: PERFORMANCE TESTS

Description

- Creation or simulation of a realistic situation that elicits specific behavior, abilities, and/or interests.

Use for Audience Research

- Testing of specific skills, strategies, and application of prior knowledge or understanding of exhibition components.

METHOD: Q-SORTS (I.E., SORTING ITEMS RELATIVE TO ONE ANOTHER ALONG A DIMENSION SUCH AS "AGREE"/"DISAGREE")

Description

- Typically include observations in the form of a checklist or rating scale.
- Create ranked categories of values, needs, and preferences.

Use for Audience Research

- Exploring preferences, priorities, and attitudes about prototypes or exhibition elements.

METHOD: USER TESTING

Description

- Work 1:1 with users as they browse an exhibition's website or an online exhibition.

Use for Audience Research

- Having users think aloud as they make decisions about navigating the exhibition's website or online exhibition and interact with sections of the site, with one researcher guiding the user through the interview questions and another recording (often in writing and on audiotape with consent from the user).

12.3.3.3 Summative Visitor Studies

METHOD: BEHAVIORAL ANALYSIS AND INVENTORY RELATED TO IN-GALLERY OBSERVATIONS

Description

- Define, observe, and code specific behaviors in the exhibition's entrance or exit, galleries or halls, and hands-on areas, during tours or programs.
- Examine specific skills or strategies, application of prior knowledge, personality traits, social interactions, and kinds and frequencies of behaviors.

Use for Audience Research

- Tracking studies of visitors' decisions about paths and stops through an exhibition and number of objects stopped at compared to number of objects in the space.
- Recording time in exhibition, and time reading text panels, labels, or captions.
- Noting use of brochures, leaflets, guides, plans, or activity cards.
- Observing use of audio guides and apps.
- Documenting interactions with docents, gallery guides, educators, hosts, or facilitators.

METHOD: WRITTEN QUESTIONNAIRES, STRUCTURED INTERVIEWS, AND SURVEYS

Description

- A series of close-ended questions or fixed-response items with predetermined categories (e.g., questions with rating scales, yes/no/not-sure options, multiple choice), or open-ended questions that will result in one or more "scores" related to visitors' responses.

Use for Audience Research

- Gathering quantifiable information about motivation for a visit, wayfinding throughout the exhibition, use of interpretive materials, and interest levels.
- Testing knowledge gain and curiosity arousal, recording general visitor behaviors and demographics, comparing responses by age, gender, language groups, and race, and assessing visitor satisfaction.

METHOD: CONTENT ANALYSIS

Description

- Examine visitor statistics or records; classify and statistically analyze content of visitor responses.
- Use Google Analytics to gather metrics for an exhibition's website, social media site, or an app.

Use for Audience Research

- Comparing visitor market segments and assessing whether the exhibition is reaching its audience targets.
- Collecting admission counts and visitor demographics.
- Analyzing visitor comment cards or books, looking for patterns in responses.
- Finding out about devices used to access content related to the exhibition, general geographic locations of users, new verses returning users, content that is getting the most "hits," and how long people are spending on specific content.

METHOD: EXPERIMENTAL OR QUASI-EXPERIMENTAL DESIGN STUDIES WITH RANDOM SAMPLES AND CONTROL GROUPS

Description

- Performance of visitors analyzed in relation to topics, ideas, or content exhibited, controlling for variables and using statistical analysis.

Use for Audience Research

- Studying a random sample of visitors to an exhibition by examining responses in exit interviews, pre- and postvisit questionnaires, and written comment cards. Variables could be leisure habits, frequency of visits to the museum, and other museums locally and internationally, why individuals visited, how long the visit lasted, what visitors think about components, and knowledge expressed about topics.

- Investigating the effectiveness of project components in a focused school field trip designed to enhance the use of an exhibition as an educational resource for students of the district's public schools (e.g., pre- and post-test of basic knowledge of target concepts, and rates of target behaviors for students and teachers).

12.3.4 Multiple Perspectives on the Visitor Experience

Most often a combination of qualitative and quantitative strategies provides multiple perspectives and the most in-depth understanding of the visitor experience in an exhibition. Together, qualitative and quantitative data can help make visitor voices heard and can help inform decision-making about exhibitions within the museum. Quantifiable information (e.g., about motivation for a visit, wayfinding, preferences for interpretive materials, and satisfaction levels) can serve as a context for more in-depth descriptive data. Evaluators working with more ethnographic or naturalistic approaches have considered "triangulation techniques" as an important way to control investigator bias and establish validity for findings. Types of **triangulation strategies** include data, investigator, and methodological strategies.

12.3.4.1 Data Triangulation

Data triangulation techniques include collection of data over a prolonged period of time and under different circumstances. In an exhibition, this may include collecting data at different times of the day/evening, week, month, or year. Analysis of the same situation may be from the point of view of the casual visitor, a tour, or a school program. The experiences of different casual visitors can be the focus of audience research, such as specific age groups, visitor groups, genders, cultural affiliations, and access needs.

For example, for an audience research component of an art exhibition visitor audit, data collected could include:

- Observing visitors during approximately fifty hours, over ten days, in meeting areas and rooms throughout the exhibition.
- Observing and interviewing visitors in as many different areas of the exhibition as possible (e.g., in front of works of art, in interactive areas, in A-V rooms, or in seating areas).
- Collecting visitor comments in writing, on email, posted on social media, or told to staff at the information desk.
- Profiling specific visitors representative of the different identified market segments to show the range of experiences for individuals and groups who visited the exhibition during the week of observation and interviews, including:
  - First-time visitors, infrequent visitors (one or two times a year)
  - Frequent and repeat visitors (three or more visits a year)
  - All age groups including families with young children, visitors eighteen to twenty-nine years and over fifty-five years
  - Residents and tourists

Any available historical documents related to exhibition development, design, and programs, and information about mandates and philosophy for collecting and public education are useful to collect (e.g., original proposals, background information, or design copy on file for objects in the exhibition). Past audience or marketing studies, related studies in the community with similar local and regional demographics, website and social media metrics, and attendance records for similar exhibitions in the museum and related exhibitions in local communities provide information about trends in visitation. Visitor comments written in books, collected in suggestion boxes, or communicated via email and at current programs or special events help to give a sense of visitor experiences.

12.3.4.2 Investigator Triangulation

Investigator triangulation provides multiple perspectives by using several investigators to collect data. The triangulation process can include either a group of outside evaluators/researchers—a combination of "outsiders" and "insiders"—or an in-house team alone. Working groups, stakeholder groups, students, and interns can collaborate in thinking about visitor evaluation and/or collecting data. The variety of individuals involved in the process helps illuminate specific data, creates a better understanding of the visitor experience in a particular exhibition, and empowers individuals to make changes that positively impact the visitor experience. An audience research or evaluation team is useful because a group of observers can share insights, continually discuss observations, and together reflect on the data gathered.

12.3.4.3 Methodological Triangulation

In methodological triangulation the audience researcher uses multiple methods to collect information. Ethnographic methods such as in-gallery observations and interviews give in-depth information about the experience of a small group of visitors. Other methods add breadth and provide statistics about, for instance, pathways a large number of visitors take through exhibitions and parts of the collections they choose to see, demographics, reasons for coming, and number of visitors who go to the retail store after time spent in an exhibition.

The following provides a list of multiple methods that have been useful for studying visitor experience in one exhibition:

- Interviewed 90 visitors
- Observed 450 individuals and groups
- Administered a minisurvey to 275 visitors during the same period to provide quantitative information about motivation for a visit, use of interpretive materials, and satisfaction levels, as a context for more in-depth, descriptive data
- Consulted Security and Information Office staff about their observations of visitor experiences
- Invited each visitor to participate in an audit and fill out a background information sheet for basic demographic information
- Conducted three focus groups with thirty regular visitors in different age groups (eighteen to thirty years, thirty-five to fifty-five years, fifty-five years and over) to find out more about how, when, and why people visited the exhibition
- Used SurveyMonkey to survey 250 members online following their visit to the exhibition

Generally, multiple methods that integrate qualitative and quantitative strategies provide a rich palette of the nature of the experience for a sample of individuals and contribute to a more holistic and reliable understanding of the meaning visitors make related to the time they spend visiting an exhibition.

Case Study

UNIVERSITY OF MICHIGAN MUSEUM OF NATURAL HISTORY FRONT-END AND FORMATIVE VISITOR STUDY USING MULTIPLE METHODS

Barbara Soren

From 2014 to 2019, the University of Michigan Museum of Natural History (UMMNH) underwent a major renovation of its permanent and temporary gallery spaces as part of the museum's relocation to the university's new Biological Sciences Building.

As part of the exhibition development process, the development team conducted a front-end evaluation and two formative evaluations to inform the exhibition planning and design process. Both qualitative and quantitative methods were used, and participant profiles were collected to gather demographics across a range of current and potential visitors. Demographic groups included:

- Relationship with the University of Michigan
- Why you would visit or wouldn't visit UMMNH
- Ages of children who might visit with you
- Age

Figure 12.4. The University of Michigan Museum of Natural History, Ann Arbor. COURTESY OF UNIVERSITY OF MICHIGAN MUSEUM OF NATURAL HISTORY/©BRUCE DAMONTE

- Highest level of schooling
- Racial/ethnic background
- Gender

PHASE I: FRONT-END EVALUATION (CONCEPT TESTING)

For the initial front-end evaluation in 2015, we recruited thirty participants for four focus groups who responded to some of the concepts described in the draft interpretive plan for the project. Participants in the focus groups were:

1. Families, represented by adults who visit the museum with young children, including members.
2. Teachers who teach kindergarten to high school.
3. University of Michigan undergraduate and graduate students across disciplines.
4. Independent adults or adults who visit the museum or participate in UMMNH programs alone or with other adults, including members.

Focus group participants responded to the visitor goals and design approach for six exhibits, which were to offer different experiences in the following three galleries:

1. Exploring the Foundations of Life: A giant interactive/immersive cell and an exhibit titled *What Am I Made Of?*
2. Exploring Evolution: Looking at the evolutionary process and our evolutionary heritage.
3. Exploring Michigan: An interdisciplinary, immersive environment and diorama on a large scale focusing on the transition from Michigan lakeshore (with marshes) to dunes to forest, and an interactive field station with minds-on questions and connections to U-M researchers.

Key findings across focus groups indicated interest in:

- New technologies: Apps, augmented reality, QR codes, interactive videos, and virtual games as effective interpretation tools, activities, and potential "wow" experiences.
- Interconnectedness: Wanting to know about similarities across Earth's life forms (past and present), interconnectedness among humans, plant life, insects, and other mammals, as well as interconnectedness across content in galleries.
- Real scientists working in the field: Opportunities to meet and learn about the work of real scientists at U-M.
- Keep it local: A focus on local flora, fauna, landscapes, and problems, specific to Michigan.
- Human variation: Emphasis on similarities more than differences in discussing human variation.
- What the future holds: What the future holds for all species (especially humans).

- Citizen scientist: How visitors can participate and contribute to current scientific studies at the museum and bring projects that they do outside the museum related to exhibits back to staff at the museum.
- Evolution: Some teachers were passionate about evolution and would love to show their students an exhibit on evolution at the museum; other teachers find evolution challenging, difficult, and might shy away from bringing a group to an evolution exhibit, in part because of conversations that may come from a visit. One independent adult wanted to see an introduction to an evolution exhibit that acknowledges there is an evolutionary perspective and a creationist perspective.

The final activity in each focus group was for each person in the group to sum up in just a few words their feelings about the plans for galleries and exhibits discussed. Final summaries gave a good sense of how this sample of thirty focus group participants, who were current visitors, felt about the ideas for the museum's new facility. Words they used were:

- Excited/exciting—old and new
- Forward thinking—fresh and fun
- Interactive and immersive
- Inspiring, engaging, and educational in the true sense of the word
- Something to remember

Three participants said that they are "anxious to see" the new facility, "*can't wait,*" and are "*looking forward to it.*" One U-M student added "*Wow.*" When asked what that meant, the response was, "*Exclamation mark!*"

People in the independent adult focus group offered a few words of caution in planning the museum's new facility:

- Focus on the adult experience, as well as experience for kids
- Have diversity, variety, and natural lighting
- Do not overemphasize education
- Keep the storylines clear and focused

Focus group participants raised a few important areas related to the content of exhibitions that resulted in a series of recommendations for the final interpretive plan:

- Local to Michigan: Including content about flora, fauna, landscapes, and problems local to Michigan is important for making exhibits and programs relevant to people from Michigan or visiting Michigan.
- "Citizen Science" projects: Integrating "Citizen Science" projects as much as possible will continue to engage visitors after their visits to the museum, bring them back to the new facility to share their findings, and help them to feel they are making a contribution as part of the Museum's research community.

- Plant, animal, and human life content: Ensuring exhibits have examples of plant life, as well as animals and humans, will show variation across species and how without plants we would not have animals living on land.

PHASE II: FORMATIVE EVALUATION (PROTOTYPE TESTING)

For the first UMMNH formative evaluation related to prototyping, we recruited a sample of thirty-two adult participants, some with their families (e.g., members, potential visitors from local communities, UMMNH visitors, and contributors to the front-end evaluation focus groups). It consisted of:

- Observing participants (individuals or groups) using a behavioral checklist, looking for whether or not the prototypes engaged them.

- Recording a group interview with participants in a focus group after they had experienced each mock-up, and after experiencing all three mock-ups about their immediate responses to experiences, as well as input into improving their experience.

Formative evaluation participants experienced mock-ups of three exhibits:

1. Exploring size interactive: A ten-minute user experience with an overhead projection using a Kinect motion sensor that perceives depth and the difference between multiple bodies. The intention was to have focus group participants just experience the interactive, the number of objects zooming in and out, with a minimum of interpretive material. The interactive was to enable them to have an intuitive sense of things that are very, very large and very, very small, and illustrate the size of the human in the universe.

2. Science forum, a storyboard outline for "The Natural History of This Place": A ten-minute pitch of storyboards with the following theme: (1) how Michigan came to be; (2) what Michigan's natural world is like today; and (3) the role humans play, how we are supported by nature, how we impact nature, and how we can participate in shaping the future. The film's storyboard outline showed the process of change and connections, habitats and organisms in situ, and visuals that are centered in "this place."

3. Michigan field station: A prototype to simulate water quality tests that are typically used to determine the health of water. Through a ten-minute browse of these tests, participants were to have a better understanding of the different types of testing and aspects of water quality, and how each contributes to a healthy environment. Activities related to species, turbidity, pH, nitrate levels, temperature, and bacteria.

Final questions for each group of participants asked about ways to improve the experience with the mock-ups, something particularly memorable about the experience with one of the prototypes, summing up in just a few words feelings about the experience, and what they would say about the new museum to family, friends, and colleagues based on sections they had seen.

Across groups, young to older kids and adults responded that they would interact with the Exploring Size Interactive and could "get something out of it." Participants sensed the "thoughtfulness" in the redesign of the museum, and that lots of hands-on opportunities is the best way for kids to learn. They liked the good variety for different educational levels, and that "there will be a lot of what's here at the museum now."

PHASE II: FORMATIVE EVALUATION (PROTOTYPE TESTING)

A second formative evaluation focused on proof-of-concept prototypes that would realistically evaluate responses to mockups of three media exhibits:

1. Biodiversity interactive exhibit
2. Epigenetics interactive called "Lick a Rat"
3. Molecules and proteins interactive

During eight time slots from Thursday through to Saturday, we recruited seventeen groups—a sample of individuals, couples, family groups, and community groups that comprised fifty visitors from eight years to over seventy years. Participants were observed and interviewed.

Each of the three media exhibits were loaded onto a thirty-two-inch touchscreens and placed at the end of a long table. Some portions of the prototype were constructed of paper. The effect of the paper prototypes was more like a PowerPoint presentation than a game. All participants were facilitated through the prototyping process. It took visitors thirty to forty-five minutes to respond to the three media exhibit prototypes. Respondents were quite engaged by the process and each person who participated received two passes for a planetarium show.

So what did respondents think?

Biodiversity Interactive

Visitors were presented with a graphic representation of a forest with a variety of trees, and a farm with two crops. They played an interactive game, choosing discrete species as the computer tallied the biodiversity index in real time, a measurement used when gauging the relative health of a particular ecosystem. The main takeaway was that a plot with a high biodiversity index (many different species) is healthier than a plot with a low biodiversity index. Across the seventeen groups, responses to interview questions indicated that visitors had a good sense of biodiversity, and not the "biodiversity index."

A trend from different sections of the interview was a desire to discuss the impact of biodiversity. Some comments were:

- The mock-up "doesn't talk about the lack of biodiversity, there are no pictures that show the impact. You need to show bugs—a forest that has been devastated, peaches washed out," so people will ask, "Why do I care at the end?" (a museum educator).
- You "could explain biodiversity in relation to climate change" (grandparents with a nine year old).
- "The biodiversity prototype makes me think about what was in Nebraska before all the farms. It makes you think about where we are going as a planet" (a Board member).

"Lick a Rat": Epigenetics Interactive

This interactive let visitors pretend they are a mother rat grooming its young. Pretending to play the game, users controlled a mother rat with newborn pups. As she "licks" her pups, the grooming changes the methylation status of the pups' GR gene. This influences how the pup grows and develops, and in turn effects how the rat responds to stress throughout its lifetime.

Visitors in all seventeen groups seemed to love the title of the interactive and playing the game. In seven of the groups (41%), visitors patted rather than poked the rats. Often there was a more nurturing response from females. The game play for this interactive was inspired by the University of Utah's online "Lick Your Rats" game.

Results

Wow! This rat pup received a lot of grooming and has an active GR gene. It will be able to bounce back from stress quickly.

This rat got some attention, but its busy mom didn't always get to it. When stressed throughout its lifetime, it will take a bit of time to recover.

This rat didn't get much attention, so its GR gene isn't very active. When it encounters stress throughout its lifetime, it will take longer to recover.

Figure 12.5. University of Utah's online "Lick Your Rats" game. COURTESY OF MARTIN BAUMGAERTNER/ANGLE PARK, INC.

An exceptional quote was: "If you are teaching, be careful, wary of thinking beyond the game—am I lesser than . . . ? Some people don't have parents. If you are specifically addressing the study of rats and pups, that is okay. I would want to be careful of extrapolating about students' lives. Maybe include some cue about how complex parenting is; parents have different ways of parenting" (a grade 1–2 teacher).

A trend from different sections of the interview was a need for more information about the GR gene and explaining more about the impact and results of the experiment. For example: I am "not sure about the exact role of the GR gene." "Do all pups have the same genetic sequence? The addition of a graphic to know what the gene is that we are talking about would be helpful" (a middle school teacher).

Molecules and Proteins Interactive

Translation is a critical part of the process of gene expression and leads to synthesized proteins from transcribed RNA. Messenger RNA is decoded in the ribosome to create a chain of amino acids, and the resulting polypeptide folds into a protein that can create structures and perform functions. This particular interactive mainly covered the process of coding the mRNA. Visitors saw a string of mRNA made up of codons (three bases, designated by three letters) and were prompted to drag from a set of corresponding amino acids to create a polypeptide.

Participants in most groups understood how proteins are created and not their importance (82.5%, fourteen groups). Some exceptional quotes were:

- "I've seen lots of visualizations of translation [or RNA . . .]—it is a hard concept to convey; it would be nice to start big with skin → cell → nucleus → chromosome → unzipped DNA and zoom in to the mRNA—it lets you know [the] scale we are looking at" (a museum educator).
- A high school student knew "the codon on a wheel; it is easier to start in the middle and go outwards, point out 1st, 2nd, and 3rd letter" (a fifteen-year-old girl who has taken biology in high school).
- A trend from different sections of the interview was wanting to know more about the importance and function of a protein. For instance: "Make a totally different game, start with three codons, add a result = proteins." "Okay, now that you have a protein, why is this important? What is the function of a protein?" Add examples of proteins and their importance (a senior male, an alum with a doctorate).

Final Interview Questions

The last questions during the interview were: Was something particularly memorable about your experience with one of these prototypes? Would you recommend visiting the new museum to family, friends, and colleagues based on the media prototypes or mockups you have seen?

The epigenetics interactive "Lick a Rat" was particularly memorable (71% of groups), and then biodiversity (59% of group). The molecules and proteins interactive was particularly memorable for four groups (23.5%). Four of the groups also liked the ability to drag and drop using a touch screen (23.5%).

In fourteen groups (82.5%), the response to recommending visiting the museum was "Yes" (the remaining three groups did not respond to this question). For instance, grandparents with granddaughters visiting from France commented, "People would enjoy" the exhibits; they are "better than static displays." They "would like to come back" to see their final form. A fifteen-year-old granddaughter would suggest to her biology teacher that the teacher brings the class, and a middle school teacher commented that the exhibits will be "especially meaningful to the seventh-grade science teachers."

NOTES

1. Barbara J. Soren, "Museum experiences that change visitors," *Museum Management and Curatorship*, 24, pt. 3 (2009): 233-51.
2. Stephen Bitgood, "Remedial Evaluation of Museum Exhibitions: Some Issues and Clarifications," Jacksonville State University, Alabama, Working Paper, accessed August 15, 2021, DOI: 10.13140/RG.2.1.2872.0882, available from, https://www.researchgate.net/publication/305725121_Remedial_Evaluation_of_Museum_Exhibitions?channel=doi&linkId=579cfebc08ae5d5e1e14c0a0&showFulltext=true.
3. Lynda Kelly, *Musing on Learning*, Seminar, Australian Museum, April 20, 1999.

PART V
HOW?

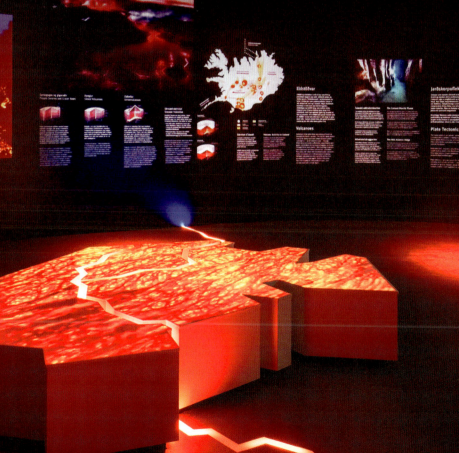

Perlan Museum of Icelandic Natural Wonders/Xibitz

An exhibition completed on time and on budget that engages with its public is an exhibition that has a successful planning team and process behind it. Although the scale of the enterprise may vary from a solo art exhibition to the coordinated efforts of the entire staff of a large museum or science center, the development process is essentially the same as illustrated in figure 1.1. This fundamental approach can be adapted to museum exhibitions of all kinds and sizes.

The following chapters explore the development process from beginning to end, starting with the appointment of an exhibition planning team. Many people—including museum professionals—tend to think either of a curator or an exhibition designer as the first or perhaps the only persons to be consulted regarding the development of an exhibition. As this manual indicates throughout, the roles of both are important, but should be seen as part of a broader development process in which the interpretive planner is just as important. This is especially critical considering the growing role of community consultation and evaluation. As such, in visitor-centered exhibitions, design should be evaluated in terms of its success in facilitating the successful communication of the exhibition's content. To accomplish this objective, comprehensive and detailed interpretive planning is essential.

Immersive and interactive digital experiences are indispensable to many exhibitions today. Multimedia has the ability to help visitors appreciate and understand more fully the meanings that the exhibition is intended to convey. Media based experiences are also major cost drivers of the budget and coordinating their production with the fabrication of other exhibit components has increased the complexity of managing exhibitions. This book devotes an entire chapter to the challenge of planning for media.

"How much will this exhibition cost?" is one of the most common questions an exhibition planner will face. Many variables and assumptions will inform an exhibition budget from size and complexity to number of objects. All too often, planners have to "design to budget." The chapter on financial planning addresses tools and techniques for developing and allocating budgets. Finally, having begun this section of the manual with a description of the exhibition development team we must end with a focus on project management—the task that draws all the many strands of the exhibition that have been identified in this book into a coherent and enjoyable visitor experience.

Chapter 13

Roles and Responsibilities

Maria Piacente

The exhibition process is a multidisciplinary one and, as such, can be challenging for individuals of diverse talents and interests to work together under the time and budget pressures of an exhibition project. The challenge is further complicated by the need to combine the abilities of museum employees with private contractors as very few museums have all related skills in-house.

13.1 WHO'S INVOLVED IN THE EXHIBITION PROCESS?

Various disciplines represent specializations that are *all* required for a successful exhibition, as shown in figures 13.1 and 13.2:

- **Audience** specialists are those team members who represent the visitor in the exhibition process. These include evaluation, education, and marketing.
- Curators, researchers, and collections management personnel are the **content** specialists.
- Designers, interpretive planners, and media developers represent the **communication** and **creative specialists**.
- The **production** specialists include project managers, conservators, preparators, finance, and specialty fabricators and multimedia producers.

An important step in the exhibition development process is assigning roles, identifying teams, and establishing how everyone will work together within the constraints of budget, time, and available personnel. Figure 13.2 provides a brief description of key roles and responsibilities that may be assigned to an exhibition project. In small museums or for small exhibition projects, a single person may wear two or more hats, and certainly some tasks may be outsourced to consultants. The case study of the Oakland Museum of California presented at the end of this chapter is an excellent example of a formalized exhibition design process with clear roles and responsibilities. The case study of the Trinidad and Tobago Central Bank Museum demonstrates how a small museum assigned roles in the course of redesigning the permanent exhibition with limited resources.

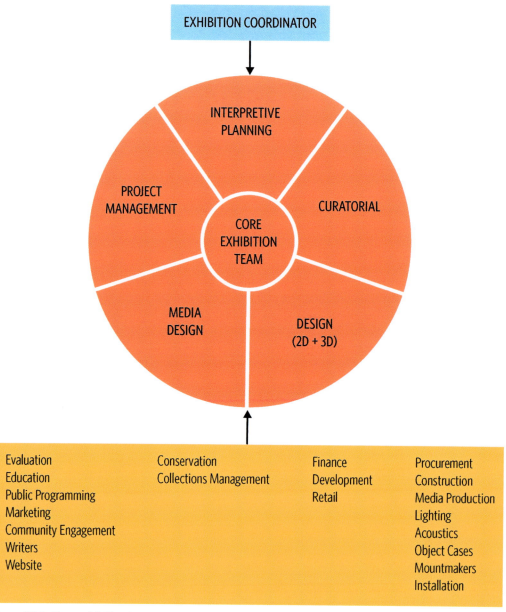

Figure 13.1. Core exhibition team. LORD CULTURAL RESOURCES

Title	Role
Project Director/ Exhibition Coordinator	This position usually belongs to an employee of the museum — an exhibition manager or director — who takes direct leadership for the project. He or she appoints teams and sub-contractors, facilitates decision-making and approvals, and takes responsibility for the project.
Curator	The curator researches the story of the exhibition and selects artifacts, specimens, and works of art. This person is responsible for authenticating the exhibition's content. Curators may be directly involved in originating the exhibition brief as well acquiring new artifacts.
Collections Manager or Registrar	The individual is responsible for preparing art, specimen, and artifact lists in consultation with the curator and managing their administration which might include updating the collections management system, moving them to temporary locations, loan agreements, insurance, valuations, and coordinating shipping if the exhibition is meant to tour.
Conservator	The conservator is responsible for assessing the condition of the collection that will go on display or any objects that will be loaned/acquired for it. The conservator will be responsible for conducting and organizing treatment, approving mount making requirements, and reviewing gallery conditions and display case design to ensure the safe display of sensitive objects. The conservator may be on hand during the installation of objects to oversee art handlers and preparators.
Community Engagement Officer	This individual develops the process for overseeing the input from BIPOC communities. Community engagement specialists will also oversee co-creation projects, advisory committees, subject matter experts, and conduct a series of events that ensure transparency in the planning process.
Designer (2D and 3D)	Designers are responsible for the creative, spatial design of the exhibition. They bring the content, collections, and interpretive plan to life. The design team includes graphic designers, wayfinding specialists, lighting designers, acousticians, and architects.

Figure 13.2. Roles and responsibilities. LORD CULTURAL RESOURCES

Title	Role
Digital Development/ Design	This individual identifies the online experience of the exhibition. Will there be a virtual exhibition companion? Online activities and programs? What content will be unique to the virtual experience versus the on-site one? As exhibition processes develop it may be that Digital Designers become part of the Core Exhibition Team.
Educator	Educators link exhibition content to relevant school curriculum so that teachers will find a reason to bring their students to the museum. Educators will create special tours and educational programs based on the exhibition content as well as represent school group needs in the exhibition process (i.e. making curriculum links).
Estimator	The cost estimator prices the design throughout the exhibition development process to ensure that the project is on budget. Estimating a project only after it has been designed can result in major delays related to value engineering and redesign.
Evaluator	Evaluators facilitate the public's participation throughout exhibition development by conducting agreed upon evaluation processes and ensuring that input is incorporated into the design. See chapter 12 for evaluation processes.
Financial Administrator	A museum employee in the finance department responsible for managing cash flow and payments to suppliers as needed. This person also ensures that exhibition projects fit within with the overall financial projections for the museum's fiscal year.
Interpretive Planner	The interpretive planner develops the interpretive plan. This individual works collaboratively with curators, designers, educators, and evaluators to ensure effective communication and visitor-centricity. The interpretive planner may also be the exhibition editor/writer.
Multimedia Design/ Technology Integrator	These specialists design and specify how complex interactive media, audio, and video experiences will deliver content and function within the exhibition. For complex media and budget control understanding the type of equipment and show control necessary to achieve the design is important early in the development process. These individuals also assess impact on museum operations for future maintenance.

Figure 13.2. *Continued*

Title	Role
Marketing Manager	The marketing team identifies opportunities for target market appeal and can assist with early topic testing. The marketing team develops the communication, advertising, and social media strategies required to generate awareness and excitement for the exhibition.
Public Programmer	The public programmer identifies aspects of the exhibition that will support special events such as lectures and films and in-gallery activities such as tours and demonstrations. Public programs enhance visitor enjoyment of the exhibition.
Procurement/Legal	A procurement officer or the museum's legal representative oversees contractual obligations for suppliers as well as enforcing the museum's procurement rules.
Project Manager	The project manager coordinates the exhibition process from beginning to end. The project manager develops communication protocols, oversees the schedule, administers quality control, and manages the budget. The exhibition coordinator may appoint project managers to support him/her or take on this role in addition to their other duties.
Retail Manager	Engaging the retail manager ensures there is time to conceive, design, test, and produce specific products for sale in the museum shop. If the exhibition is a temporary show, then participation by the retail manager will be even more significant, as shops are sometimes located within the temporary exhibition. Retail responsibilities include organizing limited edition products and catalogues that can be licensed should the exhibition go on the road.

Figure 13.2. *Continued*

13.2 TEAMS AND COMMITTEES

Museum staff, subcontractors, and specialists may be organized into teams in order to facilitate the successful implementation of the exhibition. These teams do not work independently from one another, but each has particular tasks that need to be completed. Several individuals may be on more than one team. The project manager coordinates all teams and facilitates communication between them.

- **Core exhibition team**: The core exhibition team (figure 13.1) is established at the beginning and is consistent throughout the life of the project. Other specialists and team members are brought into the process as appropriate by the project manager. At the very beginning of the project the curatorial and interpretive planning specialists will work closely together to establish the concept and core messages for the exhibition. This emphasis of focus on the project will change over time—and that is okay, but successful projects are those in which the core exhibition team works together, respecting the input and leadership of all team members to ensure a cohesive visitor experience in addition to a project that opens on time and on budget. Many positions, such as the conservator, collections manager, public programmer, retail manager, marketing manager, etc. (as per figure 13.2) may not be required on a full-time basis, but their participation ensures a holistic and institutional understanding of the project. Their expertise is brought in at the right time by the project manager.

- **Design team**: The design team includes three-dimensional designers, graphic designers, multimedia hardware specialists, lighting designers, and possibly acousticians, engineers, and architects if the exhibition involves building work or has implications for floor loading or structural issues. The designer on the core exhibition team coordinates the work of the larger design team.

- **Production team**: This team will include exhibition fabricators, artists, mount makers, case manufacturers, hardware integrators, multimedia and film producers, and many other suppliers who are responsible for building, producing, and installing the exhibition. While museums may have some of these capabilities in-house, such as mount making and art handling, these tasks are most often subcontracted to specialist suppliers through a tendering/bidding process, either separately after the design team's construction drawings are approved or as part of a design-build or turnkey assignment. In the latter case the design and construction teams are hired as one team. The work of these teams is managed by the project manager.

The project director/exhibition coordinator in consultation with members of the core exhibition team may also choose to create a series of committees. Such committees may consist of members of the various teams identified above, experts and specialists, or members of the community.

- **Advisory committee**: Large exhibition projects dealing with complex and sensitive content may benefit from the guidance of advisors, who may be subject matter experts, community stakeholders, or other professionals in the museum or academic community. Advisory committees are invited to participate in workshops or review key planning and design milestones. Advisory committees can provide an objective perspective as well as assist the museum with accountability.

To address the growing need for diversity and inclusion with BIPOC communities, the role of advisory committees becomes ever more important. Such committees or community partnerships may be part of a community engagement process that incorporates co-curation and/or co-creation.

- **Content committee**: Integrating content with design is at the heart of the exhibition development process. Content committees may consist of a mix of museum staff and outside experts. Such committees may prove useful for researching topics, selecting artifacts, procuring static and moving images, sourcing oral histories, and more. These committees may also be convened to review and approve content developed by others such as media scripts and edited label copy. The curator and the interpretive planner should meet regularly with this committee and with the designers attending specific sessions as appropriate. These types of committees are often useful for small and medium sized museums that do not have large curatorial resources in-house to do all the content work. These committees are often used to track all the content needs of an exhibition to make sure nothing is missed in the design. This is important when a museum only has one or two curators on staff.

13.3 CONTRACTING EXPERTISE

Not all museums can afford to operate with a staff that includes all the functions identified in the foregoing list of team members. By outsourcing some of the responsibilities for the exhibition process, the museum can achieve several objectives simultaneously:

- Save money on day-to-day operations
- Access world-class expertise
- Fill in skills gaps for short periods
- Bring in subject matter specialists
- Allow for the continued day-to-day operation of the museum

Hiring the right contractors for the job not only ensures that the exhibition's goals are achieved, but that the process is enjoyable for everyone. Selection of a design team or guest curator may include criteria for shared philosophy, regional awareness, and relevant experience. The most commonly outsourced functions include:

- **Design**: Individuals or firms are hired to provide creative three-dimensional, graphic, lighting, and media design. Many designers excel at particular types of exhibitions such as children's exhibits or natural history experiences; have a reputation for highly aesthetic art displays; or have more experience integrating high tech media and show control systems.
- **Interpretive planning**: Expert interpretive planners are hired to work with the museum's curators, registrars, and educators to develop powerful visitor experience plans. Their task is to make the collections and knowledge about them into a format that will communicate with the visitor.
- **Curation**: Guest curators and writers are often hired as subject matter specialists to supplement in-house expertise as well as provide short-term study of the collection or new research topic that will be featured in a temporary exhibition.
- **Project management/coordination**: Dedicated and experienced project managers or coordinators are hired to manage large and complex exhibition projects especially when exhibitions are being developed at the same time as building construction and renovation. The added complexity of coordinating with architects and general contractors can require a team of project managers and costing experts. *Tip for small- and medium-size museums: if you are outsourcing design and fabrication, include the requirement for a dedicated project manager.*
- **Production**: Although some museums continue to have some level of fabrication ability, very few have the specialized equipment and crafts workers to build and produce today's modern high-tech exhibitions.

13.4 MAKING DECISIONS

An effective exhibition planning team is one that can make decisions. Who signs off on design? Who makes curatorial decisions? Who approves text? Who will approve invoices for payment? How will comments be collected and considered during a review process? Key members of the team need to be empowered to make decisions to ensure that approvals follow in a timely manner.

Poor decision-making can result in major delays, miscommunication, and costly change orders during the implementation phase. A system of informal and formal approval processes should be agreed upon in advance and built into the overall schedule by the project manager.

- **Informal** approvals are consensus-based agreements on aspects of the project in progress. These approvals often take place by email, conference calls, workshops, and review meetings. All approvals should be carefully documented to ensure that decisions can be traced should problems arise.

- **Formal** approvals are based on key project milestones and require a formal submission and presentation. Such milestones often trigger major expenditures or fundamental decisions about design, involving the highest level of approval in the museum. Written authorization is required from the project director/exhibition coordinator in order for the exhibition process to move forward.

For most exhibitions, approval periods should not take more than two to three weeks. Projects that have committed to extensive community consultation and testing or require review from an outside advisory body will require a longer approval period that can take up to four to six weeks. A detailed project schedule must provide time for review and approval after submittal of each stage of planning or design. This ensures a realistic completion date and deadlines that all team members can work toward.

Case Study

OAKLAND MUSEUM OF CALIFORNIA EXHIBITION PROCESS WITH VALERIE HUACO, DEPUTY DIRECTOR AND CHIEF CONTENT OFFICER

The Oakland Museum of California (OMCA) was created in 1969 with the merger of three institutions: the Snow Museum of Natural History, the Oakland Public Museum, and the Oakland Art Gallery. The organization of the museum very much reflected those origins with three distinct divisions of Art, History, and Natural Sciences that operated in many ways as "mini museums." In 2010, the museum separated its operation from the City of Oakland, which inspired a reorganizational process. Here was an opportunity to create an autonomous and holistic organizational structure that would better serve the needs of the museum and its audience.

The institution is no longer based on disciplines but rather organized according to "centers" with visitor experience at the core of its structure, strategies, and processes. This change fundamentally touches upon every aspect of the museum's operation, including exhibitions.

The exhibition development process, formalized by the museum's then deputy director Kelly McKinley, demonstrates the core values of OMCA's organizational dynamic: cross-disciplinary teamwork and community engagement. Except for some consulting curators to partner with in-house curators and contract designers for smaller temporary exhibitions, a majority of OMCA's exhibitions are developed, designed, and constructed in-house to ensure delivery on the museum's mission and vision.

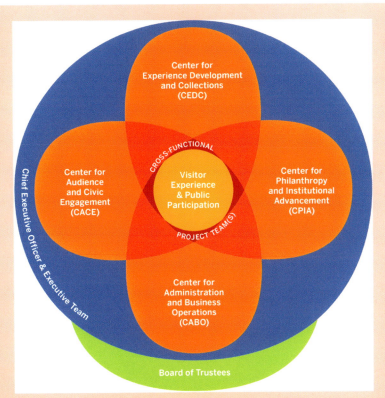

Figure 13.3. Organizational framework for the Oakland Museum of California. OAKLAND MUSEUM OF CALIFORNIA

The museum has approximately ten thousand square feet of temporary exhibition space and within its ninety thousand square feet of permanent exhibition space, there is up to five thousand square feet of flexible or changing content areas. Larger temporary exhibitions change twice a year, while multiple smaller exhibitions are presented throughout the year. As such, there are exhibitions of all sizes and scales in development at any time by OMCA's in-house team of specialists. Even on the rare occasion that exhibitions are sourced from other institutions, OMCA adapts and adds to the exhibition content to ensure stories are meaningful to its mission, audience, and community partners.

Every exhibition is assigned a core team consisting of a project manager, designer, curator, and experience developer (see figure 13.5). They are responsible for taking the approved proposal or exhibit idea generated by the curator through all phases of planning, design, and construction. The collaborative process begins with research into the subject matter and stories of the exhibition; the potential interpretive techniques that will serve visitors; and engagement with community partners in the development and design process. Community convenings are held to elicit engagement and content direction, and to build relationships with community partners. Does this exhibition require an advisory committee in a consultative role? Community collaboration to participate in outreach and content development? A co-curation process with direct community participation? The experience developer, whose focus is on the visitor experience, leads the development of the interpretive plan and community outreach process. The museum's largest temporary exhibitions, which take place in the Great Hall are often co-curated

Figure 13.4. *All Power to the People: Black Panthers at 50* temporary exhibition at the Oakland Museum of California. OAKLAND MUSEUM OF CALIFORNIA

experiences. Considering OMCA's long-time and ongoing commitment to diversity, equity, access, and inclusion and increasing commitment to becoming a truly antiracist institution, OMCA's exhibition process is designed to forefront community voices and perspectives while highlighting the stories of historically marginalized groups.

The exhibition, *All Power to the People: Black Panthers at 50*, demonstrates how OMCA's visitors are not just guests but partners in the exhibition development process. The core team engaged with a large number of current and former members of the Black Panther Party and others to ensure that the voice of the exhibition was inclusive of multiple views and first-person perspectives, thus bringing to light the often misunderstood history of the Black Panthers.

The core team is supported by an extended group of professionals drawn from the museum's staff of in-house experts including registration, preparators, public engagement, learning initiatives, marketing and communications, fundraising, conservation, and evaluation. The project manager is responsible for bringing these individuals into the process at the appropriate time and making sure that all relevant departments are engaged with the development of the exhibition.

Because the museum's focus has been on the "in person" hands-on experience of visitors with stories and objects, the role of digital has been limited and historically driven by marketing and communications. As a result of the COVID-19 crisis of 2020, OMCA (like all museums) is rethinking and repositioning digital engagement in their organization to serve community through the range of museum functions. For example, how can digital connection support membership, donors, and volunteer programs; curriculum-based activities and teacher resources; and core content related to exhibitions?

The exhibition development process at OMCA makes space for both internal and external community participation in both selection and content. OMCA is in the process of reviewing and revising its processes including exhibition development within its organizational commitment to antiracist principles as well as trends, changes in audience behavior, and new ways of working. The museum's leadership recognizes that events like COVID-19, societal confrontation with racism, and the digital revolution require a flexible organization that is open to self-reflection and change in order to ensure future success.

Core Team Roles	Key Responsibilities
Project Manager	• Manage schedule and budget • Cross discipline communication • Extended team management • Administration
Designer	• Manage design process • Establish look and feel • Lead 2D and 3D designers • Shape stories into narrative
Curator	• Generates idea for the exhibition • Research and content development • Works with community partners in development of content
Experience Developer	• Responsible for visitor experience • Interpretive Plan • Leads community outreach process

Figure 13.5. Summary of core team roles and responsibilities. OAKLAND MUSEUM OF CALIFORNIA

Case Study

ROLES AND RESPONSIBILITIES IN A SMALL MUSEUM: THE CENTRAL BANK MUSEUM, TRINIDAD AND TOBAGO

Maria Piacente

Those of you who work in small- or medium-sized museums know that in order to deliver exhibition projects, staff need to wear multiple hats. While much of the work is done in-house to save money, limited (affordable) outsourcing is also a strategy for getting bigger jobs done. The Central

Bank of Trinidad & Tobago is committed to culture and education throughout the country. It has an extensive art collection and sponsors exhibitions and cultural events. The museum, which is located on the ground floor of the Central Bank emphasizes economic literacy and the role of the bank, in addition to hosting events and exhibitions on Trinidad and Tobago art and culture.

The museum staff consists of five people: the curator, assistant curator, museum officer, research technician, and museum assistant. In addition to research and collections role, the curator is also the museum's director. This core team is supported by shared services from the bank including IT, procurement, and finance. As a branch of the bank all museum activities must be approved by the executive team.

When the Central Bank approved the curator's request to refresh the permanent exhibitions, the curator recognized that they did not have the skills or capacity to do the work. They hired a consultant to design the exhibition and reorganized their team to focus on research and collection's preparation. The bank's procurement officer acted as the project manager to control costs. The design consultant and the procurement officer came up with a tendering strategy that would take advantage of production skills on the island related to graphics and film, while sourcing museum quality cases, models, and interactives in the United States. In this way, the bank achieved its goal to create a world-class exhibition within its resource and budget constraints.

Figure 13.6. Visitors explore the new permanent exhibition in the Central Bank's refurbished exhibition gallery, Port of Spain, Trinidad & Tobago. COURTESY OF CENTRAL BANK MUSEUM, TRINIDAD & TOBAGO

Chapter 14

Preparing the Exhibition Brief

Maria Piacente and John Nicks

What is this exhibition about? The concept of an exhibition, the central idea that defines and motivates it, is fundamental to all subsequent planning and design. In chapter 3 we noted that ideas for exhibitions may be research-inspired or market-driven. What this means within the walls of a museum is that some ideas for an exhibition may be the conclusions drawn after years of research and development, while others might be the result of brainstorming by the museum's curators and exhibition staff for a series of temporary exhibitions that respond to current and popular topics. Whatever the source, the idea or concept must be formulated into a well articulated thesis and presented in the form of an exhibition or concept brief.

14.1 FORMULATING THE EXHIBITION CONCEPT

Formulation of the concept, central idea, or thesis of an exhibition is a core curatorial responsibility, although it is increasingly shared with other museum professionals (i.e., interpretive planners) as well as other stakeholders, including the museum's community as described in chapter 10. This is particularly important when the voice of those subjects cannot be fairly represented through the curatorial voice alone, as demonstrated by the permanent exhibitions at the National Museum of the American Indian in Washington, DC. In such exhibitions, presentation of the authentic voice of the people from whom the collections derive becomes the central idea.

14.1.1 Curatorship

A powerful and meaningful exhibition starts with a powerful and meaningful idea. However, the effectiveness of its realization depends in large measure on the quality of the curatorial research that supports the thesis and the collections and other materials that comprise the exhibition. There are two types of curatorial research: thematic and object.

- **Thematic research** provides a broad base of contextual information and develops the framework as well as the substance of the exhibition storyline.
- **Object research** documents, works of art, photographs, artifacts, specimens, graphics, oral histories, or audiovisuals that constitute the materials with which the exhibition is to be created.

The sequence in which this work is accomplished may vary. In many museums, both thematic and object research as part of the curatorial program are expected to lead to the formulation of exhibition ideas that are then scheduled as part of an on-going exhibition program. Much of the research of both kinds may precede the decision to develop an exhibition.

To an increasing degree, however, decisions on future exhibitions are based upon the presentation and acceptance of a powerful "big" idea that is then used to focus institutional research in order to support exhibition development. Thematic and object research pursues and elaborates the thematic idea following upon the commitment to develop the exhibition.

A well-rounded museum exhibition program will make room for both approaches. In either scenario, thematic and object research are likely to become an iterative process—first one, then the other assuming primacy, and leading back in turn to each other. A broad thematic research plan will point to the need for specific object research, either within the museum's collection or aimed outward at determining the location of relevant works of art, artifacts, or specimens in public or private collections. Object research of this kind is likely to lead back to the enhancement or alteration of the thematic research findings, and so on in an iterative circle that can remain open, inviting, and rewarding throughout the exhibition process.

14.1.2 Time Limits

The exhibition must open to the public on time so the iterative process cannot go on indefinitely. An important decision in the exhibition development process—usually forced by the exhibition schedule—is the point at which the exhibition team agrees that sufficient curatorial research has been undertaken to facilitate the next step in the exhibition development process, often with the agreement that curatorial research will continue to a certain stage while other aspects of the project, such as interpretive planning and design, are being advanced. Inevitably, a day dawns when plans and drawings become fabrication tenders or bids, after which further curatorial research findings may result in costly change orders.

14.1.3 Object Lists

Except for some science center or children's museum exhibitions, collections are the core around which good museum exhibitions very often turn. The roles of the curatorial functions—including those of curators, registrars, and conservators—are managed to ensure that collections appropriate for the proposed use are selected and prepared for exhibition. This phase of the work usually generates a list of the objects intended for display. The production of such a list is a decisive stage in the development of all collection-based exhibitions and can occur at the time of the preparation of the exhibition brief or during the concept/schematic development phase in collaboration with interpretive planners.

Curatorial judgment is required as to the extent to which the museum's collection meets the needs of the intended exhibition, the extent to which loans from other collections may be necessary, and the opportunities to add to the collection by means of donations, purchases, or fieldwork. Some exhibitions are comprised entirely of loans, such as a touring exhibition of paintings from a famous museum's collection. Others may be drawn completely from the exhibiting museum's own holdings. Most exhibitions fall between these two extremes: indeed, the exhibition concept may be precisely the opportunity to combine, compare, or contrast works of art, artifacts, or specimens from disparate sources, giving scholars and the public a once-in-a-lifetime opportunity to see the entire oeuvre of an artist whose works are held in many museums around the world.

Curatorial decisions about acquisitions, borrowing, fieldwork, or other means of collection development for the exhibition may not be easy. Quantitative considerations may be obvious if the museum's collection does not adequately represent some aspect of the culture, some range of fauna, or some period of an artist's career. But qualitative judgments may be much more subtle determining where the works of art of the highest quality are to be found, or the source of the artifacts or specimens that are most relevant to the central idea of the exhibition. Extensive research may be needed to make the selection and may extend to fieldwork aimed at discovering new artifacts or specimens for display.

An important consideration affecting the selection of objects for an exhibition is the decision as to whether outstanding or representative objects—or both—are required:

- **Outstanding objects** are very often preferred: the best examples of an artist's work, the most striking specimens, or the artifacts associated with an extraordinary historic event or person.
- **Representative objects** may also be sought to show the typical way of life, the characteristics of a species, or the necessary tools for a technology.
- **Systematic displays**, such as some visible storage exhibitions, go still further to show an example of every type or stage of development.

Of course, many large exhibitions will combine outstanding and representative objects in different parts of the show. The exhibition development process may also change the emphasis, as greater opportunities are found to make the show more representative than was originally intended. In some cases, securing key loans of specific outstanding works of art, specimens, or artifacts may determine whether the exhibition is viable or not.

A major factor affecting the selection of objects for an exhibition is the museum's capacity to borrow from private or public sources. A prestigious exhibition at a major museum may command loans from a wide range of collections, whereas a smaller institution attempting to arrange the same show is likely to have greater difficulty. This is one reason why most museums wish to provide the highest possible museum quality of environmental controls, lighting, and security to ensure that the standards of any prospective lender, public or private, may be met. An original or powerful exhibition idea can be instrumental in encouraging positive consideration of loan requests.

14.2 EXHIBITION BRIEF

Every exhibition project whether small or large, permanent or temporary, needs an exhibition brief, sometimes called a curatorial brief or concept brief. The brief assembles in one place all the information gathered by curators and other museum specialists to define the content and purpose of the exhibition. Directors and senior managers use briefs to decide whether to proceed with a project as well as plan for major capital campaigns or increases in operational budgets. Briefs can be used to describe an exhibition project to potential funders, stakeholders, and the public. It can be used to communicate scope in request for proposals. As such, an exciting and responsible exhibition brief is more than the articulation of the concept, and should include the purpose of the exhibition, core concept, schedule, budget, team responsibilities, and resource plan.

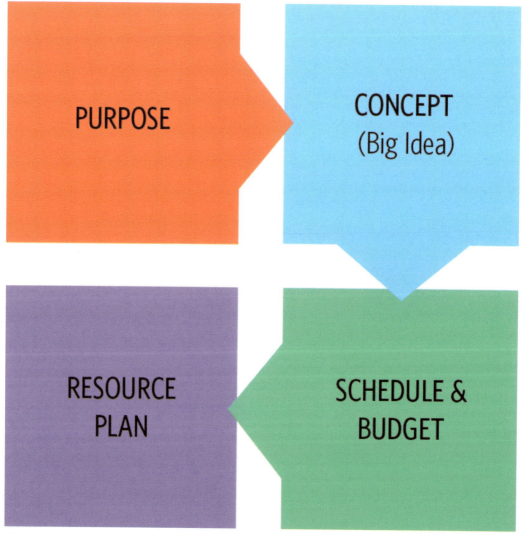

Figure 14.1. Exhibition brief. LORD CULTURAL RESOURCES

14.2.1 Purpose of the Exhibition

The exhibition brief must answer fundamental questions regarding the importance and relevance of the project. Is this exhibition necessary? Does it serve the museum's mission and vision? How does it meet the needs of the museum's audience? Does it showcase the museum's strengths in collections and research?

In 2018, the Opera di Santa Croce in Florence, Italy, embarked on the development of a temporary exhibition that would eventually be installed at the Ellis Island National Museum of Immigration. The exhibition entitled *Sisters in Liberty: From Florence, Italy to New York, New York*, would examine the intersection between ideas of liberty inspired by each country's statue of liberty: Pio Fedi's *Libertà* and Frédéric Auguste Bartholdi's Statue of Liberty. In addition, the exhibition brief identified that the long-standing cultural ties between Italy and the United States would be explored by the exhibition's content. The exhibition brief outlined how the exhibition would incorporate a 3D print of the *Libertà* and the role of key partners including Kent University and the Garabaldi Meucci Museum in New York. The purpose of the exhibition included an articulation of the exhibition's role in supporting marketing and fundraising efforts by the Opera di Santa Croce in the United States. The clear and concise brief, which included a budget and milestone schedule for completion was used to gain support from both the Opera di Santa Croce's Board and the Ellis Island National Museum of Immigration.

14.2.2 The Core Idea or Concept

The exhibition concept should be expressed succinctly as a question, thesis, or problem. For example:

- The core idea of an art exhibition might be the rediscovery of a neglected artist, or the reevaluation of a well-known one.
- The core idea of a science exhibition might be to explain the findings of a new field of research, or to provide a new way for visitors to understand the scientific method.
- The core idea of a history exhibition might be to suggest an alternate approach to our understanding of a particular period, or to reevaluate the contribution of a group or leader.
- The core idea of an ethnographic exhibition might be to reconsider our understanding and appreciation of a particular culture, or to link the heritage of a historic group with its contemporary descendants.
- The core idea of an archaeology exhibition might be to reconsider or challenge a widely accepted theory of settlement, or simply to report on the findings of an excavation.
- The core idea for a reinstallation of a museum's permanent collection exhibition may be to introduce new research, new collections, new ideas, and new means for engaging with the visitor.

The strongest exhibition ideas are those that can be expressed in dialectical terms, addressing issues on which there may very well be differences of opinion. Even if the exhibition is on a relatively arcane topic, or one of sophisticated appeal to a relatively limited audience of specialists, it is useful to express the key idea for the exhibition in terms of an issue that the exhibition will engage. A clear, succinct statement of the core idea for the exhibition will help the interpretive planners and designers to stay on track. In interpretive planning parlance, this is often called the "Big Idea" or "meta-narrative."

The concept may be defined by a preliminary **thematic framework** or structure that defines the overall scope of an exhibition or gallery. The level of detail will be determined by the amount of research completed to date. However, the concept and storyline will be further refined and defined by interpretive planning and design throughout the exhibition process.

In 2011, the North Dakota Heritage Center & State Museum in Bismarck broke ground on a major renovation and expansion that would add fourteen thousand square feet (1,300 sq m) of permanent collection exhibition space to their existing nineteen thousand square foot (1,765 sq m) gallery. The state's story beginning with its formation and ending in the present day would now be distributed among three purpose-built galleries themed according to geologic time, early peoples, and modern history. Each of the three galleries had broadly articulated concepts based on the strength of the center's collections and period of time each gallery would present. In their search for a design team to help them realize their vision for the new galleries, the center's core exhibition team clearly identified how interpretive planning would further develop these ideas into a creative storyline and design.

14.2.3 Schedule

Exhibitions need time and money to be implemented successfully. Understanding the schedule and budgetary requirements early in the exhibition process not only keeps planning teams on task, but also determines the kind of exhibition that will ultimately be constructed and what resources you will need to achieve it.

The schedule may be understood as an overall timeframe for the project—start and end dates, possibly with some reference to key planning and design milestones that need to be achieved. Is this a two-year project, a five-year project, or a ten-year project? Will it be phased? This determination is based on several factors:

- **Size**: The larger the exhibition, the more time required to plan, design, and implement it properly.
- **Permanent or temporary**: Permanent collection exhibitions usually benefit from a longer schedule—especially at the beginning. This is because permanent displays normally require larger budgets that need to be carefully spent, time for community consultation, in-depth research for content that will be displayed for more than ten to twenty years, and the integration of complex multimedia connected to the museum's content management system. In some cases, new research and new collections may need to be sourced. They need to be done right, so extra time is always advisable.
- **Funding**: Funding for an exhibition may need to be raised over time. The schedule for a project will need to reflect the availability of funds, cash flow, and incorporate logical "stopping points." The exhibition process may also contribute to fundraising, requiring design packages to attract the money that will fund their implementation.
- **Political, social, or topical occasions**: Anniversaries such as a centennial, bicentennial, or other politically and socially motivated occasion (such as the term of office of a sponsoring

government) can determine the timeframe for an exhibition project. These projects have defined "end dates" from which the project should plan backward. These are immovable dates and planning for their execution should begin as early as possible.

A general timeframe should be included in the exhibition brief. At this stage in the planning process, the schedule can be expressed in terms of Year 1, Year 2, and so on as opposed to defined dates, unless the museum is required to complete a project in time for a particular event or anniversary. They can be estimated using best practice scenarios from the profession (for museums that don't do a lot of exhibitions) or based on analysis of the museum's own history of exhibition timelines (for museums with aggressive exhibition development strategies).

Figure 14.2 illustrates ideal timeframes for exhibitions based on size, assuming that all funding is in place. These "rules of thumb" can be adapted to meet your project needs or type. Note that taking too much time to design and build an exhibition can be just as deleterious as not enough time. Technologies become obsolete, rising consultant fees and change orders set in, new research and discoveries are made, and visitor tastes and interests in topics change. An exhibition team can soon find that the work they are doing on a temporary exhibition is no longer relevant because of delays and other challenges if they take too long to develop it. Recognizing that every project is unique and that some phases might overlap, the suggested timeframes in figure 14.2 will help you get started with your planning.

Any project can be fast-tracked if additional resources and funding can be assigned to the exhibition. The core exhibition team must be committed to quick approvals and understand that some processes such as research and design will need to be shortened or adapted. Outsourcing, design-build scenarios, phasing, and an accelerated bidding processes are all strategies that can be utilized to save time and advance a project schedule.

Size	Overall Timeframe	Approximate Time by Phase
50 to 200 m² 500 to 2,000 ft²	18 months (1.5 years)	Planning - 3 months Design - 7 months Implementation - 8 months
200 to 500 m² 200 to 5,000 ft²	24 months (2 years)	Planning - 5 months Design - 9 months Implementation - 10 months
500 to 1,000 m² 5,000 to 10,000 ft²	30 months (2.5 years)	Planning - 8 months Design - 10 months Implementation - 12 months
1,000 + m² 10,000 + ft²	48 months (4 years)	Planning - 12 months Design - 16 months Implementation - 20 months

Figure 14.2. Average project timelines. LORD CULTURAL RESOURCES

14.2.4 Preliminary Budget

The exhibition brief must identify an overall budget for the project. This allocation of funds can ultimately determine the kind of exhibition the museum will produce. The budget can be determined in either of three ways:

- The first way is to identify an overall sum that senior management makes available for the project. For example, the museum administration may determine that all temporary exhibitions will have an upset budget of US$1 million, or that a major reinstallation of a ten thousand square foot permanent collection exhibition will have a $20 million budget that will be raised through a capital fundraising campaign.

- The second method for establishing a budget is based on a per square foot/square meter analysis of the proposed exhibition. Figure 14.3 identifies average costs for planning and implementing exhibitions that can be used as a tool for preliminary budgeting and controlling expectations for what can be delivered. Since the previous publication of this manual in 2014, the average cost has increased as museums incorporate more interactivity and technology. The amount of interactivity, theatrical experiences, and multimedia has the largest impact on the cost of an exhibition. Level of finish, quality of caseworks, and specialty lighting also impact the budget, but multimedia has become a critical cost driver.

- The third method for creating a budget is from the ground up instead of top-down, which the first two represent. Often, large museums with internal resources for planning and designing exhibitions will use a series of rates and comparison charts to build temporary exhibition budgets. These budgets will include other types of costs such as staff costs, marketing, conservation, programming, etc. in addition to the core costs of designing and building the exhibition.

The budget ranges identified in figure 14.3, which relate to the second method of budgeting, account only for costs directly related to the design and construction of an exhibition. Given that qualification, this rule of thumb can be used globally (as of 2021), even accounting for cheaper labor costs in some markets and temporary escalation of material and shipping costs as a result of the 2020 pandemic: exhibitions are so unique, custom-designed, and custom-built that if they are constructed by a reputable exhibition fabrication firm these averages should bear out.

Cost per m2/ft2 (USD)	Assumption
$250 to $350 per ft2 $2,700 to $3,800 m2	Didactic, low level of media and interactivity.
$350 to $600 per ft2 $3,800 to $6,500 m2	Moderate level of interactivity and media. Moderate density of museum quality cases.
$600 to $800 per ft2 $6,500 to $8,600 m2	High level of interactivity, media, and immersion. High density of museum quality cases.

Figure 14.3. Project Budget Rough Order of Magnitude Estimates.
LORD CULTURAL RESOURCES

Whichever method is chosen, at this stage of the exhibition planning process it is essential to know how much money is available for the implementation of the exhibition and how much is required to fund other tasks such as marketing, fundraising, programming, object acquisition, or conservation that are *not* included in figure 14.3. For example, an exhibition brief proposed by museum staff may identify an overall budget of US$2.5 million for a five thousand square foot (465 sq m) exhibition. This budget assumes $300 per square foot ($1.5 million) for design and implementation of the exhibition with the remaining $1 million identified for other tasks. Some comparable understanding of how "buckets" of money need to be allocated at this early stage allows for greater control throughout the rest of the exhibition process and more realistic planning.

14.2.5 Resource Plan

Finally, the exhibition brief should begin to identify the categories of staff and contract resources required to carry out the project. What staff will be assigned to the project and what percentage of their time will be dedicated to this task? Who will be the project leader? What teams and committees are required? What tasks will be contracted out and how will these firms or individuals be integrated? Will there be a catalog? Will there be accompanying curriculum-based programs or digital experiences?

Resource plans aim to show how the project can optimize the expertise of the museum without diminishing the public service and programming the museum needs to provide on a day-to-day basis. If the project is large enough, for example, leadership may determine that full or partial closure is required for a certain period to get the work done properly with internal resources and operating budgets. Alternatively, a strategy for using external resources can ensure that the museum stays open and operates normally.

Case Study

CANADA: DAY 1 TRAVELING EXHIBITION BY THE CANADIAN MUSEUM OF IMMIGRATION AT PIER 21, HALIFAX

In February 2011, Halifax's Pier 21, a site-specific museum on the dock to which many generations of seaborne immigrants had reported for processing, became Canada's sixth national museum with a mandate "to explore the theme of immigration to Canada in order to enhance public understanding of the experiences of immigrants as they arrived in Canada, of the vital role immigration has played in the building of Canada, and of the contributions of immigrants to Canada's culture, economy, and way of life" as cited in the museum's act statement. In celebration of this new national mandate, staff at the Canadian Museum of Immigration at Pier 21 (CMIP) identified a concept for an exhibition that would travel across the country. Their exhibition brief was approved by the director and the museum's Board of Trustees and became the basis for their search for designers and fabrication suppliers.

- **Purpose:** Traveling across Canada from 2013 until the 150th anniversary of Canada's Confederation in 2017, *Canada: Day 1* will be the museum's premiere exhibition. It will build awareness and raise the profile of CMIP. It will create opportunities to build and enhance the museum's digital/intangible collections. It will contribute to Canada's 150th anniversary and build new opportunities for the museum to engage with audiences across the nation.

- **Concept:** The *Canada: Day 1* traveling exhibition will reach audiences across Canada and share experiences and impressions of immigrants and refugees on their first day in Canada from Confederation in 1867 to the present day. The core idea focuses on capturing what it feels like to become a Canadian and what it means to new immigrants. What are the commonalities and differences and how are they expressed across the country, across cultures, and across time? The exhibition will use oral histories and archival collections to create a personal experience for visitors. In addition, the exhibition will incorporate original art commissioned especially for the show in order to create a compelling and visually exciting show.

- **Size:** The exhibition will be limited to 1,500 square feet (140 sq m). This is a suitably sized show that will fit in many of Canada's small- and medium-sized museums and galleries. This is a significant decision on the part of the museum. It is a conscious decision regarding whom this national museum will serve with its outreach program.

- **Budget:** A budget of $1 million was identified to research, plan, design, and build the exhibition. The budget included a juried art selection process and commissioning for new works of art, a marketing strategy, and traveling exhibition implementation plan.

- **Resource plan:** Recognizing their limited staff resources, CMIP identified a strategy to rely heavily on contracted resources: interpretive planners, designers, and fabricators. The staff's role would be limited to project oversight and sourcing and researching their own collections, which are particularly strong from 1928 to 1971—the Pier 21 period. However, in order to capture other historic periods, the present day, and stories to be collected from across the nation, additional researchers and experts needed to be hired within the project budget.

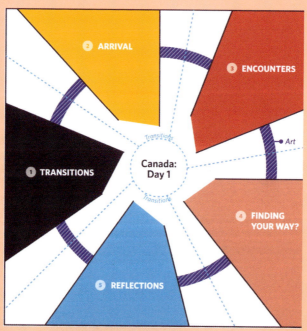

Figure 14.4. *Canada: Day 1* traveling exhibition interpretive framework.
LORD CULTURAL RESOURCES

Chapter 15

Interpretive Planning

Maria Piacente

The National Association for Interpretation defines interpretation as "a communication process that forges intellectual and emotional connections between the interests of the visitor and the meanings inherent in the resource."[1]

If, therefore, we understand that exhibitions are about meaning, communication, and affective transformation, it follows that a museum exhibition is *not* first and foremost a problem of design, but a challenge in planning for effective communication with the intended groups of visitors. The essential questions are:

- What meanings do we wish to communicate?
- To whom do we intend to communicate these meanings?
- What are the most appropriate means of communicating these meanings?

In order to answer these questions and to successfully connect objects and content found in museums to visitors emotionally and intellectually, we need an **Interpretive Plan**. Interpretive planning has emerged as a distinct and respected discipline in museology and one of the more critical tasks in the exhibition development process, as significant as design in creating high quality, educational, and engaging visitor experiences. This is the hallmark of visitor-centricity in exhibition planning. Some museums and cultural institutions have interpretive planners as part of their exhibition or public programming departments, while others have committed more firmly to the process by creating an interpretive planning division. Museums who don't have interpretive planners on staff will outsource this activity to professionals who can develop a narrative that guides design, focuses curatorial work, and puts the audience at the center of the process.

This manual focuses on *project-specific* interpretive planning—the function and products of interpretive planning in relation to exhibitions. However, it should be noted that the principles and techniques of interpretive planning can and do apply to other museum functions including institutional master plans, site master plans, and educational and public program plans, both strategic and project based. For example, interpretive master plans, which are regularly developed by the U.S. National Parks Service, apply interpretive planning principles to the entire site rather than to a specific exhibition or historic/natural feature. Such plans include expanded market analyses, staffing and resourcing strategies, budgets, public programming proposals, and implementation and phasing strategies.

There are three reasons for incorporating interpretive plans in exhibition development. The first is to be **relevant**, **meaningful**, and **relatable**. Because the majority of visitors are not artists, curators, historians, scientists, or members of a special interest group, museum professionals need to find better ways to communicate complex and unfamiliar ideas. In *Interpreting Our Heritage* Freeman Tilden outlines six principles of interpretation and summarizes that "information, as such, is not interpretation. Interpretation is revelation based upon information."[2]

The museum's task is to find ways to relate the content and character of the visitor's experience of the museum exhibition to existing visitor interests and knowledge, or if the subject matter is completely foreign, find techniques that motivate visitors to want to learn more. As Lisa Brochu describes in her *5-M Model for Successful Interpretive Planning*,[3] interpretive planning is a deliberate process for thinking about how to facilitate meaning and affective experiences for visitors.

The second reason is to be **visitor centered**. Visitors vary in age, ethnicity, and educational background among many other factors. Visitors attend as individuals or in groups as tourists, as part of a school visit, or as a family. Each grouping or type of visitor learns and behaves differently in a museum setting. Interpretive planners analyze all these diverse visitor profiles as well as the intended or "target" market for the exhibition in order to identify exhibit experiences that address disparate needs, meet curriculum requirements, and communicate effectively.

The curatorial or scientific voice is no longer the only voice in a museum exhibition. Without presenting unscientific or ahistorical interpretations as if they were authoritative, museums must find ways to acknowledge diverse and often conflicting interpretations in order to ensure that the scientific or curatorial viewpoint remains relevant to the audience. In such cases, interpretive planners will work closely with their colleagues leading evaluation and public consultation processes, as well as community based advisory committees and subject matter experts.

Interpretive planning is also a means for inviting and incorporating the community into the exhibition planning process. How do we represent opposing opinions, perspectives, and voices? How do we tell stories about our communities when our collections do not reflect them or when our curatorial and planning teams are more representative of privileged White classes? As museums continue to be more accountable to their communities, it is important for planners to find ways to inform people about an exhibition project, invite them to be a part of the process, or to actively research and collect to repair these disparities.

The third reason is **decision-making** and **monitoring**. Interpretive planning brings order to the exhibition development process and facilitates project management throughout. Interpretive plans structure process by defining/influencing the following:

- Research, collections, images, and other content needed in the exhibition. In this way an interpretive plan informs research and content coordination planning, identifies gaps that need to be addressed, and engages with the curatorial team by suggesting ways collections and research topics can be organized for visitor engagement.
- Design and creative needs. An interpretive plan outlines the scope, scale, character, and approximate anticipated number of exhibit elements and their relationships within the space. As design progresses, it becomes a tool by which to measure if design is meeting agreed interpretive and content objectives. Design may require updates and changes to the interpretive plan, which is okay. The interpretive plan is meant to be iterative and spark creativity while ensuring that the objectives for the visitor experience are maintained.
- Production requirements. The interpretive plan is one of the earliest indications of the scope of the exhibit fabrication and media production needs in a project. The approach to media use and how to realize these elements physically—from dioramas to showcases to multimedia—is first described in the interpretive plan. As such, it is an opportunity to test the project budget.
- Anticipated audiences and the nature of their experience in the exhibition environment. The descriptions found in an interpretive plan, reflecting market research and front-end evaluation, inform planning for educational and outreach services, publicity, and associated marketing initiatives.

In its role as a comprehensive qualitative description—outlining what visitors will potentially see, hear, and do—the interpretive plan can be used as part of the design brief to inform designers and other specialist suppliers, especially if design is intended to be outsourced. The interpretive strategy or interpretive plan can be used in the Request for Proposal (RFP) process to ensure you hire the right team. As well, the interpretive plan is a tool for tracking project progress, ensuring that collections, content, and communication objectives are being successfully incorporated into design and production. Is the experience balanced? Are there enough interactives? Will young people be engaged? Finally, it can be used as a tool for measuring the success of the exhibition as summative evaluation (see chapter 12) illustrates whether the documented outcomes in the interpretive plan have been achieved.

Figure 15.1 outlines the core components of the interpretive planning process. Interpretive planning is a creative, iterative, and consultative process. Each stage has specific tasks and products.

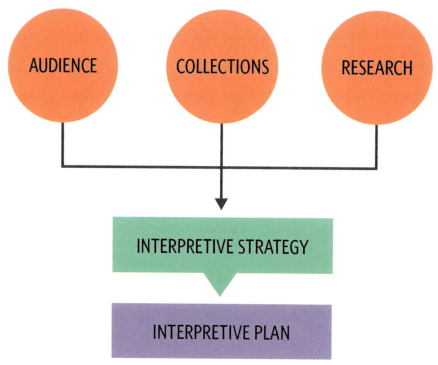

Figure 15.1. Interpretive planning process. LORD CULTURAL RESOURCES

15.1 PREPLANNING, RESEARCH, AND VISIONING

Interpretive planners begin by reviewing the research and conceptual planning that has been conducted to date as recorded in the exhibition brief or other documentation prepared by members of the curatorial team. Interpretive planners need to immerse themselves in the content of the exhibition. They are required to do the following:

1. Research, read, and learn about the subject of the exhibition. Interpretive planners will not become experts on a particular topic, but they should be able to engage more readily with curators and specialists to translate what they learn into accessible experiences for visitors. Curators and subject matter experts are academics who are intensely excited about the deep historical and scientific meaning of collections—meanings that need to be translated for the lay person who has not spent their life studying these ideas and therefore who may not be easily engaged without the intervention of an interpretive planner.

2. Review the collections that will be included in the exhibition. What is the interpretive value of the collections? What meanings can be derived from them? What stories do they tell? Interpretive plans must address how collections will be used and interpreted in the exhibition. This includes artifacts, works of art, archival materials, specimens, still and moving images, and intangible collections such as music or oral histories. Exhibition development is more effective when interpretive planners work closely with curators and scientists. Together they can create a story that unfolds for the visitor.

3. Understand the audience for whom this exhibition is being created. Existing evaluation and marketing studies as well as interviews with the museum staff will help the interpretive planner develop audience profiles. Does the museum serve mainly school children? Is the

exhibition designed to engage youth? Will the exhibition serve all audience types? At this stage in the process, the core exhibition team may engage in formative evaluation to test preliminary concepts and storylines derived from the interpretive planning process. Participating in such events ensures that the interpretive planner can more accurately represent people in the visitor experience.

In addition to this background review, interpretive planners need to conduct original research and gather information pertinent to the development of the interpretive plan, such as:

1. Compile new research regarding best practices and trends. Interpretive planners need to be aware of current trends in exhibition development and interpretive techniques. This new research allows the team to learn about successful exhibitions, creative design techniques, and what other museums are doing. The research needs to be targeted and relevant to allow the team to explore what may or may not work for the exhibition they are planning. For example, museum professionals who are not media specialists may not know about augmented reality or project mapping, and how each might function as a part of the visitor experience. Today, each of these technologies are being used in fascinating and creative ways all over the world. In the early 2000s, few museums were telling "personal stories" in their exhibitions. Today, we would be hard-pressed to find an exhibition that does not include some personal stories or other techniques to humanize objects and complex topics. The interpretive planner—just like the designer—should be on the cutting of edge of what is new, whether high tech or low tech, in order to communicate to the core exhibition teams how such techniques may or may not be suitable to the exhibition being planned.

2. Conduct and facilitate workshops to explore topics, themes, and subthemes; debate the relevance of best practices and trends; discuss communication and learning objectives; and ultimately envision what the visitor experience will be like when the exhibition opens. Dynamic working sessions build consensus and allow ideas to mature and change.

15.2 INTERPRETIVE STRATEGY

The interpretive strategy, sometimes called exhibition treatment, clarifies the purpose of the exhibition and accurately communicates a vision for the project. This strategy builds upon the exhibition brief if one exists or can influence the development of one if such a brief has not been created yet. It begins to develop the visitor experience through definition of themes and communication objectives. It consists primarily of three components: the metanarrative (the big idea), thematic framework, and communication objectives (or visitor outcomes). This is a period when the interpretive planner and curatorial team works very closely together.

15.2.1 Metanarrative or "The Big Idea"

It is important to articulate why the museum is undertaking this exhibition and the main message or "big idea" (metanarrative) that underpins the story you want to tell. While the metanarrative will be further defined by objectives, themes, and topics in the interpretive plan, early in the planning process it should be a powerful statement that inspires the story and the design.

Figure 15.2 illustrates the interpretive framework for the Perlan Museum of Natural Wonders in Reykjavik, Iceland, a natural history experience housed in a spectacular heritage building—a defunct heating plant. The metanarrative for the exhibition is "Iceland is one of the most unique geological and ecological places on earth—shaping who we are as Icelanders." The exhibition opened to the public in 2019 after a three-year planning and design process.

Figure 15.2. Interpretive framework for Perlan Museum of Natural Wonders, Iceland.

In 2020, the Niagara Parks Commission began the adaptive reuse of the stunning Canadian Niagara Power Generating Station, located in Niagara Falls Canada, into an attraction. The meta-narrative at the heart of the interpretive framework is "Harnessing the 'true power' of the Falls." Figure 15.3 demonstrates the core themes drawn from the big idea.

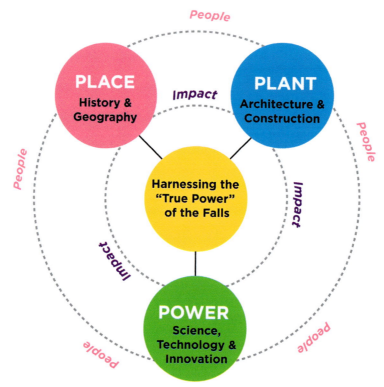

Figure 15.3. Interpretive framework for the Niagara Power Generating station, Niagara Falls, Canada.

15.3 ORGANIZATIONAL AND THEMATIC FRAMEWORKS

The organization and **thematic framework** for an exhibition, often illustrated as a bubble diagram or some other version of a relationship model, intellectually organizes the visitor experience. Thematic frameworks articulate and structure the relationship between themes and subthemes, helping visitors make sense of vast amounts of data. Frameworks also help curators to organize and group content and designers to make decisions about how the experience is laid out in physical space.

The first step in developing a thematic framework is to determine whether an exhibition will be **linear** or **nonlinear**. Linear or sequential structures have a beginning and an end. Visitors must experience content, themes, and topics in a particular order. The presentation is highly controlled and orchestrated to ensure comprehension of ideas or events as they build on each other toward a conclusion.

Chronology is the most common example of a linear organizational model as exemplified by many history exhibitions or by art museum retrospectives of artists' careers. Spatial structures are another example of a linear model in which an exhibition is based upon spatial relationships such as a trip across a country from east to west, or room by room through a reconstructed archaeological site.

Figure 15.4. Linear organizational model. LORD CULTURAL RESOURCES

Nonlinear structures are frameworks that allow visitors to explore themes and topics nonsequentially. Visitors can move between exhibit areas as they choose, according to various pathways developed by interpretive planners and designers. Such organizations, often described as thematic or contextual, accommodate more complex exhibitions. Because these exhibitions can be experienced in different ways, the role of orientation or "arrival" is crucial. Visitors need to know what choices are available to them as they navigate the content according to their interest.

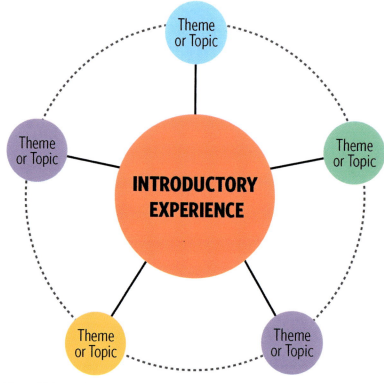

Figure 15.5. Nonlinear organizational model. LORD CULTURAL RESOURCES

Some examples of nonlinear structures include:

- **Focal specific structures** establish one major topic or theme around which are clustered a number of subthemes that radiate from the core, much like the petals of a flower or the layers of an onion. Each subtheme explores one aspect or progressively reveals aspects of a single topic. Large and complex exhibitions often string a series of focal specific structures that are contextually, thematically, or hierarchically linked together.

- **Parallel thematic structures** establish a set of themes or subthemes that are used over and over again to explore many topics. Natural history exhibitions often employ this type of interpretation where different geographical regions are interpreted by the same set of themes such as flora, fauna, and climate.

- **Independent structures** are frameworks in which individual, loosely related, or unrelated topics are addressed within a single area or gallery. An exhibit can be understood on its own, without reference to other exhibits. Such strategies are sometimes employed by science centers or children's museums.

15.4 ORGANIZATIONAL AND THEMATIC FRAMEWORKS FROM AROUND THE WORLD

15.4.1 Buddha Smriti Park, Patna, India

The thematic framework for the Buddha Smriti Park demonstrates a chronological approach to present the life and impact of Buddha on India and the world. The experience inside the museum is linear and directed, beginning in Gallery 1 and ending in Gallery 4, following key periods in Buddha's life. The twenty-two-acre park was developed by the Bihar government to commemorate the 2,554th birth anniversary of the Buddha. In addition to the museum, the park's focal point is the Stupa, a shrine that houses the holy relics of Sakyamuni Buddha. The park is a place of pilgrimage.

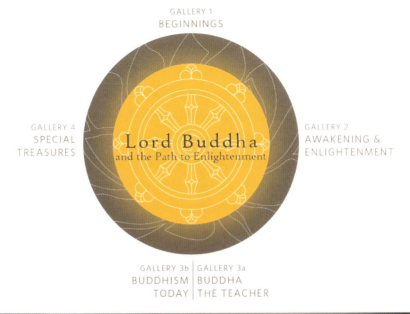

Figures 15.6 and 15.7. Thematic framework and exhibit image from the Buddha Smriti Park, Patna, India. LORD CULTURAL RESOURCES

15.4.2 Etihad Museum, Dubai, United Arab Emirates

The Etihad Museum is a history museum that celebrates the unification of the United Arab Emirates in 1971. The interpretive framework presents a hybrid solution. The chronological portion of the exhibition takes visitors on a journey through the events leading up to unification and the Constitution. Once visitors come out of the directed historical experience, a free flow gallery, thematically organized, allows for the exploration of topics demonstrating the impact of unification as well as other contemporary subjects.

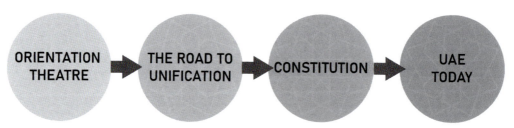

Figure 15.8. Thematic framework for Etihad Museum, Dubai, UAE.

Figure 15.9. Visitors interact with one of many of the museum's digital experiences, Etihad Museum, Dubai, UAE. DUBAI CULTURE ARTS AUTHORITY/ETIHAD MUSEUM

15.4.3 Tennessee State Museum, Nashville

Chronology is the organizing factor for the museum's permanent exhibition galleries which opened to the public in a new building in 2019. Each gallery represents a relevant period in Tennessee's history. In addition, a series of linking themes can be discovered in all galleries, creating opportunities for layered continuity and universal ideas.

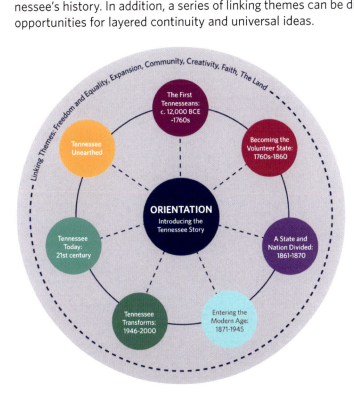

Figure 15.10. Thematic framework for the permanent galleries at the Tennessee State Museum.

Figure 15.11. Civil War Gallery at the Tennessee State Museum, Nashville. TENNESSEE STATE MUSEUM

Interpretive Planning

15.4.4 University of Michigan Museum of Natural History, Under the Microscope Gallery, Ann Arbor

Two major themes allow visitors to explore the building blocks of life in an open, discovery-based experience.

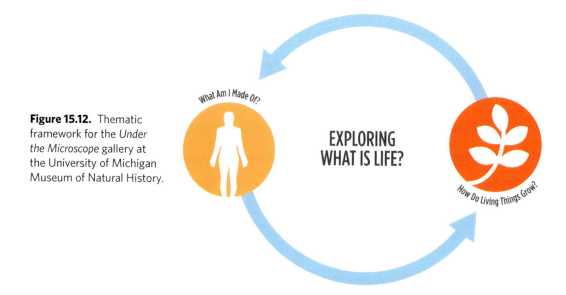

Figure 15.12. Thematic framework for the *Under the Microscope* gallery at the University of Michigan Museum of Natural History.

Figure 15.13. Under the Microscope Gallery at the University of Michigan Museum of Natural History, Ann Arbor. LORD CULTURAL RESOURCES

15.4.5 Opera di Santa Croce, Florence, Italy

The temporary exhibition, entitled *Sisters in Liberty: From Florence, Italy to New York, New York,* was installed in 2019 at the National Museum of Immigration on Ellis Island. The exhibition examined the intersection between the ideas of liberty inspired by each country's statue of liberty—Bartholdi's Statue of Liberty at Ellis Island and Pio Fedi's *Libertà* in Santa Croce, Florence. The experience is linear as each topic area builds on the stories experienced in the previous section, leading to a final conclusion.

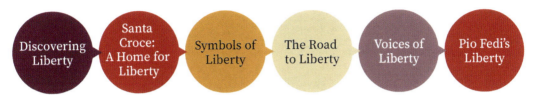

Figure 15.14. Thematic framework for the *Sisters in Liberty: From Florence, Italy, to New York, New York,* a temporary exhibit created by the Opera di Santa Croce.

Figure 15.15. *Sisters in Liberty* exhibition at the National Museum of Immigration at Ellis Island, New York, organized by Opera di Santa Croce, Florence, Italy. LORD CULTURAL RESOURCES

Interpretive Planning

15.4.6 Miraflores, Guatemala

The Miraflores Museum tells the iconic story of the ancient Mayan city of Kaminaljuyú. The new permanent exhibition completely reenvisions the story of the site, incorporates interactivity, and breathes new life into the museum's exquisite collection. The exhibition is organized thematically. Chronology will play an organizing role within each of the themes as appropriate. A linking theme called "How Do We Know?" creates opportunities to showcase the work of archaeologists and how they interpret the past.

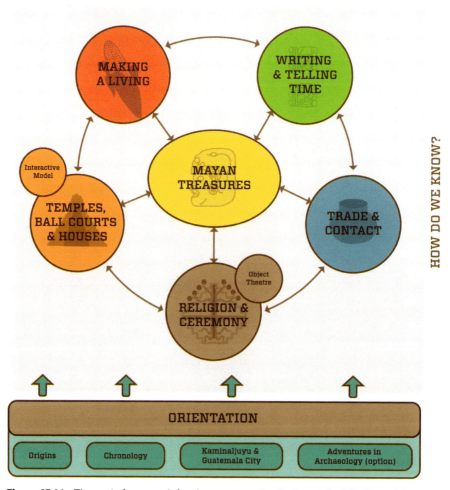

Figure 15.16. Thematic framework for the permanent galleries at the Miraflores Museum.

15.4.7 Muskoka Discovery Centre, Gravenhurst, Canada

Figure 15.17 illustrates the thematic framework for the *Misko-Aki* (Red Earth) Confluence of Cultures Exhibition. The center's new exhibition spaces represent a broader initiative of the Muskoka Discovery Center to become a more vibrant and relevant cultural hub for the community, tell the story of Muskoka's diverse cultural and natural heritage with a renewed appreciation toward Indigenous cultures and traditions, and preserve its unique marine history. Stories, content, and design are created in partnership with Indigenous communities.

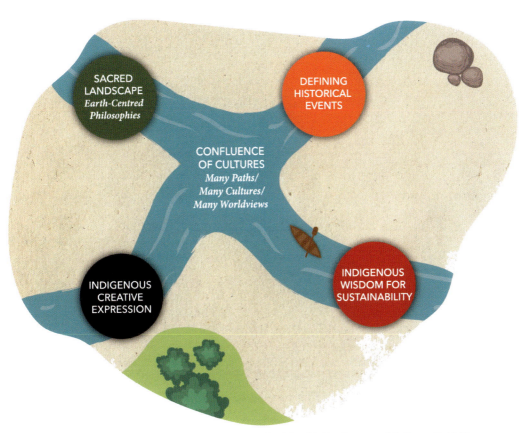

Figure 15.17. Thematic framework for the *Misko Aki* (Red Earth) Confluence of Cultures Exhibition.

Interpretive Planning

15.4.8 North Dakota Heritage Center & State Museum, Inspiration Gallery, Bismarck, North Dakota

The Heritage Center's exhibition planning team chose a nonlinear approach to telling the state's history. Visitors choose to explore history by theme after a major show and orientation experience, which helps visitors to understand how the exhibition is organized. Chronology plays a secondary role in each of the thematic areas.

This innovative approach breaks with traditional planning for permanent history exhibitions. It provides visitors with choice; creates opportunities for changing content; allows for presentation to the present day without an "end" date; and facilitates dynamic relationships between objects by theme as opposed to time.

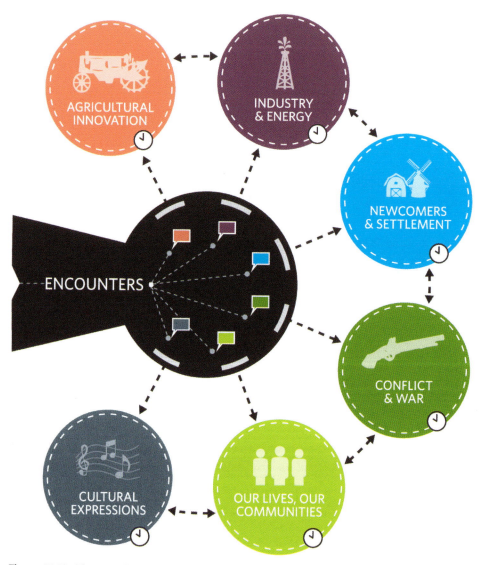

Figure 15.18. Thematic framework for the Inspiration Gallery, North Dakota Heritage Center & State Museum.

15.5 COMMUNICATION OBJECTIVES/VISITOR OUTCOMES

Communication objectives or visitor outcomes establish clear goals for the exhibition as a whole and for each of the major themes or subthemes defined by the thematic framework. These are the messages visitors will take away with them when they leave the exhibition. What do we want visitors to learn? How do we want visitors to feel? These messages identify the intended impact and outcomes for the visitor experience: cognitive, emotional, and behavioral.

These objectives guide the formulation of the storyboard. Is a didactic display of objects or a short film the best way to achieve our objectives? Well-crafted communication objectives or messages help us make decisions about the types of exhibits we need in the exhibition. As well, communication objectives influence the selection of artifacts, the writing of text, and the choice of imagery.

Communication objectives should be simply and clearly stated with no more than three objectives per theme or subtheme. Using action verbs is a great way to craft strong objectives and messages. Too many objectives will result in confusion or themes that try to accomplish too much. Most visitors can't remember or retain more than three things at a given time. This forces us to make decisions about content and exhibits that will ultimately lead to a successful interpretation.

For example, one of the exhibition themes for the National Archaeological Museum in Aruba was identified as *Contact, Exchange and Migration*. The three objectives defined for it were:

1. Visitors will explore the origins of Aruban culture.
2. Visitors will discover the ways in which different cultural groups influenced and changed each other and how that influence is recognized in the archaeological and historical record.
3. Visitors will understand the role that Aruba played in Caribbean exchange networks and the wider world of clashing empires.

Interpretive planners revisit and evaluate messaging throughout the design and content development process. If testing and summative evaluation reveal that visitors are meeting the objectives identified in the interpretive plan, we know we have been successful in achieving desired outcomes.

15.6 INTERPRETIVE PLAN

The final interpretive plan, sometimes called a visitor experience plan, is an extensive elaboration of the interpretive strategy. Each thematic area is expanded with detailed component-by-component descriptions of all the exhibits and stories that visitors will experience.

The term "storyline" is often used to describe the core of the interpretive plan—the document that identifies what visitors will see, hear, and do in an exhibition. Each theme and subtheme identified in the thematic framework is defined by a series of potential exhibits (means of expression). Here the interpretive planner describes in words how visitors will experience the content of the exhibition: didactic displays of artifacts, interactive multimedia, immersive environments, or hands-on experiments. Each exhibit is carefully selected based on the communication objectives defined for that thematic area, the collections and resources available to tell the story, and how the audience will best be able to understand and engage with that content. Budget also plays a role, as the interpretive planner is keenly aware of the amount of money that can be responsibly spent. This is a dynamic process as a large number of exhibit ideas identified in collaboration with the design team will be articulated until the best solution is determined.

One of the ways to facilitate creativity and address multiple learning styles is to identify categories of means of expression against which the storyline can be checked with reference to visitors' learning styles. For example, if using "Gardner" as a guide to understanding visitor behavior in an exhibition, consider the following:

- Didactic means of expression including text panels, cases of artifacts, and displays of works of art will appeal to visual-spatial, linguistic-verbal, and intrapersonal learners.

- Hands-on/minds-on activities are often low-tech interactives that incorporate mechanical devices, comparative exhibits, feedback stations, and open-ended questions. These types of experiences are suited to kinesthetic, interpersonal, intrapersonal, and logical-mathematical learners.

- Multimedia includes all media-based exhibits from videos to touch-screens and from augmented reality systems to simulators or even large-format theaters. Because there is such a wide variety, most media will appeal to a wide variety of learners, but in particular to visual-spatial, musical, interpersonal, intrapersonal, kinesthetic, and logical-mathematical types.

- Immersive environments include walkthrough experiences and dioramas that may incorporate sound, video, and hands-on experiences. Such exhibits appeal to most learners but especially interpersonal and visual-spatial people.

Using too much of one style may be intentional and purposeful in the case of some art and culture displays or science exhibitions, but more often than not it is not apparent. By using some form of categorization (as per above), the interpretive planner can make sure the experience is balanced, meets diverse audience needs, and is not boring!

Such categories can also be used as a budget check since some means of expression like multimedia and immersive environments tend to be more expensive than didactic displays. If the overall budget has a per-square-foot/meter cost that can accommodate only a low-to-medium level of multimedia and interactivity, then an interpretive plan that called for 75 percent media-based experiences would be over budget even before design starts. The interpretive planner and the core exhibition team should agree on categories and terminology prior to the development of the interpretive plan to help manage this process and to create support for the storyline.

Case Study

UNIVERSITY OF MICHIGAN MUSEUM OF NATURAL HISTORY

EXPLORING MICHIGAN

The University of Michigan Museum of Natural History (UMMNH) reopened to the public in 2019 after completing a move from the historic Ruthven Museum Building to the new Biological Sciences building. The new museum hosts a series of permanent galleries focusing on evolution, life sciences, and Michigan's natural history. In addition, the museum includes a new state of the art presentation space, a fully conditioned temporary exhibition gallery, and a planetarium.

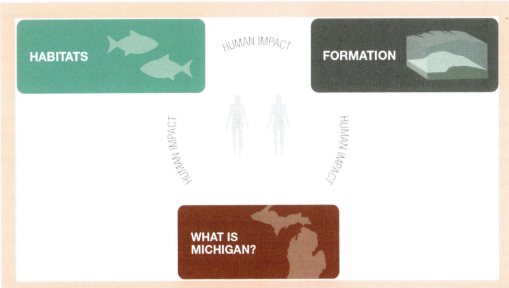

Figure 15.19. Michigan gallery thematic framework.

The *Exploring Michigan* Permanent Exhibition Gallery is organized thematically, allowing visitors to discover the state's ecology, the relationships between organisms and their environment, and the impact humans have on the environment.

The Metanarrative: "Michigan's unique habitats and diverse ecosystems are shaped by human and natural forces."

Communication objectives:

- Visitors will appreciate the diversity of Michigan's flora and fauna and how the landscape has changed over time.
- Visitors will be inspired to explore, study, and steward the local and regional natural environment.
- Visitors will understand the diversity of Michigan's ecosystems and the impact of human activity on them.

The gallery is organized into the following thematic areas:

- What is Michigan?
- How was Michigan formed?
- What are Michigan's Habitats?

Linking these themes together are stories of human interaction with the environment. These stories demonstrate the various ways humans have influenced and changed Michigan's natural history over time, and the ways the environment influences and supports us.

Design approach: The gallery is informed by stunning dioramas showcasing the museum's incredible collection of specimens. These environments are enlivened by interactive field stations as well as archaeological and paleontological materials. The following images are from the Exploring Michigan Gallery, courtesy of the University of Michigan Museum of Natural History.

Figure 15.20. Exhibits in the Exploring Michigan Gallery, University of Michigan Museum of Natural History, Ann Arbor. LORD CULTURAL RESOURCES

Figure 15.21. Exhibits in the Exploring Michigan Gallery, University of Michigan Museum of Natural History, Ann Arbor. LORD CULTURAL RESOURCES

Figure 15.22. Exhibits in the Exploring Michigan Gallery, University of Michigan Museum of Natural History, Ann Arbor. LORD CULTURAL RESOURCES

Case Study

CAPITOL VISITOR CENTER EXHIBITION HALL, WASHINGTON, DC: EXCERPTS FROM THE INTERPRETIVE PLAN

On December 2, 2008, the US Capitol Visitor Center (CVC) opened to the public. In addition to the orientation theaters, gift shops, restaurant, and a program of tours that takes visitors through the Capitol, the CVC also includes an exhibition hall where visitors explore the story of the US Congress and the Capitol. In 2014, the CVC launched a redesign of the exhibition hall with the strategic goal of addressing visitor experience and education: "Engage visitors in meaningful experiences that impart a greater understanding of our democratic process and their role in it." The redeveloped exhibition hall will launch to public in 2022.

Metanarrative: "The actions of Congress have a direct and meaningful impact on every American's life. While the institution has changed over time to reflect a changing and complex world, the role of citizens remains central to the proper functioning of our democracy."

Interpretive Planning

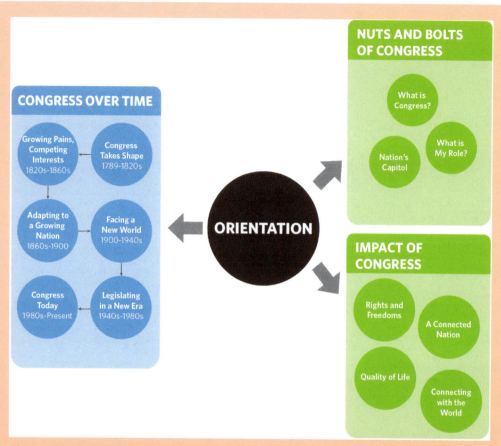

Figure 15.23. Thematic framework for the permanent exhibition, Capitol Visitor Center exhibition hall.

The framework identifies both chronology and themes to organize the visitor experience. The diagram demonstrates how content will be organized and is "relatively" proportional:

- Orientation: Visitors are drawn to the exhibition hall where their interest is piqued by the importance of Congress to the daily lives of Americans.

- Congress over Time: The story of Congress is organized chronologically, illustrating how it has changed, grown, and adapted as well as highlighting the passing of key legislation in relation to events and the changing nature of the American population.

- Nuts and Bolts of Congress: Visitors explore the function and make-up of Congress—the who, what, where, and how—and the role people play in American democracy.

- Impact of Congress: Visitors discover Congress' impact on Americans lives and the world such as rights and freedoms and quality of life.

Communication objectives for the theme "Congress over Time":

- To communicate how Congress has changed, grown, and adapted over time.
- To demonstrate how the function of the institution (over time) has and continues to influence the creation of legislation that affects our lives.
- To allow visitors to explore institutional change and congressional decision-making through primary resources; visitors make historical links or find content that is of most interest to them.
- To explore stories that demonstrate when Congress didn't act, helping visitors understand that change takes time, and that Congress is a reflection of the population.

NOTES

1. "What is Interpretation?" National Association for Interpretation, accessed November 2020, https://www.interpnet.com/NAI/interp/About/About_Interpretation/nai/_About/what_is_interp.aspx?hkey=53b0bfb4-74a6-4cfc-8379-1d55847c2cb9.
2. Freeman Tilden, *Interpreting Our Heritage*, 4th ed. (Chapel Hill: The University of North Carolina Press, 2008), n.p.
3. Lisa Brochu, *Interpretive Planning: The 5-M Model for Successful Planning Projects* (Fort Collins, CO: Heartfelt Publications, 2013).

Chapter 16

Content Development

Lisa Wright

A successful exhibition does more than convey information: it tells stories, sparks emotions, and creates memories. Beautiful design and technological flourishes, immersive environments and interactive experiences, artifacts, and touchables all should support a compelling, memorable narrative. Rich, engaging written content binds together all these other elements, unifying and clarifying the exhibition narrative. Without powerful text, the visitor experience will be flat, inauthentic, and unsatisfying. With it, visitors will come away not just with new knowledge but with new understanding.

Writing text for gallery walls and panels is a frequently underestimated undertaking. Successful exhibitions build content strategy and content creation into the entire process, developing it concurrently with concept development, research, design, interpretation, and selection and procurement of artifacts, images, video, and stories.

Depending on the institution and the nature and size of the exhibition, it is often useful to create a content development team or committee that includes key individuals with a variety of perspectives, skills, and roles. This may include museum staff from different departments, as well as external researchers, subject matter experts, and community members. While traditionally content development was the sole responsibility of the curator, museums are increasingly recognizing that the stories told in exhibitions are often best told by other experts, communities, and individuals who have lived experience of the exhibition content being presented. This is particularly true for exhibitions on Black, Indigenous, and people of color (BIPOC) stories, communities, histories, and cultures. Rethinking the "curatorial voice" and opening the content development process to those beyond the museum is important in the process of developing twenty-first-century exhibitions and committing to diversity, equity, accessibility, and inclusion.

16.1 RESEARCH PLANNING

The curator develops the core initial ideas for the exhibition in the exhibition brief. These concepts develop dynamically alongside interpretive planning, design, and content development, as illustrated in figure 1.1 in chapter 1. Content and design influence and challenge one another, ensuring each enriches the other, and providing visitors with experiences that have both intellectual depth and emotional impact.

Researching and authenticating material is necessary, but not sufficient for the success of an exhibition. Content must also be documented and packaged to make it easy for designers and fabricators to transform it into a physical experience. The content team needs the right tools to organize the research, and enough time and resources to verify facts, proofread documents, and investigate new ideas. Tools fall into two categories: organizational and documentation.

Organizational tools include schedules, tracking mechanisms, and matrices that outline content needs, responsibilities, and deadlines. Documentation tools include forms for recording all content information. Forms may be organized in a database to track the large amounts of material.

Curatorial research should be completed by the end of the design phase once plans and drawings become construction bids; content changes can become costly. Once production begins, members of the content team will be required to check content accuracy. This includes confirming factual accuracy in all text, videos, and all other verbal content, vetting production-ready graphics to ensure correct text accompanies all images, graphs and graphics, and other visual content, and that artifacts are correctly laid out and labeled.

In addition to checking for factual accuracy, the content team should also monitor for omissions and misleading, inconsistently framed, or confusing information that could diminish the effectiveness of the exhibition.

16.1.1 Research Matrix

A **research matrix** can be invaluable for organizing content development. It identifies content requirements for every exhibit and experience in the interpretive plan. It breaks exhibition content into specified categories such as:

- Artifacts (objects), specimens, or works of art
- Text and label copy
- Images
- Hands-on, or other non-media, special exhibits
- Media

Research matrices also provide project management information, including assigned roles, responsibilities, approval processes, content specifications, and deadlines. The matrix requires explicit management, as it evolves to reflect changing circumstances such as the availability of resources, design considerations, and new information. Figure 16.1 is an excerpt from the research matrix for the Centre for Freshwater Research and Education's new permanent exhibition to open at Lake Superior State University in Michigan in 2021.

Using content specifications from the research plan, the team audits resources. What research has already been completed? What new studies are required? New research can come from primary sources such as objects, archival documents, and first-person accounts, or from secondary sources such as scholarly books and articles. One member of the content team should take responsibility for developing a list of sources including those in other museums, archives, and private and corporate collections. Throughout content development, researchers must carefully

Exhibit Name and Number	Text Communication Points	Photos/Illustrations	Specimens/ Reproductions	Hands-on Interactives	Multimedia	Notes/ Comments
1. Why This Center? **Communication Points** • Freshwater is essential to our planet, from sustaining life (human, plant, other animals) to driving economies (industry, shipping etc.). We all need to be freshwater stewards. • The Center is located at the nexus of three Great Lakes, which contain nearly 20% of the world's fresh surface water. • This location makes Lake State a significant place to study and practice Great Lakes science, which is supported through cooperation from many university programs, community partners, tribal, and other government agencies and departments.						
1.1 Welcome and Orientation Map	• Brief text will convey a welcome message • Explain what the Center is and why it is located here	• Large graphic wall map beside reception desk to orient visitors, and show the Center's location at the nexus of Lakes Superior, Michigan, and Huron • OPTION: Show Ojibway perspective through Ojibway names on map. Possibly show the map oriented with East at the top, as the Anishinaabe traditionally orient themselves to the East.		• OPTION: Have the map on a turntable so that it could be turned to show Ojibway perspectives and names.		
1.2 Tribal Welcome	• Tribal elders welcoming visitors to the Center. Elders representing the four local tribes: Bay Mills, Sault Tribe, Batchewana First Nation and Garden River First Nation. • Tie water to Anishinaabe legends ("water is blood to us") • Text to be in Ojibwe, then English.	• Map showing where these tribes live?				
1.3 What We Do	• Overview for visitors about what the Center for Freshwater Education and Research is, how it came to be, and its major research areas.	• Photographs showing activities of CFRE.				
1.3.1 Other Lake State Programs	• Visitors will get an overview of other LSSU academic programs that relate to the Center and that support advancement of Great Lakes science, including but not limited to: biochemistry, biology, chemistry, conservation biology, engineering, education, environmental science, fisheries and wildlife management, geology, medical laboratory science, parks and recreation, and robotics. • Changeable graphic component so that individual academic programs can be featured on a rotating basis (profiles of students or faculty and their work)	• Photographs of students and faculty from other LSSU programs doing work related to Great Lakes science.			• OPTION: CFRE to look into getting LSSU Admissions to pay for a touchscreen here in order to profile other programs.	
1.5 What Will You Do? Visitor Pledge Interactive:	• Provide visitors with concrete actions they can take to do in their everyday lives to help preserve freshwater resources. Ask visitors to make a pledge. • Promote the Center's idea of sustainability • Touch on the Indigenous view of making decisions based on the 7th Generation (stewardship/ sustainability)	• Photos illustrating potential actions		• Visitors can pledge to do things that preserve freshwater resources. Either through a voting interactive or whiteboard/ chalkboard response.		

Figure 16.1. Sample research matrix.

track and document where information has been obtained. This allows the team to check references, investigate copyright and licensing requirements, arrange for loans where necessary, and revisit sources later in the process.

16.2 COLLECTIONS RESEARCH AND SELECTION

There is a range of exhibition collection types, including artifacts, specimens, works of art, photographs, archival documents, historic buildings, and sites, as well as intangible collections such as audio, video, and born-digital data. Each type of collection has its own challenges for research and curation—from establishing their provenance and role in the exhibition to meeting their specialized conservation and mounting requirements.

Artifacts, works of art, and specimens may play a starring or supporting role depending on the focus. An art museum exhibition on the life and work of Edgar Degas will center on the artist's paintings, drawings, and sculpture, whereas an exhibition on late nineteenth-century Paris at a history museum might feature a few Degas paintings situated among furniture, photographs, period clothing, and other vehicles of interpretation. In an artifact-heavy exhibition, some or most key pieces may be identified early in the exhibition brief phase. In exhibitions that focus less on artifacts, display items might not be identified until the interpretive plan is completed. In either case, the goal is to identify, research, and comprehensively document artifacts to create interpretive labels, case layouts, and any multimedia that incorporate digital representation or manipulation of physical objects.

When reviewing collections for artifact selection, the content team should consider:

- What collections does the museum have to support the exhibition's themes?
- What other relevant public and private collections exist? Can they feasibly be borrowed?
- Which are the "star" artifacts within these collections?
- What is the potential for telling stories around these artifacts?
- Can the artifact be displayed? Are there conservation issues? Are there cultural sensitivities that must be explored through consultation?

Once a preliminary list of artifacts has been made, consider the practicalities of these items. Key considerations for each item are:

- How big is it?
- How much does it weigh?
- Does it require special conservation or mounting?
- Is its provenance known?
- Where is it currently located?
- What does it look like?

An **artifact data sheet** is an invaluable tool for organizing information about objects and works of art. Each artifact should have its own data sheet. Museums with collections-management software can create a database of artifacts for the exhibition based on relevant fields. As artifacts are added or deleted during the content-development process, their data sheets will be added or removed from the electronic database.

Minimum information for each artifact should be organized into the following categories:

- Exhibit name/number: Artifacts are designated for specific exhibition displays identified in interpretive plans and design documentation. Designers often create a numbering system to track exhibits and design elements. These numbers should be referenced in artifact data sheets. In this manner, we know exactly where in the exhibition this artifact is supposed to be displayed.

- Artifact name: Consistent use of the correct artifact name assists in its identification and ensures that the right information appears on its display label.

- Accession or temporary number: Every artifact must have an accession number to assist in its identification during case layouts, mounting, and installation. It is also useful for tracking the location of the object in collection storerooms. If an object already has an accession number from an existing collection, that number should be used. If not, assign it a temporary exhibition-specific number.

- Dimensions: Dimensions (height, length, width, weight, and when appropriate, depth, diameter, or other parameters) are required for the purposes of exhibit design, case layout, case construction, and mounting. Dimensions should be as accurate as possible and may require members of the content team to take new measurements to ensure accuracy. Units of measurement should be clearly specified.

- Source/Location/Acquisition/Loan: This field describes the current location of the object in a collection's storage facility. If the object will be loaned from another source, this field describes the steps required to acquire the object and what special conditions will accompany the loan request.

- Description/Conservation requirements: A brief description of the object including its use, construction materials, date, and significance establish an object's provenance and reason for being included in the exhibition. Is the artifact in good condition? Is remediation required? Are there particular mounting requirements? Should its display associate it with other artifacts? Any information that can be used to write label text should be included.

- Image: Every object should be accompanied by a photograph, preferably in color. The picture not only assists in the identification of the object during installation, but also facilitates accurate case layout drawings and correct orientation of the objects in cases.

Artifact data sheets become especially important as exhibition designers and fabricators design and build display cases and mounts. Photographs and dimensions are particularly critical. For some artifacts, a written description may not clearly articulate the orientation of an artifact or accurately reflect its complexity. Should it be displayed horizontally or vertically? Do cases and platforms need additional reinforcement to support heavy objects? Good documentation immediately resolves any confusion for designers, and may avert potentially expensive errors during production, such as constructing a case that is too small. Once an artifact is identified, someone from the content team must physically find it—not just look it up in the database—to verify all the details on the artifact data sheet, including its location. It is not unheard of to discover that an artifact is not where it is supposed to be when it comes time for installation.

Object Data Sheet	
Exhibit # and Name: 3.1 Our Traditions	
Object Name and Accession Number: Hand drum and stick [shelf 5-4]	
Insert photo here 	Source: Direct Contact Details: Dimensions (LxWxH): Drum: 14 in. diameter (incl. loop) X 1.75 in. deep Stick: 12 in. L X 3.75 in. W X 5/8 in. D
Conservation/Mounting Requirement: Preferable to display item in a box-like vitrine on the introduction wall.	
Acquisition/Loan/Reproduction Details (if known):	
Credit Line Information:	
Provenance/ History of Object/Notes:	

Figure 16.2. Example of an artifact datasheet for the Forest County Potawatomi Museum and Cultural Center in Crandon, Wisconsin.

If objects are coming from remote museums, the lending institution should be responsible for checking an object's status.

In most cases, museums feature as many objects from their own collection as possible, although exhibitions can consist mostly or entirely of borrowed objects. Loan request forms outline the borrower's requirements, which typically include environmental controls, security, insurance, and professional handling procedures for the loaned object. Most forms require that these conditions be at least equivalent to those of the lending museum.

Museums must be extremely careful about provenance and authenticity of in-house and borrowed artifacts. Displaying an artifact, specimen, or work of art that is not accurately represented is embarrassing at best and can be fatally damaging to the museum's reputation. It may even result in legal action in the case of stolen artifacts. Most museums take special precautions about works of art from European collections created during the Third Reich in Germany (1933-1945) because of the large number of works the Nazis stole or extorted from Jewish owners. Additionally, artifacts of Indigenous peoples in North America, Australia, and elsewhere are culturally sensitive, and should be displayed only with the consent and involvement of the community. If artifacts are displayed alongside reproductions or replicas, the distinction should be clearly identified. It violates visitors' trust if it's unclear whether a display item is a reproduction or an original artifact.

16.3 EXHIBITION TEXT BY PATCHEN BARSS

Text is one of the most challenging tasks of any exhibition project. Writing exhibition text is unlike writing a book, essay, or newspaper article. Exhibition text comes in a range of formats: interpretive panels, image captions, artifact labels, flip panels, hands-on exhibit instructions, wall text, and digital copy for screens or monitors. It can also serve a range of functions: to inform, provoke, question, instruct, and orient. Visitors experience exhibition text within a specific experiential context.

Although each type of text is unique, there are some general best practices when it comes to drafting all forms of exhibition text. First, determine your text needs using the content team's research matrix. Eliminate all unnecessary text in cases where an image, object, or video can better convey the same message. Where text is required, consider the following:

- Research
- Core messages
- Audience
- Tone/Style
- Visual Presentation
- Word Count

Research for exhibition text may be done by the curator, writer, or someone else, depending on the institution and the nature of the exhibition. In most cases, a curator or subject matter expert performs the research, identifying key communication points for an interpretive planner or professional writer. For large exhibitions, writing responsibilities may be shared among several people. The research ensures authenticity, scientific rigor, historical accuracy, and in the case of multiple perspectives in which the community is invited to participate, the various meanings that need to be communicated. Once the final text is written, it should be reviewed against the research and core message to ensure that the editor has been true.

Core messages derive from the communication objectives and themes outlined in the interpretive plan. They guide all exhibition text and provide vital guidance on how to direct research and writing efforts. Understanding the desired outcome of each segment of writing helps the writer focus on exactly what needs to be communicated and how.

Tone and **style** should be characterized before writing begins—especially when there are multiple writers—to ensure a consistent voice. Will the tone be authoritative or conversational? Will the exhibition communicate in a third- or first-person voice? Will it be narrative or documentary? In some cases, a mix of styles may be included for exhibitions offering different perspectives and voices. The museum may publicly identify the author of exhibition text to provide the context for opinions and perspectives. The content team should create a style guide for all writers, editors, and graphic designers. Along with tone, the guide should establish spelling, grammar, and usage rules. This ensures consistency on matters such as American versus British spelling, capitalization, comma use, number styles, and target reading level.

Target audiences determine tone. Is the text aimed mainly at children, adults, or a mix? Are visitors mostly local or tourists? What languages do they speak? What is the subject matter of the exhibition and does that affect the appropriate tone? How can the text prioritize inclusiveness, diversity, equity, and accessibility? Does the text require separate interpretative sections for children or other groups? Ultimately, exhibition text should serve a broad range of visitors, but with priority placed on key audiences.

Visual presentation and writing need to be developed concurrently and seamlessly to reinforce one another. It should be possible to describe the writing and design with the same words: If the writing is informal and lively, the design should be also. If the design is epic in its grandeur, so too should be the writing. This requires writers to meet and collaborate closely with graphic designers. How will the text appear in the gallery? On what surfaces will it be presented? What font will be used and what size will it be? What color will it be printed on and what will be the color(s) of the surfaces on which it is printed? Does the design style jibe with the subject matter: be it science, history, art, politics, nature, religion, or anything else?

Word count, which is often determined by design considerations, can also be a useful tool for honing and focusing text. In general, limits reflect the minimum number of words required to get across key messages and the maximum amount of text visitors can handle reading without becoming overwhelmed. Writing to length is a skill unto itself and involves more than merely cutting content to fit. Tight constraints force the writer to ensure every word counts, reinforcing the key messages, furthering the narrative, and enhancing visitors' experience. Note that in addition to maximum word counts, many exhibitions also have minimums to help ensure a consistent, intuitive presentation.

Adhering to word count limits maintain consistency and legibility and avoids overwhelming visitors. If essential information truly cannot fit within established limits, consider breaking content up over multiple panels or reinventing it as a diagram, graphic, map, or other visual alternative.

For exhibitions involving more than one language, panels must be large enough, and word counts low enough to support each language. Some languages consistently require more space than others. For example, the same content is generally 15–20 percent longer in French than in English. Languages should be determined before content development and design begin. Some exhibitions use Braille along with printed exhibit text. At the Little White House Museum in Warm Springs, Georgia (President Franklin Delano Roosevelt's former retreat), Braille was actively incorporated into the graphic design. For polylingual exhibitions, text must be 100 percent finalized and approved in one language before being translated to avoid costly time and resources translating later edits.

16.3.1 Categories of Text

Multiple levels of text give visitors a "choice of depth" in how they experience an exhibition. Visitors with less time or interest can get the main points of the exhibition by reading headlines and primary text. Those wanting to learn more can dig deeper. Text levels can also provide multiple "entry points" into the exhibition: if a main title or primary text doesn't grab a visitor's attention, a photo caption or quote might still draw them in. Writers and designers must work together to give visitors as many reasons and opportunities as possible to read the exhibition text.

Text needs vary by exhibition, but typically fall into three categories: headline; primary, secondary, and tertiary text; and labels and captions. Some exhibition planning teams may use categories like Level 1, Level 2, Level 3, and so on. As with the former, these categories are tied to word count messaging hierarchy. These designations have a bearing on the font size, word count, leveling, and location of each category. Figure 16.3 provides commonly used word counts for each category.

Type	Description	Word Count
Headline Copy	Titles should be provocative and interesting to grab the visitor's attention as well as provide the essence of what the rest of the text will be about. It can appear on any type of textual interface from large panels to info-rails and flipbooks.	1 to 10
Primary Text	The most important message, and often the introduction to a topic, idea or exhibit area. It can be placed on its own or be supported by secondary text if a topic requires further explanation. Primary text appears on large panels or can be applied directly to walls. A large font size is recommended.	50 to 75
Secondary Text	Expands on the topic introduced by the primary statement. Secondary Text will be written in a smaller font size than primary text and may appear on panels, inforails, and monitors.	50 to 100
Tertiary Text	Provides detailed information concerning various topics, ideas, and artifacts. This type of text usually only appears in flipbooks, labels, information cards, pamphlets, or on screens. Tertiary text is not limited by number of words; however discretion is necessary considering how the text will be used. Some artifacts or items in a case will have an 'extended label' to describe the nature of the object, how it was manufactured, or some other special aspect of it. Not everyone will read tertiary text; however, it is available for visitors and students who are interested in the details and specifics of an exhibit.	100 to 200

Figure 16.3. Text categories and word counts. LORD CULTURAL RESOURCES

Type	Description	Word Count
Artifact Labels	All artifacts will have a label which is a form of tertiary text (not an extended label). Labels should be short and consistent and often keyed to a numbering system in a display case. Information that often appears on such labels includes: • Name • Creator/Culture • Date • Place of Origin • Medium • Accession Number	10 to 15
Image Captions	Images must be identified and credited at a minimum, especially if copyright requires a particular form of acknowledgement. In some cases, museums may choose to include very short descriptions about what is happening in the image.	5 to 10

Figure 16.3. *Continued*

16.3.2 Reviewing and Approving Exhibition Text

Exhibition text often goes through as many as ten drafts (if not more) for large exhibitions. A formal review process smooths this process by tracking versions and clarifying who is responsible for which aspects of content creation, editing, and approval. This process includes the following:

- Facts need to be checked and authenticated. Are dates and terms correct? Does the text tell the story it is intended to? Factual review is usually done by the curator and/or subject-matter experts.

- Tone and style are typically reviewed by an interpretive planner, educator, and/or designated editor. Is the text too academic or jargony? Is it relatable? Does it reflect the intent of the exhibition? The reviewer ensures the text serves its targeted audiences and age ranges, reads smoothly, and adheres to the style guide.

- Spelling and grammar errors are the bane of every writer's existence. An outside proofreader with fresh eyes can ensure errors are caught and corrected. This should happen before graphic designers begin final layouts and printing, as it is difficult and costly to make changes after this point.

Some exhibitions may require review by cultural advisors or community groups. This is particularly important in the case of sensitive content, such as contested history or cultural and spiritual beliefs. For example, exhibitions that present Indigenous content should welcome cultural advisors who represent relevant Indigenous peoples to review the text with the curator and interpretive planner. These reviews not only ensure that text does not use incorrect terminology or offensive language, but also that relevant narratives are treated with a spirit of respect, openness, and welcome.

Producing an exhibition is a lengthy process. It's important to establish a realistic schedule and start as early as possible. Reviewers should receive text in large sections and with advanced notice. Reviewers can set aside time to focus and absorb the entire package, helping to catch redundancies or conflicts. Reading text aloud to others is a great way to test its quality. Does it read easily? Are there awkward words or sentence structures that cause a reader to stumble? Listeners should be able to easily repeat back the key points of any exhibition text that is read aloud to them. If they cannot, text may be too long, too complicated, or not clearly written.

16.3.3 Tips for Writing Exhibition Text

Most visitors do not read all—or even half—of the text in an exhibition. They will, however, notice if the exhibition text is not well done—if there is too much or too little, or if it is confusing or poorly written. Great text might not always be appreciated, but bad text can ruin the experience and undermine the exhibition.

Writing exhibition text is a craft unlike any other form of writing. Rather than treating museum text like "a book on a wall," think of it more like oral storytelling. Engage, provoke, and delight the visitor. Here are some tips:

- "So what?" Many writers first focus on removing jargon and academic style to make concepts more understandable. But this is only half the job. The content must also be relatable. Why are you telling visitors this story? What do you want them to take away? Why will this information matter to them? Does the writing make clear not just what they should know but why they should care? If you think target audiences will read the text and think "So what?" you have refining to do.

- Less is more. If an exhibition is too text-heavy visitors will feel overwhelmed and may give up reading altogether. Stick to the word count limits, keep text in small chunks, and make sure every word is working as hard as it can.

- Text must relate to what visitors are seeing and experiencing as they read. If a label refers visitors to a bowl "to the left" ensure that the bowl ends up on the left. A last-minute switch by the installation team may invalidate your text.

- If possible, mock-up exhibit text in the actual space to get a feel for how visitors will encounter it. This can influence the content, length, tone, and more. Where will visitors read this text? At the beginning, middle, or end of the experience? Will they be sitting or standing? What relation will they be to other exhibit elements?

- Text does not exist in isolation. Visitors experience text in context with objects and images. While drafting exhibition text, include reference images and photos of artifacts that will be displayed with the text. Help visitors make experiential connections that keep them engaged and heighten the exhibition's impact.

- Layer text where possible. Provide visitors with choice of depth in their reading via different levels of text and through labels, info-cards, and supplementary digital resources.

- Avoid exclusive language such as jargon, technical information, and culture-specific references. Explain any special terms and assume neither knowledge nor ignorance on the part of visitors. Visitors will not automatically identify with the writer or with a certain group.

- Be provocative, ask questions, present challenges. Exhibit text should attract the visitor's interest and encourage them to learn more through other sources. It does not need to be the ultimate authority on a subject. Asking questions immediately pulls the visitor into a dialogue and focuses their attention on a particular subject or activity.

- Use an active, conversational voice. Write as people speak. Contractions and sentence fragments are often okay.

- Aim for a grade 7 reading level to ensure visitors of different ages and language abilities can understand. There are exceptions: text for children's museums should be written at a lower level, and university research museums may be aimed higher. But for the average museum, use vocabulary a typical twelve-year-old would understand.

- Do not assume visitors have read other exhibit text. Visitors skip sections and change directions, meaning each panel, label, or on-screen text experience should stand alone.

- When labeling audio or video experiences, indicate the length of the clip so that visitors know how long it will be.

- Avoid excessive alliteration and exclamation points. Successful exhibition text relies on the power of the words themselves rather than tricks or subterfuge to try to hold visitors' attention.

- Use humor sparingly. It does not always translate well to visitors in written form and may exclude people from some linguistic or cultural backgrounds.

- Make personal connections. Use quotations, comparisons, and personal stories. Encourage the visitor to relate to the people, events, and things in the exhibition.

- Read text outloud. Take time to read the text out loud to friends and colleagues. How does it sound? Does it flow? Are you stumbling over long and awkward sentences? Is your audience engaged? If you are struggling to read it, so will your visitors.

The exhibition *Glaciers*, from the Perlan Museum of Natural Wonders in Reykjavik, Iceland, uses a conversational tone and style to communicate the nature of glaciers. The exhibition explores the formation of glaciers, the impact of climate change on them, and how glaciers have influenced Icelandic identity. The research for all text was provided by Iceland's foremost scientists and edited by the exhibition team's interpretive planner. Figure 16.4 is of the introductory text panel to the exhibition.

16.4 IMAGE RESEARCH AND PROCUREMENT

Some say a picture is worth a thousand words. In a museum exhibition with strict limits, the right image may be worth ten thousand words. Figure 16.5 is a photograph on an outdoor interpretive panel in the Africville Park in Halifax, Canada. It shows a woman, Barbara Ross, standing with her hands on her hips, watching a group of children climbing a path in the Africville neighborhood of Halifax, Nova Scotia, c. 1965. The community of Africville was founded in the 1840s predominantly by Black American refugees of the War of 1812 and their descendants. While not provided with municipal services such as water and sewage and having to endure the location of a city dump, infectious diseases hospital, railway, and other undesirable public amenities nearby, Africville nonetheless grew into a thriving, close-knit, and self-sufficient community. However, during the 1960s, guided by the urban renewal philosophy of the time, the decision was made to relocate the residents of Africville. The last building, Seaview United Baptist Church, which had served as the spiritual and community focal point of the community, was demolished in 1967, and the remaining four hundred residents were moved to public housing, effectively destroying the community.

Himneskir jöklar
Divine Glaciers

Heillandi. Tignarlegir. Töfrandi — aðeins hluti orðanna sem lýsa stórkostlegum jöklum Íslands. Þeir sjást út um herbergisgluggann, eru virtir fyrir vatnið sem rennur frá þeim, og sem náttúrulegur sköpunarkraftur. Jöklar eru óaðskiljanlegur hluti af sjálfsmynd Íslendinga.

Hvernig leið þér í fyrsta skiptið sem þú komst nærri jökli? Spennt? Hræddur? Innblásin? Margir okkar helstu listamanna sækja hugmyndir og innblástur til jöklanna.

Fascinating. Majestic. Stunning. Just some of the words used to describe Iceland's magnificent glaciers. Seen from bedroom windows, valued for the water they provide, and respected as creative forces of nature, glaciers are integral to Icelandic identity.

How did you feel the first time you saw a glacier? Excited? Scared? Moved? Many of our nation's foremost artists are inspired by glaciers.

Figure 16.4. Introductory panel for the exhibition *Glaciers*, Perlan Museum of Natural Wonders in Reykjavik, Iceland. LORD CULTURAL RESOURCES

This image illustrates that Africville was a safe, family-oriented, and intergenerational community, where residents looked out for, respected, and helped each other. Kids were free to play, swim, skate, and pick berries on their own because someone was always keeping an eye on them. Describing the event in words is not the same as seeing Barbara Ross's watchful body language and the expressions on the children's faces. Images like this can have powerful impressions on visitors that will make for a memorable visitor experience.

Image requirements in an exhibition may be for photographs, paintings, drawings, maps, diagrams, infographics, and reproductions of artwork. Images communicate information and ideas to visitors in place of or in conjunction with exhibition text. A historic photograph of the interior

Figure 16.5. Barbara Ross watches a group of children climbing a path in Africville, Canada. THE PUBLIC ARCHIVES OF NOVA SCOTIA

of a late nineteenth-century home, for example, can communicate much more information to visitors than a textual description of the room and provide more effective context to a display of the furniture of that period. Images can communicate concepts that cannot be expressed adequately in words.

The research matrix that guides the content development process identifies all image needs for each exhibit. Specificity is important. How many graphics are needed? What form should they take? Does the exhibition require new photographs? Throughout the process, deletions and substitutions will emerge as new sources appear or expected sources don't pan out. Researchers must coordinate with graphic designers about size, quality, and format requirements to prevent resolution and quality issues. Requirements for digital-only images will be different and require consultation with multimedia producers. Occasionally, a powerful image will be of insufficient quality to meet exhibition needs.

Image research and procurement for an exhibition can be lengthy and expensive. A logical, efficient, multistep search process can help:

1. **Museum archives**: Historical photographs in the archives are the first place to start. Where these images exist, the institution likely has the rights to reproduce them at no cost.
2. **New image and illustrations**: With the right expertise and equipment, original photography is the next easiest and effective means of obtaining images. If there is a need for new illustrations, diagrams, tables, maps, or infographics that can be produced in-house, this can be done at little cost beyond staff time. The content team can also hire an external photographer, specialist illustrator/artist, or graphic designer as appropriate. The content team should

provide suppliers with specific direction, including content, season, day-or-night conditions, and overall guidelines for exhibition look and feel. New photography typically happens during exhibition production, with photography fees included in the fabrication budget. The same is true for new illustrations and art. Artist fees will be accounted for in the fabrication budget.

3. **Images from other public institutions**: Other museums, archives, and libraries have image collections that may include pertinent pictures. Public institutions will typically grant rights for other institutions to reproduce their images, often for a small fee. This process can sometimes be lengthy and administratively demanding.

4. **Stock images**: Many stock-image sites have large collections of photographs and illustrations that can be purchased for use in museum exhibitions. They're fast and convenient, but potentially costly depending on intended use. Free exhibitions typically incur smaller stock photo fees than paid shows.

5. **Private collections**: Artists, photographers, philanthropists, and other private individuals may have images that can be loaned, rented, or purchased. This may require negotiation and such deals can be expensive.

While researching images, it is best to identify redundant options in anticipation that some choices won't pan out due to costs, logistics, or quality. When selecting images, here are common industry best practices:

- Include people. Visitors find images with people more interesting.
- Add colored images. Historical exhibitions often include monochrome photographs, but color images should be included where possible.
- Show action and emotion to capture people's attention and evoke an emotional response.
- Be novel or nostalgic. Museum visitors seek out both new experiences and things that are personally familiar. Images can satisfy both.

An image data sheet helps organize and document graphic research and selections. They can be summarized in lists and electronic databases similar to the artifact research.

Every graphic should be accompanied by the following information:

- **Graphic numbers** act as a reference for chosen graphics and is original to the exhibition. They typically simply read as G-100, G-101, G-102, and so on for each exhibit element. They are important for graphic designers as they create floor plans, plot artwork, and track printing.

- A brief **description** identifying the graphic and how it will be used needs to be included. Will a panel include photographs? Who is depicted, where, and when? Descriptions are particularly important for instructions or hand drawings that are the basis of maps, tables, and infographics.

- An image's **source** indicates how or where it can be obtained. It should include full references for books, or archival information. Is an original negative or digital image available? Who owns the original? If no existing image is required, it should be indicated here with details on what the graphic needs to convey and how it should be conveyed.

- Location refers to where a graphic element is **located** (book, library, archive, etc.). This section can also refer to a specific artist, production house, or photographer who can be

Item Type	Section	Description	Location	Copyright	Thumbnail
5. Written Pieces	4. Life's Challenges	**Title:** Chronicles of Avonlea **Author:** Montgomery, L. M. (Lucy Maud) Gibbs, George **Collection:** L.M. Montgomery Institute. Ryrie-Campbell Collection. **Donor:** Ryrie-Campbell copy donated by Donna Jane Campbell. **Note:** "First impression, June, 1912"—t.p. verso Tan cloth cover with square pictorial paste-on of the "Anne" on cover ; gold lettering. Colour frontispiece illustrates "Anne Shirley". 6 p. of advertisements at back.	http://kindredspaces.-ca/islandora/object/lm-mi%3A14118?sol-r_nav%5Bid%5D=677e ab0f0b140ce46563&s olr_nav%5Bpage%5D= 0&solr_nav%5Boffset %5D=10#page/1/mode /1up	Ryrie-Campbell Book Collection	
5. Written Pieces	4. Life's Challenges	**Title:** The Golden Road **Author:** Montgomery, L. M. (Lucy Maud) Gibbs, George **Collection:** L.M. Montgomery Institute. Ryrie-Campbell Collection. **Donor:** Donated by Donna Jane Campbell. **Note:** "First impression, August, 1913."—T.p. verso Tan cloth cover with square pictorial paste-on of the "Story Girl" on cover ; gold lettering. Includes advertisements.	http://kindredspaces.-ca/islandora/object/lm-mi%3A14266?sol-r_nav%5Bid%5D=677e ab0f0b140ce46563&s olr_nav%5Bpage%5D= 0&solr_nav%5Boffset %5D=11#page/1/mode/ 1up	Ryrie-Campbell Book Collection	
5. Written Pieces	4. Life's Challenges	**Title:** Anne's House of Dreams **Author:** Montgomery, L. M. (Lucy Maud) Kirk, M.L. (Maria Louise) **Collection:** L.M. Montgomery Institute. Ryrie-Campbell Collection. **Donor:** Donated by Donna Jane Campbell. **Note:** "Copyright 1917, by Frederick A. Stokes Company."—t.p. verso Bound in dark purple cloth with picorial panel on front cover ; gilt lettering.	http://kindredspaces.-ca/islandora/object/lm-mi%3A14264?sol-r_nav%5Bid%5D=660 dbb2fbf0aefc9736f&so lr_nav%5Bpage%5D=0 &solr_nav%5Boffset%5 D=18#page/1/mode/1u p	Ryrie-Campbell Book Collection	

Figure 16.6. Example of a graphic data sheet, Green Gables Heritage Place, Prince Edward Island, Canada. PUBLIC DOMAIN; DIGITAL BOOK COVER IMAGES, COURTESY OF UPEI LIBRARY/LMMI

commissioned to work on exhibit elements. The fabricator's name may be placed in this spot if they are handling all new graphic production.

- The **copyright** field documents the image owner's rights. Can the image be licensed? For how long? At what cost?
- A **low-resolution image** should accompany every selection for easy reference.

Additional tips:

- Be diligent about copyright. Using an image without proper permission is unethical and sometimes illegal.
- Work closely with graphic designers on image quality and format. If a historical image is low-resolution, ensure that it is not reproduced large-scale.
- Research images in conjunction with writing text. Text and images must correspond and be co-developed, so they make sense together.
- Schedule sufficient time. Image research and procurement can involve online investigation, consulting books, and visiting other museums, libraries, and archives. Finding the right images should not—and often cannot—be rushed.
- Budget image procurement costs. Image costs can quickly add up for large exhibitions. The research matrix should include an estimate of image requirements, including what will need to be purchased or involve rights payments. If an exhibition is intended to travel, ensure you have budgeted for worldwide usage. Update the budget regularly to avoid surprises.

16.5 HANDS-ON EXHIBITS, MODELS, AND DIORAMAS

Special exhibits that encourage visitors to watch, build, touch, and explore often provide the most memorable museum experiences. These may include flip panels, building activities, puzzles, models, dioramas, dress-up stations, immersive environments, soundscapes, projections, computer kiosks, interactive quizzes, touch tables, and much more. Researching and developing content for hands-on and multimedia exhibits is slightly different from traditional museum displays and involves other processes and experts. The diversity of these experiences also makes it very difficult to standardize a form or documentation process. It's all about common sense and lots of descriptive material.

The number of interactive exhibits in any given exhibition depends on the subject matter and the audience. During the planning phase, interpretive planners should determine which concepts can be best expressed through special exhibits within space and budget restraints. (These types of experiences tend to be more expensive than traditional text-and-artifact, specimen, or art displays.) Challenging visitors to build a model of a bridge might be the best way to communicate certain physics and engineering concepts, while having children dress in historic clothing and undertake a household chore could communicate how people once lived. A multimedia touch table can present layered, multidimensional mixes of historical images, media, and information to satisfy different levels of visitor interest. The research matrix will identify where these special exhibits will occur and provide direction on how content needs to be gathered and documented.

Who undertakes research for special exhibits and how it is done depends on how the exhibition develops. Some large museums produce interactive and multimedia exhibits in-house, while most need to hire outside interpretive planners and producers. The latter may be the same suppliers who ultimately produce the exhibit, so collaboration with members of the content team may result in creative solutions.

For special exhibits that include physical interaction, recreated environments, models, and dioramas, it is useful to develop information packages that describe the overall features of the experience and how visitors are intended to interact with them. Anticipate every question a fabricator may have and how every visitor might use or abuse the exhibit. It's a daunting task, but worth the effort. Well-articulated information packages in addition to detailed design documentation result in successful interactives. Fabricators require detailed descriptions and information about objects and scenes. Dimensions, photos, renderings, verbal descriptions, and sketches will identify color, materials, scale, smell, and other details to ensure dramatic, authentic recreations.

Information to capture includes:

- **Description**: Verbal description of the exhibit's aims and key content. For example, if the exhibit allows visitors to touch replicas of archaeological objects, all objects should be carefully described.
- **Communication objectives/visitor experience**: Describes the intended learning, behavioral, and emotional messages of the special exhibits. How are visitors intended to interact with content? This section may include a brief narrative of the visitor experience. Example: "Visitors will approach a low table or reader rail and be able to touch three replicas of Paleo-Indian stone tools. Beside each tool will be questions to help visitors explore casts in detail."

- **Dimensions/Plans**: For models, reconstructions, and replicas, the dimensions of originals are necessary for an accurate scale reproduction. Models and scaled reconstructions require access to or copies of original plans and contour maps.

- **Photos/Sketches/Sources**: Provide all sources for photographs, sketches, reference images and other information. This will help the designer and fabricator create accurate reproductions. This field may also reference relevant sections of books, articles, videos, and websites that producers can consult.

- **Readily available/Location/Purchases/Local builder or supplier**: This final section identifies sources where media can be obtained or commissioned locally. Sometimes there are known model makers and suppliers for items like dinosaur and fossil casts who may be consulted or subcontracted. In some cases, the content and core exhibition teams may identify preferred suppliers they have worked with before, or who have previously worked on related interactives.

16.6 MULTIMEDIA EXHIBITS

Computers, videos, mobile apps, gesture-based systems, projection mapping, augmented reality, virtual reality, soundscapes—the technology available today means that almost anything an exhibition planner can envision for the visitor experience can be created if the budget allows. Putting together the right team is essential when planning for multimedia or audiovisual experiences in a museum exhibition. This means that content teams need to include researchers with expertise in sourcing audiovisual materials—capabilities that are quite different from those of traditional curators and academics. The participation of a media designer as part of the exhibition core team facilitates this work.

Audiovisual and multimedia exhibits are complex because of the need to identify content while simultaneously anticipating software and hardware requirements. The skills required to source content, develop software, and recommend hardware solutions are completely different. As a result of this complexity, the core exhibition team may choose between two alternative strategies:

1. Prepare preliminary information packages or **script treatments** during the design phase. This approach requires researchers to think not only like visitors but also like multimedia experts. This strategy results in lists of archival materials including film footage or tape that may be in antiquated formats, descriptive texts, and other forms of content that will enrich the final production. However, content teams need to be open to creativity and as such invite and pay for multimedia consultation (if the media designer is not a part of the planning team from the beginning) and review to ensure that the most creative and sensible ways of presenting the content have been explored.

2. Outsource all research for multimedia to the suppliers who will ultimately design, program, and install the systems. The content team advises and reviews the treatments and research packages created by the suppliers. This strategy relies on the expertise and diligence of the researchers who will be hired by producers to find the right content for the exhibit. Budget and ability may result in a production that is "light" on content. Is there enough money in the budget to pay for good research? Is the supplier using the budget to pay for quality research or keeping the money for programming and hardware procurement, or to pad the profit margin? What are the qualifications of the researchers they have hired? This approach does have a number of "unknowns" that cannot always be adequately controlled by the content team. Consistency may be an issue, but the strategy does relieve the content team of a

tremendous amount of research, most of which may consist of combing through public and private archival collections for relevant footage.

For large exhibitions that rely heavily on multimedia to deliver content, a combination of the two strategies may be employed. However, if the content team is primarily responsible for intellectual content and visual sourcing, a script treatment is a means for organizing this work. This document should include:

- **Curatorial brief/Intellectual content**: This identifies major themes and facts that must be presented by the audiovisual or multimedia product. It is important that researchers help to define key milestones or academic requirements of such exhibit elements. For example, interactive maps require a rough outline of a map to be reproduced with important sites represented. For a film or audio production, key sites, stories, events, and personalities must be identified that will ensure accuracy of the script and imagery. Multimedia producers and their hired researchers need this perspective and expert guidance.

- **Communication objectives**: the learning, behavioral, and emotional messages/outcomes that need to be conveyed by the multimedia exhibit. These have been identified earlier in the planning process and should be applied to the audiovisual or multimedia experiences here.

- **Narrative/Description**: A written description of the visitor experience. For example, "Children will be confronted by a series of buttons associated with images of farm animals. Visitors will press buttons and hear the sounds that each animal makes." This type of description and specificity helps the multimedia producer understand how the content needs to be delivered and experienced. During production, a producer may recommend other means besides buttons for accessing the sounds because of their knowledge of different types of hardware delivery systems, but the result will be the same.

For more complex experiences such as an interactive timeline on a touch table surface, visitors will be able to explore lots of content associated with specific dates or events. In this case the description will include the categories of content that will be accessible—audio, video, and text—with direction as to the order or amount of material that may be accessed. Again, this direction guides the producer who may in turn suggest creative ways to organize the content and recommend enhancements to the visitor experience such as "hot buttons" or tools that allow visitors to email content to themselves or friends or tag their favorite images.

- **Existing film/Video/Graphics/Audio**: Any information concerning existing films, videos, audio files, and graphics for related topics must be identified. For excerpts of moving images from longer films, researchers will need to identify where in the film producers need to "cut" the relevant footage. This field also provides producers with additional references to consult during production such as books, libraries, or important contacts.

- **New sources**: When researchers know or desire new material to be produced for the multimedia exhibit, some direction is required. This helps the producer to budget the final product as well as understand the overall intent. Does a video require custom narration and soundtrack? Do additional oral histories need to be recorded? Are special sound and light effects needed? Is original animation required?

- **Location**: This refers to where any existing sources can be located and how they can be procured. Are the sources located at the museum, a public archive, a local newspaper, a TV news station, or a website that specializes in stock sound effects?

- **Copyright**: Who owns the rights to any materials proposed to be used?

The following is an example of a multimedia treatment for the Central Bank Museum in Port of Spain, Trinidad and Tobago. The treatment, along with others, were used as a part of a Request for Proposal process to find the right multimedia producer at the right price.

C.7 Symbols Script Treatment

Description of Visitor Experience

Incorporating the Museum's current collection of bird replicas, this exhibit will explore the designs that appear on T&T banknotes and how they are symbols of the nation. A series of six (6) flip panels featuring the birds on the banknotes will be presented to visitors.

Visitors will also be able to press a button to hear each bird's call.

Performance Requirements:

- Audio experience that plays a short clip of each bird's typical call, up to ten seconds each.

Instruction to Suppliers:

- Create storyboard and/or wireframes for review as necessary.
- Supplier to recommend control and speaker system for exhibit.
- Supplier to recommend hardware and software solutions suitable for the local context (i.e., ease of maintenance and operations in Trinidad).
- Supplier to coordinate with the museum project manager to ensure design intent of exhibition is carried through multimedia design.
- Supplier to coordinate with fabrication and installation teams to ensure seamless integration of multimedia hardware with other exhibit components.

Minimum Hardware Requirements:

- Audio: Digital audio playback system with 4" speaker
- Video: N/A
- Source: PC-CPU
- Special F/X: N/A
- Control: Activated by 32 mm arcade style pushbuttons (6)
- Power: Surge protection, and cabling integrated into casework (casework by others)

Reference/Sources:

Note: Content sources identified below are a starting point. It is expected that the supplier may have to conduct additional research for the exhibit.

Birds to be featured are:

- Greater Bird-of-paradise (*Paradisaea apoda*)
  - http://www.hbw.com/ibc/sound/greater-bird-paradise-paradisaea-apoda/calls-several-birds-while-displaying-lek
- Copper-rumped hummingbird (*Amazilia tobaci*)
  - http://www.hbw.com/ibc/sound/copper-rumped-hummingbird-amazilia-tobaci/bird-initially-calls-branch-it-then-drives
  - http://www.hbw.com/ibc/sound/copper-rumped-hummingbird-amazilia-tobaci/song
- Cocrico (*Ortalis ruficauda*)
  - http://www.hbw.com/ibc/sound/rufous-vented-chachalaca-ortalis-ruficauda/groups-birds-calling-each-other-dawn-0
- Trinidad Mot (*Momotus bahamensis*)
  - http://www.xeno-canto.org/species/Momotus-bahamensis
- Scarlet Ibis (*Eudocimus ruber*)
  - http://www.bioacoustica.org/gallery/aves_eng.html
  - http://www.hbw.com/ibc/species/52774/sounds
  - http://www.xeno-canto.org/species/Eudocimus-ruber
- Red-Capped Cardinal (*Paroaria gularis*)
  - http://www.hbw.com/ibc/species/62103/sounds

Figure 16.7. Visitors engaging with the *Symbols* exhibit in the Central Bank Museum in Port-of-Spain, Trinidad and Tobago. CENTRAL BANK MUSEUM, TRINIDAD & TOBAGO

16.7 SUBJECT MATTER EXPERTS

Sometimes a museum will not have the expertise on staff to develop content for a particular exhibition. This may be because it is a small- or mid-sized museum, but it also may be that a larger museum is developing an exhibition outside of its typical sphere of expertise. In these cases, it is often a good idea to work with subject matter experts (SMEs) who can provide curatorial support in the content development process. SMEs can ensure credibility and accuracy of content as well as reflect current thinking in a particular field. This exhibition content will be developed with academic rigor that meet the educational goals of the project.

SMEs can become part of the content development team and meet regularly with the museum staff working on the exhibition, or they may be retained simply to review and provide advice on the materials being produced in-house. There are many ways that a museum may work with SMEs, depending on their need, the scale of the project, and the availability and interest of the SMEs. Typically, SMEs will need to be compensated for their work, but this may be based on an honorarium. They could also be named in any acknowledgement materials for the exhibition.

Identifying the appropriate SMEs for the exhibition project is important. Research and produce a long list of possible SMEs and rank them in order of preference in case the first-choice picks are not interested or available. You should also have an idea of the number of SMEs needed, based on the content needs of the exhibition. Places to look for SMEs may include other museums that have expertise in that subject area. Another good place to look are local universities in departments relevant to the exhibition content. Ideally, an SME would be a professor or other senior researcher in the field but depending on the project need and budget a graduate student working in that area may be acceptable and likely more cost effective. Graduate students may also value the opportunity to collaborate with the museum as part of their resume building. Depending on the subject matter of the exhibition, SMEs could also be found working in industry (e.g., scientists, artists, archaeologists, conservators, etc.).

If the exhibition is about particular community groups and histories, especially BIPOC content, the museum should look for SMEs that identify with that specific group. For example, an exhibition on African American history should ideally include an SME who is an African American historian working in that subject area. An exhibition on Inuit art should include Inuit artists as SMEs. Museums have a long history of presenting themselves as experts on other cultures and peoples, and this practice should be discontinued in the effort to decolonize museums and to support initiatives and movements such as Truth and Reconciliation and Black Lives Matter, among others. SMEs should be individuals well-respected in their fields, and ideally have some experience working on museum exhibitions or in presenting their work to the public in some other form (e.g., programs, publications, media, digital, etc.).

Once an SME has indicated they would like to be involved, it is critical to establish the terms of the relationship and obtain agreement before proceeding. Be sure to write up the specific objectives and guidelines for the SME's involvement and ask them for their input as well. The SMEs may have suggestions or ideas for working together that may not have occurred to the museum. The agreement should be signed by both parties and include the following items:

- Duration of work: How long the SMEs involvement in the project is anticipated (in weeks or months).

- Hours per week or month: If possible, try to estimate the number of hours of work required. Most SMEs will have other full-time jobs or studies and it is important to be clear about how much time they will need to devote to the project.

- Involvement expected: Will the SME be expected to attend all project meetings, or only certain ones? Will they need to participate in public or community consultations? Are they required to conduct research, write exhibit text, source images or objects? Or are they simply needed to review and comment on content produced by the museum team?

- Compensation: Will the SME be paid for their work? Will it be on an hourly basis, a fixed-fee, or an honorarium?

- Recognition: Will the museum acknowledge the involvement of the SME on exhibit panels, in publications, and/or in other marketing materials?

It is important to manage the relationship with the SMEs throughout the project and afterward as well. Make sure to thank them for their contributions and invite them to attend the exhibition opening. Maintaining these relationships after the exhibition is complete is also important in the interest of potential future work, and to ensure the museum maintains a good reputation for working with SMEs.

Case Study

WORKING WITH SUBJECT MATTER EXPERTS: CANADIAN MUSEUM OF IMMIGRATION AT PIER 21, HALIFAX, CANADA

The Canadian Museum of Immigration at Pier 21 is Atlantic Canada's only national museum. It is mandated to explore the theme of immigration to Canada to enhance public understanding of the experiences of immigrants as they arrived in Canada, the vital role immigration has played in the building of Canada, and the contributions of immigrants to Canada's culture, economy, and way of life.

Designated as a national museum in 2009, the Canadian Museum of Immigration at Pier 21 embraced its new national museum status with several exciting projects, including an expansion, reinstallation of the permanent exhibitions, and a traveling exhibition entitled *Canada: Day 1*. *Canada: Day 1* aims to explore Canada's immigration story spanning from Confederation to present day, while the permanent exhibition extends farther back to explore stories from first contact to the present. The expansion of Pier 21's mandate and scope of content meant that subject matter experts (SMEs) needed to be brought on board to accurately and appropriately tell the stories of Indigenous and newcomer cultural groups.

The development of the interpretive master plan began with a two-day visioning workshop with influential leaders in Canadian immigration. The attendees included academics, institutional leaders in refugee and immigration support, a novelist, a playwright, as well as museum staff—all of whom shared their varied experiences, insights, and perspectives.

In the detailed interpretive planning and content development phase of work for the new twenty thousand square foot permanent exhibition, the team engaged scholars in immigration, refugee, and Aboriginal affairs from across Canada to help identify gaps in the original interpretive master plan that required further development. These SMEs were selected because they brought a vital contribution to the visioning process for the museum. Their knowledge and insight in their own field were invaluable to the project. They participated in workshops, group sessions, and provided and reviewed content. They also brought to the project their approach to thinking about immigration and Canadian identity, the role of diversity, and receptiveness to new ideas. The SMEs were encouraged to debate and critique the museum's ideas, to encourage the creative tension of differing points of view on fundamental issues. The goal was to achieve consensus as a basis for planning, but also acknowledging that there may be some agreement to disagree and leave some ideas open for future development. The museum and consultant team's core team of history experts were greatly enhanced by expert researchers and advisors from across Canada to select artifacts, research stories, source oral histories, and procure images.

The permanent exhibitions are now located in the historic refurbished pier, where thousands of immigrants entered Canada. They are comprised of two exhibitions: The Pier 21 Story, which invites visitors to experience what it was like to immigrate through Pier 21 between 1928 and 1971, and the Canadian Immigration Story, which showcases the vast contributions of newcomers to Canada's culture, economy, and way of life, from past to present day. The new exhibitions opened to the public in June 2015.

Figure 16.8. Entrance to the permanent exhibition exploring the Canadian immigration story, Canadian Museum of Immigration at Pier 21, Halifax, Canada. COURTESY OF THE CANADIAN MUSEUM OF IMMIGRATION AT PIER 21

Figure 16.9. Visitors interact with personal stories about what newcomers brought with them to Canada. *Canada Day 1* traveling exhibition, Canadian Museum of Immigration at Pier 21, Halifax, Canada. TONI HAFKENSCHEID PHOTOGRAPHY/LORD CULTURAL RESOURCES

Figure 16.10. Oral history stations in the *Canada Day 1* traveling exhibition, Canadian Museum of Immigration at Pier 21, Halifax, Canada. TONI HAFKENSCHEID PHOTOGRAPHY/LORD CULTURAL RESOURCES

Content Development

16.8 COMMUNITIES AND CONTENT

Community involvement in the development of exhibition content is critical if museums want to become more diverse, equitable, accessible, and inclusive. The community should be sources of content, advisors, and active participants in the process and production of exhibition content, not just as participants in the galleries once it is complete as identified in chapter 10 of this volume. This may include focus groups, an advisory committee, co-curation, and/or community curators and collaborators.

Community involvement should begin at the very outset of the process to ensure they are part of the decision-making process and visioning for the exhibition. For example, inviting an advisory committee to participate in initial planning workshops. Alternatively, key members of the community could be invited to attend to ensure the exhibition is considering diverse voices and representations of history, culture, art, or science. As with working with SMEs, in working with communities the museum should be clear from the outset what the expectations and parameters of the working relationship will be.

Community involvement can take several different forms, including:

1. **Community consultation and public engagement**: The museum gathers content and input from a defined community to inform the development of an exhibition. This form of participation is used generally to position the institution, to gather content, and to attract new audiences. It can, however, be done in an on-going way to create more long-lasting engagement.
2. **Co-created and co-curated exhibitions**: Members of the public or a community collaborate with museum staff to develop an exhibition from selecting objects and stories to writing text and designing the exhibits. The extent of this collaboration can vary greatly, depending on the exhibition and objectives of the museum in its endeavor to be inclusive. The museum and community share authority and work together to create the final exhibition.
3. **Hosted exhibitions**: Hosted exhibitions make space within a museum for an exhibition entirely conceived and created by members of the public or a particular community. Beyond the initial invitation and selection, the museum has little control over the result. Hosted exhibitions tend to be temporary, viewing the museum as a platform and a hub for a community, however some museums are completely turning permanent galleries over to communities for their own interpretation of their culture's stories and objects.

The museum may decide to form specific community groups to advise on and help develop exhibition content, for example:

- **Advisory groups**: Museum staff may seek input into the exhibition development process using advisory groups that may be asked to generate ideas and concepts for new exhibitions or may be invited to join in a more co-creative process. Advisory groups may consist of experts or "lay people" and can act as a reference group, an informal focus group, and/or advisors on a range of matters from content to design. Advisory groups are generally guided by specific criteria for membership, protocols, and policies regarding their role, determining who can become an advisor, for how long, and the responsibilities of each member. Advisors are generally not paid; however, a stipend may be given as acknowledgment for their time and travel expenses. Advisory groups may be used when a museum wants to reach out to a specific public as a matter of institutional strategy or for a specific exhibition.

- **Community curators and participatory research**: Community curators are usually volunteers or short-term contracted personnel who are recruited to assist in content development for the exhibition for a fixed period and for a certain objective. They are trained in content collection in such media as oral history interviews, photography, videography, copywriting, or others as required by the exhibition.

Case Study

CREATING WITH COMMUNITY *THE FIRST PEOPLES* EXHIBITION AT BUNJILAKA ABORIGINAL CULTURAL CENTRE AT MELBOURNE MUSEUM, A SHARED ENDEAVOR OF MUSEUMS VICTORIA AND THE VICTORIAN ABORIGINAL COMMUNITY

Rosemary Wrench, Senior Curator, Many Nations, First Peoples *Exhibition, Museums Victoria*

The development and success of the *First Peoples* exhibition is a tribute to the powerful co-curation model undertaken with the guidance of the lead curator, Genevieve Grieves and the manager of Bunjilaka, Caroline Martin.

A key factor in this partnership was the creation and the guidance of the First Peoples Yulendj Group of Elders and community representatives from Victoria. *Yulendj* is a word from the Kulin language family meaning "knowledge" and as co-curators this group brought to the museum their cultural authority, knowledge, stories, objects, and images.

This rich collaboration signified a new era where Aboriginal peoples and museum staff worked together to unpack 150 years of museum narrative. This was not a one off "community consultation" engagement but the development of a rich and long-term partnership to create a new methodology for "seeing" the collections and the unique stories and knowledge embedded in them.

There were deep conversations to have with the Yulendj group and actions required by the museum team to show they were not only listening to the community members but importantly they too wanted meaningful change.

One early initiative was to create a shared understanding and experience of the workings and history of the museum. Alongside an extensive program of workshops, we took every opportunity to organize introductions to staff and make regular visits to the different departments across the museum. From my experience, collaborations between museums and Aboriginal communities are never equal when one side remains in control of all the access to the collections and staff. We wanted to ensure that our co-curators were not strangers to the museum, nor was the museum a stranger to them.

For their part, the Yulendj group shared their knowledge, stories, and advice across the project team from curatorial and design to conservation, photography, education, and public programs. Professional and personal connections quickly developed based on mutual respect and a willingness to explore new ways of working.

The *First Peoples* exhibition has four sections: Our Story, Generations, and Deep Listening all focus on the culture and history of Victorian Aboriginal people. The fourth section, Many Nations, highlights Victorian material culture within a display of the diverse cultures of Aboriginal and Torres Strait Islander Australians.

The Many Nations section has six showcases of material culture, the personal belongings of 500 Aboriginal men, women, and children from diverse clan and language groups, from over 250 locations across Australia. Each showcase includes objects made between the mid-1800s and 2013. The objects were made for diverse cultural practices including protection, for keeping and holding treasures, for celebration and decoration, as teaching tools for children, for hunting, for storytelling, and everyday use.

A feature of the exhibition is the inclusion of digital labels, which include multiple object and contextual images, maps, first person voice, individual narratives, and Aboriginal languages. Discussions on the use of digital labels also generated a lot of enthusiasm and support from all our contributors. Significantly, many of the narratives for the labels include Aboriginal languages and are written in first person's voice.

The tools and techniques of digital media enabled us to reconnect material culture to country, languages, families, historical events, stories, knowledge, and creators across countless generations.

For those disrupted connections we were unable to mend, members of the Yulendj group shared the responsibility for making sure the narratives and images selected celebrated and respected their owners.

Key measures of success for the co-curating model occurred quietly along the journey of developing the exhibition, a sign of trust occurring when the Yulendj members began bringing their children and family members to the workshops. Another powerful moment occurred when Eileen Harrison gifted the museum a treasured basket made by her grandmother, Thelma Carter. Eileen told me that after being part of Yulendj, she trusted us to do the right thing in looking after her basket and it was an honor to have it on display in *Many Nations*.

Museum Victoria is currently developing a First Peoples strategy to ensure that Aboriginal Australians are placed at the forefront of everything we do. The success of the co-curating model with the Yulendj group of Victorian Aboriginal community members began this significant institutional change of direction.

Figure 16.11. Yulendj member, Eileen Harrison holding the basket made by her grandmother Thelma Carter. MUSEUMS VICTORIA, 2015

Figure 16.12. *Many Nations, First Peoples* exhibition, Bunjilaka, Melbourne Museum, Australia. DIANE SNAPE, 2013

Figure 16.13. Keeping Places display in the Many Nations section of the First Peoples exhibition, Museums Victoria, Australia. MUSEUMS VICTORIA, 2015

Case Study

INDIGENOUS-LED DESIGN AND CONTENT DEVELOPMENT INDIGENOUS PEOPLES GARDEN, ASSINIBOINE PARK, WINNIPEG, MANITOBA

Monica Giesbrecht, Principal, HTFC Planning & Design

The Indigenous Peoples Garden (IPG) is the working name for an Indigenous focused landscape within the new Canada's Diversity Gardens project with the Assiniboine Park Conservancy. IPG has grown from three years of consultations with Indigenous communities through a series of visioning sessions with the aim to transform a portion of Winnipeg's Assiniboine Park into a place for healing and connecting people to each other and to the land through Indigenous approaches and traditions.

The iterative process built on numerous discussions with youth, community leaders, ethnobotanical knowledge holders, food security advocates, and elders highlighted the need for elders and youth to be further integrated into park programs.

The design and content development process for the Indigenous Peoples Garden was led by architect David Thomas and environmental designer Cheyenne Thomas, both of Peguis First Nation in Manitoba, and Mamie Griffith, an Indigenous designer with Dene, Welsh, and Scottish roots, in collaboration with landscape architecture firm HTFC Planning & Design. As part of their process, the team invited Indigenous educators, elders, youth, and members from the community to join them on several visioning exercises. On several occasions the project team and stakeholders walked the project site together to gather information and listen to the land as they planned how to share the story of the first peoples of this land most effectively and authentically within the project and the park.

Involving Indigenous designers in this project was essential to engaging the project from a personal perspective that allows for an intimate understanding and relationship to the project. The Indigenous design team had the relationships and connections with the community needed for in-depth consultation and intuitive design collaboration rooted in the cultural background of the designer. This connection and understanding would have been much more difficult for non-Indigenous designers without first-hand cultural knowledge. The cultural complexities of the project required in-depth conversations about a wide range of issues that are sensitive and require design-based decisions with cultural awareness and experience. This resulted in reclaiming a role of cultural creation through the transfer of knowledge back and forth between the designers and the community via an explorative process. Relationships explored, discovered, and rediscovered in sharing conversation and storytelling reinforce the importance of reclaiming a uniquely iterative indigenous creative process and sharing contemporary Indigenous identity through art and design.

This design process was and continues to be unique in its commitment to community engagement from for the entirety of the Canada's Diversity Garden Project. Ceremony has always been part of the project's community gatherings and design exercises. Ideas and decisions are given the respect of time and are not rushed. That is also unique to a project of this scale. There has been time for the design team to reflect on the project as the design flourished from a seed to a full-blown creation, time for the community to respond to ideas and then build on them, and time to think about the garden in the greater context of Canada's Diversity Garden project, Canada as a whole, and within the teachings and recommendations of the journey to Truth and Reconciliation.

Figure 16.14. Indigenous design team: Dave Thomas, Mamie Griffith, Cheyenne Thomas.

Figure 16.15. Fire node at Canada's Diversity Gardens Indigenous People's Garden, Winnipeg, Canada. © HTFC PLANNING & DESIGN IN COLLABORATION WITH THE FLAT SIDE OF DESIGN.

Chapter 17

Exhibition Design

Yvonne Tang and James Bruer

Design is one of the most creative and dynamic phases in the exhibition development process. This is when the project begins to take visual shape and becomes real for the first time. Until this point, the visitor experience has been articulated in words, relationship diagrams, and lists of objects difficult to envision in a three-dimensional space. Floor plans, color renderings, computer models, and other design tools bring the visitor experience to life for the planning team.

But what do we mean by exhibition design? It is easy to think it implies the obvious, the look and feel of the exhibition, but that is to think of design strictly as a noun, something which we procure, touch, and admire. But the truth is that good design is a process, a series of deliberate activities and pursuits, and as such should be considered as much a verb as a noun. This is an important distinction as it effects our understanding of what the design process is trying to achieve.

Good design should not be prescribed, timid, boring, or formulaic. It is the designer's creative challenge to take the museum team's carefully considered content and aspirations for an exhibition and make them powerful, interesting, fun, and captivating to the museum audience. The design of the exhibition can itself reflect the intentions of the content. The best designers are not intimidated by this challenge, they rather relish it.

"Design thinking" on a project begins with the formation of the interpretive plan. While the exhibition designer may be the one concerned with the translation of the interpretive plan into a three-dimensional reality, the process of its writing has already outlined many design-oriented decisions. Questions of sequence, adjacency, and means of expression are outlined and conceived at a high level. Because these decisions on their own can influence design direction, it is important for the exhibition designer to participate in the initial high-level conception of the project during the interpretive planning phase.

Exhibitions are powerful means of communication that engage and affect visitor's attitudes, values, and awareness of the world. Successful exhibition design allows visitors to be "transported." It considers the collections of an institution—both tangible and intangible—and transforms a selection of them into an experience. But whenever design takes over the agenda, imposing itself on the process, failure looms. As such, a successful visitor-centered exhibition design must be derived from a well-articulated interpretive plan.

Exhibition design has changed significantly from its earliest iterations. Long gone are the days of hushed galleries lined with heavy cases filled with artifacts, graphic panels sharing a plethora of information, and visitors thought of as inconvenient obligations. Now galleries are immersive storytelling places with visitors actively "designed in" as participants. This change necessitates collaborative efforts between various museum disciplines to address the complexity of modern exhibition design, as well as consider it within a broader than ever context. Visitors have a wider range of options at their disposal as they pursue knowledge and seek entertainment. Increasingly, the benchmarks against which an exhibition design project are held are no longer merely other exhibitions. Designs may now just as likely be compared to retail, cinematic, and entertainment benchmarks. The playing field has shifted.

Exhibition design is still a fairly young profession with limited opportunities to study in design schools. Many designers come from a range of backgrounds and philosophies from the related fields of architecture, interior design, or industrial design. Rapid changes in technology, green and sustainable design, complex multidisciplinary approaches, and the growing trend for multiple platforms of content delivery are all challenging the traditional boundaries of exhibition design, requiring designers to acquire new skills and build teams of experts with specialized knowledge to address these new challenges. It is extremely rare to find a generalist who can meet all the complex needs of twenty-first-century exhibitions.

17.1 THE DESIGN PROCESS

Design can be understood as a simple set of steps that need to be followed. First you need to understand the problem in front of you. Second, you need to explore solutions to that problem. Lastly, you need to materialize answers to that problem. This is a process in which we start broadly and proceed to the more detailed. The workflow of the design process is structured to reflect this continuum from schematic/conceptual design to detailed construction drawings.

However, like most activities in the exhibition development process, these steps do not invariably follow as neatly upon each other, as much as we would like to wrangle them into a pattern. They sometimes double-back, repeat, or fortuitously leap forward unexpectedly. It is an iterative process that allows us to test ideas, address challenges of physical space, and solve problems that only arise when we begin to explore scale, materials, and technology.

Exhibition design requires both creativity and attention to detail at each stage of the process. Designers work within a larger team throughout exhibition development and production, including those responsible for the collections, interpretation, education, and fabrication. However, once the exhibition moves from planning and development to design, the designer's role becomes critical. The designer must lead and orchestrate a group of creative specialists with expertise in lighting, graphic design, and multimedia to create the physical experience with which the visitor will ultimately engage. What are the most appropriate means for connecting visitors with content? How will visitors circulate and experience the gallery? What unique design elements will make this physical experience unlike anything they have ever done before? This is an exhilarating but decidedly careful dance that not only needs to address content and creativity, but also budget.

17.1.1 Core Design Disciplines

Within the field of exhibition design, there are five key design disciplines:

1. **Three-dimensional design**: This discipline is focused on the three-dimensional (3D) exhibition space and is the domain of the lead designer. It is here that decisions surrounding the look, feel, and character of the design are determined. This includes all facets of the exhibition including visitor circulation, the placement of objects, materials, and finishes. Three-dimensional design is responsible for any interior and industrial design elements such as cases, display plinths, platforms, and built structures. The 3D designer must respond directly to the proposed visitor experience as determined in the interpretive plan, as well as keeping an eye on the ongoing development of content, which will be progressing in pace with their design work. Elements to be considered may include specialized components such as immersive environments, dioramas, interactive or mechanical displays, models, mannequins, and other custom items unique not only to the museum field but also to the particular exhibition that is currently under development.

2. **Graphic design**: Graphic or environmental design focuses mainly on two-dimensional (2D) exhibit elements presented on panels, labels, walls, partitions, floors, and multimedia screens. The graphic designer works closely with the 3D designer to ensure a dynamic marriage of materials, colors, and textures as well as any environmental graphics that bridge both 2D and 3D design elements. Graphic design is highly significant in that it can lend an enormous amount of character as well as desired tone to an exhibition. Because of the tremendous amount of content that may be delivered by these elements, graphic designers must also provide user-friendly and accessible interfaces for the museum audience. Graphic design is considered in further detail in chapter 18.

3. **Lighting design**: Lighting within the exhibition gallery is a key factor in establishing the mood of the space, both ambient and exhibit specific. It very often works on visitors' experiences and perceptions quietly, usually without announcing itself loudly, and thus is often unappreciated. Not only must lighting address the sensitive requirements of artifacts, specimens, and works of art, it must also consider the visitor in a dramatic space. The manipulation of color, dark and light, warm and cool, hard and soft, can be significant elements in design strategies and mood setting. LED technology has changed the lighting field in recent years, allowing for broader lighting and special effects opportunities for designers, as well as leading to better conservation of objects. Lighting, when designed well, can transform an exhibition from the mundane to the spectacular.

4. **Acoustics**: The determination of the acoustics of a space is an often-overlooked aspect of exhibition design. Not only do we need to guard against the incursion of unwanted outside noise into the gallery, we also need to anticipate the spread of noise, desirable or not, from one part of an exhibition to the next. An important part of establishing a mood inside a space,

acoustics can be affected by numerous considerations: the reflectivity of hard or soft materials, the configuration of spaces, and the number of visitors passing through at any given time. A busy noisy space can discourage contemplation, while conversely an overly quiet space can be intimidating to some visitors. Acousticians are not often included on exhibit design teams, as budgets rarely cater to this degree of individual specialization, so it is incumbent upon the lead designer to consider the implications of sound transmission in their plans and to advocate when an acoustician is required.

5. **Multimedia design (software and hardware)**: There is no doubt that multimedia plays a significant role in museum spaces and exhibitions. Whereas previously it was primarily a support to more conventional means of presentation, in today's museums it can often be the star attraction itself. Multimedia is where art, design, and technology meet. As chapter 19 demonstrates, multimedia is varied and complex with hardware and control requirements that are increasingly specialized. Exhibition budgets often hinge on the amount of technology in an exhibition because it can be so expensive to conceive, produce, and install. The ongoing maintenance of multimedia also needs to be considered as museums need to ensure they have the technical support for system upkeep and content updates. As such, the role of the multimedia specialist continues to increase both in scope and significance. With such a wide range of applications and solutions, the multimedia and audiovisual specialist must work closely with the 3D designer and interpretive planner to ensure the most effective and integrated use of technology in the design. Therefore, multimedia hardware and software specialists should be considered early in the planning and design process as figure 13.1 in chapter 13 suggests.

While there are other disciplines such as mechanical and electrical that may be required and coordinated by the 3D designer and project manager, the above categories are the most common. The work of these disciplines should be directed by a lead designer who can provide both logistical and art direction. The latter refers specifically to the maintenance of the exhibition design's integrity and vision: the look, feel, and quality of the scheme.

17.1.2 Stages of Design

Generally, there are four identifiable stages in which design plays a central role. The process is cumulative as each phase and its products are built upon the last. This is the process of achieving greater detail, with opportunities to review and test, until we finally realize an exhibition that we can fabricate and install.

The **interpretive plan** is the first stage of design expression, told not through drawings but words, diagrams, and precedents. This phase considers the experience as a whole and outlines the potential means of expression through a description of the visitor experience. The interpretive plan will include information for the designer such as project parameters, best practice or comparable references, space, budget, collections, audience needs, project goals and objectives, and thematic organization. It acts as a design brief to inform the designer and may include directions outlining how components are related. An interpretive plan acts much like a script and provides designers with much needed direction. Although the designer does not lead during this stage, their participation is invaluable, as they can begin to infuse the discussion with visual references and be inspired by the content and research developed by the curatorial team. While there is no design deliverable at this stage, some exhibition planning teams and processes benefit from

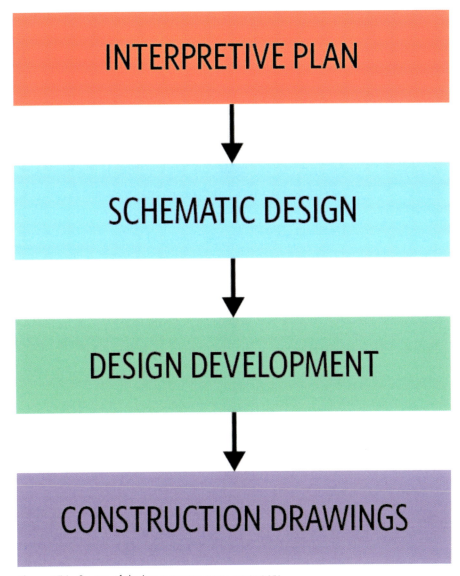

Figure 17.1. Stages of design. LORD CULTURAL RESOURCES

sketches, floor plans, and renderings. This is particularly true for exhibition design in Asia, the Middle East, and the Global South where visualization is a critical communication tool.

Once design begins in earnest, the first step is the development of a concept which may be done in parallel with interpretive planning or subsequent to it. The second stage, schematic, or concept design, begins the visualization process, providing an overall look and feel for the exhibition. This preliminary package will include layout and circulation diagrams; drawings of key exhibit components that form obvious anchors for the visitor experience such as multimedia attractions, star object display, or immersive environments; options for graphic gestures of color, font, and style; and initial references to finishes and materials. Color renderings, computer models, and virtual "fly-throughs" are most effectively used at this stage to communicate what the exhibition might

Exhibition Design

look like to members of the core exhibition team, stakeholders, and the public. Schematic design is an excellent and logical phase for planning and conducting formative evaluation studies (see chapter 12). Approval of schematic design, which may include several options for consideration, is critical as it establishes the baseline for the design of the exhibition and what all members of the exhibition team will be working toward through to opening day.

During **schematic design**, the design team may lead a series of workshops or design charettes intended to explore best practices and brainstorm ideas. Designers may choose to prepare a series of concept sketches to test preliminary solutions and make sure they are on the right track. It is an important moment in the design process, as these early images are indelible and concrete, allowing every member of the planning team to understand and define the exhibition in the same way. In other words, everyone knows what it is: words and ideas may be construed differently but visual images are objectively vivid for everyone to see, respond to, and eventually approve.

Digital visualization is a key facet of exhibition design, which has had a game-changing effect on the nature of the work. The ease with which photorealistic and stylized renderings of proposed project spaces can be created has meant that this side of design, previously the gravy at the end of the design process, is now something expected and delivered from the earliest phases through to the last. This has proven to be both a blessing and a curse for the designer. The earlier that design approaches can be communicated to a client the better. However, it also can lead to preliminary concepts, with their necessary shortcomings being viewed and judged as far more complete than they are. In short, too much too soon can undermine the creative possibilities open to the team by appearing to "cut to the chase" too soon!

A responsible schematic design package is accompanied by a preliminary budget. This is the first time that the exhibition's fabrication budget can be detailed, which allows the core exhibition team to evaluate how money is likely to be allocated. If the budget has been exceeded, now is the time to reconsider either the financial resources available to the project or the scope of the project itself. At this stage of design, the conception of the exhibition is quite "high-level," and most exhibit elements are not described in enough detail or specificity to cost individually. In this case costs are often determined on a per unit area basis (i.e., per square foot/meter or by allocation) or by comparing costs from previously built exhibitions. Industry cost standards relevant to the level of complexity of the design—higher for complex multimedia rich exhibits, lower for more straightforward didactic displays—are employed to determine budget. It is the job of the designer, with the help of an experienced cost estimator, to assess an appropriate cost matrix for the level of supply and build associated with the design.

Design development, or **detailed design**, is the next stage in the process. A series of interim packages advance the design thinking in order to resolve any and all unknowns. Elements that were not definitively described in schematic documents must now be determined in much more detail. This often occurs on two fronts: firstly, determining the specific materials, finishes, hardware, and such to be employed for every exhibit; and secondly to adjust the design to accommodate the particular content of the exhibition.

A series of iterative design packages are continuously created, building on previous decisions, providing more and more specificity until final design and fabrication solutions are realized. Design development documentation is sometimes projected as a series of "percent" completion packages such as 25 percent, 50 percent, 75 percent, 90 percent, and 100 percent. The number of packages will be determined by the project manager, size of the exhibition, and schedule for the project.

Visualization tools such as computer renderings are still used, but by the time this phase is complete, drawing packages are filled with detailed component-by-component drawings; elevations; structural, mechanical and electrical drawings; reflected ceiling plans; graphic templates; product cut sheets; and performance specifications that are often meaningful only to other designers, architects, engineers, and exhibition fabricators. A good designer will continue to find ways to communicate the design to the core exhibition team to facilitate decision-making. By the end of this stage of design all aspects of the following categories must be detailed and specified to a level that the exhibition can be built:

- Floor plans
- Elevations and sections
- Component design: all items such as cases, models, special millworks, environments, dioramas, mechanical interactives
- Case layouts: all objects in cases with mount-making requirements; for art galleries all works of art laid out to scale on elevation
- Lighting: reflected ceiling plans, equipment, light fixtures, heat and electrical loads, controls, cut sheets
- Graphics: templates, specifications, production instructions
- Materials and finishes: which may include sample boards in addition to schedules
- Performance specifications
- Architectural integration: walls, floors, partitions, doors, and other spatial interventions
- Mechanical and electrical: integration drawings as well as component specific
- Media hardware design: technical system and wiring layouts, heat and electrical loads, hardware specifications, show controls, and cut sheets
- Media software specification: experience descriptions and user flow, wireframes, screen samples, script outlines and narratives, storyboards, original versus stock material requirements

Each design package delivered during this stage must include a budget. Just as design documentation becomes more specific, so too does the budget. Greater detail provides greater confidence in pricing. It is easy to lose sight of the bottom line at this stage of a project, and much harder to reel the budget in during later stages. Depending on the scale of the project, costing can be undertaken by a professional cost consultant, by the exhibition fabricator in the case of a design-build scenario, or by experienced designers themselves. It can be the case that the design, in attempting to deliver the exhibition's ambitions, overshoots the project budget. The design must then be "value engineered," a process of simplification, reduction of scope, or substitution of elements for more affordable alternatives. It is a process of determining how to get the same value at less cost or to identify components of the visitor experience that can be removed without materially effecting the overall story that needs to be told. If this is not achievable, more money may need to be allocated to the fabrication budget.

Construction drawings (bid/tender documents) constitute the final stage in the process. Once final design has been approved at the end of design development, the team prepares a series of packages that allows the exhibition to be bid out for fabrication and production. This is sometimes called the "preproduction" phase of an exhibition project. Bid documents will consist of construction drawings and specifications that clearly illustrate how the exhibition will be built and how it must perform in the exhibition gallery. Depending on the complexity of the exhibition there may be separate drawing packages for cases and vitrines, general fabrication and millwork, models and dioramas, media hardware, media software, graphics, and mount-making. Such packaging targets specialized exhibition manufacturers and suppliers.

Alternatively, the core exhibition team may decide to proceed with the 100 percent design packages at the end of design development as the basis for contract with a fabricator who is already part of the exhibition planning team. The final decision on whether to proceed with construction drawings and how to package drawing sets and specification documents is in part reliant on the method of contract for exhibition production. Chapter 20 explores design-build and design-bid-build scenarios.

What is the RIBA plan of work? These work stages were created by the Royal Institute for British Architects (RIBA) and are most widely used to standardize architectural design and construction. In some parts of the world like Asia, the Middle East, and Europe, there is a growing desire to align exhibition design with the eight stages of the RIBA plan of work. Despite this not being an exhibition design process, if you are an exhibition planner/designer who will be working internationally, it is best to be prepared. There are many online resources that explain the RIBA process and the detailed checklists and requirements of each stage (www.architecture.com). Figure 17.2 summarizes how exhibition development and design fits within the RIBA framework.

RIBA Stage	Exhibition Development
Stage 0: Strategic Definition	An exhibition project has been identified and strategically appraised for feasibility. An exhibition proposal has been approved for design.
Stage 1: Preparation of the Brief	Aligns with the creation of the exhibition brief or project charter. At this stage, an "exhibition competition," similar to an architectural competition may take place.
Stage 2: Concept Design	The interpretive plan is created. In the RIBA process, some preliminary design documents are provided including floor plans and renderings for look and feel.
Stage 3: Developed Design	This is the schematic design and content development phase for the exhibition.
Stage 4: Technical Design	This stage is equivalent to the detailed design/design development stage of the project. In the RIBA process, exhibition deliverables at this stage need be technically designed to a high degree. The end of this stage includes the development of the construction drawings and packages for bid/tender.

Figure 17.2. RIBA and exhibition development. LORD CULTURAL RESOURCES

RIBA Stage	Exhibition Development
Stage 5: Construction	This is the construction and production period and ends with the installation of the exhibition. This is sometimes called "substantial completion".
Stage 6: Handover/Close-Out	Commissioning and testing of the exhibition occurs to make sure everything works and is compliant. This is often more commonly known as fixing errors and omissions, generating "punchlists" and training staff in the operation and maintenance of the exhibition. In some parts of the world, this means obtaining a "certificate of approval" from the client and governing authorities.
Stage 7: In Use	The exhibition is now in operation, but there is still a period of performance, project briefing, and warranty action.

Figure 17.2. *Continued*

17.1.3 Role of the Designer During Fabrication and Production

Once the exhibition is in the hands of qualified fabricators and specialist vendors, the designer takes on the role of reviewer. **Shop drawings** are usually completed by the fabrication and production teams contracted to build the exhibition. They translate final designs and construction documents into drawings that contain specific construction details that are particular to the trades who require them. This package of drawings will outline precise details such as joints, fasteners, glues, and other methods pertinent to fabricators. The designer should be retained to review these drawings to ensure quality; approve proposed alternative materials and pieces of equipment; and check that fabricators are not taking any short cuts or proposing methods that may be unsafe or unsuitable for artifacts or visitors. During this phase, there may also be queries from vendors and fabrication specialists that only the designer can answer. **Art direction** is an activity that takes place during the production phase. The designer, along with other members of the core exhibition team, will review prototypes, material samples, and graphic outputs to confirm that the original intention of the design is respected. Are the colors correct? Are objects located in the right case and positioned appropriately? Are multimedia kiosks functioning as desired?

17.1.4 Considering Accessibility

Museums have a responsibility to design exhibitions that are universally accessible, ensuring that all visitors regardless of their physical, emotional, and cognitive abilities, have the opportunity for an equally and inclusively engaging visitor experience. Accessibility can be defined in a variety of ways and should be considered early in the planning process. Accounting for inclusive design could greatly affect the project resources: timeline, budget, and space requirements. In fact, museums should have a clearly defined policy regarding accessibility standards in exhibition design.

Some countries have legislated requirements for accessibility. The United States, for example, has numerous laws including the Americans with Disabilities Act, which mandates access for buildings, programs, and services. Other jurisdictions have established standards through architectural institutes or other nongovernmental bodies. Most museum associations, such as those in the United States, United Kingdom, Australia, and Canada, have information on the relevant accessibility-related laws or requirements and provide guidelines for making museums fully accessible based on those laws or requirements. Many museums have established their own guidelines and policies for universal design, building on relevant legislation and going beyond it. The Smithsonian Institution, for example, has made its *Guidelines for Accessible Exhibition Design* available to the world museum community.

All visitors, with their diverse needs and abilities should be able to move about and interact with the exhibition without barriers. As such, consider universal design right from the beginning in the following broad categories.

Pathways and **circulation** need to be considered to ensure a barrier-free design that includes level pathways and accessibility routes, large enough for wheelchairs and other mobility aids to move and turn freely. Areas should include benches and seating that not only allow for moments of reflection, but also places to rest. Ground surfaces should be stable, firm, and slip resistant. If an exhibition has a change in floor level created by a step, a ramp will need to be incorporated at a gradient no greater than 1:15 along its centerline.

Exhibit furniture such as cases and interactive elements should be surrounded by a predictable border on all applicable sides for circulation. Wheelchair clearance requires that clear floor or ground space should be positioned for either forward or parallel approach. All visitors should be able to reach interactives and screens from a standing or sitting position. Make sure exhibit millworks aren't tripping hazards and can be detected by visitors using a cane.

Display cases should be designed so that visitors can view and interact with contents from any height. For example, cases should not be too high that young visitors or those in a wheelchair cannot see in. Keep smaller items at the front and larger objects at the back to assist with visibility. Ensure that wall mounted cases and vitrines do not be become a hazard for people as they move about the space whether they are walking by, using a cane, or in a wheelchair.

Digital media can support accessibility but must also be designed to accommodate universal access. Audio projections, such as explanations, environmental sounds, or open captioning should be incorporated. Open captions of videos benefit deaf and hearing-impaired visitors, but also help people who have difficulty hearing audio because of environmental noise. Audio-guided tours can be used by anyone and may be more flexible in the long run than media-by-media specific interventions. Consider embedding sign-language enabled experiences that visitors can select if needed, recognizing that there may be other more suitable aids in different regions and countries. Other things to consider when designing media include viewing angle, display placements, screen orientation, parallax problems, on-screen color and contrast, reflection, glare, and ambient lighting.

Lighting must be bright enough to allow people to be able to view artifacts and read labels, but still low enough not to damage sensitive objects. This can be a delicate dance. In areas of low light, ensure that fonts are larger. For sensitive objects like archival materials, adopt in-case lighting systems that only illuminate the objects upon close examination. Be aware that providing higher levels of illumination does not necessarily result in improved seeing conditions. Light can be too bright as well as too dim. A good lighting designer will adjust the design for illumination, reflection, glare, and color contrast. Color contrast is particularly important, especially for guests who have trouble distinguishing between colors.

Accessible Lighting Levels	
Ambient Lighting	50 - 300 lux
Text Panels	100 - 300 lux
Controls	100 lux
Directional Signage	200 - 300 lux
Maps, Displays	50 - 300 lux
Ramps, Stairs	100 - 300 lux
Pathways	100 - 300 lux

Figure 17.3. Accessible lighting levels. LORD CULTURAL RESOURCES

Designers should infuse **graphics** with universal design principles that address font selection, media type, use of symbols or icons, and color contrast. Graphic panels should be carefully located for ease of recognition in terms of hierarchy and un-compromised sightlines. Line drawings, infographics, silhouettes, and photographs can aid comprehension for those with reading difficulties. Consider the following:

- **Accessibility of print**: Fonts should be chosen for clarity and simplicity. The debate regarding which is more legible, serif or sans serif, is still ongoing. Determine a strategy and test it with your visitors. Over time your museum will have a body of preferred fonts for legibility.

- **Font sizes**, as discussed in chapter 19, should reflect the hierarchy of information and range in size, but the minimal 18-point font should allow people with visual limitations to read it.

- **Color** can make information more attractive and easier to follow. However, for many the wrong choice or combination of colors can make reading or understanding difficult. There is a narrow choice of colors that are easily distinguishable by most of the population. Light shades should be avoided unless paired with dark colors; reds, greens, yellows, and blues are examples of colors that can be problematic if used together because a significant proportion of visitors may have color-vision deficiencies.

- **Contrast**: When an object stands out from its surroundings because of a difference in brightness and/or color, sight activities such as separation, shape recognition, and reading are improved. Hence, there should be a strong contrast between print and background. A good rule of thumb is to ensure at least a 70 percent difference in color value.

- **Braille** is a system of reading by touch using raised dots that are arranged to represent letters. Not all blind people can read Braille so other forms of audio-based technologies should be considered.
- Symbols, graphs, photos, and other **forms of illustration** can support different means of communication and navigation within an exhibition and around the museum.

Tactile experiences such as replica artifacts, materials, models, and other touchables benefit people with visual impairments as well as engage younger visitors who are still learning to read.

The Canadian Museum for Human Rights is considered a best practice for universal design. The museum was built to feature inclusive design and sets a global standard for accessibility. From the way visitors enter the building to the way in which they interact with exhibits, the museum experience is designed to be inclusive and accessible for everyone. In addition to all the features located inside and outside the building, several gallery experiences are of particular relevance to exhibition designers. Refer to the museum's website for more information on all of the accessible features of the institution (https://humanrights.ca/visit/accessibility), which include some of the following solutions:

1. **Mobile app**: Visitors can download a fully accessible self-guided museum tour that includes sign language in English and French. The audio tour provides a description of each gallery and many exhibit highlights. It also includes text-based transcripts for the hearing impaired. The app is rich with alternatives ways of hearing, seeing, and experiencing the museum.

2. **Universal access point**: All static exhibition content, as well as audio tours, can be accessed through a tactile marker called a Universal Access Point. These markers can be found on walls and exhibit panels and are indicated on the floor using a tactile floor strip near each exhibit. The markers are digitally enabled by a device carried by the visitor and consist of raised numbers and Braille codes that trigger audio.

3. **Universal Keypad**: Near every touchscreen is a Universal Keypad. The keypads allow visitors to experience the digital content through accessible tactile controls and voiced instructions.

4. **Sign Language**: All videos with spoken words are interpreted via American Sign Language and Langes des signes Québécoise on screen.

5. **Braille**: A Braille guide contains tactile maps of the galleries and descriptions of the exhibitions in English and French Braille.

6. **Graphics**: All exhibits adhere to strict graphic standards to ensure content is accessible. Fonts were chosen for maximum legibility and clarity. Type sizes, placement, paragraph alignment, and line-lengths were all considered in the design process. Color contrast and light reflective values contrasts were designed to ensure sufficient contrast and facilitate legibility.

7. **Descriptive audio**: All videos contain descriptive audio, using a narrator to read on-screen text out loud as well as describe what is happening.

8. **Closed captioning**: All videos with spoken words have closed captioning in English and French.

17.2 EXHIBITION DISPLAY CASES BY MIKE CHAPLIN

Display cases (vitrines) form an important part of almost every museum or art gallery exhibition worldwide and are often one of the most significant investments any institution will make when developing or redeveloping their displays. The difficulty in any public space used for display is to combine an aesthetic presentation of objects or artifacts for public view, education, and enjoyment, while simultaneously protecting them from decay, damage, or theft. The advancement in glass production and processing, manufacturing techniques and technology means that more than ever, glass vitrines can be exploited not only as a protective cover for a museum's most valued objects, but that the cases themselves can form a substantial part of the visual presentation of a space.

Sometimes, institutions will request or require the use of acrylic or plexiglass vitrines. It is important to understand the purpose of this request as there are both pros and cons of using these types of cases. In some instances, there is the belief that acrylic cases are more durable and cheaper than their glass counterparts. This may not always be true and should be examined further in association with the chosen fabricator or display case provider. While it is true that acrylic will not break in the same way that glass will, it is easier to scratch or scuff the surface. Acrylic is lighter and may be chosen by smaller institutions with very few operations or facility staff. The weight may also benefit museums that desire easily changeable content and thus access to their cases for temporary exhibitions. The choice depends on budget, feasibility, operations, and design aesthetic.

17.2.1 Glass

Today, the availability and affordability of more specialist types of glass (such as laminated, tempered, etc.) can greatly enhance the viewing pleasure of audiences as well as protect a museum's most precious objects. Glass for display cases is and always should be laminated. The laminate interlayer (known as PVB), which bonds the two pieces together, forms a natural barrier against ultraviolet (UV) rays, filtering out 97 percent, between 320 and 380 nanometers. Although this alone cannot protect the artifact, it offers substantially more protection than toughened or tempered glass, which offers no UV protection or filtration. Laminated glass also offers greater security for displays than toughened or tempered glass and is inherently more difficult for thieves to break.

The thickness of the laminate PVB interlayer determines whether the glass will be classified as safety-rated or security-rated, with anything less than 1.5 millimeters PVB being classed as a safety glass only. Therefore, laminated glass with 0.4 millimeters and 0.8 millimeters PVB interlayers are not considered to have a sufficiently high security rating for the protection of valued objects.

In the United Kingdom where a Government Indemnity Scheme provides coverage for museum losses, the minimum requirement for cases is 11.5-millimeter laminated glass. While it is important to work to showcase specifications to meet the requirements of specific institutions, it is increasingly important to make sure that display cases meet the highest international standards in order for the museum to qualify for loans from other institutions.

There are two main options for glass in museum-quality cases: low iron and low reflective. Low iron laminated glass, which has several different trade names such as Optiwhite and Starfire, is now the most widely used of all glass types in the assembly of museum display cases. Low iron glass brings a greater optical purity to the visual aspect of objects and a truer viewing sense of the colors within. Another glass material that has seen a significant and sustained growth in its use for museum display cases is low reflective glass. This type of glass has a special coating applied during manufacture via a dipping or spatter process, which greatly reduces the natural reflective qualities of glass. This means the viewing pleasure for any object or painting is greatly enhanced for the visitor.

Competing products also means that the glass is much more affordable. Ultimately, the use of low iron and low reflective glass combined allows the maximum viewing pleasure for any display. Improved techniques for the surface adhesion of glass means that, visually, glass is a much more viable and attractive option for the presentation of museum objects than was previously available.

17.2.2 Case Types

Categories of display case types allow designers and planners to assess and determine the right method of display for their exhibition and objects. The options in use in museums are:

- Tabletop cases
- Freestanding case with glass top
- Freestanding case with integrated lighting hood
- Circular or curved cases
- Wall cases
- Demountable/Modular cases
- Display drawers

Tabletop cases are transparent on top and all four sides. This five-sided glass "bonnet" offers an elegant and simple way of displaying small objects such as coins, medals, or two-dimensional materials such as manuscripts. The glass corners are usually ground at a 45-degree miter, and are joined with glass cement, silicon, or an ultraviolet-resistant adhesive to form a frameless all-glass construction. The bottom edges of the glass are usually set into a U-frame, with a solid base below. Locks keep the glass hood from being lifted off the base except when required.

Access is gained by installing hinges to the glass hood and supporting it with gas or hydraulic assisters. On larger versions, electric pistons may be used to mechanically lift the entire bonnet vertically. Tabletop cases or glass bonnets that offer only a lift-off top for access are best avoided. The potential for damaging an artifact or display when lifting the glass hood back into position is too great.

Previously, acrylic, or plexiglass, was a popular choice of material for this type of case due its relatively inexpensive cost. However, this type of material is seldom acceptable today due to the lack of security it offers. Acrylic can be easily scratched and requires replacing before glass would, therefore making it a false economy.

The general aesthetic requirement for **freestanding cases with glass tops** is for any top metalwork or extrusion to be as minimal as possible and therefore the most common method of access

Figure 17.4. Tabletop case. COURTESY OF CLICKNETHERFIELD

is "pull and slide." A small U-shaped channel is bonded to the overhanging glass top allowing the door to slide within this channel. This type of case generally has locks only at the bottom of the display case. Planners should therefore consider the value of the objects being displayed inside. Hinge options are also available and usually require a top perimeter frame or patch-type hinge and lock fittings.

The freestanding case can be utilized in two ways: with glass on each side when the case is located centrally in the gallery or with a solid back or sides to the display case if the case is to be set back against a wall. The appearance and utilization of freestanding cases can be altered by using a support plinth below the case. This support plinth can be used to conceal items such as passive or active climate control systems and can be keyed to a separate maintenance suite so

Figure 17.5. Freestanding case with glass top. COURTESY OF CLICKNETHERFIELD

Exhibition Design

that the security of the display chamber is not compromised. Glass types and thicknesses would generally follow the same as freestanding light box cases.

Internal dress panels are the horizontal and vertical display surfaces within the case. These panels can be from a variety of materials depending upon required finish and method of object mounting. Today, solid surface materials and rigid PVC sheets are preferred over particle boards, but other options include steel and aluminum, which can be powder-coated. It is important that the final colors of fabric and paints are Oddy tested to ensure they are suitable for the objects to be displayed.

Due to its versatility, the **freestanding case with integral light hood** is the most common type of display case found in museums and art galleries. Like cases with glass tops, these freestanding cases can have glass on all faces or have solid sides and backs. But this case type has an integral light box that is separated from the display chamber by a lighting soffit level. The soffit can be made of glass, steel, or aluminum relevant to the lighting type chosen. The light chamber at the top must have ventilation that allows any heat gain to dissipate away from the case and it objects. The light chamber should also have a separate access to the display chamber. This means that maintenance staff can maintain lighting without having access to valuable objects in the display chamber, thus keeping the objects safe from theft or damage. This type of case can accommodate most types of lighting, whether general wash lighting or individual spotlights.

The choice of using either all glass or a solid back will impact the type of shelving that may be utilized inside the display chamber. Solid back cases provide options for cantilevered shelves or hanging rod shelving, whereas all-glass cases are generally restricted to a hanging rod-type shelving arrangement. In addition to shelves, plinths of varying sizes that sit on the base of the case can be used to display objects. Access methods for a freestanding case with an integral light box will normally be via a hinged door (with fully concealed hinges) or a pull-and-slide door configuration where the door pulls out toward the operator and then slides aside in either direction.

Glass types for upright freestanding cases should generally be laminated with a minimum thickness of 11.5 millimeters depending upon the desired height of the case. As the height of the case

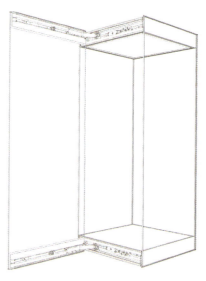

Figure 17.6. Freestanding case with integral light hood. COURTESY OF CLICKNETHERFIELD

increases, the thickness of the glass should also be increased in order to maintain the structural integrity of the display case. Glass with a thickness of 13.5 millimeters, 17.5 millimeters, and 21.5 millimeters can be used to ensure structural integrity, but the most common thickness used in this type of display case is 11.5-millimeter laminated glass.

Circular or **curved cases** are becoming increasingly popular with architects and designers. Their unique aesthetic can be used to accentuate architectural features or reflect artifact design. For the Art Gallery of Ontario in Toronto, for instance, architect Frank Gehry designed a sequence of undulating cases to display a collection of ship models, simultaneously complementing his sinuous architecture and suggesting gently rolling ocean waves. The inherent structural integrity of the curved form can also enhance the performance of frameless cases. Circular cases can be created with glass tops or with integral lighting hoods to incorporate a full range of lighting solutions. Shelving can be provided by hanging rod systems or cantilever systems from a solid back or internal support column. Hinged doors are most common with curved glass panels as they provide a better functionality than curved tracks.

There can be an element of optical distortion with curved glass, particularly concave surfaces that have a smaller radius, so it is well worth producing mockups of proposed designs to ensure that this does not affect artifact visibility. In addition, curved glass solutions can be expensive as such cases may require custom glass production solutions.

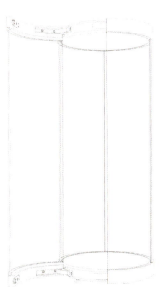

Figure 17.7. Curved case. COURTESY OF CLICKNETHERFIELD

The previously mentioned case types (and their characteristics regarding glass, lighting, and access) can be set against walls, built into walls, or mounted directly onto walls. These **wall cases** can create unique viewing patterns in wall-mounted vitrines or massive structures for the display of a large number of objects. Because of varying wall construction and the potentially heavy weights of cases and artifacts, it is preferable for cases to have a direct support from the floor—from a plinth or tubular frame—as well as being fixed back to the wall. When set into walls, it is important to consider access to the service areas of lighting and environmental control materials. The backs of wall cases generally consist of a structural panel but also an internal dress panel that is removable for reapplying a new finish.

Exhibition Design

 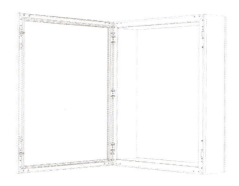

Figure 17.8. Wall case. COURTESY OF CLICKNETHERFIELD

Increased museum participation in temporary and traveling exhibitions has led to the development of **demountable** and **modular cases**, the latest generations of which can have the same levels of conservation and security as permanent cases. The key features of these cases are that they can be quickly and easily dismantled and reassembled. In addition, the modules can be formed into different case sizes and shapes to suit changing object requirements to provide maximum flexibility for the museum. These case types should have the option of a glass top or integral light hood and should be able to offer a full range of lighting and shelving options. Another important aspect of these types of cases is the provision of a secure and sturdy crate for transportation and the availability of spare parts for at least ten years.

Figure 17.9. Modular/demountable case. COURTESY OF CLICKNETHERFIELD

 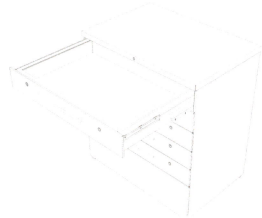

Figure 17.10. Display drawer. COURTESY OF CLICKNETHERFIELD

Many galleries and museums incorporate **drawer systems** with a locking glass top display that can be opened and closed by visitors. Drawers allow a high density of artifacts to be displayed within a small area, but also provide excellent protection from light damage as the time of exposure on display is greatly reduced. While drawers are ideal for flat materials, it is usually necessary to fit three-dimensional objects into specially sculpted trays from a material such as Plastazote to keep them from moving about when the drawers are opened and closed. For conservation reasons some types of artifacts are not suitable for display in drawers as they may be damaged by the regular and potentially rough movements from public use.

Lighting can be incorporated into drawers with a microswitch control to activate the lighting only when a drawer is open. If necessary, drawers can also contain conditioning materials such as silica gel and pollutant scavengers if required.

17.2.3 General Infrastructure and Environmental Considerations for Cases

It is important to consider the required infrastructure for cases and to incorporate it into the earliest stage of building and gallery design. In particular, cases require access to power and data:

- Electrically operated door mechanisms will require a power supply adjacent to the case and consideration must be given to case specific disaster planning requirements to define the operational characteristics.
- Lighting will require an electrical supply located at the top or bottom of the case. This should be easily switched off at night, Timed systems will require a manual override for exceptional usage such as an evening function.
- If cases are designed to incorporate active environmental control systems, then power supply on a separate circuit must operate 24/7.
- Many cases have interactive display screens and projection systems associated with them and usually require network cabling structure back to a central equipment zone.
- Alarm systems will need dedicated cabling to the case unless a wireless solution is to be used.
- Environmental monitoring equipment may require dedicated cabling to provide data to a central monitoring point.

Along with power and data, exhibition designers must also consider the weight of cases. Large cases, whether freestanding or set against a wall, will require adequate floor loading to support the case itself and the objects inside. Cases more than three meters in any dimension require thicker glass and impose significant loads on the building; it is critical to check floor loadings early, particularly with older buildings. In addition to floor loading, the cases that are expected to house heavy objects should incorporate bases and plinths that support and spread the load. This will likely affect the materials selected to frame and support the case structure.

Cases protect objects from theft and damage by keeping them safely away from visitors and staff who are not trained in handling them. They also protect them from damage that might be caused from pollutants and fluctuating environmental changes. Whereas a poorly built display case will oblige staff to continually clean the interior of the dust that will accumulate in it, well-sealed cases will keep out any dust and pollutants that are not cleared out of the gallery by a properly functioning heating and ventilation system. Cases can also be designed to provide passive and active environmental control to prevent damage that might be caused by fluctuating temperatures and humidity.

Cases with **passive-control** are well-designed and tightly constructed. They are firmly sealed, controlling the amount of air that moves through the case. In galleries where the space is conditioned to museum standards for temperature and humidity control, this is more than enough. In some instances, cases can be designed to incorporate trays for silica gel, a substance that absorbs moisture. Such trays are useful for providing extra protection, in particular for metal objects such as coins or silver or organic material such as woods and textiles that may require dryer conditions than those set by the museum's Building Management System.

Cases with **active-control** systems accommodate older museums or historic buildings that may not have the heating, ventilation, and air conditioning system to provide the necessary environmental controls in galleries. With active control museums have two options: (1) a local unit using membrane technology can be used to condition individual cases or (2) multiple cases can be conditioned from a plant located elsewhere in the building. This can require more infrastructure, including pipe being run from the plant to each of the cases. Some systems may require a water supply and a drain point.

17.3 LIGHTING DESIGN BY KEVIN SHAW

To plan and design the lighting of a museum exhibition, it is necessary to understand the basis of illumination and constraints related to the extremes of human vision. This is important in relation to the lighting of exhibitions in which conservation is a principal consideration. Essentially, the eye contains three types of characteristics for human visual perception: the response of the human eye to light, color perception, and color temperature. They need to be taken into consideration before selecting light sources, fittings, reflectors, lenses, filters, track, and control systems.

The primary consideration for lighting exhibitions must be the response of the human eye to light. The eye provides basic visual information that is processed by a surprisingly large area of the brain, which allows for the huge range of lighting conditions under which vision is possible. It also accounts for the ability to use light to suggest a great deal about the environment through relatively few clues.

The brain always makes comparisons with learned models of the environment, for example, a bright ceiling is compared with the daytimed sky; a dark ceiling represents night; warm light represents either direct sunlight or fire depending on other clues; cold, blue light may be either moonlight or an overcast dull day, again depending on other clues. The extensive involvement of the brain in the visual process accounts for our ability to discriminate detail and color under widely varying lighting conditions. This discriminative ability is the source of most visual information in the exhibition context.

Museum lighting must consider photopic (vision of the eye under well lit conditions) and scotopic vision (vision of the eye under low-light conditions). This is particularly relevant at low light levels in the region of fifty lux (e.g., five-foot candles) usually recommended for conservation reasons as the appropriate light level for works on paper or sensitive textiles. Although full color vision is possible for the majority of visitors at this level, viewing midtone objects become seriously compromised at twenty to thirty lux. It is difficult to maintain a maximum light level of fifty lux without falling into the mesopic (between photopic and scotopic) range, particularly because it is usually necessary to restrain levels twenty to thirty lux one meter above floor level in order to achieve fifty lux falling on a work of art hanging on the gallery wall.

Another peculiarity of the human visual system is the reaction to varying light levels within the field of view. Generally, the visual system does not respond like a light meter, averaging light the total area viewed. Instead, we set a response range according to the brightest point in our field of view. This response commonly causes the experience of glare, in which a single bright light can totally disable visual discrimination. This is a serious consideration for the physical design as well as the lighting design of exhibitions. Consequently, any direct view of daylight should be excluded from any field of view containing objects lit to low conservation lighting levels. Obviously, direct views of light sources must equally be avoided through judicious location and selection of fittings, which inherently contain the light source and protect visitors from glare.

It must also be remembered that the human eye takes time to adapt between significant changes in light level. Initial adaptation takes place in twenty to thirty seconds, but full adaptation can take up to thirty minutes. In the design of exhibition spaces therefore, visitor travel time between daylight exterior and comparatively low-level lighting in the exhibition must be managed to allow for adaptation through spaces with progressively lower light levels. This creates a level of comfort and avoidance of the otherwise frequent visitor complaints about "dark and gloomy" exhibitions.

The light source should always be the first decision in the development of a lighting scheme. The relative abilities of various light sources to render colors accurately are crucial in museums. The standard measure for this is the color rendering index (CRI). A CRI of 100 represents color perception under daylight at high lighting levels or incandescent light at low lighting levels.

The other factor in selecting light sources is color appearance. This is frequently expressed in kelvins as correlated color temperature (CCT) representing the color of a black body heated to the same temperature. As anyone who has observed a fire knows, the hotter a piece of carbon or metal gets, the brighter and whiter it glows. It is this principle that is codified in this measurement. But this is a poor indicator of true visual appearance, as lamps can have identical CCTs but, to the eye, can vary dramatically. In fact, the human eye has great powers of comparative discrimination, so to maintain visual continuity the same light source should be used in all areas that may be viewed simultaneously, unless a specific visual effect is required.

Exhibition Design

Sources and daylight form the basis of this measure. CRI is a relatively crude measure as it compares only eight unsaturated color samples. Since the advent of LEDs, the shortcomings of this technique have become obvious. Typically, LEDs show poor color performance at the red end of the spectrum. One way to discover if this will create issues is to get the test value for R9, which is a saturated red not included in the initial eight samples for the Ra measure (color rendering index), this value should be at least 60 percent of the Ra for the light source to get reasonable rendition of deep and dark reds.

Since the last edition of this book another color rendering scheme has been proposed, the IES TM-30. It uses a similar comparison system to CRI however using one hundred color samples. It also includes a score for color gamut, the range of colors that will be represented well. This includes a diagram that informs where in the color field there will be diminution or exaggeration of colors. This measure is slowly being adopted by light source manufacturers who are keen to demonstrate the color qualities of their systems.

LED and or solid-state lighting have now taken over from tungsten halogen as a primary light source for display lighting, principally for reasons of energy savings and in response to legislation that is limiting the availability of incandescent and tungsten halogen lamps. By their nature, LED sources are quite variable, and unfortunately CRI is not a very good indicator of how well a particular LED product will render colors. LED lamps also will change color rendition, appearance, and light output as they age, which creates significant challenges in selecting a suitable product to use. The only reliable method is by undertaking an on-site trial of different color appearance and rendering by LEDs with the particular object that you will be displaying. Since LEDs offer long service life compared to other technologies, it is important to ensure that the products you use have warranties that cover not only failure but significant variation in output, color appearance, and rendering, which are offered by only a few suppliers who generally have better products and are willing to stand by and support them. A long service life does not mean that regular maintenance is not still required; while there is no need to regularly change lamps, routine cleaning of lenses and reflectors as well as heat sinks is necessary to ensure maintenance of light quality and longevity of light fixtures. While LEDs themselves have long lives, the driver electronics are more prone to failure, therefore consideration should be given to accessibility of remote drivers even when the fixtures are at difficult locations to access.

LEDs are quite different from conventional light sources. To operate at their best, they require substantially different designs of fixture. In general, LED products intended to replace a conventional lamp should be avoided. Specific LED-based fixtures should be used for new projects or refurbishments.

Different light sources produce differing amounts of ultraviolet light (UV) and infrared (IR), which is a concern for conservators. Currently available LED sources do not emit significant UV or IR. Typically, "white" LEDs use a narrow band blue emitter and a yellow conversion phosphor. Products are coming on to the market that use violet emitters that have a shorter wavelength emission closer to UV. It is possible that some UV-driven phosphor products may emerge, however they should be treated with extreme caution in the museum environment.

LEDs vary significantly in emissions in the blue area of the spectrum. LEDs of cooler appearance, particularly of lower color rendition, can have significant spikes in the blue region. They should be avoided as research indicates that some pigments are more susceptible to damage from intense blue light. However, this should not be a problem where high-quality warm LEDs are used. In this case, a higher proportion of the blue (or violet) emission is converted to longer wavelength light, reducing the potential for damage.

Overall research indicates that good quality LED light sources are less damaging to museum objects than previous tungsten halogen and fluorescent sources at comparable warm color temperatures. The spectral distribution of the highest quality LED products is also good and even. It is worth asking for spectral distribution graphs for light sources you are considering, making sure there are no specific spikes or dips across the spectrum.

Another consideration for selecting LED products is the possibility of strobing and flickering, which is caused by the gear converting the main electricity to the controlled low voltage required to drive the LEDs. Flickering occurs more when dimming is required. It is important to ensure that the gear proposed or included in fittings is genuinely flicker-free. Apart from annoyance, flickering can cause visual disturbances and trigger migraines and other symptoms in some people. Flickering will also prevent good photography and video, which might be important with video-based interactive exhibits or for any other broadcast or enhanced reality activities.

The design of **fixtures** or fittings is a key consideration in exhibitions. Museums are a tiny fraction of the worldwide lighting market, and few manufacturers produce fittings specifically for museum use. But while few address the full requirements, some manufacturers produce variations to fittings that satisfy some of the prerequisites for museums that include:

- Positive tool-operated locking to maintain focus
- Capability to clean without moving fitting when this is necessary
- Lens options that increase flexibility
- Ability to change focus by variable optics or interchangeable reflectors or lenses
- Self-dimming capacity at the fitting to fine-tune lighting levels
- Capability of repairing the fitting and replacing gear and other essential elements on site

The **optic** (or lens) is the single most important component of a light fixture, shaping the beam and controlling any stray light. Total Internal Reflection (TIR) optics are generally injection molded from polymers and use a refractive lens inside a reflector. Optics are designed to work with specific LEDs and need to be carefully cleaned at least every two years to ensure they are operating efficiently.

At their most complicated, a **lens system** for exhibition light fittings consists of two or three elements arranged to provide a simple pattern projection similar to a theater profile spot. In fact, there are some situations where suitable theater equipment can be useful to museum lighting designers. More common in the museum environment are simpler lenses added to the front of display spotlights. Variations include sculpture lenses (or spread lenses), diffusing lenses, and filters. Sculpture lenses or spread lenses are usually pressed or ribbed cast glass or acrylic that change the shape of the light beam from the circular outline created by the primary optic to an elongated oval or elliptical pattern. This helps in lighting tall and thin or wide and long displays or with creating illuminated bands on walls to encompass a range of objects. Diffusing lenses are useful to reduce light levels and to increase the area covered by a particular fitting. They can also clean up striations or unevenness in the beam of light. They come in a variety of types, including acrylic, cast glass, or sandblasted glass.

Like lenses, **filters** are placed at the front of the fitting and are sometimes referred to as lenses. They are intended to change the quality of the light from the lamp either by coloring it for effect or, more importantly for museum applications, to remove UV from the light beam. It is essential to see a practical product demonstration of any optical system before deciding on any such products.

In recent years, manufacturers have heavily promoted **fiber optics** as the solution to all museum lighting problems. This is an exaggeration; in fact, fiber optics is merely another useful tool, a light delivery system that can be visualized as a long and thin lens on the front of a light source. Fiber optics allow the light from one lamp to be distributed over a greater area and to be subdivided. Light sources can be located some distance from the place where the light is needed. These characteristics are useful for lighting display cases where low light levels are required. They provide flexibility and allow the light source to be situated outside the case. This means that they can be maintained without the requirement to work in the vicinity of the displayed objects. For most museum applications, glass fiber, which will naturally reduce the UV content but will pass IR rays, is preferable. Acrylic fibers are available but typically less efficient.

Assuming similar light sources, fiber optic systems do not improve color rendering. If anything, glass fibers impart a green cast, and the longer the fiber harness the more apparent this becomes. Lighting large cases is problematic because fiber tends to create a large number of small pools of light within the case. Therefore, the lights must be carefully focused to prevent a scattered appearance. Fiber optic systems must be meticulously selected, and due consideration should be given to the final result. Preference should be given to systems with a large range of lens and filter options for the fiber ends, and a good locking mechanism to ensure the fiber stays in position.

The light source required at the common end of the fiber harness should also be thoroughly researched. There are many different manufacturers and designs for LED light sources for this application. Consideration needs to be given to the color appearance and rendering of the LED used, also the cooling system. Considerable heat will be generated by the LED. Sometimes fans or other mechanical devices are provided to increase air movement and cooling. If possible, avoid these as they are likely to have the shortest life in the system and any moving air is likely to increase the accumulation of dust in the light source, reducing efficiency and requiring frequent cleaning and air filter changes.

Many museums use **lighting track systems** to provide flexibility. A single type of track with common wiring standards that allows the museum to use more than one manufacturer's fittings should be selected. Three-circuit track lights provide optimum flexibility.

Positioning track lights within a gallery is usually determined by applying the "thirty-degree" rule so that a thirty-degree angle is formed between the wall and the incline of focused light from the lamp at the eye level of a five-foot, four-inch viewer. Certainly, the track should be placed to avoid frame shadow over the upper edge of a painting. The track system usually parallels the gallery walls or may be arranged in several parallel ranges or a grid in a larger gallery.

Almost all museums utilize a **lighting control system**. Centralized control of exhibition lighting is the key to creating a rational and effective means of controlling the exposure of works of art and artifacts. Programmed "switch-on" and "switch-off" at opening and closing of the public hours of the museum is essential. This may be done manually (if backed up by an effective management policy) or automatically.

Outside of public museum hours, lighting for security and cleaning staff can be controlled automatically by either timing or occupancy sensors. Of the two, the latter is more responsive to lighting requirements and is most likely to protect artifacts or works of art from unnecessary exposure to light.

Dimming control is a complex topic. Centralized dimming can provide for overall changes in light level, or for gentle transitions between different lighting states, such as transitions between daylight and artificial dusk. In this case, consideration should be given to providing automatic light sensing in the gallery spaces. It is neither realistic nor desirable to expect attendants to react appropriately and accurately to changes in lighting levels.

It is possible to provide individual control of lights through a centralized system. Typically, local control for each fitting may be easier to use when setting up an exhibition. With the advent of LEDs, it has become easier to provide complex control functions digitally, however they do not work well with traditional power control dimming systems. This means that additional data wiring is necessary to achieve control, necessitating some planning and selection of the preferred digital dimming protocol at an early stage in the design process.

Another development has been wireless lighting control. While this minimizes the need for any data wiring, the multiplicity of systems currently available are all incompatible, so a decision on the system and strategy for this is important and needs to be considered in the long term. Some systems also provide light sensors that can be placed to suit the exhibition or object to monitor the light levels and dim the relevant fittings to account for variables such as changing daylight. These systems also allow recording of the light level over time to manage the exposure of the objects while they are on exhibition. Equally, sensors for presence detection can be incorporated in these systems, allowing dimming of lights when there are few visitors, or to create a sequence of scenes to help flow visitors through the space.

It is vital that lighting maintenance retains levels for museum exhibitions at their exact design specifications. The museum environment is also unique with regard to the expected life of lighting installations. In retail establishments a lighting scheme is likely to be redesigned or replaced approximately every five years; in commercial offices every ten. By contrast, many museum installations for the display of permanent collections remain in place for periods as long as fifteen to twenty-five years without substantial changes. At the other end of the scale are temporary exhibition galleries, where lighting is changed with the exhibition as often as several times a year. It should be noted, however, that in this case the same equipment is used, so it is subject to extremes of wear and tear.

At the lighting design stage, all these factors must be given serious consideration. Selecting equipment and fittings suitable for extended use is crucial. Moreover, accurate records of fitting location, lamping details, and focusing criteria must be kept. In this way, the installation can be maintained to design specifications over the life of the exhibition.

As cost and disruption is always a consideration, one of the apparently easy methods of upgrading or changing technology is using replacement lamps that use LEDs. This is not a good long-term solution. LED replacement lamps will have an integral gear to convert the mains voltage to that required by the LED. Inevitably, the crudest circuits are used to fit in the small volume available in a lamp base and generally cheap components to keep the price low. The result is unreliability, a much shorter life than is claimed. Color quality and consistency between lamps and different batches of the same lamp are frequently seen.

Plugging new technology into legacy equipment is always going to create problems. Changing over to LEDs is a significant design exercise. The designer needs to consider the building wiring infrastructure, as digitally based control systems require a separate data connection, typically by adding wiring. Where this is likely to be a disruptive or expensive, alternate methods of control communication are now possible, including Bluetooth mesh wireless communication or data over mains. Also tying this to an existing aged lighting control system may be impossible or end up locking you into a system that is likely to be difficult to maintain in the longer term.

It is better to plan for the long term and undertake a full replacement of the lighting system, potentially phased according to the museum's permanent exhibition reinstallation rather than all at the same time. A strategic plan is definitely necessary to achieve beautiful results and a system that is easy to maintain.

17.4 GREEN DESIGN

For the most part, museums have focused **green design** efforts on the building envelope and building systems. Leadership in Energy and Environmental Design (LEED) certification developed by the US Green Building Council (subsequently adopted worldwide) primarily targets building architecture, engineering, and construction. Although LEED is not the only regulated compliance format, it is certainly popular and has been quite successful. In Europe, the BRE Environmental Assessment Method (BREEAM) is another such program, again focused on the building. Neither system is perfect, but they provide a lens through which sustainable responsibility can be examined, tracked, and addressed quantifiably. Museums are particularly challenging buildings to go "'green" due to the need to maintain environmental controls required to conserve their collections.

Exhibition design and construction is increasingly under pressure to incorporate green design solutions as well. While there are no LEED or BREEAM programs that provide guidelines for achieving sustainability goals, exhibition designers can seek to apply new technologies, materials, and best practice to incorporate sustainable solutions in their designs. A commitment to green design must be addressed as early as the exhibition brief in order to understand its potential impact on budget, schedule, interpretation, infrastructure, and operation of a proposed exhibition. Here are some issues to consider:

- **Be prepared for the cost**: Green materials, technologies, and construction methods can be expensive. Unless the exhibition budget is particularly robust, there is a risk that green components of an exhibition will be "value engineered" out of scope should the project go over budget.
- **Schedule time for research**: Green design for exhibitions is still a new field and not as regulated as building construction. Time may be required to research new materials and methods, determine what they cost, find the suppliers who deliver them, and ensure that they meet the requirements of materials for use in museums with artifacts and the amount

of visitors expected. In some cases, few suppliers will be able to deliver a green product. This may prove to be expensive and time-consuming, especially if the supplier is located in another country and lead time for procurement is simply too long.

- **Commitment**: Environmental impact should be defined early on in the process and continually assessed throughout the exhibition development process—from design to opening day and beyond. This should not be limited to material selection and production processes, but also the way the team uses resources (e.g., use less paper, reduce carbon footprint) and how materials are packed and eventually disposed during installation, as well as replaced or refurbished by the museum in the future.

- **Reuse existing resources**: The design process may begin with consideration of existing exhibition resources such as refurbishing and reusing display cases and other exhibit furniture. Recommendations on reuse should be made by both the museum staff and the design and fabrication teams to assess feasibility and suitability of reuse. Sometimes reuse of certain materials may be more expensive and less sustainable than building a new item.

- **Highlight the use of responsible materials and techniques**: Be transparent and take the opportunity to educate visitors on how the exhibition has utilized green materials and design techniques. Education staff can build a program around sustainability that uses the exhibition as a tool for interpretation and communication.

- **Use of technology**: Monitors and other electronic equipment require power and cooling systems. Consider grouping or providing integrated components so that energy can be shared and efficiently distributed. Designers should identify opportunities to save power.

- **Suitability of materials**: Just because a material is green doesn't mean it is appropriate for the exhibition. For example, the material may be sustainable but is harmful to artifacts or not durable enough to withstand repeated use by thousands of visitors over a long period of time. Repeated replacement of materials would negate the sustainable benefits for selecting it in the first place. The distance for shipping a particular product may negate the beneficial impacts of using the material. Designers need to research and understand off-gassing and the composition and type of materials that will be used in the exhibition. Sustainable materials may be more suited to temporary exhibitions which can rely on recycled materials or less durable substances as a result of a shorter exhibition period. Exhibitions that are not collection-based are likely to provide more freedom to choose a wider range of materials.

- **Construction**: Exhibit fabrication methods can be adapted to address sustainability while still meeting the particular requirements of the exhibition. The use of glues, types of joints, paints, and hardware are just some areas of exploration and research. Prototyping and testing may be required if a fabricator has never used a particular sustainable approach before.

When committing to a green exhibition, museum staff (conservators, IT, operations, and facility staff) should work closely with the design and fabrication teams to establish sustainability goals and work together to meet them. This encourages a more holistic approach that includes operational and behavioral sustainability. The following summary is based on the principles identified in a Green Paper prepared by the Society for Environmental Graphic Design (SEGD) in 2007:

1. **Education and Interpretation**: Visitors rarely understand how much work goes into producing an exhibition. It may be beneficial to educate and interpret green initiatives for visitors and allow them some insight into the process. Not only is it the role of exhibitions to be sustainable, it is also the responsibility of the museum to educate its visitors.

2. **Improvement in Air and Environment Quality**: Select products and processes that contain reduced levels of volatile organic compounds (VOCs). These products include:
   - Zero to low-VOC paints, sealants, and carpet tiles
   - Low-emission laminates and formaldehyde-free materials
   - Natural or renewable materials such as cork, wheat board, or bamboo
   - Bio-based materials such as vegetable or soy-based inks for printing
   - Adhesive-free construction methods using mechanical fasteners instead of glue

3. **Awareness of Resource and Waste Management**: Exhibition planners and designers should be aware of resource and waste management during every stage of a product's life cycle. Considerations include:
   - Modular design can establish standard dimensions. This maximizes the material and minimizes waste. It also allows the fabricators and producers to buy in bulk to minimize extra costs such as transportation, packaging, and labor.
   - What is the right balance of size and usage? Consider visitor flow and circulation but also the practicality of size for exhibits and materials used. Does it need to be that big?
   - Continue a design cycle that considers reuse of existing exhibition elements, not only reusing existing components but also the possibility of reuse after the new exhibition closes.
   - Use materials that are biodegradable or can be up-cycled or down-cycled.
   - Source local materials to reduce transportation costs and pollution.
   - Specify materials made from recycled content (such as paper instead of vinyl for graphics).
   - Reuse or recycle packaging and other materials during installation.
   - Remove harmful chemicals safely during the fabrication process.

4. **Energy and Lighting Efficiency**: Energy efficiency is measured by lighting efficiency, minimization of light bleeding into the air, and energy used in shipping and delivery of materials. Greater energy efficiency can be achieved by:
   - Efficient lighting technologies that use a fraction of the energy and generate less heat than traditional methods.
   - Motion sensors and timers to turn elements on and off, governing lighting and any electronic media in the exhibition.
   - Coordinating with architects and museum staff to find alternative power sources.
   - Adjusting climate control settings, especially in locations with no collections.

Green exhibition design is rapidly evolving and increasingly demanded by concerned citizens and responsible museum leaders. This means more and more environmentally friendly materials and construction methods that also meet the special needs of the museum environment are becoming readily available. While sustainable options often mean higher costs than traditional materials at present, these upfront costs can defray longer-run operational costs and contribute to the well-being of the museum. Such benefits cannot be quantified as they are qualitative relationships that museum staff have with each other and the communities they serve. Designers and fabricators need to address this growing trend and be ready to respond to exhibition projects where eventually green design will not be an option or a luxury but a fundamental requirement of the project.

Case Study

EXHIBITIONS AND MUSEUMS IN INDIA: CHALLENGES AND OPPORTUNITIES

Uttiyo Bhattacharya

The last twenty years have seen a massive spike in the development of museums and exhibitions in emerging economies—especially India. This has largely been led by the development of new museum projects either to rehouse existing collections or create narrative experiences that are immersive. Based on a few empirical experiences and observations, the design and development of exhibitions of a global standard has thrown up challenges as well as opportunities.

DESIGN IS THE "EASIER" PART—BUILDING IS HARDER

Conception and design of exhibitions for museums has emerged as the easier piece of the development process. Once that hurdle is overcome, public procurement processes require statutory conditions of award of work to fabricators. This often includes a least-cost bid, generating a price competitiveness that can potentially cut corners on quality.

Once a qualified fabricator and contractor is in place, developing an exhibition becomes a task of relentless and rigorous monitoring. This is in the form of constant overwatch of processes and quality—for equipment, material, and workmanship. It is safe to assume that in the event of even an *instant* of looking away, anything that can possibly go wrong will.

My recent experience with the development of the iconic Bihar Museum in Patna, as well as the permanent exhibition at the Statue of Unity (Gujarat), the world's tallest statue, I have observed the additional revelation about locally available expertise in terms of fabrication. There still remain certain human-skills and need for training in certain departments of exhibit installation, which are presently dependent on overseas talent. One example is that of specialized glass cases and display systems for housing rare artifacts and works of art. Import of these cases is a relatively simple matter, but at the time of this writing, assembly and installation still needs the presence of specialized expertise not available in India. The pandemic of 2020, and the international travel restrictions thereafter brought this constraint to the forefront.

Another skill-based expertise with the same implications is the mounting of rare artifacts and antiquities. This skill is not readily available in a country such as India. There has been a development of local talent of this very specialized museological skill over the past decade, but there is still a distance to travel before local autonomy is achieved.

That being said, there is a clear trend over the past two decades on technical skill development and training. A case in point is that of lighting and AV equipment. Installation and system integration once used to be the domain of technicians and experts who had to be specially flown in from Europe and the Middle East. Today, it is readily available in every major city in India.

A NEW TREND: DESIGN, BUILD, MAINTAIN, OPERATE

An overwhelming majority of museums and collections in India are owned and operated by the government. A new trend that has emerged recently with commissioned projects has been the appointment of a single-point entity to develop them. Conventional processes separated entities such as consultants and fabricators from the institution operating a museum. The present trend, however, aims to appoint a sole agency to design, build, and operate a new museum, sourced through a least-cost public procurement system.

There is some understandable wisdom in this approach. It ensures faster development, identifiable accountability, and reduction in costs for the government. However, it can also potentially generate an inherent conflict of interest. Cost will always trump quality in such a circumstance, and "profitability" will determine all creative and museological decisions.

OPPORTUNITIES AHEAD: COMMUNITIES AND COLLECTIONS

Most new museum projects in India that have been commissioned have been done so using the top-down approach—a single commissioning entity such as the state—creating, financing, and administering the museum. There is an immense and untapped opportunity to evolve and develop this model toward community-led and community-driven museums.

Involving local communities, as well as communities-of-interest to participate in, administer, and govern museums would be a natural progression of museums and exhibitions in India. This would potentially allow for a sustainable financial and social model for museum governance in India.

There also exist millions of rare artifacts and objects within undeveloped museums all over the country, which presently are consigned to storage. Involving communities and special-interest groups in the inventory, archiving, preservation, and curation of these objects is an opportunity to create new museums with assured operational longevity, as well as bring back to public view millions of artifacts that are nothing short of national treasures. The creation of community-driven exhibitions to house these collections and tell their stories is a hopeful next step toward the evolution of museums in India.

Chapter 18

Graphic Design

Mary Yacob and Jacqueline Tang

18.1 SEMIOTICS IN DESIGN

Graphic design is the visual language that communicates and conveys content to the public. In the context of museums, graphic design is often referred to as environmental graphic design because it facilitates communication between people and the spaces they visit and experience. This infers that environmental graphic design is applied to a 3D environment, as opposed to 2D, which includes exhibits and interpretive graphics, walls and floors, wayfinding, signage, and more. This chapter seeks to introduce semiotic principles in exhibition graphic design to demonstrate the importance and power of meanings created by the application of graphics in museum galleries. Harmony between design and semiotics can assist in the realization of an exhibition's outcomes for visitor engagement.

Meaningful visual communication can be understood through the discipline of semiotics. Semiotics is the study of signs and their signification, the way in which signs produce meaning. These "meanings" can be culturally influenced (e.g., a rose equals love in some cultures but not others) and ambiguous (e.g., a yawn could mean a person is either sleepy or bored). Furthermore, these signs are understood in a specific space and time, which contributes to the intended purpose of communication.

Peter Storkerson, in his article "Antinomies of Semiotics in Graphic Design," writes about the conflict between graphic design as a discipline and in academia.[1] He expresses the lack of applying semiotics into graphic design and explains the resistance of the scholarly knowledge, which is explicit and discursive rather than tacit within the field of graphic design. The more semiotics is applied to design, the more successful it becomes because it means that designers have thought through their design, what it means, and what it conveys.

Similarly, Jean-Marie Floch, in his book *Visual Identities*, demonstrates that a semiotician can help the analysis of a product's representation (of any design such as a logo or symbol) through greater understanding of the "sign."[2] Floch interprets the sign through the idea of "bricolage." The term "bricolage" comes from the structuralist Claude Lévi-Strauss in his book *The Savage Mind*, in which he describes the human mind as untamed with no restrictions.[3] The original term in French, *bricoleur*, translates as "handyman," which suggests a "do it yourself" approach.

The product of the bricoleur's work can be considered as a structure, as an object of meaning within its own system—and this is due to the semi-symbolic coupling of content categories and their many "sensory" qualities. By organizing and reorganizing the materials and the images provided by the signs he or she collects, the bricoleur produces meaning by establishing paradigms found in a semi-symbolic semiosis. This means that the bricoleur makes "new from old" by playing with the formal harmonies and disharmonies suggested by the sensory effects of the signs collected. Bricolage therefore presupposes that we must pay attention to the sensory world, a world already established by history and culture. A graphic designer, therefore, produces a design through a collection of pre-existing elements or meanings to create a new meaning.

Today, museum goers are exposed to an expanding array of cultural spaces and exhibitions. They are accustomed to the discourse that emerges between them as a visitor "reader" and the piece of visual design as "communicator." To position this visual communication design in a semiotic frame, let's consider the context of the complex relationship between "aesthetic" and "function" using Greimas's semiotic square.

Greimas developed the framework of the semiotic square as a theoretical foundation to map connected and disconnected relationships. "For example, if we begin by drawing a horizontal line linking two familiarly paired terms such as 'beautiful' and 'ugly', we turn this into a semiotic square by making this the upper line of a square in which the two other logical possibilities—'not ugly' and 'not beautiful'—occupy the lower corners. The semiotic square reminds us that this is not simply a binary opposition because something which is not beautiful is not necessarily ugly and that something which is not ugly is not necessarily beautiful. Occupying a position within such a framework invests a sign with meanings."[4]

To apply this to the museum setting, let's start Greimass square in the visual communication paradigm with S1 in the pure form of being "aesthetic" and in the contrary S2 being in the pure form of "function," as illustrated in figure 18.1. A museum's visual communication should be informative yet aesthetically pleasing and as a result it positions itself in a concealed zone between S1 "not aesthetic" as in unattractive, while S2 "not functional" as in impractical or nonfunctioning.

Several museums' visual communication position themselves completely in the unattractive zone moving toward S2 purely functional without considering aesthetics while some other visual communications are positioned in the impractical zone moving toward S1 purely aesthetic. The ideal for visual communication should be informative, aesthetic, and yet functional.

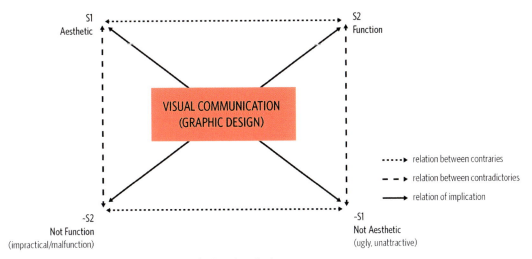

Figure 18.1. Visual communication analysis using Greimas square.

18.2 GRAPHIC DESIGN PHASES

Graphic design goes hand-in-hand with the interior 3D design phases of an exhibition project (see figure 17.1 in chapter 17). Some institutions consider graphics as an afterthought involving the graphic team at a later stage, but this is not ideal. The earlier all teams are working together the better the final exhibition. When all design teams work together from conception of the project, overall design becomes more coherent and meaningful as our discourse on semiotics suggest. In some cases, a powerful graphic design concept can impact and result in changes to interior design and architecture.

Once the interpretive plan has been developed, the design team goes through the phases of design as outlined in figure 17.1. The phasing of work allows for ever greater detail and the harmonization with content development (text, objects) as well as coordination with 3D design to allow for integrated graphics. Without this close collaboration, graphics can feel like components were added at the last moment or "pasted on" in place. The visitor's experience of graphics should be seamless.

18.2.1 Schematic or Concept Design

During this phase the graphic design team reads through the interpretive plan and the preliminary content developed to date and based on that information creates a coherent graphic concept for the exhibition. The design concept can vary broadly based on the exhibition type and gallery size. For example, a national history museum with one storyline needs to have a "sameness" with little variation deployed throughout the galleries or thematic areas within an exhibition. A children's museum or a science center could have a completely different design per theme and gallery while maintaining some common elements for coherence. To inform their work, the graphic designer will conduct research, explore references to demonstrate mood and style, and participate in workshops to test ideas.

The graphic designer will submit more than one concept showing the different directions that the design could take. This preliminary package presents the overall look and feel of the exhibition as a graphic design language. This will include:

- Proposed typography treatment and typefaces
- Proposed color palette
- A mood board demonstrating the main idea, approach, and how visitors might feel in the space
- Sample templates demonstrating how various colors, fonts, and styles may be applied

18.2.2 Design Development/Detailed Design

The graphic team creates a hierarchy of information. This includes identifying the different types of texts per space or area. For example, introductory text and titles as high-level thematic information, detailed text panels within a theme/area, and finally a labeling strategy for objects. Furthermore, within each panel a different hierarchy could be developed based on the amount of content. This could include a primary, secondary, or tertiary text. A panel is not necessarily a physical piece of material as it could be text directly applied to a wall, case, or other surface.

In this phase imagery comes into play. While in schematic design images are used to present a specific mood, here the actual images that will be used in the exhibition are manipulated to fit and inform the concept. This includes close-cropping, sizing, positioning next to text, identifying singular experiences like murals, styles of illustrations, diagrams and maps, or treatment from full-color images to monotones.

By the end of design development, which may include a series of presentations based on percentage completion, the graphic design has become very specific and includes:

- A family of graphic types, panels, and approaches directly relevant to the design and content
- Typefaces and font sizes
- Approach for new artwork, illustrations, and maps
- Refined color palette
- Hierarchy of text and applied graphics related to theme and how the story is to be communicated to the visitor
- Materials and specifications for application
- Application of the graphic design concept to the content of the exhibition to demonstrate how the story may be realized

A useful tool at this stage of design is a graphic location plan. Every graphic item in the exhibition is located on floor plans and elevations, given a graphic item number (to track production), and fully designed with final text and imagery. This is not artwork ready for production but rather a package that defines the production requirements and is used for final costing and bidding/tendering. Every graphic is accounted for and specified from panels to photomurals to quotations screened on wall surfaces.

Some exhibitions may have only a few graphics while others may have hundreds. It is always useful to create a graphics schedule (see figure 18.2) that quantifies all the different types of graphics specified. Usually organized by thematic area or location on a floor plan, each graphic is assigned a number (e.g., G-25 meaning that it is the twenty-fifth graphic panel in gallery G). The schedule should include a record of each graphic's size, substrate (materials), and other display requirements that a producer should know in order to accurately print and install it. Graphic schedules are excellent tools for pricing and tracking costs.

18.2.3 Production

Once a production firm is selected, graphic designers create what is called "production-ready artwork"—files that will go directly to print and fabrication. At this point, a complete and final graphic design solution has been specified and approved; all text will have been written and translated (if necessary); and all images and photographs will have been created or purchased at the highest resolution necessary. It is highly recommended to have the graphic designer responsible for final layouts prepare a series of "proofs." These proofs should be checked one last time by the entire team for errors prior to being sent to the printers for production. This work may be undertaken by the design team's graphic designer or the production firm's graphic designer/technical team. If the latter, the original graphic designer should be retained to review the work of the producer. Prior to final production, it is recommended that the producer prepare a series of mock-ups to confirm color, material, and print quality. Different printers and production methods can alter color hues and graphic elements in edge sharpness. As well, an idea for printing direct to a material may have sounded like a good idea during design, but the reality proves to be less than ideal. This is the time to make changes if necessary.

18.3 GRAPHIC DESIGN ELEMENTS

A successful design is one that clearly rationalizes every graphic element. Why did the graphic designer choose a specific color, typeface, and image style? What is the meaning behind them and what do they signify? Whether or not the graphic designer explicitly explains it, the idea shines through when it has a meaning as the discourse on semiotics suggests. This meaning is brought forward through the culture, the context, and the surrounding environment.

18.3.1 Typography

Typography plays a critical role in the exhibition experience. Typography is what conveys the content to the visitor and creates context for objects, specimens, and works of art. Typographic considerations for exhibition design include **typeface selection** or font, **legibility**, and **text levels** or information hierarchy. In addition, there may be other considerations that are museum specific such as addressing accessibility, multiple languages, printing methods, lighting, and more, but these three are the critical factors.

18.3.1.1 Typeface Selection

There are enormous typeface or font collections readily available and therefore it is important to know the differences between them to make the right decision. Typeface selection is usually guided by the content of the exhibition as well as the design language proposed by the design team. The graphic designer should recommend and/or select the typeface(s) that convey the nature of the content and the character of the design.

Graphic No.	Exhibit No.	Title	Graphic Type	Dimensions (inches) Width	Dimensions (inches) Height	SqFt	Substrate Material	Process	text	Sourced image/Illustration	object	custom illustration	Custom map	Custom diagram
A.1.1.INTRODUCTION														
GPL001	A.1.1.1	People and the Planet (Title and intro) The physical roots of culture How do people change the planet, and how does the planet change us? (Minds on Q)	Wall graphic	140	96	93.333	Medex	Direct Print	x	5				
GPL002	A.1.1.1	Banner 1	Printed banner	24	112	18.667	Duramesh	Direct Print	x	1				
GPL003	A.1.1.1	Banner 2	Printed banner	24	112	18.667	Duramesh	Direct Print	x	1				
GPL004	A.1.1.1	Banner 3	Printed banner	24	112	18.667	Duramesh	Direct Print	x	1				
GPL005	A.1.1.1	Banner 4	Printed banner	24	112	18.667	Duramesh	Direct Print	x	1				
GPL006	A.1.1.1	Banner 5	Printed banner	24	112	18.667	Duramesh	Direct Print	x	1				
GPL007	A.1.1.1	Banner 6	Printed banner	24	112	18.667	Duramesh	Direct Print	x	1				
A.1.2.1 LOCATION, LOCATION, LOCATION														
GPL008	A.1.2.1	People, People, Everywhere (Section intro) How resources shape culture How close do you live to where you were born? (Minds on Q) What would a culture look like that had access to	Wall graphic	147	90	91.875	Medex	Direct Print	x	1				
GPL009	A.1.2.1	A world forever transformed	Wall graphic	140	96	93.333	Medex	Direct Print	x	4	13			
GPL010	A.1.2.1	Banner 5	Printed banner	24	112	18.667	Duramesh	Direct Print	x	1				
GPL011	A.1.2.1	Banner 6	Printed banner	24	112	18.667	Duramesh	Direct Print	x	1				
A.1.2.2 DOMESTICATION														
GPL012	A.1.2.2	Taming Wild Species (Section intro) Wolves to dogs	Wall graphic	70	96	46.667	Medex	Direct Print	x	5				
GPL013	A.1.2.2	Who has the better quality of life: a wolf or a dog? (Minds on Q)	Wall graphic	128	96	85.333	Medex	Direct Print	x	3	4			
GPL014	A.1.2.2	Planet Maize	Wall graphic	84	96	56.000	Medex	Direct Print	x	2	5			
GPL015	A.1.2.2	Banner 7	Printed banner	24	112	18.667	Duramesh	Direct Print	x	1				
GPL016	A.1.2.2	Banner 8	Printed banner	24	112	18.667	Duramesh	Direct Print	x	1				
A.1.3.1 CLOTHING														
GPL017	A.1.3.1	Dress for Success (Section intro)	Wall graphic	52	90	32.500	Medex	Direct Print	x	4				
GPL018	A.1.3.1	One chilling challenge, two responses	Wall graphic	36	90	22.500	Medex	Direct Print	x		1			
GPL019	A.1.3.1	Fast fashion shakes up the planet What do your clothes say about who you are?	Wall graphic	48	90	30.000	Medex	Direct Print	x	2	3			
GPL020	A.1.3.1	Banner 9	Printed banner	24	112	18.667	Duramesh	Direct Print	x	1				
GPL021	A.1.3.1	Banner 10	Printed banner	24	112	18.667	Duramesh	Direct Print	x	1				
A.1.3.2 CULTURAL ENCOUNTERS														
GPL022	A.1.3.2	Cultural Encounters (Section intro) How does where you grew up affect who you are and how you see the world? (Minds on Q)	Wall graphic	72	90	45.000	Medex	Direct Print	x	3				
GPL023		Architects of coexistence	Wall graphic	72	96	48.000	Medex	Direct Print	x	1	7		2	

Figure 18.2. Sample graphic schedule. LORD CULTURAL RESOURCES

There are five common typeface classifications:

1. Serif historically includes Old Style, Transitional, and Modern. These typefaces are usually not linear, meaning the thickness of the letter changes. Differentiating Old Style from Transitional from Modern lies in the shape of the serif.
2. Slab serif typefaces are characterized by the square-shaped serifs, and the letters are usually linear, meaning the letter maintains the same thickness.
3. Sans serif are the typefaces that do not include serifs. Most of them are linear.
4. Script typefaces include formal script, handwriting, or calligraphy as well as blackletter and lombardic Scripts.
5. Decorative and display typefaces vary widely and have highly distinct visual form. They are mostly used for large headlines.

Figure 18.3. Typeface classification examples. LORD CULTURAL RESOURCES

The appropriate typeface for an exhibition should conform to the overall look and feel established by the design and the story the museum is trying to tell. Typefaces' visual characteristics suggest mood, emotion, historical period, and culture.

Broadly speaking, serif typefaces are known for being classical and traditional while sans serif and slabs are modern and informal. Script typefaces are commonly used with quotations while decorative and display, when chosen, are used for headlines or in fun and unexpected ways to capture visitor attention.

Often designers choose more than one typeface for an exhibition, especially if an exhibition has multiple storylines or themes. For small exhibitions with a focused theme, it is preferable to use one or maximum two typefaces to differentiate or emphasize the texts through various weights (as shown in figure 18.4), sizes, and colors. Designs that use this method are usually formal and calm.

When choosing two typefaces—one for headlines and another for body text—it is recommended to choose from two different classification groups such as a serif for the title and a sans serif for the body text. This creates a dynamic and desirable contrast that attracts visitors' eyes. While the same typeface can be used for both body text and headlines, not all typefaces are suitable for both a headline and body text. For example, you might choose a bolder, thicker typeface such as Franklin Gothic as the headline typeface while Baskerville might be selected as the body text.

Graphic Design

Thin
Light
Regular
Medium
Bold

Figure 18.4. Typeface weights. LORD CULTURAL RESOURCES

The former would be too heavy as body text and therefore difficult to read but makes a great headline. This also applies to the anticipated printing methods or substrate on which graphics will be applied. Some typefaces are well suited to traditional panels but may not be suited to three-dimensional lettering, laser cut solutions, or direct wall applications.

Too many typefaces can create a sense of chaos. However, depending on the number of languages on display, a maximum of two typefaces should be used for each language.

18.3.1.2 Legibility

The legibility of each typeface is affected by its letter form (classification), lowercase or uppercase letter formats, spacing (between letters, words, and lines), alignment (text justification), point size, line length (number of words per line), and color.

The ability of visitors to recognize individual letters or words, including visitors with aging or limited vision, is extremely important in the museum setting. This is governed by the design of the typeface. Legibility plays a more important role when selecting typefaces for body text rather than headline text as body text is smaller, so character and word recognition is more challenging. While the largest point size can vary, the smallest point size in museums should never be lower than 18-points so as to ensure legibility in a dimly lit environment and for visitors with visual impairment.

Legibility is also governed by contrast—black text on a white background or dark-color text on light-color background is best, so when using colors as creative solutions, it should be tested

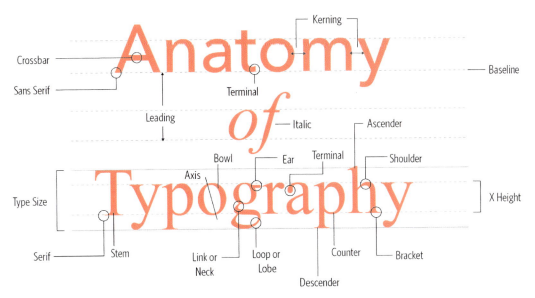

Figure 18.5. Anatomy of typography. LORD CULTURAL RESOURCES

to ensure there is enough contrast for ease of reading. A brief description of typeface anatomy that demonstrates typeface composition, and the terminology used throughout the discussion of typography can be found in figure 18.5.

As a rule of thumb, body text should always be in sans serif, serif, or slab serif and in lowercase and left aligned (for Western cultures). Studies show that it is much easier on the eye to follow the x-height, ascenders, and descenders rather than an all-caps paragraph (same height letters). Studies also show that it is easier on the eye to read a left-aligned rather than a fully justified paragraph. It is worth noting that not all typefaces of the same point size have the same x-height and for most people, especially visually impaired individuals, the larger the x-height the better. Also note that some languages like Arabic and Hebrew would be right-aligned and Chinese and Japanese letters would follow a completely different set of assumptions. When designing for multiple languages, consult with subject matter experts or designers from those cultures to ensure you are doing the language justice, and not inadvertently making cultural mistakes.

Typeface, point size, and line length are all interrelated variables. Point size can vary according to the line length, and furthermore line length can vary according to the distance the visitor is at from the text while reading. In general, line length should be between eight to fourteen words per line (ten being optimum). The farther away the visitor is expected to read the text, the longer the line length can be, and the broader the text area and point size. The guiding assumption here is the distance between the visitor and the text: the farther away, the broader range of vision. Remember to keep the visitor's eye level in mind. A child or a person in a wheelchair has a lower eye level than an adult standing. Figure 18.6 shows the ideal measurements, especially for the lowest measure from the ground.

Spacing between the letters is important. "Tracking" is when all the spaces between the letters are the same. However, that does not mean they are even visually. This becomes more noticeable in large headlines and in-between certain letter combinations in which case the designer adjusts the spacing between those letters manually. This is called "kerning."

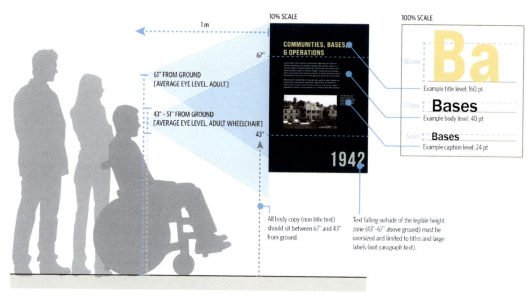

Figure 18.6. Eye level of vision range. LORD CULTURAL RESOURCES

18.3.1.3 Text Levels and Information Hierarchy

Chapter 16 (section Exhibition Text) discusses different levels of text and appropriate word counts for museum exhibitions—from headlines and introductions to detailed stories and artifact labels. To convey these content levels, the graphic designer must develop a hierarchical graphic system. This system of rules is employed to maintain consistency, make content manageable, and help visitors maneuvre through the exhibition. The variety of levels can also accommodate visitor types who are sometimes called "streakers" and "strollers." Streakers are visitors who move quickly through an exhibition because they have little time or have little interest in reading a lot of text, much preferring to look at objects and interact with media. Headlines and primary text panels provide enough information to communicate the core messages of the exhibition. Strollers, on the other hand, like to dig deep into the research and want to know more. A well-conceived hierarchical system that presents headlines clearly but also allows for detailed presentations of information ensures that both types of visitors can be enriched by the exhibition content while not becoming overwhelmed with reams of text.

There are two types of hierarchy: one is for text levels where each determines the point size (level 1 being the largest point size) and another hierarchy for information panels where each determines how large of an area it represents (introductory panel, interpretive panel, etc.). Some panels may include more than one level of text.

Creating a clear hierarchy creates a pattern in the exhibition that the visitor can discern. It guides them through the exhibition and provides a visual cue regarding the different levels of communication and depth of information that is available to be enjoyed. Creating a clear hierarchy also assists in the production process. Often the production firm ends up creating all production-ready artwork for production. They do this from a series of templates created by the graphic designer in which hierarchies are applied. These hierarchies and application standards are included in the graphic schedule and specification documentation.

Each level of text should be identified by the following information:

- Typeface and point size for each, headlines, and body text per level.
- Leading, or the amount of space between lines of text (which used to be strips of lead in mechanical typesetting, thus the origin of the term).
- Tracking and kerning, or the amount of space between words and letters.

Word counts and text level hierarchies go hand-in-hand. The point size, leading, kerning, use of images, and graphic panel size all determine the maximum number of words to be used in each text level. It is also important to note that word counts vary by language. For example, the French translation of a line of English text is typically 10 percent longer than the original English text. These factors should be considered when developing word counts.

In general, there are four levels of text a graphic designer considers in a hierarchy. Although the characteristics of each are project-specific, below are guidelines on how they are usually used:

- Level 1 is used for first level exhibition content such as titles, headlines, quotations, and introductory text to the whole exhibition. It is sized to be visible by a group and from a distance.
- Level 2 is secondary to Level 1 and is used for general overviews or introductory panels related to thematic areas or related topics in a gallery. It is sized to be visible by a group from a distance but is slightly smaller than Level 1 as it begins drawing visitors into the exhibition content. This level of text communicates main themes and topics (primary and secondary text).
- Level 3 is used for most general exhibit content related to a specific idea, story, event, or topic as well as for multimedia, diorama, model, or interactive devices. It is sized to be visible from a medium to close distance by only a few visitors at a time and communicates information that is more specific to individual works of art, specimens, or artifacts. Visitors are drawn to specific topics and objects that are related to the main themes presented by Level 2 text (tertiary text).
- Level 4 is used for the most detailed level of exhibition content: artifact label and caption text. It is detailed and explanatory and pertains to specific images, artifacts, works of art, or specimens. It is meant to be read by only one or two visitors at a time. Note that the smallest text size within an exhibition should be no less than 18-point typeface for Level 4 label text. Figure 18.7 shows an example of an actual size Level 1 and 4 while figure 18.8 shows the sample text level word counts recommended for an exhibition at the North Dakota Heritage Center & State Museum.

The final panel types and sizes are project-dependent and influenced by expected sizes of various substrates (materials on which graphics will be produced). It is important to mention that the word *panel* does not necessarily mean a physical 3D substrate, rather it could mean a designed cluster of text and images where they, as one unit, can be applied directly on a glass case (e.g., etched), a wall (e.g., vinyl letters or silkscreened), or projected on wall or floor surfaces (e.g., projectors, screens).

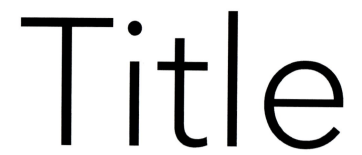

18 point label Type - Level 4 in the hierarchy of text

Figure 18.7. Actual Size Level 1 verses Level 4. LORD CULTURAL RESOURCES

The following guidelines apply:

- Introductory panels are the largest and most prominent. They may be free-standing, reproduced on large banners and scrims, or directly applied or projected on walls. Often such panels incorporate textures, 3D components and lettering, or may be dramatically backlit. These panels typically employ Level 1 and/or Level 2 text.

- Interpretive panels come in a variety of shapes and sizes to suit specific exhibition needs. These panels typically employ Level 2 and Level 3 text.

- Monitors and digital surfaces widely vary because of the different size screens and projected digital images however, they usually incorporate Level 3 and 4 text. Multimedia producers are provided with all text levels along with other specifications such as color palettes and typefaces, which they will apply accordingly.

- Labels for artifacts, works of art, or specimens can be categorized into two types: direct and indirect labels. Direct labels are extended labels placed beside each museum object. Indirect labeling involves keying museum objects to a group label. This might be facilitated by numbers located next to the object or on an illustrated key to the contents of the case. Indirect labels are suited to displays that have many small objects clustered together in which case many small labels would clutter the experience and interfere with visitor enjoyment of the objects. Captions for images may be treated in the same way, with both direct and indirect captions.

18.3.2 Color

Color plays a major role in how a design is perceived by its audience. Color is often associated with temperature or "moods." There is a wide range of literature on semiotics of color that include different meanings for the same color in different cultures and in different time periods within the same culture. In Western cultures, blues are often considered cool and calming while reds may be interpreted as hot and aggressive. Since colors can be culture-specific, it is important to understand the meanings associated with various colors in different countries to avoid offending people or incorrectly combining colors.

Color can also be derived from prominent objects or paintings within the exhibition (see figures 18.10 and 18.11). Figure 18.11 are graphic template examples from the exhibition *Sisters in Liberty: From Florence, Italy to New York, New York*. The color palette from the exhibition was derived from

LEVEL	TITLE	TEXT	USE
1	Font: Gotham Black Size: 180 pt Leading: 180 pt Kerning: Optical Tracking: 10 Word Count: 10-15	Font: Verlag Size: 65 pt Leading: 75 pt Kerning: Optical Tracking: 10 Word Count: 50-75	Level 1 titles are used for section titles on introductory panels and quotations. Level 1 text is used for content on introductory panels and quotations.
1.5		Font: Verlag Book, (i)* Size: 100 pt Leading: 120 pt Kerning: Optical Tracking: 10 Word Count: 10 to 20 words	Level 1.5 text is used for quotations.
2	Font: Gotham Black Size: 75 pt Leading: 90 pt Kerning: Optical Tracking: 10 Word Count: 5-10	Font: Verlag Book, (i)* Size: 54 pt Leading: 65 pt Kerning: Optical Tracking: 10 Word Count: 100-150	Level 2 titles are used for titles on secondary interpretive graphic panels. Level 2 text is used for content on primary and secondary interpretive graphic panels.
2.5		Font: Verlag Book, (i)* Size: 65 pt Leading: 75 pt Kerning: Optical Tracking: 10 Word Count: 100-150	Level 2.5 text is used for quotations.
3	Font: Gotham Black Size: 75 pt Leading: 90 pt Kerning: Optical Tracking: 0 Word Count: 5-10	Font: Verlag Book, (i)* Size: 35 pt Leading: 46 pt Kerning: Optical Tracking: 0 Word Count: 100-150	Level 3 titles are used for titles on extended tertiary label panels. Also used in some special contexts. Level 3 text is used for content on secondary interpretive graphic panels and on extended tertiary label panels. Also used in some special contexts.
4	Font: Verlag Bold, (i)* Size: 20 pt Leading: 25 pt Kerning: Optical Tracking: 0 Word Count: 1-5	Font: Verlag Book, (i)* Size: 20 pt Leading: 25 pt Kerning: Optical Tracking: 0 Word Count: 50-75	Level 4 titles are used for titles on artifact labels. Also used in some special contexts. Level 4 text is used for content on artifact labels and captions. Also used in some special contexts.

Figure 18.8. Levels of text for the *Innovation Gallery: Early Peoples* at the North Dakota Heritage Center & State Museum, Bismarck, North Dakota.

Figure 18.9. Sample text treatment for a label from the *Innovation Gallery: Early Peoples* at the North Dakota Heritage Center & State Museum, Bismarck, North Dakota.

Figure 18.10. Exhibition color palette and image of Michelangelo's tomb at Santa Croce, Florence, Italy.
OPERA DI SANTA CROCE/LORD CULTURAL RESOURCES

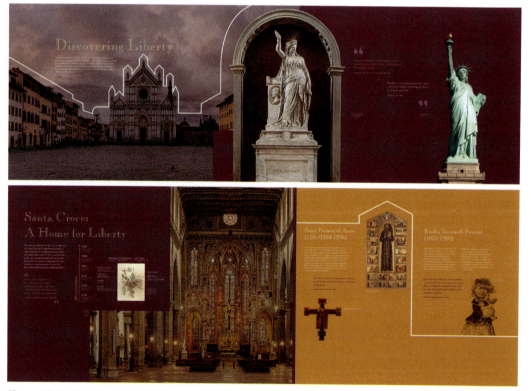

Figure 18.11. Graphic template for one of the panels in the exhibition *Sisters in Liberty: From Florence, Italy to New York, New York*. OPERA DI SANTA CROCE/LORD CULTURAL RESOURCES

a study of Michelangelo's tomb (figure 18.10). The tomb's colors included reds, purples, and soft natural tones that resulted in a rich solution for the graphic designer.

If a museum is large or if it is open-air, color can play an organizational role as it establishes a hierarchy in the exhibit text or acts as wayfinding in differentiating between thematic areas or zones in the museum.

With the different substrates and printing methods available to designers today, selecting a color that is universal across mediums and printing processes is important because colors will look different on different materials. Graphic designers typically use the Pantone Matching System, a leading provider of color systems. Colors, like typefaces, emote and communicate. Several online color tools (such as Kuler, Colour Scheme Designer, or ColourLovers) have been created to provide guidance or even to generate color schemes, depending on the criteria given to them.

18.4 IMAGERY

Illustrations, photographs, diagrams, iconography, and infographics enliven the exhibition, supporting, and in many instances, replacing text. The graphic designer must consider early in the design process how these types of imagery can be used, whether they are supports to text, primary means of communication, or backdrops for dioramas. Issues to consider include:

- Size on panels, walls, and other surfaces should be standardized for application.
- Resolution refers to the pixel count of a digital image. To ensure the highest quality graphics in an exhibition, the graphic designer should establish baseline rules for resolution requirements for photographs at the sizes they will be printed in the gallery.
- Illustration styles for new maps, graphs, infographics, and other illustrations should be consistent throughout the exhibition. This requires custom illustration of every infographic to create a clean and consistent look in the gallery. This does not apply to historic maps or illustrations, which should be treated as images to be sourced at the appropriate resolution.
- Different applications of graphic images must also be considered and communicated. Imagery can be digitally printed and applied to various substrates, produced as wallpaper, and applied to large surfaces, or even hand drawn and painted by commissioned artists.

18.5 DESIGN ESSENTIALS

Once all the necessary discrete elements for a graphic design language have been determined, the next step is to show how these elements come together to form a graphic delivery system in the exhibition.

Determining the sizes of each panel will be dependent on the amount of content (Is there a lot of text? Are there lots of images?), audience requirements, location of panels (on walls, inside cases, in flipbooks), and the available viewing space (long or short vistas).

Although the application or treatment of each graphic type may vary, there are number of design principles to follow:

- **Graphic grid**: Following (unseen) grid lines to arrange text and images on a panel creates a system to organize content hierarchies and unifies the look of the entire graphic family within an exhibition.

- **Readability**: The ability to read and comprehend the words, phrases, and blocks of text on the panel. This is determined by how type is positioned, its color contrast, point size, line length, and spacing. Legibility is a general requirement of the graphic system, but readability must be tested for each panel.

- **Substrates**: The range of possible graphic substrates appears to be infinite. Graphic applications are not limited to two-dimensional surfaces. Designers may consider three-dimensional type, printing on a curved surface, etched materials, digital projection, or printing on the floor.

- **Lighting**: The readability of text is greatly affected by lighting. Avoid typefaces with thinner line weights in dim lighting and if the text is being projected or backlit. Consultation between the lighting designer and the graphic designer is well-advised to ensure legibility. Visitors' most frequent complaint about unreadable graphics is often because the panel is in a more dimly lit location than the graphic designer assumed.

- **Content**: The type of content and how it is being displayed may affect the graphic treatment. A traditional approach may be to exhibit an artifact in a display case with its accompanying graphic panel placed adjacent to it. However, it may be possible to integrate the two to create a seamless display. This is achieved when the graphic team and the 3D design team are communicating and working together from the earliest stage of the design.

- **Text and image placement**: It is essential to consider text and images to ensure visitors understand context and the meaning of images and vice versa. Adjacencies are important.

Throughout the design process graphic elements will continue to be refined and changed until a final solution is ready for production. Testing assumptions with full scale mock-ups, prototypes or partial prints of full-size graphics is critical for decision-making.

NOTES

1. Peter Storkerson, "Antinomies of Semiotics in Graphic Design," *Visible Language* 44, no. 1 (2010): 5–37.
2. Jean-Marie Floch, *Visual Identities* (London: Continuum, 2001).
3. Claude Lévi-Strauss, *The Savage Mind* (Chicago: The University of Chicago Press, 1966).
4. See. https://www.oxfordreference.com/view/10.1093/oi/authority.20110803100454123.

Chapter 19

Multimedia

Corey Timpson

It is nearly impossible to visit any venue in person today and not experience some sort of multimedia. Supermarkets, shopping malls, sporting venues, concert halls, public transportation, government buildings, and of course museums, galleries, libraries, archives, and cultural centers all use multimedia, digital systems, and the integration of technology within their operations and in public interactions. Audiences today are informed, mobile, multitasking, and are equipped with ubiquitous access to digital technology and data. They exist in digital-physically blended environments, and their expectations reflect this reality. Planning a museum, a museum program, and/or museum services, therefore, without careful and explicit attention to multimedia, and deliberate decisions on how and how not to implement it, would be planning to fail. In our digitally enabled and integrated world, the sustainable and strategic use of multimedia is therefore critical to ensuring strong audience engagement, sustainable operations, and inclusive, welcoming, and accommodating experiences.

There are many ways to describe multimedia, and the term is often used and conflated with other terms like "new media," "digital media," and "media arts." For the purposes of this chapter, the term "multimedia" will be used in its most basic and general form: representing and encompassing linear and navigable media, emerging technologies, and the digital, analogue, and blended types of each medium.

Multimedia in exhibitions has historically referred to linear media such as film/video, audio, and any time-based media type, analogue and digital. Its expanded definition included navigable systems like kiosks, terminals, and systems accessible via a user interface of some kind. Since 2010, forms of presentation, formats of development, and surfacing mechanisms of content have evolved substantially. Part of this evolution has been due to the semantic standardization of data, the fabric of media itself. As such, multimedia has become an even more diverse landscape, as standardization presents an ability for interoperability of systems, platforms, channels, and hardware and software, and therefore has provided museums an opportunity to more accessibly, and easily, embrace emerging technologies.

19.1 STRATEGIC ROLE

Multimedia can play important strategic roles in exhibition design and development for both audience engagement and operations. The consideration of an exhibition's experiential intent, desired learning outcomes, and the ecosystem in which it will exist, are all critical variables that frame the use of multimedia in exhibitions and will help determine the prerequisites for its use. Consider that while many instances of multimedia can seem fantastical and exciting, it remains simply a suite of storytelling tools like any others used by museums to deliver content and presentation, and to satisfy objective criteria. The instances of its use should support the overall intentions of the exhibition and contribute to the experiential and learning goals, and not imperil the experience, compete with stated objectives, or create undue burden on the maintenance and operations of the exhibition. Placement, pacing, and use of multimedia should be deliberate and judicial, and always within a firm understanding of the implications of its use—implications that may require planning and accommodation on an infrastructure level in order to be most effective and sustainable.

As more museum exhibitions seek to create a mix of interaction design scenarios, increasing the active and interactive opportunities for audiences, multimedia is uniquely positioned to help satisfy these goals. Where multimedia integration in exhibitions may have once primarily referred to passive activities like watching video, listening to audio, and/or navigating a kiosk to read, watch, or listen, multimedia today can be used in far more dialogic terms: contributing user created content, users completing tasks or participating in game play, extending exhibition experiences to remote audiences, prolonging audience engagement post visit, social networking, personalizing experiences, and collaborating on shared outcomes are all examples of active and interactive experiences that can be effectively and efficiently facilitated by multimedia.

Strategic opportunities for the use of multimedia include:

- Providing more entry points to content and experience through analogue and digital blends, motion and static presentation, and ultimately a variety of how content is surfaced, presented, and interacted with.

- Extending the reach beyond the on-site visit. Use of multimedia in exhibitions can allow museums to engage with their audience's social networks, extending reach to new audiences, and allowing the museum experience to continue, within these networks, long after visitors have left the building.

- Deepening engagement and increasing learning opportunities can happen via interaction design scenarios that allow for participation and collaboration. Multimedia used in exhibitions can cost effectively facilitate dialogic interaction design scenarios.

- Distinguishing the in situ and online experiences so that each is uniquely different from one another and best suited to each context. For example, multimedia use in galleries can avoid browse, search, and view type instantiations and instead contribute to immersion and experiential events unique to in-person visits. This helps ensure online and remote audience engagement is complementary to on-site visits and that on-site visits do not replicate the same experience a visitor could have at home.
- Accessibility can be efficiently accommodated through the engagement of multiple modalities, which is greatly facilitated by the implementation of multimedia and the development of audio, visual, and even tactile affordances.

19.2 TYPES OF MULTIMEDIA

19.2.1 Linear Media

Linear media, or time-based media, has long since played a role in exhibition development. Film, video, and audio are often integrated at discreet moments and within discreet installations. Yet outside of theater settings, of 16:9, 4:3, or any rectangular format, screens, sound, and moving image can be combined with other media in the creation of multimedia installations that can provoke feelings of wonder, immersion, and develop unique place-based experiences.

Online video consumption increases 100 percent per year, and today exceeds one billion hours daily.[1] And yet viewers retain 95 percent of a message when viewed in video, compared to 10 percent when it is read via text.[2] As such, use of film and video remain important tactics within exhibition design development, however the manner in which they are used and presented can be varied and help contribute to unique experience designs, creating learning and educational experiences within exhibitions that differ to the experiences museum audiences are having within their day-to-day lives.

19.2.2 Projection Mapping

Projection mapping is a technique that involves the projection of static, time-based, or even navigable media onto a surface, turning it into a display surface. The surface being projected upon can therefore appear to come to life, a static object can present multiple states including motion, didactic and experiential content can be overlaid and mixed with one another, optical illusions can be developed, dimensionality can be played with, and within the innumerable possibilities afforded by this technology, unique and captivating museum experiences can be developed. Projection mapping can easily add 3D effects through optical illusion, however linear media being projected can also be developed in 3D, opening even further potential for unique on-site exhibition experiences.

For the *Fabric in Fashion* exhibition at The Museum at FIT in New York City (Figure 19.1), ten different textiles and fabrics were projected onto a dress. These images were projected onto the toile in rotation, mapped to the shape of the toile's skirt, bodice, and panier panels. Figure 19.2 demonstrates the tuning and aligning of the projection mapping at the Canadian Museum for Human Rights' installation on labor rights. The red lines, squares, and circles are both static and motion-based and are projected, along with white static markings, onto a three-dimensional map of the city of Winnipeg.

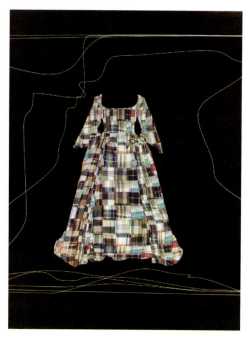

Figure 19.1. *Fabric in Fashion* exhibition at The Museum at FIT, New York. COURTESY OF MUSEWEB/ELIZABETH WAY/THE MUSEUM AT FIT

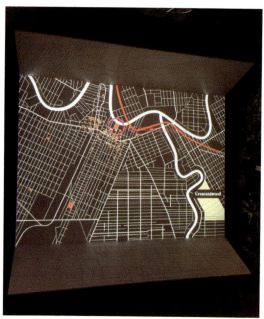

Figure 19.2. Projection mapping at the Canadian Museum for Human Rights, Winnipeg, Canada. COURTESY OF COREY TIMPSON/CANADIAN MUSEUM FOR HUMAN RIGHTS

19.2.3 Moving Image

This is not to say there is no place for the general moving image in exhibitions. Quite the contrary. Film and video play an important role in surfacing and delivering documentary information, dramatic creations, and reenactments, specific narratives, interviews and first-person testimony, oral histories, data and information visualizations, and much more.

The planning and development process for linear media remains largely the same: treatment, script and storyboard, iteration, asset research and development, shooting and recording, composing, editing, etc. Considering the unique potential of multimedia, however, allows exhibition developers and designers an opportunity to creatively and strategically consider how the linear media will be presented. While the use cases (reasons) for presenting video in a 4:3, 16:9, or any typical rectangular format on a screen or via projection is well understood, the opportunity to present video in unique shapes contributing to scenographic design, or projected with edge-blending upon multiple planes, large or nonuniform surfaces, can represent simple and effective tactics for immersion.

There is a time, place, and use case for implementing linear media within exhibitions in any number of different ways. The potential of multimedia is that its use can help facilitate engaged learning and meaningful exhibition experiences. Blended digital-analogue exhibition design, employing multimedia, can create environments that stimulate wonder, exploration, and learning in ways that audiences cannot get outside of museums. For example, the Wallpaper Room at the Cooper Hewitt Smithsonian Design Museum in New York uses simple projection of static images via two edge-blended projectors to create a unique environment. It projects the wallpaper that visitors create on the digital screen facing the corner. The experience is both interactive and

Figure 19.3. A documentary film masked into an oval shape and projected onto a non-rectangular form (a convex circular shape), to integrate the didactic material of the documentary seamlessly into the scenographic design of the immersive space. COURTESY OF COREY TIMPSON/CANADIAN MUSEUM FOR HUMAN RIGHTS

Figure 19.4. A 360-degree circular documentary film presents linear media in a format not commonly experienced outside of a museum setting. COURTESY OF IAN MCCAUSLAND/CANADIAN MUSEUM FOR HUMAN RIGHTS

Figure 19.5. The wallpaper immersion room at the Cooper Hewitt Smithsonian Design Museum, New York. COURTESY OF COREY TIMPSON

Figure 19.6. Linear media projected across an irregular shape at the Canadian Museum for Human Rights. The media is projected across a scrim and presents documentary media. When the lighting scenario changes, light passes through the scrim, instead of being reflected upon it, and objects behind the scrim become visible. COURTESY OF IAN MCCAUSLAND/CANADIAN MUSEUM FOR HUMAN RIGHTS

immersive, engaging visitors with design and patterns in a way that another technique such as a didactic display or even linear film approach could not achieve.

19.2.4 Audio

Audioscapes, audio cues, sound effects, soundtracks, and more can all be used to create immersion and atmosphere, to deliver content, to support other media, and even in the case of earcons, provide event or functionality feedback to the benefit of general usability.

Much like video, the development process for audio remains largely the same irrespective of how it will be used. Audio technology and delivery mechanisms have reached a level of sophistication where directional sound gear, synching of audio across devices and platforms, and overall integration of audio and sounds can be done with far greater fidelity than ever before. This is important as sound management remains a critical consideration with any exhibition development given the often-competing sound sources within fixed spaces.

Some museums have to manage content being presented concurrently in multiple languages. While there are a number of tactics to address content presentation in multiple languages, one specific note is in regard to technology used with multimedia. Some software and hardware have limitations upon the number of audio channels that are supported. This should be considered at the outset when designing and developing audio for exhibitions and also when considering support of multiple languages, text-to-speech applications for blind and low-vision users, and audio description.

Volume control is an important consideration in exhibition environments, especially given the need to determine how audio from one installation might interfere with another, while also ensuring visitors within all hearing ranges can perceive the intended audio. Audio, as such, can be designed and developed for multiuser and single user environments with audio control via induction technology, surfaced via mobile devices, used with headphones at the installation, and in some instances, by allowing direct volume control through an installation's interface.

Figure 19.7. The mobile device at the Canadian Museum for Human Rights is used to provide supplemental content and experience, accessibility affordances like captions and American Sign Language (synched with the media in the installation), and also provide discreet volume control. COURTESY OF IAN MCCAUSLAND/CANADIAN MUSEUM FOR HUMAN RIGHTS

19.2.5 Interactive Media

While many digital and multimedia installations are commonly referred to as "interactive," it is important to recognize the variety of media installations that sit within the range of "interactivity" and understand that this term blankets a number of different installation types and interaction design scenarios. Pushing a button on an interface to read, watch, and listen (all passive activities) are the least "interactive" type available. For example, a browser-based kiosk where users browse menus and pages to access content. As such, an important distinction should be made, when considering the development of exhibitions, as to what the intended behavior, response, and role of the user is at each installation. Requiring the user to perform a function from a predetermined set of options and returning a result from a predetermined set (typical kiosk), is certainly not the same as true dialogic interaction design that enables cause and effect, reciprocal events between user and system, and allows the user to affect the outcome of a task or scenario. Understanding that nuance will mean a more deliberate application of multimedia within exhibitions and better manage expected audience outcomes.

Multimedia can play various tactical roles in delivering experiences, presenting content, and supporting learning objectives across this range of interactive media. The multimedia component can take on any number of extremely varied forms from kiosks to responsive environments, to installations accepting the contribution of user created content and more.

19.2.6 Kiosks

The most common and general form of interactive media, which is arguably not "interactive" at all, is the kiosk/terminal style of installation presenting menu-driven content architectures. This is most commonly a digital installation that surfaces content (text, image, video, audio) through a graphical user interface allowing users to navigate an information architecture via menus, presented on a touchscreen. It is a way many exhibitions provide a depth of content in an infinite virtual space, set within a fixed physical space. Kiosks allow exhibitions to manage space and layout, create strict hierarchies of content reflecting narrative priorities, vary the media presentation style (digital vs. print/built), and can play an important role in surfacing content in an accessible format—kiosks can easily accommodate text-to-speech, zoom, high-contrast versioning, audio description, signed interpretation, and captioning.

While kiosks afford an easy opportunity to present more content within fixed spaces, it is important to consider the intended experience design and how much of the audience's time should be spent on browser-like experiences in situ when it is the same experience they can have at home. Special attention should be paid on how the kiosk/touchscreen is designed and presented within the exhibition, how it contributes to the exhibition's intended interpretation, and how it offers content, learning, and experiential objectives that contribute to the exhibition's overall goals.

19.2.7 Responsive Environments/Sensors

Responsive environments can deliver both content and experience in unique ways that contribute to rich, multisensory exhibition experiences. Infrared, motion, and microwave sensors (among other simple devices like off-the-shelf web cameras) can be used to provoke other aspects of the exhibition to respond in a range of ways: an attract sequence that transitions into core programming when someone approaches; lighting that brightens or dims; audio that begins or transitions or changes in volume; music that starts up; sound effects; projected media or effects; didactic material that plays and stops; and much more.

Combining sensor-based technology with other multimedia components can create magical environments and affect the exhibition experience in a way that is unique to being at the museum in person. These implementations are often low cost and easy to implement. For example, in the *Inuit Land and Lifeways* installation at the Canadian Museum for Human Rights blowing snow and a dog sledding attract sequence fades into a didactic program featuring documentary films projected onto a convex circular surface held up by a podium. As visitors approach the installation a microwave sensor transitions the attract sequence into the didactic programming.

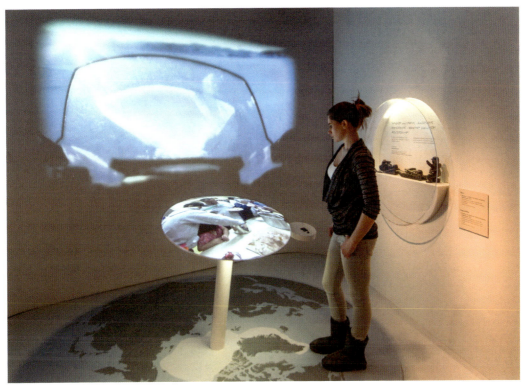

Figure 19.8. *Inuit Land and Lifeways* installation at the Canadian Museum for Human Rights, Winnipeg, Canada. COURTESY OF IAN MCCAUSLAND/CANADIAN MUSEUM FOR HUMAN RIGHTS

19.2.8 Gesture Technology

Gesture-based technology has become increasingly familiar within the general population. This technology facilitates user interaction with a system either without the need for touch or audio or using touch as a series of distinct and sophisticated gestural patterns. Home gaming systems by Microsoft, Nintendo, and Sony, and even mobile devices like the iPhone and Android platforms have a number of gesture technologies built into them. These technologies include skeletal tracking, blob detection, motion tracking, and more.

Even screen-based touch gestures (such as one, two, three, or more finger touches and the distinctions between them: press, hold, rotation, swiping, dragging, and more) are available and can

Figure 19.9. Two people use a gesture-based interface. They navigate the media by pointing and moving their arms and hands. The technology used in the installation is Microsoft Kinect. STEVE CHRONIC/ CANADIAN MUSEUM FOR HUMAN RIGHTS

be used in place of menu-driven systems. Mobile devices also contain accelerometers that sense position, orientation, and equilibrium, and can greatly facilitate rich interfacing with museum content and experience.

19.2.9 Multiuser Tables

Multiuser digital tables have become a popular multimedia intervention in exhibitions. They can facilitate opportunities for large numbers of visitors to engage with one another via human and digital facilitation, such as school groups. They can also facilitate interactive work whereby different users contribute to a collective outcome. And while there are many more use cases that can be cited, they all provide a unique in-gallery opportunity that is not readily experienced elsewhere. One unique aspect of tables is that they provide an opportunity for visitors to share space around a common object. This means visitors, even those who may not know one another, are set in a context that promotes dialogue and discussion as they literally stand or sit in adjacency to one another.

There are a number of ways in which these tables can be produced—from large multitouch screens pieced together, to rear projection, top projection, and even with patented commercial products like Christie MicroTiles. For example, figure 19.10 is a large MultiTaction table. The large, digital Breaking the Silence Study Table at the Canadian Museum for Human Rights enables up to twenty-four concurrent users to browse and navigate an information architecture via a number of interface types such as maps and controlled vocabulary-based menus. An educator can also take over the entire table and run through various guided class lessons with student groups. Figure 19.11

Figure 19.10. Breaking the Silence Study Table. COURTESY OF STEVE CHRONIC/CANADIAN MUSEUM FOR HUMAN RIGHTS

Figure 19.11. Overhead projected table game. COURTESY IAN MCCAUSLAND/CANADIAN MUSEUM FOR HUMAN RIGHTS

demonstrates an overhead projected table game. The unique shape of the table is made possible due to the projected media. Up to six players can play independently or with one another.

When designing and developing a multiuser table, consider the intended content to be surfaced and the intended interaction design. Surfacing portrait photos versus maps, for example, might require different design approaches and therefore software and hardware considerations. Gameplay versus didactic menu-driven design might also infer different requirements when it comes to interface design, function design, and therefore software and hardware selections. Many touchscreen technologies do not support true multitouch and are actually single touch. While these devices are cheaper and effective at times, this can be a constraint if the system needs to accommodate a number of different functions by a number of concurrent users. Users may also be disappointed by the responsiveness of devices that are not truly multitouch given most mobile devices are. Fiducials (static, physical objects) can also be used with multimedia tables, providing a tangible and digitally blended experience, creating unique experiences, and impacting hardware selection.

Trade-offs might be necessary based on intended use, budget, and more. Consider, for example, the use of top-down projection. While providing flexibility in overall table shape and size, and technological infrastructure, top-down projection might cause usability issues if a user reaches across the table for something "on screen" and blocks the projected image, content, or function they are trying to access. Ultimately, the use of multimedia tables can be an effective content delivery system, providing a rich in situ experience not common elsewhere. Content, learning, and experiential objectives should determine when a table is used, and what kind of table ends up being created among the many configurations and options that exist.

19.2.10 Games and Gamification

Gamification is the application of a game and/or gaming concepts, elements, and tactics, such as problem solving, rewards and token or badge gathering, points systems and leaderboards, and more to nongame contexts. Gamification has proven to build engagement, facilitate learning with some audiences, and encourage task completion across a number of disciplines from personal health goals to personal finance management, to learning and more.

In game development it is critical to develop the game design and decision trees with intended audiences/users (a diversity of users) and to iteratively prototype and test the scenarios throughout design development. While this is simply good design practice, when it comes to games and/or gamifying an installation, the margin for error and the potential for isolating the intended audience is vastly increased. Careful thought and deliberation must also be given to when it is appropriate to gamify an installation. Some subjects like those presented at sites of conscience or memorial museums might benefit from some gamified logic models but not be too "fun" in terms of interface design, on-screen feedback, or function behavior.

Figure 19.12. This game developed for the Canadian Museum of History's exhibition, *1867: From Rebellion to Confederation* by CMHR allows visitors to play against others online as well as those playing around the same table. There is a shared leaderboard available online and in the gallery. AARON COHEN/CANADIAN MUSEUM FOR HUMAN RIGHTS

19.2.11 XR

For the purposes of this chapter, XR refers to **augmented reality** (AR), **virtual reality** (VR), **mixed reality** (MR), and any technological derivatives or blends thereof. In simple terms:

- Augmented reality is the application of virtual content positioned and overlaid within the real-world view of a camera and viewer. It is most commonly used with mobile devices, but can also be used with wearables like glasses, statically positioned camera-enabled screens, or any smart devices that have a camera and a viewing screen.

- Virtual reality is most often a simulated experience that immerses the user in a virtual environment through a headset and earphones. VR experiences can be 360 degrees in view allowing the user to virtually look in all directions based on their head position and focus within the 3D environment. These experiences can be photo realistic or any graphic style, motion-based like video, or static imagery. Sound can be positioned within the 360-degree environment as well.

- Mixed reality is the mixing of virtual and real objects within virtual and real spaces, where the objects can interact with one another. For example, an action on a virtual object that provokes a reaction in a real object are all viewable within the display technology that is being used.

AR, VR, and MR can be useful tactics in exhibitions in a number of ways. VR can provide virtual yet immersive access to places not physically accessible by the public; AR can increase

Multimedia

contextualization, layer information over artifacts and spaces, and allow audiences detailed exploration of content that might be constrained by preservation conditions; and XR can facilitate the blend of historical and live events in ways not previously possible. Each one of these technologies can also facilitate greater accessibility.

As with all other instances of multimedia in exhibitions, careful consideration must be given to the use case, the content, the intended learning and experiential outcomes, and even more so in these cases than others, how the technology is being used in the first place. VR, for example, can be isolating and actually remove visitors from the exhibition and those they may be visiting the museum with, as they are virtually transported elsewhere. This can work well for transmedia storytelling experiences, but the decision should be deliberately made with a full understanding of the potential benefits and drawbacks. Each of the technologies also has operational implications beyond the typical maintenance. As fairly new technologies, and with AR and MR potentially requiring the use of a visitor's own mobile device, there is a burden on staff to ensure their effective use within the exhibition.

Figure 19.13. Visitor using augmented reality (AR) to explore an artifact that is under low lighting conditions and within a climate-controlled case. AR was used to increase detailed artifact exploration, extend the experience to remote audiences, provide supplemental content and interpretation, and increase accessibility to the artifacts for blind and low-vision audience members. COURTESY OF JESSICA SIGURDSON/CANADIAN MUSEUM FOR HUMAN RIGHTS

Figure 19.14. A transmedia storytelling installation in the exhibition, *Empowering Women* at the Canadian Museum for Human Rights includes the artifacts (dress and loom), tactile/touchable recreation of the textile, documentary images and interpretive texts, label copy, and a virtual reality (VR) experience. The artifacts were brought to the gallery from Guatemala, and the visitors were transported to Guatemala virtually via the VR installation. COURTESY OF JESSICA SIGURDSON/CANADIAN MUSEUM FOR HUMAN RIGHTS

19.2.12 Mobile Technologies

Mobile technology today is ubiquitous with people walking around with more computing power in their pocket than what NASA had in total in 1969.[3] This represents an enormous opportunity for use in exhibitions. Technologies including the accelerometer, compass, location awareness, Bluetooth, near field communication, taptic engine (vibration), camera, audio/sound system, flashlight, magnetometer, barometer, ambient light sensor, image recognition, zoom and magnifier, Lidar, Wi-Fi, telephony, radio, and more can all be used to create instances of participative, collaborative, accessible, and unique exhibition experiences and access content in different ways. Mobile devices can function as primary interfaces or can be supportive in literally hundreds of ways.

The assistive technologies natively included in mobile devices can be leveraged to increase inclusion and access of content and experience, ensuring inclusion in museum exhibitions irrespective of ability or disability.

Many users have rich suites of applications on their mobile devices that can also be effectively employed in exhibitions. Social media applications, for example, can be leveraged to extend audience reach through the social networks of visitors, allowing them to save and distribute, like and promote, and reference content from the museum, prolonging their engagement well after they have left. It isn't a stretch to note that the mobile device has changed how people engage

Figure 19.15. A visitor takes a photo of an exhibition component and uploads it to Instagram, tagging it with museum hashtags and extending the reach of the museum's content into their own social network.
COURTESY OF AARON COHEN/CANADIAN MUSEUM FOR HUMAN RIGHTS

with the world, and museums are no exception. The self-guided tour was an obvious first use of the mobile device, and that was simply the beginning.

It is important to consider hardware versions when planning for use of the mobile device in museums. It is also important when developing a BYOD (bring your own device) model, how audience members who do not have a device might engage. Many museums provide visitors the opportunity to loan a device. This requires a maintenance plan as mobile devices need to be regularly updated and charged. Increasingly however, museums are moving entirely to the BYOD model and simply offering free, robust Wi-Fi. The strategic opportunities are numerous when visitors are already logged in to their own social channels and have their own preferences, and assistive technologies enabled and customized, within their own devices.

Convergent technologies like wearables (e.g., smart watches and glasses) represent some of the same opportunities as mobile devices but might be usable in more subtle ways. When designing and developing for mobile devices, thought should be given to how convergent technologies and peripherals might be used. The field of wearable technology is an emerging one and holds great potential for seamless interfacing with systems employed in exhibitions.

19.2.13 Social Media

Social media is popularly used within some exhibitions and is deliberately avoided in others. Once again, the context and intentions of the exhibition are critical prerequisites in determining their use and integration. On the positive side, social media platforms can offset development, maintenance, and management efforts. For example, surfacing video online requires a media server, a media player, and a surfacing website or app. YouTube, Vimeo, and other online video services can provide all this with little to no cost. It can also help index the video and auto transcribe and caption the video. This can save enormous effort and holds positive budget implications. Social media platforms can also extend the reach of content and programming to remote audiences and bring more people into dialogue with one another and the museum.

It is important, however, to understand concepts like data sovereignty and the jurisdiction, custody, and intellectual property implications involved when using "free" third-party platforms. As an example, many social media platforms receive a perpetual third-party license to content uploaded to and used within their channels. This can have serious collections management implications, or rights management implications with image, quotes, video, and audio. Social media platforms also evolve and change regularly, and users have no control or say on how these platforms choose to do this. Functionality can be drastically altered with a single update, the terms and conditions can change in ways that are not aligned with organizational policy, and more. If an installation has been designed and developed to leverage a social media channel and that channel changes its database structure, for example, the installation might no longer function as intended and would require new development effort to have it function properly again.

Social media, when used deliberately and strategically, can add a dimension to exhibitions that serves a number of learning, experiential, technological, and otherwise tactical goals. It is simply imperative that its integration in exhibitions be well planned out, and the fact that it is a third-party product be mitigated through design.

19.3 OPERATIONALIZING MULTIMEDIA

Multimedia is a term that represents a broad range of technologies, media types, form factors, and more, and this range is continuously evolving and changing. As such, operationalizing the use of multimedia within exhibitions, museums, and planning processes can be inconsistent from one project to the next.

19.3.1 Team Composition

Multimedia requires unique and specialized skill sets given the variety of what the term multimedia refers to, the required skills and expertise might require multiple, individual resources. Digital media producers, A/V technicians, software developers, interaction designers, interface designers, hardware technicians, and others might all be members on an exhibition design development team. During planning, budgeting, resourcing, and when developing roles and responsibilities, determinations should be made as to which skills are required for the project, and how best to source them.

Based on the nature of the museum, exhibition policy, exhibition development style and approach, hiring certain skills that can work across projects and contribute to maintenance and management might be most efficient and cost effective, while outsourcing on a per project basis might be in other circumstances. A blended model might also be useful where certain skills are kept on staff and others outsourced. There is no right or wrong scenario and what is best for one museum might not be appropriate for another. As such, getting locked into a single model is not practical and each museum and exhibition team should research, plan, and determine for itself which structure works best for its unique instantiation.

What is fundamental though is having multimedia expertise involved as early in the exhibition development process as possible. While an interpretive planner (or exhibition developer) doesn't need to be a multimedia expert, the role of multimedia in the exhibition, the tactical and strategic goals it might help achieve, should be imagined as early as possible during the development of the interpretive plan. As the composition of collections becomes more digital, and as digital assets comprise a larger proportion of collections and/or related research databases, basic digital literacy skills are a must in research and should also affect curatorial and research practices at the very outset of the exhibition development. The involvement of specific expertise can be integrated within the design team, and multimedia opportunities included in ideation through concept and schematic design, and design development phases, before moving into media production, software development, and subsequent exhibition design-build tasks.

19.3.2 Budgeting

Discussion around budgets for multimedia can be a complex topic to unpack given the range of possibilities "multimedia" encompasses. In terms of budgeting, the same processes should be followed as with any exhibition budgeting exercise irrespective of the media that will be integrated. Begin with a cost estimate for the exhibition based on price per square foot (square m) and then work through a standard exhibition development process, and iterate and refine as plans concretize and design intent is detailed and confirmed. In some cases, like with digital scenery, the creation and installation costs of multimedia might be lower than built/fabricated scenery, whereas providing an opportunity for visitors to write comments on cards and add them to a wall might be less expensive to fabricate and install than having them add comments on an iPad and project those comments on a wall. Budgets are often segregated into project or capital budgets, and operations budgets. In the case of multimedia, it is important to consider both when making decisions on how certain content will be presented. Taking the above example, the projection of comments might cost more than comment cards but might be more efficient to moderate as staff can do it from their desk or have software do it for them. Depending on the unique circumstances for budgeting the exhibition and operations in different fiscal years, from different funding sources and models and across different organizations, it might be a better fit for some costs to be in capital budgets versus operating budgets, and/or vice versa, and this practicality should influence decisions and determinations as well.

19.3.3 Hardware and Software

Exhibitions using multimedia require decisions to be made on hardware and software. Today, much of the hardware used in exhibitions can be well integrated into IT environments, allowing for remote monitoring, debugging, tracking, and overall management and maintenance.

It is important to consider how unique the hardware is that is required for the installations being developed. Purchasing back-ups might be critical so that when a piece of hardware does fail, it can be easily swapped out and not impact the functionality of the exhibition. Standardizing the hardware landscape at the operations level can mitigate costs, simplify maintenance, and lessen the need for additional inventory. Given that lamps/bulbs are necessary and expensive perpetual maintenance costs, bulb-free laser projectors, which are more expensive, will be more cost-effective over time because they do not require bulbs or maintenance tasks that track the bulb's lifespan and replacement—a scenario that might increase a project budget but save operational budgets in perpetuity.

Software should be standardized, when it can be, as well and for the same reasons with hardware. This will not only ease maintenance and facilitate any future interoperability but will lessen the required skillset of software developers on staff, or the complexity of service agreements with outsourced providers.

With some hardware, like projectors or touchscreens, consumer versus commercial grade is an important distinction. Commercial grade projectors, for example, are meant to run for days at a time, where consumer grade projectors are not. When it comes to hardware like iPads or computers running a digital installation, it really makes little difference. Off-the-shelf hardware might also require customization such as the disabling of Bluetooth, blocking of publicly accessible ports (physical, infrared, or other), hiding/disabling the home button on an iPad, etc. There is no clear rule as to choosing consumer versus commercial grade equipment. Most museums will have a mix, and like everything else related to multimedia in exhibitions, intent should be a prerequisite in determining what is most appropriate.

19.3.4 Infrastructure

Unlike a static, built, printed exhibition, those that employ multimedia have many implications for infrastructure. They might need to be integrated with content management systems, data networks, the internet, show control systems, and more. As such, it is imperative that in the early phases of design development, IT resources are brought in when a concrete understanding is beginning to form regarding the nature of the multimedia to be implemented. IT accommodation can take time and needs to be planned for. Especially if or when user contributed content is expected, access to the cloud or external networks like the internet is required, hardware needs to be customized and/or secured, or anything that might impact IT security is being planned.

Show control systems are often used in museums, performing arts, and entertainment and amusement parks to manage lighting, A/V, and technology installations. Using show control systems with multimedia systems is effective in vastly reducing daily manual maintenance tasks while also helping preserve the lifecycle of the hardware through management of gentle start-ups, warm-ups, idle modes, and soft shutdowns. Multimedia in exhibitions should be integrated with show control systems whenever possible.

19.3.5 Content Management

It's been many years since storing content at the point of presentation was standard procedure. A content management system (CMS) model is most effective for both the short and long terms of an exhibition. The CMS is a model where content is stored in a centralized system, often the system is composed of multiple modules, and used to deliver content to and from various installation points throughout the museum. This ensures that content is not locked into any single piece of hardware or software, that exhibition maintenance staff can swap hardware components without the need to reproduce and reload content, and content can eventually be delivered to multiple end points concurrently. It also allows content edits, additions, and deletions to take place without having to touch the exhibitions. While content lives in a CMS, it should still be cached at the edge and maintain a push/fetch relationship with the CMS. This can be set to a schedule, happen upon change, or be pushed manually. Caching content at the edge will minimize network traffic, avoid any streaming/buffering issues, and has the added advantage of network failures not affecting the operations of the exhibition.

19.3.6 Data/Insights

Multimedia provides a unique aspect to exhibition management in the way of data. Multimedia systems create usage logs, integrate with various software, and ultimately can and do capture enormous amounts of data. Planning the integration of multimedia in exhibitions should include strategizing what data to collect, how to integrate it with analytics software, how it should be bundled for interpretation, and what it can inform in terms of summative evaluation, maintenance decisions, and even use of multimedia in future exhibitions. Dwell times, popular and unpopular content and/or functionalities, usability issues, and more data sets can be aggregated across the multimedia landscape and help museums make data-informed decisions.

19.3.7 Small Museums

Worthy of a special call out are the considerations and implications around small museums. For the most part, everything that has been addressed within this chapter has been conceptual, tactical, and applies across any and all size organizations within the GLAM (galleries, libraries, archives, and museums) sector. The process should remain the same, irrespective of museum size. When it comes to design development however, this is where considerations can be given toward achieving the intended outcomes, including the uses of multimedia components and creating variation in presentation through low-cost means. Some considerations called out specifically, given the resourcing and structure of museums with few full-time employees and on extremely limited budgeting, include the following.

- There are many existing resources that can save time, costs, list potential suppliers, provide case studies, and overall inform planning and strategic and design decisions available on the American Alliance of Museum's Museum Junction platform, MuseWeb's archive platform, and more.

- Loaning and rental options are often available for hardware that can be more cost-effective over the short term than outright purchases.

- Incubators, makerspaces, co-ops, colleges/universities, and communities of practice can all be important sources for valuable partnerships when working with multimedia and emerging technologies. The opportunity to work with real content and context is often of value to many groups that have access to technology but do not have rich content to work with.

- Small museums have worked together in collaboration for years when developing shared and touring exhibitions and with collection loaning. These practices can help mitigate costs that might otherwise present barriers when it comes to multimedia as well.

- In order to create a unique in-person experience, give thought to projection on substrate that is atypical, aggregation of multiple elements (some digital, some not), unique form, shape, and composition (that people would not have in their homes or encounter outside of a museum setting). Any and all of these considerations can be done with minimal expenditure, using consumer grade hardware, and requiring little to no software skills.

Figure 19.16. At James Madison's Montpelier, a simple digital terminal provides a depth of content that is not presented elsewhere in the space. Simple gobos provide silhouettes, delivering content and experience that does not detract or cover any of the primary artifacts, which in this case are the walls of the house itself. COURTESY OF PROUN DESIGN AND NORTHERN LIGHT PRODUCTIONS

Figure 19.17. At James Madison's Montpellier a collection of monitors presents a piece of linear media. This unique installation facilitates integration of accessibility affordances like captioning and American Sign Language across a larger canvass while adding dimensionality and layering. COURTESY OF PROUN DESIGN AND NORTHERN LIGHT PRODUCTIONS

Case Study

RIGHTS OF PASSAGE EXHIBITION AT THE CANADIAN MUSEUM FOR HUMAN RIGHTS

In the autumn of 2016, I was asked by the newly appointed president of the Canadian Museum for Human Rights to create a temporary exhibition dedicated to Canada's sesquicentennial, examining 150 years of Canada's human rights history. The timeline to produce this exhibition was extremely tight as it needed to open just over a year later in December 2017.

My team and I were faced with the challenge of not only designing and developing this exhibition from scratch two years after opening the museum and within a timeframe of fifteen months, but to do something different than what was already being presented in the Canadian Journeys gallery of the museum—the largest, most complex gallery, and the exhibition that was most arduous to create and ensure due diligence.

We quickly developed a unique and different design and interpretive intention. Given that we were presenting stories of Canada's human rights history over its 150-year federal existence, we created an immersive environmental design that focused on the material and medium reflective of the eras of the stories being presented and carved out a distinct zone for presenting Indigenous perspectives of sovereignty in response to these histories of colonial nationhood. We divided the exhibition into five zones reflective of those perspectives, and presented content and experience through the most common communication and technological medium of the era and built within an environment using the most emblematic materials of those eras:

- 1867–1914: Letterpress/printing press, newspaper, and wood
- 1914–1960: Steel and radio
- 1960–1982: Plastic and television
- 1982–future: Light (where medium and material have become one and the same across presentation, action, collections, and multisensory modalities)
- Indigenous sovereignty: The sacred plants and natural media (voice/sound)

This design direction proved a great fit to also push the in-situ experience through tangible/natural interfaces, further immersing visitors in the material and media of the time and encouraging a greater engagement with the exhibition's content.

The multisensory affordances not only embellished immersion but allowed for immersive inclusive design—so not only was the content and experience accessible, but inclusively accessible (where people of varying abilities share in experiences together).

The tangible interfaces of a newspaper page, radio knobs (recreating an era-specific radio using an iPad interface with tangible knobs), TV sets from the 1970s and 1980s (rear projection, Mac mini run program, synchronized video across three TVs, tangible knobs), spots of light with projected hashtags that when intersected by the visitor create a natural interface through body position within 3D space, and finally the visitor's own voice or sounds made through body movement (like clapping) acting as a natural interface.

Figure 19.18 is a close-up view of a "tangible" interface, which for this zone of the exhibition is mock newsprint—the most common medium of the time. Visitors perform an action by flipping the pages to access content, just as people did in 1867. Another exhibit (figure 19.19) uses a hollowed-out radio with an iPad inserted into it to deliver media. The insert replicates the radio model's display screen, includes captions for accessibility, and tangible knobs allow people to navigate content as they would tune a radio in the 1920s.

Figures 19.18 (top) and 19.9 (bottom). Close-up view of a "tangible" object interface: a mock newsprint and 1920s radio. COURTESY OF AARON COHEN/CANADIAN MUSEUM FOR HUMAN RIGHTS

In another exhibit, three hotspots on the floor are the interface for an experience. As visitors move into a projected hotspot, the environment brings content to that hotspot. The hotspots are social media hashtags that pull material from Twitter, Instagram, and Spotify. The hashtags are:

- #Reconciliation (red, heartbeat/pulse)
- #Equality (rainbow, linear motion)
- #Environmentalism (green, wavering motion like Aurora Borealis)

The multimedia responses provoked by engaging one of the hotspots include: LED light color and motion through the walls (responsive, personalized environment); images from Instagram are projected (masked into unique shapes) on the walls; wearables linked to Twitter, Spotify playlists; Apple and Android watches present tweets related to the hashtags; and the virtual 3D artifact changes to reflect the hashtag (e.g., the first female traffic signal from the Netherlands for equality, a beehive frame for environmentalism, the Bentwood Box from Canada's Truth and Reconciliation Commission).

Figure 19.20. Three hotspots are the interface for the experience.
COURTESY OF AARON COHEN/CANADIAN MUSEUM FOR HUMAN RIGHTS

Figure 19.21. The installation responds to the equality hashtag. The LED lights embedded in the walls project a rainbow color, the dress also projects a rainbow color, a collage of images from Instagram are projected against the wall in nonuniform shapes. COURTESY OF AARON COHEN/ CANADIAN MUSEUM FOR HUMAN RIGHTS

Figure 19.22. In this natural interface installation, visitors make a sound (speaking, singing, yelling, clapping, stomping, etc.) interacting with the projected image. The pitch and rhythm of the sounds determine the shape of what is reflected back to the visitor. COURTESY OF AARON COHEN/CANADIAN MUSEUM FOR HUMAN RIGHTS

The exhibition was truly multimedia, encompassing many different forms, types, and presentation styles. Each multimedia component served to engage the audience in different ways, complement objects and artifacts, images and text, create stimulation and rich experiences across modalities, provide a variety of entry points into the content and experience, and reinforce just how human rights discourse took place in each of the eras and contexts examined.

Case Study

MANDELA: STRUGGLE FOR FREEDOM TRAVELING EXHIBITION

The concept behind this exhibition was to show the power of individual activism and collective solidarity in the face of brutal state repression. *Mandela: Struggle for Freedom* looks at the life and legacy of Nelson Mandela and the global movement that he inspired. The exhibition follows Mandela's journey from lawyer to activist into hiding after he is declared an outlaw, then to his twenty-seven years in prison, and his emergence and role post release. Visitors learn about apartheid and the global movement to end it. They witness the approach and outcomes of South Africa's first democratic elections and about Mandela's efforts to rebuild a nation shattered by racism and injustice.

Mixed-media installations, original artifacts, immersive design, and participatory interaction scenarios help visitors understand what was happening on the streets during Mandela's lifetime. Visitors bear witness to South African children defending themselves with garbage can lids from tanks and learn about the secret plan to break Mandela out of prison. The design intention was to provoke audiences into understanding the importance each one of us holds when we choose not to be a bystander. The experience design my team and I developed is immersive through graphic and environmental design, the strategic use of digital media (linear and interactive), and the careful placement of important artifacts both personal and collective.

The exhibition was designed to be modular and for that aspect of its design (for traveling purposes) to not be apparent or in any way compromise the richness of the experience. The entire exhibition adheres to my inclusive design and accessibility methodology so that a rich, meaningful, immersive, and interactive experience is had by all.

Key multimedia installations include "Posters for Freedom" that enable visitors to create their own posters and have them projected in-situ within the setting of recreated protest signs. The remote audience is free to participate as well, developing their own posters online and having them projected in gallery.

Mandela's cell was created to be an immersive space that reacts and responds to visitors as they approach (motion sensors provoke the silhouette of Nelson Mandela training in his cell via rear projection onto the walls of the cell) and to become a canvas for short documentaries (where the linear media is projected via rear projection and takes over the two walls using them as a canvass).

The design of the Sowetto uprising forces the visitor into a narrower space where on one side are the silhouettes of the people protesting and the other the militarized police force. Replica garbage can lids were created so that visitors can handle them and be on the side of the protestors, and a full-scale Caspir tank was created on the other side. Both sides of the installation were created in order to emphasize scale, space, and contain multimodal accessibility affordances. A large-scale video projection of protesters walking in the streets adds motion, atmosphere, and sound to the immersive environmental design created by the built environment.

The use of multimedia in this exhibition was strategic in terms of varied experience design, however it also helped deliver narrative and stories supplementing original artifacts, objects, and scenographic work, which was critical given the difficulty in sourcing original artifacts from South Africa.

Figure 19.23. The digital media integrated into the scenography is a documentary film embedded in a suitcase of a child, like those used during forced relocations where families were limited to how much of their contents they were permitted to bring. COURTESY OF AARON COHEN/CANADIAN MUSEUM FOR HUMAN RIGHTS

Figure 19.24. Mini documentaries are presented across two scrim walls. COURTESY OF AARON COHEN/CANADIAN MUSEUM FOR HUMAN RIGHTS

Multimedia

Figure 19.25. The poster-making activity allows visitors to create their own protest poster. The installation of protest signs behind the people using the digital interface contain three blank picket signs that a projector superimposes user-created posters onto. The activity is available via mobile web so that the remote audiences can also participate. The entire activity is accessible via text-to-speech, description, and takes advantage of the accessibility functions that are included in all iPhones and Android operating systems. COURTESY OF AARON COHEN/CANADIAN MUSEUM FOR HUMAN RIGHTS

NOTES

Note: The author wishes to acknowledge and thank his collaborators and teammates for all their work on the projects listed within this chapter as examples of the concepts elaborated.

1. "28 Video Stats for 2018," insivia, https://www.insivia.com/28-video-stats-2018/, and "YouTube for Press, https://blog.youtube/press/, accessed January 18, 2021.
2. "50 Must Know Stats About Video & Animation Marketing 2013," insivia, accessed January 18, 2021, https://www.insivia.com/50-must-know-stats-about-video-animation-marketing-2013/.
3. "Your Smart Toaster Can't Hold a Candle to the Apollo Computer," *The Atlantic*, July 16, 2019, https://www.theatlantic.com/science/archive/2019/07/underappreciated-power-apollo-computer/594121/.

Chapter 20

Fabrication and Installation

Erich Zuern

As planning and design shifts into production, exhibition teams and project stakeholders are often energized to see the exhibition being constructed—the result of what has often been many months or years of hard work. If planning has followed a logical and responsible process, this new phase should not be one of anxiety as large amounts of money are spent, but of great excitement as confirmed designs and content decisions begin to take physical shape.

Depending on the project, the production phase can involve dozens of specialty crafts and requires experienced guidance to keep everything coordinated and working smoothly. Following are some critical elements to consider during this phase.

20.1 WHO WILL PRODUCE THE EXHIBITION?

While production and installation are among the final stages of any exhibition process, it is important to plan for these critical steps early. One of the most important planning decisions is to determine how the museum will get the work of production done. It is most commonly accomplished in one of three ways, sometimes using a combination:

1. **In-House Production**: When the capability exists within the museum (staff expertise, available time, space to work, and proper tooling), this can be a highly cost-effective way to get this work done, especially for smaller projects.

2. **Contract with Local Craftspeople**: Museums sometimes develop relationships with smaller firms and individuals who specialize in particular work, such as graphic production, fine woodworking, scenic painting, media integration, and so forth. This approach can be particularly effective at expanding in-house capacity and expertise. Working this way requires a point person at the museum who will identify appropriate resources, draw up a scope of work, and contract and then manage the work to be certain it is coordinated and completed on budget and on schedule. This approach can also be adapted to working with artists for custom installation pieces built on a brief.

3. **Contract with an Exhibit Firm**: An exhibit firm that specializes in museum exhibition work will bring to the project not only needed production expertise and capacity, but also relationships and knowledge of multiple subcontractors and vendors whose expertise will be required to complete the project. Further, an exhibit firm will have critical expertise in budgeting, scheduling, and project management, helping to ensure a smooth project. This is often a good path when undertaking a project that is unusually large or complex for the institution—even though there may be some in-house capability. Being able to contract with one entity and make them entirely accountable for the project has many advantages, but it does result in a higher level of mark-up in the budget in order to pay for this critical oversight.

20.2 DESIGN-BID-BUILD OR DESIGN-BUILD: WHAT'S THE DIFFERENCE?

When proceeding with an exhibit firm, another critical early decision is on what basis to engage the firm. There are essentially two paths to take: design-bid-build and besign-build.

20.2.1 Design-Bid-Build

Design-bid and **design-tender** strategies take place when production and installation is contracted once design is 100 percent complete. A series of bid documents or packages (such as multimedia, cases, graphics, base building fit-out, or a combination thereof) specifying various scopes of work and requirements are issued for suppliers to cost and bid against in the form of a proposal.

In order to control the large number of bids that could potentially come from firms of all levels of experience and from all over the world, the core exhibition team and project manager may decide to prequalify a group of preferred suppliers who will then submit priced proposals. In addition to this two-stage bidding process, the project manager may also recommend that the suppliers form teams under one general contractor so that the museum can enter into an agreement with only one or two firms instead of twenty.

Two key advantages of the design-bid approach include direct cost comparison and best price scenarios as a result of competition, and greater selection among a variety of suppliers whose experience suitably matches the needs of the project. In addition, design-bid projects create a natural stopping point in the exhibition schedule for fundraising, or for possible reconsideration of the project before large amounts of money are spent. Many public museums have policies that require them to participate in competitive and fair procurement processes that make the design-bid strategy mandatory.

There are some challenges with this approach:

- This process can take longer to complete, as all design and content decisions must be completed before production begins.
- The tendering or bidding process can take months if the exhibition is large or requires various stages to complete that may include shortlisting and interviewing potential firms. However, prequalification can begin prior to the completion of design to make this process more efficient.
- Despite every effort to estimate the exhibition during design, cost problems with the design may surface only after tender and after a great deal of effort has been expended on design. Redesign may then be required if tendered bids come in higher than anticipated or there is a desire to work with a particular vendor whose prices are higher than others.
- If selection criteria are overly price-focused, an adversarial relationship can be established where firms must make the lowest cost assumptions in order to successfully compete for the work without the ability to discuss trade-offs and options with the rest of the team in any meaningful way.
- When a literal interpretation of necessarily limited design documents conflicts with intent, change orders often result. As such, design documentation needs to be highly detailed and specified to ensure accurate costing.

20.2.2 Design-Build or "Turnkey" Exhibitions

In recent years, many museums have recognized the benefits of **design-build** models (or variations thereof), with the goal of establishing creative and integrated partnerships rather than vendor-oriented relationships. Sometimes called a "turnkey" contract, the design and production team is selected at the *beginning* of the project. Typically, the contract is held by one lead firm with the other team members subcontracted to that lead company, which could be either the design firm or the exhibit firm. In addition to the designer and various suppliers who will build the exhibition, some design-build agreements may also include the interpretive planner and a team of researchers. Museums have the ability to identify all the resources they need to complement and complete their in-house team. In addition, museums have the option of holding separate design contracts and build contracts, thus ensuring the turnkey approach while still maintaining direct responsibility for and control of all contractors.

Some of the advantages of this approach include:

- Increased consistency of artistic, aesthetic, and interpretive vision.
- A guaranteed price in which the entire team takes responsibility for hitting the budget from the very beginning and maintains it through all phases of work.
- Eliminates the formal solicitation packages for production and reduces the work needed to transition the project from planning and design to production, thereby reducing some design cost and shortening the time needed for the exhibition process.
- Can maximize schedule and adapt easily to fast-track processes, as design can move from concept to production more quickly.

Fabrication and Installation

- The museum retains the flexibility to begin production on certain phases of the project if other phases need a little more development time.
- The project team reaps the benefit of production team experience and expertise throughout such as specifying materials, optionally priced equipment, or methods of construction.
- Trade-offs of function versus cost are much more readily identified and quantified early in the process so that the team can make more informed and timely project decisions together.

The challenges with this approach focus specifically on cost and flexibility:

- There are no opportunities to challenge and compare prices with other suppliers who may be able to achieve the same result cheaper and at the same quality.
- In addition, it may not be easy to bring in new specialist suppliers as the lead firm under contract will want to work with their known and preferred suppliers. Building flexibility into the design-build contract is one way to mitigate this disadvantage such as novating preferred vendors or artists to the main contractor.

20.3 CONTRACTING

Whichever option is preferred, finalizing a contract with a production partner firm requires consideration of a number of items, among them scope of work, subcontractors, and bonding.

20.3.1 Scope of Work

Regardless of whether the production contract is stand-alone (design-bid) or contracted at the beginning of the project (design-build), a clearly defined **scope of work** is fundamental to understanding and contracting the work. In a design-build contract, the scope of work will be more general in the beginning and amended prior to production to identify the specific exhibition components to be provided.

As part of the scope of work there are a number of tasks for which responsibility needs to be clearly identified among the four key players: exhibit firm, designer, base building contractor, and museum. These tasks all have implications for cost (whose budget does it belong to) and schedule (when it will get done). These tasks are:

1. Lay-out of print-ready graphics for proofing and production. This work may be completed by the design team or by the production team once templates and specifications have been prepared by the design team.
2. Image and media procurement, which includes selecting, sourcing, and paying for any copyright/usage fees. Again, either the design team, museum, or the exhibit firm may be assigned this task.
3. Media hardware specification, acquisition, installation, and testing. This could be done by the exhibit firm or by a media production firm that may have been part of the design team.
4. Facility interface and gallery fit-out. While responsibility for these tasks can differ per project, this list indicates the common responsible party:
   - Accurate base building plans and measurements: architect if a new space, museum if not a new space.

- Demolition of existing exhibits, furniture, and finishes and completion of or restoration of basic ceiling, wall, and floor treatments: facility contractor or museum if existing gallery. This work can be included in the exhibit firm's scope as long as budget has been estimated for this scope.

- Utility interface and connections, in particular power and data distribution and control, sprinklers, emergency signage, way finding, and heating, ventilation, and air conditioning (HVAC): facility contractor.

- Purchase and installation for gallery track lighting, "cleaning" lights and emergency house lights: facility contractor, museum.

- Exhibit-specific lighting such as fixtures inside cases or dioramas and special effect lighting: exhibit firm.

- Exhibition security provisions as coordinated with the overall facility during production and installation (e.g., CCTV, extra guards): museum coordinating with facility contractor or security.

- Fabrication of internal gallery walls necessary for the exhibition: exhibit firm or facility contractor.

- Temporary construction barriers at the gallery entrances or in other areas: exhibit firm.

5. Code compliance: Who is responsible for fire and building codes and egress planning and marking within the gallery? What codes apply and which local officials will be responsible for interpreting them? Exhibitions are often considered "furnishings" and are thus exempt from many building code issues, but this is not always the case. This issue is often best handled as a cooperative effort between the exhibition team and the museum, since the design and exhibit firms are often not local, whereas the museum will have addressed similar issues in the past and has, ideally, developed a relationship with local code officials.

Tips for Small Museums

Even when working in-house or with a small number of local specialists, a specific, written scope of work clearly defining the project's tasks and who is responsible for each is essential. Relying on informal allocation of project responsibility will inevitably result in misunderstanding and perhaps conflict. Further, as expectations evolve through the project, a written scope document serves as a tool to manage and communicate change, allowing for and, in fact, prompting appropriate adjustments in budget, allocation of staff time, and outside agreements.

20.3.2 Subcontractors

Firms that fabricate museum exhibitions vary widely in their in-house capabilities. While some firms have more services available in-house than others, no firm has the capability to provide *all* the services needed for every project. This means that some services are **subcontracted** either to the museum directly or through the **general contractor** hired to handle all aspects of the fabrication. Here are some things to consider about subcontracting:

- Major subcontractors should be listed in any proposal, with some information provided about their background and experience. The museum should approve substitutions of major subcontractors.

- Ideally, subcontractors will have previous experience working with the main contractor or with each other. However, everyone needs to engage in new business relationships from time to time and such concerns may be secondary if key subcontractors have specific skills required for the job whether they have worked with others on the team or not.

- With allowances for extenuating circumstances, a museum should pay particular attention if the lead firm is subcontracting more than half the exhibition. Such a project will be highly dependent upon the relationships among the main contractor and subcontractors, and on the experience of the lead firm's project manager working with and organizing others to accomplish work.

20.3.3 Bonding

Some projects, but by no means the majority, require some form of **bonding** as part of the contract agreement. There are three forms of bonding generally seen in museum work, and one alternative, a holdback:

1. **Bid Bond**: Guarantees that a proposing entity will go to contract if awarded a project. This is not common in North America or Western Europe but is often a condition for bidding in many Asian and Middle Eastern countries, especially for government contracts.
2. **Performance Bond**: Guarantees that the work will be completed. In case of default by the contractor, the bond provides the funding necessary to complete the project with other suppliers.
3. **Payment Bond**: Guarantees payment of subcontractors in case of default by a prime contractor.
4. **Holdback**: In some cases, instead of a performance bond, a contractor may have 5 or 10 percent held back from every invoice. This works as a guarantee and is released to the contractor at the end of the project upon completion of the work.

Among these, performance bonds and holdbacks are by far the most prevalent. Unlike in large public works projects, where performance bonds are more often used, they are not a particularly cost-effective tool for ensuring exhibition production. The cost for providing a performance bond is added to the project budget, often as a line item. That money cannot be used to build the exhibition. While a performance bond, when used, is most often taken out for the full value of the project, most exhibition projects are produced incrementally, with finished product "stacking up" and available to the museum as the project progresses. As a result, the entire cost of the project is never at risk—assuming the contractor has sufficient insurance. Instead of spending money on bonding that otherwise could provide more or better exhibits, a museum would be well advised to construct a payment and insurance schedule that provides more targeted and appropriate protection (which might include a holdback)—often at no cost to the project.

20.4 THE PRODUCTION PROCESS

Certainly, the main event during this phase of a project is the production of all the furniture, cases, dioramas, graphics, and multimedia that comprise the exhibition. Whole books are devoted to

Figures 20.1 and 20.2.
Production at the Bluewater Studio, Grand Rapids, Michigan. COURTESY OF BLUEWATER STUDIO

construction methods, materials, and techniques, which we will not attempt to summarize here. We will simply note that this step—the physical building of components—is among the most costly and impactful of the project and needs to be directed by experienced and capable hands.

20.4.1 Site Inspections and Construction Drawings

Early in their work, the fabrication and installation team will perform a site inspection to verify all information in design drawings and architectural plans. Specifically, fabricators need to confirm exact gallery measurements and the locations of key components such as columns, walls, vents, electrical outlets, and so forth. It is vitally important to have this detailed information to ensure that all designed exhibit components will fit where they are supposed to go.

Construction drawings or shop drawings are detailed plans and specifications for how exhibition components will be fabricated, including structure, fasteners, and finishes. Some museums require sign-off on construction drawings, while others are content to have approved detailed design drawings, which are somewhat less technical and focus on the spatial relationships, size, and overall appearance of the exhibition. Determining the level of drawings to sign off will depend upon available staff resources and the level of comfort and trust with the firm doing the production.

20.4.2 Prototype Development

Prototyping needs vary widely, however a general rule is to **prototype** when trying a new interpretive technique or physical component. As well, some prototypes are needed when the designer and museum staff need verification of how something will look and work. There are two motivations for prototyping, and they happen at different times:

- **Proof of concept prototyping** is usually a rough process using inexpensive materials to test that a concept can be effectively communicated as conceived. Ideally, this should be done during the design phase, allowing the designer time to adjust as needed. Sometimes the museum may choose to get evaluators involved at this stage to test whether certain exhibits are communicating the objectives of the exhibit.

- **Production prototyping** is done after the concept has already been proven and addresses more specifically how the exhibit in question will behave when scaled up with actual materials in the specific condition in which it will be used. This step can be expensive, so it is often done using materials that will actually be incorporated in the final exhibit once all is working to satisfaction.

Prototypes are best reviewed multiple times during the exhibition process, allowing the whole team to share in learning from successes and failures. That way, everyone has a fuller understanding of what is feasible and what is not, which promotes good team decision-making.

It can also be useful to evaluate prototypes thorough direct visitor interaction. Whether through formal evaluation or informal observation (or both), information gathered by having visitors engage with prototype exhibits—and acting upon the information gathered—is a useful tool to ensure that an exhibit is reaching visitors as intended.

20.4.3 Graphics

Graphic production is a detailed and Involved process that requires careful review and coordination between the exhibit firm, designer, and museum staff. Key tasks required to ensure quality and error-free graphics during the production phase include:

1. **Layout**: While sometimes graphic layout is completed in the design phase, more often than not it happens during production, regardless of who is responsible for it. It is critical that the graphic artist doing the final layouts and the team producing the graphics communicate with each other.

2. **Proofing**: The museum should receive a final proof of each individual graphic, including all panels, labels, and murals, for review and sign-off. This is an opportunity to find those annoying spelling errors, check resolution, and quality of color saturation. This sign-off is critical, since graphics will be printed after this approval and changes would require reprinting the graphics, which quickly becomes expensive.

3. **Sampling**: It is a good idea to review samples of each major graphic type at full scale, printed using the equipment and substrate that will be used in the final graphic production. This might not include a complete graphic but should be to the correct and final scale so that the relationships among the backgrounds, type, and colors can be clearly seen and evaluated. The museum should make every effort to review these samples under lighting conditions as close as possible to those in the gallery, since colors can appear vastly different in diverse lighting conditions.

20.4.4 Mount-Making

Presenting objects in a museum exhibition in an aesthetically pleasing manner that also supports the preservation of the artifact, work of art, or specimen requires a rather unique combination of skills. An experienced **mount making** specialist is an essential member of the production team. At a minimum, the mount maker will need the following information:

- A complete list of artifacts, works of art, or specimens including photographs (ideally from more than one angle when relevant).
- Complete dimensions of each, specifying height, width, length, and relevant weight.
- Relevant notes, such as limitations on how the object may be displayed and preferred object orientation that might affect mounting. Does a textile need to lie flat or at a slight angle? Does a pot need to be supported from the inside as well as the outside?

The mount maker will be in contact with registration and conservation professionals at the museum to verify mounting and handling standards. Depending upon the nature of the objects and scale of the project, the mount maker may visit the museum ahead of time to verify certain aspects of the work. While certain work can be done ahead of time and off-site, most of the mount maker's work will be done on site with the actual objects in-hand. Such work will require a secure location at the museum.

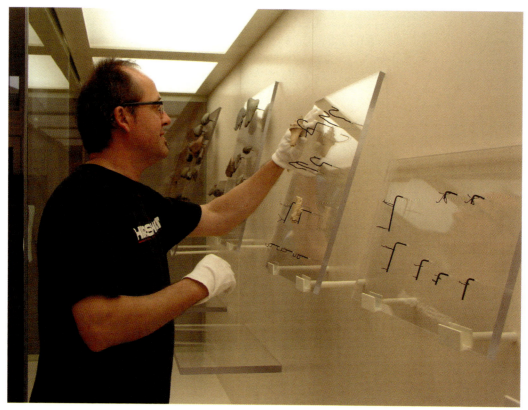

Figure 20.3. Mounting artifacts at the National Archaeological Museum Aruba, Oranjestad. LORD CULTURAL RESOURCES

20.4.5 Media Production

Media production needs to be coordinated with the overall exhibition production schedule. The three salient issues are:

1. Turnkey or separate contract: A museum may choose to incorporate media production as part of an overall turnkey production contract, or to create a separate media contract for the exhibition. The choice may be determined by the preferred working style of the museum and the available in-house expertise for managing media work. The primary advantage to a turnkey approach is that the exhibit firm handles contracting, schedule, cash flow, hardware integration, and numerous other details necessary to getting the job done. The primary advantages to a separate media contract are increased direct hands-on control by the museum, and no management fee or mark-up from an exhibit firm.

2. Monitoring: Working styles for developing media vary significantly by firm and by the type of product being produced. In general, during production a museum should review and approve some version of the media product at least at these four points:

   - Outline or storyboard: Narrative or visual depiction of the visitor experience
   - Rough cut: Components are mostly present and assembled in relationship, but not finely edited or polished

- Beta version: An edited, fairly polished version
- Final review: Complete, edited product

3. Hardware integration: Determine early in the design process whether the exhibition will have one central media hardware location (an "AV closet"), or if each exhibit component containing media will hold all hardware within that component at the location where it resides in the exhibition. **Centralized** or **decentralized control** impacts the final selection of hardware, as well as how the museum will operate it. Other considerations include ensuring that components are appropriate to the job, that they will work seamlessly together, and where possible that they will all use hardware of the same model or from the same manufacturer in order to simplify maintenance. The media producer, hardware integrator, design team, and exhibit firm must all work together to ensure seamless physical integration of media hardware into the exhibition components.

20.4.6 Installation

This is the time when the contractor and subcontractors converge on the site to install the exhibition components that have been mostly produced and built off-site. Virtually all non-traveling exhibition projects are contracted with production and installation in a single agreement. Due to the highly customized nature of the components and an often-compressed time frame, there is little to be gained financially or on the schedule by contractually separating these two phases. Traveling exhibitions often have a provision for someone knowledgeable about the exhibition to travel to the initial installation (and sometimes subsequent installations as well) to help ensure that all runs smoothly, and to tidy up any loose ends in the installation instructions.

Three salient issues affecting installation are as follows:

1. **Schedule integration** that relevant museum operations and physical activities are aligned to the exhibition schedule.
   - With facility and museum operations: Be sure to consider ongoing operations and special events when scheduling the exhibition installation. How isolated is the gallery? Is there other construction work going on at the same time? Is a special event planned for that period?
   - With site availability and accessibility: There are typically several days of significant activity on the museum loading dock (or wherever delivery will occur), which must be considered from the standpoint of other deliveries. In addition, the route from the dock to the gallery must be clear.
   - With clean and completed gallery spaces: If installation is taking place in a newly constructed or renovated facility, the galleries must be dust-free and operational. Fragile exhibits, media components, and artifacts cannot be safely installed on a site that is still under construction or has not been commissioned for operation.

2. **Staging space**: There will need to be some space for staging new components and for doing the work of installation. This can often take place right in the gallery; however, some projects may require additional space. Mount making in particular benefits from a separate workspace in order to provide the opportunity to work directly with the objects in a secure environment, not in the midst of an active installation.

Fabrication and Installation

Figure 20.4. Installing exhibits at the Canada Aviation and Space Museum, Ottawa, Canada. LORD CULTURAL RESOURCES

3. **Work hours**: Installation teams need to be aware of the hours that will be available to them to work on site. Installation teams often prefer to work longer hours than the museum might normally be open. Anticipate special arrangements that may need to be made for security, access, and supervision during this time.

20.4.7 Completion and Close-Out

A set period of time is provided for the completion of production and installation. Often this takes a few days to a week after everything is in place in order to address all outstanding items to the satisfaction of the museum. Project close-out functions include:

1. **Setting and focusing lights** is often one of the final touches for the exhibit, since all components need to be in place in order to properly focus the lights. Additionally, this usually involves a rolling scaffold or lift, which requires the gallery to be relatively clear of installation materials.
2. A sign-off process called a **punch or deficiency list** allows both the exhibit firm and the museum to reach a formal conclusion to the project. A punch list is typically created during a walk-through at the end of the installation that includes appropriate representatives from the exhibit firm, design team, and the museum. The punch list generated during this walk-through identifies any items to be corrected. Note that the punch list is not a wish list. It identifies items that are in some way not completely finished, not delivered as previously agreed to, or perhaps damaged. If the museum wishes to make changes to the exhibition

or to add items, that can certainly be discussed, but such things should be addressed in a separate process that requires a **change order** or a contract addendum.

3. Museum staff should receive **training** on the appropriate operation and maintenance of the various exhibit components. The exhibit firm will lead this training.

4. Final project **documentation** should be delivered within thirty days of the project completion, and should include:

    - Final "as-built" drawings
    - Parts lists
    - An exhibit maintenance manual
    - Warranties and product information on any purchased items (such as media hardware)

20.5 TRACKING AND SCHEDULING

The museum, design team, and exhibit firm must work together to create a schedule that integrates the work of the whole team and that properly addresses the sequence of events. This is called **critical path scheduling**. There are often multiple critical paths in exhibition creation—identified processes throughout the project where a series of tasks must occur in a certain order—wherein each step is dependent upon the step before. These critical path processes often define the schedule, since it is difficult to compress them, and the linear nature of the work means that steps must take place in sequence. Once these critical path elements are identified, assigned, and integrated, an achievable project schedule will follow. While each project is obviously unique, critical paths are often located in specific project sections such as:

- Text development, image identification and acquisition, and graphic design, layout, proofing, and production
- Facility completion or preparation, site survey, utility work, and partition wall construction
- Media planning, media hardware specification, facility integration, exhibit component integration, media prototyping, production, and completion

As the final steps in the exhibition creation process, production and installation will bear the brunt of any schedule over-runs in earlier phases. Be realistic in scheduling planning and design so that production does not get shortchanged. While it can be possible to compress a planned production window, this often ends up costing more and/or compromising the quality of the project in undesirable ways.

The frequency of reports and visits will vary with the size and complexity of the project, as well as with the museum's desire for the information. How this will be handled should be agreed upon early in the project:

1. **Progress reports**: Regular progress reports should include a general overview of work complete and photos and/or videos when applicable. These reports may be weekly, biweekly, or monthly depending upon the project and the needs of the museum.

2. **Visits**: Plans should be made to visit the location where the exhibition components are being constructed. While most exhibit firms will welcome a visit from the museum at any time during the process, the two most valuable times to visit are:

- During prototyping in order to experience testing first-hand
- Toward the end of production when there are finished and in-progress components to see and approve

20.6 WARRANTY

What should be covered in the **warranty**? Industry standard is that custom-manufactured exhibition components are warrantied for one year against defects in material and craftsmanship. Certain items may be exempt from this requirement, and those items should be spelled out contractually. Exempt items often include commercially available components manufactured by others (such as electronic components, motors, lighting equipment and so on), since such items typically carry their own warranty from the manufacturer. Be advised, however, that many such components are purchased early in order to physically incorporate them into the exhibition, and manufacturers' warranties start from the date of purchase, not from the exhibition opening. For items with a short warranty period (ninety days is not uncommon for electronics), the warranty may be expired by the time of opening.

20.6.1 Warranty Expectations and Grey Areas

When a museum experiences a problem with an exhibition during the warranty period, it is best to document the problem to the greatest extent possible (including photographs) and immediately contact the exhibit firm. Each firm will have its own process for addressing warranty claims, and it is best to follow that process closely. Warranty claims typically fall into three categories:

1. Claims for exhibits or components that are clearly a failure and need to be repaired or replaced
2. Claims that are clearly the result of intentional or accidental damage inflicted by someone or something (not typically covered)
3. Claims that inhabit the grey area between the first two

For the third type of claim, a grey area where it is difficult to ascertain the root cause of the problem, there is typically a negotiation between the museum and the exhibit firm resulting in a decision that is ideally acceptable to both. Such negotiations are one significant reason to work with a firm that the museum knows and trusts, since mutual goodwill will help in addressing future issues.

The museum should never hesitate to contact a firm after the warranty has expired. At a minimum, the firm may help to troubleshoot the problem, identifying resources, and perhaps even in solving it. Reputable firms will help to the greatest extent possible.

20.6.2 Extended Warranties and Maintenance Agreements

In certain circumstances, an institution may require a warranty period longer than offered by an exhibit firm. Such agreements are most appropriate for museums without the staff resources to operate the exhibition or for museums located in remote areas where access to parts (media hardware in particular) may be difficult.

An extended warranty can usually be made available at additional cost. It should be noted however that the vast majority of warranty issues arise during the first few weeks after installation. As with any purchased warranty protection, museum staff should carefully consider needs prior to paying for additional coverage.

While not particularly common, exhibit maintenance agreements can also be negotiated. Under such an agreement, the exhibit firm would come to the museum periodically to inspect, clean, and "tune up" the exhibits. A maintenance agreement is most useful for mechanical interactives and electronic components, including media hardware, such as big format film projection facilities, planetaria, or simulators.

Case Study

CREATIVE CONTRACTING BY THE NORTH DAKOTA HERITAGE CENTER & STATE MUSEUM

Erich Zuern and Genia Hesser

When the North Dakota Heritage Center & State Museum embarked on an expansion project that included a complete redesign of the permanent exhibition, one way that they addressed their needs was through careful attention to contract details.

Figure 20.5. Geologic Time Gallery at the North Dakota Heritage Center & State Museum, Bismarck, North Dakota. COURTESY OF NORTH DAKOTA HERITAGE CENTER & STATE MUSEUM

With an increase from nineteen thousand square feet to thirty-three thousand square feet of permanent exhibition space, three new galleries now interpret more than five hundred million years of North Dakota's history. This was, by far, the largest project that the museum team had been involved with. By addressing certain issues early in the project, the Historical Society was able to direct the project to unfold in the manner that they preferred. While this holds true for many aspects of the project, two contractual issues in particular stand out:

Fabrication and Installation

377

1. **Design build**: By working with the state to specify this as a design-build project, the State Historical Society of North Dakota (SHSND) was able to engage in this large project with a single point of accountability for the entire project and build relationships with all project team members throughout all project phases, resulting in complete and early project buy-in from all parties.

2. **Staggered schedule**: The SHSND chose to stagger the schedules for developing exhibits for each of the three galleries to accomplish two goals:

    - This schedule spread out the work of research, collaboration, and review, easing the burden on finite staff resources who were slated to perform these tasks.

    - Spreading out the work of the three galleries allowed greater diversity in the teams proposing to do the project. Specifically, smaller firms who might not otherwise have the capacity to produce a project of this scale were able to propose, resulting in a contract with a team that SHSND was pleased to work with.

By proactively incorporating these items important to them into the project contract, SHSND was able to proceed with a project fine-tuned to their advantage. Genia Hesser, former exhibitions curator at SHSND stated,

> We spent a lot of time planning the exhibition expansion. Not just the end result, but how we wanted the entire process to work. Good, early planning saved valuable time that we needed in the midst of a demanding, resource-intensive project.[1]

1. Interview with the author for this case study. Interview date October of 2020.

Chapter 21

Financial Planning

Erich Zuern

Among the many tools deemed essential in creating quality exhibitions, budgeting often takes a back seat to other functions. However, just as surely as good design and content are critical to the success of an exhibition project, when managed well a budget can enable creativity, aid in decision-making, and help to ensure a successful project. Managed poorly, a budget will be a cause for frustration and backtracking and will be a significant stumbling block to progress and the realization of the project vision.

Effective budget management requires experience, diligence, and common sense. Only as good as the information used to create and maintain it, a budget is a tool. Approached with a clear eye and not too much wishful thinking, it will help navigate the process of creating an exhibition.

21.1 CREATING AN EXHIBITION BUDGET

Exhibitions need time and money in order to be implemented successfully. Establishing a budget that is appropriate to the desired size, quality, and complexity of the exhibition at the outset of a project is of utmost importance. Therefore, it is worth spending significant time and effort on creating and maintaining a project budget and, just as important, understanding what that budget will buy you. For an exhibition of any size, consulting with colleagues experienced in budgeting is critical to success, unless the museum has in-house expertise. Alternately, it may be appropriate to consult with firms with whom you may be working, or perhaps have worked with in the past, to help establish the project budget.

21.1.1 Budgeting Basics

Initial project budgets are typically expressed in dollars per square foot (psf) or per square meter (psm). High quality, engaging exhibits can be produced for a wide range of price points. Establishing a budget is one of the first crucial steps in the project.

Cost per m2/ft2 (USD)	Description
$250 to $350 per ft2 $2,700 to $3,800 m2	Didactic, low level of media and interactivity.
$350 to $600 per ft2 $3,800 to $6,500 m2	Moderate level of interactivity and media. Moderate density of museum quality cases.
$600 to $800 per ft2 $6,500 to $8,600 m2	High level of interactivity, media, and immersion. High density of museum quality cases.

Figure 21.1. Project budget rough order of magnitude estimates.
LORD CULTURAL RESOURCES

There are many variables that can make the difference between lower costs and higher costs, for example:

- **Density**: How much exhibit material is in the space. This relationship is straightforward as greater levels of funding allow more exhibit components.
- **Exhibit cases**: Objects need to be protected both from visitors and from the environment for the long-term good of the object. The best path here is often to use the facility HVAC to create an object-friendly environment in the exhibit space. Providing this environment in the room means that each case does not have to be individually conditioned, which would add cost. The number and type of objects influences the number of cases needed. As well, the environment of the gallery influences the cost of the cases based on the need (or not) for conditioning. Each of the cases in the images below are passive, in that they do not contain internal environmental conditioning.
- **Interactivity**: The type and level of interactivity has a big effect on budget. Higher budgets generally allow higher levels and amounts of interactivity.
- **Media and technology**: Perhaps the biggest driver of exhibition budgets today is the amount and type of media in an exhibition. Media and technology can be interactive, can simply show a video or a story, or even be environmental, evoking a feeling without a specific narrative. Like other components, media budgets are related to complexity, depth, scale, and density. In the range from an all-media exhibition to a single small screen looping a video, be certain your budget aligns with your intentions in this important area.
- **Large objects**: One or two large objects in a space will not significantly skew the square foot cost for the exhibits. If, however, there are a significant number of large objects planned (think cars, trains, stagecoaches, airplanes, farm implements, and the like), those objects will occupy a lot of space and will therefore affect the total cost per square foot of creating exhibits in that space.

Figure 21.2. Tall, multilevel case at the North Dakota Heritage Center & State Museum, Bismarck, North Dakota. COURTESY OF NORTH DAKOTA HERITAGE CENTER & STATE MUSEUM

Figure 21.3. Small wall-mounted case at the Jewish Museum Milwaukee, Wisconsin. COURTESY OF JEWISH MUSEUM MILWAUKEE

- **Recreated environments**: Creating "you are there" vignettes as part of an exhibit environment can be highly effective at engaging visitors through multiple senses. Fully realized recreated environments will add cost, however partial or notional recreations can also be part of the exhibit mix in order to control costs. The ship and streetcar environments in the images below are complete recreated environments. The living room, on the other hand, is notionally recreated using a few relatively inexpensive props and furniture pieces.

Of course, everything in an exhibit is affected by budget. The above list highlights some of the major considerations and cost drivers.

Figure 21.4. This recreated streetcar with media-activated windows serves as the entry to the much-loved *Streets of Old Milwaukee* exhibit at Milwaukee Public Museum, Wisconsin. MILWAUKEE PUBLIC MUSEUM

Figure 21.5. Recreated passenger ship and 1930s living room in the *Faces of Freedom* exhibit at the National Czech & Slovak Museum in Cedar Rapids, Iowa. COURTESY OF NATIONAL CZECH & SLOVAK MUSEUM & LIBRARY

Tips for Smaller Musuems

Use square foot (sq m), budgeting with caution on smaller projects. It becomes less useful the smaller the gallery space and is of limited value below 2,000 square feet (200 sq m). In larger exhibitions, the cost is spread over many different spaces and component types, making an average cost per square foot work effective. In smaller exhibits, area-based budgeting can be a starting point or a reference, however the cost will be much more affected by what specifically is being done in the space. Identify a budget that must not be exceeded and then outline a desired scope or intent for the exhibition, prioritizing requirements such as cases and graphics over a video installation. This allows the design team to do a rough order of magnitude cost at concept design with options for review with local vendors. Check costs with previous institutional experiences, colleagues, suppliers, and other knowledgeable sources to be certain that you are budgeting appropriately for what you wish to accomplish. Using local vendors, or those you have used in the past, will ensure that you do not exceed your budget.

Figure 21.6 illustrates how a typical project budget might be divided between planning, project management, design, fabrication, and installation. Fabrication is and should be where most of the expenditure takes place, as this is the actual product that will form the visitor experience. Planning and design costs can vary depending on the amount of contracted versus in-house resources used, and the amount designers will charge. Design charges vary the most from 18 percent to 26 percent (or even higher) of total cost, depending on the reputation of the firm selected and the size and complexity of the project. Large, media rich exhibitions may require additional design consultation up front to conceptualize media components and design the technological systems and show control.

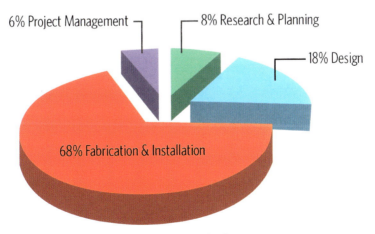

Figure 21.6. Allocation of the exhibition budget. LORD CULTURAL RESOURCES

Financial Planning

21.2 DIRECT EXHIBITION COSTS

The costs that are considered directly a part of the exhibition budget can be divided into the following broad categories:

1. **Project management**: An experienced person or team to maintain project intent, budget, and schedule throughout. This person may be in-house or contracted.

2. **Evaluation**: If the museum is committed to evaluation and consultation, the costs for conducting front-end, formative, and/or summative evaluation must be accounted for in the budget.

3. **Planning**: This includes the cost for preparing and/or contracting the interpretive plan and content development. The later may require hiring additional researchers or paying subject matter experts associated with other academic institutions, in addition to the cost of a contract for interpretive planning. Planning costs may also include a budget set aside for the creation of the initial exhibition or curatorial brief. Such budgets may be part of the museum's operating fund or be a designated fund set aside for curators and other museum staff to generate ideas for exhibitions.

4. **Collection development**: If the exhibition will require objects outside of what is available at the museum, the cost for finding, acquiring, and safely transporting the objects must be accounted for—whether the objects will be on loan or added to the museum's collections. If on loan, there will be costs of insurance, shipping, and the expenses of couriers from the lending institution, as well as the time of the museum's registrar or collections manager. If they are acquired, however, it may, for accounting purposes, be more appropriate to allocate them to the museum's acquisition budget, not its exhibition budget.

5. **Design**: This includes all phases of 3D design (concept, detail design/design development, final design), graphic design, case layouts, media design, and lighting design. Design costs may include the commissioning of special visualization tools such as a digital flythrough, which may be instrumental for fundraising.

6. **Fabrication**: The physical construction of the exhibition requires the greatest percentage of any budget. This cost allocation also includes construction drawings, sampling, and prototyping.

7. **Lighting**: Exhibit budgets typically cover design, positioning, and focus of existing lighting fixtures (usually track lighting) as well as purchase and installation of specialty lighting that may be required for the specific exhibit design (such as special f/x lighting, lighting incorporated within exhibit components, and so forth). Exhibit budgets do not typically cover installation or upgrade of a gallery lighting system (see below). However, exhibitions that are being planned and designed in parallel with new gallery construction may absorb additional exhibition lighting costs such as track, lighting control system, and specialty lights. An exhibition budget should never include tenant improvement costs such as house lighting, electrical, and base building wall construction.

8. **Installation**: The installation budget accounts for shipping and transporting all the exhibition components to the museum, as well as the labor, materials, and equipment required to mount the exhibition.

9. **Media production**: While the cost of producing the media components of an exhibition is included in the fabrication budget, the cost of producing a film to be shown in the museum's theater/auditorium is usually a separate item. The medium may be a conventional film

or could be a large-screen format such as IMAX. An allocation for a major film should be identified as a separate line item or allowance in per sf/sm budget assignment. This is good practice and ensures budget control.

10. **Remediation**: It is always a good idea to set aside some funding to address corrections, omissions, and changes. Such changes may be required as result of summative evaluation or may be changes that the museum feels are necessary to improve the visitor experience as the exhibition develops. Such changes can take place up to six months or more after an exhibition has opened.

11. **Expenses**: Expenses can be as varied as the projects being contemplated; however, this category can cover these types of items:

    - Team travel to conduct research or to do comparative studies of similar projects
    - Travel to meet with suppliers or other team members
    - Project phone, courier, document reproduction, and other day-to-day business costs if these are tracked separately in your institution
    - Travel for professionals outside your institution, such as content experts and others whom you may choose to involve in the project
    - Travel expenses for firms contracted to participate in exhibition development must be accounted for and should be addressed in individual agreements
    - In some cases the size of the project may require the set-up of a temporary office. This is particularly true of very large exhibition projects requiring daily oversight

12. **Royalties and copyright**: Any material included in an exhibition that is not owned by the museum or created specifically for the exhibition may be subject to copyright. This most commonly applies to images, media, and text. A full discussion of copyright procedures and guidelines is beyond the scope of this manual however, one must treat the creative work of others fairly. Further, it should be noted that museums are sometimes surprised to find that they do not necessarily hold copyright on items simply because they are in their collection. Similarly, museums are not automatically exempt from paying copyright fees simply on the basis of their not-for-profit status or educational mission. Museum staff should become educated on this important topic and be sure to budget to pay for the right to use materials to which the museum does not hold copyright. If the museum does not have a separate budget for this work, fees will come out of the fabrication budget. Two useful resources on this topic are *Getting Permission: How to License & Clear Copyrighted Materials Online and Off* by Richard Stim,[1] and the American Alliance of Museums' website (https://www.aam-us.org/), which contains numerous resources related to rights and reproductions in their Collections Stewardship Professional Resources section.

13. **Contingency**: Every budget needs a contingency to cover unanticipated costs that will arise in the course of the project. Even the most skilled and experienced project managers cannot anticipate every eventuality. At the outset of a project, contingency of between 10 percent and 20 percent is recommended. As the project develops and becomes more completely defined, funding reserved for contingency can be reduced or assigned to specific items and will eventually fall to zero toward the end of the project, when all exhibition components are known and firmly priced.

> ### Tips for Smaller Museums
>
> If you are producing some or all this work in-house, be certain to budget staff time appropriately. Even if there is no direct cost due to the work being completed by salaried staff, workloads need to be realistically addressed, especially overtime. If your team has past experience with multiple exhibition projects, you likely have a good sense of the time and effort this will take. If members of your team are new to this, it is common to vastly underestimate the amount of time each step will take, which can lead to problems later in the project. Be sure to consult with knowledgeable colleagues whether they be inside your institution or out.
>
> Although more work for your project manager or procurement officer, contract out fabrication as separate works because exhibition firms—even small ones—will charge anywhere from 10 percent to 15 percent markup on all works whether done in-house or through subcontracted vendors. For example, work directly with a graphics firm, purchase off-the-shelf cases rather than custom systems, and work with local craftspeople for specialty millworks such as framing and furniture. Anything you can buy off-the-shelf will ensure efficiencies in the fabrication budget and ensure that you can get replacements without having to hire a subcontractor.

21.3 RELATED EXHIBITION COSTS

Costs that are related to an exhibition project but not always addressed in direct project budget include the following categories below. The core exhibition team should decide at the outset which costs will be included in the direct project budget and which items will be assigned to other budgets.

1. **Gallery preparation** (or tenant improvement costs): This may reference space completion if the gallery is newly constructed or may involve some level of restoration if a prior exhibition was installed in the space. Preparation can include such items as:
    - Demolition of previous exhibition (when applicable)
    - Installation or restoration of basic floor, wall, and ceiling finishes
    - HVAC installation or upgrades
    - Fire suppression and security systems
    - Electrical and data distribution
    - Work (housekeeping) lights
2. **Lighting systems**: For new or renovated spaces, the exhibit design team is typically consulted on the brand, type, placement, and quantity of track, fixtures, and dimming systems, with the purchase and installation part of initial or ongoing facility cost. It should be noted that sometimes these costs are directed toward the exhibition budget,
3. **Conservation**: Typically, any conservation work that needs to be completed before an object can be put on display is the responsibility of the museum, not part of an exhibition design or fabrication scope of work, so this must be part of the museum's overall exhibition budget

when and if it applies. At a minimum, condition reports and routine cleaning will be needed for all collection objects in the exhibition; but some exhibitions are built around a conservation or restoration project, with the restored artifact, work of art, or specimen one of the star attractions. During the development of the exhibition brief, be sure to understand the conservation requirements for the exhibition so they can be addressed as a dedicated allowance for in-house preparation or outsourced specialists.

4. **Data entry and digitization**: In many exhibitions, catalogue data entry is not complete for some or all the objects to be displayed. Archival materials may need to be digitized so that their images can be used in multimedia programs in the exhibition. The registrar or collection manager's time should be budgeted for supervising loans and their documentation.

5. **Education and public programming**: A new exhibition almost always requires the development of new programs to be delivered by the education department. Planning, design, and material costs should be budgeted and managed by the appropriate museum departments.

6. **Website and social media**: Online experiences, applications, and social media bring the exhibition experience to life outside museum's walls. These projects can be quite large and complex and often have their own significant budgets and planning team separate from the core exhibition team.

7. **Publications**: These may include new books, articles, catalogues, and other offerings.

8. **Shop stock/Retail**: The development of new stock for the museum shop related to the exhibition is a potential source of revenue. However, it is also a cost item to be budgeted separately.

9. **Marketing, public relations, and advertising**: These are the tools for generating short-term and long-term interest in the project, and ultimately getting visitors through the front door.

21.4 MANAGING THE BUDGET

Budgeting for a project is not a one-time exercise. Budgets are fluid and should be adjusted regularly throughout the project to reflect new information. Most costs in a budget are estimates or allocations at the beginning of the project. As the project progresses, costs increasingly become known quantities through estimates received and contracts written. A budget should indicate which costs are known and which are only estimates or allocations so that the whole team knows which costs may be relied upon and which may change in the next round of costing.

21.4.1 Estimating through the Design Process

Once a project is underway, the largest and most malleable parts of the budget will be in the fabrication and installation phases. Costs for these phases should be established in initial budgeting and confirmed during the planning and design phases through a formal estimating process. It is critical to assign a team member who is highly experienced in museum project cost estimating to this task. Poor budgeting can and will wreak havoc with the project. Some museums have experienced estimators on staff. More commonly, estimates are provided by design and/or fabrication firms as part of their work on the project. Relatively few consultants have the necessary expertise in exhibition costs.

While cost projection, as noted above, is an ongoing task, there should be several formal points for cost review:

- **Cost allocation**: Based on the exhibition's interpretive plan, this step allocates the available funding across the components of the exhibition based upon the interpretive strategies identified in the plan. While largely an allocation, this is also when an experienced estimator can raise flags for items that may individually or, when taken as a whole, exceed the available budget.

- **Design estimates**: At the conclusion of conceptual/schematic design, an estimate should be provided based upon the known direction and identified components. While remaining a relatively "big picture" cost snapshot, certain large cost or unusual items will benefit from closer analysis by the design team, fabricating firm, or cost consultant. A detailed costing should also be provided at each formal stage of design development and again at final design. Each budget is reviewed and approved and may trigger changes to design in order to meet project budget. Because media can have such a large impact on budget, it is advisable to consult media and interactive specialty firms to provide pricing information based on known approaches early in the exhibition process.

- **Final quote/final budget**: The final quote is provided at the conclusion of design development in a design-build process or at the time of contracting with a firm that has successfully won the tender in a competitive design-bid process (see chapter 20). This is a highly detailed cost projection, accounting for every component of every item in the exhibition design. A final quote also calls for a detailed review to ensure that all costs for mounting the exhibition are covered in someone's budget, whether that someone is the fabricator, the museum, or some other entity. All assumptions, exceptions, and exclusions must be known or dealt prior to fabrication taking place.

21.4.2 What Happens When the Exhibition is Over Budget?

At some point in the project, something will almost certainly cost more than was budgeted. It is extremely important to adjust budgets to reality regularly and not depend upon hope to balance them. There are only two ways to bring a wayward budget into balance:

1. **Lower costs**: This involves working with the core exhibition and design team to determine more cost-effective ways to achieve various goals (such as finishes or types of equipment), or simplify, eliminate, or combine some tasks and exhibit components.

2. **Increase the budget**: This option is often not feasible, but sometimes a particular donor will be willing to fund a component of the exhibition that they have a particular interest in, or the museum may wish to commit funding from a different source in order to be able to achieve certain exhibition goals. If the museum has its own fabrication shop, some production tasks may be assigned to in-house resources that cost considerably less. The latter strategy must be balanced with quality, schedule, and availability. In some cases, museums hold back an overall project contingency to address potential enhancements to an exhibition. This should be kept separate from the exhibition budget and managed by the museum's project or financial manager.

Museums must resist the urge to draw from future parts of the budget to balance earlier parts or to over-spend on earlier phases of the project to the detriment of later phases. Assuming that the initial budget allocations were sound, pulling funding from future project phases only postpones the problem—and usually makes it worse since the time to effectively deal with it will have compressed. There are fewer "future" phases to draw from, and additional funding to earlier phases typically creates more work later on, not less, thus actually compounding the problem.

If, for example, during a phase of design it is determined that the project will cost more to produce than budgeted, some changes must be made from the options noted above to bring the project back to budget. Do not wait until the production phase in the hopes that a solution will magically appear. Deal with budget problems as early and as directly as possible.

Case Study

BUDGET STRETCHING WITH IN-KIND CONTRIBUTIONS

In-kind contributions can be of great help in stretching exhibition budgets. While this is not limited to smaller institutions, it can have an outsized impact on small projects. Welcome at any time, such budget boosters are most helpful if committed early in the project so that the rest of the project can be planned accordingly. Further, and this can be a delicate topic, be certain that expectations of timing, scope, and quality are clearly understood so that any such contribution does not become a burden to the project.

In-kind contributions may be almost anything, including services or reduced fees. Often this form of support involves a physical object, physical labor (a general contractor who comes in to paint walls, lay carpet, or build photo frames), an existing film, or AV equipment such as monitors, players, and projectors.

Movies are a significant theme in *Blacklist: The Hollywood Red Scare* exhibition at the Jewish Museum in Milwaukee, Wisconsin. The museum successfully solicited the donation of theater seats from a local movie house undergoing a renovation, refurbished them, and used them as both environment-enhancing props and as seating for the exhibit's introductory video.

Figure 21.7. Theater reconstruction at the Jewish Museum Milwaukee incorporates donated theater seats, Wisconsin. COURTESY OF JEWISH MUSEUM MILWAUKEE

Financial Planning

Agriculture is a core theme in the Inspiration Gallery at the North Dakota Heritage Center & State Museum. The donation of a large grain bin by a North Dakota firm provided not only the literal object, but also a large thematically appropriate setting to house agriculturally related interactive exhibits. Since the donation was secured early in the design phase, the exhibit team was able to seamlessly integrate this iconic object into the design, budget, and schedule.

Figure 21.8. A donated grain bin anchors a series of exhibits that focus on agriculture at the North Dakota Heritage Center & State Museum, Bismarck, North Dakota. COURTESY OF NORTH DAKOTA HERITAGE CENTER & STATE MUSEUM

NOTE

1. Richard Stim, *Getting Permission: How to License & Clear Copyrighted Materials Online and Off*, seventh ed. (Berkeley, CA: NOLO, 2019).

Chapter 22

Effective Exhibition Project Management

Robert LaMarre

In the years since the *Manual of Museum Exhibitions* (second edition) was published, the project management world has experienced a fundamental shift to online platforms. This progression is a natural one for a business process that involves engagement of numbers of stakeholders in disparate locations and working environments. Concurrently, the perceived accountability of individual project managers has also increased as decision makers' expectations for transparent real-time data streams to inform their work processes have grown to an "always on" state, alongside the ubiquitous presence of project information available through increasingly mobile cloud-based systems.

The fundamentals of project management remain unchanged: the development of major museum exhibitions is above all a balancing act. Balancing the needs of curators, designers, conservators, museum administrators, and other stakeholders is fundamentally a project management task—one that has a clear beginning, and theoretically ends with the successful opening of the exhibition to the visiting public, and thereafter when the final checklist items are addressed.

22.1 THE ROLE OF PROJECT MANAGEMENT AND WHY IT IS NEEDED

The role of project management in the museum exhibition context is to help ensure that it is delivered at an acceptable level of quality, on time, and on budget. Responsibility for this task needs to be all-encompassing to be effective, as every variable of an exhibition's development can and must be managed, either on a stand-alone basis or ideally as part of an effectively managed project management process to which the museum is fully committed.

Developing an exhibition is a complex undertaking involving collaboration between internal and external stakeholders, requiring the right mix of creativity and resources to be applied at the right time and in the right fashion. A defined and clear process is needed so that all participants understand the scope of work and the constraints under which the project's challenges must be met. Some basic techniques have been developed and refined over time to optimize this process and applying them and lessons learned will facilitate progress toward overall project goals on exhibition projects large or small.

An effective project management process for an exhibition must first and foremost align with the vision, mission, and mandate of the institution. The process must serve many masters and act as an impartial referee between the many disparate players involved, without choosing sides. On the safe assumption that the institution itself wishes to support the creation of an exhibition of optimal quality on time and on budget, then the process and management personnel involved must always reflect this bigger picture priority.

It may also be safely assumed that each participating department or organization may see their perspective as the highest priority. Project management must always channel this perception in the context of the core objectives of the exhibition.

In many museums curatorial departments have a particularly influential position as they have an established body of intellectual work relating to the particular field of the exhibition. Nonetheless, it is to the overall core objectives that the exhibition must adhere, balancing the intellectual rigor that may be demanded by the curatorial department with the needs and interests of the audience as interpreted by those operational departments responsible for frontline contact with museum visitors. Keeping these and many other conflicting priorities in balance is an essential function of project management.

22.2 A TEAM EFFORT

Successful exhibitions are always the result of a team effort.

At the outset of developing an exhibition, organizations large or small can benefit equally from investing in a project management process. This investment is not financial, rather it is a function that must effectively be "owned" by all concerned departments. This ownership is essential to the overall success of an exhibition development process, as the absence of participation from any responsible department may render the entire approach irrelevant.

It may be anticipated that most museum exhibitions will be developed involving dedicated human resources rather than entirely new staff teams. This reality means that each participating individual can be expected to focus initially on their areas of expertise, ensuring that their specific needs are met. It is a principal task of the appointed project manager to refocus this wide range of visions on the shared core objective.

In a museum without a full-time exhibition development team, the arduous process of bringing together the various involved departments—perhaps first into an informal committee, and thereafter into an effective team—must fall to an appointed team leader, the project manager, with delegated authority and responsibility.

In any progressive museum, administrative leadership can support the exhibition development process through the appointment or designation of the project manager. They may be a current participant in the exhibition development process or may originate from outside the organization. As there are often no specific background or training requirements for project management, candidates from any involved department within the organization may be considered. It is helpful if the candidate has had some previous exposure to at least part of the exhibition development process, however, the museum director or other appointing authority may choose to underline their priorities for a particular exhibition by supporting candidates from a design background for one type of exhibition, candidates from a curatorial background for another, and media specialists or professional project management consultants for still other exhibition projects. If project managers are being appointed on contract, it is essential that they have museum exhibition experience; there are many other types of project management, and their methods may or may not be suitable to the exhibition process, so it is important to specify the need for a consultant or external candidate with specific experience in exhibition project management. However appointed, the priorities of the project manager should always reflect the overall core objectives of the institution.

22.2.1 Attributes of a Successful Project Manager

Successful exhibition project managers often have several attributes in common. Typically, these individuals:

- Are detail-oriented and methodical
- Possess a good spatial awareness and an ability to visualize
- Are comfortable with technology
- Are ready and willing to embrace and facilitate change
- Are patient, supportive, and good team players themselves
- Have a demonstrated commitment for the duration of the project
- Are sensitive to the needs of eventual users (i.e., visitors)
- Are aware of the importance of the content in exhibitions

On larger exhibition projects, it is also quite common to see more than one project manager. This approach will facilitate coordination between components, with each participating department or unit designating one key contact to coordinate their specific contributions to the exhibition development process. Together these individuals then channel their respective units' work into the process, guided by the primary project manager or project director. Each key participant must be empowered to commit their respective units to timelines, budgets, and effective completion of specific tasks. The lines of delegation and reporting must be clear.

Although turnover in key participants and project managers will naturally occur in most projects, continuity is always an important consideration, such that lessons learned early in the process can be applied throughout the project life cycle. This workplace reality of turnover underlines the need for the continuity of a clear and comprehensive approach to project documentation to minimize the prospect of abortive work.

22.3 APPLYING PROJECT MANAGEMENT METHODOLOGY

At any stage in the exhibition development process, the application of effective project management methodologies can be considered. It is never too late to begin, as the process itself adds only a layer of order to any stage. Thus, at all stages:

- Effective project management of the content development stage can help ensure that all needed content is captured and accurately represented in the design stage.
- Effective project management of the design stage can help ensure that both new exhibition elements and base-building factors are properly coordinated.
- Effective project management of the production/fabrication and installation process, both off-site and on-site, can help ensure that the finished exhibition reflects both the required content and design.

Effectively realizing the purpose of project management—to facilitate on-time and on-budget completion of the exhibition at the highest level of quality—relies on four fundamental project management tools:

1. Undertaking project coordination meetings
2. Adopting standardized forms and templates
3. Developing and managing comprehensive task lists and project schedules
4. The provision of timely project overview or dashboard reports

22.3.1 Project Coordination Meetings

The most important activity in effective project management is the traditional coordination meeting. The best and clearest schedules and reports have little meaning if face-to-face communication does not occur so that all aspects of a particular challenge can be explored by project participants. Most important at the outset of a project, and again toward its completion, coordination meetings are sometimes the only way that project participants can meet and report on progress and task completion.

There is no set agenda for such meetings and review processes, however most such processes tend to begin with broad topics and move to specific exhibition site matters as exhibition design moves into exhibition production/fabrication and eventually installation. Individual team members participate as needed for their areas of responsibility and all participants are fully expected to take responsibility for the proper execution of agreed tasks within agreed budgets and timeframes. As with any effective internal organization and process, project participants must be fully empowered to act within their respective areas and not be continuously returning to their line supervisors for authorization.

To minimize meeting fatigue and to promote cooperation, the effective project manager must ensure that no unnecessary meetings take place, or their importance to individual team members will understandably wane. It can be expected that individual project participants have many such departmental or administrative meetings to attend, and everyone's time is equally precious and cannot be squandered for a project manager to retain credibility. In a typical two-year planning cycle for a museum exhibition, it could be fairly anticipated that the following will occur:

- A series of start-up coordination meetings may be needed within a short period of time.
- They would be followed by regular, perhaps monthly, coordination meetings booked well in advance for a period of at least a few months.
- Thereafter, increased frequency to meetings every two weeks will likely take place at a logical point in the schedule.
- As the opening day approaches, weekly coordination meetings become the norm, along with more regimented topic-by-topic meetings that may allow some individuals to attend for only their requisite (e.g., twenty minutes out of a two-hour meeting) on a scheduled basis, facilitated by the project manager.
- Checklist meetings where the baseline management activities move from general and location-based discussions to individual issues to be addressed one at a time may continue well after opening day as owner concerns, consultants, and contractors' potential claims are addressed on an item-by-item basis.

Communication is the key to successful project management, and meetings are a critical tool for maintaining team coordination and cooperation.

22.3.2 Standard Forms and Templates

Project management did not originate in the museum sector, for many functions there is no need to reinvent the wheel. Many standard forms and templates exist within organizations—or are otherwise freely available on the internet—that can be effectively adapted for use in exhibition project management. Such forms may include:

- Meeting attendance sheets
- Meeting minutes templates
- Management authorization forms
- Content/Design approval forms
- Building/Gallery handover inspection forms
- Material/Sample submittal forms
- Prefabrication approval forms
- Request for Information forms

Effective Exhibition Project Management

- Contract Change/Variation approval forms
- Installation inspection approval forms
- Deficiency lists/Deficiency forms
- Final sign-off forms

Assigned personnel and their respective superiors can change during implementation, and human memory has its limits. Regular and routine signoffs as well as detailed documentation of the project help to ensure that progress can continue unhindered toward the core objectives of realizing a world-class exhibition.

22.3.2.1 Developing the Task List (Work Breakdown Structure)

Exhibition project management is one of only a few processes where those responsible for implementation can effectively choose when to stop managing. In theory, a project manager could continue delineating tasks at greater and greater levels of detail to the point where the information becomes overwhelming and the timeframes too short to effectively progress the work. The project manager must always keep the bigger picture and core objectives in mind, and not overwhelm either the tools or the project participants with too much detail. This risk of overdetailing applies most specifically to the identification of activities or tasks within a given scope of work, and the organization of that work into manageable components. To be most effective, an agreed hierarchy of tasks at a manageable scale should be determined as early in the process as possible so that those overseeing the project manager are satisfied with the levels of detail in project reports.

The entire exhibition development process can be broken down into intelligent step-by-step phases and the project manager can decide just how detailed that breakdown should be. Early in the exhibition development process, it is generally recommended that primary level activities or tasks are identified, such as:

- Exhibition planning
- Exhibition design
- Exhibition off-site production/fabrication
- Exhibition on-site installation/commissioning

Following such an approach will allow a logical progression of secondary and tertiary level tasks to eventually be added to each primary task, such as:

- Exhibition planning
    - Develop interpretive plan
    - Identify objects for display
    - Draft exhibition text
- Exhibition design
    - Verify available space

- Develop initial concept
- Develop schematic design
• Exhibition off-site production/fabrication
  - Order materials
  - Fabricate components
  - Assemble exhibition modules
• Exhibition on-site installation/commissioning
  - Undertake site survey
  - Install basic floor, wall, and ceiling finishes
  - Install exhibition modules

This approach may continue with fourth, fifth, and sixth level-plus tasks as may be required to reflect the desired level of detail in managing the process, creating a skeleton work breakdown structure to which time requirements and resources can eventually be attached. The possibility of overmanaging the work becomes more evident as these task levels cascade into work breakdowns of ever-greater detail, such that managing the task list itself becomes unwieldy and consumes too much time for the project manager. A disciplined project manager will choose a level of detail that allows for sufficient clarity on project and contractual progress and satisfies stakeholders who are outside the day-to-day involvement in the project but may have accountability for its successful completion.

Garbage in, garbage out! Any task list or work breakdown structure will only be as useful as the information entered into it. It should always be recognized that developing the task list is only an organizational tool when used in moderation; the real work of actually completing the tasks remains ahead. Building and maintaining this work breakdown structure is an ongoing priority for the project manager as it provides a complete picture of the overall process—a picture that is relatively easy to understand for others not involved in the project—individual tasks can be added at any time to reflect new information about the project or new levels of detail desired in reports.

22.3.2.2 Developing a Gantt Chart

Once a skeleton work breakdown structure has been developed, then the task list can be readily integrated into one or more management and reporting tools in common use, such as a **Gantt chart**. The Gantt chart is used widely in the project management field, across many industries throughout the private and public sectors worldwide. Capturing key project data and displaying it in a useful and relatively easy-to-understand format is what makes the Gantt chart the de facto standard in project management.

The Gantt chart was first developed by mechanical engineer and management consultant Henry L. Gantt in the first quarter of the twentieth century. It is essentially a type of bar chart that illustrates a project schedule. It includes the start and finish dates of the terminal elements and summary elements of a project, including assigned resources.

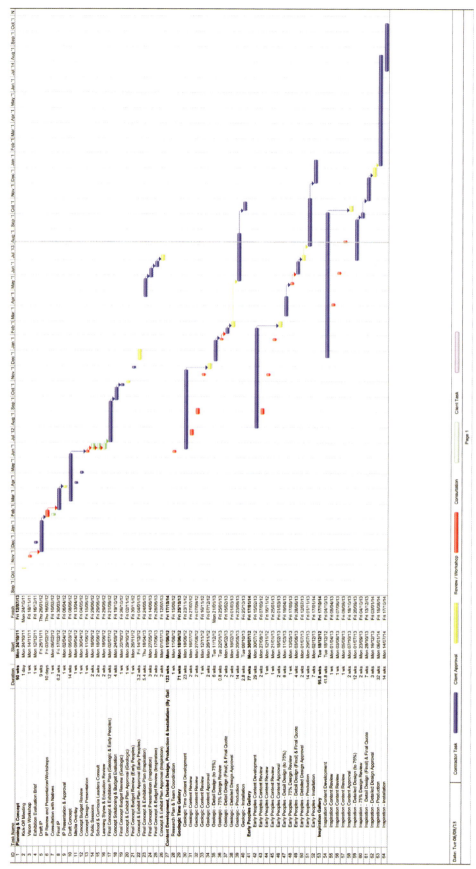

Figure 22.1. Sample Gantt chart. LORD CULTURAL RESOURCES

The creation of a Gantt chart typically facilitates the assignment of timeframes and resources to individual tasks. When used in real time as a management tool, rather than only as a look-ahead reporting tool, a complete Gantt chart with resources assigned can provide a project manager with an effective high-level picture of the entire project. When presented on one single chart, this picture allows a project manager to interpret impending deadlines, new task starts, and resource requirements—all essential to keeping a project on schedule and on budget.

Key variables that an effective Gantt chart for an exhibition project would feature include:

- Current date
- Task name
- Task level (according to the hierarchy of tasks; original data entry should allow all primary tasks to be represented on page one of the Gantt chart, with secondary or tertiary tasks on subsequent pages)
- Task start date
- Task duration
- Milestones (e.g., reference dates)
- Dependencies across tasks
- Financial resources
- Human resources
- Material resources

Other key data points that can be extrapolated from the above variables include, perhaps most importantly, **task finish date(s)**. If a task start date and task duration are known, then the task finish date appears automatically when these first two variables are entered. Conversely, if a task finish date is absolute (e.g., an announced opening day) and a required task duration is known, then the Gantt chart can be used effectively to work backward to calculate a task start date in order to achieve the required task finished date. These principles apply to all tasks that might be included in a Gantt chart, be they primary or subsidiary tasks.

More simplified Gantt charts can be produced manually or using basic productivity computer software packages such as Microsoft Office or freeware such as Google Docs. These manual techniques can effectively demonstrate the status of a project, what proportion of the overall scope is yet to be completed, and how much time is available to complete the work. In addition, in such charts dependencies can be readily shown through simple color coding or basic graphics. In project management terms, dependencies are relationships between tasks that require an individual task to be started, progressed, or completed for another dependent task to progress. In a complete work breakdown structure for a given project, it is the management of these dependencies that is best represented on a Gantt chart, and it is the ability to effectively automate these dependencies that has created a demand for dedicated project management applications and collaboration suites.

22.3.2.3 Project Management Software and Collaboration Tools

More experienced users and those engaged on more complicated exhibition projects may wish to consider dedicated project management applications such as Microsoft Project or Smartsheet and/or online collaboration tools such as Basecamp or Asana that can be implemented on exhibition projects of any scale. Each application offers varying degrees of user-friendliness for all skill levels, and the ability to integrate and import data from/export data to other applications for higher level project review or reporting. Key to the practicality of collaboration suite applications are macro-type custom interfaces and functionality that can effectively assign tasks to participants within the system, which then tracks and logs task completion, changes in dependencies, and similar project developments with notification functions for both participants and supervisors helping to ensure performance is nominal to profile.

Once again, a key challenge for the project manager can be deciding when to stop managing—finding the right level of detail in identified tasks and ensuring that the scope and parameters for each task can be effectively identified and managed. As mentioned above, the real-time automation capabilities of project management software have made it possible for project managers to apply the capabilities of the software more effectively as a management tool. The software can quickly recalculate data points such as task end dates when task durations change, or through clear display of task dependencies, which demonstrate the knock-on effects of missing key project milestones. Implementing even a minor change in a manual Gantt chart created with Microsoft Excel can mean laborious and painstaking double-checking and methodical review, whereas one created in Microsoft Project can be changeable in seconds with only a few keystrokes.

Another benefit of project management software or online collaboration suites is the easy ability to dedicate resources to individual tasks—be they financial, material, or human resources. Once baselines are established and the resource data entered, a project manager can see at a glance how much time or money has been spent on one particular task, or how many additional specialist personnel may be required to be engaged to undertake another, at what point in the future they may be required, and for what duration.

On large projects, such as the development of an entirely new gallery wing or entirely new museum, it is not uncommon to see five hundred primary tasks with five thousand or more subsidiary tasks identified and managed, Enterprise-level project management software packages such as Oracle Primavera P6 and Oracle Aconex Project Controls are in common use on such larger scale initiatives, especially in the engineering and construction sector. A variety of dedicated project management software packages are available in the marketplace, catering to all experience and skill levels and all require some degree of hands-on user training or practice in order to be effective. In general, the more sophisticated the software package, the more diverse the data management capabilities, and the larger and more complex the projects that can be more effectively managed with the help of these tools.

As the project management sector has developed, so have the software tools created to support it. Today, it is common on major projects that all stakeholders are invited to collaborate online in a project's development through cloud-based collaboration tools. With these tools not only Gantt charts and related reports are available online, but also contracts and correspondence between project participants are available to all authorized users at any time, a valued primary function of enterprise-scale applications such as Oracle Aconex Project Controls in particular.

The successful project management of any exhibition of more than one month's duration would likely benefit from the availability of project management software or online collaboration tools. Any computer-literate project manager can typically begin using the software after a short seminar or a series of online tutorials, and the time saved by using the software will more than make up for the up-front investment in software, acquiring the license, and undergoing the necessary training. One software license can be used to manage multiple projects concurrently as well as new projects in the future. Ultimate project needs, abilities of the project manager, and common sense should prevail when selecting such tools.

As online collaboration applications are becoming more ubiquitous across enterprises, the following is generally recommended:

- When working within larger organizations, project managers may wish to consider any legacy or enterprise-wide collaboration suites that feature project management/reporting functionality, as it may be anticipated that a large proportion of project participants may already be familiar with their functionality and limitations, and resultantly the project management outputs can effectively integrate with enterprise-wide reporting structures.

- In smaller organizations, or organizations with no legacy systems to consider, the exact functionality of a selected project management or collaboration application should be fit-for-purpose. If it is likely that only the project manager(s) themselves would be entering key project management data and/or producing project management reports, then the simplest and resultantly less-expensive tools would perhaps be the most suitable, as in no circumstance should working with the application suite being considered become more complicated than the project being managed.

22.3.2.4 Project Overview or Dashboard Reports

As one of the key purposes of engagement of an exhibition project manager is to assure the museum's leadership that a given exhibition project is being undertaken on time, on budget, and at an agreed level of quality, the reality of most projects is that task lists and their integration into charts are most often used only as reporting tools, rather than management tools. As project managers typically need to undertake many of the detailing of individual tasks themselves, as well as managing the process, this is not a bad thing, as long as the information presented in the reports is accurate.

Perhaps one of the most important and popular innovations that has been driven by generations of development of online project management and reporting tools is that of the project overview or dashboard report. These reports have become a fundamental part of project reporting across multiple industries wherein external nontechnical committees, and commercial managers in particular, can effectively assess a project's adherence to contractually agreed milestones, while project managers can underline key project risks and compliance with project terms by all participants, both client side and contractor side as appropriate.

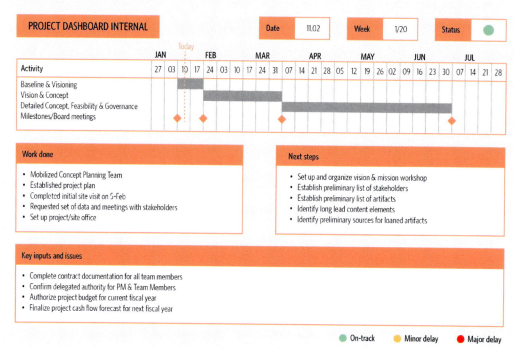

Figure 22.2. Example project dashboard (internal). LORD CULTURAL RESOURCES

Figure 22.3. Example project dashboard (commercial). LORD CULTURAL RESOURCES

22.4 CERTIFICATIONS AND CONTINUOUS LEARNING

As the project management sector matures, Project Management Institute (PMI), Prince2, or similar certifications remain a requested minimum qualification by employers or clients looking to fill full-time, large-scale project management positions. In the case of the engineering and construction sector PMI certification is commonly a "must have" for serious candidates.

The ever-changing nature of project management, typically undertaken in a high-energy atmosphere, has made it an attractive career option for line managers in museums looking to make a change within their respective organizations. In general, the larger and more complicated the project, the more senior level the professional that is required in the project management chair. As the largest projects often require the services of multiple project managers, all led by a project or program (group of projects) director, formal management training may indeed boost a candidate's project management aptitudes simply through exposure to different ways of thinking and case study explorations of how to improve effectiveness in a project management role.

Undergraduate, graduate, and postgraduate level degrees exist for project management, as such a practical option for midcareer professionals would involve certification through one or more project management industry organizations. At present, no internationally accepted certification exists for project management; however, in North America the PMI offers a wide range of certifications, as does the Six Sigma Organization through its program "Lean Project Management." In the United Kingdom, Prince2 was originally developed as a national government standard, and as such its certification is widely recognized and available.

22.5 COMPLETING THE TASKS

Depending on the scale of the project, the project manager may be required to undertake all the necessary planning, management, and reporting on progress to the museum's leadership as well as to execute individual tasks. Assuming the project manager is qualified to do so, issuing the necessary instructions to other project participants to execute their respective scopes, which together make up the entire project, might also be part of the project manager's responsibilities. Contrary to the popular saying, in exhibition project management the whole is precisely the sum of its parts—with the "parts" being the tasks identified as necessary to complete the project. A great Gantt chart showing a clear task list and clear dates and dependencies serves little purpose if the work itself does not get completed.

An effective project manager will allow individual specialists and subject matter experts to do what they do best within a project framework that works to achieve the core objectives. Individual participants in a project may or may not see their own strengths and weaknesses in executing their respective tasks, and it is the job of the project manager to ensure that each participant has the necessary support to meet the project goals and execute assigned tasks within agreed timeframes and resource allocations. A continuous process of task prioritization is a big part of the juggling act of an effective exhibition project manager, for example, finalization of an exhibit text that is to form part of one graphic panel may only affect the production of that panel, or the exhibit text may need to be translated so that it also becomes part of a multimedia exhibition that needs to be produced in multiple languages, edited, and programmed into a touchscreen system, in which case delay of that exhibit text can be a show stopper. It is the responsibility of the effective project manager to balance priorities on the project from start to finish.

The effective project manager helps to set the scene for every member of the team to achieve their individual goals in the context of overall project success. Within the project scope it is the project manager's role to:

- Prioritize to achieve the core objectives
- Establish the project framework
- Ensure adequate wiggle room (in the schedule and the budget)
- Dacilitate communication between participants
- Acknowledge and embrace bureaucratic checks and balances
- Remove roadblocks to cooperation
- Support individual goals and engender mutual respect
- Identify and manage dependencies
- Analyze all opportunities for improvement
- Optimize the use of project management tools

As Harold Kerzner wrote in his 1985 textbook, *Project Management: A System Approach to Planning, Scheduling and Controlling*:

> The Project Manager's job is not an easy one. Project managers may have increasing "responsibility," but very little authority. This lack of authority can force them to "negotiate" with upper-level management as well as functional management for control of company resources. They may often be treated as outsiders by the formal organization.[1]

The priorities of the administrative leadership of a museum are effectively demonstrated by their choice of project managers—be they internal candidates, outsiders, long-term employees, or term contractors. No matter their background, skill set, or previous priorities, the effective exhibition project manager must embrace the core objectives and build their management approach to achieve them.

NOTE

1. Harold Kerzner, *Project Management: A Systems Approach to Planning, Scheduling and Controlling*, 11th edition (New York: Wiley, 2013).

Chapter 23

Conclusion

The Future of Exhibition-Making

Gail Dexter Lord

In the seven years since the previous edition of *The Manual of Museum Exhibitions*, we all have a shared experience of a deadly pandemic, economic hardship, social reckoning,[1] and periodic closing of museums and many other valued organizations, places, and events. We have also witnessed a massive surge of skepticism of experts, denial of facts, and the confounding of subjective belief with objective fact. At the same time, museums retained their place as one of society's more trusted organizations.[2] This experience challenges us to think about museum exhibition-making from some different perspectives.

EXHIBITIONS FROM EVIDENCE TO MEANING-MAKING

Museums, while slow moving, have proven over their brief history to be adaptable. The unique function of museums is to preserve physical evidence in every field of human knowledge: historical records whether on tablets or the rings of trees; specimens in glass jars and glass slides; objects from original works of art to steam locomotives; and the less tangible expressions of cuisine, music, dance, and traditions. It's clear that in a digital age when many of our decisions, ideas, and attitudes are guided by algorithms that are based on words, preserving the physical evidence is more important than ever.

This evidence is continually being studied and reevaluated because human knowledge is always growing. Furthermore, the questions posed by researchers, students, and the general public change as society changes. There is a sense in which questions are social in origin. For example, gender equality has given rise to questions about where the great art by women is produced. Just a few decades ago, the question was not asked because it was socially accepted that there were no great women artists. Exhibition-making responds to questions that arise in society by research that leads to connecting and reconnecting the evidence museums collect in response to new questions that people pose based on their interest and experience. The much sought after "relevance" of museums derives from an institutional understanding and willingness to tackle interesting and important questions. This mode of museum expression is often referred to as storytelling; but I prefer the term "meaning-making" to distinguish what museums do from fiction.

The delicate balance of this meaning-making process—evidence, research, social questions, research, selection of artifacts, creation of narrative—can be destabilized by many forces: on one side, lack of funding to preserve the evidence and conduct research;[3] and on the other, failure to hear and respond to new questions arising from social change. This failure (or refusal) to hear the questions from new social forces leads to an inevitable result: the same old exhibition stories being dressed up in new clothing and technology. Is it any wonder that many people do not attend?

Those who enjoy the old stories and who have acquired the skills to make their own connections and meanings enjoy going to museums over and over. Thanks to increasing levels of education and mass travel (until the pandemic) this has led to rising museum participation rates, which is a very good thing indeed.

MUSEUM EXHIBITIONS BOTH ON-SITE AND ONLINE

The requirements of social distancing due to the pandemic, closures, and fear of public space radically speeded up the transition of museum exhibitions from the three-dimensional space of the gallery to two-dimensional screen space. Many museum activities were offered online including tours of permanent galleries and some blockbuster exhibitions, most notably *Artemisia* at the National Gallery in London.[3] In city history and culture museums like The Historic New Orleans Collection, website visits for programs and illustrated stories of current relevance soon outnumbered on-site visits.[4] Given the success of these initiatives, it is highly likely that in the future postpandemic, museum exhibitions will circulate equally online as on-site, making them more accessible to more people and maximizing the benefits of the large investment that changing exhibitions require. Many exhibitions are limited in the number of venues they can tour due to high transportation and insurance costs and limitations on artifact loans—both of which can be overcome through "virtual tours." The online exhibition represents both quantitative and qualitative transformation for museum exhibitions.

The quantitative aspect is that many more millions of people who live far from where museums are located will be able to experience exhibitions. As broadband access and speed increases, people living in rural areas (and people living in cities who find going to the museum too expensive and intimidating or those who cannot visit for reasons of health and mobility) will have access to great museum storytelling, possibly in 3D, but most certainly in 360-degree high definition. Those of us in the Global South will be able to see important exhibitions without traveling to former colonial capitals. Those of us in the Global North can begin to understand how objects and their meanings are communicated by people in the places where they were created. We might gain some humility around our aesthetic and ideological presumptions, which would not be noticed unless you saw the objects in the exhibition setting.

Seeing collections in the exhibition setting is the key. The online exhibition will be a qualitative change because the museum exhibition creates a whole new layer of content—new content being the meaning that is created when the museum connects the evidence, the knowledge about the evidence, and the societal questions they to choose to answer.

The first step was when museums began to put their collections online in the early 1990s,[5] which has been very helpful especially in giving people the world over the agency to access this inventory of human achievement for many uses such as research, restitution, inclusion in exhibitions, and enjoyment. Today, access to collections is even more sophisticated as demonstrated by the V&A Museum's online exploration of Raphael's Cartoons.[6] In 2019, the V&A worked with the Factum Foundation for Digital Technology in Conservation to carry out an ultra high resolution recording of the seven cartoons in color, 3D, and infrared. Online visitors can interact and manipulate the digital recordings to see beneath the layers and what is visible to the naked eye; compare and contrast the cartoons; and discover the faint adjustments Raphael made as he perfected his art.

Placing exhibitions online is even more transformative because it transmits the stories museums tell when they connect the object, specimens, and works of art; it opens a new level of content that is beautiful, exciting, dynamic, and perhaps controversial because every exhibition tries to answer some questions that came from some people somewhere.

SHIFTS IN MUSEUM THINKING

One of the major shifts in museological thinking of the last forty years has been characterized as "the rise of the visitor." Museums are places that not only preserve collections but serve valuable educational and community-building functions by creating spaces for reflection, conversation, and creative and critical thinking.

Engaging twenty-first-century museum exhibition visitors both on-site in the galleries and remotely online requires some shifts in museum thinking, such as:

- Incorporating partnerships with both local and global community stakeholders and professionals in the exhibition planning process
- Ensuring that the questions to be answered by the exhibition reflect a diversity of perspectives
- Insisting that museum exhibition staff include Black, Indigenous, and people of color
- Creating an empathetic environment and social spaces for on-site and online exhibitions where participants of all ages and abilities can connect and probe more deeply
- Situating museum exhibitions as part of a broader learning ecology that includes schools, home, libraries, public health and wellness, media, and social services
- Linking exhibitions to mass media story-telling vehicles such as webisodes, streaming service, radio, and television
- Enabling participation, co-creation, and collaboration in the planning and experience of museum exhibits

Since the pandemic of 2020, which saw both the closing of museums and reduced on-site attendance as well as the explosion of online educational and entertainment content, many museums are struggling to find the right place for their content. The message is clear: people are looking for an exhibition experience that is worth their attention—an experience that is personal, responsive, changing, and changeable, with inclusive content that values their input on-site or off through social media and crowdsourcing. Ever increasing attendance at blockbuster exhibitions tells us that visitors still want visual access to the rare, famous, and infamous stories of humanity that are told on a giant three-dimensional platform that only the largest museums can provide. The technology is almost there for these exhibitions to be experienced online around the world. Museums of all sizes can engage with the online world and take their experiences to people who may never have entered their doors and now can gain confidence in doing so from prior digital access.

Historically, museums have always been early adapters of new technology, from electric lights to iPods, and that is largely because museum workers have a unique quality: we are equal part scholars, educators, and entertainers. If we did not value scholarship, we would not be the trusted source of information that we are. Study after study has demonstrated that museums are trusted more than the internet, more than TV, more than university professors, and more than books.[7] Museum exhibitions not only reflect scholarship, but they are also profoundly committed to conveying the complexity of meaning, often from multiple perspectives. Studies on the impact of the internet reveal that it is becoming a tool for reinforcing our personal opinions as algorithms push us from link to link rather than challenging them. Creativity and innovation depend crucially on the critical thinking space provided in museum exhibitions. If we were not entertainers as well as educators, we would not create exhibitions with all their opening excitement, risk, and novelty. There are easier ways to communicate new discoveries in archaeology than working with exhibition designers and fabricators, not to speak of the lighting experts and exhibition evaluators. But three-dimensional museum exhibitions reinforced by digital media are more than worth the trouble they take.

In closing, I encourage all readers to find in themselves the balance between commitment to evidence, dedication to research, and openness to different perspectives—mixed in with a big dose of "shameless entertainer." Easy to say, but hard to do in times of rapid change and financial constraints. But has it ever been an easy path in this unusual field of museum exhibitions? Museum exhibitions have always succeeded in attracting top talent from every field of human endeavor. That talent pool has now expanded locally and globally to communities, regions, and countries where museum exhibitions are relatively new, which means that the public will challenge us in more ways than ever, but we must listen, hear, and respond to their questions. The basic requirement for a positive future for museum exhibitions is that museum leadership, governance, and staff embrace new voices and perspectives.

NOTES

1. Referencing social justice movements including truth and reconciliation with Indigenous people, Black Lives Matter, and climate change and the growth of authoritarianism both locally and among elected governments worldwide.
2. See chapter 2 by Brad King
3. The National Gallery, London, had its long-planned exhibition of the great seventeenth-century artist Artemisia Gentileschi interrupted by pandemic closures. This show was of exceptional interest because her works have been appreciated recently due to feminist voices in formerly male-dominated

art world that basically ignored them. Artemisia is seen as a hero for the bravery in her life, her subject, and her outlook as well as the beauty of paintings. The National Gallery responded by making curatorial tours available online and successfully charging for them. See www.nationalgallery.org.uk/exhibitions/artemisia.
4. The Historic New Orleans Collection, www.hnoc.org
5. Maria Piacente, "Surf's Up: Museums and the World Wide Web," (master's thesis, University of Toronto, 1996). Museums were just beginning to explore the power of the internet and early experiments with outreach, interactivity, and visitor information.
6. "Explore the Raphael Cartoons," V&A, https://www.vam.ac.uk/articles/explore-the-raphael-cartoons.
7. See Brad King, chapter 2.

Glossary

Access: in the context of exhibition facilities, access refers to the various means of ingress and egress for people, collections, materials, supplies, and refuse; often used to refer to the need for inclusive access for all visitors, including those with disabilities.

Accession Number: the unique identifier assigned to every artifact in a museum's collection.

Adjacency: refers to museum spaces that need to be adjoining or near each other for the proper ordering of activities relating to all aspects of exhibitions.

Affective Learning: an attribute of human experience that describes feelings or emotions and sometimes attitudes or values; often used to describe learning objectives or outcomes in opposition to formal learning that takes place in a classroom.

Artifact Data Sheet: a tool for documenting and tracking objects and works of art selected for an exhibition.

Associative Collecting: museum objects that are acquired only when they have a direct association with a specific location, person, or event.

Audience Fragmentation (also Audience Segmentation): refers to the categorization of visitor motivation driven by preference, personality traits, attitudes, lifestyles, and values.

Audience Research: The systematic gathering of information (descriptive, psychological, contextual) about visitors or audiences.

Augmented Reality (AR): a technology that superimposes a computer-generated image on a user's view of the real world, thus providing a composite view

Bid Bond: guarantees that a proposing entity will go to contract if awarded a project. Bond is usually a percentage of the project budget.

Benchmarking Study: a management tool that examines "best practices" in other museums regarding such elements as exhibition philosophy, decision-making systems, resource allocation, and evaluation.

Building Management System (BMS): is a system with related controls and monitoring devices that manages ventilation, lighting, power systems, and fire and security systems.

Business Plan: a document that projects the viability of a project under certain conditions or assumptions, which in the museum context may include collections analysis; a public programming plan; statements of mission, mandate, and purpose; recommendations as to institutional status and structure; space and facilities requirements; staffing requirements; market analysis; marketing and operational recommendations; projections of capital and operating expenditure and revenues; and an implementation schedule.

Capital Costs: in the context of exhibition development refers to the one-time cost of designing and building an exhibition; includes interior fit-out, demolition costs, along with new construction or renovation costs of a gallery space.

Centralized Control Installation: in the context of audiovisual hardware, that type of installation in which all the main sources of media delivery are centrally located within one room adjacent to but separate from the galleries.

Change Order (or Variation Order): a contract document issued by the client to the contractor or contractor to the client, authorizing an alteration in the original design or specifications of a building or exhibition under construction or installation.

Circulation: refers to the efficient flow of people and materials between all the spaces in which exhibition activities take place.

"Clean" Workshops: areas located in a museum's nonpublic collection zone where art, artifacts, and specimens are cleaned, mounted, or (in the case of artworks) matted or fitted to frames.

Cocreated/Cocurated Exhibitions: are projects for which members of the public collaborate with the museum to develop an exhibition.

Collection Analysis: quantitative and qualitative study of the contents of a museum collection in meaningful groups or classifications, and of the spatial and facilities requirements of the collection, including projection and provision for its future growth over a stated time.

Collection Policy: statement of the subject matter of a collection, its temporal and geographical limits, and any requirements as to material, conditions, size, or other factors for inclusion in the collection, together with the terms, procedures, and forms under which acquisition (gift, loan, bequest, purchase) or deaccessioning may occur.

Color Perception: refers to social, emotional, and cultural meanings communicated by color.

Color Rendering Index (CRI): the degree to which a museum's lighting system can render colors accurately. A CRI of 100 equals daylight.

Commissioning: the process of verifying that building systems have been constructed according to contract documents, work properly at the time of substantial completion, and continue to function as designed within their periods of warranty; additionally, commissioning ensures that all warranty information and operating manuals have been given to the museum's building supervisors and that they have been appropriately trained to operate all systems.

Community Consultation (or Public Engagement): a process that involves gathering content and input from a defined community or broad public to inform the development of an exhibition.

Compactor Storage: a museum storage system employing storage units that can be moved to allow access when required and then "compacted" to occupy a minimum floor area.

Competitive Bidding: comparison of tenders submitted by contractors for work specified; the tender selected usually being the lowest in other sectors, but not always in the museum field due to the need for museum standards of quality.

Conceptual Design: a design stage that describes the concepts and general layout of the design, as well as how the design will meet program needs.

Condition Report: a highly detailed statement of the condition of a borrowed work of art or artifact, prepared immediately upon its extraction from the packing crate by the curator, conservator, or registrar who oversees the temporary exhibition. Condition reports should also include photographs.

Conservation: maximizing the endurance or minimizing the deterioration of an object through time, with as little change to the object as possible.

Contingency Budget: an allocated sum or percentage of the budget to account for unanticipated costs, changes, and escalations throughout the life of the project.

Construction Budget: the sum established by the owner as available for construction of the project, including contingencies for bidding to contractors and for changes during construction.

Construction Documents: drawings and specifications created by a designer that set forth in detail requirements for the construction of the project.

Content Management System: software (authored) that allows the input, editing, and modifying of content. This is usually performed from a centralized or remote location but may also be local (located on the same machine as the interactive).

Contractor (or General Contractor): individual or company who undertakes to fulfill a contract to build or renovate a structure.

Correlated Color Temperature (CCT): a measure of the color appearance of a light source, expressed in kelvins and determined by comparing that source with a theoretical black body radiator. Various types of discharge lamps, especially fluorescent lamps, are classified according to their CCT.

Couriers: museum personnel—usually curators, registrars, or conservators—who often accompany major works of art that have been loaned out to other institutions as part of a traveling exhibition program.

Critical Path Scheduling: the process of scheduling tasks and milestones that must occur in a certain order.

Crowdsourcing: the practice of obtaining needed services, ideas, or content by soliciting contributions from a large group of people, and especially from an online community, rather than from sources.

Curatorship: that aspect of a museum's functions that is centrally concerned with the development, preservation, and interpretation of its collections.

Decentralized Control Installation: in the context of audiovisual hardware, that type of installation in which all the equipment is located within the exhibition galleries (i.e., there is no separate control center).

Decolonization: a process that institutions undergo to expand the perspectives they portray beyond those of the dominant cultural group, particularly white colonizers

Deficiencies List: a process whereby the contractor and client (museum) identify any items in the exhibition that need to be corrected prior to final sign-off and payment.

Desiccant: a chemical compound that tends to attract and hold moisture from surrounding moist air and liberating moisture in the presence of dry air; useful in controlling environments within a vitrine.

Design Artifact: also known as **Design Specimen** or **Design Work of Art**, is the largest object that a museum expects to store or display.

Design Brief: a document that informs potential designers, specialists, and contractors of the requirements of a project.

Design-Build: a method of project delivery in which the owner contracts directly with a single entity that is responsible for both design and construction services for a construction project. Also known as a **Turnkey Project or Contract**.

Design Criteria: a set of principles that describe, first, the desired result about a museum's spaces and facilities, and second, the means of evaluating success in achieving that result. *Subjective* design criteria suggest the character of the building and its interior spaces in conceptual and qualitative terms; *objective* design criteria provide a quantitative or instrumental guide to the architects, engineers, building contractors and exhibit designers working on the project.

"Design Day" Figure: the number of people likely to be in the building on a busy day.

Design Development or **Detailed Design:** The designer prepares more detailed drawings and finalizes all plans and specifications for construction of the exhibition. Also included is an outline of the construction specifications listing the major materials to be used.

Design Noise Criteria: a rating (expressed NC) that allows comparison of allowable noise levels in various building spaces. For example, a rating of NC 30 is usual for exhibition and research areas, NC 35 for related public areas, and NC 25 for auditoria.

Didactic Displays/Exhibits: displays that are primarily static such as cases filled with artifacts, paintings hung on walls, and large-scale graphics.

"Dirty" Workshops: areas located in nonpublic, non-collection zones of a museum where carpentry, painting, and other processes that might be detrimental to the museum objects are undertaken.

Display Density: expressed either as how many objects are on display per square foot or meter of gallery space, or vice versa, how many square feet or meters per object on display. Display density varies not only with the size of the objects on display, but also with the mode of exhibition used and the mode of visitor apprehension that is preferred for each section of the collection.

E-Learning: learning conducted via electronic media, typically the internet.

Evaluation: staff assessment of an exhibition's likelihood of, or actual, success. The process runs according to an iterative cycle of front-end, formative, and summative evaluation.

Exhibition Brief: states the primary subject matter of the exhibition, the main communication objectives, and the projected target audience and provides a summary of the overall interpretive and visual strategies. Sometimes called a **Curatorial Brief**.

Exhibition Concept: the core idea or thesis for the exhibition.

Exhibition Policy: a comprehensive statement of the purpose and philosophy of a museum's permanent and temporary exhibition program.

Fabrication or **Exhibition Construction:** refers to the process of producing and constructing exhibitions.

Facilities Programming: a broad planning activity usually undertaken by a specialist consultant to determine the facilities required by an institution undergoing physical expansion or alteration, including the design and performance criteria of those facilities, as well as social and behavioural factors.

Fit-Out: a term that describes the interior finishing of a gallery in preparation for installation of exhibits. This may include floor and wall finishes, electrical points, and lighting.

Floor Loading Standards: the standard to which a museum must be built to withstand the downward forces, measured in kN/m^2, produced by artifacts, exhibits, displays, furniture, etc.

Formative Evaluation: provides information about how a program or exhibit can be improved and occurs while a project is under development. It is a process of systematically checking assumptions and products in order to make changes that improve design or implementation.

Footcandle: nonmetric unit for measuring light intensity (10.76 lux = 1 footcandle).

Free-Standing Case: a five-sided case in which one of the sides serves as a door, mounted on a base, or on tubular legs. The case top can be glass or acrylic and may or may not include integrated lighting.

Front-End Evaluation: provides background information for future project planning and development. It is typically designed to determine an audience's general knowledge, questions, expectations, experiences, learning styles, and concerns regarding a topic or theme.

Functional Brief or **Functional Program:** a brief, written in nontechnical user language, describing the functions required for the building and its systems and facilities. "Brief" and "Program" are British and American terminologies, respectively.

Functional Requirement: the facilities required for a project, stated in nontechnical user language.

Gantt Chart: a form of project management tool that identifies tasks, resources, and timeframes.

Geolocation: the process or technique of identifying the geographical location of a person or device by means of digital information processed via the internet.

Gesture Technology: technologies that facilitate user interface without the need for touch or audio. Visitors use gestural patterns (such as arms and hands) to interface with media systems.

Graphic Data Sheet: a tool for documenting and tracking all images and graphics to be used in an exhibition.

Graphic Design: the art of communication, stylizing, and problem-solving using type and image.

Green Design: in the context of exhibitions, a process that identifies sustainable materials and constructions methods.

Gross Area: total of all the space allocations in a building program or brief space list, multiplied by a percentage factor to allow for thickness of walls, mechanical-electrical service areas, and both horizontal and vertical circulation space. The proportion of gross to net area is often in the range of 1.3 or 1.4 to 1.

Hands-On Displays/Exhibits: low-tech interactive exhibits that incorporate mechanical devices to deliver content and invite visitor feedback.

Holdback: a percentage of the value of a construction or renovation contract withheld from the contractor until substantial completion.

HVAC: heating, ventilation, and air conditioning.

IES: Illuminating Engineering Society; professional society for lighting designers and engineers.

Installation: the process of setting up exhibits in a museum gallery.

Image Resolution: refers to the pixel count of a digital image.

IMAX: a motion picture system that uses a film frame ten times the size of a conventional 35 mm photographic frame and three times larger than a normal 70 mm movie frame.

Informal Learning: life-long process whereby every individual acquires attitudes, values, skills, and knowledge from daily experience and the educative influences and resources in his or her environment—from family and neighbors, work and play, the marketplace, library, and mass media. Related words or phrases include free-choice learning and self-directed learning.

Intangible Collections: collections that cannot be touched or stored but rather refer to the non-physical representation of culture such as songs, folk tales, traditions, etc. that are passed on from one generation to the next.

Interpretative Planning: a communication process that forges intellectual and emotional connections between the interests of the visitor and the meanings inherent in the resource. The process results in an interpretive plan.

Legibility: the ability of viewers to recognize individual letters or words.

Licencing: an agreement in which the owner or owners of a copyrighted image, logo, trademark, etc. rent the right to use that image, etc. to museum stores, which then use it on their own products in return for a royalty, allowing museums to access markets they normally could not reach on their own.

Linear Media: time-based media such as film, video, and audio.

Linear Sequence Exhibitions: exhibitions that must be organized and physically and intellectually experienced in sequence (i.e., chronology).

Loading Requirements: the strength needed in a museum's support structure to take the weight of artifacts or exhibits without structural deterioration over time and also the structural stiffness required to prevent undue vibration from affecting the stability of both exhibit elements and the objects they house.

Lumen output: measure of the quantity of light produced by a lamp.

Luminaires: light fixtures.

Lux: metric unit for measuring the intensity of light (10.76 lux = 1 footcandle).

Lux Level: the amount of visible light to which a museum object is being exposed; most accurately calculated as lux-hours per annum, being the lux level at any given time multiplied by the number of hours the lights with that lux level are turned on the object.

Maker Spaces: designated places within a museum with equipment that supports participants creating and designing their own projects with or without a link to the museum's content.

Market Analysis: a study of the characteristics of current and potential visitors to the museum with a view to increasing attendance.

Market Segmentation: analysis of the potential visitors to a museum into groups sufficiently homogeneous so that the institution can effectively plan programs to meet the needs of each segment and prioritize its development of facilities accordingly.

Market-Driven Exhibition: an exhibition program that arises from public interest or demand, as interpreted by the museum. Not to be understood as being in opposition to **Research-Based Exhibitions**, since good exhibitions should have elements of both.

Marketing: in the context of museums, is defined to include all ways and means to increase attendance, length of stay, visitor satisfaction, expenditures, and repeat visits.

Microclimate: the climate generated inside an enclosed environment within an exhibition gallery (such as inside a display case, vitrine, or diorama) that is different from the ambient climate.

Minds-On Displays/Exhibits: low-tech interactives that use open-ended questions and comparative devices to engage visitors with content.

Mixed Reality (MR): the mixing of virtual and real objects within virtual and real spaces, where the objects can interact with one another.

Mobile Application "App": a software application designed to run on smartphones, tablet computers, and other mobile devices.

Modes of Apprehension: the various mental processes by which visitors discover meaning in the objects on display. There are four general modes of apprehension: contemplation, comprehension, discovery, and interaction.

Modes of Presentation: methods by which exhibits assist with visitor comprehension. Examples of modes of presentation are the *systematic* mode, where comprehension is built through the visitor's exploration of many examples ranged together, or *contextual/thematic* mode, where the visitor's comprehension is aided through contextualization of the artifacts or specimens on view.

Modular Case: mass-produced case made to a set of standard specifications and designed to be free-standing and self-supporting. Also known as **System Case**.

Multimedia: in the context of museum exhibitions, the term refers to any audio-visual, computer, photographic, or video program. These may be small computer kiosks or large format theatres.

Multiuser Tables: systems that allow for groups of users to engage with digital content at the same time. This can be accomplished via multitouch screens pieced together, rear projection, top projection, or other patented technologies.

Museum Planner: a museum professional specializing in the planning of museum space, facilities, functions, services, operation, and/or administration.

Museum Planning: the study and practice of facilitating the preservation and interpretation of material culture by ordering all the components that comprise a museum into a constructed or renovated whole that can achieve its functions with optimal efficiency.

Nonlinear Exhibition Structures: frameworks that allow visitors to explore topics and themes nonsequentially (physically and mentally) according to choice and interest.

Objective: A statement of a specific, measurable, and observable result desired from an educational or interpretive activity or experience; a stated expectation about audience, behavior, condition, and degree that will result from a learning experience.

Open Access Exhibitions: exhibitions that allow the visitor to explore the connections between the exhibits for themselves, whether apprehended by surveying specimens or artifacts ranked in visible storage or a cluster of exhibits in the interactive or comprehension mode illustrating aspects of a theme that do not require consecutive experience.

Operating Costs: ongoing expenses of an institution, including salaries and benefits, maintenance, and the cost of public programming.

Opportunistic Collecting: museum objects acquired as they become available, provided they fit the collection mandate.

Outcomes: achievements or changes brought about by a program, exhibit, or activity that helps lay the foundation for longer-term impacts or benefits. Outcomes can involve changes in behavior, skills, knowledge, attitudes, values, or condition after participating in a learning activity or experience.

Payment Bond: Guarantees payment of subcontractors in case of default by a prime contractor.

Performance Bond: guarantees that the work will be completed. In case of default by the contractor, the bond provides the funding necessary to complete the project with other suppliers.

Phototropic Effect: the phenomenon that causes the human eye to be attracted to the brightest object in the field of view.

Platform (Digital): refers to the digital host for virtual exhibition and digital experiences. Examples include websites, microsites, content aggregators, and social media.

Print Ready Graphics (or Artwork): graphic files that are ready for final production.

Procurement: the process of soliciting or obtaining goods and services.

Program Evaluation and Review Technique (PERT) Chart: project management communication tool that identifies the likely path of tasks or set of tasks graphically. It addresses timeframes, dependencies, and decision-making milestones.

Project Budget: the sum established by the owner as available for the entire project, including the construction budget, land costs, costs of furniture, furnishings and equipment, financing costs, compensation for professional services, cost of owner-furnished goods and services, contingency allowance, and similar established or estimated costs.

Project Management: the act of planning, organizing, and managing resources to successfully complete specific project goals and objectives.

Project Manager: an individual or company, independent of or on the museum staff, whose function is to bring under a single coordinating authority all those involved in a project's implementation, to ensure that the project objectives are achieved and that it is completed on time, within budget, to an agreed level of quality, and with minimum disruption to other functions.

Projection Mapping: refers to the technique of projection of static, time-based, or even navigable media onto a surface, turning it into a display surface

Pop-Up Exhibition: temporary, short-term exhibitions located in off-site locations to create exciting, alternative, and fun exhibitions in nontraditional venues such as shopping malls, bus stations, outdoor kiosks, etc.

Prototype: a preliminary version of an exhibit, product, or device that is tested for effectiveness and quality.

Punch List (or Deficiencies List): see Deficiencies List.

QR Code (or Quick Reference Code): a machine-readable code consisting of an array of black and white squares, typically used for storing URLs or other information for reading by the camera on a smartphone.

Qualitative Audience Research: type of audience research in which information is collected about visitor behaviors and words (spoken or written).

Quantitative Audience Research: type of audience research in which numerical data is collected and in which a standardized approach and predetermined response categories are used to measure the reactions of many individuals to a limited set of questions.

Quantity Surveyor (or Cost Consultant): a professional consultant specializing in the estimation of quantitative requirements to achieve qualitative goals, and therefore projecting capital cost and occupancy cost estimates for exhibitions, buildings, systems, facilities, and functions.

Readability: the ability to read and comprehend worlds, phrases, and blocks of text.

Relative Humidity (RH): the ratio, expressed as a percentage, of the absolute humidity of sampled air to that of air saturated with water at the same temperature.

Remedial Evaluation: conducted after the installation of an exhibition, when all the exhibit displays are placed on the exhibition floor. Remedial evaluation can look at, for example, circulation flow, sight lines that capture attention, and visual competition among objects.

Request for Information (RFI): a formal document that identifies the need for additional information or clarity.

Request for Proposal (RFP): a solicitation made, often through a bidding process, to procure a commodity, service, or valuable asset to potential suppliers to submit business proposals.

Request for Qualification (RFQ): a solicitation that asks interested businesses to submit their experience, corporate profile, and resumes in order to be considered suitable for service or construction project. An RFQ often precedes an RFP process.

Research-Based Exhibition: an exhibition program that arises from the discipline itself, from an analysis of the museum collection, or from the interests of the museum's curators. Not to be understood as being in opposition to **market-driven exhibitions**, since good exhibitions should have elements of both.

Research Matrix: a tool for organizing the content and research needs of an exhibition.

Research Policy: establishes the museum's commitment to research, confirming that time, money, personnel, and facilities will be dedicated to it in keeping with the museum's mission.

Responsive Environments: refers to the use of infrared, motion, and microwave sensors (among other simple devices like off the shelf web cameras) to provoke other aspects of an exhibition to respond in a range of ways.

Risk: possibility of occurrence of an event that may adversely affect the normal functions of an institution.

Risk Analysis: calculation of the priority of security needs in terms of the possibility of a threat and the vulnerability of the institution to that threat.

Schematic Design: the stage of planning of an exhibition that follows on the design concept phase by developing drawings that indicate the contours and character of the building or exhibition according to the general requirements of the interpretative plan.

Search Engine Optimization (SEO): the process of maximizing the number of visitors to a particular website by ensuring that the site appears high on the list of results returned by a search engine.

Semiotics: refers to the study of signs and their signification, the way in which signs produce meaning.

Shop Drawings: the drawing component of the construction documents that, together with the specifications, are issued for use in actual construction.

Social Media: the means of interactions among people in which they create, share, and/or exchange information and ideas in virtual communities and networks.

Sound Transmission Class: a numerical rating that expresses the amount of sound "leakage" between spaces in a museum building.

Sponsorship Policy: a museum's ethical position regarding external sponsorship of exhibitions, part of the museum's overall **exhibition policy**.

Summative Evaluation: conducted after an interpretative program or exhibition is completed and provides information about the impact of that project. Assessment should be tied to project goals and objectives.

Sustainability: development that meets the needs of the present without compromising the ability of future generations to meet their own needs.

System Case: see **Modular Case**.

Systematic Collection: museum objects selected as examples of significant types or variants within collection categories.

Tabletop Case: a shallow, five-sided case used for displaying relatively flat objects or materials.

Tagging (in Social media): or social bookmarking is a term to describe the marking, saving, and archiving of certain websites. Internet users can use social tagging tools to track and organize their favorite websites and access them from any computer with an internet connection.

Terms of Reference: requirements set by the Board or its committees for a capital project or for a planning study, making explicit the extent and limitations of the study or project, used as a basis for submitting tenders on a planning project by planning consultants.

Text Levels/Categories: the hierarchy of text in an exhibition that results in diverse visual representation and depth of content explored by that text.

Thematic Exhibition: a display of specimens or artifacts arranged to illustrate a theme, subject, or "storyline."

Thematic Framework: the intellectual organization of the exhibition and is often the visual expression of the exhibition's storyline.

Track Lighting System: a flexible system for hanging and organizing light fixtures in a gallery.

Triangulation Strategies: a method of audience research that combines quantitative and qualitative approaches to eliminate the inherent biases of each. Types of triangulation strategies include data, investigator, and methodological triangulation.

Typography: the style and appearance of printed matter; the art technique of arranging type to make written language legible.

Turnkey Project or Contract: See **Design-Build**.

Universal Accessibility: the ability of users to have equal opportunity and access to services, products, systems, and environments, regardless of economic or social situation, religious or cultural background, gender, or functional limitation.

User Interface: in the context of exhibitions, the mechanical or digital means by which visitors (or users) access content in multimedia and interactive displays.

Value Engineering: a systematic method to improve the "value" of any products or services—a building or an exhibition, for example—by subjecting them to an examination by function. Also known as "cost cutting."

Variation Order see **Change Order**.

Virtual Exhibition: exhibitions created online for the internet and are not physical experiences. Such exhibitions may only be experienced online or via a digital interface.

Virtual Reality (VR): a computer-generated simulation of a three-dimensional image or environment that can be interacted with in a seemingly real or physical way.

Visible Storage: provision of public access to part or all of a complete museum collection by means of systematic presentation of artifacts, specimens, or works of art as in closed storage, but presented in a public gallery, normally on shelves or in drawers behind or under glass, with publicly-accessible catalogues providing interpretation either by means of laminated flip-cards of entire catalogue entries, or computer screens where similarly detailed information is available.

Warranty: guarantee provided by the contractor to correct deficiencies as defined by particular criteria.

Wall Case: wall-mounted cases built with varying degrees of sophistication, sometimes equipped with light boxes. Access is by a sliding or hinged door.

Word Count: in a museum exhibition, refers to the number of words in a text panel or display.

Select Bibliography

This updated bibliography selects and comments on those of the many recent books about museum exhibitions that are most relevant to the subjects discussed in this Manual.

Ames, Kenneth L., Barbara Franco, and L. Thomas Frye, eds. *Ideas and Images: Developing Interpretive History Exhibits*. Nashville, TN: American Association of State and Local History, 1992. This collection of case studies by academics and curators analyzes the theories behind several innovative history museum exhibitions.

Anderson, Gail, and Adrienne Horn. "Charting the Impact of Museum Exhibitions and Programs: Understanding the Public's Perspective," *AASLH Technical Leaflet #204*, included in *History News*, Vol. 54, No. 1 (Winter 1999). The authors present a concise explanation of exhibition evaluation, including information on types and methods of evaluation and its role in the museum decision-making process. They also provide a useful bibliography.

ASHRAE Handbook: Heating, Ventilating, and Air-Conditioning Applications. Atlanta, GA: American Society of Heating, Refrigerating, and Air-Conditioning Engineers, Inc., 1999. Chapter 20 of the 1999 edition outlines new standards for environmental controls for museums, libraries, and archives.

Barclay, Robert L., et al. *Mount-Making for Museum Objects*. Ottawa and Québec: Canadian Conservation Institute and Centre du conservation du Québec, 1998. Provides practical information on the mounting of museum objects for conservators, designers, and display technicians.

Belcher, Michael. *Exhibitions in Museums*. Leicester; London; and Washington, DC: Biddle, Ltd., 1991. An introductory survey of the basics of exhibition development, considering all phases of the processes of planning, design, and presentation.

Bertram, Brian. *Display Technology for Small Museums*. Ultimo, N.S.W., Australia: Museums Association of Australia (NSW), 1982. A "how-to" book with detailed sections on fixture construction, exhibit production, and display installation techniques.

Bienkowski, Piotr. "Soft Systems in Museums: A Case Study of Exhibition Planning and Implementation Processes," *Museum Management and Curatorship*, Vol. 13, No. 3 (Sept. 1994),

233-50. The author describes the application of "soft systems management" methods to the planning and implementation of the *Jordan: Treasures From An Ancient Land* exhibition at the Liverpool Museum in 1991.

Bitgood, Stephen. "Remedial Evaluation of Museum Exhibitions: Some Issues and Clarifications" (working paper, Jacksonville State University, July 2016), https://www.researchgate.net/publication/305725121_Remedial_Evaluation_of_Museum_Exhibitions?channel=doi&linkId=579cfebc08ae5d5e1e14c0a0&showFulltext=true [accessed Aug 15 2021]. DOI: 10.13140/RG.2.1.2872.0882. This article discusses the brief history how remedial evaluation became part of a visitor evaluation model and the arguments for inclusion in a classification system of visitor evaluation.

Blais, Andrée, ed. *Text in the Exhibition Medium*. Quebec: La Société des Musées Québécois and Musée de la Civilisation, 1995. The book is divided in two sections: the first on the theories of perception and learning and the second on the practical implications for those theories with regard to the creation of meaningful label text, including that disseminated by audio and other electronic media.

Bogle, Elizabeth. *Museum Exhibition: Planning and Design.* Walnut Creek, CA: AltaMira Press, 2013. A detailed reference on the exhibition planning and design process including an introduction to key elements of effective design, a guide to building materials, and a helpful glossary of terms.

Bridal, Tessa. *Effective Exhibit Interpretation and Design.* Walnut Creek, CA: AltaMira Press, 2013. Bridal argues for the importance of integrating the planning and creation of live interpretation as a key part of the exhibition development process.

Brochu, Lisa. *Interpretive Planning: The 5-M Model for Successful Planning Projects.* Heartfelt Publications, Fort Collins, CO: 2013. A useful framework for guiding interpretive planning projects based on the five m's: management, markets, message, mechanics, and media.

Carr, David. *Open Conversations: Public Learning in Libraries and Museums.* Santa Barbara, CA: Libraries Unlimited, 2011. Carr invites readers to "think with me" about the vital roles cultural institutions can play in fostering learning, discourse, and democracy. He advocates for social cohesion through empathy and a renewed era of public thought led by museums and libraries.

Caputo, Paul, Shea Lewis, and Lisa Brochu. *Interpretation By Design: Graphic Design Basics for Heritage Interpreters*. Fort Collins, CO: InterpPress, 2008. An introduction to the basics of creating and evaluating effective graphic design for those working in exhibition and interpretive contexts.

Catlin-Legutko, Cinnamon and Stacy Klingler. *Interpretation: Education, Programs, and Exhibits.* Walnut Creek, CA: AltaMira Press, 2013. Book five of the *Small Museum Toolkit,* this volume provides strategies for planning, researching, and designing exhibitions, tours, and public programs appropriate for the resources and unique challenges faced by smaller institutions.

Casciani, Stefano. "Lightweight Exhibit Design", *Abitare*, No. 338 (Mar. 1995), 123-30. Reviews new trends in exhibition design philosophy and in exhibit installation methods through a case study of the *Museum fur Gestaltung* in Zurich, Switzerland.

Caulton, Tim. *Hands-On Exhibitions: Managing Interactive Museums and Science Centres*. London and New York: Routledge, 1998. A work from an expert in interactive exhibition design, aimed at museum professionals interested in making their institutions competitive as entertainment venues.

Cherry, Kendra. "Howard Gardner Biography and Theories," *Verywell Mind.* (https://www.verywellmind.com/howard-gardner-biography-2795511). A comparison of multiple intelligences or different mental abilities and learning styles related to personality and learning preferences.

Crysler, Greig. "Angels in the Temple: The Aesthetic Construction of Citizenship at the United States Holocaust Museum," *Art Journal*, Vol. 56, Pt. 1 (Spring 1997), 52-64. Considers the aesthetics of the museum's presentation of the Holocaust and the ways in which the museum promotes American values and the belief that the state can guarantee individual liberty.

Davidson, Betty. *New Dimensions for Traditional Dioramas: Multisensory Additions for Access, Interest, and Learning.* Washington, DC: American Association of Museums, 1991. This book is a case study of how Boston's Museum of Science transformed its static diorama exhibit, *New England Habitats*, into a multisensory experience that became more accessible to a broader segment of the population.

Dean, David. *Museum Exhibition: Theory and Practice.* London and New York: Routledge, 1994. This book helps museums develop entertaining yet educational exhibitions and is particularly strong on the role of human perception and psychological considerations in exhibit design.

Dernie, David. *Exhibition Design.* New York: W. W. Norton & Company, 2006. A collection of exhibition case studies from around the world, this book also overviews creative approaches and techniques to exhibition design, including lighting, color, and graphics.

Diamond, Judy. *Practical Evaluation Guide: Tools for Museums and Other Informal Educational Settings.* Walnut Creek, CA, and Nashville, TN: AltaMira Press and American Association for State and Local History, 1999. Shows how evaluation can help museum professionals design more effective exhibitions and programs and examines visitor learning styles in museum settings.

Dickenson, Victoria. "Indiana Jones and the Exhibit Development Process," *Muse* (Summer/Été 1995), 29–35. Dickenson sketches out a three-stage, step-by-step process of exhibition development—planning, design, and production—with an emphasis on teamwork and collaboration.

Dierking, Lynn D. and John H. Falk. *The Museum Experience Revisited.* Walnut Creek, CA: Left Coast Press, 2013. An update in thinking about visitors' reasons for going to museums, activities they engage in at museums they visit, and free-choice learning related to their experiences.

Dierking, Lynn D. and John Falk. *The Museum Experience.* Washington, DC: Whalesback Books, 1992. The authors discuss visitors' reasons for going to museums, the activities they engage in once they get there, and the things they learn in the process.

Dierking, Lynn D. and Wendy Pollock. *Questioning Assumptions: An Introduction to Front-End Studies in Museums.* Washington, DC: Association of Science-Technology Centers, 1998. A discussion of the front-end evaluation process and what it can contribute to exhibition and program design.

Dilenschneider, Collen. "People Trust Museums More Than Newspapers. Here Is Why That Matters Right Now (DATA)." 2017. (Accessed www.colleendilen.com). The data and analysis in this article contribute to several debates taking place in the visitor-serving industry right now from crowd-curated exhibits and the "education versus entertainment" debate. Knowing how much people trust museums is important information for developing relevant and sustainable organizations.

DiMaggio, Gino. "A Flexible System of Exhibition," *Ottagono*, Vol. 31, No. 19 (June–August 1996), 68–72. The article discusses the relationship between the planning of exhibition spaces and the design of the exhibition as a whole.

Dingus, Lowell. *Next of Kin: Great Fossils at the American Museum of Natural History.* New York: Rizzoli International Publications, 1996. A lavishly illustrated account of the major facilities renovation and exhibition design project undertaken by the American Museum of Natural History in the late 1980s and early 1990s.

Dubin, Steven C. *Displays of Power: Memory and Amnesia in the American Museum.* New York and London: New York University Press, 1999. The author examines the growing importance of "symbolic politics" and shows how museums have become arenas for political contests.

Durbin, Gail, ed. *Developing Museum Exhibitions for Lifelong Learning.* London: The Stationery Office, 1996. A collection of essays dealing with aspects of the educational function of a museum exhibition, presented from a theoretical perspective.

Exhibitionist. National Association for Museum Exhibition (NAME): Washington, DC. A journal dedicated to the intellectual aspects of exhibition practice. Published biannually by the

National Association for Museum Exhibition, an organization recognized by the AAM as the Standing Professional Committee on exhibitions.

Exhibition Planning and Management: Reprints from NAME's Recent and Recommended. Washington, DC: American Association of Museums Technical Information Service, 1992. Drawn from various sources, the book is a compendium of previously-published articles that provide an introduction to the basics of exhibition planning and management.

Falk, John H. *Identity and the Museum Visitor Experience.* Walnut Creek, CA: Left Coast Press, Inc., 2009. A detailed description of identity-related motivations that are useful for attracting visitors and marketing.

Falk, John H. "Testing a Museum Exhibition Design Assumption: Effect of Explicit Labeling of Exhibit Clusters on Visitor Concept Development," *Science Education*, Vol. 81, No. 6 (November 1997), 681–89. A research paper describing the impact of exhibit labels on the learning process, concluding that labels often do facilitate learning.

Floch, Jean-Marie. *Visual Identities.* London: Continuum, 2000 (originally published in French in 1995 by Presses Universitaires de France). The six essays of visual identities are an important contribution to the growing field of industrial semiotics. Floch's major strength is his analysis of signs in a way which is both industrially relevant and textually precise.

Gardner, Howard. *A Synthesizing Mind: A Memoir from the Creator of Multiple Intelligences Theory.* Cambridge, MA: MIT Press, 2020. Current thinking about multiple ways in which individuals understand and learn through multiple modalities, which can be useful for museum workers planning exhibitions and programs. In his recent book, Gardner reflects on his ability to survey experiences and data across a wide range of disciplines and perspectives.

Golinelli, Paolo. "The Detail and the Whole," *Ottagono*, Vol. 31, No. 121 (December 1996–February 1997), 126–29. Discusses a permanent exhibition of antique coins at the *Museo Archeologico* in Aquileia, Italy, focusing on the role of display cases, lighting, and space allocation.

Greenberg, Rosa, Bruce W. Ferguson, and Sandy Narine, eds. *Thinking About Exhibitions.* London and New York: Routledge, 1996. A collection of scholarly essays addressing the concerns and debates that surround the exhibition development process. Questions of curatorship, spectatorship, narrative, and forms of staging and spectacle are considered.

Greenhaulgh, Paul. "Education, Entertainment, and Politics: Lessons From the Great International Exhibitions" in Peter Vergo, ed., *The New Museology* (London: Reaktion Books, 1989), 74–98. The author believes that museum exhibitions can become more relevant to the public at large if they reflect the sociopolitical climate of their times in the fashion of their nineteenth-century predecessors.

Hall, Margaret. *On Display: A Design Grammar for Museum Exhibitions.* London: Lund Humphries, 1987. A textbook for exhibition designers that establishes a "grammar" or set of ground rules for exhibitions with the goal of striking a balance between aesthetics and scholarship. Contains information on "basic principles, the participants and their roles, the steps which they take, and the major hazards of exhibition design," along with suggestions for handling artifacts.

Harris, Neil. "Exhibiting Controversy," *Museum News* (September–October 1995). Harris reviews some controversial museum exhibitions with a view to uncovering the reasons for our current interest in "controversy" per se.

Hébert, Louis, "Tools for Text and Image Analysis: An Introduction to Applied Semiotics2. The Semiotic Square." London and New York: Routledge, 2019. In his series Hébert, a professor from the Université du Québec à Rimouski, describes the way in which Greimas Square can be applied.

Helkama, Iris. "To Design a Museum Exhibition," *Form Function Finland*, Pt. 2 (1997), 40–42. Reviews the basic criteria of good exhibition design with particular reference to Finnish museums.

Henderson, Amy and Adrienne L. Kaeppler, ed. *Exhibiting Dilemmas: Issues of Representation at the Smithsonian*. Washington, DC and London: Smithsonian Institution Press, 1997. A series of provocative essays by various authors describes the social, political, ethical, and cultural challenges inherent in mounting exhibitions in the 1990s and how Smithsonian personnel have responded to this new complexity.

Henriksen, Ellen Karoline. "Environmental Issues in the Museum: Applying Public Perceptions in Exhibition Development," *Curator: The Museum Journal*, Vol. 41, No. 2 (June 1998), 90–105. The article explores the value of constructivist theory, which "implies that exhibitions should build on visitors' expectations" for exhibition development through a case study of the *Our Radiant World* exhibition at the Norwegian Museum of Science and Technology.

Hood, Adrienne. "The Practice of [American] History: A Canadian Curator's Perspective," *The Journal of American History*, Vol. 81, No. 3 (December 1994), 1011–19. The article discusses successful and unsuccessful attempts to make history relevant to the general public through museum exhibitions, including the Royal Ontario Museum's ill-fated 1989 *Into the Heart of Africa* exhibition, a case study of the pitfalls inherent in the communication of complex ideas.

Hooper-Greenhill, Eilean. *Museums and Education: Purpose, Pedagogy, Performance*. London: Routledge, 2007. A discussion of the power of experiential learning that can include performance, enactment, participation, active engagement, or involvement with active participants and result in "real knowing."

Hooper-Greenhill, Eilean. *Museums and the Interpretation of Visual Culture*. London and New York: Routledge, 2000. Hooper-Greenhill engages with theoretical questions about the nature of museums, their role in the construction of knowledge, and how that has changed over time. She also coins the term "post-museum" to describe constructivist institutions and approaches that challenge the "transmission" model of modernist museums.

Hooper-Greenhill, Eilean. *Museums and Their Visitors*. London and New York: Routledge, 1994. Shows how museums have reordered and revamped their organizational cultures to respond to their new roles as active learning centers. Many practical examples are provided.

Howarth, Shirley Reiff. *Guide to Traveling Exhibition Organizers*. The Humanities Exchange, Inc., 1999. A listing of more than eighty organizations that offer traveling exhibitions to museums, art galleries, and other display spaces.

Humphrey, Thomas and Josh Gutwill. *Fostering Active Prolonged Engagement: the Art of Creating APE Exhibits*. San Francisco: Exploratorium, 2005. This book outlines the findings of the Exploratorium's Active Prolonged Engagement project and includes the goals, approaches, results, and lessons learned from fifteen constructivist-style science exhibitions.

Hunter, Carol. *Everyone's Nature: Designing Interpretation to Include All*. Billings, MT: Falcon Press, 1994. This book explains the requirements of the Americans with Disabilities Act and includes practical ideas for making visitor centers, interpretive displays, nature trails, and other outdoor facilities accessible for everyone.

Janes, Robert, R. and Richard Sandell. *Museum Activism*. London and New York Routledge, 2019. The book explores the potential for museums as key intellectual and civic resources to address inequalities, injustice, and environmental challenges.

Jenkins, Henry, Ravi Purushotma, Margaret Weigel, and Katie Clinton. *Confronting the Challenge of Participatory Culture: Media Education for the 21st Century*. Boston, MA: MIT Press, 2009. This report analyzes questions and challenges related to how young people access and engage with participatory cultures.

Joffee, Elga and Mary Ann Stiller. *Reaching Out: A Creative Access Guide for Designing Exhibits and Cultural Programs for Persons Who Are Blind or Visually Impaired*. Video: American Foundation for the Blind, 1998. A two-part video designed to help museum professionals improve accessibility for visually-impaired visitors.

Karp, Ivan and Steven D. Lavine, eds. *Exhibiting Cultures: The Poetics and Politics of Museum Display*. Washington, DC, and London: Smithsonian Institution Press, 1991. An interdisciplinary approach to the problems of meaning and representation raised by mounting exhibitions in a multicultural society, presented as a series of essays by scholars from various disciplines.

Kelly, Starr, Angela Raup, and Cinnamon Catlin-Legutko. "Discomfort in Learning: Museum Audiences React to Decolonizing practices." *Museum* (July–August 2019): 25–29. Presents a decolonizing framework informed by the research of Ho-Chunk scholar Amy Lonetree and outlines a case study of decolonializing methodologies put into practice by the Abbe Museum, Bar Harbor, Maine.

Kennedy, Jeff. *User-Friendly: Hands-On Exhibits that Work*. Washington, DC: Association of Science-Technology Centers, 1994. The author shows how to improve the quality of interactive exhibits through attention to the "human factors" or ergonomics of exhibit design. Useful solutions to common design problems are included.

Klobe, Tom. *Exhibitions: Concept, Planning and Design*. Washington, DC: American Association of Museums, 2012. Klobe outlines the basic principles of exhibition design, lighting, graphics, as well as managing budgets and resources.

Korn, Randy and Laurie Sowd. *Visitor Surveys: A User's Manual*. Washington, DC: American Association of Museums, 1990. A do-it-yourself guide to the design of visitor surveys.

Kurin, Richard. *Reflections of a Culture Broker: A View From the Smithsonian*. Washington, DC, and London: Smithsonian Institution Press, 1997. A discussion of the "brokering process" by which cultural understandings are translated into museum exhibitions. Contains a useful case study section.

Leftridge, Alan. *Interpretive Writing*. Fort Collins, CO: InterpPress, 2006. A useful guide to writing and editing interpretive text that is both engaging and accessible.

Lockett, Christine. "Ten Years of Exhibit Evaluation at the Royal Ontario Museum 1980-1990," *ILVS Review* (Spring 1991), 19–47. The author examines how front-end, formative, and summative evaluation procedures have been carried out at the ROM between 1980 and 1990 and discusses the impact of those procedures on that museum's exhibition practices. Case studies are included.

Lord, Gail Dexter and Ngaire Blackenberg. *Cities, Museums and Soft Power*. Washington, DC: AAM Press, 2015. Explores how cultural institutions can activate their societal influence to amplify civic discourse and accelerate cultural change. Features thirteen essays by a variety of experts exploring the significance of soft power and museums in cities worldwide.

MacDonald, Sharon, ed. *The Politics of Display: Museums, Science, Culture*. London and New York: Routledge, 1998. An academic work highlighting the previously ignored political undercurrents present in science museums and the role of such museums in the "culture wars" of the 1990s.

Maekawa, Shin, ed. *Oxygen-Free Museum Cases*. The Getty Conservation Institute, 1998. A summary report of experience gained through conservation projects including the royal mummies of Egypt, the original Constitution of India, and the charter for the Hudson's Bay Company.

Magelssen, Scott. *Living History Museums: Undoing History through Performance*. Lanham, MD: Scarecrow Press, 2007. An examination of the contemporary practices and theoretical dilemmas facing living history museums in the United States and Europe.

Majewski, Janice. *Smithsonian Guidelines for Accessible Exhibition Design*. Washington, DC: Smithsonian. A thorough and practical handbook for developing physically and intellectually accessible exhibition based on standards from the Americans with Disabilities Act. Also includes a useful list of sources and resources.

Majewski, Janice. *Part of Your General Public is Disabled*. Washington, DC: American Association of Museums, 1987. This book presents eight major groups of disabilities that visitors may have and how these disabilities affect them. It also presents practical information in planning and delivering tours.

Marincola, Paula, ed. *What Makes a Great Exhibition?* Clerkenwell, London, UK: Reaktion Books, 2007. This collection draws together some of the world's leading curators and art historians in a discussion on the role and purpose of art exhibitions today.

McKenna-Cress, Polly and Janet Kamien. *Creating Exhibitions: Collaboration in the Planning, Development, and Design of Innovative Experiences.* Hoboken, NJ: Wiley, 2013. A guide to the key phases of the exhibition development and design process, including practical problem-solving techniques and illustrative case studies.

McLean, Kathleen. *Planning For People in Museum Exhibitions.* Washington, DC: Association of Science-Technology Centers, 1993. McLean presents the fundamentals of exhibition design with a view to improving the visitor's experience.

McLean, Kathleen and Catherine McEver, eds. *Are We There Yet? Conversations about Best Practices in Science Exhibition Development.* San Francisco, CA: The Exploratorium, 2004. This book includes descriptions of twelve "noteworthy" science exhibitions, including budgets, timelines, goals, process, techniques, and outcomes.

McLean, Kathleen and Wendy Pollock, ed. *Visitor Voices in Museum Exhibitions.* Washington DC: Association of Science and Technology Centers, 2007. An overview of both low- and high-tech techniques for engaging visitor interaction and incorporating visitor-contributed content.

McManus, Paulette and Roger Miles. "United Kingdom: Focusing on the Market," *Museum International*, Vol. 45, Pt. 2 (1993), 26–32. The article shows how visitor studies can be useful in designing new exhibitions and in improving older ones.

Melton, Arthur W. *Problems of Installation in Museums of Art.* Washington, DC: American Association of Museums, 1935, 1988, 1996. A reprint of a seminal 1935 work that discusses the ways in which human behavior, and the actual installations themselves, influence visitors' experiences in museums.

Miles, R. S., in collaboration with M. B. Alt, D. C. Gosling, B. N. Lewis, and A. F. Tout. *The Design of Educational Exhibits*, 2nd ed. London: Unwin Hyman, 1988. A practical manual for the development of educational exhibitions, useful for its systematic approach.

Mintz, Ann and Selma Thomas, eds. *The Virtual and the Real: Media in the Museum.* Washington, DC: American Association of Museums, 1998. A series of articles discussing the effects of museum media on the visitor and on the museum itself.

Mola, Francesc Zamora. *Affordable Exhibition Design.* New York: Harper Design, 2011. Mola draws on case studies from around the world, including material, cost, and design details, and provides a wealth of creative and cost-saving solutions for planning and designing effective exhibitions on a tight budget.

Moore, Kevin. *Museums and Popular Culture.* London and Washington, DC: Cassell, 1997. The author examines the democratization of museums through a study of recent attempts to display and interpret popular culture.

Muscat, Marcie M. "The Art of Diplomacy: Museums and Soft Power," *E-International* November 9, 2020. The article explores how museums employ classic methods of public diplomacy, transmitting messages in ways that allow recipients to arrive at their own conclusions. The museum emerges as a consummate agent of soft power.

Museum and Art Gallery Lighting: A Recommended Practice. The Illuminating Engineers' Society of North America (IESNA) Committee on Museum and Art Gallery Lighting, 1996. A practical guide for exhibition lighting designers and others interested in the ways in which good lighting can improve understanding and communication in museums.

Museum Exhibition Design, Part VI, Exhibition Evaluation, published independently by Museum Planning, LLC. This online material discusses the four phases exhibition evaluation: front-end evaluation, formative evaluation, remedial, and summative evaluation. Museum exhibitions are a form of communication and museum evaluation is a method to analyze the communication of an exhibition or answer "What is the exhibition communicating to visitors?"

Neal, Arminta. *Exhibits for the Small Museum: A Handbook.* Nashville, TN: American Association for State and Local History, 1976. Aimed at the small history museum, this book explains the technical details of case construction, floor display, and other practical aspects of exhibition development.

Nigam, Mohan Lal. "Creating a Context: A Challenge to Indian Museums," *Museum International*, Vol. 47, Pt. 1 (January–March 1995), 21–24. Considers the challenges facing exhibition designers in a country where large portions of the potential audience are semiliterate or illiterate.

O'Doherty, Brian. *Inside the White Cube: The Ideology of the Gallery Space*, expanded edition. Berkeley, Los Angeles, and London: University of California Press, 1999. Originally published in 1976, this groundbreaking work explores the effect of the gallery's context on art objects and on the viewers themselves.

Oudsten, Frank. *Space.Time.Narrative: The Exhibition as Post-Spectacular Stage.* Burlington, VT: Ashgate Pub Company, 2011. The author examines contemporary exhibitions as unique and complex narrative spaces, drawing from a variety of philosophical, museological, curatorial, and other interdisciplinary perspectives, as well as interviews with six leading exhibition designers.

Pearson, Clifford A. "Exhibit design: breaking out of the display case, exhibits reach out and touch," *Architectural Record*, Vol. 182 (September 1994), 28–33. Discusses the trend toward subject-based approaches to museums and their exhibitions, citing the examples of the Holocaust Museum, the American Museum of Natural History, and the Rock and Roll Hall of Fame and Museum.

Pekarik, Andrew J., James B. Schreiber, Nadine Hanemann, Kelly Richmond, and Barbara Mogel. "IPOP: A Theory of Experience Preference," *Curator: The Museum Journal*, vol. 57, no. 1, (January 2014), 5–27. A Theory of Experience Preference, which evolved from structured observations and interviews with visitors to the Smithsonian Institution museums in Washington, DC, from the 1990 to 2014. The authors discuss four key dimensions of experience: ideas, people, objects, and physical experiences.

Pieterse, Jan Nederveen. "Multiculturalism and Museums: Discourse About the Other in the Age of Globalization," *Boekman Cahier*, Vol. 8, No. 28 (June 1996), 172–89. The author believes that exhibition designers often display outmoded attitudes toward other cultures in their exhibitions and that alternative approaches to exhibition design are needed to eliminate cultural biases.

Phillips, David. *Exhibiting Authenticity.* Manchester and New York: Manchester University Press, 1997. The book deals with the problem of authenticity in museum exhibitions from a theoretical perspective.

Rabinowitz, Richard. "Exhibit as Canvas," *Museum News*, Vol. 70, Pt. 2 (March–April 1991), 34–38. The author discusses the need for history museums to design exhibitions that reflect historical context. Collections must be interpreted so that the museums themselves become works of art that reveal the identities of the various societies with which they are concerned.

Roberts, Lisa. *From Knowledge to Narrative: Educators and the Changing Museum.* Washington, DC and London: Smithsonian Institution Press, 1997. Noting the augmented role for educators in the more audience-centered museum environment of the 1990s, the author examines the ways in which educators can contribute to the exhibition development process.

Rosenberg, Pnina. "A Question of Time and Space," *Museum International*, Vol. 47, Pt. 1 (January–March 1995), 6–8. The author considers exhibition design considerations with a view to the relationship between the museum and its surroundings and the spatial organization of exhibits.

Roth, Stacy. *Past into Present: Trends & Techniques in First Person Interpretation.* Chapel Hill: University of North Caroline Press, 1998. Roth explores effective trends and techniques relevant to using live historical interpretation to bring history to life at museums, historical sites, and other venues.

Salman, John P. S. *Everyone's Welcome: The Americans with Disabilities Act and Museums.* Washington, DC: American Association of Museums, 1998. This manual outlines the ADA's legal requirements for museums in the United States, provides practical and specific information on making museum exhibitions accessible.

Screven, C. G. "United States: A Science in the Making," *Museum International*, Vol. 45, Pt. 2 (1993), 6–12. Screven asks whether educational exhibitions have become more accessible to the general public in recent years. He finds that such exhibitions could benefit from the inclusion of contributions from educators and others who are not strictly museum specialists.

Serrell, Beverly. *Judging Exhibitions: A Framework for Assessing Excellence.* Walnut Creek, CA: Left Coast Press, 2006. A useful framework for assessing and improving the quality of museum exhibitions from a visitor experience perspective, including key criteria like comfort, engagement, and meaningfulness.

Serrell, Beverly. *Exhibit Labels: An Interpretive Approach.* Walnut Creek, CA: AltaMira Press, 1996. A comprehensive treatment of label planning, writing, design, and publication.

Serrell, Beverly. *Paying Attention: Visitors and Museum Exhibitions.* Washington, DC: American Association of Museums, 1998. A research report detailing visitor behavior in museums, with implications for exhibition design.

Serrell, Beverly. *Exhibit Labels: An Interpretive Approach* (2nd ed.). Lanham, MD: Rowman & Littlefield, 2015. An updated description of learning styles, types of labels, evaluation during development and after opening an exhibition, as well as writing, design, production, and digital interpretive devices.

Silverman, Lois. *The Social Work of Museums* London, UK: Routledge, 2010. Drawing on visitor studies, recent trends, and case studies, Silverman argues that museums should and do provide an important social service for their visitors and their communities.

Simon, Nina, *The Art of Relevance.* Museum 2.0, 2016. A guide to how museums can matter more to more people.

Simon, Nina. *The Participatory Museum.* Museum 2.0, 2010. Nina Simon's book (and accompanying blog, *Museum 2.0*) provides real-world techniques and strategies for engaging visitors and communities in meaningful ways as active participants and co-creators in the exhibition experience and the design process.

Sixsmith, Mike, ed. *Touring Exhibitions: The Touring Exhibitions Group's Manual of Good Practice.* Oxford: Butterworth-Heinemann Ltd., 1995. A practical manual dealing with all aspects of touring exhibitions.

Skolnick, Lee, Jan Lorenc, and Craig Berger. *What is Exhibition Design? (Essential Design Handbooks).* Hove, East Sussex, UK: RotoVision, 2007. A visual introduction into the various types and functions of exhibitions, this book includes portfolios of projects from sixteen leading design firms.

Skotnes, Pippa, ed. *Miscast: Negotiating the Presence of the Bushmen.* Cape Town, South Africa: University of Cape Town Press, 1996. Companion volume to the *Miscast* exhibition at the South African National Gallery in Cape Town in 1996, which examined representations of Bushmen since colonial times, especially the relationship between colonizers and colonized. The book contains a series of essays by scholars from various academic disciplines.

Smithsonian Guidelines for Accessible Exhibition Design. Washington, DC: Smithsonian Institution, Smithsonian Accessibility Program. The Smithsonian Institution has developed a working manual for its museum staff to provide guidelines in creating accessible exhibitions.

Soren, Barbara J. "Museum experiences that change visitors," *Museum Management and Curatorship,* vol. 24, pt. 3 (2009), 233–51. This often-cited article looks at transform, transforming, and transformative as common terms for describing museum spaces, the creation of objects on display, and experiences for visitors. The author questions whether there is evidence that museums profoundly change visitors through their objects, collections, exhibitions, public programs, and websites.

Soren, Barbara, in collaboration with Gail Lord, John Nicks, and Hugh Spencer. "Triangulation Strategies and Images of Museums as Sites for Lifelong Learning," *Museum Management and Curatorship*, Vol. 14, No. 1 (1995), 31–46. Provides a detailed description of various triangulation methods, used to help museum professionals learn more about museum visitors' "meaning making" and learning activities. Case studies are included.

Sousa, Jean L. *Telling Images: Stories in Art*. Chicago: The Art Institute of Chicago, 1997. The catalogue for the *Telling Images* exhibition at The Art Institute of Chicago, which is presented as a case study of the process of exhibition development.

Spencer, Hugh. "Get It? Got it? Good! A Model for Exhibit Communication," *Museum Quarterly*, Vol. 17, No. 2 (May 1989), 8–15. Spencer discusses the communication gaps that can cause an exhibit's intended message to be garbled or lost. He offers methods to overcome those gaps that are based on theories of communication developed by Lev Vgotsky.

Standards Manual for Signs and Labels. Washington, DC: American Association of Museums and the Metropolitan Museum of Art, 1995. The book establishes standards for signs and labels with a view to increasing accessibility, particularly for the disabled and the visually impaired.

Staniszewski, Mary Anne. *The Power of Display: A History of Exhibition Installations at the Museum of Modern Art*. London and Cambridge, MA: MIT Press, 1998. A survey of influential avant-garde exhibitions held at MoMA throughout the twentieth century.

Steiner, Christine, ed. *A Museum Guide to Copyright and Trademark*. Washington, DC: American Association of Museums, 1999. A guide for museum professionals grappling with the intricacies of copyright, trademark, licensing, and other issues surrounding intellectual property rights. Includes a useful section on the online content.

Stim, Richard. *Getting Permission: How to License & Clear Copyrighted Materials Online & Off*. Berkley, CA: Nolo, 2010. Stim gives a comprehensive overview of the process of acquiring permissions for the use of copyright materials, including text, photographs, artworks, music, and online content.

Stocker, Michael. "Exhibit Sound Design for Public Presentation Spaces," *Museum Management and Curatorship*, Vol. 13, No. 2 (June 1994), 177–83. An article on an oft-neglected aspect of exhibition design: the soundscape.

Stolow, Nathan. *Conservation and Exhibitions: Packing, Transport, Storage, and Environmental Considerations*. London and Boston: Butterworths, 1986. Still the standard reference on this vital subject.

Storkerson, Peter. "Antinomies of Semiotics in Graphic Design." *Visible Language,* 2010. The paper assesses the roles played by semiotics in graphic and graphic design education.

Tepper, Steven and Bill Ivey, ed. *Engaging Art: The Next Great Transformation of America's Cultural Life*. London, UK: Routledge, 2007. Drawing on the perspectives of experts from diverse fields, this book explores key trends in citizen participation in the arts. A useful resource for thinking about the importance of participation and engagement in exhibitions and museums.

Taylor, Samuel. *Try it! Improving Exhibits Through Formative Evaluation*. Washington, DC: Association of Science-Technology Centers, 1992. A series of essays describing how formative evaluation can contribute to exhibition development. Case studies and examples are used throughout.

Thompson, Steven L. "The Arts of the Motorcycle: Biology, Culture, and Aesthetics in Technological Choice," *Technology and Culture*, Vol. 41, No. 1 (Jan. 2000), 99–115. Interesting for its use of the Guggenheim Museum's *The Art of the Motorcycle* exhibition as an illustration of changing ideas about "art" and the impact of those ideas on museum exhibitions.

Tilden, Freeman. *Interpreting Our Heritage.* Chapel Hill: The University of North Carolina Press, 4th edition, 2008. A key foundational text for those who plan and deliver interpretive programs, the most recent edition includes new essays on the art and craft of interpretation and reflections on the present and future of historical interpretation.

The Empathetic Museum. "Empathetic Museum Maturity Model." The Empathetic Museum represents the collective work of museum professionals who explore the ways institutions can better reflect and represent the values of their communities. The Empathetic Museum Maturity Model is a rubric that museums can follow to work toward becoming more inclusive, diverse, relevant, and responsive organizations.

Vergo, Peter. "The Reticent Object" in Peter Vergo, ed., *The New Museology* (London: Reaktion Books, 1989), 41–59. A theoretical piece in which Vergo presents his view of the exhibition as educative device; museum professionals must choose objects that contribute to the didactic theme of the exhibition, but they must also design that exhibition with the intended audience in mind.

Veverka, John. Interpretive Master Planning: Volume 1–Strategies for the New Millennium and Volume 2–Selected Essays: Philosophy, Theory and Practice. Edinburgh, UK: Museumsetc, 2011. Two comprehensive volumes dedicated to all aspects of the planning and design of a wide variety of interpretive contexts, illustrated with case studies.

Weaver, Stephanie. *Creating Great Visitor Experiences: A Guide for Museums, Parks, Zoos, Gardens & Libraries.* Walnut Creek, CA: Left Coast Press, 2007. Practical advice, exercises, resources, and case studies aimed at improving visitor satisfaction throughout the entire visitor experience.

Wells, Marcella, Marianna Adams, and Judith Koke. *Interpretive Planning for Museums: Integrating Visitor Perspectives in Decision Making.* Walnut Creek, CA: Left Coast Press, 2013. A comparison of formal, nonformal, and informal learning experiences across the learning landscape and a range of sites, as well as the concept of lifelong learning.

Wilk, Christopher. "The Victoria and Albert Museum at the Grosvenor House Fair," *Apollo*, Vol. 145, No. 424 (June 1997), 3–10. Describes the proposed reorganization of the collection of British art and design at the Victorian and Albert Museum. The reorganization aims to provide a comprehensive account of the development of British design from 1500 to 1900.

Wilkening, Susie. "Curiosity, Empathy, and Social Justice: A Data Story." Independently published by Wilkening Consulting, 2019. Draws on research results intended to help museum professionals understand different types of curiosity to inform visitor engagement practices.

Witteborg, Lothar P. *Good Show! A Practical Guide to Temporary Exhibitions*, 2nd ed. Washington, DC: Smithsonian Institution Traveling Exhibition Service, 1991. A practical guidebook for those interested in the basic steps involved in exhibition planning, design, fabrication, installation, security, accessibility, and conservation.

Index

Abbe Museum, Maine, 155, 157
Aboriginal peoples, 283, 284
access, 133; to collections for traveling exhibitions, 134; installation, 374; public, 64; service, 56–57; Universal Access Point, 300; virtual exhibitions, 108
accessibility: Americans with Disabilities Act, 297; back-of-house space relationship diagram, *58*; Braille, 300; closed captioning, 300; CMHR and mobile devices for, *341*; color, 299; contrast, 299–300; controlling, 55–56; DEAI, 152, 154, 155, 157, 158, 160–63; descriptive audio, 300; digital media, 298; Digital Museums Canada Accessibility Values and Standards, 99; exhibition design, 297–300, *299*; exhibition facilities, 55–58, *58*; font sizes, 299; forms of illustration, 300; graphics, 299, 300; *Guidelines for Accessible Exhibition Design*, 298; lighting, 298, *299*; mobile apps, 70, 300; nonpublic support spaces, 57–58; pathways and circulation, 298; print, 299; requirements, 56; service, 56–57; sign language, 300; Universal Keypad, 300; virtual exhibitions, 98–99; W3C Guidelines, 99
accession number, 261
acoustics, 45, 291–92
activating change, 160–63
active-control display cases, 308
active microclimates, 36, 44
activist institutions, museums as, 10–12
activists, women, 155

Adams, Barbara, 171
Addison, Laura, 114, 115
adjacency, exhibition facilities, 55–58, *58*
admissions, virtual exhibitions, 108
advertising, related exhibition costs, 387
advisory committee, exhibition process, 216
advisory groups, 282–83
aesthetic displays, *66*, 66–67
affordability, traveling exhibitions, 135
Africa, 148, 160
African Americans, War of 1812 veterans, 159, 268
Africville Park, Halifax, 268–69, *270*
agreements: extended warranties and maintenance, 376–77; loan, 125–26, 138–39
air cleanliness, 30, 33–34
air filters, efficiency ratings, 33–34
air movement, 30, 31, 33, 312
air quality, green design, 316
Alaska Native culture, 69
Alaska Native Heritage Center, Anchorage, 55
Alexander Girard virtual exhibition, MOIFA, 114, *114*, 116, *116*
Alexander McQueen temporary exhibition, The Costume Institute at the Met, 127, *128*
All Power to the People temporary exhibition, OMCA, 220, *220*
ambient light, 34, 44, 52, 298, 349
American Alliance of Museums, 97, 149, 354, 385
American Federation of Arts, 124
American Museum of Natural History (AMNH), New York City, 122, *123*, 133, 134

437

American Sign Language, 298, 300, *341*, *355*
American Society of Heating, Refrigerating, and Air Conditioning Engineers (ASHRAE), 31, 32, 35
Americans virtual exhibition, Smithsonian National Museum of the American Indian, 105
Americans with Disabilities Act, 297
AMNH (American Museum of Natural History), New York City, 122, *123*, 133, 134
Anchorage Museum, Alaska, 69
anniversaries, traveling exhibitions, 134
Annual Survey of Museum-Goers (American Alliance of Museums), 97
"Antinomies of Semiotics in Graphic Design" (Storkerson), 319-20
antiracism, 155
apps: mobile, 70, 300; museum, 101-2
AR (augmented reality), 106-7, 347, *348*
archaeology museums, 68
architecture, 12, 26, 62, 296, *296-97*
archives, 26, 270, 354
art, 67; direction, 297; handlers, temporary exhibitions, 125; museums, 11-12, 18, *19*, 74, *75*, 78, *91*, 91-92, 105, 113-16, *114*, *116*, 119-21, 127, *128*, 157, 159, 218, 305; new media exhibition spaces for, 26
Artemisia exhibition, National Gallery, 406
Art Gallery of Ontario, Toronto, 18, *19*, 78, 305
artifact case, preparators with traveling, *141*
artifacts: AR used to explore, *348*; data sheet, 260-61, *262*; macro, 69-70; mounting, *372*
artists, women, 406
arts, 26, 102, 108, 124
Artsy.net, 102
artwork, production-ready, 323
Asana, 400
ASHRAE (American Society of Heating, Refrigerating, and Air Conditioning Engineers), 31, 32, 35
Asian Collection, musée du quai Branly-Jacques Chirac, 66
asset building, vision-driven design criteria, 28
Association of Children's Museums, 76
ATMs, 56
audiences: demand, expectations and attracting new, 95; development for traveling exhibitions, 134; digital, 89, 95-99, 220; exhibition text and target, 264; experiences and exhibition preferences, 171-75; fragmentation, 173-75; research, 169, 187-200; specialists for exhibition process, 211; virtual exhibitions, prolonged closures and maintaining, 93-95
audio, 45, 291-92, 300, 341, *341*
audio/film/video/graphics, multimedia exhibits, 275
audiovisual multimedia exhibits, 274

augmented reality (AR), 106-7, 347, *348*
Australian National Maritime Museum, Sydney, 122
authority, shared, 9, 154
Ayala Museum, Manila, 94, *94*

back- and front-of-house separation, security levels, 53
back-of-house spaces, *58*
banners, for *Turner, Whistler, Monet* exhibition, *19*
Barrie, Ontario, 157, 159
Bartholdi, Frédéric Auguste, 227, 245
Basecamp, 400
Beausoleil First Nation, Ontario, 159
behaviors, digital audiences, 96-97
benefit of membership/subscription, 108
bid bond, 368
bid documents, 295-96
Big Idea (metanarrative), 224, 228, 237-38, *238*
Bihar Museum, Patna, 317
biodiversity interactive, 205
Biological Sciences Building, UMMNH, 250
Black, Indigenous, people of color (BIPOC) communities, 154-55, 157, 158, 216, 257-58, 278
black box galleries, 26
Blacklist (film), 389, *389*
Black Lives Matter, London exhibition, Museum London, *156*
Black Lives Matter movement, 149, 157, 278
Blackman, Cheryl, 160-63
Black Panthers, 220, *220*
Blankenberg, Ngaire, 10
blockbusters, 127, 136, 148, 149, 150, 406, 408
Bluewater Studio, Grand Rapids, *369*
blue whale skeleton, ROM, 121, *121*
Boijmans van Beuningen Museum, Rotterdam, 69, 71
bonding, contracting, 368
born-digital virtual exhibitions, 100
borrowers, traveling exhibitions and, 144, *144*
Boston Children's Museum, 77, 157
Bowie, David, 129, 130
Boyd-Shafer, Colin, 157
Braille, 264, 300
branches, temporary exhibitions and museum, 131
branding, 28, 134
Breaking the Silence Study Table, 344, *345*
BREEAM (BRE Environmental Assessment Method), 314
bricoleur (handyman), 320
brief: curatorial, 275; functional, 30, 111
brief, exhibition: budget, *230*, 230-31; *Canada Day 1*, 231-32, *232*, 279, *281*; with concept formulated, 223-25; core idea, 227-28; outline, *226*, 226-31;

438   Index

project timeline, *229*; purpose, 227; resource plan, *231*; virtual exhibitions, 111
bring your own device (BYOD), 350
British Museum, London, 45, 153
Brochu, Lisa, 234
Brooklyn Children's Museum, 76
Brooklyn Museum, 106, *106*
Buck, R. D., 31
Buck, Rebecca, 134
Buddha Smriti Park, Patna, India, 241, *241*
budgets: basics, 380–83; costs and, 30, 41, 104, *104*, 108, 109–10, *110*, 314–15, 380–89; design process, final quote and, 388; exhibition, 379–83, *383*, 388; exhibition brief, *230*, 230–31; going over, 388–89; in-kind contributions and, 389–90; management, 387–89; operationalizing multimedia, 352; with rough order of magnitude estimates, *230*, 380; staffing, 386; temporary exhibitions, 130–31; virtual exhibitions, 109–10, *110*. *See also* financial planning
budgets, exhibition: allocation of, *383*; creating, 379–83; rough order of magnitude estimates, *380*. *See also* financial planning
builder, local, 274
building systems, gallery shell, 38
Bunch, Adam, 102, *102*
Bunjilaka Aboriginal Cultural Centre, Melbourne Museum, 283–86
Burman, Chila, 124
Business for the Arts, 108
BYOD (bring your own device), 350

Canada Aviation and Space Museum, Ottawa, *374*
Canada Day 1 traveling exhibition, CMIP, 231–32, *232*, 279, *281*
Canada's Diversity Gardens project, 287–88, *288*
Canadian Conservation Institute, Ottawa, 45
Canadian Museum for Human Rights (CMHR), Winnipeg, 74, 300, 337, 344; *1867*, *347*; *Empowering Women*, *349*; *Inuit Land and Lifeways* installation, 343, *343*; linear media projected across irregular shape, *340*; *Mandela*, 124, *124*, 360–62, *361-62*; mobile device for accessibility affordances, *341*; *Rights of Passage*, 356–59, *357-59*
Canadian Museum of History, Gatineau, *347*
Canadian Museum of Immigration at Pier 1 (CMIP), Halifax: *Canada Day 1*, 231–32, *232*, 279, *281*; entrance to permanent exhibition, *280*; oral history stations, *281*; visitors interacting with personal stories of newcomers, *281*; working with subject matter experts, 279–81, *280-81*
Canadian Museum of Nature, Gatineau, 122
Canadian Niagara Power Generating Station, *238*
Canadian War Museum, Ottawa, 70, *70*, 105, *105*

capital costs, 30, 41
Capitol Visitor Center (CVC), Washington DC, 253–55, *254*
carbon dioxide sensors, 33
carbon filters, activated, 33
Carlsson, Rebecca, 8–9
carousel (slideshow) virtual exhibitions, 104–5
Carr, David, 169
Carter, Karen, 157–59
Carter, Thelma, 284, *285*
cases: active climate-controlled, *36*; climate-controlled, *348*; costs with exhibit, 380; preparators with traveling artifact, *141*. *See also* display cases
case/security hardware, security levels, 53
CCT (correlated color temperature), 309
ceilings: exhibition spaces, 26–27; functionality and appearance, 41; load requirements, 38–39
celebrate, 88
Central Bank Museum, Trinidad and Tobago, 212, 221–22, *222*; multimedia treatment for, 276–77; visitors with *Symbols* exhibit, *277*
centralized, hardware integration, 373
Centre for Freshwater Research and Education, 259
Le Centre Pompidou, Metz, 132
certification: continuous learning and, 403; LEED, 314
Chagal, Marc, 84
change orders: with completion and close-out, 375; decision-making, 218
Cherry, Kendra, 173
Chicago History Museum, 75, 76
Chicago Museum of Science and Industry, 82, *82*
children, 268, 269, *270*; exhibitions, 76–79, *78*; museums, 6, 27, 42, 76, 77, 157
China, temporary exhibition spaces, 135
choice of depth, 265, 267
Christie MicroTiles, 344
chronology, 239, 243, 248
circular display cases, 305, *305*
circulation: accessibility, 298; exhibition facilities, 55–58, *58*; vertical, 42
"The Citizen Design tool kit," 166
Civil War Gallery, Tennessee State Museum, *243*
claims, warranties, 376
classification, typeface, *325*
cleaning, 52
clerestory window systems, 43
climate: change, 8, 18, 21, 120, 205, 268; control, 31–33, *36*, 348; microclimate, 30, 35–36, *36*, 44
closed captioning, 99, 300
closed tour, traveling exhibitions, 136
close-out, production process, 374–75
CMHR. *See* Canadian Museum for Human Rights

Index **439**

CMIP (Canadian Museum of Immigration at Pier 1), Halifax, 231-32, *232*, 279-81, *280-81*
CMS (content management system), 353
cocreated exhibitions, 282
cocuration, 9, 74, 154, 216, 219, 282, 283
code compliance, 367
collaboration: multidisciplinary and cross department, 154; tools and software for project management, 400-401
collections: development and direct exhibition costs, 384; ethnographic, 155, *156*; exhibitions and museums in India, 318; First Nations, 71; gaps an biases in, 154; Girard, 113-16; The Historic New Orleans Collection, 103, *103*, 406; intangible, 61, 75, 154, 231, 236, 260; interpreting, 64-66, *65*; with living history exhibitions, 79; natural history museum, 67; permanent or temporary exhibitions, 228; private, 271; research, 260-63, *262*; traveling exhibitions and access to, 134; virtual exhibitions, 62, 92-93. See also permanent collection displays
collections manager, temporary exhibitions, 125
Colonial Williamsburg, Virginia, *80, 81*
color rendering index (CRI), 309-10
colors: accessibility, 299; BIPOC, 154-55, 157, 158, 216, 257-58, 278; CCT, 309; graphic design, 330-33, *332*; IESTM-30 rendering system for, 310; Michelangelo's tomb, *332, 333*; Pantone Matching System, 333; perception, 309; *Sisters in Liberty*, 330, *332, 333*
Coming Home exhibition, Abbe Museum, 155, 157
commercially driven separate division, traveling exhibitions, 136
commissioning: period, 45-46; virtual exhibitions, 111
commitment, green design, 315
committees, exhibition process teams and, 215-16
communication: exhibition space with power and, 44-45; interpretive planning and, 248-49; multidirectional, 9, 14; multimedia exhibits and, 275; objectives and visitor experience, 273; powers of art, 67; specialists and exhibition process, 211; visual, 319-20, *321*
communities: BIPOC, 154-55, 157, 158, 216, 257-58, 278; consultation, 1, 154, 210, 218, 228, 279, 282; content development and, 282-88, *285-86, 288*; curators, 283; exhibitions and museums in India, 318; outreach, 78, 119, 219
Community Through Making virtual exhibition, MOIFA, 116
competition, traveling exhibitions, 135
completion, production process, 374-75
concept, exhibition, 223-25
concept design, 290, 321-22

condition report: temporary exhibitions, 125; traveling exhibitions, 137, 142-43
conservation, 45, 47; reasons for, 64; related exhibition costs, 386-87; staff, 56
conservators: temporary exhibitions, 125; traveling exhibitions, 137
construction: drawings, 295-96, 370; green design, 315
Contact, Exchange and Migration exhibition theme, National Archaeological Museum, 249
contact relationship management, 137
contemporary art, grand exhibition spaces, 26
content: aggregators and virtual exhibition platforms, 102; committee and exhibition process, 216; coordination and virtual exhibitions, 111; design essentials, 334; specialists and exhibition process, 211; virtual exhibitions, 97, 99-100
content development: collections research and selection, 260-63, *262*; communities and, 282-88, *285-86, 288*; exhibition text, 263-68, *265-66, 269*; *First Peoples* exhibition, 283-86; hands-on exhibits, models, dioramas and, 273-74; image research and procurement, 268-72, *270, 272*; IPG, 287-88; multimedia exhibits, 274-78, *277*; research planning, 258-60, *259*; subject matter experts, 278-81
content management system (CMS), 353
contextual displays, *67*, 67-68
contextual galleries, 26
contingency, direct exhibition costs, 385
contracting: bonding, 368; craftspeople locally, 364; with exhibit firm, 364; expertise and exhibition process, 217; fabrication, 366-68, *377*, 377-78; scope of work, 366-67
contractors: general, 367; project coordination meetings and, 395; sub-, 367-68
contrast, accessibility, 299-300
control system, lighting, 312-13
Cooper-Hewitt Smithsonian Design Museum, New York, 166, *167-68*, 338, *340*
copyright: image research and procurement, 272; multimedia exhibits, 275; royalties and, 385
core exhibition team, exhibition process, *212*, 215-16
core idea, exhibition brief, 227-28
core messages, exhibition text, 263
corporate partnerships, 12
corporate sponsorship, 12-13
correlated color temperature (CCT), 309
Cosmopolis Toronto exhibition, Myseum of Toronto, 157
costs: allocation and design process, 388; budgets basics and, 380-83; capital, 30, 41; direct exhibition, 384-86; exhibition budget and lower,

388; exhibition production, 108; going over budget, 388–89; green design, 314–15; hosting virtual exhibitions, 104; operating, 30; related exhibition, 386–87; virtual exhibitions, 109–10, 110. *See also* budgets; financial planning

costumes, 64, 81

The Costume Institute at the Met, 127, *128*

couriers: direct exhibition costs, 384; traveling exhibitions, 138, 143

COVID-19 pandemic, 11, 84, 93, 95, 157; digital audiences, 220; planning, 29, 42, 55; revenue and, 12; traveling exhibitions and, 147–48; traveling exhibitions post-, 149–50. *See also* virtual exhibitions

craftspeople, local, 364

creative specialists, exhibition process, 211

CRI (color rendering index), 309–10

critical path scheduling, 375

cross department collaborations, multidisciplinary and, 154

crowdsourcing, social media and, 408

The Crown (TV show), *106*

cultural history museums, 27

culture: Alaska Native, 69; Bunjilaka Aboriginal Cultural Centre, 283–86, *285–86*; Forest County Potawatomi Museum and Cultural Centre, *262*; Google Arts and Culture, 102; *Misko-Aki Confluence of Cultures Exhibition*, 247, *247*; Shaanxi Provincial Cultural Relics Bureau, 122; Wabanaki, 155, 157

curation, contracting expertise, 217

curatorial brief/intellectual content, 275

curatorial voice, 223, 258

curators, 125, 154, 283

curatorship, exhibition concept, 224

curiosity: audience experiences and exhibition preferences, 171–75; cultivating, 165–69; with improved outcomes, 165; learning and exhibitions, 169–71; learning types compared across museums, *170*; motivation and, *174*; museum experiences and fostering, 169; *Process Lab*, 166, *167–68*; types, 166–68

Curiosity (Wilkening), 165–66

current issues, timely exhibiting of, 154–55

curved display cases, 305, *305*

customs broker, traveling exhibitions, 142

CVC (Capitol Visitor Center), Washington DC, 253–55, *254*

dances, 61

Darwin Centre, NHM, 69

dashboard reports, 401–2, *402*

data entry, related exhibition costs, 387

data/insights, operationalizing multimedia, 354

data sheet, 260–61, *262, 272*

data triangulation, 198–99

David Bowie Is exhibition, Victoria and Albert Museum, 129

Da Vinci, Leonardo, 92

DEAI (Diversity, Equality, Accessibility, and Inclusion), 152, 154, 155, 157, 158, 160–63

DEAI, exhibitions: *Black Lives Matter, London*, 156; Blackman on activating change, 160–63; Carter, Karen, on, 157–59; with cocuration, shared authority and curators, 154; community consultation and, 154; cross department and multidisciplinary collaborations, 154; current issues, 154–55; development schedules, 155; ethnographic collection, 155, *156*; evolution of roles and responsibilities, 155; funding for sustainable engagement, 155; implications for, 154–57; Sloane and British Museum, 153

decentralized control, hardware integration, 373

decision-making: exhibition process, 217–18; interpretive planning, 235

decolonization, 155, 158

decorative arts, exhibition spaces for small-scale, 26

decorative typeface, 325, *325*

deficiency (punch) list, 374

Degas, Edgar, 260

democratic societies, 169

demountable display cases, 306, *306*

density, costs, 380

Depot Boijmans van Beuningen, 69

design: compact and easy to ship, 140; concept, 290, 321–22; content coordination phase and, 2; contracting expertise, 217; criteria, *27*, 27–37, *29, 34, 36*; detailed, 294; development, 294; direct exhibition costs, 384; easy to assemble, take apart and pack, 140; essentials, 333–34; estimates, 388; of exhibition spaces for small-to medium-sized works, 26; green, 314–17; indigenous-led, 287–88, *288*; Interaction Design Foundation, 98; of light fixtures, 311; modular, simple and durable, 140; object, 30, 42, 57; process and budgets, 387–88; schematic, 290, 293–94, 321–22, 397; semiotics in, 319–21, *321*; stages and construction drawings, 295–96; team, 125, 216; three-dimensional, 291; traveling exhibitions, 139–41, *141*; virtual exhibitions, 111–12. *See also* graphic design

design, exhibition: accessibility, 297–300, *299*; acoustics, 291–92; core disciplines, 291–92; display cases, 301–8; fabrication, production and designer role, 297; graphics, 291; green, 314–17; *Guidelines for Accessible Exhibition Design*, 298; interpretive plan and, 289–90; lighting and, 291, 308–14; multimedia, 292; museums in India, 317–18; process, 290–300;

RIBA and development, 296, *296-97*; stages of, 292-97, *293*; three-dimensional, 291; value engineered, 295, 314
design-bid-build, 364-65
design-bid strategies, 364
design-build: assignment and exhibition process, 216; fabrication, 365-66; models, 365; SHSND, 378
designers, with fabrication and production, 297
Design Noise Criteria (NC) ratings, 45
design-tender strategies, 364
detailed design, 294
Deutsches Museum, Munich, 81
development: audience, 134; design, 294; exhibition process, 1-2; process and virtual exhibitions, 111-12; schedules, 155. *See also* content development
development process, exhibition: design and content coordination phase, 2; development phase, 1-2; evaluation in, *180*; formative evaluation, 183-85; front-end evaluation, 181-83; implementation phase, 2; from initial concept to opening day, *2*; RIBA, 296, *296-97*
devices: BYOD, 350; virtual exhibitions, 96
didactic: means of expression, 250; virtual exhibitions, 104, 115
Dierking, Lynn, 9
digital audiences: behaviors and expectations, 96-97; content, 97; COVID-19 pandemic and, 220; devices used, 96; location, 89, 96-97; platforms, 97; user experience, 97; virtual exhibitions and, 95-99
digital divide, 97-98
digital first virtual exhibitions, 100
digital immersive exhibitions, 83-84, *83-84*
digital media, 298, *361*
Digital Museums Canada, 99, 109
digital resources, microsites for, 101, *101*
digitization, related exhibition costs, 387
Dilenschneider, Colleen, 8
dimensions, hands-on exhibits, 274
dimming, lighting design, 313
dinosaurs, 62, 127, 147, 149, 274
dioramas, 273-74
direct exhibition costs, 384-86
direct revenue, traveling exhibitions, 134
disabilities, people with, 56, 79, 98, 157, 297, 349
dispersal, traveling exhibitions, 140, 144
display cases: active-control, 308; curved or circular, 305, *305*; drawer systems, 307, *307*; exhibition design, 301-8; freestanding with glass top, 302-3, *303*; freestanding with integral light hood, *303*, 304; glass, 301-2; infrastructure and environmental considerations, 307-8; modular/demountable, 306, *306*; passive-control, 308; tabletop, 302, *303*; types, 302-7; wall, 298, 305, *306*, 381
displays: aesthetic, 66, *66-67*; contextual, *67*, 67-68; modes of, *66-68*, 66-71, *70-71*; permanent collection, 61-71, *63-65*; process, 68, *68*; visible storage, 69-71, *70-71*, 225
display typeface, 325, *325*
disposal, traveling exhibitions, 140
Diversity, Equality, Accessibility, and Inclusion (DEAI), 152, 154, 155, 157, 158, 160-63
DIY (do it yourself) approach, 320
documentary films: *Mandela* exhibition with mini, *361*; masked into oval shape, *339*; 360-degree circular, *339*
documentation, completion and close-out, 375
documents, 88, 295-96
do it yourself (DIY) approach, 320
doors: gallery shell and exterior, 37-38; stairs, ramps and, 41-42
drag load, 39
Dragons, Unicorns, and Mermaids temporary exhibition, AMNH, 122, *123*
drawer systems display cases, 307, *307*
drawings: construction, 295-96, 370; shop, 297
ductwork, 26, 37, 38
Duplessis, Antoinette, 173
dynamic virtual exhibitions, 105

Earth's Treasures (visible storage display), 70, *71*
education, 20, 21, 129, 137, 259, 315, 387
1867 exhibition, Canadian Museum of History, *347*
electronic surveillance, 53-54
elevators, 38, 41, 42, 45, 56, 57, 140
Eliasson, Olafur, 124
Ellis Island National Museum of Immigration, New York City, 227, 245, *245*
embedded operation, traveling exhibitions, 136
emergencies, 52-53
Empowering Women, CMHR, *349*
Encore Media Partners, 129
energy: LEED certification, 314; lighting efficiency and, 316
Engagement Group, NHM, 146
English, Jan, 145-48
environment: display case considerations with infrastructure and, 307-8; LEED certification, 314; materials and finishes, 45-51, *47-51*; quality and green design, 316; SEGD, 315-16; standards, 30-37
equality hashtag, *359*
ethics, sponsored content and, 12
ethnographic collection, Tropenmuseum, 155, *156*
Etihad Museum, Dubai, 242, *242*
European Museum of Modern Art, Barcelona, 105

evaluation: direct exhibition costs, 384; exhibition development, 180; formative, 154; front-end, 1, 154-55, 180-84, 186, 203, 235; front-end, formative, remedial and summative, 179-87; museum specific criteria, 178-79; qualitative and quantitative audience research, 187-200; with success measured, 177-79; UMMNH front-end and formative visitor study, 200-207; virtual exhibitions with monitoring and, 112; visitor, 169

Evolution at Eindhoven, Netherlands, 81

execution, design criteria, 28

execution-driven design criteria, spaces, 30; air cleanliness, 33-34; air movement and outdoor air, 33; climate control, 31-33; light levels, 34, 34-35; microclimates, 35-36, *36*; movement and vibration, 37; pest management, 36-37

exhibition director/manager, temporary exhibitions, 125

exhibition-making, future of, 405-8

exhibition planning, MIs theory and, *172*

exhibition process: contracting expertise, 217; core team, *212*, 215-16, *221*; decision-making and, 217-18; Huaco and OMCA, 218-21; principals in, 211-15; roles and responsibilities, *213-15*; small museum roles and responsibilities, 221-22

exhibitions: as agents of transformation, 7, 8-10, 12; audience experiences preferences in, 171-75; children's, 76-79, *78*; corporate sponsorship, 12-13; digital immersive, 83-84, *83-84*; ideas for, 17-21, 73-76, *75-76*; learning and, 169-71; light levels recommended for, *34*; living history, 79-81, *80-81*; permanent collection, 61-63, 227-28, 230; physical, 90-92; play-based, *77*, *78*; renewal costs, 62; research-based and market-driven, 18, *19*, 20-21; research planning, 18-21; science, 81-83, *82*. *See also* temporary exhibitions; traveling exhibitions; virtual exhibitions

exhibits: content development and multimedia, 274-78, *277*; hands-on, 273-74; objectives of, 370. *See also specific exhibits*

expectations, digital audiences, 96-97

expenses, direct exhibition costs, 385

experts: content development, 278-81; exhibition process and contracting, 217; subject matter, 279-81, *280-81*

Exploratorium, San Francisco, 81

Exploring Michigan Permanent Exhibition Gallery, UMMNH, 201-2, 250-53, *252-53*

expo booth virtual exhibitions, 107

exposed ceiling, 41

extending life: of physical exhibitions, 90-91; of traveling exhibitions, 113-16, *114*, *116*

exterior doors, gallery shell, 37-38

external perimeter, security levels, 53

eye level of vision range, graphic design legibility, *328*

fabrication: contracting, 366-68, *377*, 377-78; design-bid-build, 364-65; design-build or turnkey exhibitions, 365-66; designer role during production and, 297; direct exhibition costs, 384; exhibition production and, 363-64; production process, 368-75; tracking and scheduling, 375-76

Fabric in Fashion exhibit, The Museum at FIT, 337, *338*

Facebook, 87, 92, 193, 195

Faces of Freedom exhibit, National Czech & Slovak Museum, *382*

facilities, exhibition: accessibility, adjacency and circulation, 55-58, *58*; criteria for spaces, 27-37; gallery security, 51-55; shortfalls, 25-26; space, utility and size, 26-27; space characteristics, 37-51, *39*, *47-51*

Facing Freedom exhibition, 75, *76*

Factum Foundation for Digital Technology in Conservation, 407

Falk, John, 9, 173

family: activities, 77, 92; Weston Family Innovation Centre, 78, 82-83, *85*, 85-88

Fantastic Beasts touring exhibition, NHM, 147

Fedi, Pio, 227, 245

fenestration, natural light and, 42-44

Fernbank Museum of Natural History, Atlanta, 122

fiber optics, 312

Field Museum, Chicago, 122

film/video/graphics/audio, multimedia exhibits, 275

filters: air, 33-34; carbon, 33; lighting, 312

final dispersal, traveling exhibition, 144

final quote/final budget, design process, 388

financial planning: budget management, 387-89; direct exhibition costs, 384-86; exhibition budgets, 379-83; related exhibition costs, 386-87

finishes: exhibition space with material and, 45-51; summary of gallery materials and, *47-51*

fires, detection and suppression, 54-55

firm, exhibit, 364

First Nations collections, 71

First Peoples exhibition, Bunjilaka Aboriginal Cultural Centre, 283-86; Harrison holding basket, *285*; Keeping Places display, *286*; Many Nations section, 284, *285*, *286*

5-M Model for Successful Interpretive Planning (Brochu), 234

Five D Media, 115

fixtures, light, 26, 310, *311*

Index 443

flexible, vision-driven design criteria, 28
flip experience, 175
Floch, Jean-Marie, 320
floors, gallery: load requirements, 38-39, *39*; systems, 40
Floyd, George, 155
focal specific structures, 240
font sizes, 299
footcandle (lux), 43
Forensic Architecture, 12
Forensic Architecture exhibition, 12
Forest County Potawatomi Museum and Cultural Centre, Wisconsin, *262*
formal approvals, decision-making, 218
formative evaluation, 154, 181, 183-85
formative studies, front-end and, 191-92
formative visitor studies, 196
formats, virtual exhibitions, *105, 106*; AR, 106-7; carousel or slideshow, 104-5; didactic, 104, 115; dynamic, 105; expo booth, 107; 3D virtual walkthrough, 105-6, 115; VR and immersive renderings, 106
forms of illustration, accessibility, 300
Frames of Mind (Gardner), 171
framework, core idea and thematic, 228
free admission, 108
freestanding display cases: with glass top, 302-3, *303*; with integral light hood, *303*, 304
free with registration, 108
friends, 77, 131, 204, 206
Frist Art Museum, Nashville, 119
front-end evaluation, 1, 154-55, 180-84, 186, 203, 235
front-end studies, formative and, 191-92
front-end visitor studies, 195-96
functional program, 30
funding: for long-term engagement, 155; schedule, 228; temporary exhibitions with resourcing and, 130-31
furniture, exhibit, 298

galleries: building systems, 38; exhibition space characteristics, 37-51, *39, 47-51*; exterior doors, 37-38; libraries, archives, and museums sector, 354; load requirements for, 38-39, *39*; moisture, 38; preparation and related exhibition costs, 386; purpose-built, 24, 26, 76, 83, 228; security, 51-55; shell, 37-38; wall within wall, 37
galvanizing, vision-driven design criteria, 28
Game of Thrones exhibition, 18, *19*
games, gamification and: multimedia with, 346-47, *347*; overhead projected table, *345*; systems, 343
Gantt chart: development, 397-99; with Microsoft Project, 400; sample, *398*; task finish dates, 399
Garabaldi Meucci Museum, Staten Island, 227

garden, sculpture, 27
Gardner, Howard, 171-73, *172*, 249
Gehry, Frank, 24, 305
general contractor, 367
Geologic Time Gallery, North Dakota Heritage Center & State Museum, *377*
GES Events, 18
gesture technologies, 83, 343-44, *344*
Getting Permission (Stim), 385
Getty Conservation Institute, Los Angeles, 45
Gilmore, Jean Allman, 134
Girard, Alexander, 113-15
Girard, Susan, 113
Girard Collection, 113-16
Glaciers exhibition, Perlan Museum of Natural Wonders, 268, *269*
GLAM (galleries, libraries, archives, and museums) sector, 354
glass display cases, 301-2
glass top, freestanding display cases with, 302-3, *303*
global market, gaps and inequalities in, 148-49
Google Arts and Culture, 102
Google Docs, 399
Google Sites, 101
government indemnity program, 126
Government Indemnity Scheme, 301
grand exhibition spaces, 26
graphic data sheet, from Green Gables Heritage Place, *272*
graphic description, 271
graphic design: color, 330-33, *332*; development/detailed, 322-23; elements and typography, 323-30, *324-28, 330*; essentials, 333-34; exhibition and, 291; imagery, 333; legibility, 323, 326-28, *327-28*; process, 321-23; production, 323; schematic or concept, 321-22; SEGD, 315-16; semiotics, 319-21, *321*; text levels and information hierarchy, 323, 328-30, *330-31*; typeface selection, 323-26, *324-26*
graphic grid, design essentials, 333
graphic numbers, 271
graphics: accessibility, 299, 300; production process, 371
graphics/audio/film/video, multimedia exhibits, 275
Great Exhibition, Hyde Park (1851), 157-58
Great Whales exhibition, ROM, 121
green design, 314-17
Green Gables Heritage, Prince Edward Island, *272*
Greimas, Algirdas Julien, 320
Greimas square, 320, *321*
Grieves, Genevieve, 283
Griffith, Mamie, 287, *288*
Guggenheim Museum, New York City, 24, 35, 131-32

Guidelines for Accessible Exhibition Design (Smithsonian Institution), 298
Gujarat (Statue of Unity), 317

Hamdun, Ghaida, 155
hands-on exhibits, 273–74
hands-on/minds-on activities, 250
handyman (*bricoleur*), 320
hardware: integration and media production, 373; multimedia design, 292; operationalizing multimedia with software and, 352–53
Harrison, Eileen, 284, *285*
Harvard University, 157
hashtags, *350, 359*
HBO, 18
Herman Miller Inc., 113, 114
hierarchy, information, 323, 328–30, *330–31*
Hillbilly Elegy (film), 12
The Historic New Orleans Collection, 103, *103*, 406
Historic Threads website, *80*
history museums, 75, *76*; display/storage ratios, 63; natural, 6, 21, 27, 63, 67, 69
holdback, 368
hosted exhibitions, 282
hosting, virtual exhibitions, 103–4
hotspots interface, *Rights of Passage* exhibition, *358*
HTFC Planning & Design, 287
Huaco, Valerie, 218–21
human rights violations, 12
humidity, 31–35, 37, 38, 56
Huron-Wandat peoples, 159
HVAC system, 32, 37
hybrid model, traveling exhibitions, 136

idea exhibitions, 73–76, *75–76*
ideas, IPOP framework, 175
Identity and the Museum Visitor Experience (Falk), 173
identity motivations, 173
IESTM-30 color rendering system, 310
illustrations: accessibility and forms of, 300; image research and procurement, 270–71
image research: content development with procurement and, 268–72, *270, 272*; Ross watching children climbing path, 268, 269, *270*
imagery, graphic design, 333
images, *359*; low-resolution, 272; moving, 338–41, *339–40, 361*; from other public institutions, 271; placement and design essentials with text, 334; source, 271; stock, 271
Imaginate traveling exhibition, Ontario Science Centre, 87
immersive experience, 83–84, *83–84*, 109, 250
immersive renderings, VR and, 106
Immersive Van Gogh exhibition, 84, *84*

implementation: phase of exhibition development process, 2; virtual exhibitions, 112
inclusivity, virtual exhibitions, 98–99
An Incomplete History of Protest exhibition, 74, *75*
independent structures, 240
India, exhibitions and museums in, 317–18
indigenous design team, 287–88, *288*
Indigenous peoples, 153–55, 159, 263, 266, 283, 284
Indigenous Peoples Garden (IPG), 287–88, *288*
industrial museums, 6
infants, 77
Infinity Mirrors (Kusama), 81
informal approvals, decision-making, 218
informal learning, 77
information hierarchy, graphic design, typography, 323, 328–30, *330–31*
information pamphlet stations, 56
infrared light (IR), 310
infrastructure: display cases with environmental considerations, 307–8; operationalizing multimedia, 353
in-house production, 363
in-kind contributions, budgets and, 389–90
Innovation Centre 2.0, 87
Innovation Gallery, North Dakota Heritage Center & State Museum, *331*
Inspiration Gallery, North Dakota Heritage Center & State Museum, 248, *248*, 390, *390*
Instagram, 103, *103*, 129, 193, *350*, 358, *359*
installation: access, 374; art and grand exhibition spaces, 26; direct exhibition costs, 384; of exhibits at Canada Aviation and Space Museum, *374*; manual for traveling exhibitions, 141, 143–44; production and, 3, 363, 364, 367, 373, 374, 375; production process, 373–74, *374*; staging space and, 373; work hours and, 374
installations hall, special, 26
intangible collections, 61, 75, 154, 231, 236, 260
intangible-interactive interpretive displays, 64–65
integration, 68, *68*; installation and schedule, 373; programming, 70; vision-driven design criteria, 28
integrative planning, 249–50
intellectual content/curatorial brief, 275
intelligences, multiple, 171–73, *172*
Interaction Design Foundation, 98, 99
interactive media, 342
interactivity, costs, 380
International Coalition of Sites of Conscience, 74
international shipping, traveling exhibitions, 142
interpretation: collections-based, 64–66, *65*; green design with education and, 315
interpretative plan: process, 171; virtual exhibitions, 111

Index   **445**

interpretive plan, 2, 63, 109, 125, 171, 184, 186; communication objectives/visitor outcomes and, 248-49; contracting expertise, 217; critical role of, 233-34; CVC, 253-55, *254*; decision-making and monitoring, 235; exhibition design and, 289-90; *Exploring Michigan*, 201-2, 250-53, *252-53*; metanarrative or Big Idea, 224, 228, 237-38, *238*; organizational and thematic frameworks, 239-40, *239-40*; process, *236*; project-specific, 234; relevant, meaningful and relatable, 234; with research and visioning, 236-37; story line, 249-50; strategy and, 237-38; thematic framework examples, 241-48; visitor centered, 234-35

Interpretive Planning for Museums (Wells, Adams and Koke), 171

interpretive planning team, temporary exhibitions, 125

interpretive strategy, planning and, 237-38

Inuit Land and Lifeways installation, CMHR, 343, *343*

investigator triangulation, 199

IPG (Indigenous Peoples Garden), 287-88, *288*

IPOP framework, 173, 175

IR (infrared light), 310

ivory, 64

Jamaica, slave plantations, 153

James Madison's Montpelier, *355*

Janes, Robert R., 11

Jewish Museum Milwaukee, Wisconsin, *381*, 389, *389*

Kaminaljuyú (Mayan city), 246

Keeping Places display, Many Nations section of *First Peoples* exhibition, *286*

Kent University, 227

kerning, typography, 327

Kerzner, Harold, 404

kindergarten-aged children, 77

kiosks, multimedia, *71*, 297, 342

Klimt, Gustav, 84

knowledge, creation of new, 178

Koke, Judith, 171

Kolko, Jon, 8

Kusama, Yayoi, 81

label, from *Innovation Gallery*, *331*

Le Laboratoire, Paris, 119

Lake Superior State University, Michigan, 259

language: American Sign Language, 298, 300, *341*, 355; changing, 87

large objects, costs, 380

layout, graphics, 371

Leadership in Energy and Environmental Design (LEED) certification, 314

"Lean Project Management," Six Sigma Organization, 403

learning: exhibitions and, 169-71; objectives, 1, 100, 237, 342; project management, certification and continuous, 403; types compared across museums, *170*

LED lights, 310, 311, *359*

LEED (Leadership in Energy and Environmental Design) certification, 314

legibility, graphic design, 323; anatomy of typography, *327*; eye level of vision range, *328*; typography, 326-28, *327-28*

lens system, lighting, 311

Lévi-Strauss, Claude, 320

Libertà (Fedi), 227, 245

"Lick a Rat" epigenetics interactive, UMMNH, 205-6, 207

"Lick Your Rats" online game, University of Utah, 205, *205*

light: ambient, 34, 44, 52, 298, 349; fixtures, 26, 310, 311; freestanding display cases with integral hood, *303*, 304; IR, 310; LED, 310, 311, 359; levels, 34, 34-35, 52; natural, 42-44; phototropic effect and, 43; setting and focusing, 374; skylight, 33, 37, 42, 43, 44; sunlight, 43, 44, 82, 309; UV, 310; working, 35

lighting: accessibility, 298, *299*; control system, 312-13; design, 291, 308-14, *313*, 334; direct exhibition costs, 384; exhibition, 34; fenestration and natural, 42-44; fiber optics, 312; filters, 312; green design with energy efficiency and, 316; lens system, 311; maintenance, 313; sidelighting, 43; systems and related exhibition costs, 386; toplighting, 43; track, 35, 312; traveling exhibitions with power and, 140; upgrading or changing technology, 313-14; wireless control, 313

light installation (Burman), 124

linear exhibitions, thematic frameworks, 239

linear media, 337, *340*

linear organizational model, *239*

line load, 39

Little White House Museum, Warm Springs, 264

living history exhibitions, 79-81, *80-81*

load requirements, for galleries: floors, 38-39, *39*; walls, ceilings, 38-39

loan agreements: temporary exhibitions, 125-26; traveling exhibitions, 138-39

location: graphic element, 271-72; hands-on exhibits, models, dioramas, 274; multimedia exhibits, 275; virtual exhibitions, 89, 96-97

Lord, Barry, 7

Lord Cultural Resources, *2, 27, 34, 36, 39, 47, 58, 65, 68, 70. 71, 82, 110, 123, 126, 144, 180, 188, 191, 212, 213, 226, 229, 230, 232, 236, 239, 240, 241,*

244, 245, 252, 253, 265, 269, 281, 293, 296, 299, 324, 325, 326, 327, 328, 330, 332, 372, 374, 380, 383, 398, 402
Lord, Gail, 10
Louvre Abu Dhabi, 132
Louvre Lens, 132
Louvre Museum. *See* Le Musée du Louvre, Paris
low-resolution image, 272
Lowry and the Painting of Modern Life exhibition, Tate Britain, 121, *122*
lux (footcandle), 43

MacLaren Art Centre, Barrie, 157, 159
macro artifacts, 69-70
Magna Carta exhibit, 126, *126*
maintenance, lighting, 313
maintenance agreements, extended warranties and, 376-77
makerspace, 86
management: CMS, 353; contact relationship, 137; financial planning and budget, 387-89; green design and waste, 316; pest, 36-37; temporary exhibitions, 125-27; tour for traveling exhibitions, 141-44. *See also* project management
Mandela, Nelson, 360
Mandela exhibition, CMHR, 124, *124*, 360-62; digital media integrated into scenography, *361*; mini documentaries presented on scrim walls, *361*; "Posters for Freedom" activity, 360, *362*
Manila, 76
Manuels River Hibernia Integration Centre, Newfoundland, 68, *68*
Many Nations section, *First Peoples* exhibition, 284, *285*; Keeping Places display, *286*
market-driven exhibition, 18, *19*
market-driven imbalance, traveling exhibition, 149
marketing, 2; related exhibition costs, 387; temporary exhibitions, public relations and, 129-30; traveling exhibitions, sales and, 137
Martin, Caroline, 283
materials: exhibition space with finishes and, 45-51; green design, 315; summary of gallery finishes and, *47-51*
meaningfulness, interpretive planning and, 234
media, 26, 115, 129; costs, 380; digital, 298, *361*; interactive, 342; linear, 337, *340*; with sponsored content, 13; trust factor and, 12. *See also* multimedia; social media
media production: direct exhibition costs, 384-85; hardware integration, 373; monitoring, 372-73; turnkey or separate contract, 372
meetings, project coordination, 394-95
Melbourne Museum, Australia, Bunjilaka Aboriginal Cultural Centre, 283-86

membership benefits, 108
metanarrative (Big Idea), 224, 228, 237-38, *238*
methodological triangulation, 199-200
Metropolitan Museum of Art (the Met), New York City, 120-21, 127, *128*
Mexico City, 76
Michelangelo's tomb, Santa Croce, Florence, *332*, 333
microclimate, 30, 35-36, *36*, 44
microsites, for digital resources, 101, *101*
Microsoft, 343
Microsoft Excel, 400
Microsoft Office, 399
Microsoft Project, 400
middle school children, 77
Milwaukee Public Museum, *382*
Miraflores Museum, Guatemala, 246, *246*
MIs (Multiple Intelligences), 171-73, *172*
Misko-Aki (Red Earth) Confluence of Cultures Exhibition, Muskoka Discovery Centre, 247, *247*
mistakes, making, 87
mixed reality (MR), 347, 348
M+ Museum, Hong Kong, 94-95
Mnjikaning First Nation, Ontario, 159
mobile applications, 70, 300
mobile device for accessibility affordances, CMHR, *341*
mobile technologies, multimedia, 349-50, *350*
mock-up, exhibition text, 267
models, content development, 273-74
modular display cases, 306, *306*
MOIFA (Museum of International Folk Art), Santa Fe, 113-16, *114*, *116*
moisture, gallery shell, 38
molecules, proteins interactive, 206
Mona Lisa (Da Vinci), 92
Monet, Claude, 18, *19*, 84
monitoring: interpretive planning, 235; media production, 372-73; virtual exhibitions with evaluation and, 112
motion sensors, 83, 203, 316
motivations, identifying, *174*
mount-making, 371-72, *372*
moveable gallery walls, 40-41
movement, execution-driven design criteria, 37
move people around, 88
moving images: *Mandela* exhibition with mini documentaries, *361*; multimedia, 338-41, *339-40*
MR (mixed reality), 347, 348
multidirectional communication, 9, 14
multidisciplinary collaborations, cross department and, 154
multimedia, 70, 250; audio, 341, *341*; defined, 335; exhibition design and, 292; games and gamification, 346-47, *347*; gesture technology,

Index 447

83, 343-44, *344*; interactive media, 342; kiosks, *71*, 297, 342; linear media, 337, *340*; *Mandela* exhibition, 360-62, *361-62*; mobile technologies, 349-50, *350*; moving image, 338-41, *339-40*; multiuser tables, 344-46, *345*; operationalizing, 351-55; projection mapping, 337-38, *338*; responsive environments/sensors, 342-43, *343*; *Rights of Passage* exhibition, 356-59, *357-59*; social media, 350-51; specialists, 3, 292; strategic role, 336-37; types of, 337-51; XR, 347-49, *348-50*

multimedia, operationalizing: budgeting, 352; content management and infrastructure, 353; data/insights, 354; hardware and software, 352-53; small museums, 354-55, *355*; team composition, 351-52

multimedia exhibits: content development and, 274-78; outsourcing research, 274-75; visitors engaging with *Symbols*, *277*

Multiple Intelligences (MIs), 171-73, *172*
multiple-perspective approach, 10, 12
multiple perspectives, 71
MultiTaction table, 344, *345*
multiuser tables, 344-46, *345*
Multiversity Gallery visible storage exhibition, 71
Muscat, Marcie M., 10
Musée d'Orsay, Paris, 18, 44
musée du quai Branly-Jacques Chirac, Paris, *66*, 67
Le Musée du Louvre, Paris, 92, 132
The Museum at FIT, New York City, 337, *338*
Museo Guggenheim Bilbao, 24, 35, 131-32
Museum Activism (Sandell and Janes), 11
museum archives, 270
museum experiences, curiosity and, 169
Museum Junction platform, American Alliance of Museum, 354
Museum London, Ontario, 155, *156*
MuseumNext (website), 8-9
Museum of Anthropology, UBC, 71
Museum of Art and Design, Miami Dade College, 11-12
Museum of International Folk Art (MOIFA), Santa Fe, 113-16, *114*, *116*
Museum of Modern Art, New York City, Tim Burton exhibition, *91*, 91-92
Museum of Science and Industry, Chicago, 81
Museum of Tolerance, Los Angeles, 74
museum planner, 30
museums: as activist institutions, 10-12; art, 11-12, 18, *19*, 74, 75, 78, *91*, 91-92, 105, 113-16, *114*, 116, 119-21, 127, *128*, 157, 159, 218, 305; corporate sponsorship, 12-13; hashtags, *350*; India with exhibitions and, 317-18; *Interpretive Planning for Museums*, 171; learning types compared across, *170*; soft power, 10-11, 146, 169; trust factor and, 8, 12-14, 74; as truthful storytellers for humanity, 6, 13-14. *See also specific museums*

museums, small: budgeting for staff, 386; exhibition budgets, 383; exhibition process roles and responsibilities, 221-22; how to go digital for, 112-13; James Madison's Montpelier, *355*; operationalizing multimedia, 354-55, *355*; with project tasks and written scope of work, 367
Museums of New Mexico Foundation, 115
Museums Victoria, Australia, 283-84, *285*, *286*
MuseWeb, 354
Música Buena virtual exhibition, MOIFA, 116
Musico, Olivia, 155
Muskoka Discovery Centre, Gravenhurst, *247*, 247
Myseum of Toronto, 157

nailable gallery walls, 40
narrative/description objectives, multimedia exhibits, 275
NASA, 349
National Archaeological Museum, Aruba, 249, *372*
National Association for Interpretation, 233
National Awareness, Attitudes and Usage Study of Visitor-Serving Organizations (2017), 8
National Czech & Slovak Museum, Cedar Rapids, *382*
National Gallery, London, 92, 406
National WWII Museum, New Orleans, *67*, 67
Native Youth Program, 71
Natural History Museum (NHM), London: Darwin Centre, 69; Engagement Group at, 146; English with, 145-48; *Fantastic Beasts*, *147*; *Treasures of Life* touring exhibition, *145*; *Treasures of the Natural World*, 146
natural history museums, 6, 27, 69; collections, 67; display/storage ratios, 63; research planning, 21
natural light, 42-44
Nazis, 263
NC (Design Noise Criteria) ratings, 45
Neon Signs virtual exhibition, M+ Museum, 95
Netflix, 106, *106*
Neue Pinakothek, Munich, 92
new media exhibition spaces, 26
new sources, multimedia exhibits, 275
The New York Times (newspaper), 69
NHM. *See* Natural History Museum, London
Niagara Parks Commission, *238*
1999 ASHRAE Applications Handbook, 31, 32, 35
Nintendo, 343
nonlinear exhibitions, thematic frameworks, 239
nonlinear organizational model, *240*
nonpublic support spaces, 57-58, 128
North Dakota Heritage Center & State Museum, Bismarck, 228, 248, *248*, 329; levels of text for *Innovation Gallery*, 331, 377, *377*-78, 390, *390*;

sample text treatment for label from *Innovation Gallery*, 331
north light, 43
Nye, Joseph, 10

Oakland Art Gallery, California, 218
Oakland Museum of California (OMCA), 212; *All Power to the People*, 220, *220*; core team roles and responsibilities, *221*; exhibition process, 218–21; organizational framework for, *219*
Oakland Public Museum, 218
object handlers, traveling exhibitions, 138
objectives, of exhibit, 370
object lists, exhibition concepts, 224–25
object research, curatorship, 224
objects: costs with large, 380; IPOP framework, 175; outstanding, 225; representative, 225; tangible interface, 357
occupancy levels, 52
Oddy tested, 304
offer package, traveling exhibitions, 137
off-gassing, 45–46
OMCA (Oakland Museum of California), 212, 218–21, *219–21*
Ontario Science Centre, Toronto, 81, 82–83, *85*, 85–88
On the Road Again (Buck and Gilmore), 134
opening, virtual exhibitions, 107, 112
Opera di Santa Croce, Florence, 227, 245, *245*
operating costs, 30
optic, lighting fixtures, 311
Optiwhite glass, 301–2
Oracle Aconex Project Controls, 400–401
Oracle Primavera P6, 400
oral histories, 61, 74, 75, 216, *281*
organizational framework, for OMCA, 219
organizational frameworks, interpretive planning, 239–40, *239–40*
organizers: summary of responsibilities, *144*; traveling exhibitions with borrowers and, *144*, *144*
Oro Townships, Ontario, 159
Our Heritage (Tilden), 234
outcomes, curiosity and improved, 165
outdoor air, movement, 30, 33
Out of the Depths exhibition, ROM, 121
outsourcing research, multimedia exhibits, 274–75
outstanding objects, 225

paid admission, 108
paintings: exhibition spaces for small-scale, 26; exhibition spaces for small- to medium-sized, 26; grand exhibition spaces for large-scale, 26
Pantone Matching System, 333
paper, works on, 24, 26, 42, 64, 309

parallel thematic structures, 240
participatory research, 283
passive-control display cases, 308
passive microclimate, 35
Past into Present (Roth), 79
past practices, questioning, 87
PA (public address) system, 45
pathways, accessibility, 298
payment bond, 368
pay what you can/suggested donation, 108
Peabody Essex Museum, Salem, 157
Peabody Museum of Archaeology and Ethnology, Harvard University, 157
Peguis First Nation, Manitoba, 287
Pekarik, Andrew, 173, 175
people, IPOP framework, 175
performance art, grand exhibition spaces for, 26
performance bond, 368
Perlan Museum of Natural Wonders, Reykjavik, 237, *238*, 268, *269*
permanent collection displays: changing, 63–64, *64*; display/storage ratios, *63*; exhibition planning for, 61–63; expansion, 63; interpreting, 64–66, *65*; modes of, 66–71; rotating, 64, *64*
permanent collection exhibitions, 61–63, 227–28, 230
pest management, execution-driven design criteria, 36–37
Philadelphia Museum of Art, Pennsylvania, 92
photography: exhibition spaces for small-scale, 26; hands-on exhibits, 274
phototropic effect, 43
physical, IPOP framework, 175
physical exhibitions, 90–92
Picasso, Pablo, 120–21, 147
Picasso exhibition, the Met, 120–21
planning: content development and research, 258–60, *259*; COVID-19, 29, 42, 55; design criteria, 28–30, *29*; direct exhibition costs, 384; for exhibition research, 18–21; interpretive, 171, 217; for permanent collection exhibitions, 61–63. *See also* financial planning; interpretive plan
planning-driven design criteria, spaces, 28–30, *29*
platforms, virtual exhibitions, 97; apps, 101–2; content aggregators, 102; microsites, 101, *101*; *Prohibition*, 103, *103*; social media, 102–3; Toronto Dreams Project, 102, *102*; website of museum, 100–101
play, 77, 87
play-based exhibitions, 77, *78*
Plymouth Plantation, Massachusetts, 81
PMI (Project Management Institute), 403
point load, 39
policies: research, 20–21; temporary exhibitions, 120–22, 124, 130

Index   **449**

political occasions, schedules, 228-29
polylingual exhibitions, 264
pop-ups, 105, 132
"Posters for Freedom" activity, *Mandela* exhibition, 360, *362*
power: exhibition space with communication and, 44-45; traveling exhibitions with lighting and, 140
preparators: temporary exhibitions, 125; traveling artifact case opened by, *141*; traveling exhibitions, 138
preparing, traveling exhibitions, 139-41, *141*
Prince2 certification, 403
print, accessibility of, 299
private collections, 271
process displays, 68, *68*
Process Lab exhibition, Cooper-Hewitt Smithsonian Design Museum, 166, *167-68*
procurement, image research and, 268-72, *270*, *272*
production: at Bluewater Studio, *369*; contracting expertise, 217; designer role during fabrication and, 297; exhibition costs, 108; fabrication and exhibition, 363-64; graphic design, 323; in-house, 363; installation and, 3, 363, 364, 367, 373, 374, 375; media, 384-85; prototyping, 370; specialists and exhibition process, 211; virtual exhibitions with prototyping and, 112
production process: completion and close-out, 374-75; fabrication, 368-75; graphics, 371; installation, 373-74, *374*; media, 372-73; mount-making, 371-72, *372*; prototype development, 370; site inspections and construction drawings, 370
production-ready artwork, 323
production team, exhibition process, 216
progress reports, tracking and scheduling, 375
Prohibition virtual exhibition, The Historic New Orleans Collection, 103, *103*
project coordination: contracting expertise, 217; meetings with project management, 394-95
projection mapping, 337-38, *338*
project management: certification and continuous learning, 403; dashboard reports or project overview, 401-2, *402*; direct exhibition costs, 384; evolution, 391; Gantt chart, 397-99, *398*, *400*; with methodology applied, 394-402; project coordination meetings, 394-95; role and purpose, 392; software and collaboration tools, 400-401; standard forms and templates, 395-96; task completion, 403-4; task list development, 396-97; team effort, 392-94
Project Management (Kerzner), 404
Project Management Institute (PMI), 403
project manager: attributes of successful, 393-94; contracting expertise, 217; temporary exhibitions, 125; traveling exhibitions, 137

project-specific interpretive planning, 234
proofing, graphics, 371
proof of concept prototyping, 370
proofreader, exhibition text, 266
prospectus, traveling exhibitions, 137
proteins, molecules interactive, 206
prototype, 43, 370
prototyping: production, 370; virtual exhibitions with production and, 112
provoking, vision-driven design criteria, 28
psychographic segmentation, audience fragmentation and, 173-75
public: access, 64; engagement, 282; libraries, 98, 157; Milwaukee Public Museum, *382*; nonpublic support spaces, 57-58, 128; Oakland Public Museum, 218; programming, 129, 387; relations, 129-30, 387
public address (PA) system, 45
publications, related exhibition costs, 387
public institutions, images from other, 271
public safety, security, 52-53
punch (deficiency) list, 374
purpose-built galleries, 24, 26, 76, 83, 228

qualitative audience research, 187-200
quantitative audience research, 187-200
The Queen and The Crown virtual exhibition, Brooklyn Museum, 106, *106*
The Queen's Gambit (TV show), *106*

racism, 14, 155, 166, 171, 221
Rain Room (Random International), 83
ramps, doors, stairs and, 41-42
Random International, 83
Raphael's Cartoons, V&A Museum, 407
read, 88
readability, design essentials, 334
reality, multimedia exhibits, 274
re-created environments, costs, 382
registrars: temporary exhibitions, 125; traveling exhibitions, 137
relatable, interpretive planning and, 234
relative humidity, 31-35, 37, 56
relevance, interpretive planning and, 234
remedial evaluation, 181, 185-86
remediation, direct exhibition costs, 385
renewal costs, exhibitions, 62
representative objects, 225
reputation, traveling exhibitions, 134
Request for Proposal (RFP), 235
research: audience, 169, 187-200; Centre for Freshwater Research and Education, 259; content development and collections, 260-63, *262*; content development with procurement and image, 268-72, *270*, *272*; exhibition text,

263; green design, 314-15; interpretive planning with visioning and, 236-37; matrix, 258-60, *259*; object, 224; participatory, 283; planning for exhibition, 18-21; planning with content development, 258-60, *259*; policy, 20-21; space, 69; thematic, 224
research-based exhibition, 18, *19*, 20-21
resources: green design and reusing existing, 315; green design with waste management and, 316; microsites for digital, 101, *101*; plan with exhibition brief, 231; traveling exhibitions with staff and professional, 137-38; Verywell Mind, 173
resourcing, temporary exhibitions and, 130-31
responsibilities: borrowers and organizers, 144; DEAI exhibitions and evolution of roles and, 155
responsible, vision-driven design criteria, 28
responsible materials, green design, 315
responsive environments/sensors, multimedia, 342-43, *343*
Réunion des Musées Nationaux, 18
reusing existing resources, green design, 315
revenue: COVID-19 pandemic and, 12; direct, 134; temporary exhibitions and generating, 131-32
RFP (Request for Proposal), 235
RIBA (Royal Institute for British Architects), 296, 296-97
Rights of Passage exhibition, CMHR: with equality hashtag, LED lights, Instagram images, *359*; hotspots as interface for, *358*; multimedia and, 356-59; tangible object interface, *357*
risk: without environmental standards, 30-37; of hardening soft power, 11; innovation and, 87; security, 51-55
Roberts, Kiera, 155
Rodriguez, Antonio, 148-50
ROM (Royal Ontario Museum), Toronto, 36, 70, *71*, *121*, 121-22, *123*, *141*
room level-internal gallery perimeter, security levels, 53
Ross, Barbara, 268, 269, *270*
Roth, Stacy, 79
Royal Institute for British Architects (RIBA), 296, 296-97
Royal Ontario Museum (ROM), Toronto, 36, 70, *71*, *121*, 121-22, *123*, *141*
royalties, copyright and, 385
Ruthven Museums Building, UMMNH, 250

safety, public, 52-53
Sakyamuni Buddha, 241
sales, traveling exhibitions, marketing and, 137
sampling, graphics, 371
Sandell, Richard, 11
San Diego History Center, 101, *101*

San Jose Public Library, 98
sans serif typeface, 325, *325*, 327
The Savage Mind (Lévi-Strauss), 320
schedules: integration and installation, 373; sample graphic, *324*; staggered, 378
scheduling: critical path, 375; fabrication and, 375-76; time for green design research, 314-15
schematic design, 290, 293-94, 321-22, 397
scholarship, under attack, 8
Schultz, George, 8, 13
science: under attack, 8; Biological Sciences Building, 250; centers, 27, 42, 122, 130; Chicago Museum of Science and Industry, 82, *82*; exhibitions, 81-83, *82*; Ontario Science Centre, 81, 82-83, *85*, 85-88
Science Storms exhibition, 82, *82*
scope of work, contracting, 366-67
script treatments, multimedia exhibits, 274
script typeface, 325, *325*
sculpture garden, 27
sculptures: exhibition spaces for small-scale, 26; exhibition spaces for small- to medium-sized, 26; grand exhibition spaces for large-scale, 26; monumental, 62
Seaview United Baptist Church, Halifax, 268
security: electronic surveillance, 53-54; exhibition gallery, 51-55; fire detection and suppression, 54-55; guards, 54; human, 127; levels, 53; public safety, 52-53
SEGD (Society for Environmental Graphic Design), 315-16
segmentation, psychographic, 173-75
Seiji Togo Memorial Sompo Japan Nipponkoa Museum of Art, Tokyo, 92
self-directed experiences, 178-79
Selfridges, 130
semiotics, in design, 319-21, *321*
sensors: carbon dioxide, 33; motion, 83, 203, 316; responsive environments, 342-43, *343*; timing, 313
serif typeface, 325, *325*, 327
Serota, Nicholas, 63
Serra, Richard, 24, 132
service access, 56-57
Shaanxi Provincial Cultural Relics Bureau, 122
shared authority, 9, 154
shipping, temporary exhibitions, 142
Shoenberger, Elisa, 153
shop drawings, 297
shop stock/retail, exhibition costs, 387
SHSND (State Historical Society of North Dakota), 378
sidelighting, 43
Siegel, Nina, 69
signage, 64, 95, 185, 319, 367

sign-off process, completion and, 374
Simcoe County, Ontario, 159
Simon, Nina, 9
Sisters in Liberty temporary exhibition, Ellis Island National Museum of Immigration, 227, 245; color palette, 330, *332*, 333; thematic framework, 245
Sisters in Liberty temporary exhibition, Opera di Santa Croce, 227, 245, *245*, 330, *332*, 333
site inspections, construction drawings, 370
SITES program, Smithsonian Institution, 133, 148
Six Sigma Organization, 403
size, schedule, 228
sketches, 274
skylight, 33, 37, 42, 43, 44
slab serif typeface, 325, *325*, 327
slaves, 153, 159
slideshow (carousel) virtual exhibitions, 104-5
Sloane, Hans, 153
Smartsheet, 400
Smeds, Kersten, 9-10
SMEs (subject matter experts), 278-81, *280-81*
Smithsonian Arctic Studies Center, Anchorage Museum, 69
Smithsonian Institution, Washington DC: *Guidelines for Accessible Exhibition Design*, 298; security guards at, 54; SITES program, 133, 148; Temporary Exhibition Service, 124
Smithsonian National Museum of the American Indian, *Americans* virtual exhibition, 105
smoke detectors, 41, 55
Snow Museum of Natural History, Oakland, 218
social media: crowdsourcing and, 408; hashtags, *350*, *359*; multimedia, 350-51; related exhibition costs, 387; virtual exhibition platforms, 102-3
social occasions, schedules, 228-29
Society for Environmental Graphic Design (SEGD), 315-16
soft power, museums, 10-11, 146, 169
software: multimedia design, 292; operationalizing multimedia with hardware and, 352-53; project management collaboration tools and, 400-401
songs, 21, 61, 65
Sony, 343
sound control, acoustics and, 45
Sound Transmission Class (STC), 45
source, image, 271
sources, photos, sketches and, 274
South Africa, 360
South America, 148
Southeast Asia, 148
space characteristics, exhibition: acoustics and sound control, 45; doorways, stairs, ramps, 41-42; gallery ceilings, 41; gallery floors, 38-39, *39*, 40; gallery shell, 37-38; gallery walls, 40-41; load requirements, 38-39, *39*; materials and finishes, 45-51, *47-51*; natural light and fenestration, 42-44; power and communication, 44-45
spaces: back-of-house relationship diagram, *58*; exhibition, 26-51, *39*, *47-51*; nonpublic support, 57-58, 128; research, 69; staging, 373; temporary exhibitions and making, 127-29; virtual exhibitions with unlimited, 90. *See also* facilities, exhibition
special events, traveling exhibitions, 134
special measures, security levels, 53
"A Specification for Museum Air-Conditioning" (Buck), 31
sponsored admission, 108
sponsored content, ethics and, 12
sponsorship policy, temporary exhibitions, 130
sprinkler systems, 37, 38, 40, 41, 55, 367
staff: budgeting for, 386; conservation, 56; traveling exhibitions with professional resources and, 137-38
staggered schedule, SHSND, 378
staging space, installation and, 373
Stained Glass Navigator, York Minster Cathedral, 92
stairs, doors, ramps and, 41-42
standard forms, project management, 395-96
Starfire glass, 301-2
State Historical Society of North Dakota (SHSND), 378
Statue of Liberty (Bartholdi), 227, 245
Statue of Unity (Gujarat), 317
STC (Sound Transmission Class), 45
Stim, Richard, 385
stock images, 271
Stolow, Nathan, 138
storage: display/storage ratios, *63*; visible displays, 69-71, *70-71*, 225
Storkerson, Peter, 319-20
story line, interpretive planning, 249-50
storytelling installation, CMHR, *349*
strategies: design-bid and design-tender, 364; interpretive plan, 237-38; multimedia, 336-37; temporary exhibition, 120-22, 124; traveling exhibitions and success, 135-37
streakers, visitor types, 328
Streets of Old Milwaukee exhibit, Milwaukee Public Museum, *382*
strollers, visitor types, 328
study spaces, 27
Stupa, Buddha Smriti Park, 241
style, exhibition text, 264, 266
subcontractors, 367-68
subject matter experts (SMEs), 279-81, *280-81*
subscription benefits, 108
substrates, design essentials, 334

success, measuring, 177–79
suggested donation/pay what you can, 108
summative evaluation, 181, 186–87
summative visitor studies, 192–95, 196–98
"Sun Flowers" (Van Gogh), 92
Sunflowers 360 exhibition, 92
Sunflowers Virtual 360 Gallery, Van Gogh Museum, 92, *93*
sunlight, 43, 44, 82, 309
supplier, local, 274
suspended ceiling, 41
sustainability of materials, green design, 315
Symbols exhibit, Central Bank Museum, *277*
A Synthesizing Mind (Gardner), 173
systematic displays, object lists, 225
systemic racism, 155

tables, multiuser, 344–46, *345*
tabletop display cases, 302, *303*
Tank Galleries, Tate Modern, 28, *29*
target audiences, exhibition text, 264
tasks, 367; completion and project management, 403–4; finish dates with Gantt chart, 399; lists for project management, 396–97
Tate Britain, London, 18, 63, 64, 121, *122*, 124, 132
Tate Gallery, London, 63, 132
Tate Liverpool, 132
Tate Modern, London, 28, *29*, 63, 124, 132
Tate St Ives, Cornwall, 132
teams: composition with multimedia, 351–52; core exhibition, *212*, 215–16; design, 216; effort with project management, 392–94; exhibition process committees and, 215–16; exhibition process roles and responsibilities of core, *221*; interpretive planning and design, 125; production, 216; virtual exhibitions, 111
technicians, traveling exhibitions, 138
technologies: BYOD with, 350; costs, 380; Factum Foundation for Digital Technology in Conservation, 407; gesture, 83, 343–44, *344*; green design, 315; lighting and changing, 313–14; multimedia and mobile, 349–50, *350*; wearable, 350, 358
temporary collection exhibitions, 228
temporary exhibitions: *Alexander McQueen*, 127, *128*; *All Power to the People*, 220, *220*; benefits of, 119–20; blue whale skeleton, 121, *121*; China, 135; *Coming Home*, 155, 157; *Dragons, Unicorns, and Mermaids*, 122, *123*; funding and resourcing, 130–31; *Great Whales* exhibition, 121; *Lowry and the Painting of Modern Life*, 121, *122*; Magna Carta, 126, *126*; making space for, 127–29; managing, 125–27; *Mandela*, 124, *124*; marketing and public relations, 129–30; *Out of the Depths*, 121; policy or strategy, 120–22, 124; public and educational programming, 129; revenue, 131–32; shipping, 142; *Sisters in Liberty*, 227, 245, *245*; types of, 120–24; *The Warrior Emperor and China's Terracotta Army*, 122, *123*
Temporary Exhibition Service, Smithsonian Institution, 124
temporary gallery walls, 40–41
temporary number, 261
Tennessee State Museum, 243, *243*
text, exhibition: categories of, 265–66; content development, 263–68; for *Glaciers* introductory panel, 268, *269*; reviewing and approving, 266–67; word counts and categories, 264, 265–66; writing, 267–68, *269*
text, with design and image placement, 334
textiles, 26, 64
text levels, graphic design, 323; actual size Level 1 versus Level 4, *330*; for *Innovation Gallery*, *331*; sample treatment for label, *331*; typography, 328–30, *330–31*
theater reconstruction, Jewish Museum Milwaukee, 389
thematic exhibition, 26
thematic frameworks: Buddha Smriti Park, 241, *241*; core idea, 228; Etihad Museum, 242, *242*; interpretive planning and, 239–40, *239–40*; Miraflores Museum, 246, *246*; Muskoka Discovery Centre, 247, *247*; North Dakota Heritage Center & State Museum, 248, *248*; Opera di Santa Croce, 245, *245*; Tennessee State Museum, 243, *243*; University of Michigan Museum of Natural History, 244, *244*
thematic galleries, 26
thematic research, curatorship, 224
Things That Matter exhibition, Tropenmuseum, 155
thinking, shifts in museum, 407–8
Third Reich (1933–1945), 263
Thomas, Cheyenne, 287, *288*
Thomas, Dave, 287, *288*
3D virtual walkthrough exhibitions, 105–6, 115
360-degree circular documentary film, *339*
three-dimensional design, exhibition and, 291
Tilden, Freeman, 234
Tim Burton virtual exhibition, *91*, 91–92
time: limits and exhibition concept, 224; virtual exhibitions and, 90
timing, 107, 389. *See also* opening, virtual exhibitions
timing sensors, 313
TIR (Total Internal Reflection) optics, 311
toddlers, 77
tone, exhibition text, 264, 266
tools, project management software and collaboration, 400–401
topical occasions, schedules, 228–29

Index 453

toplighting, 43
Toronto Dreams Project (Bunch), 102, *102*
Toronto Public Library, 98
Torres Strait Islander Australians, 284
Total Internal Reflection (TIR) optics, 311
touring exhibitions. *See* traveling exhibitions
tour manager, 137, 141-44
tours, traveling exhibitions: closed, 136; managing, 141-44
tracking: fabrication and, 375-76; typography, 327
track lighting, 35, 312
traditional ways of life, 61
training, with completion and close-out, 375
transformation, exhibitions as agents of, 7, 8-10, 12
transformative experiences, 178
transparency, exhibition viewpoint, 179
traveling (touring) exhibitions: affordability, 135; borrowers and organizers, 144, *144*; *Canada Day 1*, 231-32, *232*, 279, *281*; competition, 135; condition report, 137, 142-43; COVID-19 pandemic and, 147-48; designing and preparing, 139-41, *141*; disposal and dispersal, 140; extending life of, 113-16, *114*, *116*; *Fantastic Beasts*, 147; gaps and inequalities in global market, 148-49; *Imaginate*, 87; lighting and power, 140; loan agreements, 138-39; *Mandela*, 124, *124*, 360-62, *361-62*; NHM with, 145-48; in post-pandemic world, 149-50; purpose of, 135; reasons for developing, 134; Rodriguez on, 148-50; role of, 148; size, 135; staff and professional resources, 137-38; strategize for success, 135-37; target market, 135; tour management, 141-44; *Treasures of Life*, 145; *Treasures of the Natural World*, 146
Treasures of Life touring exhibition, NHM, 145
Treasures of the Natural World touring exhibition, NHM, 146
triangulation, 198-200
Tropenmuseum, Amsterdam, 155, *156*
trust factor, 8, 12-14, 74
Truth and Reconciliation movement, 278
Turner, J. M. W., 18, *19*
Turner, Whistler, Monet exhibition, 18, *19*
turnkey: assignment with exhibition process, 216; exhibitions, 365-66; media production, 372
Twitter, 102, *102*, 193, 358
typeface selection, graphic design: classification examples, *325*; sample graphic schedule, *324*; typography, 323-26, *324-26*; weights, 326, *326*
typography, graphic design: anatomy of, *327*; legibility, 323, 326-28, *327-28*; text levels and information hierarchy, 323, 328-30, *330-31*; typeface selection, 323-26, *324-26*

UBC (University of British Columbia), 71
ultraviolet light (UV), 310

UMMNH (University of Michigan Museum of Natural History), 200-207, 250-53, *251-53*
Underground Railroad, in Barrie, Ontario, 159
Under the Microscope Gallery, University of Michigan Museum of Natural History, 244, *244*
Universal Access Point, 300
Universal Keypad, 300
University of British Columbia (UBC), 71
University of Michigan Museum of Natural History (UMMNH), Ann Arbor, 244, *244*, 250-53, *251-53*; biodiversity interactive, 205; final interview questions, 206-7; formative evaluation, 203-4; front-end and formative visitor study, 200-207; front-end evaluation, 201-3; "Lick a Rat" epigenetics interactive, 205-6, 207; molecules and proteins interactive, 206
University of Utah, "Lick Your Rats" online game, 205, *205*
upgrading, lighting, 313-14
user experience, virtual exhibitions, 97
user interface, virtual exhibitions, 97
UV (ultraviolet light), 310

V&A East, London, 69
value engineered, exhibition design, 295, 314
V&A (Victoria and Albert) Museum, London, 69, 71, 129, 133, 134, 407
Van Gogh, Vincent, 84, *84*, 92, 127
Van Gogh Museum, Amsterdam, 92, *93*
vertical circulation, 42
Very Early Warning Smoke Detection Apparatus system, 55
Verywell Mind (online resource), 173
vibration, execution-driven design criteria, movement and, 37
Victoria and Albert (V&A) Museum, London, 69, 129, 133, 134, 407
Villela, Khristaan D., 116
Vimeo, 351
virtual exhibitions: access and admissions, 108; *Alexander Girard*, 114, *114*, 116, *116*; *Americans*, 105; audiences maintained during prolonged closures, 93-95; be responsive, tell more stories, stay relevant, 93; *Community Through Making*, 116; considerations, 99-110; content, 97, 99-100; costs and budgets, 109-10, *110*; defined, 89-90; demand, expectations and new audiences, 95; development process, 111-12; digital audiences and, 95-99; digital divide, 97-98; digital first or born-digital, 100; formats, 104-7, *105*, *106*; hosting, 103-4; inclusive and accessible, 98-99; *Música Buena*, 116; *Neon Signs*, 95; opening, 107, 112; payment options, 108; platforms, 97, 100-103; present distant,

iconic and sensitive collections and sites, 92–93; *Prohibition*, 103, *103*; *The Queen and The Crown*, 106, *106*; reasons to develop, 90–95; Tim Burton, *91*, 91–92; time and, 90; tips for smaller museums going digital, 112–13; *Women in Service*, 105, *105*; *Yokai*, 116
virtual reality (VR), 106, 347, 348, *349*
visible storage, displays, 69–71, *70–71*, 225
vision, design criteria, 27, *28*
visionary, design criteria, 28
vision-driven design criteria, spaces, 27, *28*
visioning, interpretive planning with research and, 236–37
visitors: AR used by, *348*; centricity, 2, 9, 233; at CMIP interact with personal stories of newcomers, *281*; collections and expectations of, 62; engagement with full diversity of, 179; evaluation and audience research, 169; experience, 273; *Identity and the Museum Visitor Experience*, 173; intangible-interactive interpretive displays, 64–65; interpretive planning centered around, 234; objectives with interpretive planning, 248–49; streakers and strollers, 328; studies, 195–98; with *Symbols* exhibit, *277*; virtual exhibitions and user experience, 97
visits, tracking and scheduling, 375
visual communication, 319–20, *321*
Visual Identities (Floch), 320
visual presentation, exhibition text, 264
Vitra Design Museum, Germany, 114
VOCs (volatile organic compounds), 45, 316
VR (virtual reality), 106, 347, 348, *349*

W3C (World Wide Web Consortium) Accessibility Guidelines, 99
Wabanaki culture, 155, 157
walkthroughs, 3D virtual exhibitions, 105–6, 115
wall-mounted cases, 298, 305, *306*, *381*
Wallpaper Immersion Room, Cooper-Hewitt Smithsonian Design Museum, 338, *340*
walls, galleries: load requirements, 38–39; nailable, 40; permanent, temporary, moveable, 40–41
wall within wall, gallery shell, 37
War of 1812, African American veterans, 159, 268

warranties: expectations and grey areas, 376; maintenance agreements and extended, 376–77
The Warrior Emperor and China's Terracotta Army temporary exhibition, ROM, 122, *122*
waste management, green design, 316
wearable technologies, 350, 358
The Weather Project (Eliasson), 124
weaving demonstration, Colonial Williamsburg, *80*, *81*
websites, museum, 100–101, 387
WebXR, 106
weights, typeface, 326, *326*
Wells, Marcella, 171
Weston Family Innovation Centre, Toronto, 78, 82–83, *85*, 85–88
whales, 121, *121*
Whistler, James Abbott McNeill, 18, *19*
Whitney Museum of American Art, New York City, 74, *75*
Wilkening, Susie, 165–66
windows. *See* fenestration, natural light and
wireless lighting control, 313
women, 80; Aboriginal, 284; activists against systemic racism, 155; artists, 406; *Empowering Women* exhibition, *349*
Women in Service virtual exhibition, Canadian War Museum, 105, *105*
word counts, exhibition text, 264, *265–66*
work hours, installation and, 374
working lights, 35
works on paper, 24, 26, 42, 64, 309
World Wide Web Consortium (W3C) Accessibility Guidelines, 99
writing text, for exhibitions, 267–68, *269*
Wu Kingdom Helv Relics Museum, Wuxi, China, *83*, 83–84

XR, multimedia, 347–49, *348–50*

Yokai virtual exhibition, MOIFA, 116
York Minster Cathedral, 92
YouTube, 351
Yulendi group, 283–84, *285*

Zoom! Kindermuseum, Vienna, 76, *78*

About the Editor

Maria Piacente has spent more than twenty-five years in the global cultural sector, specializing in exhibition planning and development, interpretive planning, and project management for cultural projects of all sizes, ranging in scope from art to science to history. Formerly the Vice President of Exhibitions and Events with Lord Cultural Resources, Maria is currently the Senior Vice President for Exhibition and Gallery Planning at the Royal Ontario Museum in Toronto, Canada.

About the Contributors

Jackie Armstrong is associate educator of visitor research experience at The Museum of Modern Art where she works cross-departmentally planning, conducting, and sharing the results of visitor research and evaluation. Jackie is interested in how museums connect with diverse publics, create thoughtfully designed experiences, and empower people to make personal meaning through their encounters with art and one another.

Patchen Barss is a journalist, author, and communications consultant. He has worked on content strategy and development for many museums and other cultural institutions across North America and in Europe. He specializes in transforming complex, multidisciplinary ideas into relatable, accessible stories for diverse audiences.

Cheryl Blackman is the director of museums and heritage services for the City of Toronto. Cheryl is an expert in visitor experience development, audience research, community engagement, fundraising, business development, working with volunteers, and more. Cheryl is a leader in diversity, inclusion, accessibility, and equity initiatives for museums.

James Bruer is a partner with WeatherstonBruer Consultants and a graduate of the Ontario College of Art and Design. He has more than thirty years' experience designing exhibitions for museums and galleries internationally.

Karen Carter is the executive director of MacLaren Arts Centre and an associate at Lord Cultural Resources. Karen is an exemplary arts executive whose transformational leadership with C-Art Caribbean Art Fair, BAND, Myseum, and Heritage Toronto reflects her commitment to community building, innovative programming, and artistic excellence.

Mike Chaplin is the managing director of Click Netherfield, one of the premier display case suppliers to museum and galleries. He has gained more than thirty years' experience in the industry working with conservators, curators, designers, and architects on small and large projects around the world.

Jan English specializes in strategy and planning, partnership building, financial management, international relations, touring exhibitions, visitor experience, marketing, and communications, as well as exhibition development for museums, science centers, and cultural institutions. Jan is currently the Collections and Public Engagement Director at the American Museum & Gardens, Toulouse.

Duncan Grewcock is the director of the MA Museum & Gallery Studies and MA Heritage programs at Kingston University, London. His background is in art history and he has a PhD in museum studies from University College, London.

Sarah Hill has spent more than fifteen years serving the cultural sector in Canada, the United States, and the United Kingdom and holds an MA in arts and culture management from Queen Margaret University, Edinburgh. Formerly a senior consultant with Lord Cultural Resources, she was the practice leader responsible for the firm's digital services and thought leadership. She now acts as a senior program advisor for the Department of Canadian Heritage.

Valerie Huaco has more than twenty-five years' experience in strategic planning and change management of Museum Collections and Exhibitions at the national and international levels, including museums, galleries, and associations. Valerie is the deputy director and chief content officer at Oakland Museum of California.

Brad King is vice president for strategy at Lord Cultural Resources. Based in Toronto, he has led or contributed to some 250 museum planning projects in fifteen countries since 2000. He holds a PhD in history from the University of Toronto.

Robert LaMarre has spent more than thirty years in planning, development, and operations of attractions, museums, exhibitions, world expositions, and cultural tourism initiatives across Asia, Europe, and North America. Working with Lord Cultural Resources, Robert has contributed to major museum and exhibition projects around the world since 1994.

Leslie Lewis was the CEO of the Ontario Science Centre from 1998 to 2014. She is the past president of the board of directors of the Washington-based Association of Science and Technology Centers and has been a vocal advocate for public engagement with science. Leslie is currently an independent consultant for the museum and science center sector.

Gail Lord is president and cofounder of Lord Cultural Resources. With Barry Lord, she is coeditor of *The Manual of Museum Planning* (1991, 1999, 2012) and coauthor of *The Manual of Museum Management* (1997, 2009) and *Artists, Patrons and the Public: Why Culture Changes?* (2010). She is coauthor with Kate Markert of *The Manual of Strategic Planning for Museums* (2007) and *The Manual of Strategic Planning for Cultural Organizations* (2017). She is coauthor with Ngaire Blankenberg of *Cities, Museums and Soft Power* (2015). Gail has led exhibition, planning, and management assignments for museums, galleries, and cities as well as cultural and tourism plans for cities throughout Canada, the United States, the United Kingdom, Europe, and Asia. Gail is a member of the Order of Canada (2016), and Officier de l'Ordre des Arts et des Lettres de France (2014). In 2016 she was awarded an Honorary Doctor of Letters by McMaster University.

Heather Maximea, formerly a senior consultant with Lord Cultural Resources, specializes in collections management and facilities planning. She has more than thirty-five years of experience in the museum field.

Katherine Molineux is a principal consultant with Lord Cultural Resources. Katherine received a bachelor of arts and a master of arts in history from the University of Western Ontario. An experienced educator and communicator, she has international experience developing and facilitating exhibitions through interpretive planning, research, content development, coordination, and project management.

Antonio Rodriguez is an accomplished professional with more than twenty years' experience in arts management, nonprofit organization and museum management, strategic planning, international traveling exhibitions, and public relations and fundraising. Antonio develops strategic alliances with governments, private sector organizations, foundations, nonprofit organizations, academic and research institutions, and embassies.

Kevan Shaw (ELDA, IALD), is principal of Kevan Shaw Lighting Design and has practiced in the lighting industry for more than twenty-five years. Founded in 1989, Kevan Shaw Lighting Design is based in Edinburgh and Geneva and has extensive experience of lighting for architecture, exteriors, museums, and exhibitions.

Barbara Soren is an educator with a PhD in education and a master of science in teaching. Barbara works as an audience research consultant and has recently retired after lecturing for twenty years in the Master of Museum Studies program at the University of Toronto. Barbara has undertaken visitor research, consulting, and teaching related to evaluation of learning experiences across North America and in the United Kingdom.

Sean Stanwick is an experienced facilities planner and programmer with more than twenty years of experience in the field. As director facilities planning at Lord Cultural Resources, Sean contributes to collections, exhibition, and facilities projects. He is the author of three books on contemporary architecture and contributed to numerous journals and periodicals.

Jacqueline Tang has been telling stories through experiential graphic design for over a decade. As creative director with Entro Communications, she designs spaces that engage its users and inspire them to form meaningful connections with each other and the spaces they inhabit.

Yvonne Tang is director of visitor experience with Lord Cultural Resources and cofounder of the nonprofit organization Link Coalition Toronto. With a background in visual arts and design, Yvonne has led many planning, design, and installation projects and programs around the world. She believes that cultural spaces should provide all visitors with a safe and welcoming environment that seamlessly integrates content and design.

Corey Timpson is an active collaborator and thought leader in the experience design and museological discourses within the cultural sector. Having collaborated with more than eighty museums internationally, Corey's primary focus is to facilitate meaningful experiences among audiences (on-site and online) through mixed-media, digital technology, multisensory, and inclusive design.

Kevin von Appen is the Ontario Science Centre's director of science communication. He oversees the center's science writing and translation for exhibitions and online science communication initiatives. Kevin also oversees the operations for the Weston Family Innovation Centre.

Lisa Wright is a senior consultant with exhibitions and events with LORD Cultural Resources where she has worked on exhibition planning and development for a range of cultural institutions. She holds a bachelor of arts in history from Queen's University and a master's degree in museum sudies from the University of Toronto.

Mary Yacob has conceptualized twenty-plus museums across four continents with a focus on the visitor experience. In her work with museum and exhibition design sector, Mary builds on the connection between visitor experience and brand loyalty. Mary is supremely sensitive to the visitor's experience of an exhibition's cultural identity and aesthetic quality. Mary has completed a master of cultural studies degree at KU Leuven in Belgium where she analysed semiotics' influence in design.

Erich Zuern is a producer for Bluewater Studio. Erich has more than thirty-five years of experience guiding museum and theatrical projects through planning, design, fabrication, and installation. Currently focusing on interpretive exhibitions for museums and other institutions of informal learning, Erich produces projects across the United States and internationally.